THE GREAT WAVE

THE GREAT WAVE

Price Revolutions and the Rhythm of History

David Hackett Fischer

New York Oxford
Oxford University Press
1996

Oxford University Press

Oxford   New York
Athens   Auckland   Bangkok   Bogotá   Bombay
Buenos Aires   Calcutta   Cape Town   Dar es Salaam
Delhi   Florence   Hong Kong   Istanbul   Karachi
Kuala Lumpur   Madras   Madrid   Melbourne
Mexico City   Nairobi   Paris   Singapore
Taipei   Tokyo   Toronto

and associated companies in
Berlin   Ibadan

Copyright © 1996 by David Hackett Fischer

Published by Oxford University Press, Inc.
198 Madison Avenue, New York, New York 10016

Oxford is a registered trademark of Oxford University Press

Library of Congress Cataloging-in-Publication Data
Fischer, David Hackett, 1935–
The great wave: price revolutions and the rhythm of history /
David Hackett Fischer.
p.cm.   Includes bibliographical references and index.
ISBN 0-19-505377-X
1. Prices—History.   2. Business cycles—History.
3. Economic history.   I. Title.
HB231.F48   1996
338.5'2—dc20   95-52161

9 8 7 6 5 4 3 2

Printed in the United States of America
on acid-free paper

For my parents, with love
Norma and John Fischer

CONTENTS

APPENDICES

FIGURES
❧ Charts, Maps, and Graphs

THE REVOLUTIONARY CRISIS

THE VICTORIAN EQUILIBRIUM

THE PRICE REVOLUTION OF THE TWENTIETH CENTURY

PREFACE
ᔥ "Something Like a Seismograph . . ."

> Of all the recording devices that can reveal to an historian
> the fundamental movements of an economy, monetary phe-
> nomena are without doubt the most sensitive. But to recog-
> nize their importance merely as symptoms would do them
> less than full justice. They have been and are, in their turn,
> causes. They are something like a seismograph, which not
> only measures the movements of the earth but sometimes
> provokes them.
>
> —Marc Bloch, 1933[1]

QUANTITATIVE METHODS find many uses in modern historical research. In some hands, they are tools of descriptive
measurement. In others, they become a calculus of conceptual
relationships. A few work with them mainly as rhetorical devices, to
"enlarge the historian's vocabulary."[2]

Not everyone is comfortable with these applications. History
teachers know that when the dreaded word quantification is mentioned
in a classroom, undergraduate eyes glaze over. Numbers too often
become numb–ers of young and restless minds.

It need not be so. If one makes a leap of the imagination, numbers
come alive. They do so both in what they allow us to know and in how
they help us to think. Numbers make it possible for us to put the pieces
together. They allow us to compare events that are otherwise incompa-
rable. They tell us which way the world is moving. They help us to
think in general terms about particular events, and then to test our
generalizations against the evidence of empirical indicators.

Many indicators of that sort exist for the study of recent events, but few reach very far into the distant past. Only one type of source-material spans the entire range of written history: the record of prices. We carry these humble documents about with us every day, in the tattered receipts that accumulate in our wallets and purses. They seem so ephemeral that we scarcely think of them in historical terms, and yet they survive in greater abundance than any other quantifiable material.

Price-records come down to us from ancient civilizations of Asia, India, Rome, Greece, Egypt, Palestine and Mesopotamia. In the dust of old Babylon, archeologists have found large numbers of clay tablets and cylinders that yield price-series as early as the reign of Hammurapi (*circa* 1793–1750 B.C.). In the deserts of Egypt, scholars have found papyri that record the cost of living in the time of the Pharaohs. The civilizations of Greece and Rome, China and India all generated a large body of price-records.

Even for the early Middle Ages, where the sources are not as strong, scholars have been able to put together primitive price-lists (as distinct from price-series) for an astonishing variety of medieval commodities. We can follow the price of peasant grain, monkish cowls, knightly armor, and even sacred relics from the sixth to the twelfth centuries. These sources allow us to reconstruct price movements in a rough way through the darkest period of European history.[3]

From the twelfth century to the present, historians have compiled more sophisticated price-series of very high quality. These data now exist for all European nations, and many cities and towns.

Since the mid-nineteenth century, complex price-indices have been constructed by governments throughout the world, in a vast labor of data-gathering that grows ever more elaborate and precise. Every month, the latest price movements are front-page news in our morning papers, and lead stories on the evening broadcast.[4]

With all of this material in hand, it is possible to follow the movement of prices through nearly four thousand years of recorded history. The interpretive opportunities in these sources are limited only by the reach of our imagination.

There are as many ways to study a price series as to read a text. On the surface, prices are a running record of the cost of commodities as they change hands in the market. This is their most common and familiar meaning. At the same time, they may also be studied in a different way, as evidence of the changing value of money—which is how some economists prefer to think of them. On a third level, prices tell us about systems of production, and especially about structures of exchange—a subject of growing historical importance, as scholars begin to discover that processes of exchange may have played much of the role that Marx attributed to the means of production.

On a fourth plane of abstraction, prices become a source for the study of broad historical movements. To look at the movement of prices in the United States during the nineteenth century, for example, is to see many things through that one particular lens. In the ebb and flow of American prices we may observe the cultural effect of the Jacksonian movement, the social impact of the Civil War, the chronology of the industrial revolution and the geography of the westward movement. Historical happenings as evanescent as moods of hope and fear may be measured with high precision by a study of prices. In the history of the American Civil War, a sensitive indicator of northern hopes was the changing price of government bonds from 1861 to 1865. A barometer of southern fears was the price of slaves as it rose and fell through the same period. Price movements are a powerful source of inferential knowledge about changing historical conditions and events.

At a still higher level of abstraction, prices may be studied as clues to the nature of change itself. That is the purpose of this inquiry. Every period of the past has been a time of change. The world is always changing—but not always in the same way. We shall find empirical evidence of distinct "change-regimes" in the past that were often highly dynamic, but stable in their dynamism. Sooner or later, even the strongest of these change-regimes broke down in moments of what might be called "deep change." When it did so, one system of change yielded to another. Deep change may be understood as a change in the structure of change itself. In the language of mathematics, deep change is the second derivative. It may be calculated as a rate of change in rates of change.

The method of this inquiry is to describe and hopefully to explain the rhythm of change regimes and deep change in price movements during the past eight hundred years. The purpose is to enlarge our understanding not only of prices in particular, but also of change in general.

Large questions about the nature of change have tended to belong more to philosophers than historians, and have been studied mostly by methods of deduction. The growing accessibility of quantitative evidence allows us to convert a metaphysical conundrum into an empirical question. Dr. Samuel Johnson would have understood. He once observed, "That, sir, is the good of counting. It brings everything to a certainty, which before floated in the mind indefinitely."

Wayland, Massachusetts   D. H. F.
June 1996

THE GREAT WAVE

INTRODUCTION
❧ Great Waves in World History

> Upswing in the thirteenth century . . . downswing in the later middle ages . . . upswing in the sixteenth century which breaks in the seventeenth century; a third upswing in the eighteenth century . . . what is the meaning of these movements?
> —Wilhelm Abel, 1935[1]

> History doesn't repeat itself—but it rhymes.
> —attributed to Mark Twain

THE HISTORY OF PRICES is a history of change. A helpful perspective on the troubles of our time is a remarkable record of English "consumable" prices since the year 1264, compiled with great care by Henry Phelps-Brown and Sheila Hopkins. This index shows that market prices of food, drink, fuel and textiles in the south of England have tended to rise for more than seven hundred years, at an average rate of about one percent each year.[2]

Price-inflation has been a continuing problem in the past, but it has not been constant in its rhythm, rate, or timing. Some eras have been more inflationary than others. A few have experienced long-term price-equilibrium, and even deflation.

If we study the Phelps-Brown-Hopkins index and others like it, we find that most inflation in the past eight centuries has happened in four great waves of rising prices. The first wave continued from the late twelfth century to the early fourteenth century, and has been called the medieval price-revolution. The second was the familiar "price-revolution of the sixteenth century,'' which actually began in the fifteenth century and ended in the mid-seventeenth. The third wave started *circa* 1730, and reached its climax in the age of the French Revolution and the Napoleonic Wars. It might be called the price-revolution of the eighteenth century. The fourth wave commenced in the year 1896, and

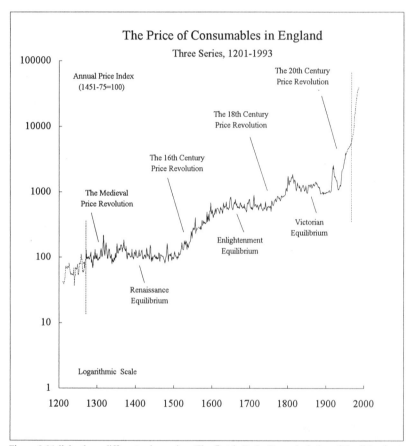

The Price of Consumables in England
Three Series, 1201-1993

Figure 0.01 links three different price series. The first is D. L. Farmer's index of English wheat prices in shillings from 1210 to 1275. The second is the Phelps-Brown-Hopkins price index of consumables (grains, vegetables, meat, fish, butter, cheese, drink, fuel, light and textiles) in shillings for southern England from 1264 to 1954. The third is the Ministry of Labor index of British retail prices in pounds sterling, 1952-93. All are converted to a common base of 1451-75=100. Sources include D.L. Farmer, "Some Livestock Price Movements in Thirteenth Century England," *Economic History Review*, 2d ser., 22 (1969) 15; E. H. Phelps-Brown and Sheila Hopkins, "Seven Centuries of the Prices of Consumables, Compared with Builders' Wage-Rates," *Economica* 23 (1956) 297-314; B. R. Mitchell and Phyllis Deane, *Abstract of British Historical Statistics* (Cambridge, 1968) 740-41; *idem, Second Abstract of British Historical Statistics* (Cambridge, 1971); B. R. Mitchell, *International Historical Statistics: Europe, 1750-1988* (New York, 1992); *Annual Abstract of Statistics* (London, 1972-1994).

has continued since, with a short intermission in some nations during the 1920s and early 1930s. It is the price-revolution of the twentieth century.

These great waves were punctuated by periods of a different nature—when prices fell a little, then found an equilibrium and fluctuated on a fixed plane. One such era, which might be called the equilibrium of the twelfth century, coincided with the climax of medieval civilization. Another could be named the equilibrium of the Renaissance (ca. 1400–1480). A third may be thought of as the equilibrium of the Enlightenment (1660–1730). The fourth might be remembered as the Victorian equilibrium, for it coincided with the life of Queen Victoria herself. All of these periods of equilibrium were marked by fluctuations of high complexity. None experienced long-term price-inflation.

This alternating rhythm of price-revolutions and price-equilibria was discovered as early as the eighteenth century. It was studied during the 1930s by French economist François Simiand, by Italian scholar Jenny Griziotti-Kretschmann, and by German agrarian historian Wilhelm Abel.[3]

Abel's work is still in print after fifty years, and strong in its empiricism. His purpose was different from that of other scholars. Phelps-Brown and Hopkins had wanted to know about the movement of monetized wages and prices. Abel was more interested in agricultural conditions. He studied the price of grain alone, and converted it to kilograms of pure silver, rather than measuring a market-basket of "consumables" in monetary units.

Abel found a wave-pattern that was similar in timing to the Phelps-Brown-Hopkins series, but different in its trend. His revolutions in price of grain rose more steeply than did consumables in general, and were followed by periods of sharp decline rather than by price-equilibrium. Even so, the same long waves appear in both series. They have been documented in many studies, and are the most robust pattern of secular change in the history of prices—more so than Kondratieff cycles or any other cyclical rhythm, which must be derived by "detrending" the data.

This wave-pattern is familiar to European scholars, but it is not well known in the English-speaking world. The reason why makes a story in its own right, and one that appears in an appendix to this work. Suffice to say that when French historian Fernand Braudel mentioned early modern wave-movements in a history of capitalism, American reviewers responded with expressions of surprise, bewilderment, and outright disbelief.

Most historians in the United States are familiar only with one great wave, the price-revolution of the sixteenth century. Its successor, the inflation of the eighteenth century, has been much discussed by French scholars in relation to the revolution of 1789, but it is little known in America or Britain where its effects were less dramatic. The medieval price-revolution is even more obscure, because it is distant

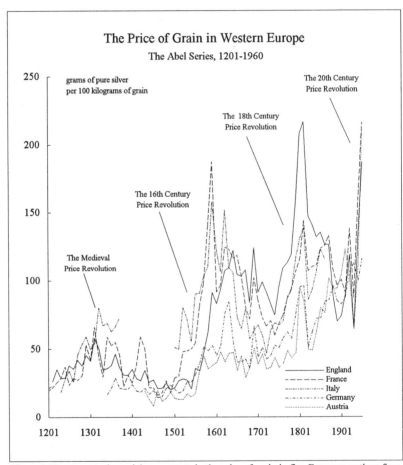

Figure 0.02 represents decennial movements in the price of grain in five European nations from 1201 to 1960. It includes wheat in England, France, and Italy; and rye in Austria and Germany. Prices are decennial means, converted to silver equivalents (grams of pure silver per 100 kilograms of grain). The source is Wilhelm Abel, *Agrarkrisen und Agrarkonjunktur: Eine Geschichte der Land und Ernährungswirtchaft Mitteleuropas seit dem höhen Mittelalter* (1935; Hamburg and Berlin, 1966), appendix. The raw data are from price lists of Rogers, d' Avenel, Barolini, Parenti, Magaldi, and Fabris, listed in the bibliography.

from our time and its sources are inaccessible. The price-revolution of the twentieth century is misunderstood for opposite reasons: the data are overwhelming, and the event is so close to us that we have trouble thinking of it in historical terms.[4]

Economists in the United States also have little memory of these historical events, except for the price-revolution of the sixteenth century, which is distantly remembered as proving the truth of the axiom that inflation is "always and everywhere primarily a monetary phenomenon," as the American economist Alan S. Blinder wrote in another context. Otherwise, the author has found that price-revolutions in general are (with some exceptions) entirely unknown to most economists, political leaders, social planners, business executives, and individual investors, even as they struggle to deal with one price-revolution in particular.[5]

This collective amnesia is partly the consequence of an attitude widely shared among decision-makers in America, that history is more or less irrelevant to the urgent problems before them. An exception shows the power of this rule. In 1980, American economist Lester Thurow advised his colleagues that they could not understand the inflationary surges of that era without entering the distant realm that he quaintly called "the long ago." By "the long ago," he meant the year 1965.[6]

There are signs that these attitudes may be changing. So turbulent and unpredictable have been the events of the late twentieth century, that even the most atemporal minds have begun to realize that history is happening to them. Academic interest in this subject also has a strong wave-like rhythm of its own. The discipline of price history, which flourished during the 1930s, is now in the early stages of revival.

The purpose of this inquiry is to stimulate growing interest in this subject, by studying each price-revolution in turn, and then by comparing one with another. We shall describe the four great waves in their most important aspects: first, their timing, magnitude, rhythm, volatility, and the sequence of secular change in price levels; second, the pattern of price relatives for different types of commodities; third, the movement of real wages; fourth, the pattern of change in rent and interest. The same questions will be asked about periods of price equilibrium, one of which may be approaching.[7]

The second task is to explore the question of cause. Braudel himself believed that these great waves were the strongest secular pattern in modern economic history, but he thought that the task of explaining them was the "most neglected" problem in historiography, and "impossible" to solve.

Even so, price historians in Europe have suggested seven causal explanations, which might be called the monetarist, Malthusian, Marxist, neoclassical, agrarian, environmental, and historicist models. Monetarists understand movements in the "general price level" as changes in the value of money, caused mainly by variations in its quantity and velocity. Malthusians think of price movements in a different way as a material representation of the changing value of commodities that money might buy, caused primarily by imbalances between demographic and economic growth. Marxists think that price movements represent the changing terms of transactions within social systems, mainly between social classes. Neoclassical models perceive prices as indicators of change in the flow of supply and demand, and explain price-revolutions as the result of imbalances in market-relations, caused by various demand-centered or supply-side events, or by changes in the structures of market-conditions themselves. Agrarian approaches link prices mainly to harvest conditions. Environmental models understand price-movements as ecological indicators which register imbalances between human activity and its natural environment. Historicists explain things in their particulars, and think of each price-revolution as a unique event with its own *ad hoc* explanation.

Each of these approaches has taught us something useful about their common subject. All are flourishing today. The differences between them rise in large part from their assumptions about what prices are, and what the world is made of. They are theoretical constructions, but all of them also make strong empirical claims that can be tested against historical evidence. This inquiry will attempt to frame another model that might combine their strengths and correct their weaknesses.

The third assignment is consider the consequences of price-movements, or more precisely the consequences of movements that prices represent. These consequences have been profound, and never more so than in our own time. The darkest tendencies of our troubled era—the growth of violence and drug use and family disruption which many people identify as the most urgent social problems of our age—are closely connected to price movements (or, again, the movements that prices represent). Most students of these social problems are entirely unaware of these linkages, which bring a new perspective to an understanding of the causes of our present discontents.

Some of the brightest moments in modern history have also been linked to the rhythm of material events. This was so for the renaissance of the twelfth century, the renaissance of the fifteenth century, the age of the enlightenment, and the Victorian era.

ʲ⍥ A Caveat for the Critical Reader

Before we begin to study these relationships, a caveat is necessary. It should be understood clearly that the movements we are studying are waves—not cycles. To repeat: not cycles, but waves.

Cyclical rhythms are fixed and regular. Their periods are highly predictable. Great waves are more variable and less predictable. They differ in duration, magnitude, velocity, and momentum. One great price-wave lasted less than ninety years; another continued more than 180 years. The irregularities in individual price-movements make them no more (or less) predictable than individual waves in the sea.[8]

Even so, all great waves had important qualities in common. They all shared the same wave-structure. They tended to have the same sequence of development, the same pattern of price-relatives, similar movements of wages, rent, interest-rates; and the same dangerous volatility in later stages. All major price revolutions in modern history began in periods of prosperity. Each ended in shattering world-crises and were followed by periods of recovery and comparative equilibrium.

These great waves also differ from cycles in their epistemic status. We know about them in different ways. Cycles must be teased from the data, commonly by statistical inferences in which the evidence is "filtered" and "detrended" by various techniques. The great waves are different in that respect. They appear on the surface of the evidence. To observe them no filtering or detrending of the data is required. Each great wave is the major price-trend in its own era. No theoretical models or statistical massages are needed to summon them from recalcitrant sources. To discover these secular trends in the data, it is necessary to do something that is very simple, and yet immensely difficult for many academic scholars. One must learn to look the evidence in the face, without fixed ideological, theoretical or epistemological preconceptions. We are sometimes told that this is impossible. So it is—for some people.[9]

This book is written mainly for general readers who share the author's interest in understanding patterns of historical change for their own sake. It also has a message for practical business leaders, journalists, investors, and ordinary citizens. Today, we are living in the late stages of the price revolution of the twentieth century. Disaster does not necessarily lie ahead for us. This book does not predict the apocalypse. It does not attempt to tell the future. To the contrary, it finds that uncertainty about the future is an inexorable fact of our condition.

But it also finds evidence that what happens in the future is contingent on our choices in the present, which derive from our memory of the past. The result of this inquiry strongly suggests that when we make our economic choices, we would do well to improve our powers of recall, and to remember some very hard-won lessons of historical experience. If our purpose is to master the dangerous dynamics of our contemporary world, or merely to survive them, then we must remember the past—even the distant past. We must also learn to think of the present and future as part of an historical continuum.

Many readers who are literate in economics will remember the special meaning of the Keynesian dictum that in the long run we are all dead. The events of the twentieth century should have taught us that this idea, in its most common application, is very much mistaken. American economist Herbert Stein, after a term of service in Washington, wrote ruefully in 1979, ''we woke up to discover that we were living in the long run, and were suffering for our failure to look after it.''[10]

To that end, this history begins more than seven centuries ago, on a market day in a medieval cathedral-town. The date was September 8, 1224. The place was Chartres.

THE FIRST WAVE
≈ The Medieval Price Revolution, 1180–1350

Greet prees at market maketh deere ware.
—Chaucer's wife of Bath

CHARTRES, September 8, 1224, the festival of the Virgin's Birth. For more than a week, the country roads to this cathedral town were clogged with crowds of pilgrims. Some were pious peasants who wished to thank the Virgin for hearing their prayers. Others were worldly merchants who came to buy and sell at the great market-fair called the Septembresce.

Their journey brought them to the golden plain of Beauce, prosperous wheat country in the heart of France. In early September, the rolling fields were bright with ripening grain, and the last scarlet poppies of the summer were still in bloom beside the dusty roads. In the distance, footsore travellers could see their destination long before they reached it. The beautiful blue silhouette of Chartres Cathedral soared high above the horizon, and was visible for many miles across the open countryside.

The great building that loomed before them, and still stands today, was the seventh cathedral of Chartres. The fate of the other six made a catalogue of medieval miseries. The first had been wrecked by the Duke of Aquitania in 743, and the second had been ruined by the Vikings in 843. The third cathedral had been destroyed in 962, and the fourth had been pulled down in 1020. The fifth and sixth had burned in 1134 and 1194.

After each of these catastrophes, the people of Chartres acted quickly to rebuild a structure that was vital to their faith and fortunes. In 1134 and again in 1194, they unhitched animals from their carts and placed themselves in the traces to haul stone for the new cathedral. That act of piety was remembered as the Cult of the Carts.

"At Chartres," one chronicler wrote, "men began with their own shoulders to drag wagons loaded with stone, wood, grain and other materials to the workshop of the church, whose towers were then rising . . . one might observe women as well as men dragging [carts] through deep swamps on their knees, beating themselves with whips." People of every rank joined in the Cult of the Carts. "Whoever heard in all the generations past," another chronicler wrote, "that kings, princes, mighty men of the world puffed up with honors and riches, men and women of noble birth, should bind a bridle upon their proud and swollen necks and submit themselves to wagons."[1]

The new cathedral that they built at Chartres was one of Christendom's holiest shrines. Its sanctuary held the tunic that the Virgin Mary was thought to have worn when Jesus was born. Many pilgrims purchased replicas of this garment. Others bought sacred shirts called *chemisettes* which soldiers wore beneath their armor and pregnant women draped over their swollen bellies. During the festival of the Virgin's birth, the sale of these sacred articles brought a large income to the people of Chartres.

In the year 1224, this cathedral town was the capital of Europe's richest province—an area of 13,000 square miles and a thousand churches. It was called the "great diocese" even in Rome. The town had become a center of trade and industry, specially renowned for textiles, weapons, and leather goods.

The hub of this thriving economy was the Cathedral itself. During the festival, much buying and selling took place within the church. Food and firewood were sold inside the south door. Manufactured goods were available at the north door, where buyers and sellers haggled over prices. The side aisles of the nave became a labor-exchange, where artisans gathered in anxious circles around employers. The crypt was given over to the wine merchants. The south cloister was opened to the stalls of the money-changers. So lucrative were the rents paid by these much-hated men that a lively competition developed for their business between the Cathedral's canons and deans, who controlled different parts of the building. The great cathedral was both a religious and an economic institution.[2]

At the same time it was vital to its community in another way. Every great work of architecture is a cultural symbol. Chartres was a case in point. The beautiful cathedral perfectly symbolized an era that

Charles Homer Haskins called the Renaissance of the twelfth century.[3] This was the period when medieval civilization reached its highest level of cultural achievement. In the twelfth century, Romanesque architecture attained its peak of perfection. At the same time, the new Gothic style appeared full blown in the cathedrals of Paris (1163) and Canterbury (1175), as well as Chartres itself (1194). The people of France constructed more than eighty new cathedrals, 500 abbeys and 10,000 parish churches during this era—a building program that consumed more stone than the pyramids of Egypt, and more labor than the roads of Rome.[4]

Great universities were founded at Paris, Oxford, Bologna and Salerno. Rapid progress was made in the revival of classical learning. Immortal works of Europe literature were recorded in the vernacular— *Le Cid* in Spain, the *Nibelungenlied* in Germany, the *Chansons de Geste* in France, and the *Arthurian Legends* in Britain.

The twelfth century was also an epoch of high importance in political history. It was an era of great kings. Henry II of England (1154–89), Frederick Barbarossa of Germany (1152–90), Philip Augustus of France (1180–1223), and Alfonso II of Castile (1126–57) all claimed the title of Emperor, and enlarged their power and dominions. The twelfth century was also the great age of feudalism, when complex rules of chivalry and heraldry and primogeniture were elaborately codified. It was a time when new charters were granted to towns, gilds, and corporations. The twelfth century in Europe was marked by the simultaneous development of monarchy, aristocracy and popular government in open and pluralistic systems that were unique to the Western world. Power was broadly distributed among kings, clergy, nobles and commons.

The twelfth century was an age of European expansion. The last major invasions by Magyars, Saracens, and Moslems had come to an end by the year 1050. Thereafter, the population of Europe slowly began to increase. It did so in northern Italy and southern France as early as the year 1000. In Spain, historians still speak of the great *repoblación* that commenced about 1150.

Europeans began to move outward. The first crusade began in 1096, and was followed by many others in the 12th century. This also was the time of the *Drang nach Osten*—the movement by Teutonic Knights into eastern Europe. It was the age of the great Scandinavian migrations, west from Norway to North America, and east from Sweden to Russia.

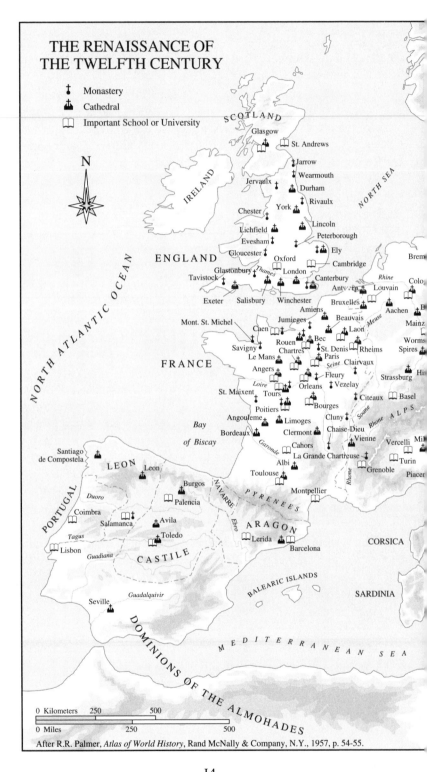

THE RENAISSANCE OF
THE TWELFTH CENTURY

✝ Monastery

⛪ Cathedral

📖 Important School or University

SCOTLAND

Glasgow

St. Andrews

N

IRELAND

Jarrow
Wearmouth
Jervaulx
Durham
Rivaulx
Chester
York
Lincoln
Lichfield
Peterborough
Evesham
Ely
Gloucester
ENGLAND
Oxford
Cambridge
Brem
Glastonbury
Thames
London
Tavistock
Canterbury
Rhine
Colo
Antwerp
Louvain
Exeter
Salisbury
Winchester
Bruxelles
Aachen
B
Amiens
Mont. St. Michel
Jumieges
Beauvais
Meuse
Mainz
Caen
Laon
Rouen
Bec
Worms
Savigny
Chartres
St. Denis
Rheims
Spires
Le Mans
Paris
FRANCE
Angers
Seine
Clairvaux
Strassburg
Hi
Fleury
Loire
Orleans
Vezelay
St. Maixent
Tours
Citeaux
Basel
Poitiers
Bourges
Angouleme
Cluny
Limoges
Bay
Chaise-Dieu
A L P S
Bordeaux
Clermont
Vienne
Vercelli
Mi
of Biscay
Garonne
Cahors
La Grande Chartreuse
Turin
Santiago
Albi
Grenoble
Piacer
de Compostela
LEON
Leon
Toulouse
PORTUGAL
Duoro
Burgos
Montpellier
Coimbra
Palencia
PYRENEES
Salamanca
Avila
ARAGON
Tagus
Toledo
Lerida
CORSICA
Lisbon
Guadiana
CASTILE
Barcelona

NORTH SEA

Rhone

Rhone

Soane

Ebro

BALEARIC ISLANDS

SARDINIA

NORTH ATLANTIC OCEAN

Seville

Guadalquivir

D
O
M
I
N
I
O
N
S

O
F

T
H
E

A
L
M
O
H
A
D
E
S

MEDITERRANEAN SEA

0 Kilometers 250 500

0 Miles 250 500

After R.R. Palmer, *Atlas of World History*, Rand McNally & Company, N.Y., 1957, p. 54-55.

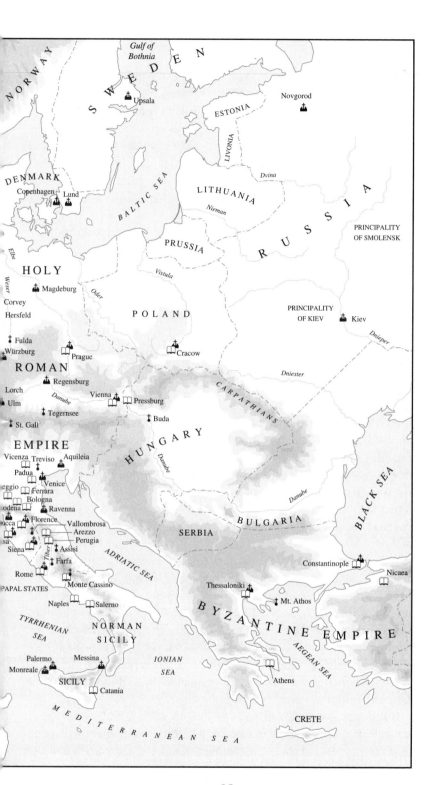

All of these movements rose from an expanding demographic base. Families, cities, markets, gilds, and fairs multiplied everywhere in Europe. Centers of commerce and industry grew at a great rate. As late as the year 1100, Paris had been a small settlement, largely confined for its own security to an island in the Seine. By 1215 it had become a city of perhaps 50,000 souls. The economy of medieval Europe rapidly developed from a comparatively primitive system of barter exchange toward a more complex system of market relationships.

The growth of population and the increase of wealth were roughly in equilibrium during the twelfth century. Prices remained comparatively stable throughout this period. The only major economic problem was the so-called "money-famine" of the eleventh and twelfth centuries—an event that would occur in most eras of price equilibrium throughout modern history. The growth of population and prosperity had created demand for a larger circulating medium. With precious metals in short supply, the people of Europe began to use what historian David Herlihy calls "substitute money"—not barter or commodity money, but liquid assets of high value called *mobilia,* such as silver jewelry, furs, fine textiles and even books.[5]

By the year 1100, the hunger for specie was so great that the canons of Pistoia's St. Zeno Cathedral melted down their great crucifix and used it for money. German princes sold their imperial seals. English nobles exchanged their silver sword mounts, and French bishops converted their golden chalices into cash. The theologian Fulbert of Chartres justified these practices with the casuistry that it was better to sell sacred vessels to Christians than to pawn them into the hands of Jews.[6]

This money-famine was only a hint of economic trouble in a period of high prosperity throughout Europe. The architecture of Chartres Cathedral perfectly captured the soaring optimism of its age. The geometry of its great rose windows symbolized a dynamic equilibrium that had appeared in the economy of Europe. The solid strength of the cathedral building embodied a union of social order and spiritual harmony. The bustle of commerce within its walls represented the prosperity that seemed to have become a permanent part of western culture in the early thirteenth century.

But it was not to be. Ironically, the era when Chartres was built was a time of a deep change in European history—a moment when one change regime yielded silently to another. Even as the great vault of the

Cathedral was completed in the year 1224, dangerous stresses were beginning to develop within the structure of medieval civilization.

A symptom of trouble, and also in part its cause, was a movement that might called the medieval price revolution. This was a long wave of rising prices that began late in the twelfth century, and continued to the middle of the fourteenth century.

In its earliest stage, the new trend was nearly imperceptible. It first appeared as a minor price-flutter in medieval market-fairs such as the Septembresce. By the festival of 1224, the pilgrims of Chartres would have noticed that prices were a little higher, especially for firewood and food that was for sale inside the south door. Manufactured goods at the north door were also up a little, but not as much as food and fuel. The money-changers were getting more for their services, and the laborers who anxiously sought employment in the nave would have noticed that wages were beginning to lag behind the rising cost of living.

All of these changes were still of minor magnitude in the year 1224. The price-revolution had barely begun. But once underway, it would continue for more than a century. Many years later it would end in a catastrophe so complete that scarcely anything of medieval civilization survives today except the beautiful blue silhouette of Chartres Cathedral, which still soars triumphantly above the scarlet poppies on the golden plain of Beauce.

The Medieval Price Revolution Begins, circa 1180–1230

Many years ago, the brilliant British polymath William Beveridge hypothesized that there had been a "price-revolution of the middle ages." That idea was at first ignored or rejected by medieval historians, who regarded its author as a trespasser on their turf.[7]

Trespasser or not, Lord Beveridge was correct in his belief. Toward the end of the twelfth century, prices began to rise throughout medieval Europe in a new trend that was destined to continue for more than a century. In England where evidence is most abundant, the inflection-point of this new trend appears to have come about the year 1180.[8]

By the measure of modern movements, the medieval price-revolution advanced at a very slow pace. Economic historian Michael Postan estimates that "the secular rise of prices between say 1225 and 1345 proceeded at a rate not higher than 0.5 per cent per annum."[9]

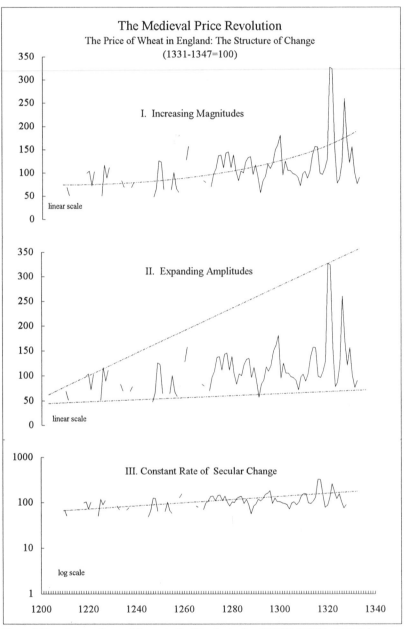

The Medieval Price Revolution
The Price of Wheat in England: The Structure of Change
(1331-1347=100)

I. Increasing Magnitudes

linear scale

II. Expanding Amplitudes

linear scale

III. Constant Rate of Secular Change

log scale

Figure 1.02 analyzes patterns of change in English wheat prices (1330/1-1346/7 =100). Prices are for harvest years (e.g., 1347 = Michaelmas, Sept. 29, 1346, to Michaelmas, Sept. 29, 1347). Data are from a price series by D. L. Farmer in H. E. Hallam, ed., *The Agrarian History of England and Wales, vol. 2, 1042-1350* (Cambridge, 1988), 779-91. Trends are fitted with an Excel 5.0 program.

Even so, this great inflation of the medieval era was great because
it was general throughout the Western world, and because it continued
for a very long time. It happened in England, France, Italy, Germany,
Iberia, and every other part of Europe where prices have been studied.[10] Throughout that broad region, its impact was not perfectly uniform. The pace of inflation was comparatively rapid in the north of
Italy, moderate in England and France, and slowest in eastern and
northern Europe; but no part of the Western world is known to have
escaped it.[11]

Why did medieval prices go up? Some historians find the cause in
an expansion of the money supply; others, in the growth of population.
Both factors were involved, but population appears to have been the
prime mover. Before 1150, as we have seen, the population of Europe
had been slowly increasing. After 1170, its rate of gain accelerated. In
Picardy, the rural population doubled during the last quarter of the

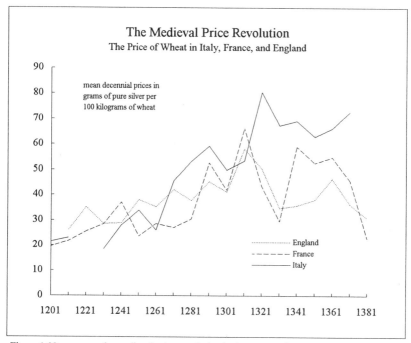

Figure 1.03 compares the medieval price revolution in three parts of Europe, where trends were
much the same in the thirteenth century, but different in the play of contingent events during the
crisis of the fourteenth century. These data were compiled by Wilhelm Abel from price series of
Rogers (England); d'Avenel (France); Bartolini, Fabris, Magaldi and Parenti (Italy). The source
is Abel, *Agrarkrisen und Agrarkonjunktur*, appendix.

twelfth century (1175–1200), and kept growing rapidly for three generations thereafter. Similar trends appeared in England, France and Germany.[12]

   During the thirteenth century, large parts of rural Europe became
more densely settled than they would ever be again until the twentieth
century. One study of the Lincoln fens on the east coast of England
finds that the number of inhabitants reached a level in 1287 that would
not be exceeded until 1950. Similar patterns have been discovered in
the English counties of Devonshire, Gloucestershire, Leicestershire,
Cambridgeshire, Warwickshire and Norfolk.[13]

   The cause of medieval population-growth was mainly an increase
in fertility, not a decline in mortality. After a long period of comparative stability and growing prosperity, women throughout Europe married at earlier ages and decided to have more children. The result was a
medieval baby boom that began in the twelfth century and continued
for many years.[14]

   This medieval baby boom had important economic consequences.
It changed the age-structure of the population. As long as it continued,
a larger proportion were dependent children. Fewer were mature adults
in the prime of their productive years. This happened at the same time
that people needed more food, fuel, houses and land. Demand for life's

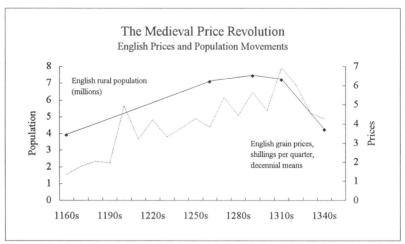

Figure 1.04 finds a strong association between prices and population growth in medieval
England. The sources for population are point estimates by H. E. Hallam (1983) and E. Miller
(1991); and for grain prices a series by D. L. Farmer, all in *The Agrarian History of England
and Wales*, II, 537; III, 4-5.

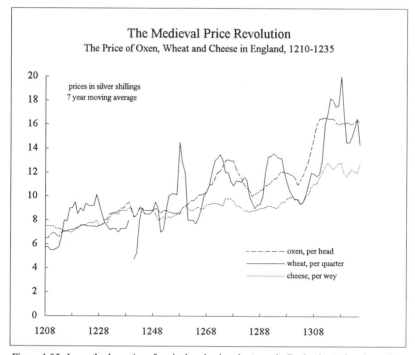

The Medieval Price Revolution
The Price of Oxen, Wheat and Cheese in England, 1210-1235

prices in silver shillings
7 year moving average

----- oxen, per head
——— wheat, per quarter
·········· cheese, per wey

Figure 1.05 shows the long rise of agricultural prices in Angevin England. As in other price revolutions, the price of staple foodstuffs and energy led the advance, and were also the most volatile. The source is D. L. Farmer, "Some Livestock Price Movements in Thirteenth Century England," *Economic History Review* 2d ser., 22 (1969) 15.

necessities expanded more rapidly than supply could increase. Inexorably, prices went up.[15]

Not all prices increased at the same rate. The most rapid rises appeared in the price of energy, food, shelter and raw materials— items most heavily in demand during a period of population growth, and least elastic in their supply.[16] Specially striking was the price of energy. In England from 1261 to 1320, the price of firewood and charcoal rose faster and farther than that of any other commodity. The cause was not hard to find. During the late twelfth and thirteenth centuries, Europe rapidly cut down its forests, consumed its timber, and burned its brushwood for fuel. Timber and charcoal began to be imported over increasing distances, and the great coal fields of England, Belgium and France began to be exploited on a large scale during this period. London suffered severely from smoke pollution in the thirteenth century.[17]

Close behind the soaring cost of energy came price-rises for food-

stuffs of various kinds—particularly for grain, meat, and dairy products that were the staples of life in medieval Europe. This trend was
evident everywhere in the Western world, where a grain market was
well established by the early thirteenth century.[18]

By contrast with energy and food, the price of finished manufactures such as cloth and nails increased comparatively little—less than
the cost of raw materials such as wool and iron. The inflation of
industrial prices was moderate, because the supply of manufactured
goods could be expanded more easily to meet rising demand.

A case in point was the cost of armor. This, the leading "consumer durable" in medieval Europe, was mainly designed to make a
more durable consumer. Iron skullcaps called coifs were worn not
merely by soldiers but also by traveling merchants who lived in a world
where consumer complaints were forcefully expressed. The price of
iron coifs and body armor in the thirteenth century behaved very much
like that of washing machines and refrigerators in the twentieth century. It rose in nominal terms, but fell in relation to other commodities
for which supply was less elastic.[19]

Altogether, historian Michael Postan observes that "movements
of agricultural and industrial prices did not synchronize" with one

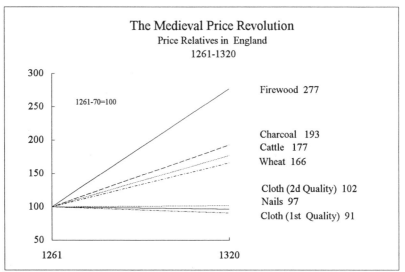

Figure 1.06 represents the relative movement of commodity prices in England from 1261-70 to
1311-20. As in most price revolutions, the cost of energy and food rose most rapidly.
Manufactured goods lagged behind. Prices are decennial means, computed from raw data in J.
E. Thorold Rogers, *A History of Agriculture and Prices in England,* I, 1259-1400.

another during the medieval price-revolution. This distinctive pattern of price-relatives was typical of a demand-inflation. It appeared in every great wave without exception.[20]

This population-driven inflation was reinforced by material pressures of many other kinds. An economic consequence of population-growth was an expansion of trade. In England, the number of weekly markets licensed by the Crown grew at an accelerating rate from 1180 to 1274. These medieval markets were mainly places for the local exchange of firewood, grain, livestock, bread, ale, cloth and "chapman's wares" such as coal, salt and fish.[21]

The growth of commerce stimulated industrial development, at such a pace that medieval historian Jean Gimpel speaks of an "industrial revolution of the thirteenth century." Dye works, fulling mills and iron works multiplied throughout Europe. Some operated on such a scale that the effects of environmental pollution by medieval industries still scar the landscape of Europe seven centuries later.[22]

The growth of commerce and industry had major consequences for monetary systems. Expanding markets increased the velocity of money in circulation. This added a monetary inflation to a demand inflation, and caused prices to keep on rising, once the increase had begun.

♔ Cultural Responses to the Medieval Price Revolution

In the mid-thirteenth century, the medieval price-revolution entered a new stage. Inflation rose beyond the limits of previous price fluctuations. As it did so, people began to think about it in a different way—not as a sequence of fluctuations, but as a secular trend. Many years ago, a German scholar discovered that during the middle decades of the thirteenth century (*circa* 1230–60), medieval writers changed their language of economic description. When they referred to rising grain prices, they shifted their Latin terms from *fames* to *caristia*. *Fames* meant famine, hunger, short harvests. *Caristia* (from the adjective *carus,* costly, dear) meant high prices in general and the high cost of living.[23]

This change of terms from *fames* to *caristia* meant that the increase in the price of food was no longer perceived to be mainly a matter of fluctuations in the size of the harvest. It was now recognized as a general inflation. People had begun to awaken to the fact that the rising cost of living was not a short-run disturbance but a long-term movement.

This discovery set in motion a series of cultural responses that caused prices to rise higher. One of the most important of these inflationary responses was an expansion of the money supply. Silver was the most common coin in commercial exchanges within Europe during the thirteenth century. Gold tended to become the leading currency in international trade.[24]

The supply of these precious metals was remarkably small in the medieval West. Scholars have estimated that as late as the year 1500, all the gold in Europe would have fit within a two-meter cube (that is, eight cubic meters in all).[25] The supply of silver was much larger, but still very small by modern standards. As late as 1200, England's silver stock totaled only about 300 tons, and would have fit into a fourteen-meter cube. Altogether, it amounted to only a few ounces of sterling for every man, woman and child in the realm.[26]

At the same time, there were also heavy losses of silver from Europe. France's unfortunate King Louis IX (1214–70) was captured on a crusade in the year 1250. His royal ransom (together with expenses of the crusade itself) cost his nation 240 tons of silver—a heavy burden on a medieval economy.[27]

During the thirteenth century, a major effort was made to expand the supply of silver in Europe. Old mines opened again in Hungary and the Harz Mountains. New mines were brought into operation. Output was increased by new technologies.[28] By the end of the thirteenth century, production may have risen as high as fifty tons a year.[29] Much of this metal was turned into currency. Mints throughout Europe coined money on demand; merchants commonly appeared with a supply of silver, and asked to have it converted into coin, which was done for a fee.[30]

Silver stocks expanded throughout Europe in the thirteenth century. One study finds that silver coins minted in England rose from 200,000 pounds in the period 1210–18, to more than 500,000 in the 1240s, and above 1,000,000 pounds in the 1280s. As the quantity of money increased, its value declined. The effect was to drive prices higher.[31]

Gold, which had drained away from Europe during the early Middle Ages, now began to flow in again. Some of it was stolen by Venetian pirates, Teutonic knights and French crusaders. More was gained in trade, and large quantities of bullion were imported from the mines of Africa. In the mid-thirteenth century, the Italian city-states became the first in the West to mint gold coin since the fall of Rome. Genoa may have been the earliest trading town to do so, as early as 1249. The people of Florence followed with gold florins in 1252. Venice began to issue gold ducats in 1284. The ducat became renowned for its stability, by keeping its gold content unchanged for more than five hundred years, from 1284 to the fall of the Venetian republic in 1797. The quantity of gold and silver in circulation, and probably their velocity as well, increased during the late thirteenth century, and added to inflationary pressures.[32]

Despite these increases, historian Carlo Cipolla observes, "the supply of precious metals proved to be relatively inelastic throughout the whole period, and the growth of the demand for silver for monetary purposes exceeded the supply." To solve this problem, a variety of other monetary expedients were adopted. Commodities were used as money in addition to gold and silver. Pepper, for example, became a form of currency in the seaport cities of southern Europe. New credit instruments such as contracts of exchange and bank transfers expanded rapidly.[33]

Metal coins were also systematically debased. In Italy and France particularly, mint-masters reduced the content of silver in their coins, and increased the quantity of base metal. Individuals acted in other ways to diminish the value of money that passed through their hands. Coins were clipped, filed, scraped, and washed despite ferocious penalties. Cipolla finds evidence that debasements "became more rapid between the middle of the thirteenth century and the fourteenth century."[34]

The continuing rise in commodity prices during the later stages of the price-revolution was linked to these monetary factors. Deliberate increases in the quantity of precious metal, debasements of various kinds, and the development of other instruments of exchange all sent prices higher. But the money supply was not a *deus ex machina* that descended inexorably upon the economy. It was an artifact of human will and purpose. People responded to the discovery of *caristia* by deliberately expanding the quantity of money. In cultural terms their actions helped individuals and institutions to cope with high prices, but had the collective effect of driving prices higher. The price-revolution thus became a self-reinforcing process. High prices increased demand for money. When the demand was met by increased supplies of money, and growing velocity, prices were driven higher.

Figure 1.07 explores the impact of money on prices. It finds an association in movements around the central tendency. Recoinages lowered prices; debasements inflated them. The source is D. L. Farmer, "Some Livestock Price Movements in Thirteenth-Century England," *Economic History Review*, 2d ser., 22 (1969) 21.

Other responses to rising prices appeared in the movement of wages, rents and interest. In the early stages of the great wave, wages had kept pace with prices, and during some decades even increased more rapidly. But as inflation continued in the mid-thirteenth century, money wages began to lag behind. As a consequence real wages fell, slowly at first, then with growing momentum. By the late thirteenth and early fourteenth centuries real wages were dropping at a rapid rate. In 1320 real wages in western Europe were 25 to 40 percent lower than they had been a century before.[35]

At the same time that real wages fell, rents and interest rose sharply. Returns to landowners generally kept pace with inflation and even exceeded it. The old notion that feudal and manorial lords were

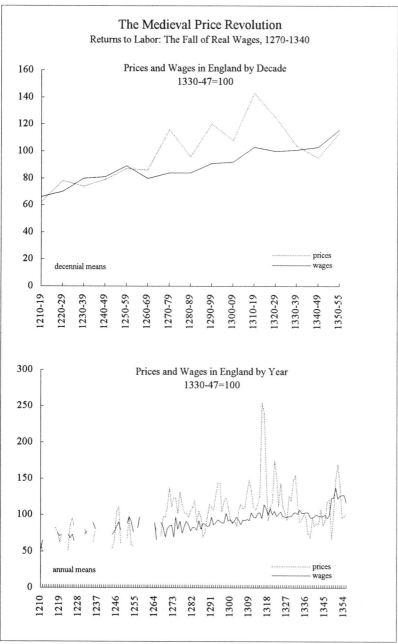

The Medieval Price Revolution
Returns to Labor: The Fall of Real Wages, 1270-1340

Prices and Wages in England by Decade
1330-47=100

decennial means

.... prices
——— wages

Prices and Wages in England by Year
1330-47=100

annual means

.... prices
——— wages

Figure 1.08 finds that returns to labor kept up with the rising cost of living in the beginning of the medieval price revolution, but lagged behind in the later stages (circa 1265-1330). The data are in D. L. Farmer, "Prices and Wages," in H. E. Hallam, ed., *The Agrarian History of England and Wales, Volume II, 1042-1350* (Cambridge, 1988) 777.

hard pressed by falling real income during price-revolutions has been contradicted by much research. In many parts of Europe, rents and land values increased even more rapidly than the price of energy and food. The pioneering French price historian Georges d'Avenel may have been the first to discover that rents reached very high levels during the late thirteenth century—the "highest recorded levels in all of the Middle Ages." Subsequent research has solidly confirmed d'Avenel's findings. The rate of increase in rent appears to have been greater than 2 percent a year—twice the inflation of grain prices in the later stages of the price-revolution.[36]

Manorial lords had many ways of protecting their income against inflation. They could impose new fines and feudal dues upon the peasantry, and often did so. They also possessed monopolies of milling—in effect, owning the water and even the wind in their territories. The chronicle of Jocelin de Brakelond tells of a free spirit named Herbert the Dean who built himself a mill, and defended it with an argument that "free benefit of the wind ought not to be denied to any man." His

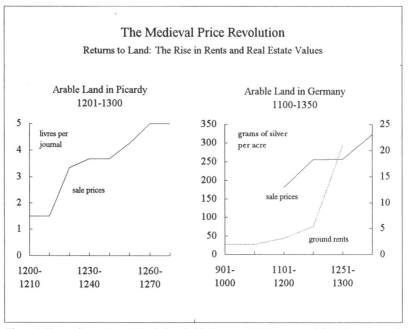

The Medieval Price Revolution
Returns to Land: The Rise in Rents and Real Estate Values

Arable Land in Picardy
1201-1300

Arable Land in Germany
1100-1350

Figure 1.09 examines returns to landed capital in France and Germany, and finds that rents and real estate values rose more rapidly than wages and the general price level. Sources include Robert Fossier, *La terre et les hommes en Picardie,* 1:581; Karl Lamprecht, *Deutsches Wirtschaftsleben im Mittelalter* (Leipzig, 1886) 2:614-615.

lord was reduced to paroxysms of fury, and swore that "by God's face I will never eat bread till that building be thrown down." Conflicts of this sort commonly ended in the triumph of the lord.[37]

In the late thirteenth century, manorial lords aggressively expanded their economic privileges. At St. Albans, just north of London, the Abbey constructed its own grist and fulling mills, and forbade the inhabitants to take their grain and cloth anywhere else or even to process them in their homes. The result was an insurrection in 1274. When Queen Eleanor passed through St. Albans, she was met by a vast throng of weeping women, reaching out their hands in supplication and crying "Domina, misere nobis." The Queen tried to help them, but the Abbot of St. Albans took his case to the King's court and won. Strife continued at St. Albans for many years, while the abbots waxed fatter and the peasants grew thinner. Similar scenes were enacted throughout Europe.[38]

At the same time, rates of interest also rose very high. In the Italian city states, interest charged in actual transactions increased from 12 percent a year before 1230, to 20 percent later in the century. This rise was greater than the average increase of commodity prices. Real interest rose at a time when real wages were falling.[39]

Men of wealth were able to profit by the price-revolution in many ways. Powerful Italian merchants, for example, obtained laws that allowed them to insist on being paid in gold florins or ducats which held their value, but permitted them to pay wages and taxes in silver coins which were much debased. As a consequence, rich merchants grew richer, and the poor sank deeper into misery and degradation.[40]

This growing gap between returns to labor and capital was typical of price-revolutions in modern history. So also was its social result: a rapid growth of inequality that appeared in the later stages of every long inflation. A case in point was the commune of Santa Maria Impruneta, six miles south of Florence in the hills of Tuscany. In 1307, the richest tenth of Impruneta's families held about 33 percent of its wealth. By 1427, their holdings had increased to 50 percent. At the same time the poor sank deeper into distress. The wealth of the bottom half of the population sharnk from 21 percent to 6 percent. The rich were growing richer. At the same time, much evidence survives of the rapid growth of rural poverty and homelessness during the late thirteenth and fourteenth centuries.[41]

Yet another set of cultural responses to inflation created disparities of a different kind: fiscal imbalances between public income and expenditures. Governments fell deep in debt during the middle and later

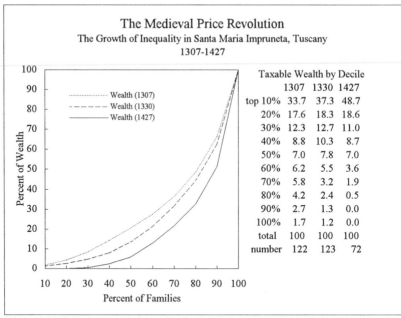

The Medieval Price Revolution
The Growth of Inequality in Santa Maria Impruneta, Tuscany
1307-1427

Taxable Wealth by Decile			
	1307	1330	1427
top 10%	33.7	37.3	48.7
20%	17.6	18.3	18.6
30%	12.3	12.7	11.0
40%	8.8	10.3	8.7
50%	7.0	7.8	7.0
60%	6.2	5.5	3.6
70%	5.8	3.2	1.9
80%	4.2	2.4	0.5
90%	2.7	1.3	0.0
100%	1.7	1.2	0.0
total	100	100	100
number	122	123	72

Figure 1.10 finds that wealth inequality increased in the late stages of the medieval price revolution, and the early years of the Renaissance equilibrium. The cause appears in figures 1.08 and 1.09: a rise in real returns to capital and a fall in real returns to labor. The evidence consists in the distribution of assessed wealth in the Italian commune of Santa Maria Impruneta, six miles south of Florence. Data are from the *èstimi* of 1307 and 1330, and the *catasto* of 1427, in David Herlihy, "Santa Maria Impruneta: A Rural Commune in the Late Middle Ages," in Nicolai Rubenstein, ed., *Florentine Studies* (Evanston, 1968), 242-76. The data are organized in a Lorenz Curve which measures wealth shares in the population by decile.

years of the thirteenth century. As spending outran revenues, monarchs borrowed heavily from domestic and foreign merchants. In Constantinople, the last Latin Emperor Baldwin II (1217–1273), was so hard pressed for ready cash between 1237 and 1261 that he surrendered the Crown of Thorns as collateral for loans by Venetian bankers. Public deficits began to grow out of control—another dangerous tendency that developed in the later stages of every price-revolution and gravely weakened the spring of government.[42]

?➤ The Third Stage: Growing Instability

In the late thirteenth century, the medieval price-revolution entered another stage, marked by growing instability. Prices rose and fell in wild swings of increasing amplitude. Inequality increased at a rapid rate. Public deficits surged ever higher. The economy of western Europe became dangerously vulnerable to stresses that it might have managed more easily in other eras.

In the late thirteenth century, the growth of population was pressing very hard against resources. Many people found themselves living precariously near the edge of survival. As the number of people increased, lands of lesser quality had been brought into cultivation. Farmers on these poor lands had to work much harder to scratch a living from the soil. Production and productivity fell for both land and labor. Many were driven to the margin of subsistence.[43]

For peasant farmers in that situation, the most immediate perils arose from changes in the weather. Throughout western Europe, the size of the harvest had always varied from one season to the next. Rainfall was the vital factor. In Europe, unlike other parts of the world, the great danger was too much rain rather than too little. Heavy rains in midsummer beat down the ripening grain and rotted it in the fields. Wet years, more than dry ones, brought short crops and soaring prices.

There had been seasons of scarcity even in the best of times. Most years had their dreaded *disettes,* which were the intervals that came after the last grain crop had run out, and before the new crop came in. *Disettes* occurred even in normal years. When things went wrong there were *grand disettes,* and scarcity became starvation. From 1260 to 1320, the rhythm of grain prices in England and Wales showed that *grand disettes* increased in frequency, severity and duration. Similar patterns appeared in greater or lesser degree throughout western Europe. In a time when people were living closer to the margin, the effect of harvest fluctuations was to create dangerous instabilities.[44]

Even in normal times, the margin was so narrow that a shortage of only 10 percent in the harvest caused severe suffering among impoverished peasant families. A shortfall of 20 percent meant starvation. And these were not normal times. The social effect of even small variation in the climate was enlarged by a growing imbalance between population and resources.

Within the villages of medieval Europe, the effect of harvest fluctuations on farm prices was compounded by other problems in medieval markets. Agricultural conditions were apt to vary from one region to another, even from one village to the next. The transportation of bulk-commodities such as wheat or barley across the countryside was not easy in the thirteenth century. Scarcity and surplus often existed within a few miles of one another. In Normandy during the year 1180, wheat fell to one livre at Norrancourt where the market was glutted. At the same time, the price was ten livres at Mortain and sixteen livres on the Cotentin peninsula, which suffered a shortage. These places were only a few miles apart.[45]

Added to market problems were monetary disturbances. As prices rose in western Europe, governments manipulated their coinage with an increasingly heavy hand: sometimes debasing it by reducing the quantity of silver; sometimes restoring its value by recoinages. These repeated acts had an impact upon price levels. Debasements drove prices up; recoinages brought them down again. Economic historian David L. Farmer has shown that the price of oxen fell after each recoinage in England during the thirteenth century.[46]

The effect of repeated recoinages and debasements in the thirteenth century was to increase the instability of markets and prices. When one medieval state debased its coinage, merchants responded by carrying their silver to another kingdom and having it reminted in a currency that held its value. In France, for example, Philip the Fair debased his silver coins so severely that Geoffroi de Paris protested that "the king was playing the magician, transforming 60 into 20 and 90 into 30."[47]

Moneyed men carried their silver across the channel, and had it struck as English sterling. In 1305, John de Everdon, England's Warden of the Exchange, reported that the "merchants were daily bringing silver there in great quantities," so much so that the mint was running six weeks behind. The quantity of England's money supply surged from 1305 to 1310, and prices of even the most humble commodities increased sharply. Eggs, which had cost less than four pence a hundred before 1305, suddenly rose above sixpence in 1306. The price of a laying hen doubled, from one penny to more than twopence. A historian of this sudden inflation concludes that the leading cause was a change in the size of the money supply.[48]

Exchange rates also became highly unstable in the fourteenth century. Governments tried to stabilize their fragile economies by imposing export controls. The effect was often the opposite of what was intended. England's Edward I, for example, tried to make things better by forbidding the export of English coins in 1299. By 1307, he had prohibited the removal of foreign money as well. He also pegged gold at an artifically high level relative to silver. These policies caused

increasing distortions in exchange rates, which in turn created dislocation in English trade.[49]

Other sources of instability were financial in their nature. In the
late thirteenth century, a major crisis led to the disruption of credit and
banking in the western world. The great Italian banks dangerously
overextended themselves by lending heavily to monarchs and private
borrowers. These loans were highly lucrative—for a time. They
brought prosperity to the north of Italy, and especially to the city of
Siena, which in the words of one leading historian was "for seventy-
five years the main banking center of Europe." As Siena flourished in
the thirteenth century, its citizens began to build a great cathedral
which was intended to be the largest in Europe. The magnificent architecture of its central square, which today delights so many tourists, was
created by the prosperity of this era.[50]

In the year 1298, Siena's banking boom came suddenly to an end,
with the failure of its greatest bank, the Gran Tavola of the Buonsignori. This was a world bank, with agents throughout Europe and
the Mediterranean basin. Among its borrowers were great merchants,
cities, nobles, kings and even the Pope himself. Increasing numbers of
these loans went sour. In the year 1298, a banking panic began in
Siena. The Buonsignori managed to hold things together for nearly a
decade, but finally in 1307 the great bank collapsed. Many lesser
enterprises failed with it.

The economy of Siena did not recover from this disaster for many
years. Work on the great cathedral was abandoned. The building stands
today in the same unfinished state as when workers downed tools in the
fourteenth century. The city's magnificent central square is still frozen
in time—a fiscal Herculaneum that had been engulfed by the great
wave of the thirteenth century.[51]

Siena's loss was at first a gain for the city of Florence. In the early
fourteenth century there were three great Florentine banks—the Bardi,
Peruzzi and Acciaiuoli—and many smaller ones such as the Mozzi,
Franzesi, Pulci, Rimbertini, Frescobaldi and Scali. Some of these enterprises grew even larger than the Sienese houses that had preceded
them. The bank of the Peruzzi, for example, had fifteen branches
throughout the world, and was bigger than the Medici Bank would ever
become.

The big Florentine banks made foreign loans to the kings of
England and Naples. This was a dangerous business. Once it had
begun, the loans grew inexorably larger. The banks could not call

them in, for fear of default or confiscation. The results were inexorable.

Early in the fourteenth century Florentine banks began to fail. The Mozzi went under in 1302, the Franzesi in 1307, the Pulci and Rimbertini in 1309, the Frescobaldi in 1312, and the Scali in 1326. Six houses failed in 1342. Then, in 1343 and 1346, the three great houses of the Peruzzi, Acciaiuoli and Bardi all collapsed with a great crash. Not for many years would banking enterprise recover in Tuscany.

Behind these events, many factors were operating at the same time: climatological, demographic, monetary, commercial, fiscal and financial. Together they unsettled social relationships throughout Europe, and caused deep suffering among the poor.

Monarchs attempted to impose price regulations with little success. In the fourteenth century, powerful elites condemned price controls as unnatural, ineffectual and immoral, much as other economic moralists would do in the twentieth century. The Canon of Bridlington wrote in 1316, "How contrary to reason is an ordinance on prices, when the fruitfullness or sterility of all living things are in the power of God alone, from which it follows that the fertility of the soil and not the will of man must determine the price."

The arguments of medieval theologians differed in detail from those of modern neoclassical economists, but the conclusions were much the same. Price controls were condemned in the fourteenth century both as constraints upon the free market, and as violations of the will of God. In every price-revolution, as we shall see, propertied and powerful elites would oppose economic controls and profit by their absence.

As prices rose and fell and rose again, complex linkages and multipliers began to operate. Rising prices led to a need for larger stocks of silver and gold, which drove prices higher still. Great kingdoms and small city states teetered on the edge of bankruptcy. They struggled to survive by borrowing heavily at ruinous rates of interest, and by debasing their money, thereby introducing powerful instabilities into the price system of western Europe. Manorial lords maintained their incomes by raising rents. A growing peasant population brought marginal lands into cultivation, causing productivity to fall. More workers competed for fewer jobs, and wages lagged behind price increases. As real wages fell, the margin of subsistence became paper-thin. There was less security against any sort of trouble, at a time when danger was increasing. Medieval Europe had come to the edge of disaster.

ᴥ The Crisis of the Fourteenth Century

The first years of the fourteenth century were a time of dark foreboding for the suffering peasantry of Europe. The economy of the Western world was in deep disorder. Material inequalities had dangerously increased. The growth of population far outpaced the means of its subsistence. The cost of food and firewood surged to high levels. Poverty and hunger increased in many parts of the Western world.

Then, in the summer of 1314, the weather turned cold and very wet. Rain fell incessantly. Crops rotted in the fields. Grain harvests were late and desperately short. In England, Parliament asked King Edward II to impose price controls on farm products. He speedily did so. Royal sheriffs rode through the realm proclaiming maximum prices for food, poultry and livestock.

These disturbances seemed at first to be merely another routine disaster of a sort that had often afflicted medieval Europe. Crops had fallen short before. In the winter of 1314, people tightened their belts and prayed for better times.

But the next harvest was worse. The spring of 1315 brought heavy rain throughout Europe. Stormy weather lashed the continent for months. Dikes collapsed in England and the Low Countries. Entire fields washed away in France. Villages were destroyed by rising rivers in Germany. Once again grain and fodder crops failed. This was not merely a set of local shortages. It was, in the words of historian Henry Lucas, "a universal failure of crops in 1315 . . . from the Pyrenees to Slavic regions, from Scotland to Italy."[1]

In England during the year 1315, the price of wheat rose eightfold, from five shillings to as much as forty shillings. Hungry livestock sickened and died. The chronicles tell of a "great murrin" which took a heavy toll of domestic animals. Impoverished peasants ate cats, rats, reptiles and insects. Many tried to survive on animal droppings. Others ate the leaves from the trees. In London, Paris, Ypres, Breslau and Utrecht, the streets were littered with dying people. Gangs of starving laborers roamed the countryside in search of food. Crime became widespread—mostly the theft of food, or anything that could be exchanged for food.[2]

The economy of Europe, already dangerously fragile, disintegrated under a stress that it might have survived at another time. People sought scapegoats for their suffering. Millers and bakers became favorite targets. In France, the people of Paris staged a mass punishment of

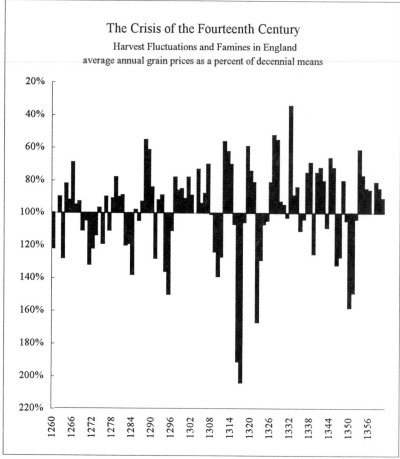

Figure 1.11 measures annual harvest prices as a percent of decennial means. Abundant crops drove prices down; scarcity sent them up again. The impact of scarcity grew more severe as the price revolution continued, reaching a peak in 1315-17, the worst famine in European history. This graph is created from price series in James E. Thorold Rogers, *A History of Agriculture and Prices in England,* vols. I & II.

bakers who had been found guilty of mixing their flour with animal droppings. Sixteen bakers were lashed to wheels in public squares and made to hold bits of rotten bread in outstretched hands, while they were beaten and reviled by the multitude.[3]

In England, even the King felt the famine. One chronicle recorded that "when Edward II with his household stopped at St. Albans at the Feast of St. Laurence [August 10], it was practically impossible to procure bread for his court.'' But large hoards of grain remained in the hands of kings and noblemen in the west, and Teutonic Knights in the east, and great abbeys throughout Europe. The ruling few of Europe were slow to open their granaries to feed the starving many. All of these things happened in the year 1315.[4]

Then, inconceivably, torrential rains came again in 1316. The grain crop failed a third year in a row. Europe began to experience the worst famine in its history. When other sources of food ran out, people began to eat one another. Peasant families consumed the bodies of the dead. Corpses were dug up from their burying grounds and eaten. In jails the convicts ceased to be fed; we are told that starving inmates ''ferociously attacked new prisoners and devoured them half alive.'' Condemned criminals were cut down from the gallows, butchered, and eaten. Parents killed their children for food, and children murdered their parents.[5]

The death toll in this famine is unknown. It must have been very large. The town of Ypres, with a population of perhaps 25,000 souls, counted 2,794 burials at public expense from May to October, 1316, not including many others whose families paid for their interments. More than 10 percent of the population died *in pauperis* within the span of less than six months. Many other deaths must have gone unrecorded. Ypres was not unique in its suffering. Some historians estimate that a tenth of Europe's teeming population perished in the years 1315 and 1316.[6]

In the wake of famine, epidemics began to break out. Both people and animals suffered from a nameless pestilence that spread swiftly through the continent. Some of its symptoms were similar to those of modern anthrax; others were more like ergotism and dysentery. Probably this was a polydemic of many different diseases, including some that may be unknown to modern science.

Famine, epidemics and oppression were followed by an increase in crime. As price-movements became more volatile, every surge in the cost of living was accompanied by a sudden increase in criminal violence. Most of these crimes were thefts and robberies by desperate men and women. Many were homicides, assaults and acts of rage against the cruel suffering that had been visited upon so many people.

There were also acts of collective violence and insurrection. In rural France, a movement called the Pastoureaux spread rapidly through the countryside. A great mass of peasants and laborers gathered in the northwest, and began marching south and east toward

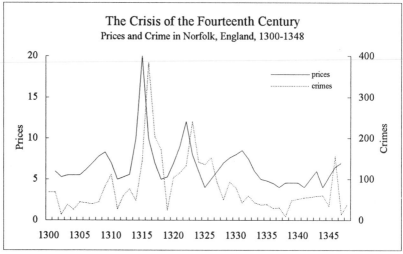

The Crisis of the Fourteenth Century
Prices and Crime in Norfolk, England, 1300-1348

Figure 1.12 compares the price of wheat in Norfolk (silver shillings per quarter) with criminal indictments in the same county. Crimes (in order of frequency) include larceny, burglary, homicide, robbery, receiving stolen goods, treason, counterfeiting, arson, and rape. The source is Barbara Hanawalt, *Crime and Conflict in English Communities* (Cambridge, Mass., 1979), 243, 279.

the Holy Land, gaining numbers as they went. On the way, the Pastoureaux attacked castles, sacked monasteries, burned archives, released convicts, slaughtered Jews, murdered Lepers, and settled scores with the nobility for many centuries of oppression. They spread terror among the possessing classes, until finally they were dispersed and hanged by the hundreds. Their gaunt bodies dangled from the branches of trees throughout the south of France.

While these disorders spread through the western world, yet another misery was inflicted upon the people of Europe. As if famine, pestilence, and social violence were not suffering enough, this period became a time of bloody war between the sovereign states of Europe. "Wars are not evenly distributed throughout the centuries," writes A. R. Bridbury, "they come in clusters." He observed that one such run of conflicts began in the year 1294, and continued for fifty years. Major wars occurred between Scotland and England, England and France, France and Flanders; many smaller conflicts broke out between German, Swiss and Italian city-states. Warfare had been endemic in medieval Europe, but Bridbury and others find that its incidence greatly increased after the year 1294.[7]

Incessant wars caused economic dislocation—both directly by the destruction that they visited upon the countryside, and indirectly by their heavy costs as well. A large part of public spending went for war at the moment when Europe could least afford it.[8]

Domestic insurrections also occurred in many parts of Europe, with similar result. In Rome a rebellion broke out against Boniface VIII, a pope who was hated for his despotism and despised for his impiety. The people of Rome took him prisoner and forced him to resign his office. He died shortly afterward—of humiliation, the faithful believed. Others suspected poison. His successor Benedict XI was murdered, and the papacy fled to Avignon in 1305. There it remained in opulent exile for more than seventy years.

Even Venice, the most stable of Italian city-states, suffered the only major insurrection in its thousand-year history—an uprising called Tiepolo's Rebellion in 1310. It was suppressed by a vigilante group called the Council of Ten, which made itself a permanent part of the Venetian government, along with secret police, anonymous informers, savage torture, arbitrary imprisonment, and an apparatus of official terror which today is exhibited to tourists in the Doge's Palace. This system of repression was the price of stability in the Venetian republic.

In the monarchies of northern Europe, nobles turned against their kings and toppled them from their thrones. An aristocratic revolution was organized against England's Edward II and his supporters of the hated Despenser family, whose name had become a byword for avarice and oppression. In September 1324, when the people of England were groaning under the weight of their accumulated miseries, the young Hugh Despenser had accumulated large deposits in Italian banks. This money had been extracted from starving peasants on his estates and from the profits of his offices. Despenser and his father so outraged their countrymen that they were seized by the rebels and summarily executed. Young Hugh Despenser's head was triumphantly displayed on London Bridge, "with much tumult and the sound of horns."

For England's much-hated King Edward II, a worse fate was in store. He was forcibly deposed and cast into a deep dungeon at Berkeley Castle in the west of England. His captors faced a dilemma. They could not let him live, but neither could they appear to kill their sovereign. They solved their problem by inventing a unique method of execution that left no visible marks. The king was seized and tightly bound. A red-hot iron was driven slowly upward through his anus until it penetrated his brain. It is said that his dying screams could be heard for miles across the Severn Valley. The folk memory of this event is still alive in Gloucestershire. Some swear that the death cry of Edward II can still be heard in the silence of a moonless night.

That savage act of regicide was not an isolated horror. The people of Flanders rose against their hated French masters in 1302, and killed many of them in an epic slaughter called the Matin de Bruges. Then they defeated the French nobility in the Battle of the Spurs at Courtrai. In France, King Louis X (remembered as Louis the Quarrelsome) was deposed in 1316. Twelve years later, the Capetian dynasty collapsed after more than three centuries in power.

In Sweden after 1290, a civil war between royal brothers ended in a popular insurrection, in the expulsion of King Birger in 1319 and in the collapse of royal authority. Denmark dissolved into anarchy after 1332, when King Christopher II was deposed by Gerhard Count Holstein, who was murdered in his turn. The Holy Roman Empire suffered a protracted civil war between contending parties called Guelfs and Ghibbelines. The popes were driven into exile for seventy years, and in Rome a popular revolution led by Cola di Rienzi overthrew the city's patriciate. The Italian city-states were consumed by internal conflict. Florence, unable to govern itself, invited a tyrant named Walter of Brienne, Duke of Athens, and soon found its liberties crushed beneath his heel.

Order also collapsed throughout eastern Europe. In the year 1304, an army of 6,000 Catalonian mercenaries laid waste to broad areas of Thrace and Macedonia. The Ottoman Turks first appeared in the early years of the fourteenth century, attacking the Byzantine Empire and capturing Greek cities in Asia Minor. The Tartars rode eastward from the steppes as far as the plains of Hungary, and for a time gained effective control of Russia.

These disorders, cruel as they may have been, were not the worst of Europe's sufferings. Famine, pestilence, war and insurrection returned repeatedly to Europe during the 1320s and 1330s. Some places—Tuscany for example—suffered worse famines in the period 1328–30 than in 1315–20. Prices surged and declined in great swings. The rural population shrank, arable lands began to be abandoned, and peasants grew poorer.

At the same time, some of the rich continued to grow richer. This was the period when the French popes lived in high luxury at Avignon. Pope John XXII (1316–34) spent vast sums for jewels and ornaments and gold cloth for his vestments. Papal banquets were served on gold plate beneath gilded frescoes and ceilings. Petrarch protested that even the papal horses were "dressed in gold, fed on gold, and soon to be shod in gold if God does not stop this slavish luxury." The cardinals accumulated great wealth; one Prince of the Church required 51 houses for his servants. Similar scenes were enacted in royal courts and noble households.

At the same time, many small *seigneurs* were caught up in the general misfortunes. A study of the Norman seignury finds evidence of a "sharp collapse of rents" in the fourteenth century, caused mainly by the decline of population, after the long rise of the thirteenth century.[9]

Meanwhile, the peasants suffered and the poor starved. The generation born in this age of crisis was so debilitated by hunger, disease, exploitation, war and disorder that a few years later it succumbed to a still greater catastrophe, the worst in world history.[10] In 1346 a Tartar army besieged the Genoese town of Caffa (now Feodosia) in the Crimea. The attackers were stricken by plague, and converted their misfortune into a weapon of war—catapulting their dead into the city in a deliberate attempt to spread the infection. This tactic succeeded so well that the Genoese abandoned the city and fled in their galleys through the Black Sea, the Aegean and the Mediterranean, carrying with them the plague that came to be called the Black Death.

By October 1347, the Black Death had established itself in Sicily, and spread swiftly to Africa, Sardinia, Corsica and the mainland of Europe. In January 1348, it reached Venice, Genoa and Marseilles, where 56,000 people died. By June it crossed the Alps and Pyrenees. England was infected by December, and Scotland and Scandinavia by 1349. A few cities miraculously escaped—Milan, Nuremberg, Liège, and several fortunate regions such as Bearn, as well as much of eastern Germany and Poland where the population was sparse.

But most of Europe felt the full force of the epidemic. Great centers of commerce and culture suffered severely. The plague found a vulnerable population that had outstripped the means of its subsistence and was already beginning to decline. Historian Philip Ziegler writes, "Whatever one's thesis about the inevitability of the Black Death, it cannot be denied that it found awaiting it in Europe a population singularly ill-equipped to resist. Distracted by wars, weakened by malnutrition, exhausted by his struggle to win a living from his inadequate portion of ever less fertile land, the medieval peasantry was ready to succumb even before the blow had fallen."[11]

We shall never know how many people died in the Black Death.

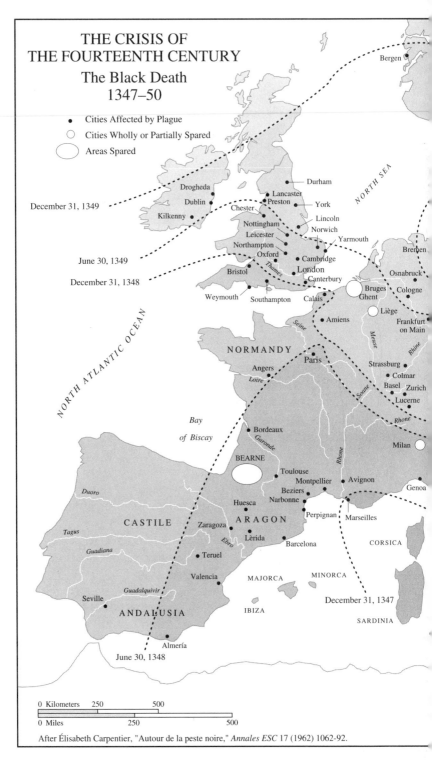

THE CRISIS OF
THE FOURTEENTH CENTURY
The Black Death
1347–50

- • Cities Affected by Plague
- ○ Cities Wholly or Partially Spared
- ⬭ Areas Spared

Bergen

December 31, 1349

Drogheda
Dublin
Kilkenny

Durham
Lancaster
Preston
Chester
York

NORTH SEA

June 30, 1349

December 31, 1348

Nottingham
Leicester
Northampton
Oxford
Bristol
Weymouth
Southampton

Lincoln
Norwich
Yarmouth
Cambridge
London
Canterbury
Calais

Bremen
Osnabruck
Bruges
Ghent
Cologne
Liège
Frankfurt
on Main

Amiens

Meuse
Rhine

NORTH ATLANTIC OCEAN

NORMANDY

Seine

Paris

Angers
Loire

Strassburg
Colmar
Basel Zurich
Lucerne

Saône

Bay
of Biscay

Bordeaux
Garonne

Rhône

Milan

BEARNE

Toulouse
Montpellier
Beziers
Narbonne

Avignon

Genoa

Duoro

Huesca

Rhône

Perpignan
Marseilles

CASTILE

Tagus

Guadiana

Zaragoza
Lèrida

ARAGON

Teruel

Ebro

Barcelona

CORSICA

Valencia

MAJORCA

MINORCA

December 31, 1347

Guadalquivir

Seville

ANDALUSIA

IBIZA

SARDINIA

Almería

June 30, 1348

0 Kilometers   250   500

0 Miles   250   500

After Élisabeth Carpentier, "Autour de la peste noire," *Annales ESC* 17 (1962) 1062-92.

42

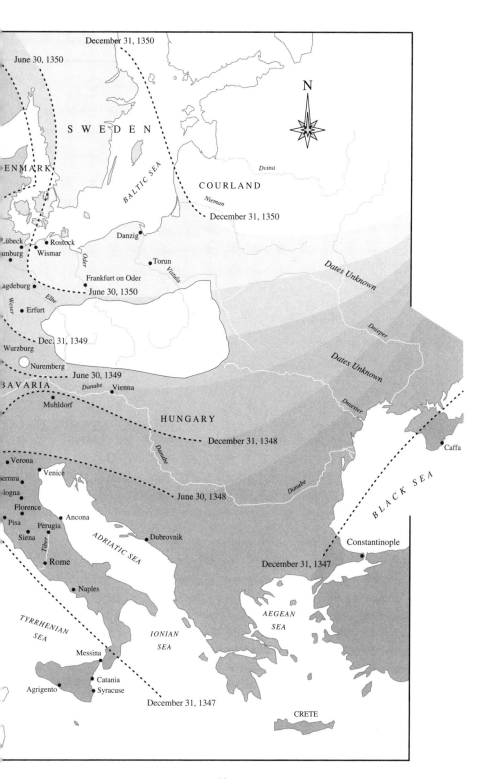

December 31, 1350

June 30, 1350

S W E D E N

BALTIC SEA

DENMARK

Dvina

COURLAND

Nieman

December 31, 1350

Lübeck
Rostock
Hamburg
Wismar

Danzig

Oder

Torun

Vistula

Dates Unknown

Frankfurt on Oder

Magdeburg

Elbe

June 30, 1350

Weser

Erfurt

Dnieper

Dec. 31, 1349

Wurzburg

Nuremberg

June 30, 1349

Dates Unknown

BAVARIA

Danube

Vienna

Dniester

Muhldorf

HUNGARY

Caffa

December 31, 1348

Danube

Verona

Venice

Ferrara

Bologna

June 30, 1348

Danube

BLACK SEA

Florence

Ancona

Pisa

Perugia

Siena

Tiber

ADRIATIC SEA

Dubrovnik

Constantinople

Rome

December 31, 1347

Naples

TYRRHENIAN
SEA

AEGEAN
SEA

Messina

IONIAN
SEA

Catania

Agrigento

Syracuse

December 31, 1347

CRETE

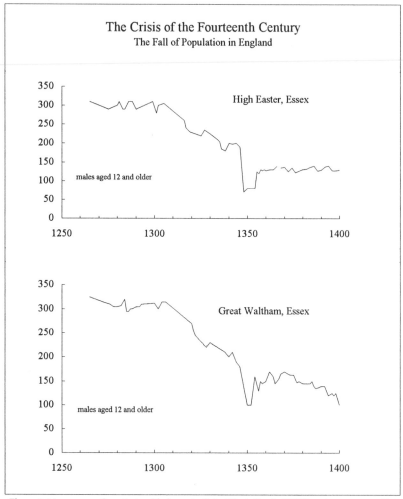

Figure 1.14 measures the catastrophic impact of the Black Death (1348) on two communities 25 miles northeast of London. A meticulous study by L. R. Poos also finds that the fall of population began as early as 1310 and continued in Great Waltham as late as 1400. The source is L. R. Poos, "The Rural Population of Essex in the Later Middle Ages," *Economic History Review* 2nd ser., 38 (1985) 22.

Among England's parish clergy, whose deaths were comparatively well recorded, something like 45 percent are known to have perished. Most scholars believe that the death toll in the general population was smaller, but still very large. Many historians estimate that Europe lost between 25 and 40 percent of its inhabitants. Altogether, the European population fell from approximately 80 million at its peak in the early fourteenth century to 60 million or less after the Black Death—the largest decline in the cruel history of that continent.[12]

This great depopulation had many economic consequences. The price of food rose sharply during the epidemic years, then began to fall very rapidly as there were fewer mouths to feed. At the same time prices of manufactured goods tended to rise, partly because artisans and craftsmen could demand higher wages, and also because of dislocations in supply. These countervailing trends—falling agricultural prices and rising industrial prices—were called by Thorold Rogers a ''price scissors.'' Their effect was particularly severe after the catastrophe of the fourteenth century, but they were not unique to this period. Similar movements would also occur in every other price-revolution. In the years that followed the Black death, the ''price scissors'' added much to Europe's miseries.[13]

The catastrophe of the fourteenth century was followed by cultural disintegration. Jews and foreigners were massacred. Among Christians, the practice of flagellation spread rapidly in cities and the countryside. Processions of Christians scourged one another until their bare backs ran red with blood. Entire villages and towns were abandoned, the doors and shutters of the vacant buildings creaking sadly in the wind. Empty churches and deserted castles fell into ruin. Grass grew in the marketplaces, and the country roads that had been thronged with pilgrims were reclaimed by weeds and brush.

In the period from 1314 to 1348, the great wave crested and broke in a shattering catastrophe. As it did so, the people of Europe suffered through the darkest moment in their history: a terrible time of starvation and pestilence, insurrection and war, persecution and political chaos. This was more than merely the collapse of the medieval economy. It was the death of medieval civilization.

❧ The Equilibrium of the Renaissance, 1400–1470

The time of troubles continued in western Europe for many years. It was a long, grinding misery that lasted a lifetime, and must have seemed an eternity to those who were condemned to suffer through it.[1]

The Black Death did not strike merely a single blow. It was one of a family of epidemics that returned again and again to Europe. In many places the first visit was not the worst. The Tuscan city of Pistoia, for example, suffered its first great plague in 1339. This was not the Black

Death but another pestilence, which came after famines had weakened the population for twenty-five years. The epidemic of 1339 probably killed a quarter of Pistoia's population in the city itself and the surrounding countryside. Eight years later, in 1347, another pestilence returned to that region. In 1348 the Black Death arrived, and did its work so thoroughly that the keeper of the city's chronicle remembered that "hardly a person was left alive." Slowly the survivors struggled to their feet, only to be struck by other epidemics of "mortal fevers" (not the Black Death but different diseases) in 1357, 1389 and 1393. Then, in 1399, bubonic plague came back to Pistoia and destroyed half of the city's inhabitants in one final visitation.

Thereafter, conditions began at last to grow better, but even this period of improvement was punctuated by lesser epidemics that overswept the town in 1410, 1418, 1423, 1436 and 1457. No other community experienced the same sequence of misfortunes as did the city of Pistoia, but similar events occurred in most European towns and in much of the countryside as well.[2]

While epidemic disease continued to ravage Europe, many parts of the continent were laid waste by war. This was the period of the Hundred Years War (*ca.* 1337–1453) between France and England.

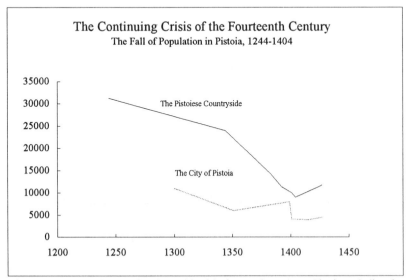

The Continuing Crisis of the Fourteenth Century
The Fall of Population in Pistoia, 1244-1404

Figure 1.15 shows the impact of the long crisis of the fourteenth century on Pistoia, an Italian city state thirty kilometers northwest of Florence. The source is David Herlihy, *Medieval and Renaissance Pistoia: The Social History of an Italian Town, 1200-1430* (New Haven, 1967), 70.

Each campaign reduced large areas to anarchy, and left in its wake wandering gangs of mercenaries and freebooters who preyed upon the peasantry. Some of these bands were as big as a modern infantry brigade. When they passed through a rural region, they left a wide swath of devastation.

For self-defence, French peasants converted their stone churches into castles. The clang of bells that had summoned families to worship in time of peace now sounded a warning *tocsin* when raiders were in the neighborhood. In the beautiful Loire Valley, peasants retreated at night to islands in the river. In Picardy, they moved underground into tunnels and caves with hidden entrances. Another dark age had descended upon Europe.[3]

One consequence was a continuing decline of population. The number of inhabitants did not merely fall during the great plague year of 1348. In many parts of Europe it kept on falling, in a long contraction that persisted from 1315 to 1400. A careful Danish study of farms on the manors of the Bishops of Roskilde near Copenhagen found that the proportion of abandoned houses increased steadily for sixty years after the Black Death. The decline of rural population reached its nadir not in 1348 but half a century later, in the period 1401–20.[4]

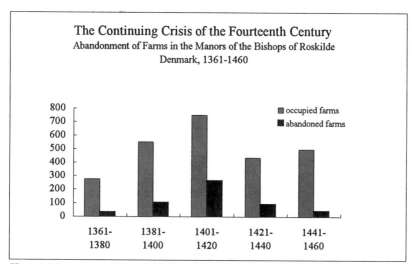

The Continuing Crisis of the Fourteenth Century
Abandonment of Farms in the Manors of the Bishops of Roskilde
Denmark, 1361-1460

Figure 1.16 measures the impact of falling population on farm tenancy in Denmark. Here again we find evidence not of a single catastrophe but of a long decline that reached its nadir circa 1400. A large literature on the *Wüstungsproblem* ("lost village question") finds similar trends throughout Europe. The source is C. A. Christensen, "Aendringerne i landsbyens Økonomiske og sociale strukur i det 14. og 15. århundrede," *Historisk Tidsskrift* 12 (1964) 346.

At the same time that Europe's population continued to fall and social unrest continued, an economic problem developed. Money began to disappear. Europe's stock of silver and gold contracted sharply during the late fourteenth century. Historian John Day writes, "for the better part of two decades the European economies were scourged by a genuine scarcity of money." In the violence of the fourteenth century, much silver and gold had been lost. Some of it disappeared into forgotten hordes that are being rediscovered even today. At the same time the West had an unfavorable balance of trade with Asia, and specie drained rapidly away. Imports of gold from Africa also declined, and many silver mines in central Europe were abandoned or became less productive.

After 1390, a severe monetary famine developed. In France, the low point was reached during the year 1402, when the minting of money virtually came to an end. In Florence, the minting of silver coins ceased entirely from 1392 to 1402. In London, the entire output of the Royal Mint was merely eight pounds in silver pennies during the year 1408. The mints of Flanders closed altogether. Only Venetian gold ducats, which have been called "the dollar of the middle ages," continued to be struck in quantity; and even in Venice silver was in short supply. This money famine was part of a deep economic depression that continued to the end of the fourteenth century.[5]

The decline of population and scarcity of money had a powerful effect on European prices.[6] In Pistoia, famine and plague had reduced the population from more than 40,000 souls in the late thirteenth century to less than 14,000 by the early fifteenth. Houses and estates fell empty; rents and land values declined roughly in proportion to the loss of population. Grain prices also came down, but the growing scarcity of labor caused wages to rise.[7] The money-income of unskilled workers in Pistoia doubled from 1349 to 1400, and real wages (measured in terms of purchasing power) increased in even greater proportion. These trends appeared generally throughout Europe.[8]

In the midst of these many tendencies, an important social transformation began to take place. From the long travail of the fourteenth century, a new society was born. Forms of status and obligation were altered in fundamental ways. England and western Europe underwent an economic process that historian M. M. Postan summarizes as the "commutation of labour services and the emancipation of serfs." Similar trends also occurred in the cities of northern Italy, where urban workers improved their material condition. A major cause was the scarcity of labor that allowed workers to bargain for better terms. This process continued for nearly a century after the Black Death.

Angry social conflicts broke out as a consequence of this assertiveness. Among them was the *Jacquerie* in France (1358), a rebellion of peasants against their masters. Another was the revolt of the *Ciompi* in Florence (1378), when the *popolo minuto* rose violently against the ruling families of that city.[9] A third was England's great Peasant Rebellion (1381). In that year there was a insurrection in East Anglia, and the Kentish Rising of Wat Tyler who led his followers into the streets of London. In many places, peasants burned the manorial rolls that recorded their servile obligations.[10]

These rebellions were suppressed, but the conditions that produced them had lasting consequences. In Postan's words, a "rapid withering away of servile dues and disabilities" transformed social relationships. Vestiges of the old obligations remained for many generations, but Postan concludes that "in general rural serfdom had gone out of the land, and was all but forgotten by the time Queen Elizabeth ascended the throne of England [in 1558]."

This transition would have momentous consequences in English history during the early modern era. England was ahead of France and Germany, and eastern Europe lagged far behind, but similar trends were stirring in many parts of the Western world.[11]

At the dawn of the fifteenth century, economic conditions began at last to stabilize in Europe. Prices ceased falling and began to fluctuate in a more regular way. A long period of comparative equilibrium followed in the fifteenth century.

Once again, the city of Pistoia represented the general trend. Historian David Herlihy writes, "After about 1400, Pistoia's agricultural economy was attaining a new equilibrium, and was achieving a real if moderate prosperity. Declining commodity prices bespeak a returning abundance, and profits to investors, reaching 12 percent by the century's end, registered a distinct if modest gain. Among the factors which contributed to the new rural prosperity was the stabilization and then steady growth of the rural population. . . . Population and social tumult was largely, if not finally, calmed. . . . The new agricultural system of the fifteenth century . . . provided Pistoia's Renaissance society with a firm and stable basis for its political life and for its cultural growth."[12]

Similar trends appeared throughout northern Italy. Outbreaks of mortal disease continued, but they happened less frequently after 1400, and their effects were less severe. The size of harvests continued to fluctuate from year to year, but the magnitude of price-variations slowly diminished during the fifteenth century. The Italian city-states entered a long period of slow recovery, stable growth and dynamic equilibrium in economic and demographic movements (*circa* 1405–80). The urban populations of Venice, Florence and Siena began to

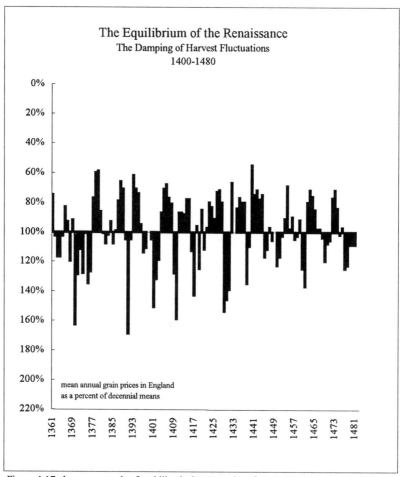

Figure 1.17 shows a growth of stability in harvest prices from 1390 to 1480. Fluctuations continued, but magnitudes diminished through nearly a century. Major shortages became progressively less severe. This annual series (as a percent of decennial means) is computed from data in J. E. Thorold Rogers, *A History of Agriculture and Prices in England,* vol. 2.

increase again, though still remaining smaller than before the Black Death. Commerce and industry revived, real wages rose buoyantly, and commodity prices continued to decline and stabilize.[13]

Italy was more advanced in these tendencies than other parts of Europe. North of the Alps, disorder and instability persisted for another generation or longer. The people of France suffered through three terrible periods of anarchy, pestilence, war and famine in the early

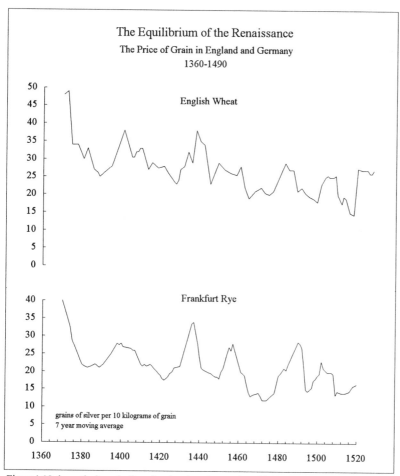

The Equilibrium of the Renaissance
The Price of Grain in England and Germany
1360-1490

English Wheat

Frankfurt Rye

grains of silver per 10 kilograms of grain
7 year moving average

Figure 1.18 shows the long decline of grain prices that continued from 1360 to 1480 in most parts of Europe. The central tendency was stable for more than a century. The source is Wilhelm Abel, *Agrarkrisen und Agrarkonjunktur*, 66; for similar trends in France, see d'Avenel, *Histoire économique*, 2:518.

fifteenth century. During the years from 1413 to 1420, France was
afflicted with an insane monarch (Charles VI), an impotent government, an English invasion, and an internal rebellion led by a skinner
named Simon Caboche. French prices rose to a great height during
these disorders. They went even higher in 1428–30, when an English

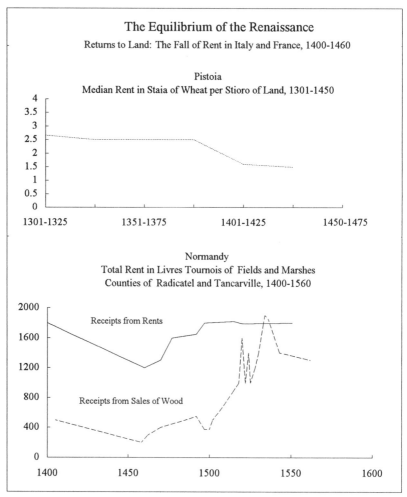

Figure 1.19 shows a long decline in rent from 1360 to 1460, when wages were rising. It also
shows a rise in rent after 1460, when the next price-revolution was underway. Sources include
David Herlihy, *Medieval and Renaissance Pistoia* (New Haven, 1967), and Guy Bois, *Crise
du feodalisme: Économie rurale et démographie en Normandie orientale du début du 14e
siècle au milieu du 16e siècle* (Paris, 1976).

army besieged Orleans and burned a Saint, Jeanne d'Arc, at Rouen in 1431. A third time of troubles in France occurred during the years 1437–39, a period of *grand disettes*, the return of plague, and the anarchy of the *ecorcheurs*. In each of these three eras, French prices surged to very high levels.[14]

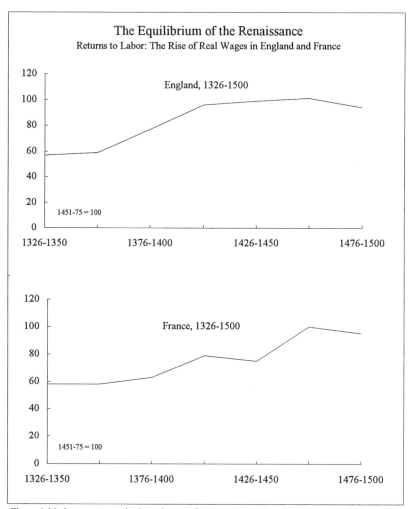

Figure 1.20 shows a strong rise in real wages from 1351 to 1475, while prices were falling. After 1476, when the next price revolution began, real wages began to come down. The source is Henry Phelps-Brown and Sheila V. Hopkins, *A Perspective of Wages and Prices* (New York, 1981), 28-31; Georges d'Avenel, *Histoire économique de la propriété, des salaires, des denrées, et de tous les prix en générale, depuis l'an 1200 jusqu'en 1800* (7 vols., Paris, 1894-1926).

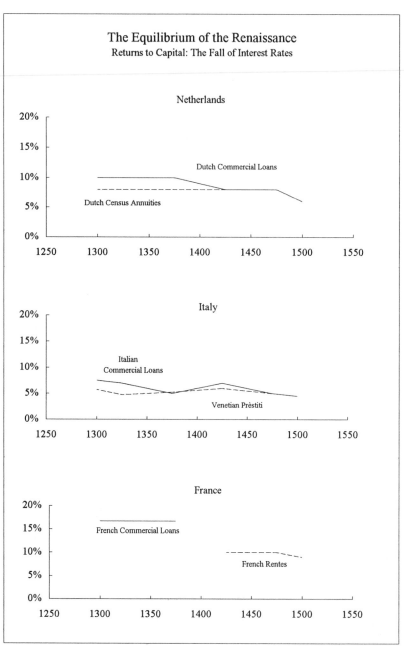

The Equilibrium of the Renaissance
Returns to Capital: The Fall of Interest Rates

Netherlands

Dutch Commercial Loans

Dutch Census Annuities

Italy

Italian Commercial Loans

Venetian Prèstiti

France

French Commercial Loans

French Rentes

Figure 1.21 shows the fall of interest rates in the fifteenth century. Levels differed widely: public securities such as Venetian *prèstiti*, French *rentes* and Dutch census loans combined higher security with lower rates. Commercial loans carried higher rates, but trends were much the same. The source is Sidney Homer, *A History of Interest Rates* (2d ed., New Brunswick, 1977), 104-43.

After 1440, conditions began at last to improve in France. During the reigns of Charles VII "the Well Served" and Louis XI "the Bourgeois," order was restored, the English were defeated and anarchy was suppressed. From 1437 to the end of the fifteenth century, prices stabilized throughout France. Annual price fluctuations diminished, and the cost of grain remained roughly on the same level for nearly half a century.[15]

As France lagged behind Italy, so England lagged behind France. That unhappy island became a byword for political strife in the fifteenth century. A cruel and sordid conflict, inappropriately named the Wars of the Roses, persisted into the late fifteenth century. So also did economic instability. But even in England, the amplitude of price fluctuations steadily diminished after 1440 and real wages improved.[16]

While real wages increased, returns to capital diminished. Rates of interest fell by 50 percent in France and the Low Countries in the century from 1370 to 1470. Italian rates also came down, though not so

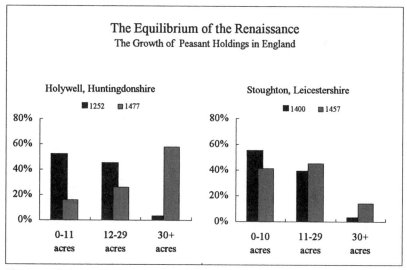

The Equilibrium of the Renaissance
The Growth of Peasant Holdings in England

Figure 1.22 finds that when wages rose and rents fell during the fifteenth century, the peasantry of Europe enlarged their holdings. These English villages are cases in point. In Holywell, landholders included both customary and leasehold tenants; in Stoughton, they were freeholders as well as leaseholders and customary tenants. The number of holders fell: in Stoughton from 62 to 24, and in Holywell from 59 to 49. Sources include Edwin B. Dewindt, *Land and People in Holywell-cum-Needingworth: Structures of Tenure and Patterns of Social Organization in an East Midlands Village, 1252-1457* (Toronto, 1972), 114; and Christopher Dyer, *Standards of Living in the Later Middle Ages* (Cambridge, 1989), 141.

much as in northern Europe. Rents also came down during the same period, from 1370 to 1460. The same combination of rising wages, falling rents and falling interest rates also appeared in every period of price equilibrium from the fifteenth to the nineteenth centuries.

This was a difficult time for people who lived on rents and interest. But for most ordinary folk who earned their bread by daily labor, life was better. Real wages increased. Rents fell. Returns to labor outpaced rewards to land and capital. New trends slowly began to emerge in the distribution of wealth. In England, many studies have found that peasants and small proprietors enlarged their holdings in the fifteenth century.

At the same time that these patterns of equilibrium began to appear in the European economy, new political trends emerged as well. The second half of the fifteenth century became an age of strong and successful state-building. This was the era of Poland's great king Casimir IV, who united his grand duchy and drove out foreign invaders. In Russia it was the time of Ivan the Great (1462), the first truly national ruler. It was also the era of Hungary's greatest king Mathias Corvinus (1458); of France's Louis XI (1461), who transformed a medieval kingdom into a great national monarchy; and of England's Henry VII (1485), who founded the Tudor dynasty.

These patterns of demographic equilibrium, economic recovery and political stability developed in every part of Europe, but not all at the same time. They first appeared in the territories that bordered the Mediterranean Sea. The early fifteenth century might be remembered as the Mediterranean moment in modern history. It was an era of prosperity and proud achievement from the straits of Gibraltar to the Golden Horn.[17]

In Spain, a new nation was born. Nobody could have predicted it. The future of Iberia seemed very bleak as late as the year 1410, when the death of Aragon's King Martin I was followed by the collapse of Spain's strongest dynasty. But in 1412 the throne of Aragon passed to a cadet branch of the family that ruled Castile, and the two strongest kingdoms in Spain were governed by members of the same clan. Contacts between these kingdoms steadily increased. In 1469, the foundation of a new national state was created by a marriage of two Spanish stepcousins, Ferdinand of Aragon and Isabella of Castile. A single national religion was forcibly imposed by the Spanish Inquisition (founded in 1478), and the Spanish church was protected from interference by a papal concordat in 1482. A system of national law was established in the *Libro de Montalvo* (1485). The Moors were expelled from Spain in the great *reconquista* which ended triumphantly with the liberation of Granada in 1492, the same year when Columbus sailed for America.

These national events were closely linked to economic trends. The Spanish economy flourished during the fifteenth century. Its increasing stability supported the new political trends and was in turn reinforced by them. The result was the creation of the strongest nation-state in the Western world—one that was destined to dominate Europe and America through the sixteenth century.

At the opposite end of the Mediterranean, another empire was created in a different way. The greatness of the Ottoman Empire rose not from the imposition of cultural unity on a single nation, but from the reconciliation of cultural diversity within an imperial frame. In company with their Christian neighbors, the Ottoman Turks had suffered many vicissitudes during the fourteenth century. After 1413 a new trend appeared. Turkish armies captured Byzantium, ravaged the Balkans, and conquered the Crimea. They battered Greek cities into submission with marble cannonballs made from ancient monuments. The Ottoman empire was formed by conquest during the three reigns of Mehmed I (1413–21), Murad II (1421–51) and especially Mehmed II the Conqueror (1451–81).

The new Ottoman Empire was a mixture of light and shadow. It was created by slaughter and maintained by terror. Sultan Mehmed II alone was thought to have been responsible for the murder of more than 800,000 people. But brutal as the Turks may have been, they were humanitarians by contrast with some of the despots whom they destroyed. One of their enemies was the sadistic Vlad Dracul of Wallachia—the original Dracula who ordered mass murders merely for amusement, and once impaled and crucified 20,000 captives in a single orgy of violence. The Turks drove Dracula from power.

Once created by violent acts, the Ottoman Empire was tolerant of ethnic and religious minorities—more so than Christian states. In its prime, the Ottoman state was remarkable for administrative enlightenment, rational economic policies and ethnic pluralism. Throughout the eastern Mediterranean it forcibly imposed a *pax ottomanica* that lasted many centuries.[18]

At the same time, the most remarkable achievements occurred in the center of the Mediterranean basin, mainly among the Italian cities of Florence, Siena, Genoa, Modena, Lucca, Milan, Padua and Venice.

Here there was no single nation-state or despotic dominion, but something very different in structure and spirit. The sovereign cities of northern Italy, in rivalry with one another, invented a new institution which they named *lo stato*. We know it as the modern secular state. They also created the idea of a modern state system in which a political equilibrium was maintained by a balance of power, by spheres of influence, by the exercise of diplomacy and by the sway of international law.

Some of these Italian city states also developed complex internal systems of republican liberty and self-government. Political stability was achieved in the stronger cities, and linked to a material equilibrium that prevailed throughout northern Italy in the fifteenth century.

A leading example was the history of Venice in the *quattrocento*. From 1405 to 1484, this maritime republic annexed much of northern Italy: Padua, Vicenza, Verona, Treviso, Bergamo, and Brescia. Even to this day in many small Italian villages throughout these regions, the lion columns that symbolized Venetian sovereignty still stand in the town squares.[19]

Venetian ships controlled the inland waterways of Italy, as far as the Lago di Garda. Venetian settlers occupied many Mediterranean islands that had belonged to the Byzantine Greeks and the Crusader States. They added Corfu in 1386, Saloniki in 1423, and Cyprus in 1489 to their medieval possessions of Crete in the Mediterranean and Negroponte in the Aegean Sea.

These acquisitions made Venice into a great seaborne empire which dominated trade between West and East. Within the city of Venice itself, the *arsenale* became the largest industrial complex in Europe and the basis of the city's naval power. Here the Venetians developed assembly lines and standardized parts, from which an entire galley could be manufactured in a single day. So secret was the *arsenale* that anyone who entered without permission could be blinded or put to death. Its great walls, bearing the date 1460, still stand today.

After 1450, the Turks began to make inroads on the eastern fringes of Venetian empire, but the economy of Venice remained prosperous throughout the fifteenth century and prices were highly stable. Historian Frederic Lane finds an indicator of this new stability in the price of pepper, which had long been an exceptionally volatile commodity in medieval markets. After 1415, the price of pepper stabilized and fluctuated remarkably little until 1499—the result of Venetian commercial hegemony and of more fixed and regular trading conditions between East and West.[20]

By the late fifteenth century, the Venetians were extracting from their territories a public revenue of a million gold ducats a year, and much private wealth as well. The immense prosperity of Venice appeared in its 200 opulent churches, in its Ducal palace that was rebuilt on a magnificent scale in the fifteenth century, and in the private *palazzi* that still line the Grand Canal. Venice became the golden city of the west. Its purse-proud merchants looked with envy upon the *palazzo ca d'oro*, a palace covered entirely with gold. They prayed in the Cathedral of San Marco before the *pala d'oro*, a screen of gold. They dreamed of gold, lived for gold, and at St. Mark's they even appeared to worship gold.

Very different in spirit was the city of Florence, which also became a great center of commerce, industry and finance during this period. The Medici Bank, with branches in London, Geneva, Bruges and Avignon, became highly profitable. The city's silk and woolen industry also flourished in the fifteenth century. Prosperity came to great families such as the Medici themselves, and also to the *popolo minuto* of most social ranks and occupations.[21]

Prices in Florence remained stable through much of the fifteenth century, and wages were relatively high. Historian Richard Goldthwaite observes that "the stability of wages was the result of a general equilibrium" in this period. Prices also fluctuated within a fixed range from 1380 to 1470. Politics and social relations were comparatively orderly. In those years, Florence experienced nothing like the great revolt of the *Ciompi* in 1378.[22]

After many centuries of strife, the political and social institutions of Florence became more stable in the fifteenth century. The central figure was Cosimo de Medici. Without holding high office himself, Cosimo dominated his city from 1434 until his death in 1464. He gave Florence an enlightened and humane government, a more progressive system of taxation, a long period of prosperity at home, and a successful policy of peace abroad, which was maintained by complex diplomatic alliances. He also began a dynasty that continued under the leadership of his son Piero and his grandson Lorenzo de Medici.

The strength and confidence of Florence during the fifteenth century was captured by its culture. The soaring spirit of the *quattrocento* simultaneously appeared in the exquisite beauty of Donatello's sculpture, in the symmetry and grace of Brunelleschi's great Duomo (1420–

THE RENAISSANCE OF
THE FIFTEENTH CENTURY

- School of Art
- Early Printing Press and Date
- Birthplaces of Artists and Writers

N

NORWAY

SWEDEN

SCOTLAND

Edinburgh

IRELAND

Dublin

DENMARK

Coverdale 1488

NORTH SEA

Cranmer 1489

Agricola, 1443   Lübeck

ENGLAND

HOLY

Tyndale 1490   Colet, 1466   Leiden 1483   Bremen
Malory   Oxford 1478   More, 1478   London 1477   Wittenberg
15th Cent.   Thames   Utrecht 1473   Weser
Caxton, 1422   Bruges 1476   Rotterdam   Gouda 1477   Oder
Erasmus, 1466   Cologne 1466
Canterbury   Louvain   Luther, 1483
Linacre, 1480   Van de Wyden,   Massys, 1460   Ulrich   Elbe
1400   Gossart,   von Hutten, 1488
Le Favre 1445   Comines,   1470   Mainz by 1454   Frankfurt   Erfurt
d' Étaples,   Melanchthon, 1497   Bamberg 1460   Cracow 147
1455   Nicholas of Cusa, 1401   Trier   ROMAN   Prague
Seine   Würzburg   Nuremberg 1470   Pilsen 1468
Paris 1470   Mannheim   Behaim, 1480   Regensburg
Heidelberg   Dürer, 1471   Altdorfer, 1480

FRANCE   Blois   Fontainebleau   Strassburg   Reuchlin, 1455   Danube
Amboise   Villon, 1430   1460   Augsburg   Vien
Loire   Chambord   Basel   1468   Holbein, 1497   147
Azay-le-Rideau   Dijon   1462   Constance
Bay   Rabelais, 1490   Tours   Saone   Zurich   Zwingli, 1484
Jean Fouquet, 1415   Paracelsus, 1493   EMPIRE   Budapest 147
of Biscay   Angouleme   ALPS
Marguerite de Navarre,   Geneva
1492   Milan   Venice
Bordeaux   Garonne   Lyon 1473   1470   Venice 1469

PORTUGAL   Genoa   Ferrara
Loyola, 1493   Avignon   Bologna   ADRIATIC SEA
Magellan, 1480   NAVARRE   PYRENEES   Florence 1471
Duoro   Marseilles   Pisa   Perugia
Ximenes, 1438   Zaragoza 1475   Siena
Tagus   Madrid   Ebro   CORSICA   PAPAL STATES
ARAGON   Barcelona   (Genoa)   Rome 1467   Subiaco 1465
Guadiana   CASTILE
Valencia 1474   BALEARIC ISLANDS   Naples
Guadalquivir   (Aragon)   TYRRHENIAN SEA
Seville   1480   SARDINIA
Las Casas, 1474   (Aragon)
GRANADA
MEDITERRANEAN SEA   Palermo

SICILY
(Aragon)

0 Kilometers   250   500
0 Miles   250   500

After R.R. Palmer, *Atlas of World History*, Rand McNally & Company, N.Y., 1957, p. 58-59.

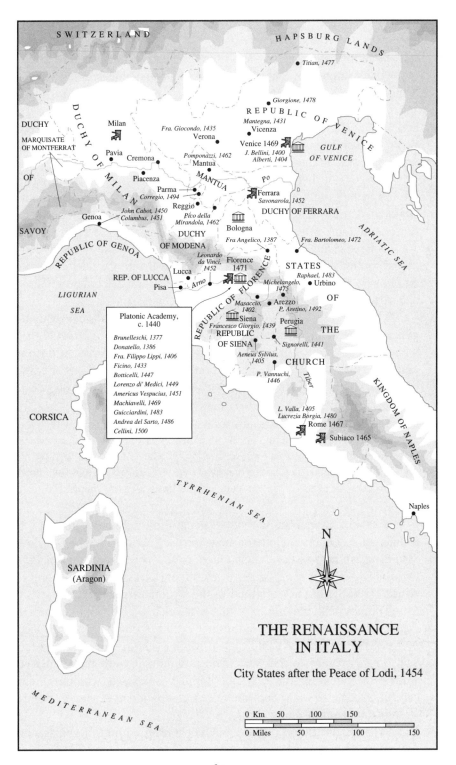

SWITZERLAND

HAPSBURG LANDS

● Titian, 1477

● Giorgione, 1478

REPUBLIC OF VENICE

DUCHY OF MILAN

DUCHY

Milan

Fra. Giocondo, 1435
Verona

Mantegna, 1431
Vicenza

MARQUISATE
OF MONTFERRAT

Pavia ● Cremona

Pomponazzi, 1462
● Mantua

Venice 1469
J. Bellini, 1400
Alberti, 1404

GULF
OF VENICE

OF

Piacenza

MANTUA

PO

Parma ●
Corregio, 1494

Ferrara
Savonarola, 1452

SAVOY

John Cabot, 1450
Columbus, 1451

Reggio ●
Pico della
Mirandola, 1462

DUCHY OF FERRARA

ADRIATIC SEA

Genoa ●

Bologna

REPUBLIC OF GENOA

DUCHY
OF MODENA

Fra Angelico, 1387

Fra. Bartolomeo, 1472

Leonardo
da Vinci,
1452

Florence
1471

STATES

LIGURIAN
SEA

REP. OF LUCCA

Lucca
Pisa ●

Arno

REPUBLIC OF FLORENCE

Raphael, 1483
Michelangelo, ● Urbino
1475

OF

Masaccio,
1402

● Arezzo
P. Aretino, 1492

Platonic Academy,
c. 1440

Siena
Francesco Giorgio, 1439

Perugia

THE

Brunelleschi, 1377
Donatello, 1386
Fra. Filippo Lippi, 1406
Ficino, 1433
Botticelli, 1447
Lorenzo di' Medici, 1449
Americus Vespucius, 1451
Machiavelli, 1469
Guicciardini, 1483
Andrea del Sarto, 1486
Cellini, 1500

REPUBLIC
OF SIENA

Signorelli, 1441

Aeneus Sylvius,
1405

CHURCH

P. Vannuchi,
1446

Tiber

CORSICA

L. Valla, 1405
Lucrezia Borgia, 1480
Rome 1467

Subiaco 1465

KINGDOM OF NAPLES

TYRRHENIAN SEA

Naples ●

N

SARDINIA
(Aragon)

THE RENAISSANCE
IN ITALY

City States after the Peace of Lodi, 1454

MEDITERRANEAN SEA

0 Km   50   100   150

0 Miles   50   100   150

24) above the cathedral, in the austere grandeur of the Medici Palace, in the quiet serenity of San Marco's convent cells, and especially in the beautiful frescos that were painted there by Fra Angelico (1439–45). The striking contrast between the celebrations of St. Mark in Florence and Venice could scarcely have been more complete. In very different ways, both cities captured the general mood of confidence and certainty that flourished in the north of Italy during the fifteenth century.

Throughout that region, a remarkable transformation occurred in the life of the mind during the *quattrocento*. "Ever since the humanists' own days," writes historian Hans Baron, "the transition from the fourteenth to the fifteenth century has been recognized as a time of big and decisive changes." During the early decades of the fifteenth century, Florentine humanists such as Leonardo Bruni, Coluccio Salutati and Poggio Bracciolini produced a literature which celebrated republican virtue, the rule of law, and the power of reason.

This intellectual movement culminated in the rhetorical extravagance of Pico della Mirandola's *Oration on the Dignity of Man* (1486), which argued that the greatness of man consisted in his freedom from material constraints. In Pico's oration, the following words are addressed by God to Adam:

> You may have and possess whatever abode, form and functions that you might desire. The nature of all other beings is limited and constrained within the bounds of law prescribed by us. But you, constrained by no limits, in accordance with your own free will, in whose hand we have placed you, shall ordain for yourself the limits of your nature.[23]

Pico's idea of human life without external limit was one aspect of the Renaissance. Others included a new spirit of civic humanism, a new idea of republican virtue, a new classicism, a new conception of Platonic idealism, and most of all a new dream of symmetry and order, which Hans Baron has described as the "geometric spirit."

The physical expression of this new spirit was the architecture of the Renaissance palaces that multiplied in Florence—the Medici palace north of the Duomo; the Pitti palace south of the river Arno, and the vast Strozzi palace to the west. These buildings, with their massive walls, rusticated masonry, heavy cornices, exposed windows, and careful symmetries all communicated a confident sense of order, strength and equilibrium.

Whether one thinks of the neoclassical proportions of Renaissance architecture, or the rules of perspective in Renaissance painting, or the idea of balance in Renaissance statecraft, or the Platonic system-building of Renaissance philosophy, these expressions shared an assumption that the world was a place of harmony, symmetry, proportion and balance. They expressed a mood of cosmic optimism that arose during an era of comparative stability in the material culture of the West—an era that might well be remembered as the equilibrium of the Renaissance.[24]

THE SECOND WAVE
ぞ❧ The Price Revolution of the Sixteenth Century

I can get no remedy against this consumption of the purse;
borrowing only lingers and lingers it out, but the disease is
incurable.
—Shakespeare's Sir John Falstaff
Henry IV, Part 2, 1.2.216 (1597)

LORENCE, June 24, 1491, the festival of San Giovanni. On this
happy summer day, the citizens of a great and prosperous city
honored their patron saint, John the Baptist. Every year the
Florentines spent months in preparation for an event which they believed to be "unparalleled in the world."

The festival of St. John was a joyous holiday for people of every
rank. Servants received new livery, and a day of freedom. Masters and
mistresses appeared in extravagant new costumes and jewels. The *ma-
gnati* of the city, who in years past had met in mortal combat at the
city's piazza, now competed for honor in contests of material display.
The morning was marked by tournaments, by fights between wild
animals, and by demonstrations of martial arts called *armeggerie.*
Great crowds gathered to watch the *palio,* a wild and dangerous horse
race through the streets of the city. There was a lively parade of the
gonfalonieri, marching proudly with their billowing flags. The evening
of the festival was a traditional time for weddings, which had been
postponed for weeks to honor the occasion. The grand climax was a
solemn religious procession of colorful floats called *trionfi,* which celebrated scenes from the life of Christ and St. John.

Those things had been done for as many years as anyone could remember. But this year a change was made. In place of the religious floats, the first citizen of Florence Lorenzo de' Medici ordered the construction of fifteen *trionfi* on a classical rather than a Christian theme. The new floats celebrated the triumph of Roman consul Lucius Aemilius Paulus Macedonicus, whose victories had brought so much treasure to Rome that its citizens were freed from some of their taxes for forty years.[1]

These new Florentine *trionfi* were drawn through the streets by 100 oxen, and escorted by five squadrons of war horses from the Laurentian stables. An historian at the time observed that this display "was considered the worthiest thing ever done on the day of San Giovanni." A parallel was pointedly drawn between the largesse of Paulus Macedonicus and the generosity of Lorenzo de' Medici, whose family had spent more than a million florins in acts of philanthropy. In the process, an old religious procession was turned into a secular event that celebrated the prosperity of the city, the stability of its institutions, the generosity of the Medici family, and the glory of their young leader who was called Lorenzo il Magnifico.[2]

In 1491, the city of Florence had much to celebrate. "The city enjoyed perfect peace," its historian Guicciardini wrote, "the citizens in power were united and close, and their regime was so powerful that no one dared oppose it. Every day, the people were treated to shows, feasts, and novelties; provisions abounded in the city, and all the trades prospered. Genius and ability flourished, for all men of arts, letters, and ability were welcomed and honored. At home, the city enjoyed complete order and quiet; and abroad, the highest glory and reputation."[3]

The city was at the very pinnacle of its power. It had enlarged its domain in Tuscany, and had so strengthened its alliances that it appeared to be "the fulcrum of all Italy."[4] Money flowed into its coffers at such a rate that only three days before the Feast of St. John, the commune announced that citizens would be allowed to pay their public obligations at only a fraction of the usual rate. A month before the festival, the mint-masters issued a new Florentine coin that "was thought [to] work miracles with the economy." Throughout the city, the great Renaissance palaces and especially Brunelleschi's majestic *duomo* above the cathedral symbolized an era of prosperity and stability.[5]

So it seemed in 1491, when the people of Florence celebrated the day of their patron saint. But beneath the surface, things were not as they appeared. Once again, at the very moment when it was least expected, a deep change was silently stirring in Florence itself and throughout the Western world. After nearly a century of equilibrium, new trends were beginning to develop in Italy and other parts of Europe.

An early sign was the movement of prices. During the last quarter of the fifteenth century, the cost of living had begun to rise in Italy and Germany. The magnitude of its increase was not very great, but in retrospect we are able to recognize the silent beginning of a new change-regime that was destined to continue for many generations.

The people of Tuscany sensed the new trend long before they saw it clearly. Within nine months of the Feast of St. John, the cultural mood began to change in Florence. It started with an omen of a sort that Florentines took very seriously. On the fifth of April, in the year 1492, the sky suddenly turned black above the city. A brilliant bolt of lightning streaked down from the heavens and struck Brunelleschi's soaring *duomo* with a mighty crash.[6]

As if on cue, a sinister friar named Girolamo Savonarola emerged from his cell at the convent of San Marco and delivered a dark prophecy to the people of Florence. "Tell Lorenzo to do penance for his sins," Savonarola warned, "for God will punish him." Before a vast crowd, the friar prophesied the death of il Magnifico himself and an ordeal of suffering for his city.[7]

Within months, both prophecies came true. In 1492, the magnificent young Lorenzo died suddenly of a strange illness. The *coup de grace* may have been administered by his own physicians, who ordered this great sybarite to drink a potion of powdered pearls as a last desperate remedy for his mysterious affliction. He was barely 43 years old.

After Lorenzo's death, the peace and prosperity of Florence collapsed. His carefully crafted foreign policy was destroyed by his reckless son and heir, Piero di Lorenzo de' Medici. As the Italian states resumed their ancient quarrels a French army seized the moment, crossed the Alps and occupied Florence. An angry mob sacked the Medici palace, and Piero di Lorenzo was banished from the city. After a brief revival of republican liberty, Florence passed under the sway of Friar Savonarola, who ruled the city from 1494 to 1498.

Savonarola tirelessly lectured the people on their sins, and blamed their troubles on spiritual corruption and love of luxury. He persuaded them to do penance for their prosperity. In an orgy of remorse they built a huge bonfire of their beloved Renaissance paintings, books, furniture and musical instruments in the Piazza de Signori. Just before the pile was set alight, an incredulous Venetian merchant offered to remove the offending vanities for 20,000 gold ducats. His reward was to have his own portrait instantly painted, and thrown into the flames.[8]

The burning of the vanities in Florence on February 7, 1497, became one of the best remembered scenes of the Italian Renaissance. Not so well known, even to professional historians, was its close conjunction with economic events. Prices surged very high in the 1490s, and the economy began to fail. On February 19, 1497, only twelve days after the burning of the vanities, there was a riot in the old Piazzo del Grano, the site of the city's public granary. The starving poor, driven to desperation by rising food prices, gathered before the granary in such numbers that some were crushed and others were suffocated. The surging crowd broke down the doors and attacked the granary, crying "Palle, palle," the nickname of the Medici who had so often helped them in the past.[9]

Hungry peasants crowded into the city from the hills of Tuscany. The streets and hospitals were filled with dying people. Famine was followed by epidemic disease, and Florence found itself once again in the grip of the plague. Savonarola wrote his brother, "Every day we see nothing in Florence but crosses and corpses." The city itself was described as "a living corpse." What remained of it was consumed by foreign war and domestic disorder until self-government was destroyed.[10]

In 1498, the people of Florence began to blame Savonarola himself for their misfortunes, and turned savagely against their spiritual leader. On the eve of Ascension Day they burned him at the stake while the mob jeered, "Prophet, now is the time for a miracle."[11]

These events were a pivot-point in Italian history. After the death of Savonarola, Italy became a bloody cockpit for the great powers. Foreign armies laid waste to Tuscany. Venice was despoiled of her empire by the French in the west and by the Turks to the east. Rome itself was brutally sacked in 1527. In 1530 the proud republic of Florence became a dark and wretched despotism, which called itself the Grand Duchy of Tuscany. These happenings ended the equilibrium of the Renaissance. They marked the beginning of a new material process which economic historians call the price-revolution of the sixteenth century.[12]

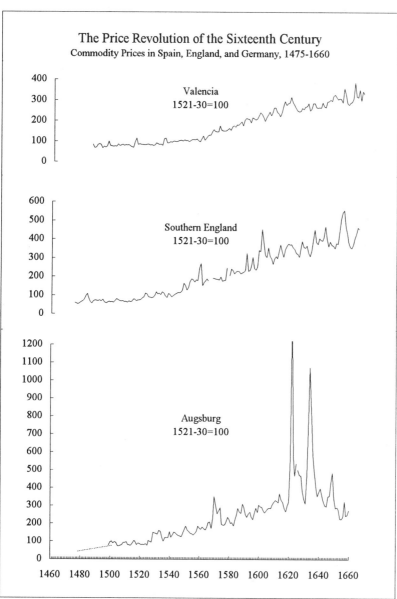

The Price Revolution of the Sixteenth Century
Commodity Prices in Spain, England, and Germany, 1475-1660

Valencia
1521-30=100

Southern England
1521-30=100

Augsburg
1521-30=100

Figure 2.01 shows the main lines of this price revolution from its beginning in the late fifteenth century to its climax in the mid-seventeenth century. Annual indices of consumable prices in England, and commodity prices in Germany and Spain, are converted to a common base (1521-30=100). The sources are Henry Phelps-Brown and Sheila Hopkins, *A Perspective of Wages and Prices* (London, 1981), 28-31, 94-98; Moritz J. Elsas, *Umriss eine Geschichte der Preise und Löhne in Deutschland* (2 vols., Leiden, 1936-40); Earl J. Hamilton, *Money, Prices, and Wages in Valencia, Aragon, and Navarre, 1351-1500* (Cambridge, 1936); *idem, American Treasure and the Price Revolution in Spain, 1501-1650* (Cambridge, 1934), 191, 200, 216.

69

❧ The Price Revolution Begins, circa 1470–80

The first signs appeared in the north of Italy and southern Germany. The price of grain in Florence began to rise about the year 1472. In the south German cities of Wurzburg, Munich and Augsburg, the new trend started about the same time. Throughout France and England, the inflection-point came a little later, approximately 1480. In Spain and Portugal, the price-revolution did not appear until after 1490. Parts of eastern Europe were not affected until 1500.[13]

Once begun, the new trend continued for a very long time. Historians call it the price-revolution of the sixteenth century—a name that is not precisely accurate. This very long wave began as early as 1470, and continued as late as 1650. Altogether, it had a run of 180 years—the longest price-revolution in modern history.[14]

Through that long period, the annual rate of inflation was very moderate by the measure of our own time. From 1490 to 1650, price increases averaged only about 1 percent each year. The speed of their advance seems very slow by modern standards, but it was twice as fast as the medieval wave and it was compounded for a very long time. An historian observes that "the most remarkable feature of the Price Revolution was not the pace at which prices rose, but the fact that a rising trend was sustained for so long."[15]

The underlying rate of change was remarkable for its stability. A striking pattern appears in that respect. When the price of grain in the Italian city of Modena is plotted on a semilog scale (which represents a constant rate of change as a straight line, the central trend was perfectly straight from the late fifteenth century to the early seventeenth.

There was much movement around that central trend. From year to year, the price of grain in Modena fluctuated sharply, mainly because of changes in the size of harvests. But these gyrations also showed stability in their rhythm and scale. Trendlines drawn through the peaks and valleys of annual price-fluctuations make two more straight lines. Here was another set of constants in the parameters of change, and a classic example of a change-regime that combined dynamism with stability in high degree.

The experience of Modena was not representative of the price-revolution as a whole. Patterns varied in detail from one city to another. But in general, the price-revolution of the sixteenth century showed a similar tendency in much of the Western world.[16]

What set this change-regime in motion? There are many answers

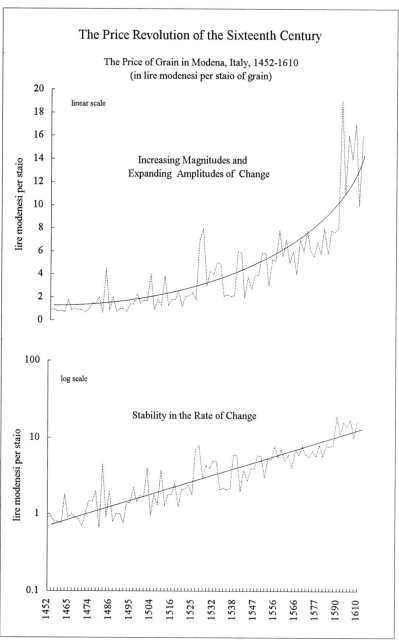

The Price Revolution of the Sixteenth Century

The Price of Grain in Modena, Italy, 1452-1610
(in lire modenesi per staio of grain)

linear scale

Increasing Magnitudes and
Expanding Amplitudes of Change

log scale

Stability in the Rate of Change

Figure 2.02 examines components of change in this price revolution: increasing magnitudes, expanding amplitudes, and stability in the underlying rate of change. The source is Gian Luigi Basini's elegant monograph *Sui mercato di Modena tra cinque e seicento: Prèzzi e salari* (Milan, 1974). Trend lines are fitted with an Excel 5.0 program.

in the literature: monetarist, Malthusian, Marxist, and more. As the evidence continues to grow, many historians (including this one) have come to believe that prime mover of the price-revolution was a revival of population growth, which placed heavy pressure on material resources.

This demographic tendency began during the late fifteenth century, when parallel tendencies appeared in England, Italy, Spain, Germany, France, the Low Countries, Switzerland, Scandinavia and eastern Europe. Most nations experienced the same sequence of change: catastrophe in the mid-fourteenth century, continuing decline of population to the end of the fourteenth century; stagnation and slow growth in the early and mid-fifteenth century; acceleration after 1460 or 1470.

England was a case in point. That country had approximately two million inhabitants in 1430, and not many more in 1470. Thereafter, the population of England began to grow more rapidly. It reached 2.8 millions by 1541, and more than four millions by the end of the sixteenth century. Historian Michael Postan found evidence that this de-

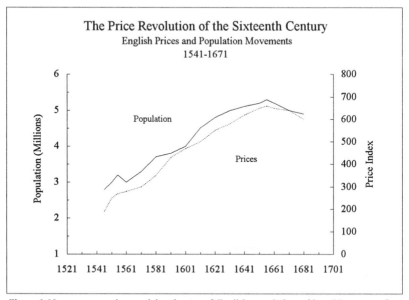

Figure 2.03 compares quinquennial estimates of English population with a 25-year moving average of the Phelps-Brown Index of English consumable prices. The source is E. A. Wrigley and R. S. Schofield, *The Population History of England, 1541-1871; A Reconstruction* (Cambridge, 1981), 403.

mographic trend began *circa* 1470, and continued through the sixteenth century.[17]

The cause of population growth after about 1460 is not difficult to discover. The prolonged period of economic equilibrium in the fifteenth century had been a time of increasing real wages, and a revolutionary rise in expectations. Many years after the catastrophe of the fourteenth century, the world at last seemed to be a better place in which to raise a family. This change of attitude was broadly cultural rather than narrowly material. In the period from 1460 to 1510, millions of men and women throughout Europe freely decided for their own purposes to marry earlier and have more children. The general trend emerged from a web of individual choices.[18]

The consequences were much the same as in the thirteenth century. German writer Sebastian Franck remarked in his *Deutschen Chronik* (1538) that "there are so many people everywhere, no one can move." In Italy, England, and France there were complaints of overcrowding in cities and the countryside. Similar observations were repeated throughout Europe.[19]

The effect of population growth was to undercut the cultural expectations that set it in motion. But this was not precisely a Malthusian process. Neither Malthus nor Marx can explain what happened in the sixteenth century. Long before population outstripped the means of its subsistence in a Malthusian manner, complex imbalances of other kinds began to develop.

As the demand for food increased, people began to bring marginal lands into cultivation, with large labor and small return. French historian Emmanuel Le Roy Ladurie described that process at work in Languedoc. That region had a thin and stony scrubland called the *garrigue* which had been abandoned since the Black Death. Now it began to be plowed and planted once again. This process began in the mid-sixteenth century. "By 1576," Le Roy Ladurie writes, "the rape of the *garrigue* was well underway. . . . Demographic pressure, the rise in demand, and the increase in prices had made their combined effect felt. One had to resign oneself to the working of poor, rocky soils."[20]

Many years before Malthusian "positive checks" came into operation, these more subtle mechanisms came into play. The growth of population caused the price of food to rise, faster and farther than that of other commodities. Industrial products and wages lagged behind. In Spain, economic historian Earl Hamilton found that "throughout the first three-quarters of the sixteenth century, agricultural prices rose faster than non-agricultural.'' Similar patterns appeared in England, France, Germany. This pattern of price-relatives was much the same as in the long wave of the thirteenth century.[21]

Once food prices began to rise, the cost of energy also started to climb at a rapid rate. In the early years of the price-revolution, energy prices increased slowly, then began to accelerate. In an environment that was rapidly losing its forest cover, the rising price of firewood and charcoal soon outstripped even the cost of food. After 1530 or thereabouts, the price of wood in all its forms (including charcoal) increased more rapidly than that of grain or meat or any other commodity.[22] Wood prices rose sharply in England, France, Germany and Poland. Energy prices were among the most volatile in the long inflation of the sixteenth century.[23]

The movement of price-relatives revealed differences not merely of magnitude but also of timing. The secular rise in farm prices began before the increase in the cost of manufactured goods. In England, the price of grain began to rise as early as 1470–89, forty years before most

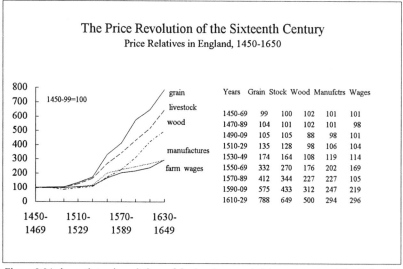

The Price Revolution of the Sixteenth Century
Price Relatives in England, 1450-1650

Years	Grain	Stock	Wood	Manufctrs	Wages
1450-69	99	100	102	101	101
1470-89	104	101	102	101	98
1490-09	105	105	88	98	101
1510-29	135	128	98	106	104
1530-49	174	164	108	119	114
1550-69	332	270	176	202	169
1570-89	412	344	227	227	105
1590-09	575	433	312	247	219
1610-29	788	649	500	294	296

Figure 2.04 shows that price relatives of food and raw materials rose most rapidly. Industrial prices and farm wages lagged far behind. This pattern appeared in every price revolution. Sources include D. C. Coleman, *The Economy of England, 1450-1750* (Oxford, 1977), 23; and P. Bowden, "Statistical Appendix," in Joan Thirsk, ed., *The Agrarian History of England and Wales* (Cambridge, 1967) IV, appendix.

industrial products, which started to climb *circa* 1510–39. In Poland, the price of Torún rye was rising from about 1495, and Cracow oats from 1505; Polish manufactures began to go up later.[24]

The price of manufactures also rose at a slower pace than those of food and fuel. Throughout Europe, the slowest rates of increase were for industrial goods which could be produced most easily in larger quantity. In England, the price of food and fuel rose by a factor of six or eight, while industrial prices merely trebled. That pattern of price relatives has appeared in every great wave.

The timing and magnitude of these changes in price-relatives is an important clue to the cause of the price-revolution. The earliest and most rapid increases appeared in the cost of life's necessities such as food and fuel and shelter, which were most in demand when population was accelerating, and least elastic in supply. Here was strong evidence of a demand-driven demographic determinant at work. A monetary cause alone should have been more even-handed in its effect.[25]

The Second Stage: Discovery and Cultural Response

In the early and middle years of the sixteenth century, the price-revolution entered another phase. It did so when the long inflation broke through the boundaries of the old price system that had prevailed in the mid-fifteenth century. As it rose beyond the range of fluctuations in the preceding equilibrium, it became visible as a new trend. Individuals and governments began observe that prices were rising in a secular way. Their responses added another dynamic which carried the price-revolution to a different stage.

When the price-revolution became visible, people sought explanations. Many looked for someone to blame. In England, members of Parliament attributed rising prices to "covetous and insatiable persons seeking their only lucre and gain." Others blamed the price-revolution on export merchants, who were thought to have sent so many goods abroad that "corn, victual and wood are grown unto a wonderful dearth and extreme prices." In 1555, Parliament forbade exports of food and wood when prices rose above a fixed level.[26]

These laws had less effect than did the individual actions of ordinary people. Their responses to inflation caused more inflation. The daily choices that people made in the face of rising prices, tended to drive prices even higher. This happened in many ways—some highly

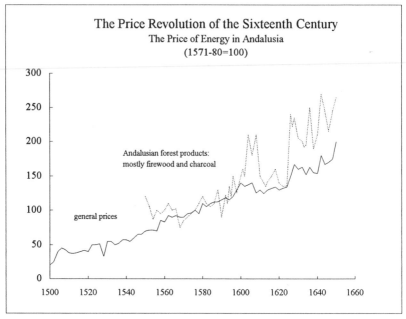

The Price Revolution of the Sixteenth Century
The Price of Energy in Andalusia
(1571-80=100)

Figure 2.05 shows another feature of most price revolutions: in late stages, sharp surges in the cost of energy. In these Spanish data, forest products include ashes, firewood, charcoal, resin and pitch. General prices are a weighted commodity index, averaged among four regions of Valencia, Andalusia, Old Castile and New Castile. Prices of forest products rose higher in Andalusia than in Valencia but lower than in Old Castile or New Castile. The source is Earl J. Hamilton, *American Treasure and the Price Revolution in Spain, 1501-1650* (Cambridge, 1954), 224.

rational, others not. One response was the hoarding of goods. Another was speculation. A third was panic buying. A fourth was the degradation of commodities.

Farmers kept grain from the market in fear of famine in their own households. Millers hoarded flour in hope of profits to come. Communities and entire states blocked the movement of grain beyond their boundaries. Merchants cornered local markets. Bakers added sawdust (and worse things) to their bread, and defied the market-assizes by selling smaller loaves for larger prices. These responses caused prices to climb higher, and also increased their volatility.

ﺽ Social Imbalances

Some people, more than others, were able to respond to rising prices. As a consequence, social imbalances began to develop. At the beginning of the price-revolution, wages had risen more or less together with the cost of food and shelter. While they did so, there was a heady sense of high prosperity. In later stages of the price-revolution that pattern changed. Money-wages lagged behind the rising cost of living, and real wages fell sharply. By 1570 real wages were less than half of what they had been before the price-revolution began.[27]

This decline of real wages, once begun, continued into the early seventeenth century. Most vulnerable were workers who had few skills and no capital of their own. "The real victims of economic forces in this age," writes Peter Ramsay, "were the evicted agrarian small-holder and the landless laborer of both town and country."[28]

By comparison, landlords and capitalists tended to do better. Re-turns to capital kept pace with commodity prices and even leaped ahead in some decades of the sixteenth century. Overall, rates of interest rose during the sixteenth century despite a proliferation of usury laws and condemnations by Catholic and Protestant moralists. The Hapsburgs were forced to pay their bankers annual interest as high as 52 percent. These were exceptionally high rates, but in the developing money markets of early modern Europe, rates of interest rose during the six-teenth century.[29]

Returns to landowners also increased during the price-revolution. A landlord who was secure in the possession of his property held many private remedies for rising prices firmly in his own hands. Manorial customs provided landlords with a broad range of opportunities for increasing their own income in rents, fees, fines, forfeitures and obliga-tory services. There was more than one way for a feudal lord to in-crease his income from tenants. Most of all, he could raise the rent. During part of the sixteenth century, rents and land prices rose even more rapidly than food and fuel. One study finds that English rents increased ninefold from 1510 to 1640, while grain went up by a factor of four and wages barely doubled. In Belgium, land prices increased elevenfold; in Holstein, they multiplied by a factor of fourteen during the same period.[30]

Contemporary observers counted the movement of rent itself as a leading cause of rising prices. A husbandman in Hales's *Discourse of the Common Weal* was made to say to landowners, "I think it is long of you gentlemen that this dearth is, by reason you enhance your lands to such a height, as men that live thereon must need sell dear again, or else they were not able to make the rent."[31]

Increases in rent caused much rural unrest. In England, a leading demand in Kett's Rebellion (1549) was that copyhold rents should be

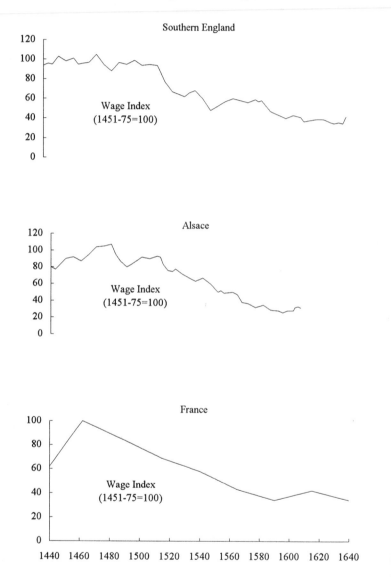

The Price Revolution of the Sixteenth Century
Returns to Labor: The Long Fall of Real Wages, circa 1480-1640

Southern England

120
100
80
60
40
20
0

Wage Index
(1451-75=100)

Alsace

120
100
80
60
40
20
0

Wage Index
(1451-75=100)

France

100
80
60
40
20
0

Wage Index
(1451-75=100)

1440 1460 1480 1500 1520 1540 1560 1580 1600 1620 1640

Figure 2.06 shows that real wages (deflated by consumable prices) fell throughout Europe from the late fifteenth century to the mid-seventeenth century. The data are eleven-year moving averages for Southern England and Alsace, and twenty-five-year fixed averages for France. The source is Phelps-Brown and Hopkins, *A Perspective of Wages and Prices*, 62.

Figure 2.07 compares rents per acre on landed estates with an index of consumable prices in England. The source is Eric Kerridge, "The Movement of Rent, 1540-1640," *Economic History Review* 2d ser., 6 (1953-54) 16-34.

rolled back to rates that had prevailed 65 years earlier, during the first year of Henry VII (1485). Similar complaints were heard throughout western Europe.[32]

As always, some of the worst exploitation occurred in the east, where serfdom and forced labor had persisted. "In Poland," writes historian Stanislas Hoszowski, "landowners benefitted most, while the disadvantages fell on the peasants. . . . The rise in cereal and food prices encouraged landowners to change feudal cash payments into labor rents. They created new demesnes, forcing their peasants to work on them unpaid. Minimum production costs and the large profits to be derived from the system encouraged the nobility to extend the estates at the expense of peasant farms and to exploit peasants on an ever increasing scale." Hoszowski concludes that the price-revolution actually strengthened the feudal system in eastern Europe. Everywhere, it made the dominant elites richer and stronger than they had been before.[33]

The growing gap between returns to labor and rewards to capital was one of the most important social consequences of inflation in the sixteenth century. These trends caused inequality to grow, in a society that was grossly unequal before they began.

Great wealth and grievous poverty increased in the mid-sixteenth

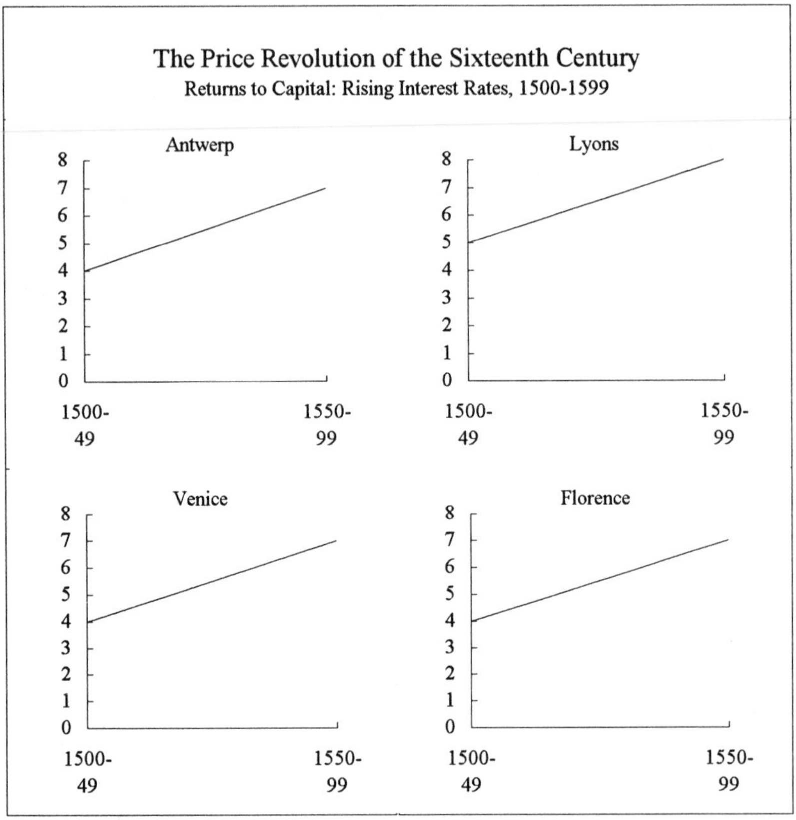

Figure 2.08 finds evidence in fragmentary data that interest rates nearly doubled in the mid-sixteenth century, outpacing the rise of prices in the same period. The source is Homer, *A History of Interest Rates,* 121, 137, 140.

century. In England, the numbers of beggars and vagabonds and homeless people were observed to rise rapidly during the price-revolution. The growth of inequality created a set of social imbalances that grew increasingly dangerous throughout the western world.[34]

❧ Monetary Imbalances

Another imbalance developed in the monetary system. Once again, as in the medieval price-revolution, individuals and institutions responded to inflation by taking actions which expanded the supply of money. In western Europe, historian Georg Wiebe estimated that the supply of silver increased from approximately 10,000 tons in 1550, to more than 23,000 tons by 1600, and above 34,000 tons in 1660. Subsequent research challenged these numbers in detail, but confirmed the general trend.[35]

The largest part of this increase was American silver and gold, that flowed abundantly into Europe after 1500. The cause of the price-revolution of the sixteenth century has often been attributed to this single factor: large imports of American metal, which increased the quantity of money in circulation, and reduced its purchasing power by expanding its supply.

In light of much historical research, this monetarist explanation must be revised, without being rejected. American treasure could not have been the first cause of a price-revolution. Prices began to go up as early as 1480, many years before American silver and gold arrived in Europe. In England and Germany, prices nearly doubled during the half century before American silver could have had a significant effect on their economies.[36]

Further, major fluctuations in the flow of treasure from America did not correlate with variations in price-movements, in time or space. In Spain, where the impact of American treasure was comparatively large, the pace of inflation actually lagged behind other parts of Europe. Moreover, the largest proportionate increases in Spanish prices occurred during the first half of the sixteenth century—not the second half, when American treasure had its greatest impact.[37]

Similar disparities also appeared in northwestern Europe, where one of the largest inflationary surges occurred during the period from 1552 to 1560, when imports of gold and silver were comparatively small. From 1570 to 1590, on the other hand, silver imports from America rose at a rapid rate while prices actually fell a little.[38]

Yet another difficulty for a monistic monetary model appears in recent collaborative research by chemists and historians on the diffusion of American silver in Europe. The largest trove of American treasure was found in the fabulous silver mountain at Potosí, which became a monument to earthly abundance, cruelty, and greed. Spanish conquerors discovered the silver of Potosí in 1545, and forced Indians to mine a vast quantity of precious metal, at terrible cost in human suffering. Nearly half of all the silver produced in America from 1521 to 1610 came from Potosí alone.

The silver of Potosí was highly distinctive in its chemical composition, which allows a metallurgical test of its diffusion. The results are

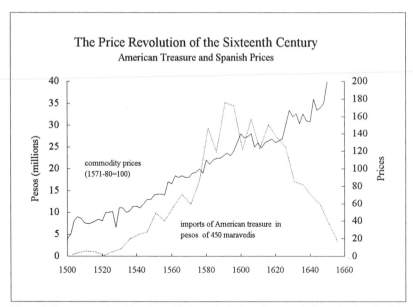

The Price Revolution of the Sixteenth Century
American Treasure and Spanish Prices

commodity prices (1571-80=100)

imports of American treasure in pesos of 450 maravedis

Figure 2.09 compares Spanish prices with the arrival of precious metals from the New World. The evidence shows that American treasure contributed in a major way to the momentum of the price revolution, but did not set it in motion, or sustain it to the end. The data are from Hamilton, *American Treasure and the Price Revolution in Spain*, 35, 228.

instructive for students of this event. Silver from Potosí appeared in the coinage of Spain, Genoa, Milan, and Venice, but not until after the mid-sixteenth century. It was found on the Atlantic coast of France, but not in large quantity until the 1590s, more than a century after the price-revolution began. None was discovered in Belgium, England, the Netherlands or most other parts of France. The inventors of this test concluded, perhaps prematurely, that South American silver had little impact on the coinage of northern Europe in the sixteenth century. It would be more accurate to say that its impact was not felt until the later stages of the price-revolution.[39]

In short, the price-revolution came first; American treasure followed later. The test of timing is decisive here. One of the few clear and simple laws of historical causality is that the effect cannot precede the cause. The old idea that American treasure was the first cause of the price-revolution in Europe during the sixteenth century will not do.

Nevertheless, the monetary model retains its relevance in other forms. It does so in ways that are more complex and also more interesting than a simple monetarist idea. The gold and silver of America did not set the price-revolution in motion, but powerfully reinforced its momentum. The effect of vast new supplies of gold and silver was to support an existing economic trend and to intensify its effect.[40]

Further, one may observe in the timing of this complex relationship an historical pattern that monetarism alone is powerless to explain. Monetary theory explains why an increase in the supply of money drives up prices. It cannot explain why the money-supply increases in the first place, except by introducing the monetarist's favorite *diabolus ex machina* in the form of corrupt and incompetent politicians who are believed to be too stupid or weak to understand the monetarist's favorite remedies.

To approach the price-revolution in broadly historical terms is to discover a more mature explanation. In every price-revolution, one finds evidence of frantic efforts to expand the supply of money, after people have discovered that prices are rising in a secular way. The price-revolution of the sixteenth century caused the rulers of Spain (who were hard-pressed to keep up with inflation) to redouble their efforts to extract gold and silver from their American dominions. Two

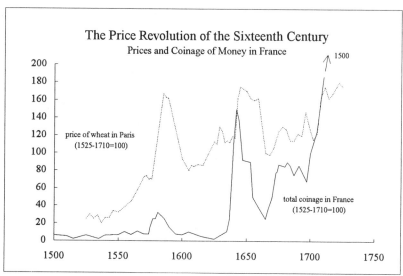

Figure 2.10 compares prices and coinage in France. It finds more evidence that expansion of the money supply contributed strongly to price-inflation in the middle and late years of the sixteenth century, but was not as important in early stages of the price-revolution. Fluctuations in coinage also caused movements around the central trend, but had less effect on the central tendency. The source is Frank Spooner, *The International Economy and Monetary Movements in France, 1493-1725* (Cambridge, Mass., 1972), 273.

tendencies powerfully reinforced each other. Together they created a dynamic of high importance in the history of that troubled age.

The same processes worked in other ways. Another monetary factor (small by the measure of American treasure but still important) was the mining of precious metals within Europe, which also expanded during the sixteenth century. The great inflation created a voracious hunger for a larger circulating medium. Old mines were reopened at heavy expense. Once again, most of this activity came after the price-revolution had begun.[41]

In Russia, the Tsars made major efforts to encourage production of gold and silver. In 1567, Ivan IV actively recruited mining experts abroad. Thirty years later, Tsar Fedor Ivanovich asked his ambassador in Italy to pay any price for miners. There was an air of desperation in these acts. Increased supplies of European and Russian silver also contributed to rising prices.[42]

It is important to observe that the correlation between the rise of prices and the minting of money in western Europe was itself variable through time— another vital clue. The association was comparatively weak in the early sixteenth century. It became stronger in the period from 1550 to 1610. This finding strongly suggests that monetarist factors operated as historical variables. They were more powerful in the second stage of the price-revolution than in the first.[43]

After the mid-sixteenth century, intelligent observers began to discover that a relationship existed between prices and the size of the money supply. The quantity theory of money was invented during the second stage of this price-revolution. In 1556, Spanish scholar Martin de Azpilcueta proposed the thesis that ''money is worth more when and where it is scarce than when it is abundant.'' Further, he perceived that ''in Spain, in times when money was scarcer, saleable goods and labor were given for very much less than after the discovery of the Indies, which flooded the country with gold and silver.'' Twelve years later, French writer Jean Bodin developed the same idea. Other monetarist models were invented by the Polish scientist Nicolaus Copernicus, by the Florentine Davanzatti, by many English observers, and by other writers throughout Europe during the middle decades of the sixteenth century. These discoveries were made at a particular moment in the price-revolution.[44]

At the same time that these monetarist theories appeared in the mid–sixteenth century, other observers came to a different conclusion that the primary cause of rising prices was the growth of population. An example was England's Alderman Box, who wrote to Lord Burghley in 1576, "Now the time is altered . . . for the people are increased and ground for plows doth want, corn and all other victual is scant, [and] many strangers [are] suffered here, which make corn and victual deare." He recommended that "waste grounds" should be given to husbandmen—a remedy that found little favor among the possessing classes.[45]

A few people argued a third proposition that the cause of rising prices was an increase in both population and money. Thus George Hakewill wrote, "The plenty of coin and multitude of men . . . either of which asunder, but much more both together, must needs be a means of raising prices of all things." This was the most accurate explanation, but also the most complex. It had less appeal than simple monetary or demographic models.[46]

∂⬤ Fiscal Imbalances

The response of governments to rising prices created a third sort of imbalance, fiscal in its nature. By the mid-sixteenth century, large deficits were growing in the public accounts of European states. The problem was compounded by regressive taxation, and by the persistent tendency of the rich to shift the weight of taxes to poor and middling people.

By and large, the heaviest tax burdens fell upon the peasantry. In many parts of Europe the nobility were exempt from the most onerous forms of taxation. In Spain, for example, the privileged class called *hidalgos* were released from some taxes, though they were still compelled to pay a sales tax. During the sixteenth century, the *hidalgos* preserved and even expanded their special privileges at a time when the poor were groaning under their heavy burden and the government was unable to pay its bills.

As the price-revolution continued, the revenues of European states fell far behind expenditures. In desperation, governments borrowed heavily. The Spanish government kept going by mortgaging its annual treasure fleet before the ships arrived, to foreign bankers at ruinous rates of interest. Spain also issued annuities called *juros,* pledging an income to private lenders for many years into the future. By 1543, a

large part of Spanish revenue went to pay the interest on a public debt
that was soaring out of control. The effect was to weaken the spring of
government itself.[47]

These many responses to rising prices—social, demographic, economic, monetary, fiscal—interacted in combinations of increasing
power. For example, the price-revolution caused falling real wages and
rising returns to land and capital, which caused the growth of inequality,
which increased the political power of the rich, which led to regressive
taxation, which reduced government revenues, which encouraged currency debasements, which drove prices higher. This was merely one of
the more simple linkages in a causal web of high complexity.

As the web thickened, the price-revolution came to be elaborately
embedded in entire economic systems, and social conflicts began to
grow. The Protestant Reformation and Catholic Counter-Reforma-
tion shattered the most important unifying institution in the Western
world—the Christian church. Religious conflicts of great violence
broke out, and continued through a period that corresponded almost
exactly to the years of the price-revolution. These two movements—
Reformation and price-revolution—were connected. In Germany,

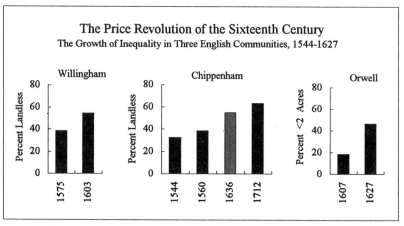

The Price Revolution of the Sixteenth Century
The Growth of Inequality in Three English Communities, 1544-1627

Figure 2.11 shows that in the period from 1544 to 1627 a growing proportion of English tenants
became landless (or held less than two acres) in three villages of Cambridgeshire: Chippenham
on chalk soil in East Cambridgeshire, Orwell on clay soil in West Cambridgeshire, and
Willingham in the fens near the Isle of Ely. All percentages are computed from Margaret
Spufford's tabulations of survey data except Chippenham in 1636, which is estimated from a
survey of landowning in that year and evidence of total population. The source is Margaret
Spufford, *Contrasting Communities: English Villagers in the Sixteenth and Seventeenth
Centuries* (Cambridge, 1974), 73, 100, 149.

many historians have found evidence that the rapid spread of the Protestant Reformation and also the Peasants' War were closely linked to
increasing economic stress, caused by population growth and price
inflation.[48]

These linkages appeared in Belgium and the Netherlands during
the 1560s, when Calvinism suddenly spread from one city to the next in
the so-called Iconoclast disorders. Mobs of newly converted Calvinists
attacked Catholic churches, smashing the sacred artifacts that were
hated symbols of the old religion.[49] Historians have concluded that the
Iconoclast movement was directly linked to economic instabilities, and
particularly to a sudden surge in grain prices in the Netherlands from
1564 to 1566.[50] Similar connections between religious conflicts and
economic fluctuations were also observed in England, France, Switzerland and Scandinavia from 1558 to 1640.[51]

The causal connection between economic and religious movements was highly complex. In some instances, price disturbances operated as a direct determinant of religious events—as with the Dutch and
Belgian Iconoclasts. In others, religious disturbances led to price fluctuations during the major wars of the Protestant Reformation. In general, it might be said that both the Reformation and Counter Reformation on the one hand, and the price-revolution on the other, were
parallel expressions of deep imbalances in European society.

?? From Imbalances to Instability

In the late sixteenth century, dangerous instabilities began to develop in
European society. Prices surged and declined in broad swings of increasing amplitude. A case in point was the price of grain in England,
which rose very sharply in great surges during the 1540s, 1570s, 1590s
and 1620s. Intervening decades were marked by periods of sudden
price-decline, which were sometimes equally disruptive. Similar patterns appeared in the prices of many commodities throughout Europe.
The effect on social and economic relationships was profoundly unset-
tling.

Historian Y. S. Brenner observes that ''while grain prices continued to rise gradually as the sixteenth century progressed, their yearly
fluctuations became more severe.'' He concludes that this pattern was
''consistent with the price behavior which is to be expected if a market's equilibrium between supply and demand is upset.''[52]

The price of grain rose and fell sharply from one harvest to the next, in a manner that was similar to price movements in the thirteenth century. As early as 1529, a major famine occurred throughout Europe. Its effects were especially severe in northern Italy. The city of Venice, with its huge granaries, was overrun by hungry peasants from the countryside. A Venetian wrote, "Give alms to two hundred and as many again appear. You cannot walk down a street or stop in a square or church without multitudes surrounding you to beg for charity: you see hunger written in their faces, their eyes like gemless rings, the wretchedness of their bodies with skins shaped only by bones. . . . many villages in the direction of the Alps have become completely uninhabited."[53]

Conditions worsened toward the end of the century. The greatest suffering occurred in the period from 1594 to 1597, when four harvests failed in a row. Much of Europe experienced a cruel famine which was long remembered as "the great dearth."

With famine came epidemic disease. Rates of mortality fluctuated through the long period of the price-revolution. When death rates fell several years running, prices increased and wages declined. On the other hand, when death rates rose, prices declined and wages increased. This happened in England during the 1550s, when epidemics took an exceptionally heavy toll— killing as many as 20 percent of the population in a five year period.[54]

Some were quick to profit from these misfortunes by speculation and the hoarding of scarce commodities. A dramatic example occurred in the cities of Ghent, Antwerp, and Lille during the years 1565 and 1566, when the Danish sound was closed to grain ships, and a major famine occurred in the Low Countries. One of Antwerp's richest merchants, Pauwels van Dale, bought large quantities of grain and kept it off the market to drive its price still higher. In September, 1565, while the poor were literally starving in the streets of Antwerp, the warehouse of Pauwels van Dale was so packed with grain that the building collapsed. A wild riot broke out and spread through the city.

Similar events occurred elsewhere. At Malines, the houses of grain speculators were marked with blood. Riots occurred in Ghent, Lille and other towns—an expression of popular rage against speculators and *monopoleurs* who not only profited from price fluctuations, but also made them worse.[55]

Hoarding and speculation spread widely through Europe in time of scarcity. They were done not only by merchants, but also by noble

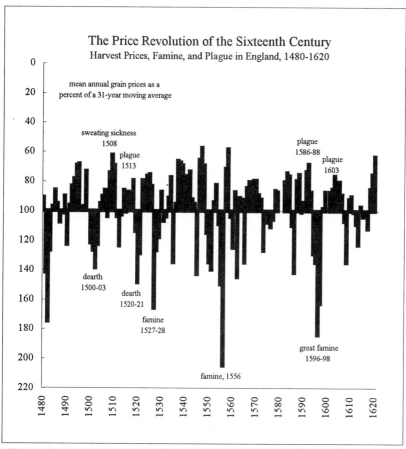

The Price Revolution of the Sixteenth Century
Harvest Prices, Famine, and Plague in England, 1480-1620

mean annual grain prices as a
percent of a 31-year moving average

sweating sickness
1508
plague
1513
plague
1586-88
plague
1603
dearth
1500-03
dearth
1520-21
famine
1527-28
great famine
1596-98
famine, 1556

Figure 2.12 compares wheat prices with major famines and plagues in England. The sources are the Bowden series of wheat prices in England, in W. G. Hoskins, *The Age of Plunder* (London, 1976), 87, 246-47; and Andrew Appleby, *Famine in Tudor and Stuart England* (Stanford, 1978), 95-154.

families and even monarchs. In Russia, historian Jerome Blum writes, "the price rise of this period was aggravated by the engrossing of goods by wealthy men, including the Tsar, who sought to benefit financially from the shortage."[56]

Monetary factors became yet another source of instability. European states and sovereigns tinkered endlessly with their coinage during the sixteenth century, sometimes inflating the value of their coins, sometimes deflating them again. In England, an inflationary "great debasement" from 1541 to 1551 drove prices higher. This was followed by a "great recoinage" in 1561, which had the opposite effect. By and large, debasements became more common than recoinages. The monetary policies of the European monarchs added momentum to the price-revolution, and increased its instability. A dangerous cyclical relationship developed. High prices forced governments to debase their currency; debasement in turn drove prices higher. The wheel kept spinning round and round.

Moralists preached against these practices. Merchants protested angrily. Even satirists added their mite. When the weight of silver in English testons was reduced by a third, the coins were ordered to be "blanched" or washed with a wafer-thin coat of silver so that the portrait of Henry VIII would remain bright and shiny. As they passed from hand to hand, the copper core quickly showed through, and gave the king a distinctly ruddy complexion. A poet wrote:

> These testons look red, how like you the same?
> 'Tis a token of grace; they blush for shame.[57]

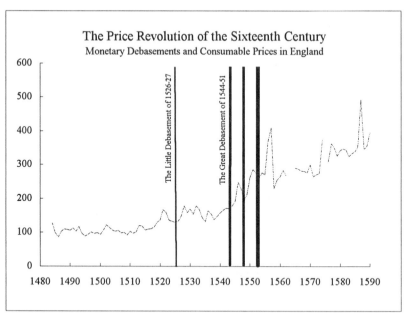

Figure 2.13 compares debasements of English money with the Phelps-Brown-Hopkins index of consumable prices in southern England (1451-75=100). The evidence indicates that debasements caused inflationary surges but did not drive the underlying trend. Sources include G. D. Gould, *The Great Debasement* (Oxford, 1970); C. E. Challis, *The Tudor Coinage* (Manchester, 1978); and Henry Phelps Brown and Sheila V. Hopkins, *A Perspective of Wages and Prices* (New York, 1981).

A related source of instability arose from international flows of specie. Europe in the late sixteenth century was awash with money, which sloshed back and forth from one sovereignty to another. Many contemporaries attributed the movement of prices primarily to international trade and the balance of payments. Sir Francis Drake's raids had a similar effect by different means. They removed from the Spanish economy between one and two million pounds (of which £600,000 were silver and gold bullion) and brought it to England between 1577 and 1580.[58]

Economic imbalances engendered political instabilities. Spain in the reigns of Charles V (1516–1556) and Philip II (1556–1598) was the strongest state in Europe. Like many other great powers, even to our own time, it fell into the fatal habit of deficit spending, and was finally reduced to a fiscal condition that historian J. H. Elliott describes as "chronic bankruptcy." At least six times between 1557 and 1647, the Spanish government went bankrupt, and found itself unable to meet its obligations or to borrow further. These fiscal crises occurred every twenty years with remarkable regularity—1557, 1575, 1596, 1607, 1627, 1647. Spanish historian Vicens Vives writes, "the vicious cycle was complete: the larger the state's debts became, the harder it was to meet them."[59] Other states were caught in the same cycle. Deficit financing was not invented in the twentieth century. In England, France and Germany, rulers became chronic debtors.[60]

These instabilities were deepened by the effect of war. The two steepest surges of inflation in the 1540s and 1590s were periods of heavy military spending. Here was yet another vicious circle between economic imbalances, political instability, and war.[61]

₰ The Crisis of the Seventeenth Century

During the decade of the 1590s, the price-revolution entered a new stage—a prolonged and very painful period that historians call the "general crisis of the seventeenth century." They use that name with good reason. This was the darkest era in European history after the catastrophe of the fourteenth century.[1]

The first signs were similar to those of the medieval crisis. During the last quarter of the sixteenth century, the economy of Europe was afflicted by the same cruel combination of rising prices and falling opportunities that neoclassical economists would call "stagflation" in the late twentieth century. The economy of England was a case in point. Historian Barry Supple writes, "the last years of Elizabeth's reign can no longer be considered as a prosperous era of economic expansion." He finds evidence of a deep economic depression in the 1580s and 1590s. At the same time, prices of consumables rose even more rapidly than before.[2]

Conditions differed in detail throughout Europe, but the general trends were much the same. Real wages and industrial prices were depressed, while the cost of food and fuel climbed higher, and also became highly unstable—rising and falling in sharp surges of increasing amplitude. The real wages of artisans and laborers fell farther behind the cost of living, while returns to land and capital continued to advance. Wealth became increasingly concentrated in a few hands. That tendency engendered Francis Bacon's epigram: "Money is like muck, not good except it be spread around." But the wealth of Europe was not spread around in the late sixteenth century. The rich grew richer, while increasing numbers of the poor were driven very near the edge of starvation.[3]

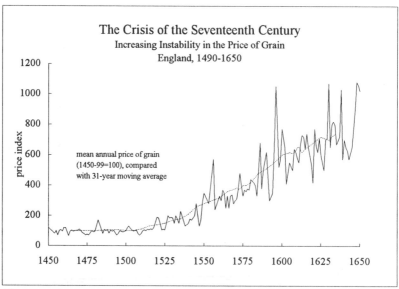

The Crisis of the Seventeenth Century
Increasing Instability in the Price of Grain
England, 1490-1650

mean annual price of grain
(1450-99=100), compared
with 31-year moving average

Figure 2.14 shows that harvest prices became more dangerously volatile as the price revolution approached its climax. It compares average annual prices of wheat, barley and oats with a 31-year moving average. The source is C. J. Harrison, "Grain Price Analysis and Harvest Qualities, 1465-1634," *Agricultural History Review* 19 (1971) 135-55, building on W. G. Hoskins, "Harvest Fluctuations and English Economic History, 1480-1619," *ibid.*, 12 (1964) 28-46; and "Harvest Fluctuations and English Economic History, 1620-1759," *ibid.*, 16 (1968) 15-31; and P. Bowden, "Statistical Appendix," in Joan Thirsk, ed., *The Agrarian History of England and Wales*, IV, 814-70.

As these very dangerous trends continued, the western world experienced a major disaster. In 1591, the weather turned wet and cold. European peasants watched helplessly as their wheat and rye were beaten down in the fields, and their hay crops rotted in the meadows. The same thing happened the next year, and the year after that, and altogether seven years running. In France, the wine harvest was late and small from 1591 to 1597. Grain crops fared even worse. English historian W. G. Hoskins observed, "the 1594 harvest was bad; 1595 was even worse; 1596 was a disaster; 1597 was bad too."

This was more than merely a short spell of bad weather. It was a shift in the climate—one of several sharp downturns in the early modern era that have been called collectively the "little ice age." The decade of the 1590s was so cold that Alpine glaciers began to send rivers of ice through inhabited valleys. In 1595 the Giétroz glacier buried the villages of Martigny and killed seventy people. Disasters of the same sort happened at Grindelwald and Chamonix and the Val d'Aosta.[4]

Similar events had happened before, but in the 1590s they came at a time when the economy was dangerously overstrained. Families had little in reserve. Food riots broke out in many parts of Europe. As the troubles continued, people began to starve. A season of scarcity grew into a massive famine that was called the "great dearth." There were terrible scenes of suffering in many parts of Europe. A Swede wrote in 1597:

> People ground and chopped many unsuitable things into bread such as mash, chaff, bark, buds, nettles, hay, straw, peat moss, nutshells, peastalks, etc. This made people so weak and their bodies so swollen that innumerable people died.
>
> Many widows, too, were found dead on the ground with red hummock grass, seeds which grew in the fields, and other kinds of grass in their mouths.
>
> People were found dead in the houses, under barns, in the ovens of bath houses and wherever they had been able to squeeze in, so that, God knows, there was enough to do getting them to the graveyard, though the dogs ate many of the corpses.
>
> Children starved to death at their mothers' breast, for they had nothing to give them suck.[5]

Similar scenes were described in England, Scotland, France, Germany, Scandinavia, Hungary, Russia and Spain.

The great dearth fell cruelly upon the poor, while the rich remained secure in their plenty. In London's affluent central neighborhoods, the number of burials increased very little during these years; but outlying parishes inhabited by the poor suffered severely. The effect of scarcity was to deepen the material inequalities that were already very great in European culture, and to contribute to growing social instability.[6]

Another consequence of scarcity was an increase in crime. The pattern was much the same as in the fourteenth century. When the price of food surged, crime increased sharply. When prices fell, criminal acts declined. This correlation was very strong in the later stages of every price-revolution from the Middle Ages to our own time.

These troubles were compounded by the growth of disease. During the great dearth many parts of Europe reported much trouble with the "bloody flux." This was perhaps not dysentery as many have surmised; similar symptoms are caused by malnutrition. Soon other epidemic diseases spread swiftly through a weakened population. The plague returned to Europe, ravaging its cities and many parts of the countryside. One of the worst outbreaks was the Cantabrian Plague,

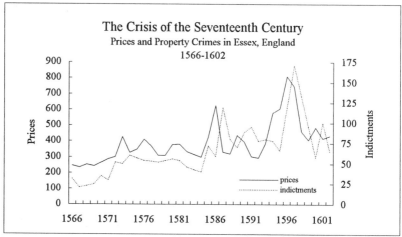

Figure 2.15 compares annual indictments for crimes against property in the English county of Essex, with an index of mean annual wheat prices in England (1470-79=100). Indictments are missing for the years 1568, 1575, 1577, 1583, 1596, and 1598-99, and have been added by linear interpolation. The source for indictments is J. S. Cockburn, "The Nature and Incidence of Crime in England, 1559-1625," in *idem*, ed., *Crime in England, 1550-1800* (Princeton, 1977), 68. Wheat prices are from Joan Thirsk, ed., *The Agrarian History of England and Wales, IV, 1500-1640* (Cambridge, 1967), statistical appendix, 865.

which killed half a million people in Iberia from 1597 to 1602, then spread to England and other parts of Europe.

As in the fourteenth century, plague did not strike a single blow. It returned again and again, with shattering effect. The region of Angers was an example. In the diocese of Murienne, it was introduced by soldiers returning from a military campaign (a common means of infection). Repeated epidemics followed in 1583–84, 1598, 1626, 1631 and 1639. Of 62 parishes in the diocese, 56 were severely infected. Two parishes (Modane and Aiguebelle) lost more than 40 percent of their inhabitants. In the diocese as a whole, the death rate rose to 80 per thousand—much below the toll of the Black Death in 1348, but twice the normal level.

This was merely one of many epidemic diseases that spread through Europe, which suffered much from visitations of smallpox, diptheria, typhus and other nameless infections. One historian writes that "no century since the fourteenth has a worse record for epidemic disease."[7]

At the same time that mortality increased, rates of fertility declined. From northern Germany to southern Spain, the number of inhabitants fell sharply after a long period of growth. In the cathedral of Toledo a clergyman named Sancho de Moncado studied his baptismal registers and found that the number of births dropped from the midsixteenth century to 1617 by 50 percent. Moncado observed that this decline happened not because of pestilence or migration, but "because the people cannot support themselves," as a consequence of scarcity and the soaring cost of food.[8]

The combined effect of rising mortality and falling fertility caused a reversal of demographic growth in the seventeenth century. This was the only period after the Black Death when the population of Europe actually declined.

As if these sufferings were not enough, a major economic collapse occurred in the period from 1610 to 1622. This was more than merely a cyclical downturn. It was a major break in the secular trend. Historian Ruggiero Romano observed its effects almost everywhere in Europe. In the Baltic, the number of ships passing through the Danish Sound reached its peak near the year 1600, and then after a period of fluctuation declined steadily for more than fifty years. In the Spanish port of Seville, a major entrepot for American trade, the monumental research of Huguette and Pierre Chaunu yielded evidence that total tonnage entering and leaving Seville harbor rose steadily through most of the

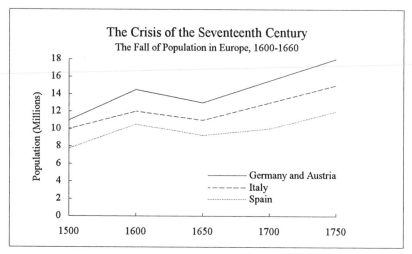

The Crisis of the Seventeenth Century
The Fall of Population in Europe, 1600-1660

Germany and Austria
Italy
Spain

Figure 2.16 shows a decline in population during the general crisis of the seventeenth century, the only period after the fourteenth century when the population of Europe declined. Sources include Colin McEvedy and Richard Jones, *Atlas of World Population History* (New York, 1978); Massimo Livi-Bacci, *A Concise History of World Population* (Cambridge and Oxford, 1992); J. Nadal, *La población Española* (Barcelona, 1984).

sixteenth century to a peak in the year 1610; then it fell sharply, and kept on falling for many decades. In Venice, Ragusa, Leghorn and Marseilles, customs duties and anchorage taxes peaked in the early seventeenth century, then declined catastrophically after 1618. In Danzig, the grain trade collapsed after 1619. In England, Italy and Spain, the sale of wool and textiles peaked in the decade 1610–20, then entered a deep depression that continued for half a century. Even the prosperous Low Countries—an exception to many seventeenth-century trends—were caught in this economic collapse. Industrial production began to decline in Amsterdam and Rotterdam after about 1620.[9]

Famine, pestilence, and economic depression were accompanied by war. During the entire century from 1551 to 1650, peace prevailed throughout the continent only in a single year (1610)—a record unmatched since the fourteenth century. These conflicts were remarkable not only for their frequency but also their ferocity. By far the most destructive was a cluster of religious and political conflicts that historians call the Thirty Years War (1618–48). This great conflict was a catastrophe for central Europe. Historian Gunther Franz estimates that the population of Germany declined by 40 percent from 1618 to 1648—a larger proportion than were killed by the Black Death. Other scholars think that losses was not so high, but all agree that the human cost of the Thirty Years War was very great. Large sections of middle Europe were laid waste. There was also a brutalization of the spirit in the Thirty Years War; appalling atrocities routinely occurred.[10]

Germany was not alone in her suffering. Broad areas of France, England, Scotland, Ireland and the Low Countries were also ravaged by war in this period. Flanders became once again the charnal house of Europe.

A few regions escaped the general carnage. Switzerland managed to keep war at bay. Many of its young men went off to fight and never came home again, but the Swiss republics themselves remained secure in their Alpine redoubts. They were so much the exception that a German visitor in Switzerland wrote, ''The country appeared to me so strange . . . as if I had come to Brazil or China. There I saw a people going about their business in peace. . . . Nobody stood in fear of the foe; nobody dreaded pillage, nobody was afraid of losing his property, his limbs or his life.''[11]

During the early seventeenth century, the armies of Europe reached their largest size since the Roman era. Their upkeep imposed heavy costs at the same time that public revenues were reduced by the combined effect of famine, pestilence, war, depression, regressive taxation and monetary inflation. They also were put to frequent use in most of Europe. War became highly destructive of life and wealth and happiness during this period. Historian John Nef writes, ''For suspicion and hatred, devastation and hardship, there was to be nothing quite like it again until the twentieth century.''[12]

Needy governments resorted to all the usual forms of fiscal folly. Some tried deficit financing on a large scale. Others systematically debased their coinage. Many tried to wring more taxes from sullen and resentful populations. As governments desperately attempted to increase their revenues, the suffering people of Europe were goaded to acts of violent resistance.

The result was an age of revolutions in virtually all European states. Most of these overturnings were caused by fiscal problems. In Iberia, major revolutions broke out in Catalonia and Portugal (1640) when Spanish ministers tried to raise large revenues. In England, an ill-fated attempt by Charles I to obtain more money from his subjects led to full-scale civil war, which ended in the execution of the king himself. In France, a series of rebellions called the Frondes developed from 1648 to 1654, primarily as a result of fiscal disputes between the

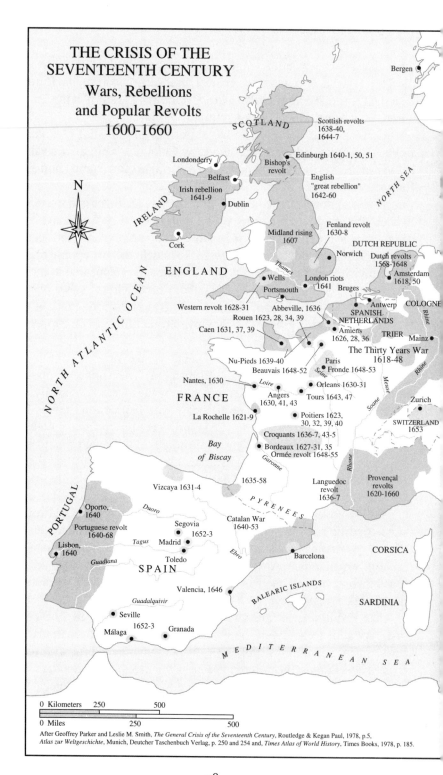

THE CRISIS OF THE
SEVENTEENTH CENTURY
Wars, Rebellions
and Popular Revolts
1600-1660

N

SCOTLAND

Bergen

Scottish revolts
1638-40,
1644-7

Edinburgh 1640-1, 50, 51

Londonderry
Bishop's
revolt

Belfast
Irish rebellion
1641-9
Dublin

English
"great rebellion"
1642-60

NORTH SEA

IRELAND

Cork

Midland rising
1607

Fenland revolt
1630-8

DUTCH REPUBLIC

Norwich

Dutch revolts
1568-1648

ENGLAND

Wells
Portsmouth

London riots
1641
Bruges

Amsterdam
1618, 50

NORTH ATLANTIC OCEAN

Western revolt 1628-31
Rouen 1623, 28, 34, 39
Caen 1631, 37, 39

Abbeville, 1636

Antwerp
SPANISH
NETHERLANDS
Amiens
1626, 28, 36

COLOGNE

TRIER

Mainz

Nu-Pieds 1639-40
Beauvais 1648-52

Paris
Fronde 1648-53

The Thirty Years War
1618-48

Nantes, 1630

Loire

Orleans 1630-31

FRANCE

La Rochelle 1621-9

Angers
1630, 41, 43

Tours 1643, 47

Poitiers 1623,
30, 32, 39, 40
Croquants 1636-7, 43-5

Bay
of Biscay

Bordeaux 1627-31, 35
Ormée revolt 1648-55

Zurich

SWITZERLAND
1653

1635-58

Languedoc
revolt
1636-7

Provençal
revolts
1620-1660

PORTUGAL

Vizcaya 1631-4

Oporto,
1640

Duoro

PYRENEES

Catalan War
1640-53

Segovia
1652-3

Portuguese revolt
1640-68
Lisbon,
1640

Tagus

Madrid

Guadiana

SPAIN

Toledo

Barcelona

CORSICA

Valencia, 1646

BALEARIC ISLANDS

Guadalquivir

Seville

SARDINIA

Málaga

1652-3

Granada

MEDITERRANEAN SEA

0 Kilometers   250   500

0 Miles   250   600

After Geoffrey Parker and Leslie M. Smith, *The General Crisis of the Seventeenth Century*, Routledge & Kegan Paul, 1978, p.5,
Atlas zur Weltgeschichte, Munich, Deutcher Taschenbuch Verlag, p. 250 and 254 and, *Times Atlas of World History*, Times Books, 1978, p. 185.

98

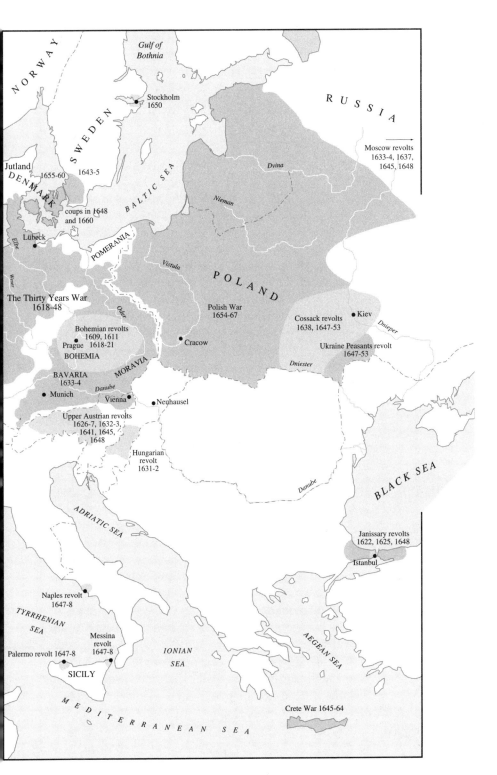

Gulf of
Bothnia

NORWAY

SWEDEN

RUSSIA

Stockholm
1650

Moscow revolts
1633-4, 1637,
1645, 1648

Dvina

Jutland

DENMARK

1655-60   1643-5

coups in 1648
and 1660

BALTIC SEA

Nieman

Lübeck

Elbe

POMERANIA

Vistula

POLAND

Weser

The Thirty Years War
1618-48

Oder

Polish War
1654-67

Cossack revolts
1638, 1647-53

Kiev

Dnieper

Bohemian revolts
1609, 1611
Prague   1618-21
BOHEMIA

Cracow

Ukraine Peasants revolt
1647-53

Dniester

MORAVIA

BAVARIA
1633-4

Danube

Munich

Vienna

Neuhausel

Upper Austrian revolts
1626-7, 1632-3,
1641, 1645,
1648

Hungarian
revolt
1631-2

Danube

BLACK SEA

ADRIATIC SEA

Janissary revolts
1622, 1625, 1648

Istanbul

Naples revolt
1647-8

TYRRHENIAN
SEA

Messina
revolt
1647-8

IONIAN
SEA

AEGEAN SEA

Palermo revolt 1647-8

SICILY

MEDITERRANEAN SEA

Crete War 1645-64

Parlement of Paris and the Crown. In Naples, the revolt of the fisherman Masaniello occurred after the kingdom had been drained of its
wealth by the Spanish government (1647). In Sicily a revolution began
at Palermo (1647); its rallying cry was "Long live the King and down
with taxes."[13] Denmark experienced a revolution from the right that
created an absolutist monarchy in 1660, as a direct consequence of a
fiscal crisis.

Even in Switzerland, there was a Peasants' Revolt (1654), which
happened after the government ordered a major depreciation of its
currency. The Ukraine had its "Great Ukrainian Revolution" from
1648 to 1654. In Hungary, there was the Durucz movement. The
Netherlands experienced a bloodless coup d'état which broke the
power of its ruling Stadtholders (1650). Sweden went through a constitutional crisis (1650). The people of Scotland and Ireland suffered a
series of bloody rebellions and repressions from 1638 to 1660.

Smaller peasant risings also occurred throughout Europe in exceptionally large numbers. In the south of France alone, one historian has
counted no fewer than 264 insurrections between 1596 and 1660—a
larger number than in any other period of that region's history. Most
were protests against intolerable economic conditions.[14]

The general crisis of the seventeenth century left its mark upon the
culture of an age. The greatest works of literature, painting, philosophy
and theology in this era commonly expressed a mood of increasing
pessimism and despair. After 1601, Shakespeare turned from his Elizabethan comedies and histories to his great tragedies—*Hamlet* (1600–
01), *Othello* (1604), *Macbeth* (1605–06), *King Lear* (1605–06). These
works were dark visions of a disordered world that seemed to conspire
against human hope and happiness. At the same time, Cervantes produced perhaps the greatest masterpiece of Spanish literature, *Don
Quixote* (1605, 1615), which for all its mordant humor was a sad and
bitter description of a world that had dissolved into social chaos.

The great painting of the period captured the same themes in
different ways—in the demonic fantasies of Pieter Brueghel (1564–
1638), the spiritual suffering of El Greco (1548?–1614?), the brooding
melancholy of Rembrandt (1606–69), the sensual violence of Rubens
(1577–1640), and the bizarre grotesqueries of the Italian mannerists.

The philosophy of the period was similar in tone. The leading
example was the work of Thomas Hobbes (1588–1679), with its organizing assumption that the natural condition of man was "poor and
solitary, nasty, brutish and short." Another dark vision of the world
flowed from the pen of Oxford clergyman Robert Burton (1577–1640),

in his treatise on sadness and disappointment called *The Anatomy of Melancholy*. There were always a few hopeful voices who cried out against despair. This was also the age of Descartes (1596–1650), and his affirmation of enduring values in an unstable world. But Descartes described his intellectual journey as that of "a man who walks alone in the darkness."[15]

In theology this was the era of neo-Calvinism—the narrowest, darkest, bleakest, and most pessimistic form of Christianity that has ever been invented, more so even than the theology of Calvin himself. As formally defined by the Synod of Dort (1618–19), the "five points" of neo-Calvinism asserted that most people and all infants were irretrievably sunk in a state of total depravity and inexorably condemned to eternal damnation; that Christ died not for everyone but only for a chosen few; that human beings were utterly without power to achieve their own salvation. Here was yet another cultural expression of an era in which people felt that the world was entirely beyond their power to control. In a later and happier age neo-Calvinism would make no sense at all, but in the early seventeenth century it seemed to fit the facts of the human condition.

The crisis of the seventeenth century was marked by a revival of religious strife. Protestants and Catholics became increasingly militant and uncompromising; the result was angry and bloody conflict in virtually all European states. In England, the Puritans combined religious and political ideas in a single movement that overturned the government. In Poland, Catholic nobles destroyed most of the Protestant churches in that nation. In the Ukraine, the revolt of the Cossacks was in part a religious movement.

Throughout central and eastern Europe, the people of Russia, Poland, and Germany expressed their unhappiness in the customary way, by slaughtering the Jews. Chmielnicki's rebellion in Poland was wildly antisemitic. From 1648 to 1658, more than 700 Jewish settlements were destroyed; perhaps 100,000 Jews were killed.[16]

The suffering of Europe in the general crisis of the seventeenth century was comparable to that of the fourteenth century. But this time Europe suffered in a different way. The seventeenth century was a period of falling population, but the magnitude of its decline was much smaller than in the fourteenth century. The scale of misery did not approach the demographic disaster that had been caused by the epic famines and Black Death of 1348.

The economic collapse was also not as severe as before. The pace of price-inflation was greater this time, but the magnitude of price fluctuations was less extreme than in the medieval price-revolution. The variance of prices fell by half from one of these great waves to another. Periods of scarcity were less severe in their impact upon prices, and they occurred less frequently. Even the worst years of this period were not nearly comparable with the famines of the fourteenth century.

Beyond doubt, a long-term improvement had taken place during the intervening years in productivity, production and per capita income. Markets had become larger and more tightly integrated. Even the worst miseries of this dark era were measures of material progress. During the crisis of the fourteenth century, high medieval civilization had collapsed. In the crisis of the seventeenth century, the civilization of early modern Europe was shaken to its deepest foundations. But it survived.

ꙮ The Equilibrium of the Enlightenment, 1660–1730

In the middle decades of the seventeenth century, the great crisis came to an end. After a period of transition, a new equilibrium appeared

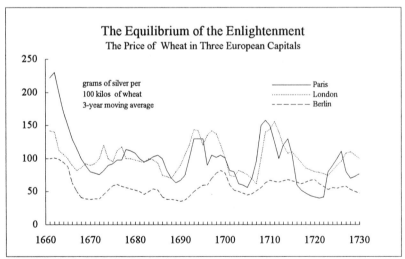

Figure 2.18 follows the price of grain in Paris, London and Berlin. In all three cities it fell sharply after 1661, then fluctuated on fixed level from 1670 to 1730. The source is Wilhelm Abel, *Agrarkrisen und Agrarkonjunktur: eine Geschichte der Land und Ernahrungswirtschaft Mitteleuropas seit dem höhen Mittelalter* (1935, Hamburg and Berlin, 1966).

throughout Europe. It established itself, more or less at the same time, in France, England, Germany, Italy, Russia, Spain and Scandinavia, and also in European colonies throughout the world.[1]

This new change-regime might be called the equilibrium of the Enlightenment. Its historical dynamics were similar in many ways to the equilibrium of the Renaissance. This was not a system at rest. It was a complex structure of countervailing movements, much like the counterpoint of Johann Sebastian Bach (1685–1750), or the baroque harmony of George Frederick Handel (1685–1759), whose lives and music perfectly captured the cultural spirit of an age.

The material components of this equilibrium may be summarized in a few sentences. The price of grain ceased rising, fell sharply, and then began to find a level. Food and energy came down, manufactures went up, and the general price level began to fluctuate on a fixed and level plane. Wages rose. Rents and interest fell. The distribution of wealth and income became a little more equal. Population, production, and productivity grew slowly. There were many local variations—

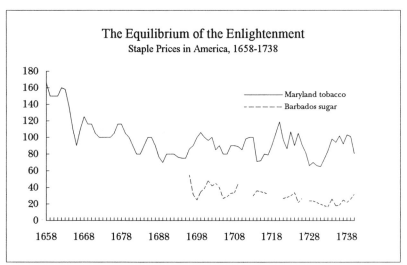

The Equilibrium of the Enlightenment
Staple Prices in America, 1658-1738

——— Maryland tobacco
– – – – – Barbados sugar

Figure 2.19 follows the price of Maryland tobacco (pence sterling per pound), and Barbadian sugar (shillings per hundredweight). Their movements were broadly similar to those of wheat prices in Europe during this period. The sources are Russell Menard, "Farm Prices of Maryland Tobacco, 1659-1710," *Maryland Historical Magazine*, 68 (1973) 80-85; Carville Earle, *The Evolution of a Tidewater Settlement: All Hallow's Parish, Maryland, 1650-1783* (Chicago, 1975), 16; Richard B. Sheridan, *Sugar and Slavery: An Economic History of the British West Indies, 1623-1775* (St. Lawrence, Barbados, 1974), 496-97.

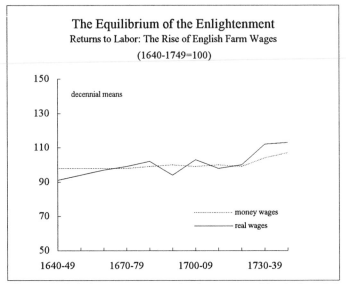

Figure 2.20 finds that money wages and real wages were rising in the period from 1650 to 1740, while rents and rates of interest were falling. The source is Peter J. Bowden, "Statistics," in Joan Thirsk, ed., *The Agrarian History of England and Wales*, vol. 5.2, 879.

price-inflation in Chile, wage-declines in Germany—but the major trends were strong and consistent.

Some historians of agriculture have perceived this period as a time of rural depression. So it was at the start. Reports from the European countryside told a story of falling farm prices and growing poverty among landowners. In 1685, the intendant of Rouen wrote, "The poverty is such that a farmer who bought a woollen garment had to do without a linen one. The peasant women, who used to love wearing red and blue petticoats, seldom have them now. They are very poorly dressed and mostly make do with white linen."[2]

But throughout the period from 1650 to 1730, returns to labor slowly increased. In England and France, nominal wages went up for manual laborers and skilled artisans alike. Real wages increased even more rapidly, nearly doubling for laborers and building craftsmen in the south of England from 1650 to 1740. Continental workers did not fare as well as their English counterparts; wages fell in parts of Germany. But throughout western Europe, farm laborers and artisans tended to improve their material condition.[3]

At the same time that wages rose, rents came down. France's

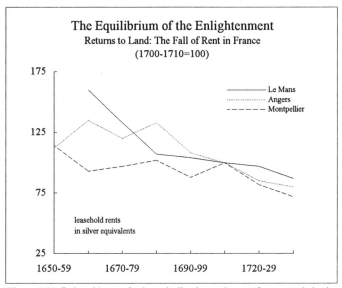

The Equilibrium of the Enlightenment
Returns to Land: The Fall of Rent in France
(1700-1710=100)

Figure 2.21 finds evidence of a long decline in rural rents, from a peak in the 1660s to a trough in the 1730s. Similar trends appeared throughout Europe. The source is Abel, *Agrarkrisen und Agrarkonjunktur.*

pioneering price historian the Vicomte d'Avenel calculated that the rent of one hectare of farmland fell from the equivalent of 12.8 francs in 1651–75 to 7.5 francs by 1701–25. Subsequent research by academic specialists has confirmed his general findings in France, England, Italy, Germany and most parts of Europe.[4] Interest rates also declined in this period. The maximum lawful rate of interest in England fell from 10 to 6 percent in the seventeenth century. Further, economic historian H. J. Habakkuk discovered that interest actually charged by money-lenders declined even more sharply than the legal maximum. During the general crisis of the seventeenth century, English creditors had tended to charge the highest allowable rate. By the century's end, actual rates had fallen below the statutory limit.[5] French *rentes* declined from 10 to 4 percent. In England by the year 1735, the yield on long annuities sank as low of 3 percent. Dutch commercial loans drifted downward to 2 percent or even less in this period.[6]

While interest rates were falling and wages were rising, commodity prices tended to fluctuate within a fixed range from 1650 to 1735. The price of grain fell in nearly all European countries, but other prices rose a little. Overall, the general price level remained approximately the same—a pattern typical of price movements in every period

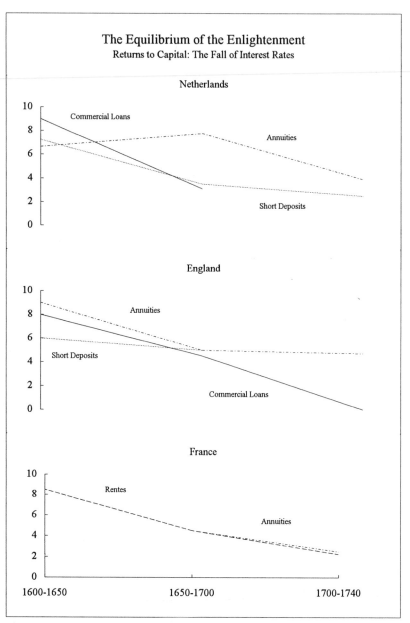

The Equilibrium of the Enlightenment
Returns to Capital: The Fall of Interest Rates

Netherlands

Commercial Loans

Annuities

Short Deposits

England

Annuities

Short Deposits

Commercial Loans

France

Rentes

Annuities

1600-1650   1650-1700   1700-1740

Figure 2.22 shows that interest rates declined in western Europe in the period 1600-50 to 1700-40. The source is Homer, *History of Interest Rates*, 156-58, 161-65, 172-78.

of equilibrium. Henry Phelps-Brown and Sheila Hopkins observed of their own price series in this period there was "constancy in the general level, and this surprising stability, as it seems to us, was maintained through fluctuations of two or three years' span, due no doubt mostly to the harvest, whose violence seems no less extraordinary."[7]

Both scholars were startled by the strength and resilience of these persistent patterns, which often were violently disrupted by extraneous events, and yet always recovered their equilibrium through a period of seventy years. "What was the secret of this stability," they asked, "and how was it held through such vibration?"

The violence of vibration was sometimes very great. Changes in the weather continued to cause sharp and sudden fluctuations in harvest prices. The people of France suffered severely when shortages drove grain prices very high in the *grand disettes* of the mid–1670s, and again in 1694–99, 1708–09, and 1713.

The worst crisis occurred in the years from 1694 to 1700. The weather turned wet and very cold. Once again, the glaciers advanced through alpine valleys. Arctic icefields expanded so far to the south that Eskimos in their kayaks appeared in Scotland. A major famine occurred in Finland, and northern parishes in Scotland lost a third of their population. The south of England was less severely affected, but everywhere in the English-speaking world these cruel years were remembered as "King William's Dearth" and "the barren years."[8] In Languedoc, food was so desperately short in 1694 that the poor were reduced to eating grass—a thin bread made of couch-weed and sheep entrails. In Narbonne, a priest wrote that the people looked like "skeletons or spectres" (*des équelletes ou d'espectres*), as they wandered far from their parishes, in searching of some way to "prolong their listless lives."[9]

The climatic stresses much the same as in the crisis of the 1590s, but this time the cultural and economic consequences were very different. Grain prices briefly surged to record levels in the 1690s, but when the weather improved price levels fell as rapidly as they had risen, and equilibrium was restored. After 1700, scarcities came less often and were less severe, but they kept on coming in the early eighteenth century without ending the material equilibrium. Altogether, the economics of the ancien regime resembled the movements of an eighteenth-century carriage on a rough country road. The vehicle jolted violently from rut to rut. The irritable passengers were thrown painfully

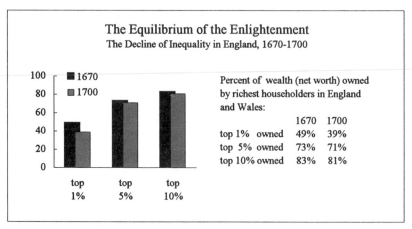

The Equilibrium of the Enlightenment
The Decline of Inequality in England, 1670-1700

Percent of wealth (net worth) owned
by richest householders in England
and Wales:

	1670	1700
top 1% owned	49%	39%
top 5% owned	73%	71%
top 10% owned	83%	81%

Figure 2.23 shows the consequences of the long fall in returns to capital and the rise in real wages during this period. Wealth inequality declined. One study finds that the wealth-shares of the richest 1 percent in England shrank 20 percent in the years 1700-30. The source: Peter H. Lindert, "Toward a Comparative History of Income and Wealth Inequality," in Y. S. Brenner, Hartmut Kaelbe, and Mark Thomas, eds., *Income Distribution in Historical Perspective* (Cambridge, 1991) 212-31, 220.

against one another. The carriage itself swayed dangerously with every strain—but it continued to advance.[10]

The passengers themselves perceived their economic situation in different ways, according to their station. The possessing classes described this era as one of prolonged depression. So it was for propertied elites, who were caught in a web of falling rents, rising labor costs and low prices. But for ordinary people, the times were more favorable. Wages increased at the same time that the cost of grain and shelter actually declined, and prices in general remained on the same level. A period that seemed a depression to manorial lords and rural proprietors (as well as to historians who read their letters and shared their perspective) was an age of improvement for artisans and laborers and the great majority of Europe's population. Wealth and income were more broadly distributed. Inequality diminished.

Still, the question posed by Phelps-Brown and Hopkins demands an answer. What was the "secret of stability" in this age of equilibrium? A simple monetarist model, that seeks an explanation of price movements primarily in terms of the quantity of money in circulation, works no better for this period than for any other. New research by Michel Morineau finds evidence that American treasure flowed abundantly into Europe during the period 1660–1730, in quantities almost (but not quite) equal to the price-revolution that preceded it. But this time there was no long-term inflation.[11]

In France, a large increase occurred in the supply of silver and gold in circulation during this period. Voltaire estimated that the quantity of silver money increased from five hundred million livres in 1683 to twelve hundred millions in 1730. Modern economic and social historians generally agree that the quantity of gold and silver doubled or trebled in France during this period. But the cost of living did not go up.[12]

Further, the French monetary system in particular also suffered many debasements between 1660 and 1730. One scholar writes that "recoinage after recoinage so altered the value of the real money of France that it caused serious economic difficulties at home and abroad. . . . Only with the great monetary reform and consolidations of 1726 did this era end." But prices did not rise.[13]

Other monetary systems were more stable than that of France. Dutch guilders and rixdollars remained perfectly stable from 1691 to the nineteenth century. British guineas, Venetian ducats and Portuguese crusados also preserved their value. In Europe as a whole, however, price stability in this period was achieved not because of monetary factors but in spite of them.[14]

A better explanation for the price equilibrium of this period may be found in the pattern of population growth, which was modest in the period 1650–1730. In England, for example, the number of inhabitants had increased more rapidly before this era—from 2.8 millions in 1541 to 5.3 millions in 1657. In the mid-seventeenth century, that trend broke. Population ceased rising and began to fall unsteadily for thirty years, reaching its nadir in the year 1686, at approximately 4.9 millions. Thereafter, it began to fluctuate, rising a little but remaining on the same plane. Not until after 1730 did it resume a pattern of rapid and sustained increase. This trend matched a thirty-year moving average in consumer prices with uncanny precision. The correlation was very close, with price movements lagging a few years behind demographic trends through most of the sixteenth, seventeenth and eighteenth centuries.[15]

Population movements were marked by many fluctuations. A slow rolling rhythm in fertility and sudden surges in mortality caused by outbreaks of epidemic disease. But the secular movements of prices and population were closely linked. This was the basis of the equilibrium in that period.[16]

In economic terms, that equilibrium should be understood as a period not of stasis but of stable growth. Production and productivity increased. Commerce flourished throughout Europe. Handsome neoclassical exchanges were constructed throughout the Western world. They symbolized improvements that were made in many sorts of markets. Labor markets, capital markets, land markets, commodity markets all were made to work more efficiently.

Banks multiplied rapidly: the Bank of England (1694), the Royal Bank of Scotland (1727), and many others.[17] Every European country improved its roads, enlarged its ports and constructed canals and bridges. The growth of colonies also increased the wealth of Europe and improved its productivity. Marginal returns to capital and labor tended to be higher in the staple industries of colonial economies than in the mother-country.[18]

The great cities, as always the barometers a civilization's health, prospered throughout Europe in this period. London was rebuilt to the taste of Christopher Wren and Inigo Jones, and took on the neoclassical character that it preserves to this day. Paris became the metropolis of Europe—its beautiful squares and broad boulevards began to be laid out in this period. Berlin as late as 1654 had been a small river settlement of about 5,000 inhabitants; by 1740 it had become a stately city with nearly 100,000 people. Vienna was transformed from a grim medieval fortress town into an imperial capital of great beauty. The Schönbrunn palace was begun in 1695 and the Belvedere in 1717. The city's great baroque churches and state buildings date from this period.

At the opposite end of Europe, the people of Edinburgh constructed their "new city" in this era. In the words of David Daiches, the heavenly city of the eighteenth-century philosophers was realized in Scottish stone. As the cities were rebuilt, urban architecture flourished everywhere in Europe, from the baroque glory of Dresden to the Georgian grace of Dublin. The handsome colonial cities of Philadelphia, Calcutta and Batavia arose on the banks of the Delaware, the Hooghly and the Tjiliwong.

Social life became more orderly in this period. By the evidence of arrests and prosecutions, rates of violent crime diminished from the late 17th century well into the eighteenth century.

The equilibrium of this era also expressed itself in politics. The

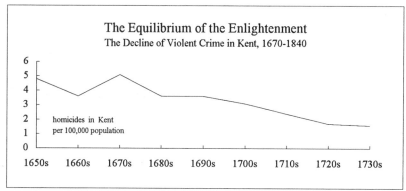

The Equilibrium of the Enlightenment
The Decline of Violent Crime in Kent, 1670-1840

homicides in Kent
per 100,000 population

Figure 2.24 shows the same sustained decline in crime that occurred in every period of price equilibrium, after a sharp rise during the late stages of every price revolution. The downward trend that appears here in Kent's homicide rates has also been found in many other English counties during the same period. The source is J. S. Cockburn, "Patterns of Violence in English Society: Homicides in Kent, 1560-1985," *Past and Present* 130 (1991) 70-106.

turbulence of the early and mid-seventeenth centuries came to an end in many European states during the period from 1660 to 1740. English historian J. H. Plumb observes that "political stability, when it comes, often happens to a society . . . as suddenly as water becomes ice." That metaphor—a "change of phase" in the language of chemistry— perfectly describes a transition that happened in the politics of England, France, Germany, and Russia during the late seventeenth and early eighteenth centuries. These four nations achieved stability in different ways, but all experienced a change of phase in this age of equilibrium.

Particularly striking was the growth of political stability in England. "The contrast between political society in eighteenth and seventeenth century England is vivid and dramatic," Professor Plumb writes. "In the seventeenth century men killed, tortured and executed each other for political beliefs; they sacked towns and brutalized the countryside. They were subjected to conspiracy, plot and invasion. This uncertain political world lasted until 1715, and then rapidly began to vanish. By comparison, the political structure of eighteenth century England possesses adamantine strength and profound inertia."

Plumb was wrong about inertia. In politics, as in economics, the equilibrium of the Enlightenment was a dynamic process, with many moving parts. But he was right about its stability and strength.[19]

Political stability was also achieved in France during the long reigns of Louis XIV (1643–1715) and Louis XV (1715–1774). Its form was very different from that of the English-speaking nations. While England moved toward toleration and parliamentary government, France traveled in the opposite direction. Religious dissent was savagely repressed, the *Etats généraux* were ignored, the *Parlements* were reduced to judicial and administrative bodies, and the fetters of royal absolutism were riveted upon the body politic of a great nation.

Prussia created a stable polity in yet a third form. This was a militarist monarchy that derived its power from the Prussian army, and developed steadily under Frederick the Great Elector of Brandenberg (1688–1713), and his successors Frederick Wilhelm I (1713–1740), and Frederick the Great (1740–1786).

In Russia, Peter the Great (1682–1725) founded a fourth type of European state. It has been well-described as an autocracy "enserfed from top to bottom . . . in which all strata of the population without exception were required to perform service and pay dues to the ruler."[20]

Many rulers were called "great" in this era: Louis Le Grand, Frederick the Great Elector, Frederick the Great, Peter the Great, Catherine the Great. These leaders were no more able than many of the failed monarchs who preceded them in the seventeenth century. The enlightened despots of Europe were consumed by vanity and greed. They quarreled incessantly with other princes, and squandered both the wealth of their nations and lives of their subjects on petty and destructive rivalries. But an age of equilibrium is kind to reigning kings. A reputation for greatness in a monarch often owes more to circumstance than to character.

The equilibrium of this era expressed itself not only in economics and politics, but also in a philosophical system that was called *Die Aufklarung* in Germany, *Illuminismo* in Italy, and the Enlightenment in England. Ironically, the only people of Europe who did not have a single word for this movement were the French, who did more than any others to create it. The Enlightenment is remembered in France not as an idea, but as an era and a set of individuals—the *siècle des lumières*.

The man who personified this era better than any other was François Marie Arouet (1694–1778), better known by his pen name, Voltaire. He thought of his own generation the epigoni of an age that he called the *siècle de Louis XIV*. This epoch he defined as the time when "human reason in general was brought to perfection." The young Voltaire recognized that this era was not "exempt from crimes and misfortunes." He fought against evil all his life, and suffered many defeats. Nevertheless, his history of this era was suffused with a sense of satisfaction in the events of the recent past, and a feeling of confidence for the future.[21]

Voltaire's way of thinking about history was different from our own. He did not think in modern terms of "material base" and "cultural superstructure." If anything he tended to reverse that causal relationship, but he had no doubt of a close connection between economic and cultural processes. His history of this era was a paean to progress in both realms. He celebrated the era of Louis XIV not so much as the apotheosis of a great king, but as a time when "the middle classes enriched themselves by industry," and the condition of peasants and laborers became much improved. In his mind these material events were connected to the great intellectual achievements of his age—to the science of Newton (1642–1727) and Halley (1656–1742), the literature of Racine (1639–99) and Molière (1622–73), the philosophy of Locke (1632–1704), Bayle (1647–1706) and Leibniz (1646–1716).

The work of these men had a fundamentally different texture from those who had preceded them by only a generation. They believed that the universe was a place of order and symmetry; that the world was within man's power to understand and even to control.

These attitudes came to be shared by many people in the early eighteenth century. The great historian Edward Gibbon wrote complacently in his autobiography, "My lot might have been that of a slave, a savage, or a peasant, nor can I reflect without pleasure on the bounty of Nature, which cast my birth in a free and civilized country, in an age of science and philosophy."[22]

The same spirit was expressed in many different ways by English literati such as Pope (1688–1744), by the German composers Bach (1685–1750) and Handel (1685–1759), by French social philosophers Montesquieu (1689–1755) and Quesnay (1694–1774), by scientists such as the Swedish Linnaeus (1707–1778) and the American Franklin (1706–1790), and by theologians such as Edwards (1703–1758) and Zinzendorf (1700–1760).

These men of the Enlightenment were keenly aware of evil in the world. But even as they struggled against injustice, and suffered from its effects, the world appeared to them as a place of order, harmony, equilibrium and balance. Their mechanical metaphors represented the

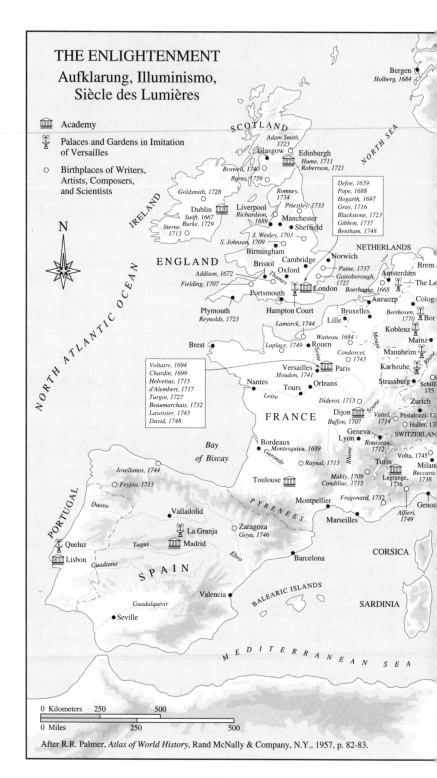

THE ENLIGHTENMENT
Aufklärung, Illuminismo,
Siècle des Lumières

🏛 Academy

♊ Palaces and Gardens in Imitation
  of Versailles

○ Birthplaces of Writers,
  Artists, Composers,
  and Scientists

N

Bergen ●
Holberg, 1684

SCOTLAND
Adam Smith,
1723
Glasgow ○ Edinburgh
  Hume, 1711
Boswell, 1740 ○ Robertson, 1721
Burns, 1759 ○

NORTH SEA

Goldsmith, 1728
○
Dublin 🏛 Liverpool Romney,
Swift, 1667 Richardson, 1734
Sterne, Burke, 1729 1689 Manchester Priestley, 1733
1713 ○ ● Sheffield
S. Johnson, 1709 ○ J. Wesley, 1703 ○

IRELAND

Defoe, 1659
Pope, 1688
Hogarth, 1697
Gray, 1716
Blackstone, 1723
Gibbon, 1737
Bentham, 1748

NETHERLANDS

Birmingham
ENGLAND Bristol Cambridge Norwich
Addison, 1672 Oxford ○ ○ Paine, 1737 Brem
Fielding, 1707 Thames Gainsborough, Amsterdam
Portsmouth 🏛🏛 London 1727 ○ ● The L
  Boerhaave, 1668 ♊
  Antwerp ● Colog

Plymouth Hampton Court Bruxelles Beethoven, ♊
Reynolds, 1723 Lamarck, 1744 Lille ● 1770 ♊ Bor
  Koblenz ○

Brest ● Watteau, 1684 Mainz
  Laplace, 1749 ● Rouen Mannheim
  Seine Condorcet, ○ 1743
Voltaire, 1694 Versailles 🏛♊ Paris Karlsruhe ♊
Chardin, 1699 Houdon, 1741 Strassburg ● Schill
Helvetius, 1715 Nantes Orleans 175
d'Alembert, 1717 Tours ● Diderot, 1713 ○ Zurich
Turgot, 1727 Loire Dijon 🏛 Vattel, ● Pestalozzi, 17
Beaumarchais, 1732 FRANCE Buffon, 1707 1714 ○ ○ Haller, 17
Lavoisier, 1743 Geneva SWITZERLAN
David, 1748 Lyon ● Rousseau,
Bay Bordeaux 1712
of Biscay Montesquieu, 1689 Volta, 1745○
  Garonne Turin Milan
Jovellanos, 1744 ○ Raynal, 1713 Rhone Becceri
○ Feyjóo, 1713 Toulouse 🏛 Mably, 1709 Lagrange, 1738
  Condillac, 1715 1736
PORTUGAL Duoro Montpellier Fragonard, 1732
  Valladolid ○ Genoa
  PYRENEES Marseilles Alfieri,
  ○ Zaragoza 1749
♊ La Granja Goya, 1746
♊ Queluz Tagus 🏛 Madrid
🏛 Lisbon Guadiana Barcelona CORSICA
  SPAIN
  Valencia ● BALEARIC ISLANDS
Guadalquivir SARDINIA
● Seville

MEDITERRANEAN SEA

NORTH ATLANTIC OCEAN

0 Kilometers 250 500
0 Miles 250 500

After R.R. Palmer, *Atlas of World History*, Rand McNally & Company, N.Y., 1957, p. 82-83.

Gulf of
Bothnia

St. Petersburg

Lomonosov, 1711
(Near the White Sea)

Tsarskoe Selo

Peterhof   Slutsk

S W E D E N

Upsala

Stockholm

Swedenborg, 1688

R U S S I A

Moscow

Radichev, 1749

Linnaeus, 1707

Dvina

N O R W A Y

D E N M A R K

Copenhagen

B A L T I C   S E A

Nieman

H O L Y   R O M A N

Klopstock, 1724

Königsberg
Kant, 1724

Handel, 1685

Bach,

Winckelmann, 1717

Herder,
1744

Vistula

P O L A N D

Charlottenburg

Göttingen

Berlin

Potsdam

Dnieper

Weimar

Erfurt   Dresden

J.S. Bach, 1685

Lessing,
1729

Breslau
Wolff, 1679

Goethe,   Gluck,
1749   1714   Prague

Cracow

Frankfurt

Dniester

Nuremberg

Würzburg

E M P I R E

A U S T R I A

Nymphenburg

Danube

Munich

Vienna   Schönbrunn

C A R P A T H I A N S

Salzburg

Haydn, 1732

Mozart, 1756

Buda   Pest

A L P S

H U N G A R Y

Canova, 1757

Verona

Danube

Colorno

Venice
Tiepolo,
1696
Goldoni, 1707

Bologna

B L A C K   S E A

Florence

A D R I A T I C   S E A

I T A L Y

Galiani, 1728

Constantinople

Tiber

Rome

Caserta

Naples
Vico, 1668
Filangieri, 1752

O T T O M A N   E M P I R E

T Y R R H E N I A N
S E A

A E G E A N   S E A

Palermo

I O N I A N
S E A

SICILY

Athens

M E D I T E R R A N E A N   S E A

CRETE

union of dynamism and stability, a belief in the possibility of progress and order.

The Enlightenment was an era with major social problems, but it was also a time when people believed that problems could be solved. The savants of this age disagreed in their solutions, but they shared a stubborn optimism that set them squarely apart from earlier generations. That attitude was a *zeitgeist* in the strict sense, a spirit grounded in the historical conditions of the age.[23]

The philosophical gentlemen of the enlightenment invented many of our modern social sciences—including the science of economics. Their economic ideas commonly took two countervailing forms. One would later be called mercantilism. It encouraged the active intervention of the state in economic processes, and was given its classical expression by the ministers of Louis XIV, notably Jean Baptiste Colbert. The other economic ideology would later be called *laisser faire*. It was developed in this period by the French physiocrats, and in particular by François Quesnay. There is a story, perhaps apocryphal, of a conversation between Quesnay and the Dauphin:

> "What would you do if you were King?" the Dauphin asked.
> "Nothing," said Quesnay.
> "Then who would govern?"
> "The law," Quesnay replied.[24]

Many enlightened thinkers shifted back and forth from one of these economic ideas to the other. One historian has remarked upon their "characteristic oscillation between mercantilist and laisser faire thought."[25] Others became fierce partisans of a single ideology. But even as they differed with one another, the *philosophes* of the enlightenment shared a common cosmology.

The central assumption in this cosmology was an idea that Jean Ehrard calls *la nature-horloge,* the world as a piece of clockwork. Some believed that the machinery needed constant tinkering. Others thought that the machine would go of itself. But the major premise was the same: *un univers-horloge, un Dieu horloger.*[26]

These assumptions came to be widely shared in the early eighteenth century because they seemed to fit the empirical facts. The prevailing ideas of balance and equilibrium in the enlightenment were not merely a philosopher's dream. They represented the world as it actually was—for a time.

THE THIRD WAVE

さ The Price Revolution of the Eighteenth Century

> People of the same trade seldom meet together, even for
> merriment or diversion, but the conversation ends in a con-
> spiracy against the public, or in some contrivance to raise
> prices.
>
> —Adam Smith, *Wealth of Nations* (1776)

PARIS, September 3, 1729, the grand festival of the Dauphin's
birth. At Versailles, a little past three o'clock in the morning, the
Queen was delivered of a healthy son, who became at birth
heir-apparent to the throne of France. A royal messenger was ordered
to carry the happy news to Paris. He spurred his horse forward, galloping toward the first light of dawn in the eastern sky. The sleeping city
lay open before him.

In the year 1729, Paris was the capital not merely of a country but
of a civilization. It was a city of dramatic contrasts. Some of its narrow
and crooked streets had changed little since the thirteenth century. In
other neighborhoods a great rebuilding was underway. The ancient city
walls had been pulled down, and in their place royal engineers had laid
out the first tree-lined boulevards. The old fortified gates had been
replaced by open *arcs de triomph*. The Champs d'Elysses had been
extended from the Tuileries as far as the Place d'Etoile. The Place des
Victoires and Place Vendôme had been created, and those noble spaces
were already surrounded by huge private *hotels* of the aristocracy and
nouveau riche.[1]

Paris had many *nouveaux riches* in 1729. The city had become a great center of trade and finance. Only a few years earlier its hated *usuriers* had been confined behind heavy iron grilles in the serpentine passages of the rue Quincampoix. Now the richest *usuriers* were called *financiers,* and their mansions were scattered through the city. A great *banque* had recently been founded, and a new *bourse* had opened for the exchange of securities. Our modern language of finance was invented in the early eighteenth century. Much of it is French.

Paris had grown rich, but many Parisians remained desperately poor. Extravagant wealth and grotesque poverty lived side by side. Beggars died of hunger in the streets, while the rich rode past in gilded chairs on the shoulders of other human beings. The suffering poor crowded miserably into a maze of medieval tenements. Many lived like animals on close-built bridges above the river Seine, while the great families of France resided in magnificent mansions only a few streets away.

The cultural contrasts were equally dramatic. Paris in 1729 was the city of light, the seat of the Enlightenment, the heavenly city of the eighteenth-century philosophers. Its great libraries in the Bibliothèque Royal, the Bibliothèque Mazarin and the Bibliothèque Ste. Geneviève were the among the best in the world. Its elegant salons set the intellectual fashion for enlightened people everywhere.

At the same time Paris was also a capital of despotic darkness. It was the controlling center of an absolutism that ruled by terror, cunning, and brutal force. High above the city's fabled rooftops rose the walls of the Bastille, where state prisoners were held for life without the slightest shadow of legality. Next to the river Seine stood the dark and silent mass of the Châtelet, the prison where ordinary Parisians were confined without warrant and punished without trial. In the center of the city was the Place Greve, where huge crowds gathered every week before the City Hall to watch obscene tortures inflicted upon shrieking victims.

Paris in 1729 was a city divided against itself. Its restless population was kept in order by a garrison of Swiss mercenaries and by large numbers of informers, spies, detectives and agents provocateurs. Our modern language of espionage and surveillance is French, and much of it was invented in this era. A regime of great and terrible cruelty dominated its people by methods that were profoundly hostile to the ethics of Christianity and the dreams of the Enlightenment.

But on the day of the Dauphin's birth, September 3, 1729, all this was forgotten. The people of Paris put aside their differences and joined freely in a festival of joy. When news of the infant's arrival reached the city, the tocsin was sounded and cannon were fired. Every house was ordered to be illuminated for three nights, and every shop was commanded to be closed for three days, while preparations began for a grand celebration. Each evening bonfires burned in the open squares. Casks of wine were opened to all who wished to drink. The poor were given free sausages and small loaves of bread, baked specially for the occasion.

On September 7, at exactly 5:30 in the afternoon, the royal father of the newborn child proudly entered the city. Louis XV was a handsome youth, barely nineteen years old. He proceeded in high pomp to the Cathedral of Notre Dame, escorted by two companies of Musketeers and the Royal Company of Falconers, with birds of prey perched on their gloved fists. The princes of the blood and the great nobility followed in a long line of gilded carriages.

When the King reached the Cathedral, the great guns of the royal artillery fired a salute in his honor. The infantry discharged three volleys of a *feu de joie*. Flashes of flame and clouds of smoke rippled down their long ranks from the Tuileries to Notre Dame. Inside the crowded cathedral three Cardinals led the singing of a Te Deum. Afterwards, the King traveled in great state to the city hall for dinner and a display of fireworks. His meal was served by the *prévôt des marchands* Jacques-Etienne Turgot himself, as obsequious as the lowest lackey. At 11:30 the King rose from his table and made a tour of the city. The houses were ablaze with light. Each neighborhood competed for the honor of the best display. The Place Vendôme was judged the winner: its buildings were illuminated with perfect symmetry, and its street lamps were replaced by glittering chandeliers.

The celebration of the Dauphin's birth continued for a week. It spread to every city of France, and to many other nations. By all reports, people of every rank joined wholeheartedly in these events. What they celebrated was not merely the arrival of the little Dauphin himself, but the promise of order, prosperity, peace and continuity. The people of France still keenly remembered the cruel disorders of the last century. They recalled the terrible uncertainties of a time, not very long ago, when the last king in his grave and the next was in his cradle, and nobody knew what the future might bring.

The people of Europe welcomed the birth of the Dauphin as a sign that order, stability and equilibrium would continue for many years to come. In 1729, France was at peace with all the great states of Europe.

Her harvests were good, her commerce was flourishing, and her arts were the envy of every nation. The people of this great kingdom looked forward to a future of prosperity and peace with increasing confidence.[2]

But it was not to be. In the very hour of the Dauphin's birth, a deep change was silently occurring in the dynamics of European history. Once again, an important indicator was the movement of prices. At Paris in approximately the year 1729, the price-equilibrium of the Enlightenment quietly approached its end. A new movement began, which might be called the price-revolution of the eighteenth century.

≈ The Price Revolution Begins

The new trend started slowly and silently, in much the same manner as the great waves that had preceded it. Its epicenter was Paris. In the grain markets of the French capital, the price of wheat began to rise about the year 1729.[3] Other cities followed close behind. Grain prices began to climb at Winchester in 1731–32; Amsterdam, 1732–33; Bruges, 1733–34; Cologne, 1735–36; Philadelphia, 1738–39.[4] In the eighteenth century, urban markets had become more closely linked throughout the Atlantic world.

The countryside lagged behind the cities. In England and Wales, one very broad index of farm prices found that the advance did not begin until the early 1740s. Another English price-series showed no increase until after 1750. But by the early 1740s, agricultural prices were rising throughout most of Europe. Similar patterns appeared for the price of wheat in Belgium, France and Italy; and for rye in Germany, Austria, and Poland.[5]

Once begun, the new trend spread swiftly from Europe to the New World. American historian Winifred Rothenberg made the startling discovery that farm prices in remote parts of rural Massachusetts synchronized with market fluctuations in London and Paris during the eighteenth century. This linkage was all the more remarkable in that very little gold and silver circulated in New England. The small farmers of Massachusetts did business without hard money, maintaining among themselves a system of mutual charge-accounts that has been called bookkeeping barter. Even so, the changing values in their account books closely matched the vibration of prices throughout the Atlantic world.[6]

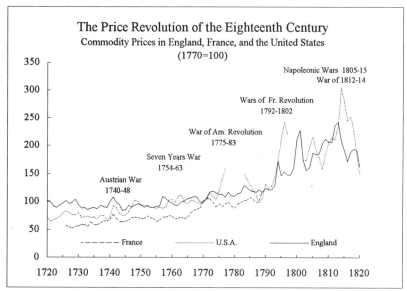

The Price Revolution of the Eighteenth Century
Commodity Prices in England, France, and the United States
(1770=100)

Figure 3.01 shows the profile of the eighteenth century price revolution in three nations. Sources include for England, the Schumpeter-Gilboy price index of 32 commodities, in B. R. Mitchell, *British Historical Statistics,* 719-20; for U. S. A., the Bezanson index of prices of 140 commodities in the Philadelphia market, *Historical Statistics of the U.S.,* series E111; for France, an unweighted index of agricultural prices in Ernest Labrousse et al., *Histoire économique et sociale de la France,* II, 386-87. All series are converted to a common base of 1770=100.

Similar movements also appeared in French Canada, but in Latin America, the trends were more complex. Agricultural prices in the Spanish and Portuguese colonies fell or remained on the same level until 1750, and kept on falling in some places (such as Salvador and ironically Potosí) as late as the 1780s. But in Mexico, Chile, and other parts of Latin America, prices were generally rising from the 1760s. By the late 1780s, the price-revolution of the eighteenth century was operating broadly there. Historian John Coatsworth writes of Latin America in general that ''in all cases for which there are data, commodity prices were rising in the 1790s and during the war years that followed.''[7]

The same pattern also appeared in Asia and the Middle East. The movement of Chinese grain prices during the eighteenth century was similar in trend, but smaller in magnitude. The Ottoman Empire also experienced a long wave of rising prices. The price-revolution of the eighteenth century was truly a world event.[8]

At first, the new trend advanced slowly and unsteadily. For a time,

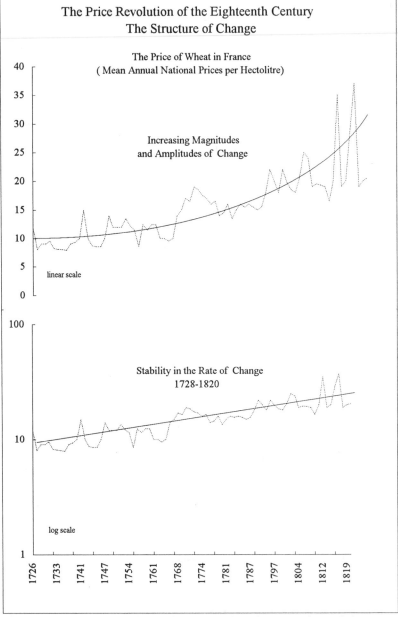

The Price Revolution of the Eighteenth Century
The Structure of Change

The Price of Wheat in France
(Mean Annual National Prices per Hectolitre)

Increasing Magnitudes
and Amplitudes of Change

linear scale

Stability in the Rate of Change
1728-1820

log scale

Figure 3.02 finds evidence in French grain prices that the 18th century price-revolution was an exponential process, dynamic in its expanding magnitudes and amplitudes, but stable in its underlying rate of change. The data are from C. E. Labrousse, Ruggiero Romano and F. G. Dreyfus, *Le prix du froment en France au temps de la monnaie stable (1726-1913)* (Paris, 1970), xiv. Trendlines are fitted with an Excel 5.0 program.

contemporaries took it to be merely another market-flutter. In retro-spect, however, the profile of a price-revolution was clearly evident from the start, especially in the distinctive pattern of price-relatives which were much the same as in the thirteenth and sixteenth centuries. Once again, the most rapid movements occurred in the price of energy and food. Of nine basic commodities in France, the largest increase occurred in the cost of firewood and charcoal.[9] Close behind the soaring cost of energy came the price of food. Foodstuffs in general rose rapidly during the eighteenth century, as in every other price-revolution. The largest increases appeared in staple commodities that were the staff of life among the poor—the cheaper grains and beans. Rates of inflation were more moderate for meat and wine. The smallest gains were in the price of manufactured products, which lagged behind as they had done in every other great wave.[10]

The prime mover of this price-revolution was the increasing pres-sure of aggregate demand, caused by an acceleration in the growth of population. In England, demographic historians Anthony Wrigley and Roger Schofield discovered that the rhythm of price-movements corre-

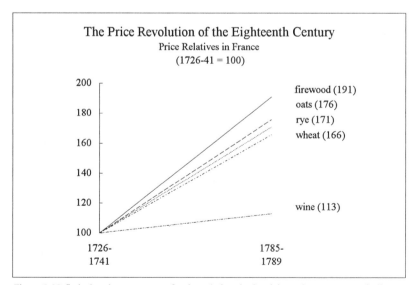

The Price Revolution of the Eighteenth Century
Price Relatives in France
(1726-41 = 100)

firewood (191)
oats (176)
rye (171)
wheat (166)

wine (113)

1726-
1741

1785-
1789

Figure 3.03 finds that the movement of price relatives in the eighteenth century was similar to those in other price revolutions. In France, the cost of energy went highest, closely followed by food and raw materials. Processed products, manufactures, and wages lagged far behind. The data are from Ernest Labrousse, *Esquisse du mouvement des prix et des revenus en France au XVIIIe siècle* (2 vols., Paris, 1933), II, 98.

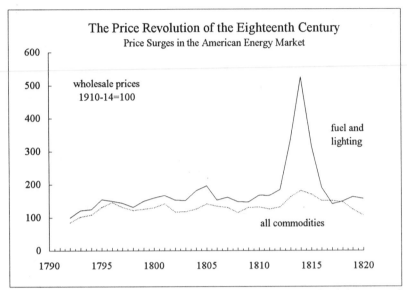

Figure 3.04 shows a recurrent pattern in price revolutions: surging energy prices in late stages of the long wave. This was the case in Europe and even in America during the late eighteenth century. The source is George F. Warren and Frank A. Pearson, *Prices* (New York, 1933), 11-27; reprinted in part in the *Historical Statistics of the United States, Colonial Times to 1970* (Washington, 1976), series E52-57.

lated closely with rates of population-increase in the eighteenth century. After a long pause from 1660 to 1720, the population of England began to grow more rapidly during the late 1720s, at precisely the same moment when the price-revolution also started. The correlation could not have been more exact.[11]

A similar association between rising prices and increasing population also appeared in other European states. In eastern Europe, the number of inhabitants who lived within the old boundaries of Brandenberg-Prussia rose from less than 1.6 million people at the death of Frederick William the Great Elector (1688) to nearly four million by the death of Frederick the Great (1786). Large increases occurred in most parts of Europe, with a few exceptions such as the Netherlands. The trend of prices matched this upward curve of population-growth.[12]

Why did population grow in the eighteenth century? In demographic terms, it happened mainly because of a decline in age at marriage and a small rise in rates of intramarital fertility. In many parts of rural Europe, the average age at first marriage for women fell from 27 in the mid-seventeenth century to 24 or even 23 in the mid-eighteenth.

Once married, women tended to reduce intervals between births, and began to bear children more frequently. The average age of a woman at the birth of her last child also rose a little—evidence of a deliberate decision not to limit the size of families as narrowly as had been done in the mid-seventeenth century.

There was also a modest improvement in life expectancy for infants and women during the eighteenth century, and a moderate stabilization of death-rates. But the primary cause of population growth in this period was a rise in fertility, not a fall in mortality.[13]

Why did men and women choose to marry earlier and have more children? An improvement in material conditions was part of the answer, but not the whole of it. Husbands and wives decided to have more children because the world appeared to have become a better place in which to raise a family. Always that sort of judgment has been made in terms that are broadly cultural rather than narrowly material.

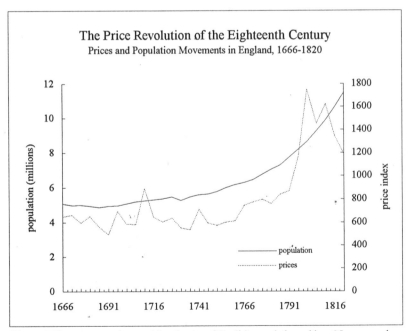

The Price Revolution of the Eighteenth Century
Prices and Population Movements in England, 1666-1820

Figure 3.05 compares quinquennial estimates of English population with a 25-year moving average of the Phelps-Brown-Hopkins index of consumable prices in the south of England. The source is E. A. Wrigley and Roger Schofield, *The Population History of England, 1541-1871; A Reconstruction* (Cambridge, 1981), 403

The growth of population in the eighteenth century created inflationary pressures in several ways. Most important was a demand inflation that developed from increasing need for life's necessities—food,
fuel, shelter and land. The supply of these commodities did not expand
as freely as demand; in consequence, prices went up. Industrial
products, on the other hand, could be turned out more easily in ever
larger quantities. As a result, prices of manufactured goods tended
to be more stable than those of farm crops and raw materials. This
demand-induced inflation was not the only economic consequence of
population growth. The increase of rural population also caused what
in the twentieth century would be called "cost-push" inflation, especially in farm prices. In the agrarian economies of Europe and
America, increases in food supplies were obtained in part by bringing
marginal lands into cultivation. Production increased, but productivity
diminished. Farmers worked harder to extract a smaller crop from
stubborn fields of poor fertility. The same sad story was played out on
the stony hillsides of New England, the bleak moors of Devon, the chill
Schnee Eifel of Germany, and the barren lands of Bourbonnais where
hamlets bore such names as *Tout-y-fait* (All's Wanting), *Pain-perdu*
(Lost Bread) and *Petit-gain* (Small Reward).

English economist David Ricardo (1772–1823) was one of the
first to observe and describe this mechanism from his own experience.
It was clearly at work during the eighteenth century, as it had been in
every previous price-revolution. The classic Ricardian processes of
rising population and falling productivity served as an important source
of price-inflation.[14]

Some people responded to these problems by introducing new
methods of farm management that have been called the agricultural
revolution. In the process, farming tended to become more intensive,
but it did not at first become more productive. Economist Esther Boserup has taught us that levels of productivity tend to fall in the early
stages of agricultural revolutions during the twentieth century. Similar
patterns also appeared in the eighteenth century.[15]

₴ Discovery and Cultural Response

The rise of prices was felt keenly throughout Europe, but it was not
perceived as a new secular tendency for many years. As long as the
magnitude of price increases remained within the range of previous

fluctuations, the new trend was invisible to contemporaries. There was no "inflationary psychology" in the period from 1725 to 1755. Price stability was assumed to be natural and normal in the world. As so often in history, perception was contemporary with the event, but understanding lagged behind. The intellectual climate remained largely unchanged even as the material order was beginning to be transformed in a new way.

The second stage began during the middle years of the eighteenth century when prices rose above the range of fluctuations in the equilibrium of 1650–1720. As they did so, contemporary observers could at last recognize the great wave for what it was: a sustained and powerful long-term tendency that profoundly changed the conditions of ordinary life.

Governments and individuals responded to this discovery much as they had done in earlier waves. As prices rose, pressures mounted for monetary expansion. In this relationship, the quantity of money (and the velocity of its circulation) was not an independent variable. In the face of rising prices, deliberate efforts were made to expand money in circulation. The supply of gold and silver in the Western world may have doubled or trebled during this period.[16]

A large expansion also occurred in commercial paper, which served increasingly as a circulating medium in the eighteenth century. Private notes and bills of exchange (a sort of eighteenth century M-3) became widely used as money in many Western cities, and passed from hand to hand in multilateral transactions.[17]

At the same time, paper currency began to appear in Scandinavia and North America, where shortages of specie were severe. The Swedish Wexelbank had issued paper notes as early as the 1660s, primarily as a carrying convenience. Swedish money was made of copper. The largest coin weighed forty-three pounds, and must have had a sluggish circulation. The American colonies issued paper money for the opposite reason: not because their metal coins were too heavy to carry around, but because they took wing and flew out of the country. New France adopted paper money in the 1680s; New England, in 1690. During the eighteenth century many other colonies issued paper currency.[18]

These tendencies increased the quantity of money in circulation and added to inflationary pressures, especially in the second stage of the price-revolution. The inflationary effect of monetary expansion was felt most powerfully during the last four decades of the eighteenth

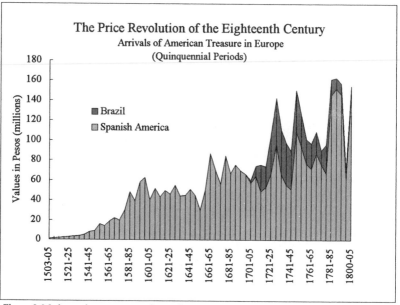

Figure 3.06 shows the movement of American treasure from 1503 to 1805. It reinforced the momentum of the price revolution in the eighteenth century, as it had done in the sixteenth century, but the largest increases occurred during the price equilibrium of 1660-1730. The source is Michel Morineau, *Incroyables gazettes et fabuleaux métaux: les retours des trésors américains d'après les gazettes hollandaises (XVIe-XVIIIe siècles)* (Paris, 1985), 482, 562.

century. Once again, monetary factors reinforced the momentum of the great wave, but did not set it in motion.

Governments responded to the price-revolution with various fiscal expedients that were also inflationary. As public spending tended to exceed income, the gap was filled with borrowing on a heroic scale. The government of France resorted to perpetual annuities called *rentes.* So large was the French national debt in the eighteenth century that it spawned a capitalist class called *rentiers.* Major European wars were financed by these securities in large volume, and by unfunded borrowing as well.

Similar trends also occurred in Britain, where the government met its obligations by issuing "consolidated annuities," or "consols" for short. These securities paid a nominal 3 percent, but in most years they traded below par and the yield rose in that proportion. The market-value of British consols fell sharply during periods of war, when large quantities were issued and public confidence declined. In 1745, after the effect of rebellion in Scotland was added to a general European

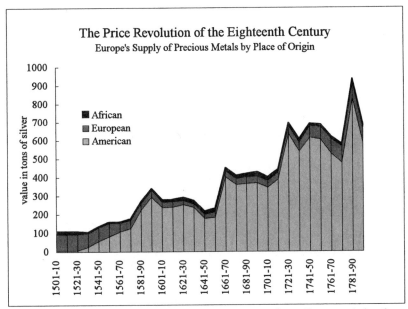

The Price Revolution of the Eighteenth Century
Europe's Supply of Precious Metals by Place of Origin

Figure 3.07 estimates the flow of gold and silver to Europe from all sources during three centuries. The increase in the price revolution (1730-1800) was smaller than in the preceding price equilibrium (1660-1730). Overall the rhythm in both periods was much the same. The source is Michel Morineau, *Incroyables gazettes et fabuleux métaux: les retours des trésors américains d'après les gazettes hollandaises (XVIe-XVIIIe siècles)* (Paris, 1985), 578.

war, London's security market suffered its first "Black Friday." The price of Consols dropped below 75. A similar crisis occurred during the Seven Years War (1754–63), when Britain's national debt rose to the then unimaginable level of 100 million pounds, and consols fell below 80. The worst of these fiscal crises developed during the American Revolution, when Britain's national debt rapidly expanded and consols plummeted as low as 54 before recovering after the peace of 1783. Whenever they did so, interest rates surged.[19]

Returns to commercial capital also increased rapidly in this period. A good barometer was the rate of interest. In the Netherlands, market-rates for short-term loans on the capital-rich Amsterdam Exchange had fallen as low as 1³/₄ percent during the period from 1700 to 1725. From this nadir, interest rates rose steadily during the eighteenth century. By 1738, the British Parliament was informed that interest-rates in the Low Countries were normally 2 to 3 percent. They climbed to 3 or 4 percent during the War of American Independence (1775–83), and 4 to 6 percent by the early 1790s.

Dutch interest rates tended to be the lowest in Europe, but similar trends appeared in every financial center. These movements were highly volatile, fluttering up and down in Europe's still very small capital markets. Heavy wartime borrowing sent interest rates soaring; periods of peace brought them crashing down again. These fluctuations occurred on the curve of a rising secular trend. Through the eighteenth century, interest rates climbed higher and higher.[20]

As the price-revolution continued, the rich and powerful generally did well for themselves. The mid-eighteenth century was a golden age for country gentry and landowning elites. The English agricultural reformer Arthur Young observed that rents increased sharply during the Seven Years War, and kept on increasing thereafter. In France, farm rents doubled during the middle decades of the eighteenth century. Land prices increased even more rapidly; the cost of real estate quadrupled in many parts of Europe during the eighteenth century. Here was another process that David Ricardo studied at first hand. Ricardian theories of rent and wages should be read not as timeless economic truths, but as highly perceptive historical descriptions of the eighteenth century price-revolution, in its middle and later stages.[21]

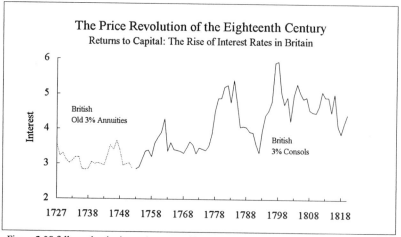

The Price Revolution of the Eighteenth Century
Returns to Capital: The Rise of Interest Rates in Britain

Figure 3.08 follows the rise in market rates of interest on British public securities. The evidence shows a pattern of surges during major wars, and a long upward trend that matched the price revolution. Dutch interest rates rose from a range of 1.75 to 2 percent (1700-25) to a range of 8 to 10 percent (1798). In France, yields on *rentes* were highly volatile, rising from 2 percent in 1720 to 34 percent in 1798. Source: Sidney Homer, *History of Interest Rates* (1963, 2d ed., 1977, New Brunswick, N.J.), 161-62.

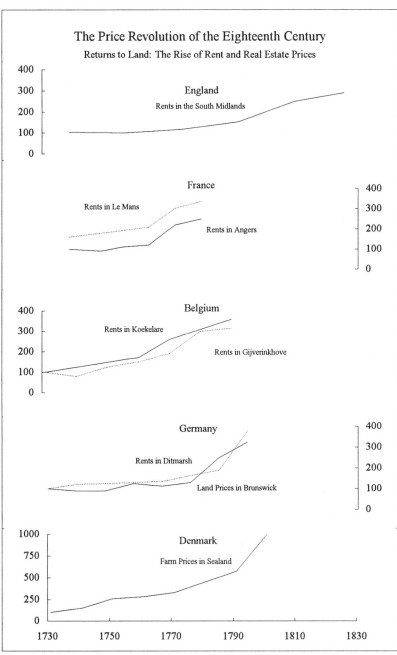

The Price Revolution of the Eighteenth Century

Returns to Land: The Rise of Rent and Real Estate Prices

England
Rents in the South Midlands

France
Rents in Le Mans
Rents in Angers

Belgium
Rents in Koekelare
Rents in Gijverinkhove

Germany
Rents in Ditmarsh
Land Prices in Brunswick

Denmark
Farm Prices in Sealand

Figure 3.09 finds that rent and real estate rose more rapidly than consumer prices. Values for England are in silver shillings per acre (1725-49=100); and for Europe in silver equivalents of local coinage (1731-40=100). Sources: Abel, *Agrarkrisen und Agrarkonjunktur*; and R. C. Allen, "Freehold Land and Interest Rates" *Economic History Review* 2d ser. 41 (1988) 33-50.

While rent and interest kept up with inflation, wages fell behind. Money wages tended to increase a little, but did not keep pace with commodity prices. In consequence, real wages fell from as early as the 1730s to the nineteenth century. This trend appeared in England, France, Germany, Austria, Poland, and Denmark during the eighteenth century. It was the case both for free laborers in western Europe and serfs in eastern Europe. The same cause—increasing population—that drove up commodity prices also depressed real wages by expanding the size of the work force. Wilhelm Abel concluded from thirty years' study of this subject that "with few exceptions, western and central European wages between 1740 and 1800 were left far behind by the rising price of cereals."[22]

The result of this decline in real wages in the eighteenth century was different from earlier price-revolutions. It caused much suffering among the poor, but no epidemic famines as in the fourteenth century and no decline of population as in the seventeenth. Here is a striking paradox in the history of price-revolutions. As one of these great waves followed another, rates of inflation increased but human suffering diminished. How could this have been the case?

One important factor, beloved of classical economists, was the expansion and integration of world markets. Another was the improvement of income per capita, which meant that fewer people were living near the edge. A third was the growth of welfare which, however limited, helped to prevent starvation. The price of all these improvements was acceleration in rates of inflation, and diminution of its cruelest consequences.

A case in point was the history of welfare. The great Hungarian scholar Karl Polanyi identified an important event in this long process. In 1795, the justices of Britain's Berkshire County met at the Pelikan Inn in Speenhamland, and agreed to make a change in their system of poor-relief. They ordered that "subsidies in aid of wages would be granted in accordance with a scale dependent upon the price of bread, so that a minimum income should be assured to the poor irrespective of their earnings."

This "Speenhamland system" spread rapidly across England, and was practiced during the next three decades, until abolished in 1834. It contributed to rising prices, even while controlling their effects. All of these events were part of the response to the price-revolution, after it was discovered as a secular trend.

The Price Revolution of the Eighteenth Century
Returns to Labor: The Fall of Real Wages

England (1451-75=100)

annual means

Naples (1740-44=100)

quinquennial means

Germany (1740-49=100)

decennial means

Figure 3.10 finds evidence of a long decline in real wages. It began as early as 1740 and continued through the full span of the price revolution, accelerating after 1775 in Italy, after 1780 in Germany, and after 1800 in England. Sources include E. H. Phelps-Brown and Sheila Hopkins, "Seven Centuries of the Prices of Consumables, Compared with Builders' Wage Rates," *Economica* 23 (1956) 296-315); Ruggiero Romano, *Prezzi e salari e servizi a Napoli nei Secolo XVIII (1734-1806)* (Milan, 1965); and Abel, *Agrarkrisen und Agrarkonjunktur.*

❧ Cultural Responses

Soon after the price-revolution became clearly visible in the middle years of the eighteenth century, a change began to occur in the cultural mood. Intellectual historians have long noted this event without being able to explain it in a satisfactory way. In 1756, a massive earthquake destroyed a large part of the city of Lisbon. This disaster inspired an outpouring of literature throughout Europe, which expressed a new spirit of scepticism, confusion, pessimism and even cultural despair. The optimism of the young Voltaire's *Age of Louis XIV* suddenly gave way to the darkness of his *Poème sur le désastre de Lisbonne* (1756) and the bitter satire of *Candide* (1759). Intellectual historians have suggested that the cause of this transformation was the Lisbon earthquake itself. This is an error. Natural catastrophes of that sort had occurred in every era. What was new was the response. In the mid-eighteenth century events began to be perceived in a different way.

Another intellectual event in this era was a religious movement that overspread the Protestant world during the mid-eighteenth century. In English-speaking America it was named the Great Awakening, and began with the preaching of Jonathan Edwards in 1734. In Britain it was known as the evangelical movement and dated from the conversion experiences of John and Charles Wesley and George Whitefield in 1738. A similar movement developed in Scandinavia and Germany, where it was called *pietismus*. There were many names in different nations, but they referred to a great international movement that revived the "religion of the heart," and rejected the optimism of the Enlightenment. Pietism in this sense flourished throughout Protestant Europe during the 1740s and 1750s, and continued to the end of the century.

These intellectual trends were not mechanical reflexes of material processes. Their dynamics were more complex. One might hypothesize that cultural and material trends simultaneously expressed underlying imbalances in the Western world during the mid-eighteenth century.

❧ "A Scrambling among Ourselves:" Growing Instability

Continuing imbalances created instabilities. Throughout Europe, commodity prices began to surge and decline, climbing sharply in the years

1739–41, 1755–58 and 1776–81, and falling rapidly in between. These movements coincided with major European wars, a series of dynastic rivalries which expanded into world wars and people's wars during the eighteenth century.[23]

In 1739, a bizarre conflict called the War of Jenkins' Ear began between Britain and Spain. This was a commercial dispute that grew into one of the first Jingo-wars in modern history. It started after Spanish officials mutilated an English interloper named Captain Robert Jenkins by cutting off his ear. Captain Jenkins presented the severed ear to Parliament in a handsome mahogany box. It became a cause of war between two great powers.[24]

The affair of the unfortunate Captain Jenkins was followed by the War of the Austrian Succession (1740–1748), a dynastic conflict between the larger states of Europe. Fighting continued for a nearly decade in Europe and America, and prices rose sharply as a consequence of heavy military spending.

An interval of peace followed that conflict, but the powers of Europe were soon at war again, in a larger struggle that German historians misnamed the Seven Years War. It actually lasted nine years from 1754 to 1763, and began in the wilderness of western Pennsylvania, when an obscure young Virginia officer named George Washington got into a fight with a French party, and was defeated. This small event led to a great world war, with heavy fighting in America, Asia, and central Europe. One of its many consequences was a surge in world prices. The price of grain rose sharply in London, Paris and Boston, and remained very high until the war ended.[25]

The peace of Paris in 1763 was followed by a short but painful period of price deflation and economic depression. Twelve years later, the great powers went to war again, in a still larger world conflict that started on Lexington Green in Massachusetts, and drew in many nations. Great armies and fleets were set in motion around the world. The cost of war caused another sharp surge of inflation.

As individuals and governments tried to cope in various ways, cultural stresses of high intensity began to develop in western society. The pattern was similar to that which had occurred in the great waves of the thirteenth and sixteenth centuries. Instabilities of many sorts developed. One of the most dangerous was the growth of inequality. This trend appeared in both Europe and America, where wealth became more concentrated in a few hands during the period from 1750 to 1790. Similar tendencies appeared in Britain and France, Scandinavia and Germany, Massachusetts and Virginia.[26]

For the rich this was the best of times, an age when the lives of the privileged few were marked by what Talleyrand called the *douceur de vie*. In the twilight of the old regime, many European states experienced what has been called an aristocratic resurgence during the third and fourth quarters of the eighteenth century. In France, the nobility arrogated to itself an increasing share of what economists call "positional goods," that is, goods that are limited in supply by their very nature: the top jobs, the most powerful offices, the highest honors. Major offices were increasingly restricted to the *noblesse*. After 1781, new army officers were required to have at least four "quarterings" of nobility in their ancestry. The effect of this rule was to expand opportunity for a narrow elite, and to restrict it for others. In the 1780s, all French bishops (135 in all) were of the nobility. Nearly all royal ministers were nobles. In retrospect, we know that this aristocratic resurgence was what German historian Martin Göhring calls a triumph *der ständischen Idee,* a triumph for the moment only. But within that moment the nobility seemed to carry everything before them. In a time of widespread suffering, they awakened intense resentment against themselves.[27]

At the bottom of French society, the poor sank deeper in misery and degradation. Between a third and half of the people of France lived near the margin of subsistence, spending as much as 80 percent of their income on food alone. In the late eighteenth century, the numbers of the poor multiplied. Homelessness increased. Public roads were thronged with aged beggars, abandoned children, broken families, and able-bodied men without work.

The disruption of families also increased. Through the period from 1730 to 1810, many studies have found a rapid rise in the proportion of children conceived and born outside of marriage. The same pattern appeared in European rates of illegitimacy and American rates of prenuptial pregnancy. Historians have struggled to explain these trends in various ways. None appear to have noticed that they correlated closely with rising prices, and with the social disruption that the price-revolution caused.

Contemporary observers in the late eighteenth century were keenly aware of these trends. They remarked on the growth of social tensions and class conflict during the 1780s. In France, the American diplomat Thomas Jefferson observed that every man seemed to be either a hammer or an anvil, either a sheep or a wolf. He was describing a period as well as a place.

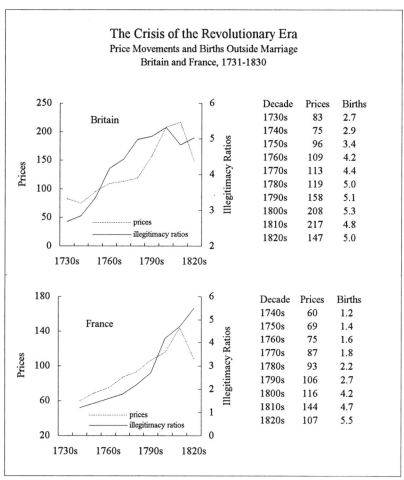

The Crisis of the Revolutionary Era
Price Movements and Births Outside Marriage
Britain and France, 1731-1830

Decade	Prices	Births
1730s	83	2.7
1740s	75	2.9
1750s	96	3.4
1760s	109	4.2
1770s	113	4.4
1780s	119	5.0
1790s	158	5.1
1800s	208	5.3
1810s	217	4.8
1820s	147	5.0

Decade	Prices	Births
1740s	60	1.2
1750s	69	1.4
1760s	75	1.6
1770s	87	1.8
1780s	93	2.2
1790s	106	2.7
1800s	116	4.2
1810s	144	4.7
1820s	107	5.5

Figure 3.11 compares ratios of births outside of marriage to all births by decade in 98 English parishes, with the Abel index of decennial wheat prices in England (grams of silver per 100 kilograms of wheat); and also illegitimacy ratios for France with the Abel series of French wheat prices. Sources are Abel, *Agrarkrisen und Agrarkonjunktur*, appendix; Yves Blayo, "Mouvement naturel de la population française de 1740 à 1829," *Population* 25 (1970) 15-64; Peter Laslett, Karla Osterveen and Richard M. Smith, eds., *Bastardy and Its Comparative History* (Cambridge, 1980) 14-15.

The growth of class conflict was attributed to "scarcity" and soaring prices. An anonymous English pamphleteer wrote in 1766:

People not perceiving a scarcity, are apt to be jealous of one another; each suspecting another's inequality of gain to rob him of his share, every one will be employing his skill and power, the best he can, to procure to himself the same plenty as formerly. This is but scrambling amongst ourselves, and helps us no more against our want, then the struggling for a short coverlet, by those who lie together, till it is pulled to pieces, will preserve them from the cold.

The laborer's share being seldom more than a bare subsistence, never allows that body of men time or opportunity to raise their thought above that, or to contest with the richer for their's;—unless when some uncommon and great distress, uniting them in one universal ferment, makes them forget respect, and emboldens them to serve their wants with armed force; and then sometimes they break in upon the rich, and sweep all like a deluge. But this rarely happens, but in the MALADMINISTRA-TION OF NEGLECTED AND MISMANAGED GOVERNMENT.[28]

The growth of inequality was an international trend in the late eighteenth century. It appeared in Europe, Great Britain and even in the new United States, where many studies have found a rapid increase in the concentration of wealth during the period from 1760 to 1830.

The effect of growing inequality was to disrupt the moral economy of the western society, and to destabilize its material order. The humanitarian ethics of Christianity, which the Enlightenment had done much to reinforce, compelled the nations of western Europe to spend larger sums on social welfare than ever before. In France during the 1780s the poor received more than 20 million livres in government assistance alone, plus larger sums from the church and private individuals. This vast effort prevented the famines that had occurred in the fourteenth century, but intensified social tensions. In place of starvation there was hunger. Instead of despair there was rage—an emotion far more dangerous to the standing order.

Inequality also created material strains within western society. As poor families devoted more of their income to bread, less remained for other things. The result was shrinkage of demand, which caused sharp contractions in markets for industrial goods. The economies of western Europe in the 1780s experienced the same combination of inflation and stagnation that marked the penultimate stage of every other price-revolution.

Governments, caught in a spiral of increasing instability, struggled to maintain their solvency by raising taxes, as Britain did throughout its empire in 1763–75, and France attempted to do in 1783–88. Entrenched elites were able to shift these burdens away from themselves. The new taxes, like the old ones, fell heavily on those who were least able to bear them. In England, the resistance of the country gentry to a trivial tax on cider in 1763 compelled the government to try the dangerous expedient of taxing America, with disastrous results for the empire. In France, the crown had long conciliated the nobility and *haut bourgeoisie* by exempting them from various taxes. The Marquis de Lafayette inherited an estate that paid him 140,000 livres a year, but he was exempt from the *taille* which took a large part of a peasant's small surplus. Many rich bourgeois were also released from the *taille*. By and large it was paid by the people of middling estates, and by the working poor. There were other taxes, such as the *capitation* (a cross between a poll tax and an income tax) and *vingtieme* ("the twentieth"). Both were nominally paid by everyone, but the rich and strong could reduce these obligations by payment of a lump sum, which was much diminished by inflation. Indirect taxes such as customs duties, excise taxes

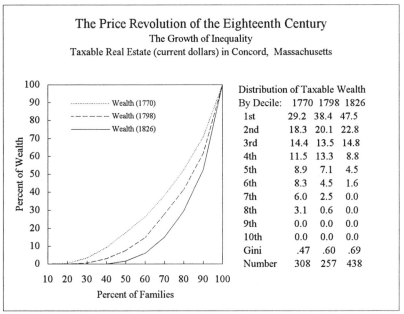

The Price Revolution of the Eighteenth Century
The Growth of Inequality
Taxable Real Estate (current dollars) in Concord, Massachusetts

Distribution of Taxable Wealth			
By Decile:	1770	1798	1826
1st	29.2	38.4	47.5
2nd	18.3	20.1	22.8
3rd	14.4	13.5	14.8
4th	11.5	13.3	8.8
5th	8.9	7.1	4.5
6th	8.3	4.5	1.6
7th	6.0	2.5	0.0
8th	3.1	0.6	0.0
9th	0.0	0.0	0.0
10th	0.0	0.0	0.0
Gini	.47	.60	.69
Number	308	257	438

Figure 3.12 is one of many studies that find growing inequality in the period 1750-1830. It surveys the distribution of taxable wealth in real estate (current dollars), for the town of Concord, Massachusetts, twenty miles west of Boston. The data are taken from town valuations in 1770 and 1826, and from the federal direct tax assessment in 1798. The source is D. H. Fischer, ed., *Concord: The Social History of a New England Town, 1750-1850* (Waltham, 1983) 91, 222. Similar trends, with higher levels of inequality, appear for personal wealth, total wealth, and the distribution of real estate by acres.

and the hated salt tax were paid by all, but tended to be passed on to the consumer. Again, it was the poor and middling who bore the weight. Other taxes in kind, notably the *corvée* and the *transport militaire,* fell heavily upon the peasantry. This system of regressive taxation simultaneously increased social resentments, diminished the moral authority of the standing order, and shrank the government's income.[29]

As public revenue lagged behind expenditures, public debt began to grow rapidly, trebling in fifteen years from 1773 to 1788. In France by 1789, nearly half of national spending went for interest payments on the national debt. Europe's greatest power, with its massive military spending, became a heavy debtor. But it was not the heaviest. In relative terms, other countries such as the Netherlands had an even larger national debt than France during the late eighteenth century.[30]

Britain's national debt also grew at a formidable rate, rising during the Seven Years War, falling in the peace that followed, then rising again during the American War of Independence. These fluctuations gave rise to heavy speculation in public securities. There were many angry complaints against speculators, whose operations added to fiscal instability. But one of this group responded, "There is only one way to get rid of us; pay off the national debt."

This, Britain was unable to do. Stock speculation, originally conducted furtively in alleys and coffee houses, institutionalized itself. By the year 1773, a favorite meeting place called New Jonathan's Coffee House posted a sign saying "The Stock Exchange" above its entrance, and admitted only those who paid for the privilege.

Speculators found opportunities in the growing economic instabilities of this era, and created further instability in their turn. A case in point was Sir George Colebrooke, scion of a prominent English banking family and "a great adventurer in . . . articles of speculation." Colebrooke attempted to corner the English market in hemp, a strategic commodity for the Royal Navy. One of his rivals unkindly observed that his purpose was "so that if he should be ordered to be hanged, no one will have hemp enough to find him a halter."

When his national hemp corner failed, Colebrooke tried in 1771–72 to make a world corner on alum, a substance used in the dying of textiles. He actually succeeded in buying up the output of most major suppliers, but drove the price so high that new producers suddenly appeared. The market for alum was glutted and Colebrooke was ruined, dragging down other speculators with him. His fall contributed to a massive credit crisis throughout Europe.[31]

There were many financial collapses in the second half of the eighteenth century. One of them began in the Netherlands with the failure of the Dutch firm of de Neufville (1763), and spread quickly to Germany, France, Britain and America. Another panic started in Scotland with the failure of a Scottish banker and speculator named Alexander Fordyce, who had taken a short position in East India stock and was ruined by a sudden rise in the market. He fled to Europe, leaving a disaster in his wake. The reverberations spread throughout the Atlantic world.[32]

There were also growing political tensions, which in the 1760s and 1770s began to develop into armed insurrections. The Swiss city of Geneva experienced a bourgeois revolution in 1768 and a counter-revolution in 1782. A close student of these events concludes that they rose partly from the writings of Jean-Jacques Rousseau and partly from price movements in Switzerland.[33]

In Russia, a great rebellion was led by Cossack private Emilian Pugachev, who killed members of the gentry and captured many towns. Pugachev's Rebellion grew in large part from economic grievances that had been exacerbated by rising prices. Other rebellions broke out in the Netherlands, Corsica, and Ireland.

The largest of these insurgencies developed in England's American colonies, in response to repeated attempts by the British government to raise taxes in the Revenue Act of 1764, the Stamp Act of 1765, the Townshend Acts of 1767 and the Tea Act of 1773.

The American rising was not unique. The regiments of British infantry that were sent to restore order in Boston after the Tea Party had been employed on many similar missions throughout the British Empire. The history of their service was a record of the rising spirit of rebellion throughout the western world. The 23rd Foot (Royal Welch Fusiliers) had been used to "restore order" throughout Devon and Cornwall. The 18th Foot (Royal Irish) had been putting down riots against press gangs in Whitehaven. The 43rd and eight other regiments had been assigned to suppress agrarian risings through twelve counties of the South Midlands and East Anglia in 1766. The 4th Foot had been suppressing smugglers along the Channel coast, and the British Marines had been dispatched on the same mission into Romney Marsh. Many regiments had served in Ireland, which was in a state of insurrection in 1771 and 1772. In England itself there were at least 159 major riots between 1740 and 1775, and minor ones beyond counting.[34]

At the same time, the nobility from Poland to France demanded more advantages for themselves. Statesmen struggled to hold the system together, while short-sighted elites destroyed the props of their own privilege. By 1783, the long inflation was turning class against class. The old regime was on the edge of disaster.

❧ The Revolutionary Crisis, 1789–1820

After 1783, the great wave approached its climax, in a crisis that overswept the western world. In some ways this event was remarkably similar to the troubles of the fourteenth and seventeenth centuries. In others, it was entirely new.

The crisis began during the decade of the 1780s. It was triggered by change in the weather. During the late eighteenth century, the climate of western Europe became highly variable. The years from 1778 to 1781 were exceptionally warm, with long hot summers and unusually mild winters. Then the pattern reversed. From 1782 to 1787, Europe and America suffered hard winters, wet summers and short harvests. In 1788, the weather was even worse. Throughout western Europe, crops rotted in the fields. In France that year the final blow was a fantastic hailstorm that dropped stones as heavy as eight pounds, killing animals and ruining what remained of the ripening grain. The harvest was very short, and food prices soared during the winter of 1788–89. Shortages became more severe in 1789. Farmers had yet another dismal crop year, and a very poor harvest.[1]

These events were not unique. Prolonged spells of bad weather had happened many times in Europe during the eighteenth century: 1711–17, 1739–52 and 1769–77. But the hard years of the 1780s were different. They came after half a century of rising prices, falling wages and growing instability. In the countryside, a long run of short harvests meant less work for country laborers and a surge in rural unemployment. In the cities, small crops caused grain prices to surge. Even in good times, the wages of working class families went mostly for food. In the period from 1726 to 1791, an average wage-earner in France spent 50 percent of his income to feed his family. In 1789, that proportion rose to 88 percent.[2]

In France, these troubles coincided with a fiscal crisis. By 1787, Europe's most powerful government was on the edge of bankruptcy. Annual expenditures of 300 million livres and revenues of merely 140 millions left a deficit of 160 million livres—more than half of total national public spending.

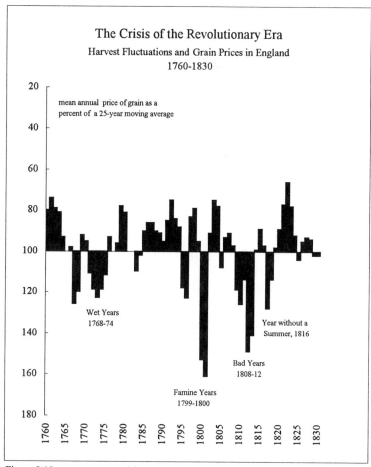

The Crisis of the Revolutionary Era
Harvest Fluctuations and Grain Prices in England
1760-1830

mean annual price of grain as a
percent of a 25-year moving average

Wet Years
1768-74

Year without a
Summer, 1816

Bad Years
1808-12

Famine Years
1799-1800

Figure 3.13 represents annual harvest prices in England as a percentage of a 25-year moving average. It shows an increase in the severity of harvest shortages, peaking *circa* 1799-1816. Thereafter, the trend reversed. The source is Henry Phelps-Brown and Sheila V. Hopkins, *A Perspective of Wages and Prices* (London, 1981), 59.

Ministers tried desperately to balance their books. Economies were enacted. The king himself, Louis XVI, set an example by reducing his household expenses from 22 million livres to 17 million, largely by consolidating the royal stables. But this was merely 3 percent of the deficit. Much of the budget went for irreducible military and social spending. Half of it was needed for service on the debt.

The financial ministers of Louis XVI pleaded desperately for more revenue, and were refused. The possessing classes refused to accept new taxes. Many demanded more privileges and exemptions. This combination of public need and private greed was fatal to the old regime. In scenes reminiscent of fourteenth century England, sixteenth century Spain, and twentieth century America, the national credit of the most powerful nation in the world was systematically wrecked by the selfishness of its affluent citizens.[3]

The effect of fiscal crisis in France was compounded by a world depression in commerce and industry. From 1782 to 1789, the output of the French textile industry fell by 50 percent. Employers ruthlessly laid off workers. In the town of Troyes alone, it was reported that 10,000 people lost their jobs. Conditions were much the same throughout western Europe and North America during the 1780s. Unemployment rapidly increased among silkworkers in Italy, shipbuilders in Massachusetts, and miners in Germany. Those who kept their jobs lost much of their income, as real wages declined.[4]

Benjamin Franklin toured a textile factory in Norwich and observed a cruel and bitter irony. He was amazed to see that the English clothmakers were themselves "half-naked or in tatters." The factory owner pointed proudly to his inventory and said, "those cloths are for Italy, those for Germany, the ones over here for the American islands, and those for the continent." Franklin replied, "Have you none for the factory workers of Norwich?"[5]

When wages fell and the price of food surged throughout the western world, crime increased sharply—especially crimes against property. The poor in desperation took what they could get no other way. The long downward trend in crime reversed during the later stages of the price-revolution, as it had done in every other great wave. Crimes against property surged to high levels.

Local and national governments made a major effort to provide relief on an unprecedented scale, and succeeded in doing so. The French minister Necker suspended grain exports in 1788, bought heavily abroad, and compelled merchants to sell their stocks. In consequence, there was nothing like the epidemic famines of the fourteenth century, nor even a demographic contraction as in the seventeenth century. Few people starved in the 1780s, but many were hungry, and more were angry.

The politics of hunger were very different from those of starvation. In the early fourteenth century, starving peasants had been too weak to rebel. In the late eighteenth century, hungry peasants were outraged against feudal lords and seigneurial dues. They were infuri-

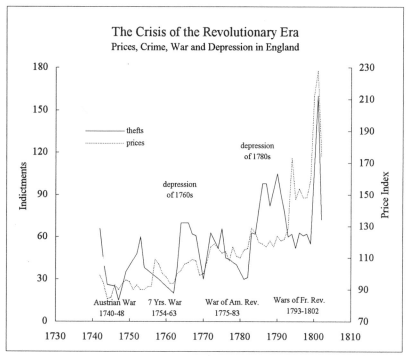

The Crisis of the Revolutionary Era
Prices, Crime, War and Depression in England

Figure 3.14 compares prosecutions for theft in the Staffordshire Assizes with the Schumpeter-Gilboy price index, and with periods of war and depression. It shows that crime increased in periods of inflation and depression. Wars caused crime rates to fall in their early years, then to rise in later years and to rise higher in immediate post-bellum periods. The greatest increases in crime occurred when these conditions coincided in post-bellum periods of stagflation. The source for the data shown here is Douglas Hay, "War, Dearth and Theft in the Eighteenth Century: The Record of English Courts," *Past & Present* 95 (1982) 125, which offers a different interpretation. The Schumpeter-Gilboy index is in Mitchell and Deane, *Abstract of British Historical Statistics*, 468-69.

ated by the prosperity of bourgeois speculators with their bulging granaries. They felt oppressed by bullying tax-gatherers and corrupt officials.

Few people in France blamed their amiable King Louis XVI, but many hated his Austrian Queen, Marie Antoinette. While hunger stalked the countryside she amused herself in an endless whirl of fashion. She made a game of peasant life, building a play-cottage of the finest materials and tending miniature fields and flocks with silver tools that seemed to mock the misery of her suffering subjects.

Marie Antoinette never said "let them eat cake," but similar expressions were heard from high officials. When a royal officer in

Touraine was told in 1788 that the peasants had no grain, he did actually say, "Let them eat grass." An officer employed by the Duc de Deux Ponts observed contemptuously of the local peasantry in 1786, "It is our interest to feed them, but it would be dangerous to fatten them." An old Alderman of Orleans was arrested after the Revolution began for allegedly saying, "If all the little girls died, there would be plenty of bread."[6]

A sense of outrage against the arrogance and imbecility of ruling elites developed rapidly throughout Europe. That emotion was specially strong in France. The most powerful nation in Europe was in some respects the most vulnerable. It had no social safety-valve comparable to the virgin land of Russia and America, and no outlet such as the heavy emigration from Britain and Germany. In France during the late 1780s, anger and frustration overflowed into acts of violence.

First came individual acts of rage—the burning of a speculator's house in Paris, the beating of a bailiff in Languedoc, the stoning of a bishop in Manosque, the theft of grain everywhere. By 1788, gangs of desperate men were roaming the countryside, stealing what food they could find and assaulting tax collectors. In the Spring of 1789, food riots broke out in the cities and towns, and the spirit of resistance spread swiftly through the countryside. The authorities made the worst possible response—sporadic acts of symbolic violence that were just harsh enough to stimulate resistance, but not sufficient to repress it. From time to time, beggars and petty thieves were rounded up in large numbers, but there were not jails and galleys enough to hold them. Increasingly, soldiers whose families were themselves suffering refused to act against the people. As food prices surged in 1789, these various insurrections suddenly exploded into revolution.[7]

There were no fewer than four French Revolutions in 1789: a continuing aristocratic revolt against royal ministers; a bourgeois revolution against the aristocracy, a rising of urban workers against the high bourgeoisie, and a peasant insurrection against all of their oppressors. Each of these movements was set in motion by rising prices. All were responses to the fiscal and economic crisis of the 1780s.

In Paris, urban workers began their revolution by attacking the *barrières* where internal customs were levied on food coming to the city. They went on to ransack the monastery of St. Lazere, not in an orgy of anti-clericalism but in search of something to eat. A vast hoard of food was found in the cellars. Then they turned their wrath against that hated symbol of injustice, the Bastille. Historians Ernest Labrousse and Georges Lefebvre discovered that the Bastille was attacked on precisely the same day when grain prices reached their cyclical high in Paris. The men who assaulted the Bastille were not the *canaille* of the city. The great majority were artisans, masters, journeymen, and shopkeepers who were driven to desperate acts by the high cost of living, and by their rage against a government that had turned away from the people.[8]

At the same time, the peasants' revolution broke out in the countryside. Complaints centered on feudal dues, seigneurial ovens, high rents, the hated hunting parties, cruel moneylenders, the loss of collective rights and the imposition of individual exactions. Specially resented were unequal taxes that fell heavily upon the poor and rose in proportion to soaring prices—the *taille, champart, gabelle, picquet de farine,* and taxes on wine and beer.

Throughout France many vestiges of privilege were attacked, sometimes with great violence. Chateaux were burned, convents attacked, mills pulled down, warehouses looted. Archives became a

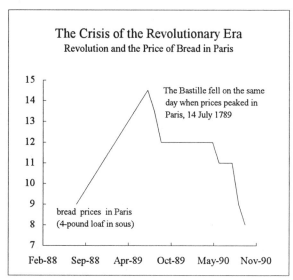

The Crisis of the Revolutionary Era
Revolution and the Price of Bread in Paris

The Bastille fell on the same day when prices peaked in Paris, 14 July 1789

bread prices in Paris
(4-pound loaf in sous)

Figure 3.15 shows the association between prices and revolution in Paris. The sources are George Rudé, "Prices, Wages and Popular Movements in Paris during the French Revolution," *Economic History Review* 2d ser., 6 (1953-54) 246-67; and Georges Lefebvre, "Le mouvement des prix et les origines de la Revolution française," *Annales Historiques de la Revolution Française* 14 (1937) 289-329.

common target. Rent rolls and debt books were systematically destroyed. The streets of provincial capitals were strewn with official papers.

A third bourgeois revolution, which claimed to be "The Revolution," was a syncretist movement dominated by the middle class who attempted to give France a system of constitutional and representative government under a new National Assembly. The leaders of this body at first pursued two economic ideas: free trade and the sanctity of private property. The new regime did not repudiate the national debt, which was held by many bourgeois *rentiers*. Instead, it tried to solve the nation's fiscal problems by other means—partly by seizing the assets of the church and selling them to private buyers. It extinguished monopolies and guilds, and abolished collective rights that had been cherished by the peasantry.

For two years from 1789 to 1791, the prospects were encouraging for this bourgeois revolution. The weather improved in Europe. Business revived throughout the western world, and the price of provisions fell sharply. This was the moment when it seemed that France might succeed in creating a stable constitutional monarchy for itself.

But it was not to be. The problem, once again, was the cost of living. From 1791 to 1793 there was another economic crisis. Food prices surged again, in a volatile movement that was typical of the last stage in every price-revolution. Food riots once more became common in Paris. The result was a second and more radical French Revolution. The king was deposed and later executed; the Jacobins seized power and the Terror began.

Robespierre's Jacobin regime tried to deal with the problem of price surges by imposing a *maximum*. This measure briefly halted inflation by a highly effective system of price controls, but it was accompanied by food-rationing and wage-restraints which proved to be intensely unpopular. When Robespierre fell from power, he was brought down by a riot against wage-controls.[9]

Then came the counter-revolution called "Thermidor" which took its name from the month in the revolutionary calendar when the wage riots occurred. A new and highly corrupt regime called the Directory gained control of the government and relaxed the system of wage and price controls. The result was yet another period of soaring prices, falling wages, extreme suffering for the poor, and high prosperity for speculators. More riots occurred, and were met this time by harsh repression, which ended in the fall of the Directory.

From 1789 to 1799, every twist and turn of fortune in the French Revolution was closely tied to the movement of prices. Market fluctuations and political events were linked together.[10]

Meanwhile, the revolutionary spirit spread rapidly to other nations. Everywhere in Europe and America, prices had risen and real wages had declined. The concentration of wealth increased. Elites became more assertive of their privileges, and social tensions grew more intense. These were international events, and so also was the response. The revolutionary rallying cry of liberty, equality and fraternity was invented not in France but in the Netherlands. Those powerful ideas were not disembodied abstractions, but concrete solutions to urgent problems. The result was a wave of revolutions, unprecedented in breadth and violence.

In rapid succession, revolutions broke out in what is now Belgium (1789), Switzerland (1792), the Netherlands (1794), Poland (1794) and Ireland (1798). Revolutionary French armies toppled the old oligarchies of Genoa (1797), Venice (1797), Berne (1798), and many other Italian cities and Swiss cantons. Assassination was the fate of Sweden's King Gustavus III (1792), and Russia's Czar Paul I (1801). England's prime minister Spencer Perceval (1812) was murdered by a bankrupt broker, John Bellingham. In the new republic of the United States, a peaceable revolution occurred when the Jeffersonian movement transformed a whiggish Federalist oligarchy into a representative democracy. Revolutions broke out in French and Spanish colonies of America. Others spread to every corner of the world. On the Comoro Islands in the Mozambique Channel, the African inhabitants marched against their Arab masters with banners that read ''America is free! Cannot we be?''[11]

Defenders of the old regime reacted by organizing counterrevolutionary movements that were more violent than the revolutions themselves. During the 1790s, the worst scenes of social violence in the western world were the work of conservative mobs in Spain who sought to purge that country of radical elements.[12]

By the winter of 1792–93, Prussia, Austria, Britain, Spain, and Holland were at war against the revolutionary government of France. To pay its heavy military costs, the French government printed large quantities of unsecured money called *Assignats* which lost as much as eighty per cent of their face value in five years—a classic hyperinflation.[13] Conservative regimes were also hard pressed. After war began, the Bank of England ceased to redeem its banknotes in specie. For a

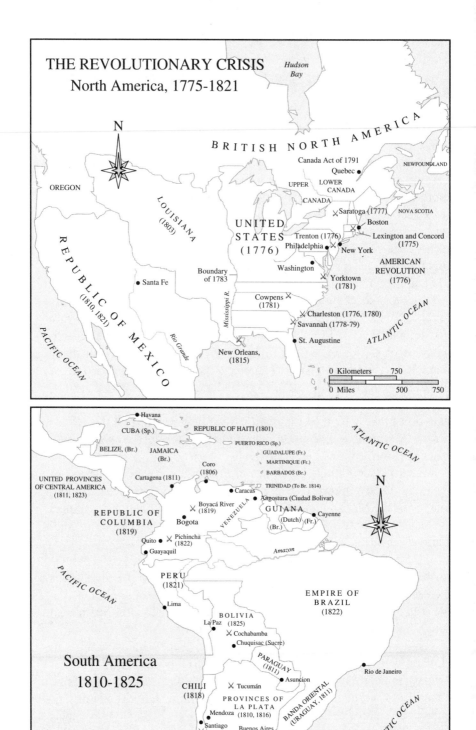

THE REVOLUTIONARY CRISIS
North America, 1775-1821

Hudson Bay

N

NORTH AMERICA

BRITISH NORTH AMERICA

NEWFOUNDLAND

Canada Act of 1791
Quebec

UPPER | LOWER CANADA

OREGON

CANADA

Saratoga (1777)   NOVA SCOTIA

Boston

LOUISIANA (1803)

UNITED
STATES
(1776)

Trenton (1776)
Philadelphia
New York

Lexington and Concord
(1775)

REPUBLIC OF MEXICO
(1810, 1821)

Santa Fe

Boundary
of 1783

Washington

AMERICAN
REVOLUTION
(1776)

Yorktown
(1781)

Cowpens
(1781)

Charleston (1776, 1780)
Savannah (1778-79)

Mississippi R.

Rio Grande

New Orleans,
(1815)

St. Augustine

ATLANTIC OCEAN

PACIFIC OCEAN

0 Kilometers   750
0 Miles   500   750

Havana

CUBA (Sp.)

REPUBLIC OF HAITI (1801)

ATLANTIC OCEAN

BELIZE, (Br.)   JAMAICA
(Br.)

PUERTO RICO (Sp.)

GUADALUPE (Fr.)
MARTINIQUE (Fr.)

Coro
(1806)

BARBADOS (Br.)

UNITED PROVINCES
OF CENTRAL AMERICA
(1811, 1823)

Cartagena (1811)

TRINIDAD (To Br. 1814)

Caracas

Angostura (Ciudad Bolivar)

Boyacá River
(1819)

GUIANA

REPUBLIC OF
COLUMBIA
(1819)

Bogota

VENEZUELA

(Dutch) (Fr.)   Cayenne
(Br.)

N

Quito   Pichincha
(1822)

Guayaquil

Amazon

PERU
(1821)

PACIFIC OCEAN

Lima

EMPIRE OF
BRAZIL
(1822)

BOLIVIA
La Paz   (1825)

Cochabamba

Chuquisac (Sucre)

South America
1810-1825

CHILI
(1818)

PARAGUAY
(1811)

Tucumán

Asuncion

Rio de Janeiro

PROVINCES OF
LA PLATA
Mendoza   (1810, 1816)

Santiago

Buenos Aires

BANDA ORIENTAL
(URAGUAY, 1811)

Montivideo

ATLANTIC OCEAN

Maipú (1818)

0 Kilometers   750
0 Miles   500   750

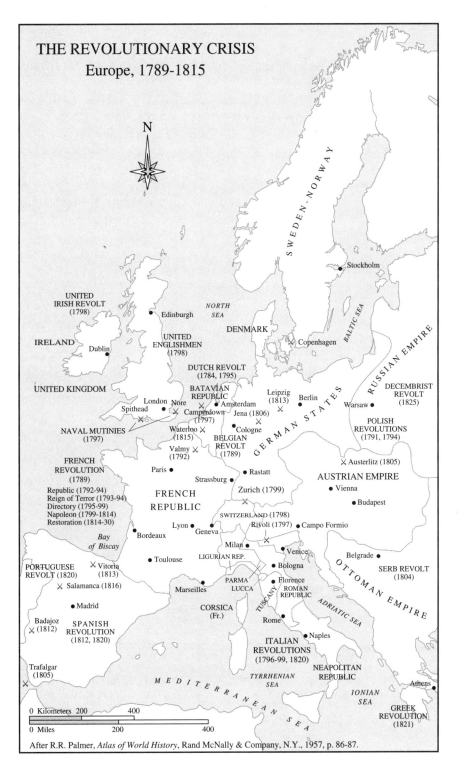

THE REVOLUTIONARY CRISIS
Europe, 1789-1815

N

SWEDEN-NORWAY

• Stockholm

BALTIC SEA

RUSSIAN EMPIRE

UNITED
IRISH REVOLT
(1798)

NORTH
SEA

• Edinburgh

DENMARK

× Copenhagen

IRELAND
Dublin
•

UNITED
ENGLISHMEN
(1798)

DUTCH REVOLT
(1784, 1795)

UNITED KINGDOM

BATAVIAN
REPUBLIC

London Nore × Amsterdam
Spithead × × Camperdown
× (1797)

Leipzig
(1813)

Berlin

GERMAN STATES

Warsaw •

DECEMBRIST
REVOLT
(1825)

NAVAL MUTINIES
(1797)

Jena (1806) ×

Waterloo ×
(1815)
Valmy ×
(1792)

Cologne ×

POLISH
REVOLUTIONS
(1791, 1794)

BELGIAN
REVOLT
(1789)

FRENCH
REVOLUTION
(1789)

Paris •

× Rastatt

× Austerlitz (1805)

AUSTRIAN EMPIRE

Republic (1792-94)
Reign of Terror (1793-94)
Directory (1795-99)
Napoleon (1799-1814)
Restoration (1814-30)

Strassburg •

FRENCH
REPUBLIC

Zurich (1799)

SWITZERLAND (1798)

× Rivoli (1797)

• Vienna

• Budapest

Lyon •
Geneva

• Campo Formio

Bay
of Biscay

Bordeaux •

Milan •

• Toulouse

LIGURIAN REP.

• Venice

• Bologna

Belgrade •

OTTOMAN EMPIRE

PORTUGUESE
REVOLT (1820)

× Vitoria
(1813)

PARMA
LUCCA

× Salamanca (1816)

Marseilles •

• Florence
ROMAN
REPUBLIC

TUSCANY

ADRIATIC SEA

SERB REVOLT
(1804)

• Madrid

CORSICA
(Fr.)

Rome •

Badajoz
× (1812)

SPANISH
REVOLUTION
(1812, 1820)

• Naples

ITALIAN
REVOLUTIONS
(1796-99, 1820)

Trafalgar
(1805)
×

MEDITERRANEAN
SEA

TYRRHENIAN
SEA

NEAPOLITAN
REPUBLIC

IONIAN
SEA

Athens •

0 Kilometers 200   400

GREEK
REVOLUTION
(1821)

0 Miles   200   400

After R.R. Palmer, *Atlas of World History*, Rand McNally & Company, N.Y., 1957, p. 86-87.

time Britain went off the gold standard, with a consequent decline in the purchasing value of its currency.[14]

Prices soared in many nations. From 1790 to 1815, rates of increase were greater than in any previous price-revolution. Every European nation and monetary system was caught up in it, and the Americas as well. From Boston to Buenos Aires, the price of consumables trebled between 1794 and 1814. Grain prices rose sharply in Canada, the United States and Mexico during the same period. Between 1767 and 1839 the Middle East, the Balkans and Turkey experienced what has been called "the most inflationary period in Ottoman history." The timing varied in detail, but the trends were almost everywhere the same.[15]

This surge drove the overall rate of inflation above earlier long waves. The average annual increase had been one half of one per cent in the medieval price-revolution, and a little more than one per cent in the sixteenth century. The great wave of the eighteenth century averaged about 1.7 percent in England, mainly because of sharp increases in the period from 1793 and 1815.[16]

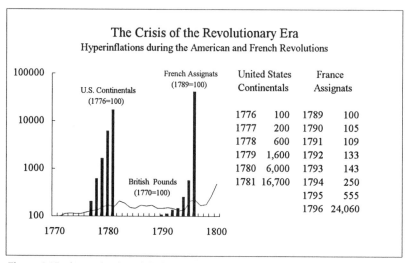

The Crisis of the Revolutionary Era

Hyperinflations during the American and French Revolutions

United States Continentals		France Assignats	
1776	100	1789	100
1777	200	1790	105
1778	600	1791	109
1779	1,600	1792	133
1780	6,000	1793	143
1781	16,700	1794	250
		1795	555
		1796	24,060

Figure 3.17 shows the hyperinflations that were caused by the monetary policies of revolutionary regimes in France and the United States. The price trend in a more stable hard currency appears in the change in purchasing power of British sterling. Sources for Continentals are E. James Ferguson, *The Power of the Purse: A History of American Public Finance, 1776-1790* (Chapel Hill, 1961); for Assignats, A. Bailleul, *Tableau complet de valeur des Assignats* (Paris, 1797); for British Pounds Sterling, B. R. Mitchell, *British Historical Statistics* (Cambridge, 1988).

Those years were a period of war—not the dynastic quarrels of the mid-eighteenth century, but social upheavals that combined abstract appeals to high principle with savage violence such as the western world had not experienced since the crisis of the seventeenth century. Entire populations went to war with one another. In Russia, Canada and the United States, national capitals were looted and burned. In Spain, atrocities beyond imagining became commonplace during the Napoleonic Wars. Goya's drawings captured the horror of war more powerfully than any western artist had done since Collot in the general crisis of the seventeenth century.

The effect of war was to deepen the revolutionary crisis. Every age of glory in military history is an agony for ordinary people. So it was in the time of Napoleon and Nelson. The worst suffering came during the decade from 1805 to 1815, when after a brief interlude of peace the great powers went to war once again. Britain's Royal Navy won mastery of the sea at Cape Trafalgar (1805), and the imperial army of France gained a hegemony on the European mainland in the battles of Austerlitz (1805) and Jena (1806).

Thereafter the struggle changed. Two rival nations, each secure in its own sphere, turned to economic warfare. Britain imposed a vast blockade on Napoleonic Europe, while France closed the ports of the continent to British commerce. As the great wave approached its catastrophic climax, the two strongest nations in the western world went systematically about the business of wrecking each other's economy. In this consummate act of human folly, markets were deliberately disrupted throughout western Europe. The price of food in Britain and France rose to unprecedented heights. Real wages plummeted, and poverty increased so rapidly that by 1812 more than half of all English families were dependent on some sort of poor relief.[17]

The cost of economic warfare was a heavy burden even for non-combatants. The United States had flourished as a neutral trader from 1793 to 1805. Now its ships were seized by both Britain and France. The carrying trade of New England was destroyed, the staple commerce of the southern states was disrupted, and the United States was drawn inexorably into the vortex of war. Its economy slipped into a deep depression and yet prices soared, reaching their peak in the 1814 when commerce was at its lowest ebb. Massive surges occurred in the price of food and energy.[18]

But the worst suffering was in the old world. In 1812 Napoleon recruited a huge army from his European dominions and sent it headlong to destruction in Russia. At the same time, the Peninsular War between Britain and France reached its climax of barbaric violence. Yet another war broke between the United States and Britain. Institutions everywhere were strained to the snapping point. The British government came the edge of insolvency in 1812; the American republic came close to disintegration in 1814. Finally it was the Napoleonic Empire that collapsed in bloody ruins.

This general crisis, like those that had preceded it, was also an intellectual event. The certainties of the Enlightenment were destroyed by the disorders that overtook the Western world. Confidence in reason and progress was lost. Their apostles became martyrs.

A case in point was the career of the Marquis de Condorcet, a kind, gentle, and highly principled gentleman-philosopher who embraced the Enlightenment, welcomed the Revolution, and became an early convert to its humanitarian ideals. He voted against the execution of Louis XVI and opposed the arrest of the Girondins. For those acts of humanity he was denounced as a traitor and driven into hiding, where as a fugitive he wrote an astonishing book called *A History of the Progress of the Human Spirit.* Pursued by the Jacobins, he lived like an animal in woods and abandoned quarries. Finally, he was caught by the peasants whose cause he had championed. Thrown into prison, abandoned by his friends, bleeding and in rags, this great apostle of progress took his own life on April 8, 1794.

The melancholy fate of Condorcet was shared by the Enlightenment that he personified. The Revolution devoured not only its children but also its intellectual parents. During the period from 1790 to 1815, the dream of reason evaporated in the fires of war, and another mood began to dominate the intellectual life of the West. Its vehicle was the complex cultural ideology called romanticism, which had long been gestating in eighteenth century Europe. During the period from 1800 to 1815, romanticism rapidly gained strength and power, and became the dominant aesthetic movement in the western world.

Romanticism was most of all a new epistemology. It valued feeling above reason, intuition above empiricism, and ambiguity above clarity. It tended to look backward to the past rather than forward to the future. It had little faith in reason or hope for human progress. In Europe it often expressed a mood of melancholy, drifting even to despair. Romanticism was Goethe's sorrowful Young Werther, and the literature of *Sturm und Drang.* It was Stendhal's tragic vision of society, and Wordsworth's great escape into the company of clouds and daffodils. In America it was Poe's tale of Gothic horror, Hawthorne's scarlet letter, and Melville's Captain Ahab. In England it was Byron's Manfred and Childe Harold, hero-symbols of alienation from society and even from one's self. The general crisis became a cultural revolution that transformed the values of the western world.

The great wave reached its crest and broke with shattering violence during the Napoleonic Wars (1796–1815). With uncanny precision, prices reached their peak in each nation during the moment of its greatest military peril—Germany in 1808, Russia in 1812, Britain in 1812–13, the United States in 1814. The battles of Leipzig and Waterloo, Baltimore and New Orleans proved to be pivotal for the history of prices, as they were for politics and war.

Thereafter, the secular trend suddenly broke and prices began to fall. This transition was not a clean and simple break. The new trend had barely begun when its progress was suddenly interrupted by one of the most severe moments of climate-stress in modern history. The years from 1814 to 1818 were marked by extremely harsh winters and cold wet summers. The worst came in 1816. In Europe, the summer of that year was cold, dark, wet and gloomy. A party of literati spent their ruined Swiss vacation indoors, writing horror fantasies that captured the prevailing mood. Mary Shelley invented *Frankenstein* and Lord Byron's physician Dr. Polidori created *The Vampyre*. In the northern United States, 1816 was the "year without a summer." Killing frosts occurred in every month, and crops were widely ruined. In Ohio folklore 1816 was called "eighteen-hundred-and-froze-to death." New England remembered it as the Mackerel Year.

Crop shortages were more severe in 1816–17 than in 1788, and food prices surged to high levels. But the cultural consequences were different than before. Grain poured into western Europe—Ukrainian grain from the new port of Odessa, American grain from Baltimore, Egyptian grain from Alexandria, Turkish grain from Constantinople. The growing integration of a global food market saved Europe from starvation.

Governments had become more efficient in providing social welfare. As a consequence the poor did not starve in a period of scarcity. Mortality increased very little. In New England, the death rate actually declined during the coldest years.

The new nation-states had also learned from hard experience how to control social violence before it reached the flashpoint of revolution. Standing armies, national guards, and new professional police forces throughout the western world prevented popular insurrections and food riots from overturning governments. The crisis of 1816 passed without major unrest.[19]

After 1816 the weather improved, but the western world suffered yet another heavy blow. In the United States, a commercial panic began in 1819, and grew into a full-scale depression. Prices plummeted, pauperism increased, and unemployment became a more serious social problem than it ever been before. Once again, the new charitable organizations prevented starvation, and professional peacekeepers preserved order.

Full economic recovery did not occur until the 1820s, a decade after Waterloo and half a century after revolutions had shattered the old regimes of many western nations. Only then did the crisis come to an end. A new equilibrium at last emerged.

❧ The Victorian Equilibrium, circa 1820–1896

This new change-regime might be called the price equilibrium of the Victorian era. It coincided almost exactly with the life of Queen Victoria herself (1819–1901), and was closely linked to the cultural values that she represented. Its character was most clearly evident in Great Britain. Prices in that nation fell sharply from 1813 to the early 1820s, then fluctuated within a fixed range for more than fifty years. They fell again during the depression of 1873, and stabilized once more until nearly the end of the nineteenth century. There was no sustained inflation in Britain from 1820 to 1896.[1]

Similar patterns also appeared in other nations, with variations that reflected their different histories. In Germany, prices came down rapidly during the period from 1815 to 1830. Thereafter, the general price level fluctuated on a flat plane for the rest of the nineteenth century. Here again, the equilibrium was not static. Every major political event in German history left its mark upon price movements. None changed the underlying pattern in a fundamental way, and some reinforced it.

A case in point was the creation of the *Zollverein,* the customs union that began with a treaty between Prussia and Schwarzburg-Sondershausen (1819), and gradually expanded to include most of Germany by 1844. This economic union removed barriers to internal commerce, and created a more free and open national market. Between

1819 and 1844, prices in Germany became more stable than before, and more orderly even than in Britain.

During the late 1840s, a period of bad weather and widespread crop failures briefly disrupted that stability, and caused a surge in prices through Germany and central Europe. These disturbances were partly responsible for the revolutions of 1848, which were set in motion by short crops and surging costs. After 1849, equilibrium rapidly returned.[2]

Another period of price-volatility in Germany was caused by three wars of national unification: the Danish War (1864), the Austro-Prussian War (1866) and the Franco-Prussian War (1870). Prices rose sharply during these events. After 1871 they reverted to the general trend.[3]

In the United States, the Civil War (1861–65) caused a burst of inflation that disrupted the underlying equilibrium, and departed from economic trends in Europe. In the northern states, the combined impact of the Civil War on supply and demand, marketing and manufactures, fiscal policy and the monetary system all combined to drive prices to higher.[4]

An even greater disruption occurred in the southern Confederacy, which experienced extreme hyperinflation during the Civil War. So primitive was the economy of the slave states in 1861 that they lacked artisans with sufficient skills to engrave notes and bills. Lacking other resources, the Confederacy paid for the war by issuing unsecured paper currency: at first in small amounts and large denominations, later in many millions of little bills. Confederate dollars were so crudely lithographed that counterfeit money was detected by its superior quality. For a time, the value of this money was sustained by southern patriotism, and by high hopes of victory to come. As late as the spring of 1863, Confederate currency still held much of its value: the normal rate of exchange was two southern dollars to one Yankee greenback. After the Battle of Gettysburg, however, the exchange rate fell abruptly to four for one. Still, southern patriots continued to accept Confederate money at face value as late as 1865. The Confederacy never declared its notes to be legal tender; their value was a function of the loyalty of the people who accepted them. Nearly a billion dollars were issued during the conflict.[5]

The Civil War and its painful aftermath were followed by rapid price deflation. By 1880 the effect of the war on American price levels had entirely disappeared. Thereafter, price trends in the United States

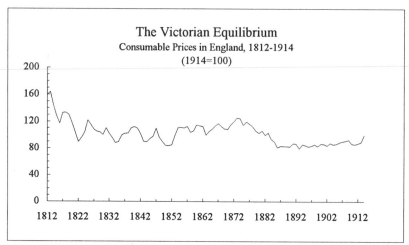

The Victorian Equilibrium
Consumable Prices in England, 1812-1914
(1914=100)

Figure 3.18 traces the movement of consumable prices in England from 1812 to 1914. A period of falling prices (1812-22) came after the crisis of the previous price-revolution. This deflation was followed by fluctuations on a fixed plane (1822-73), then by a second sharp deflation (1873-82), and yet another period of stability. The source is E. H. Phelps-Brown and Sheila Hopkins, "Seven Centuries of the Price of Consumables," *Economica* 23 (1956) 740-41.

rejoined the general equilibrium in the Western world. By the early 1890s, wholesale price indices in Britain, Germany and the United States moved almost as one.

The equilibrium of the Victorian era was highly complex in its dynamics. Its underlying stability increased the visibility of many cyclical rhythms. There were harvest cycles in farm prices, inventory cycles in manufactures, and commercial cycles of many different lengths. There were diurnal cycles, weekly cycles, seasonal cycles, annual cycles, generational cycles and perhaps a fifty-year cycle. Many of these vibrations were highly regular in their complex cadence. As the equilibrium continued, the amplitudes of short-cycle movements (harvest fluctuations in particular) tended to diminish through time. This dampening process was typical of price equilibria in general, and very different from the expanding amplitudes that developed in price-revolutions.[6]

Prices of specific commodities varied through space as well as time, but here again the variance tended to be highly stable and regular in its patterns. The price of grain was comparatively high in the urban-industrial heartland of western Europe and also in the more densely settled parts of the eastern United States. It was lower in central Europe

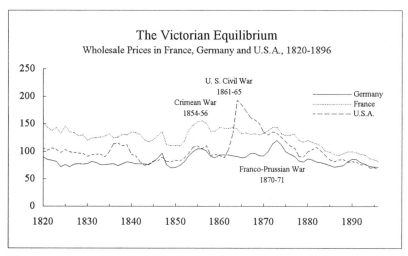

Figure 3.19 surveys wholesale prices in Germany (1913=100), France (1901-10=100), and the U.S.A. (1910-14=100). The pattern was similar in all three nations: stable or declining prices from 1820 to 1896, punctuated by short surges of inflation (mostly war-related) that disrupted the prevailing equilibrium only for a few years. The sources are A. Jacobs and H. Richter, *Die Grosshandelpreise in Deutschland von 1792 bis 1934* (Berlin, 1935); A. Chabert, *Essai sur les mouvements des prix et des revenus en France de 1798 à 1820* (Paris, 1945); *Historical Statistics of the United States* (1976) series E40, 52.

and American midlands, and lowest in eastern Russia and the American West. This classic ring-pattern persisted through the nineteenth century, but differences between core and peripheral prices tended to diminish as world grain markets became more integrated.[7]

Other complex patterns appeared in the relative movement of prices, wages, rent and interest. While prices fluctuated on the same plane or even declined, real wages rose buoyantly—as in other periods of equilibrium. By one measure (an index constructed by Henry Phelps-Brown and Sheila Hopkins), the real wages of English building craftsmen increased more than 400 percent from 1801 to 1899. That comparison overstated the magnitude of change: 1801 was an exceptionally hard year; 1899 was a time of high prosperity. Other benchmarks showed smaller magnitudes of increase—a doubling of real wages rather than quadrupling. But always the same upward trend appeared. Both money wages and real wages increased in Britain, France, Germany, Sweden and every other European nation where data has come to hand. In this respect the equilibrium of the Victorian era

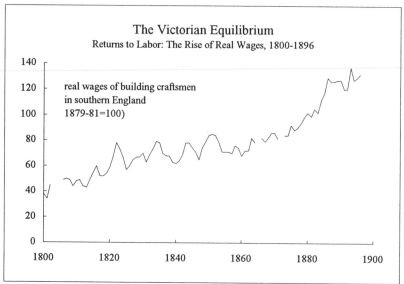

The Victorian Equilibrium
Returns to Labor: The Rise of Real Wages, 1800-1896

real wages of building craftsmen
in southern England
1879-81=100)

Figure 3.20 reports evidence of a sustained rise in real wages, which for British builders trebled during the nineteenth century. The source is E. H. Phelps-Brown and Sheila Hopkins, "Seven Centuries of the Prices of Consumables, Compared with Builders' Wage-Rates," Economica 23 (1956) 296-315.

was similar to those of the twelfth century, the Renaissance and the Enlightenment.[8]

Wages also rose in the United States, but the American pattern was less stable than that in Britain. Real earnings of workers fell sharply during the Civil War, reaching their nineteenth century nadir in 1866, largely as a consequence of the price inflation in that period. Panics and depressions in 1873 and 1893 also drove wages down, but these dark intervals were the exceptions. Long-term improvement was the rule for both highly skilled artisans and farm laborers.[9]

These generalizations, it must be emphasized, refer to the income of workers only during periods of employment. "The great difficulty," writes Stephan Thernstrom, "lies not in estimating the daily wage, but in judging how many days each year the laborer was likely to find work." He estimated that unskilled laborers in Massachusetts were unemployed two or three months in every year during the mid-nineteenth century. Whether this proportion increased or diminished during the course of the nineteenth century we are unable to discover. Thernstrom believes that it changed little from mid-century to the

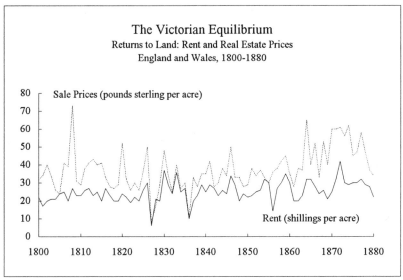

The Victorian Equilibrium
Returns to Land: Rent and Real Estate Prices
England and Wales, 1800-1880

Figure 3.21 finds a long, slow decline in sale prices of English and Welsh real estate from 1812 to 1864, followed by a brief rise from 1864 to 1877. The secular trend in rent was stable through the nineteenth century. The source is E. M. Carus-Wilson, "A Century of Land Values: England and Wales," *Essays in Economic History*, III, 128-31.

1870s, but even a small alteration would have made a major difference in real income, as distinct from real wages.[10]

Further, a rise in the cost of labor was not always a return to laborers themselves. An example was the slave economy of the American South before the Civil War, with its combination of a free market and unfree labor. The price of slaves in the southern states moved in parallel with real wages in Europe and the northern States, as it had done in earlier periods. During the late eighteenth century slave prices had fallen sharply in America, at the same time that real wages for free workers had been declining rapidly in western Europe. That trend reversed during the 1790s. Slave prices began to rise from $300 (or less) in 1795 to $1200 in Virginia and $1800 in New Orleans on the eve of the Civil War.

The increase in slave prices was greater in its magnitude than the rise of real wages for free labor. Nevertheless, the direction of change was similar in both labor systems. The long secular rise of slave prices from 1815 to 1860 was not unique to the "peculiar institution" of the American South, nor was it driven primarily by the economics of slavery itself, as historians have mistakenly believed. The trend in slave prices was part of a much larger movement throughout the Western world.[11]

The Victorian equilibrium was not a golden era of prosperity for everyone. All felt the bite of hard times some of the time; some suffered all of the time. Grain farmers were in deep trouble throughout the world after the panic of 1873, with political consequences that included the Populist movement in the United States, the "revolt of the field" in Britain, and rural unrest in Europe. But in general real wages rose for most workers.

At the same time that real wages were rising, returns to capital (as measured by rates of interest) fell steadily during the nineteenth century, as they had done in other periods of price equilibrium. This trend clearly appeared in the city of London, the epicenter of international capitalism in the nineteenth century, where bonds were called "stocks," and stocks were "shares," and public securities were "funds." Their annual performance was carefully monitored in a publication called *Fenn on the Funds,* a Victorian equivalent of *Moody's Manual* which showed a striking pattern of stable change for nearly a century.

The most important funds were the "consols" that the United Kingdom had long issued for its national borrowing. In 1812, when Britain was simultaneously fighting separate wars against France and the United States, the average yield of Consols rose to 5.08 percent. Thereafter, the rate of return declined for 85 years, reaching bottom at 2.25 percent in 1897. This downward trend was not perfectly constant. The Crimean War drove up interest rates and commercial depressions brought them down again, but through these many fluctuations the pattern of secular change was stable for a century.[12]

The same tendency also appeared in the public securities of other western nations. Yields on French *rentes,* Dutch perpetuals, Prussian bonds and New England municipals all showed similar patterns of secular decline. There were a few exceptions. The government of France had to pay more for its money after its revolutions in 1830, 1848 and 1871. But these fiscal disturbances were remarkably shallow and short-lived. Even the French government, despite a persistent reputation for political disorder, was able to meet its public obligations with 3 percent securities during the late nineteenth century.[13]

Interest rates in private transactions were higher, and also more variable, than those for public funds. The Bank of England charged its

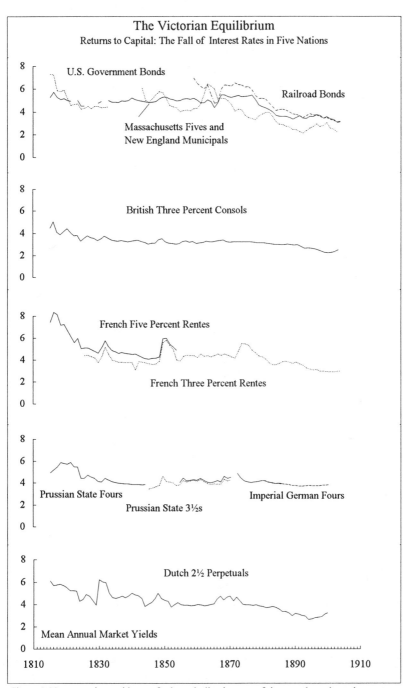

The Victorian Equilibrium
Returns to Capital: The Fall of Interest Rates in Five Nations

U.S. Government Bonds

Railroad Bonds

Massachusetts Fives and
New England Municipals

British Three Percent Consols

French Five Percent Rentes

French Three Percent Rentes

Prussian State Fours

Imperial German Fours

Prussian State 3½s

Dutch 2½ Perpetuals

Mean Annual Market Yields

1810   1830   1850   1870   1890   1910

Figure 3.22 summarizes evidence of a long decline in rates of interest throughout the western world from 1820 to 1896. The source is Homer, *History of Interest Rates,* 196-209.

individual customers different rates, after ranking them on a scale that was more moral than material, from "dealers in greatest respectability and opulence" to "persons in low estimation." Each borrower was offered a discount to match the measure of his depravity. Private debtors of high eminence but dubious reputation were compelled to pay interest that would shock even a twentieth-century sensibility. In 1840, Britain's future prime minister Benjamin Disraeli was charged annual interest of 40 percent for a loan to cover a "pressing liability." In general, however, interest rates tended to decline in private lending as well as public finance during the Victorian equilibrium. The trend was consistently downward throughout the long equilibrium of Victorian era.[14]

Returns to land—both rent and real estate prices—also fell, then stabilized and fell again in the early nineteenth century. A history of land in Saxony-Anhalt showed a very close correlation between real estate values and the price of rye from 1820 to 1895. Land prices and rents also moved together in Prussia, England and the United States.[15]

These trends were full of trouble for rural estate-owners, and in time their tribulations would be visited upon the world. The landowning classes faced falling rents, rising wages and depressed agricultural prices all at the same time. England's county families, Prussian Junkers and southern planters in the United States all shared that same predicament. These landholders traced their descent (in spiritual terms at least) from Europe's old feudal elites, and raised their sons to a warrior ethic. As the *pax victoriana* wore on, more than a few of these energetic young men were bankrupt, bored, and bloody-minded—a dangerous combination. Some sought adventure overseas in "splendid little wars" and distant conquests; the British Empire has been called a system of outdoor relief for the upper classes. Others pursued politics and diplomacy as an equivalent of war, which was still more menacing to world peace—all the more so when the horrors of the last great European slaughter were forgotten, or half-remembered in a haze of glory. In the sunny afternoon of the Victorian era, the dark clouds began to gather on the distant horizon.

Altogether, the relative returns to land, labor, and capital were much the same in the Victorian equilibrium as they had been during the Renaissance and Enlightenment. They were also similar in their social results. In the middle and later stages of every price equilibrium (but not in the early stages), the distribution of wealth tended to stabilize, or even to become a little more equal. There was a lag-effect here. In the

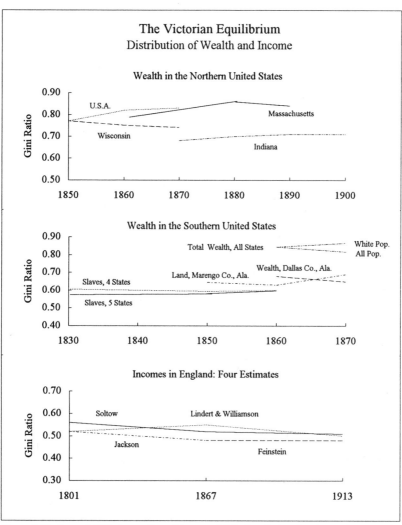

The Victorian Equilibrium
Distribution of Wealth and Income

Wealth in the Northern United States

Wealth in the Southern United States

Incomes in England: Four Estimates

Figure 3.23 shows stability in wealth and income distribution during the nineteenth century in Britain and the United States. This was the net effect of stable rents, falling returns to capital and rising real wages. Sources include Lee Soltow, "Long-Run Changes in British Income Inequality," *Economic History Review,* 21 (1968) 17-29; Peter Lindert and Jeffrey Williamson, "Revising England's Social Tables," *EEH,* 19 (1982) 385-408; Charles Feinstein, "The Rise and Fall of the Williamson Curve," *Journal of Economic History,* 48 (1988) 699-729; R. V. Jackson, "Inequality of Incomes and Lifespans in England since 1688," *Economic History Review,* 47 (1994) 508-24; Lee Soltow, *Men and Wealth in the United States, 1850-1870* (New Haven, 1975); *idem, Patterns of Wealthholding in Wisconsin since 1850* (Madison, 1971); Roger Ransom and Richard Sutch, *One Kind of Freedom* (Cambridge, 1977); Jonathan M. Wiener, *Social Origins of the New South: Alabama, 1860-1885* (Baton Rouge, 1978).

early nineteenth century, inequality continued to increase, as it had done during the later stages of the price-revolution of the eighteenth century. But after 1850 wealth and income tended to become more equal in their distribution or to remain on the same plane of inequality. This tendency appeared in the later stages of all other equilibria, and the lag pattern was always the same.

In other respects, however, the Victorian era was unique. It was more dynamic in its structure than any comparable period. During the equilibria of the Renaissance and the Enlightenment, population had increased very little. A balance was achieved between low rates of economic development and a lower pace of demographic growth. This was not the case in the Victorian era. In Europe, America, and throughout the world, population grew at an exponential rate through the nineteenth century. Rapid population rises had often occurred before— always with the same inflationary effect upon price levels. As Labrousse wrote, an *inflation des hommes* had been accompanied by *inflation d'argent* and *inflation des prix* as well.

In the nineteenth century something else happened. Population went on increasing, and prices fluctuated on the same plateau. English historians Anthony Wrigley and Roger Schofield write, ''If there was a notable uniformity in the behavior of the two series relative to each other until the beginning of the nineteenth century, however, there was a remarkably clean break with the past thereafter. . . . The historic link between population growth and price rise was broken; an economic revolution had taken place.''[16]

Wrigley and Schofield were right in one way, but wrong in another. It is true that a simple, surface correlation between prices and population disappeared, just as they said. But the link was not broken altogether. A deeper association persisted in the second derivative of change. The rhythm of change in rates of population increase during the nineteenth century continued to correlate very closely with price movements. The Victorian equilibrium was indeed something new in the world—a dynamic balance between rates of change in rates of change.

The Victorian equilibrium also derived its stability from magnitudes of change in economic growth. Real output (per capita) of the American economy, for example, had grown only about 0.6 percent each year before 1790. After 1825, it grew at a rate of approximately 1.6 percent a year—enough to double national product per capita every forty-three years. This rate was maintained throughout the nineteenth

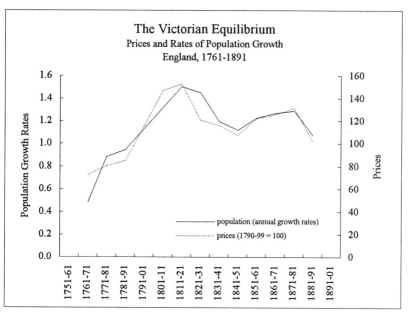

The Victorian Equilibrium
Prices and Rates of Population Growth
England, 1761-1891

— population (annual growth rates)
········· prices (1790-99 = 100)

Figure 3.24 compares price movements with rates of population growth in Britain. Both series are decennial means of annual data. Sources include E. A. Wrigley and Roger S. Schofield et al., *The Population History of England, 1541-1871: A Reconstruction* (Cambridge, 1981), table A3, column 3 (estimated values of compound annual growth rates); and Henry Phelps-Brown and Sheila V. Hopkins, *A Perspective of Wages and Prices* (New York, 1981).

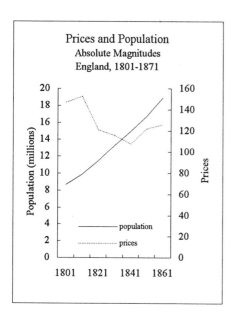

Prices and Population
Absolute Magnitudes
England, 1801-1871

—— population
········· prices

Figure 3.25 makes a different comparison between price levels and absolute magnitudes of population size. Wrigley and Schofield found that between 1811 and 1871 English population doubled while prices fell. They concluded that "the historic link between population growth and price rise was broken; an economic revolution had taken place" (pp. 403-4). This statement is correct in its own terms, but if one compares rates of growth rather than magnitudes of change, a strong link between the dynamics of demographic and economic change continued through the 19th century. An economic revolution had indeed taken place, but the association between population growth and price movements remained very important.

century. Similar trends (with differences of timing) occurred in European nations.[17]

Equilibrium at higher levels of economic growth was achieved in many ways. A revolution in transportation created broader markets, which allowed larger units of production. An agricultural revolution released many workers from the soil and allowed them to shift to other sectors where their labor was more productive. An industrial revolution increased the productivity of labor and capital. A commercial revolution radically improved the efficiency of exchange.

Other factors included the emigration of Europeans in large numbers to other parts of the world where the marginal return on their labor and capital was higher than at home. Also important was the economic development of new regions which produced commodities in unprecedented quantity: Mississippi cotton, Argentine beef, Australian wheat, New Zealand mutton, African ore and Canadian timber. Perhaps the most important factor was the integration of a world market through the nineteenth century, which created vast economies of scale.

The Victorian equilibrium was a great whirring machine with many moving parts. It did not always run smoothly. The economy of the western world moved through alternating periods of prosperity and depression, but even these disturbances were remarkable for their regularity. In the United States, major panics and depressions tended to recur at twenty-year intervals: 1819, 1837, 1857, 1873, 1893. The rhythm of these economic fluctuations remained remarkably stable for nearly a century.

Far from disturbing the Victorian equilibrium in any fundamental way, this pattern was part of the process by which the balance was maintained. In an era of equilibrium, the market operated as a self-correcting mechanism—a process that prompted contemporary observers such as John Stuart Mill (1806–73) and Alfred Marshall (1842–1924) to develop the timeless axioms of classical economics.

But the conditions that inspired them were not eternal. They did not operate in the same way before 1815 or after 1896, or in any other period of modern history. The dynamic stability of the Victorian equilibrium was unique. It was maintained by an unprecedented set of balances between rapid population growth and even more rapid economic growth, between industrial transformation and agricultural revolution, between massive international migration and still more massive domestic movements, between overseas development and commercial integration of a world economy.[18]

A few economists have attempted to explain the Victorian equilibrium primarily in monetarist terms. Monetary factors did indeed have an impact on prices throughout the period, but they did not create the equilibrium itself. In the United States, for example, annual fluctuations in price levels and the money supply (that is, specie, banknotes and bank deposits) tended to correlate closely, and were much the same in timing. But magnitudes and secular trends were very different. Large changes in the supply of money caused price movements that were comparatively small, by the measure of other periods. Money supply in the United States increased enormously during the 1820s and 1830s, more than trebling in a period of fifteen years, according to estimates by Peter Temin. But price levels remained remarkably stable, rising and falling only about 15 percent in that same period. A similar pattern also appeared during the 1840s and 1850s, when large swings in the supply of money coincided with very small movements in price levels. Clearly a close relationship existed between the quantity of money and the level of prices in the American economy. All things being equal, that relationship was strong and intimate, but *ceteris non paribus* is the iron law of economic history.[19]

In this age of equilibrium, monetary and demographic factors might be understood as strong centrifugal forces, acting to pull prices off their stable base. Those elements were balanced by equally strong centripetal forces of expanding production and exchange, which drew them in again. The dynamic equilibrium of the nineteenth century might be envisioned as a Tenniel engraving of a tug-of-war between two teams of muscular Victorian athletes, each of approximately equal strength. On one side were the wiry Centrifugals, with currency symbols embroidered on their old school caps. On the other side were the brawny Centripetals, straining mightily in the opposite direction. With much tumult and shouting, the rope moved slightly one way and then the other, but the white rag remained in the middle until 1896, when the exhausted Centripetals collapsed in a heap.

The dynamic equilibrium of the Victorian era was not entirely self-generating. It found support from exogenous factors of various kinds—in particular from favorable climatic conditions. After a period of very nasty weather which historians call the "little ice age," the climate of western Europe and North America grew warmer through much of the nineteenth century. English meteorologist H. H. Lamb observes that "the price rise around 1800 could be attributable largely to the interference of the Napoleonic wars with supplies and with trade,

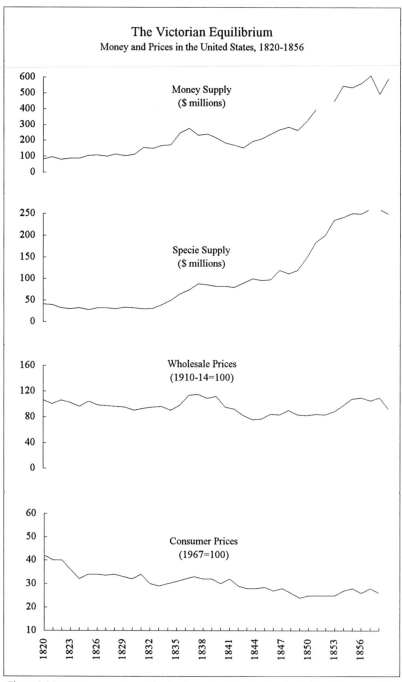

The Victorian Equilibrium
Money and Prices in the United States, 1820-1856

Money Supply
($ millions)

Specie Supply
($ millions)

Wholesale Prices
(1910-14=100)

Consumer Prices
(1967=100)

Figure 3.26 compares monetary estimates from Peter Temin, *The Jacksonian Economy* (New York, 1969), 71, 159; and price indices from *Historical Statistics of the U. S.*, E52, E135.

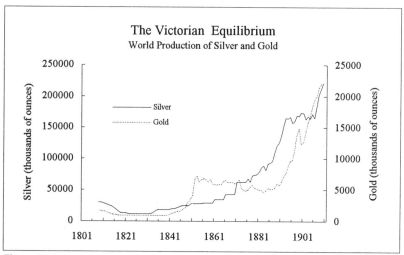

Figure 3.27 surveys world stocks of gold and silver, which rapidly increased during the nineteenth century, while prices remained stable or declined. The source is Pierre Vilar, *A History of Gold and Money, 1450-1520* (London, 1984), 352.

but the time does coincide with the latest of the great periods of advance of the glaciers and the Arctic Sea ice about Iceland.'' There were no major climatic anomalies in the next century of remotely comparable magnitude. The amelioration of climate may have made a difference in price levels, but it was not a major factor. Long changes in climate do not correlate with long waves in the history of prices.[20]

Whatever the cause of the Victorian equilibrium may have been, its consequences were abundantly clear. A period of comparative political stability developed in Europe. The century from 1815 to 1914 was one of the few periods in that continent's long and bloody history when there was no general war. The only exception was the Crimean War, which was kept securely in bounds. The nineteenth century was an era of many smaller wars, some of which were very costly in life and treasure. There were wars of national integration such as the Prussian wars against Denmark, Austria and France, the American Civil War, and the conflicts of the Italian *Risorgimento*. Small imperialist wars were also very numerous. In the reign of Queen Victoria, the British army fought six Ashanti wars, five Basuto wars, three Afghan wars, three Burmese wars, two Maori wars, two Matabele wars, two Boer Wars, two Sikh wars, two Sudanese wars, and altogether 230 colonial wars, punitive expeditions, and insurrections.[21]

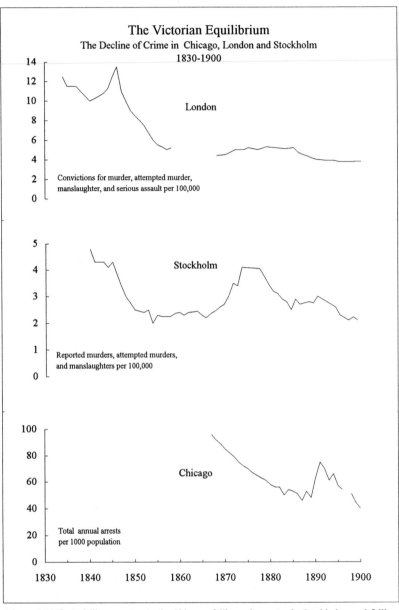

The Victorian Equilibrium
The Decline of Crime in Chicago, London and Stockholm
1830-1900

London

Convictions for murder, attempted murder,
manslaughter, and serious assault per 100,000

Stockholm

Reported murders, attempted murders,
and manslaughters per 100,000

Chicago

Total annual arrests
per 1000 population

Figure 3.28 finds falling arrest rates in Chicago, falling crime rates in Stockholm, and falling conviction rates in London (five-year moving average of convictions in Middlesex County, 1834 58, and the Metropolitan Police District, 1869-1900). Sources include Ted Robert Gurr, *Rogues, Rebels, and Reformers: A Political History of Urban Crime and Conflict* (Beverly Hills and London, 1976), 38-40, 63; Wesley G. Skogan, *Chicago since 1840: A Time-Series Data Handbook* (Urbana, 1975); Theodore N. Ferdinand, "The Criminal Patterns of Boston since 1849," *American Journal of Sociology* 73 (1967) 688-98, and Gurr, 39-46.

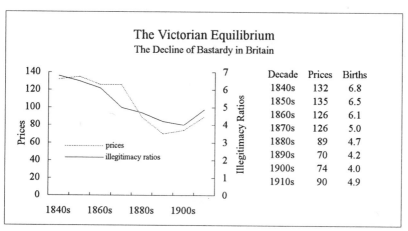

The Victorian Equilibrium
The Decline of Bastardy in Britain

Decade	Prices	Births
1840s	132	6.8
1850s	135	6.5
1860s	126	6.1
1870s	126	5.0
1880s	89	4.7
1890s	70	4.2
1900s	74	4.0
1910s	90	4.9

Figure 3.29 shows that rates of illegitimacy declined in close association with the price of wheat during the nineteenth century. This long trend followed an earlier rise in bastardy during the price revolution of the eighteenth century, and preceded another sustained increase in the price revolution of the twentieth century. Plotted here are decennial ratios of illegitimate births per 100 live births in England and Wales (civil registration), compared with the Abel index of English wheat prices (decennial averages in grams of pure silver per 100 kilograms of grain). Sources include Peter Laslett, Karla Oosterveen and Richard M. Smith, eds., *Bastardy and Its Comparative History* (Cambridge, 1980), 17; and Wilhelm Abel, *Agrarkrisen und Agrarkonjunktur*, appendix.

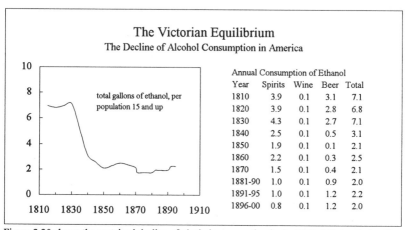

The Victorian Equilibrium
The Decline of Alcohol Consumption in America

Annual Consumption of Ethanol

Year	Spirits	Wine	Beer	Total
1810	3.9	0.1	3.1	7.1
1820	3.9	0.1	2.8	6.8
1830	4.3	0.1	2.7	7.1
1840	2.5	0.1	0.5	3.1
1850	1.9	0.1	0.1	2.1
1860	2.2	0.1	0.3	2.5
1870	1.5	0.1	0.4	2.1
1881-90	1.0	0.1	0.9	2.0
1891-95	1.0	0.1	1.2	2.2
1896-00	0.8	0.1	1.2	2.0

Figure 3.30 shows the sustained decline of alcohol consumption in the United States during the nineteenth century. Estimates include spirits, wine, and beer, converted to ethanol equivalents. Beer includes hard cider, the leading alcoholic beverage in early America. The source is Merton M. Hyman, et al., *Drink, Drinking, and Alcohol Related Mortality...* (New Brunswick, 1980) Many other studies have replicated these findings.

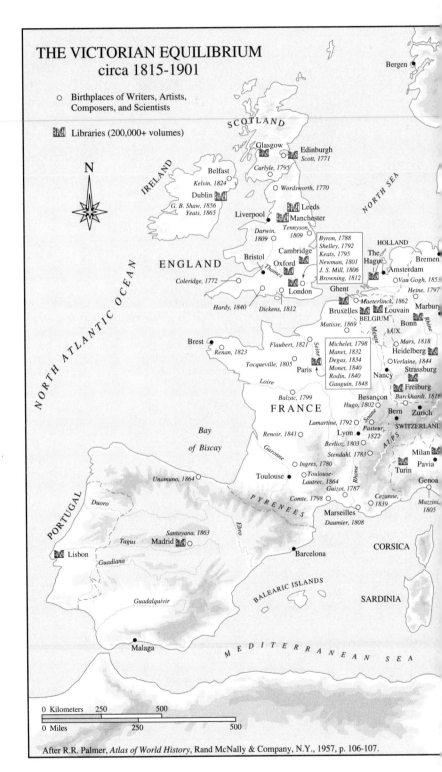

THE VICTORIAN EQUILIBRIUM
circa 1815-1901

Bergen ●

○ Birthplaces of Writers, Artists,
   Composers, and Scientists

📚 Libraries (200,000+ volumes)

SCOTLAND

N

IRELAND

Glasgow 📚
Edinburgh 📚
Scott, 1771

Belfast
Kelvin, 1824 ○
Carlyle, 1795

Dublin 📚
G. B. Shaw, 1856
Yeats, 1865

NORTH SEA

○ Wordsworth, 1770

Liverpool ○
Leeds 📚
Manchester 📚

Darwin, 1809 ○
Tennyson, 1809 ○

Byron, 1788
Shelley, 1792
Keats, 1795
Newman, 1801
J. S. Mill, 1806
Browning, 1812

HOLLAND
The Hague
Amsterdam 📚
○Van Gogh, 1853

Bremen ●

Bristol ●
Cambridge
Oxford 📚

ENGLAND

Coleridge, 1772 ○

Thames
London 📚

Ghent

Maeterlinck, 1862 ○
Heine, 1797 ○

Marburg 📚

NORTH ATLANTIC OCEAN

Hardy, 1840 ○
Dickens, 1812 ○

Bruxelles 📚 📚 Louvain
BELGIUM
Matisse, 1869 ○
Bonn 📚
LUX.

Brest ●
Renan, 1823 ●

Flaubert, 1821 ○
Tocqueville, 1805 ○
Balzac, 1799 ○

Seine
Paris

Michelet, 1798
Manet, 1832
Degas, 1834
Monet, 1840
Rodin, 1840
Gauguin, 1848

Marx, 1818 ○
Heidelberg 📚
○Verlaine, 1844
Strassburg
Nancy 📚
Freiburg 📚
Besançon Burckhardt, 1818

Loire

FRANCE
Hugo, 1802 ○
Lamartine, 1792 ○
Bern
Zurich

Bay
of Biscay

Renoir, 1841 ○
Lyon ●
Berlioz, 1803 ○
Stendahl, 1783 ○

Garonne

Pasteur, 1822 ○
SWITZERLAND
ALPS
Milan 📚
📚 Pavia
Turin

○ Ingres, 1780
Toulouse ●
○ Toulouse-
Lautrec, 1864
Guizot, 1787 ○

Rhone

Genoa ●

PORTUGAL
Duoro

Unamuno, 1864 ○

Comte, 1798 ○
Marseilles ●
Daumier, 1808

Cezanne, ○
1839
Mazzini,
1805

PYRENEES

Santayana, 1863 ○
Tagus   Madrid 📚 ○
Lisbon 📚
Guadiana
Ebro

CORSICA

Barcelona ●

Guadalquivir

BALEARIC ISLANDS

SARDINIA

Malaga ●

MEDITERRANEAN SEA

0 Kilometers   250   500

0 Miles   250   500

After R.R. Palmer, *Atlas of World History*, Rand McNally & Company, N.Y., 1957, p. 106-107.

174

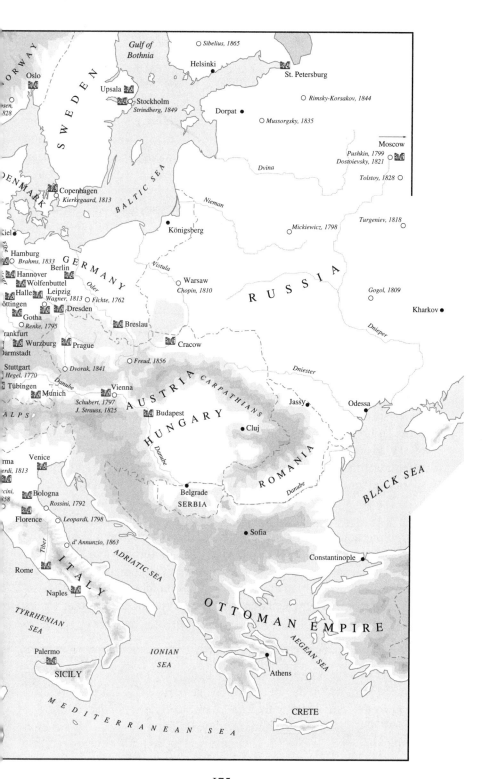

Gulf of Bothnia

○ *Sibelius, 1865*

Helsinki

St. Petersburg

Oslo

Upsala

Stockholm
Strindberg, 1849

Dorpat

○ *Rimsky-Korsakov, 1844*

Moscow

Mussorgsky, 1835

Pushkin, 1799
Dostoievsky, 1821

Dvina

Tolstoy, 1828 ○

SWEDEN

NORWAY

BALTIC SEA

DENMARK

Copenhagen
Kierkegaard, 1813

Kiel

Nieman

Königsberg

Mickiewicz, 1798

Turgeniev, 1818 ○

Hamburg
Brahms, 1833
Berlin
Hannover
Wolfenbuttel
Halle
Wagner, 1813 ○ *Fichte, 1762*
Leipzig
Dresden
Göttingen
Gotha
Renke, 1795
Frankfurt
Wurzburg Prague
Darmstadt

GERMANY

Elbe

Vistula

Oder

Warsaw
Chopin, 1810

R U S S I A

Gogol, 1809
○

Kharkov

Breslau

Cracow

Dnieper

Freud, 1856

Stuttgart
Hegel, 1770
Tübingen
Munich

Dvorak, 1841

Danube

Vienna

A U S T R I A

CARPATHIANS

Dniester

Jassy

Odessa

ALPS

Schubert, 1797
J. Strauss, 1825 Budapest

H U N G A R Y

Cluj

Danube

Venice
erdi, 1813

cini,
58
Bologna
Rossini, 1792
Florence ○ *Leopardi, 1798*

R O M A N I A

Belgrade
SERBIA

Danube

BLACK SEA

Parma

Tiber

d'Annunzio, 1863

ADRIATIC SEA

Rome

I T A L Y

Sofia

Naples

TYRRHENIAN
SEA

Constantinople

O T T O M A N   E M P I R E

Palermo

IONIAN
SEA

AEGEAN SEA

SICILY

Athens

M E D I T E R R A N E A N   S E A

CRETE

The economic effect of these conflicts was to integrate an ever larger proportion of the world's population into national and even global markets, and monetary systems. Many scholars have written about the effect of European contact on primitive monetary systems that Europeans called "pseudo-money." French historian Fernand Braudel observes, "The fate of this pseudo-money after the European impact (whether cowries in Bengal, wampum after 1670 or the Congo zimbos) proves identical in every case where it can be investigated—monstrous and catastrophic inflation, caused by an increase in reserves, an accelerated and even hectic circulation, and a concomitant devaluation in relation to the dominant European money."[22]

But economic chaos was merely the first effect. The second result was economic order. Local markets were incorporated in a larger system, where price movements became progressively more stable. The price equilibrium of the Victorian era promoted political stabilization and integration, which further increased price equilibrium, which in turn brought more stability and integration.

The effect of price equilibrium upon society was also to promote another sort of social integration. This was a period when crime declined throughout the western world, after a period of sharp increase in the crisis of the eighteenth century. In London, Bombay, and even in Chicago life became more orderly during the Victorian era. Indicators of social deviance and family disruption also declined: alcohol consumption fell sharply; so also did rates of prenuptial pregnancy and sexual deviance. All had risen during the eighteenth century.

The most important cultural correlate of the Victorian equilibrium was what Walter Houghton calls the Victorian frame of mind. Houghton (not the best guide on this question, for he went to excessive lengths to stress similarities between the Victorians and ourselves) defined the Victorian mind-frame in terms of optimism, anxiety, the will to believe, dogmatism, rigidity, the commercial spirit, earnestness, enthusiasm, hero worship, love and hypocrisy. Different words appear in other lists—liberalism, improvement, confidence, strength, faith and certainty.

Historian G. M. Young approached the subject in a different way. He organized the Victorian era into a chronology of thinkers, arranged by the year in which they reached the age of 35. This list of "floruits" began in the year 1830 with Arnold and Carlyle. It ended in 1901–2 with Wells, Galsworthy, and Stanley Baldwin. It is a list of high complexity, and cannot be encompassed by unitary generalizations.

But in the phrase of one eminent Victorian, F. W. Maitland, there is in every era a "common thought of common things." On this level, which the Victorians themselves called their *zeitgeist*, we may find elements of cultural unity.[23]

In the Victorian era, as in the Enlightenment and the Renaissance, creative thinkers in many fields drew their conceptual models from their historical condition. Similar textures of thought appeared in the biology of Darwin (1809–82), the geology of Charles Lyell (1797–1875), the historiography of Leopold von Ranke (1795–1886), the economics of Karl Marx (1818–83), the politics of William Ewart Gladstone (1809–98) and the statecraft of Abraham Lincoln (1809–65).

However different their ideologies may have been, these Victorians all thought of the world in dynamic terms as a process rather than a static state. All of them understood that world-process as a sequence of conflicts which were progressive, coherent, self-regulating and self-sustaining. The Darwinian principle of natural selection, the Rankean idea of historicism, the Marxian model of dialectical materialism, the Lyellian concept of geologic stratiology, the Lincolnian creed of liberal conservatism and the Gladstonian ideology of conservative liberalism shared those qualities in common.

These large ideas resembled the Victorian equilibrium itself, which was a dynamic, progressive, self-balancing and self-sustaining structure of countervailing forces. Most of these thinkers (with a few exceptions such as Lincoln) also shared a spirit that H. G. Wells called "optimistic fatalism." This, too, was an expression of the Victorian equilbrium, and an instrument by which it was maintained.

THE FOURTH WAVE
&. The Price Revolution of the Twentieth Century

Wages chase prices, prices chase wages, and both
chase their past history.
—Clyde Farnsworth, 1977

L ONDON, June 22, 1897, Diamond Jubilee Day. The rain-washed streets of this proud imperial city sparkled in the summer sun, as the people of Britain prepared to celebrate the sixtieth anniversary of Queen Victoria's accession to the throne. At precisely eleven o'clock in the morning, the Queen repaired to her Royal Message Room in Buckingham Palace and sent a telegram of congratulations to her subjects throughout the world—370 million of them. Then she put on an ostrich-feathered bonnet, unfurled a small parasol of white silk, and traveled in an open carriage to St. Paul's Cathedral. Her escort included 50,000 troops in brilliant uniform from every part of the Empire. Above the rooftops of the city, thousands of Union Jacks flew in the summer breeze. In the narrow streets happy crowds doffed caps, waved white handkerchiefs, and cheered their aged Queen.

In many ways, the London that Queen Victoria looked upon that morning still seems remarkably the same today. Buckingham Palace and the great Cathedral of St. Paul are outwardly the same, despite the depredations of the Luftwaffe and the London smog. The red coats of the Queen's Brigade of Guards, and the scarlet tunics of their officers, are still the same—and so are the class-distinctions that those subtle shadings represent. The Household Cavalry in their gleaming cuirasses

179

and high flowing plumes still look and sound the same as they clatter down the Mall on jet-black horses. The Royal Horse Artillery still dress in the same dark blue shell jackets and red busby bags on state occasions, as when they saluted their Queen-Empress on her anniversary a century ago.

But these superficial resemblances are apt to be deceiving. The city of London today is far removed in time and mood and social circumstance from the metropolis that celebrated Queen Victoria's Diamond Jubilee on June 22, 1897. The most profound differences are not to be found in the many material transformations: not in the swarms of small cars that choke the narrow streets of the City, or the hideous modern buildings that sprout like concrete weeds in Mayfair, or the shoals of tourists in shorts and tee-shirts at Piccadilly, or the muffled Arab women in Rolls Royces, parked three deep outside the shops of Knightsbridge.

London is more profoundly different in less tangible ways—most of all, in its memories of the past and its expectations for the future. In 1897, nearly all of its inhabitants had lived their entire lives in an era of stability and comparative peace. No general war had marred the peace of Europe since 1815, except the brief unpleasantness in the Crimea. Every ten or twenty years the British economy had drifted into a commercial depression, but prosperity had rapidly returned. Real wages had risen for nearly a century, and prices had remained remarkably stable for many years. The purchasing power of the pound sterling was actually greater on Diamond Jubilee Day than it had been in 1819, when the old Queen was born. In 1897, a gilt-edged government security paid a steady 2 percent, which was thought to be an entirely reasonable return on capital. Inflation was regarded as a distant horror that was visited upon less deserving nations as divine punishment for their economic sins.

On Diamond Jubilee Day in 1897, eminent Victorians contemplated the future with the same confidence that marked their memories of the past. Peace, progress, and stability were thought to be natural and normal in the world. They were firmly expected to continue.

But it was not to be. The Victorian certainties that London celebrated on Diamond Jubilee Day had already begun to be left behind by events. When we look back on the economic indicators for the year 1897, they reveal to us in retrospect a pattern that was still mercifully invisible to those whose lives it would transform. Beneath the surface of events, the equilibrium of the Victorian era had come quietly to an end. On the day that the Queen and her subjects commemorated sixty years of stability and peace, a deep change was silently occurring in the structure of change itself. That sunny June morning in 1897, the Western world was entering a new era, which would be filled with horrors that the Victorians could scarcely have imagined, much less foretold. This new epoch has continued to our own time. One of its many material manifestations was a long movement that might be called the price-revolution of the twentieth century.

❧ Slow Beginnings, 1896–1914

In the year 1896, wholesale commodity prices in Britain and the United States reached their lowest level in more than a century. Then, during the year of the Diamond Jubilee, they began to rise a little—not very much, not enough for anyone to notice. The increase was only about 1 percent that year, smaller than the range of annual fluctuations. But we may observe a large significance in that small advance. It marked the beginning of a price-revolution that would continue for more than a century.[1]

Students of American history will observe an irony in the timing of this event. It began immediately after the presidential election of 1896. The major issues in that campaign were low prices and scarce money. The cost of living in the United States had shown no long-term secular increase since 1814. Commodity prices had actually fallen after 1870. It is not easy for us, the children of a long inflation, to understand that our ancestors in the 1890s felt as deeply threatened by falling prices as we have been by rising ones.

The American presidential election of 1896 centered on that economic problem. Democratic candidate William Jennings Bryan terrified the possessing classes by proposing a bimetallic monetary standard, and ''free and unlimited'' coinage of silver, mainly to encourage higher farm prices and wages. Republican nominee William McKinley defended the gold standard, maintained a moderate position on silver, and pledged to protect the sanctity of property. McKinley won the election, and the possessing classes breathed a collective sigh of deliverance.[2]

Ironically, they did so at the moment when prices began to creep upward. The same inflection-point simultaneously appeared in the price records of many Western nations: Austria-Hungary (1896–97),

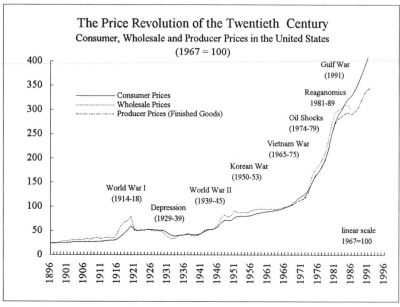

Figure 4.01 surveys annual price movements in the United States. Sources include *Historical Statistics of the United States* (1976), series E23, E135; *Statistical Abstract of the United States* (1988), table 735; *Statistical Abstract of the United States* (1993), tables 756, 764.

Belgium (1895–96), Britain (1896–97), Germany (1896–97), Italy (1897–98), Norway (1897–98), Spain (1896–97), Sweden (1895–96) and the United States (1896–97). Each of these countries had its own monetary system. All of them began to experience the price-revolution at the same time.[3]

Once begun, the new inflation continued at a moderate pace from 1896 to 1914, averaging between 1 and 2 percent each year. The rate of gain was variable: comparatively small in Britain and the United States; larger in Spain and Germany. But almost everywhere, the same upward tendency appeared.

Rising prices were at first welcomed as a timely correction of a recent deflation that had caused many social problems. During the depression year of 1894, the wholesale price of wheat in the United States had fallen to fifty-six cents a bushel, the lowest since the eighteenth century. Rising prices promised relief for farmers, merchants, and manufacturers alike. The authoritative *Financial Review* commented, ''A retrospect of 1897 is much more pleasing than was a similar retrospect of 1896. The year was marked by a decisive recovery

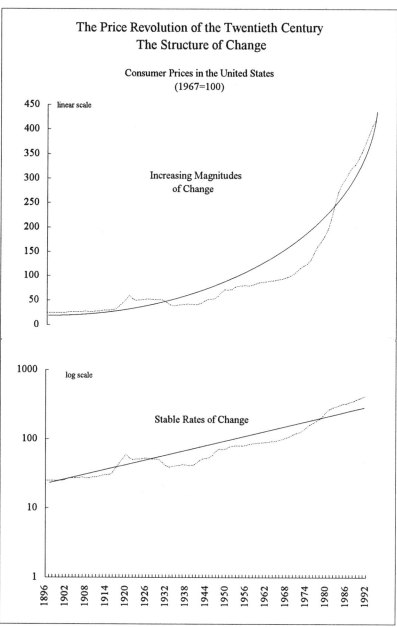

The Price Revolution of the Twentieth Century
The Structure of Change

Consumer Prices in the United States
(1967=100)

Figure 4.02 finds that the structure of change in the twentieth century was similar to other price revolutions, but not entirely the same. As before, magnitudes increased exponentially and the underlying rate of change remained stable. But this great wave showed less annual variability, and little expansion of amplitudes. Sources include *Historical Statistics of the United States* (1976), series E135; *Statistical Abstract of the United States* (1988-94). Trend lines are fitted with an Excel 5.0 program.

of business . . . and at the year's close we find the outlook more hopeful than for many years past.''[4]

The decade that followed, from 1897 to 1907, was marked by the same sense of sustained prosperity. A few short downturns did not disrupt the prevailing optimism. In the United States, a "rich man's panic" in 1903 caused stock prices to drop sharply after the U.S. Steel Corporation missed a dividend and a merger plan collapsed in the American shipbuilding industry. But that disturbance was largely limited to Wall Street, and the speed of the recovery encouraged the general mood of confidence.

A larger panic in 1907 caused a short but very sharp contraction. In the United States, unemployment surged from 2 to 8 percent in 1908. Producer prices fell a little in America, Britain, France, and Germany that year. But within a few months prosperity returned. By 1909, everything was moving up again. Wages were up. Profits were up. Employment was up. Farm income reached record levels.

At first, the great wave of the twentieth century remained invisible to contemporary observers, much as every other price-revolution had done. But as early as 1904, the continuing rise of prices began to be recognized as a secular trend. A few alert contemporaries searched for an explanation.

Some attributed the increase in price levels to an expansion in the supply of gold and silver. In 1886, the fabulous gold mines of Johannesburg had been discovered, entirely by accident. In 1890, gold was found on Cripple Creek in Colorado; the lucky finder, William Stratton, made a fortune of $125 million within a few years. Canadian gold began to flow from the Klondike in 1896. The Alaskan gold rush began in 1898. But these events were part of a long continuum of gold discoveries that had happened through the nineteenth century without raising prices. The rate of growth in gold production throughout the world was roughly the same before and after 1896. Moreover, the pace of secular increase in silver production actually declined during the 1890s.[5]

After the fact, another monetarist explanation has been suggested by American economists who believe that the rise of prices after 1896 was caused by acceleration in the growth of the money supply within the United States—from 6 percent in the period 1879–97, to 7.5 percent in the years 1897–1914. That idea is mistaken. Another economist, Arthur Lewis, has demonstrated that the estimates on which it rests are an artifact of periodization—that is, on the choice of years that

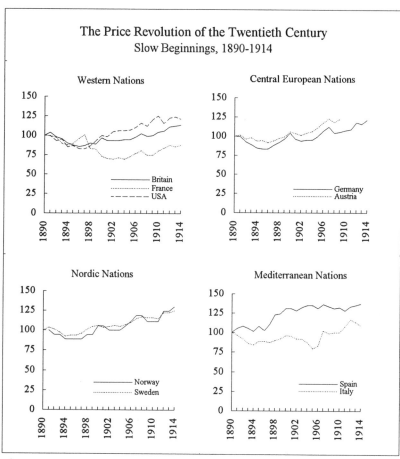

The Price Revolution of the Twentieth Century
Slow Beginnings, 1890-1914

Figure 4.03 surveys wholesale prices in nine nations from 1890 to 1914. Most show similar trends: stasis or decline in the last years of the Victorian equilibrium, a turning point circa 1896, and sustained increase (circa 1896-1914). These common trends marked the beginning of the price revolution of the twentieth century. The data are from B. R. Mitchell, *European Historical Statistics* (2d rev. ed., New York, 1981), 772-75. All are converted to a common base (1890=100).

frame the temporal generalization. Annual fluctuations were large enough to make a major difference in that respect. Lewis finds that the growth of money (and national product) in the United States occurred at virtually the same pace, before and after 1896. Further, an expansion in the American money supply alone could not have set the price-revolution in motion. This was an international event. Prices began to rise simultaneously in most currencies and monetary systems throughout the world.[6]

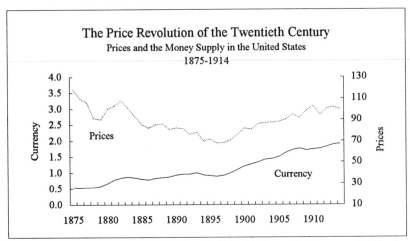

The Price Revolution of the Twentieth Century
Prices and the Money Supply in the United States
1875-1914

Figure 4.04 compares wholesale prices (1910-14=100) with the supply of currency held by the public (in billions of dollars) in the United States. It shows strong similarities in the timing of short-term fluctuations: prices and currency all rose in the boom of the 1880s and declined in the panic and depression of 1893. But differences appeared in the direction of secular trends. Patterns of growth in the money supply were similar before and after the depression of 1893, while price movements were fundamentally transformed from a deflationary to an inflationary trend. The source is *Historical Statistics of the United States* (1976), E40, E52, E410, X417.

Monetary factors would play a major role in the price-revolution of the twentieth century, but the great wave itself grew mainly from a different root. It was primarily (not exclusively) the result of excess demand, generated by accelerating growth of the world's population, by rising standards of living, and by limits on the supply of resources, all within an increasingly integrated global economy.

The accelerating growth of world population was a driving force in the price-revolution of the twentieth century. After 1890, death rates began to decline rapidly, with the conquest of major epidemic diseases such as tuberculosis, typhoid, typhus, diphtheria and malaria. These events derived from the discoveries of German bacteriologist Robert Koch between 1876 and 1890, and from a "public health revolution," that spread swiftly throughout the world.

Fertility declined in western Europe and North America, but rose higher in most other parts of the world. As a result, the growth of global population began to accelerate. Its annual rate of increase in the early twentieth century (1900–1950) was nearly double what it had been in the late nineteenth century (1850–1900).[7]

Economic production and productivity also rose after 1896, but so did living standards and cultural expectations. The major European nations were rapidly becoming industrial democracies. Men of all classes received the right to vote in unprecedented numbers. Women began to be enfranchised, first on the national level in New Zealand (1893), then in other nations. These new electors demanded that governments serve the interest of the many, not merely the few. National legislatures enacted far-reaching systems of social welfare, health care, old age security, mass education, and unemployment insurance. The effect of these innovations was to increase aggregate demand.

Through the twentieth century, there was also a continuing revolution in material expectations among people of every social class—a cultural event that added to the growing pressure of demand on limited resources. The Canadian economist John Kenneth Galbraith wrote, "Even in the United States there is now a persistent feeling . . . that the poor should have access to a doctor. . . . The economic effect of this release of consumption from occupational and class restraint is to

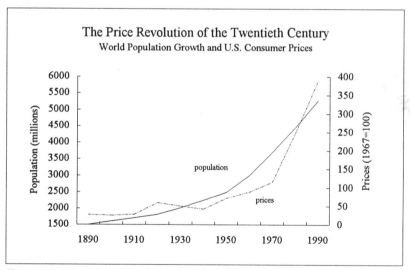

The Price Revolution of the Twentieth Century
World Population Growth and U.S. Consumer Prices

Figure 4.05 compares consumer prices in the United States with the growth of world population. Sources include McEvedy and Jones, *Atlas of World Population History,* 343; *Statistical Abstract of the U.S.* (1993), table 1372; United Nations *Demographic Yearbook* (1993); A. M. Carr-Saunders, *World Population* (Oxford, 1936); consumer prices (1967=100) are from *Historical Statistics of the United States* (1976) ser. E135; *Statistical Abstract of the U.S.* (1993), table 756.

put a strong, even relentless, pressure on the supply of both private and public goods and services.''[8]

At the same time that demographic and social pressures of that sort were building throughout the world, the supply of what Frederick Jackson Turner called ''free land'' was beginning to be exhausted. In 1890, after a survey of population was completed in the United States, the superintendent of the census reported that the American frontier was closed.

In the 1890s, frontiers were closing in many parts of the world. The expansion of Europe was beginning to meet its natural limits. Russia had largely completed the conquest of its built-in Asian empire. India and its border states to the north and east had been brought under the British Raj. The island-spoils of Oceania had been divided among the great powers. The European ''scramble'' for Africa was largely completed by 1896. The Australian outback, New Zealand sheep runs, Argentine pampas and North American prairies all had been converted to the production of meat and grain for the world market. The continuing incorporation of these areas into the Western economy had been the dynamic basis of the Victorian equilibrium. By the late 1890s, that great process was largely completed, and world population was multiplying more rapidly than ever.

Late in the nineteenth century, the nations of the world were also becoming integrated in a single economy at a rapid and accelerating rate. That process had begun as early as the fifteenth century, but a quantum leap occurred in the late nineteenth century, when, as Geoffrey Barraclough has demonstrated, the flow of goods from one nation to another suddenly and greatly expanded. The first effect of this integration had been to stimulate supply; the second was to increase aggregate demand.[9]

The price-revolution of the twentieth century was not peculiar to any national economy or monetary system. It was a global event. Like every great wave that preceded it, this great movement began primarily because the acceleration of demand outstripped the increase of supply.

In other ways, however, the price-revolution of the twentieth century was different from its predecessors. In its early and middle stages real wages increased, and kept on increasing until the late 1960s. This pattern was differed from other price-revolutions. In the twentieth century, the role of trade unions, democratic politics, and welfare states had a major impact on returns to labor.

At the same time, the distribution of income and wealth tended in

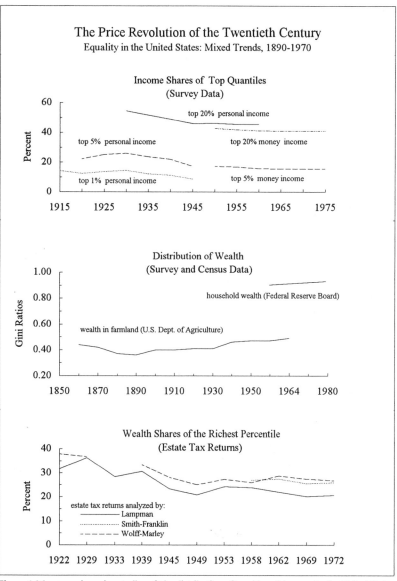

The Price Revolution of the Twentieth Century
Equality in the United States: Mixed Trends, 1890-1970

Figure 4.06 summarizes nine studies of the distribution of wealth and income in the United States. Most show mixed trends from 1890 to 1929, then growing equality from 1929 to 1968, and growing inequality thereafter (see figure 4.23). Sources: Lee Soltow, *Men and Wealth in the United States, 1850-1870* (New Haven, 1975); Robert E. Lipsey and Helen Stone Tice, eds., *The Measurement of Saving, Investment, and Wealth* (Chicago, 1989), 765-844; Lee Soltow, "Distribution of Income and Wealth," in Glenn Porter, ed., *Encyclopedia of American Economic History* (3 vols., New York, 1980) I, 1116; *Historical Statistics of the United States* (1976), series G319-36; *Statistical Abstract of the United States* (1976-1993); Jeffrey G. Williamson and Peter H. Lindert, *American Inequality* (New York, 1980).

The Price Revolution of the Twentieth Century
Returns to Labor: The Rise of Real Wages in the United States
1900-1960

Figure 4.07 follows the upward movement of money wages and real wages from 1900 to 1960.
In this respect, the price revolution of the twentieth century differed from its predecessors--for a
time. These estimates by Stanley Lebergott include mean annual earnings of all employees in the
United States except members of the armed forces. To correct for unemployment Lebergott
added another series which reduced money wages and real wages by 11 percent in 1900 and by 7
percent in 1960. The source is Stanley Lebergott, *Manpower in Economic Growth: The
American Record since 1800* (New York, 1964).

general to become a little more equal, especially in the period from the
1920s to the 1950s. This equalizing tendency had also appeared in the
first stages of other price-revolutions. In the twentieth century, however, it continued for a longer period than before.

?❧ Price Surges and Declines, 1914–45

From 1896 to 1914, prices continued their slow, steady rise. Then
suddenly a new trend appeared. The outbreak of war in 1914 shattered
not only the peace of Europe but also its economic stability. A symptom and cause of that disruption was a massive surge of inflation in
every western nation. From 1914 to 1919, wholesale prices doubled in
the United States, trebled in Britain, quadrupled in Germany, and
sextupled in Italy.

The great powers were unprepared to bear the heavy cost of war,
or to manage its economic consequences. Each nation responded in its

own way. The British government dealt at first with rising prices and shortages in a traditional Anglo-Saxon way. It asked the clergy to read proclamations from church pulpits, urging voluntary limits on consumption. Slowly and reluctantly, Prime Minister David Lloyd George improvised a system of piecemeal price controls and rationing. He added fiscal and monetary measures that restrained inflation more effectively than in any other combatant nation. [10]

In Germany, things were done differently. Effective control of the war economy passed to military officers under the old Prussian Law of Siege. The entire nation was divided into "army corps districts." In each district Deputy Commanding Generals imposed rationing, allocated goods, and controlled prices. They did so with a heavy hand, and ultimately with disastrous consequences for their nation. Low farm prices discouraged production. Germany's inability to feed itself became a fundamental cause of its defeat. Further, the war was paid for by huge loans and taxes on the middle and lower classes. The rich were protected from income and profits taxes. [11]

In Russia, the economy collapsed totally under the strain of the war. The distribution of food was so disrupted by 1917 that the army was forced to live off the land, even within its own country. Major shortages developed in the cities. Prices of food soared. On March 8, 1917, when hungry mobs attacked bakeries throughout the capital and were fired on by police, the Russian Revolution began. Like the French Revolution in 1789, the immediate cause was a combination of high prices and extreme scarcity, which also occurred in many parts of Europe during World War I.

Even after the fighting ended in 1918, the economic troubles continued. Britain, for example, imposed milk rationing for the first time in 1919—a step that it had been able to avoid during the war. In France and many other nations the most rapid inflation occurred not during the war itself, but in the first years of peace. Germany was reduced to economic chaos after the armistice. Russia moved from revolution to a bloody civil war. Major outbreaks of epidemic disease, notably the so-called influenza epidemic of 1918 (probably a polydemic of several diseases), caused heavy mortality in Europe, America, and especially Asia. High prices and scarcities persisted.

In 1920, these trend lines broke. A severe economic depression occurred throughout the world. Prices plummeted in a great deflation that was as disruptive as the previous rise had been. Commodity markets were glutted. In Britain, wholesale prices fell by half in two years from

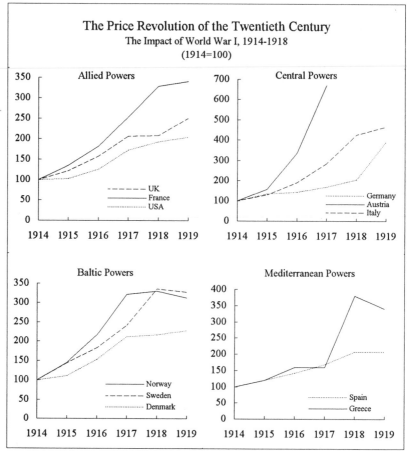

The Price Revolution of the Twentieth Century
The Impact of World War I, 1914-1918
(1914=100)

Figure 4.08 shows the impact of World War I on prices. Rates of inflation were highest in the Central Powers (400-600 percent), and lower in most Allied powers and neutral nations (200-350 percent). Data are from B. R. Mitchell, *European Historical Statistics* (2d rev. ed., New York, 1981) pp. 774-75. All are wholesale prices, except Austria and Greece which are consumer prices. Each is converted to a common base (1914=100).

1920 to 1922. Wages also came down, and unemployment rose rapidly. Broadly similar tendencies appeared in the United States and western Europe. Price and wage deflation were reinforced by the economic policies of conservative governments, and by rigid adherence to the gold standard. This was a period of deep suffering among the poor, but business conditions slowly improved, and stock markets began to boom.[12]

In central Europe, more dangerous trends developed. Germany's new and very shaky Weimar Republic inherited a vast burden of debt and the crushing weight of heavy war reparations to France. When a heroic attempt at tax reform by Matthias Erzberger failed, public credit was exhausted. The German government felt compelled to pay its debts by printing money. It did so at first with some restraint in 1921–22, but soon lost control of its currency. The result was one of the most extreme hyperinflations in history. An American dollar was worth 40 marks in July 1920, 493 marks in July 1922, 4 million marks in the summer of 1923, 4.2 trillion on November 15, 1923. This became the classic monetary hyperinflation, caused by a vast expansion in the quantity of currency in circulation. By late 1923, the German government required 1,783 printing presses, running round the clock, to print money.

Germany was not alone in its travail. Monetary hyperinflation also occurred in Austria (1921–22), Russia (1921–22), Poland (1923–24), and Hungary (1923–24). Similar causes operated through much of central and eastern Europe.

These monetary crises were severe, but very short-lived. German inflation was brought to a sudden end in 1924, and prices were generally stable thereafter. But the experience of hyperinflation had a shattering effect on an entire German generation. The Weimar Republic received much of the blame for problems it had inherited, and none of the credit for solving them. Confidence in open, democratic institutions was weakened fatally in central Europe.

These economic events in the postwar era created profound instabilities. Concentration of wealth remained very high. In Britain, two-thirds of the national wealth in the 1920s was owned by 1 percent of the population. One-third was owned by 0.1 per cent. The twenties were a decade of high prosperity for the rich, and an Indian summer of the old regime. They were also a time of desperate poverty in Scotland, Appalachia, rural Europe, and urban slums throughout the world.

Inequality put narrow limits on consumption. In the United States during the late 1920s, major industries began to suffer from excess capacity and insufficient demand. By 1927, purchases of houses, cars, and consumer durables were in decline. Commodity prices turned downward. Industrial production began to fall. In October 1929, the American stock market crashed, and the world slipped into the Great Depression.

Once again, as in the early 1920s, suffering was deepened by fiscal and monetary policies of conservative governments. After the Crash, American secretary of the treasury Andrew Mellon proposed to

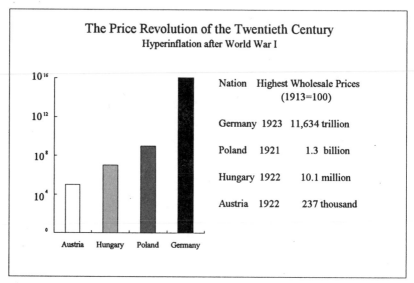

Figure 4.09 represents on a logarithmic scale the hyperinflations that followed the First World War in central Europe. Sources include B. R. Mitchell, ed., *International Historical Statistics; Europe, 1750-1988* 3rd ed. (New York, 1992), 837-51; Thomas J. Sargent, "The Ends of Four Big Inflations," in Robert E. Hall, ed., *Inflation: Causes and Effects* (Chicago, 1982), 99-110; Gerald D. Feldman, *The Great Disorder* (New York, 1993). Prices are in German marks, Polish zlotys, Hungarian krone, Russian rubles, and Austrian krone.

''liquidate labor, liquidate stock, liquidate the farmers.'' Congress gave relief to the rich by cutting income taxes, but offered little assistance to the poor. The Federal Reserve Board pursued a policy of tight money that made things worse. The ultimate folly was President Herbert Hoover's proposal for a large increase in taxes in 1932. As wages fell and unemployment surged, wholesale prices fell by a quarter in Britain, by a third in the United States and Germany, and by half in France.

The Western nations responded to the Great Depression in very different ways. The international gold standard was abandoned by Britain in 1931 and by the United States in 1934. Protectionist walls were raised around national and imperial economies by the American Smoot-Hawley tariff (1930) and the British Ottawa Agreements (1932).

In the United States, President Franklin Roosevelt's New Deal launched the American republic on a sea of economic experiments, which included ''pump priming'' of the private economy by public spending, tighter regulation of business, and an attempt to diminish material inequalities. The results were mixed. Production, wages, and prices began to rise after 1933, only to be driven down again by another sharp recession in 1937–38.

Britain followed a more conservative course with no better success—retrenchment, a balanced budget, subsidies to business, and economic nationalism. These policies were pursued by Prime Minister Ramsay MacDonald (1931–35), who carried retrenchment to the point of reducing the dole in the depth of the Depression, and was expelled from his own Labour party. They were adopted also by Conservative Prime Ministers Stanley Baldwin (1935–37) and Neville Chamberlain (1937–40). By 1937, British prices and wages had nearly returned to 1929 levels, but then they fell again in the second recession of 1938. Throughout the Western world, recovery came very slowly, and at a terrible price.

In France, forty governments held office between 1918 and 1939, five in 1933 alone. Politics were reduced to a chaos of competing factions. In the mid-1930s, French industrial production fell to its lowest level since 1913. Unemployment surged to painfully high levels. The money supply was expanded and prices surged, doubling in merely four years from 1935 to 1939.

Italy and Germany took the dark road to fascism, which in economic terms was an unstable combination of private ownership and public control, feudal fiefdoms and bureaucratic regulation, national autarchy and international conquest. Fascist economies were stimulated by public works and military spending, but German prices remained depressed throughout the 1930s. Old economic problems persisted and new ones were added. The economics of European fascism and Japanese militarism, as well as their ideologies, drove their leaders to embark upon ever more desperate adventures.

In 1937, Japan went to war against China, mainly to secure markets and resources on the Asian mainland. Historian R. A. C. Parker observes that "Japanese civilian authorities in Tokyo were more belligerent than the army." This was a war of economic ambition; it continued in Asia for eighteen years. In 1939, Germany attacked Poland, mostly in search of *Lebensraum,* living space, which meant land for German farmers and raw materials for German factories.[13]

From 1939 to 1941, military victory went to armed forces of Germany and Japan, but the balance of economic power moved in another direction. The beginning of the Second World War at last brought the great depression to an end. Prices, wages, employment and production surged throughout the world. The economies of Germany

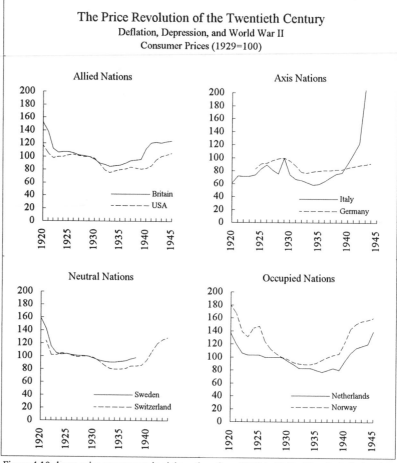

Figure 4.10 shows price movements in eight nations from 1920 to 1945. After the inflation that followed World War I, prices tended to fall from the early 1920s to the early 1930s. The nadir was reached in most nations circa 1934. Thereafter, prices resumed their upward climb, accelerating during World War II (1939-45). Hyperinflation developed in Italy after 1943, and in many European nations after 1945 (see figure 4.12); but controls were successful in Britain and the United States. Sources are B. R. Mitchell, *European Historical Statistics* (2d rev. ed., New York, 1981), 778-83; *Historical Statistics of the United States* (1976), E135.

and Japan experienced growth without development—a vast expansion of resources by conquest and of workers by enslavement. Their swollen economies became in some ways more primitive than before.

In the United States, President Franklin Roosevelt assembled a team of exceptionally able managers who made the American economy into the decisive weapon of the war. Productivity soared. National product per capita (in constant dollars) nearly doubled in the United States from 1938 to 1944, the strongest surge of economic growth in modern American history.[14]

In the United States, a regulatory system that included rationing and price controls worked remarkably well to stabilize the booming economy. A black market developed for scarce goods, but most Americans willingly accepted a more highly regulated economy as part of the war effort. Economists such as John Kenneth Galbraith, who worked for the Office of Price Administration during the war, always remained more supportive of price controls than colleagues who had not shared that experience. The contribution of economic regulation in World War II was both material and moral. It fostered a sense of fairness and justice, and sustained collective effort in a nation that was united as never before.

Britain also used price controls with high success during World War II. The cost of living in the United Kingdom rose only about 20 percent from 1939 to 1945, and increased scarcely at all from 1940 to 1947. The record of the Axis nations was more mixed. In Nazi Germany, prices were kept very stable, increasing 9 percent from 1939 to 1944. This was done in part by requiring citizens and corporations to freeze their liquid assets in compulsory savings accounts, which in turn were confiscated by the state. This plundering of private assets effec-

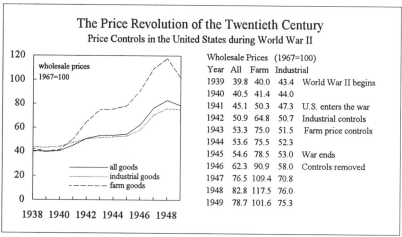

The Price Revolution of the Twentieth Century
Price Controls in the United States during World War II

Wholesale Prices (1967=100)			
Year	All	Farm	Industrial
1939	39.8	40.0	43.4	World War II begins
1940	40.5	41.4	44.0
1941	45.1	50.3	47.3	U.S. enters the war
1942	50.9	64.8	50.7	Industrial controls
1943	53.3	75.0	51.5	Farm price controls
1944	53.6	75.5	52.3
1945	54.6	78.5	53.0	War ends
1946	62.3	90.9	58.0	Controls removed
1947	76.5	109.4	70.8
1948	82.8	117.5	76.0
1949	78.7	101.6	75.3

Figure 4.11 shows the impact of price controls in the United States during World War II. Industrial prices were controlled in 1942; farm prices, in 1943. Controls were removed in 1946. The source is *Historical Statistics of the United States* (1976) E23-25.

tively reduced demand and diminished inflation, but it also contributed to the total destruction of the German economy. Fascist Italy cheerfully resorted to the printing press, and suffered severely from an inflation that continued at a rapid rate from 1934 to 1948. Through much of occupied Europe, prices rose sharply during the war. The Soviet Union also had very high inflation during World War II; official estimates put the increase of prices at 325 percent. The true number was probably higher.[15]

After the war, many European nations suffered severe hyperinflations, similar to the aftermath of World War I. The worst problems were in eastern and southern Europe, during the years from 1947 to 1949.

In the United States, price controls were removed in 1945. What followed was similar in some respects to the period after World War I. In the immediate postwar years, inflation increased to double-digit levels—high by the measure of the American experience, but low by comparison with contemporary trends in Europe. Wholesale commodity prices rose 14 per cent in 1946, and 23 per cent in 1947.

Then the American economy slipped into a short recession. National income declined, rates of unemployment increased, and in 1949 consumer prices actually fell. The decline was small and shortlived: less than 1 percent, in little more than one year. Underlying inflationary pressures were strong. By early 1950, prices were climbing again.

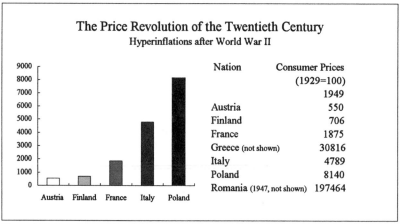

Figure 4.12 shows levels reached by hyperinflations in Europe during 1947-49. The sources are consumer price indices (1929=100) in B. R. Mitchell, ed., *International Historical Statistics: Europe, 1750-1988* (New York, 1992), 848-49.

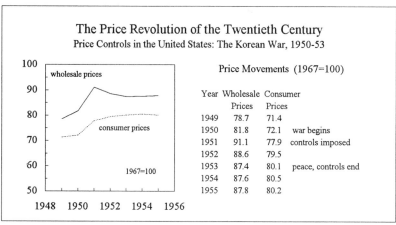

The Price Revolution of the Twentieth Century
Price Controls in the United States: The Korean War, 1950-53

Price Movements (1967=100)

Year	Wholesale Prices	Consumer Prices	
1949	78.7	71.4	
1950	81.8	72.1	war begins
1951	91.1	77.9	controls imposed
1952	88.6	79.5	
1953	87.4	80.1	peace, controls end
1954	87.6	80.5	
1955	87.8	80.2	

Figure 4.13 shows the effect of price controls in controlling inflation in the United States during the Korean War. When the war began in 1950, wholesale prices and consumer prices surged to double-digit levels. Controls were imposed in 1951-53. Prices immediately stabilized and did not increase when controls were lifted. The source is *Historical Statistics of the United States* (1976) E23, E135.

Inflationary pressures mounted in the United States during the summer of 1950, when a Communist regime in North Korea suddenly attacked its southern neighbor, and yet another major war began. By 1951, most of the world's great powers had men in combat on the Korean peninsula. Military forces rapidly expanded throughout the world. More Americans were in uniform during the Korean War (1950–53) than during World War I.

In its economic impact of the Korean War was similar to the world wars that had preceded it. Once again inflationary pressures surged throughout the world. In 1950, wholesale prices jumped 12 percent in the United States, 18 percent in Germany, 21 percent in Britain, 28 percent in France, 32 percent in Sweden.

In the United States, President Harry Truman acted decisively, and revived price controls with high success. As a short-run emergency war measure, the regulation of the American market during the Korean conflict proved to be highly effective, more so even than in World War II. After controls were imposed in 1951, prices and wages became remarkably stable. There was no inflationary surge from 1951 to 1954, and no explosion of repressed demand when controls were removed. Price-regulation kept inflation within narrow bounds. It also diminished the dangerous social instabilities that often accompany price-surges. The side effects of short-term price controls in 1942–45 and 1950–53 were much less destructive to the social fabric than neo-classical anti-inflationary policies of 1980s and 1990s. Those who believe that "price controls don't work," even in the short run, will find strong evidence to the contrary in the history of the American economy during World War II and the Korean War.

ॐ The Discovery of Inflation, 1938–63

Through all of these turbulent events, global prices continued to rise in peace as well as war. Even as price surges were restrained in some nations by strict controls, the secular trend moved inexorably upward. In the United States from 1938 to 1963, consumer prices rose every year but two. During the span of an entire generation, inflation was the rule in twenty-three years out of twenty-five. One result was a growth of what Americans called an "inflationary psychology." The existence of inflation as a secular trend began to be discovered by individuals, corporations, and governments throughout the world.[16]

American historian Eric Goldman lived through this period in the United States. "Inflation jabbed people wherever they turned," he remembered. "Trolleys and subways went up two cents, then a nickel. The ten-cent Sunday newspaper was disappearing in America. Still more irritating were things that were hard to buy at any price. A public with billions of dollars stored up in war bonds and savings accounts . . . found itself queuing up in long nerve-jangling lines. Women had trouble getting furniture, nylons, a new electric iron; men found clothing, even a razor blade that would shave clean, in short supply. . . . As the summer of 1946 closed, the food shortages were reaching their climax. First came a meteoric rise in prices. . . . Gradually the store shelves began to fill; within months of the election of 1946, steaks and roasts were no longer drawing crowds. . . . Prices kept on climbing. Even the kids of Cape Cod resort towns, who for years had dived to retrieve pennies thrown in the water by vacationers, now refused to budge except for nickels. But the public was learning to live with inflation."[17]

In the years after World War II, this underlying inflationary psychology firmly established itself in North America and western Europe. People tried to make light of the problem. American humorist Max

Kauffman observed, "Among the things that money can't buy is everything it used to." Vaudeville comedian Henny Youngman remarked, "Americans are getting stronger. Twenty years ago, it took two people to carry ten dollars' worth of groceries. Today, a five-year-old can do it."

The inflation jokes of the 1950s expressed a growing mood of fatalism about price movements. That attitude encouraged pessimism about the possibility of restraining inflation and caused people to seek other remedies. These new responses caused more inflation and increased its momentum. They also institutionalized its dynamics within entire cultural systems.

This had happened in every other price-revolution, but during the twentieth century, the institutional machinery of modern society had grown stronger and more complex than before. Institutional responses to rising prices reinforced inflation more powerfully than in earlier waves.

Industrial democracies began to create elaborate systems of institutional price-inflators, which economist Robert Heilbroner described as regulatory "floors without ceilings." Price floors were constructed in many sectors of the American economy. In some industries, "administered prices" became commonplace. In others, prices were formally fixed by regulatory agencies, and by "fair trade" statutes that forbade merchants to sell below the manufacturer's "suggested retail price."

The dynamic American responses to price floors were not price ceilings, but wage floors. In 1938, the Congress enacted the Fair Labor Standards Act, which set the first national minimum wage. It also briefly considered a maximum wage, but that idea was quickly forgotten. Thereafter, the minimum wage was frequently raised, and extended more broadly through the economy. Similar laws were enacted in other nations. This legislation helps to explain one of the distinctive features of the price-revolution in the twentieth century—its exceptionally high rate of advance.[18]

In the period from 1938 to 1968, many inflationary floors were built into the American economy: floors under wages, pensions, and compensation for the unemployed; floors beneath farm prices, steel prices, liquor prices, and milk prices; floors for airline fares, trucking charges, doctors' bills, and lawyers' fees. Not all of these floors were erected by public authorities. Many were imposed by corporations, labor unions and professional associations. The creation of regulatory floors without ceilings accelerated a dynamic process called the wage-price spiral by conservatives, and the price-wage spiral by liberals.

The institutionalization of inflation in the twentieth century was not limited to price and wage regulation itself. Systemic restraints were placed also upon supply. Many nations imposed limits on production: farm products in the United States, oil in Saudi Arabia, coffee in Colombia, gold in South Africa, and many other commodities throughout the world. International cartels pursued the same policy where they were able to do so. The classic example was the price of diamonds, which the De Beers syndicate inflated to many times their market value by restrictions on supply and other methods. From a functional perspective, it mattered not at all whether these policies were imposed by a national government, or an international cartel, or a corporate manager. The impact on prices was the same. Wherever supply was held down, prices tended to rise. The integrated international economy of the twentieth century created many opportunities, and put them in the hands of small groups who profited by their application.

Other new structural causes of inflation began to operate in the mid-twentieth century. One of them was invented by American businessmen. Economist David Slawson called it "competitive inflation." Two rival sellers of the same commodity, instead of competing in the classical manner by seeking to offer a better product at a lower price, learned in the twentieth century to operate in other ways. They discovered that they could increase profits and expand market-share by degrading their product, advertising relentlessly, packaging it in a different form, and raising its unit price.

As a case in point, Slawson studied the price history of American candy bars. During the late 1950s, the going price of a candy bar was five cents. By 1983, it had risen to thirty-five cents. The price was deliberately raised in a series of small five-cent increments by manufacturers. Slawson found that "each increase was disguised by making the bar larger at the same time—the size of the bar having been gradually decreased since the time of the last price rise. People generally choose candy bars on the basis of taste and size, neither of which encourages them to make close distinctions on the basis of price. Moreover, the manufacturers, one assumes deliberately, make size difficult to assess by making the wrappers larger than the bars inside, and by using a wide variety of shapes."[19]

The laws of neo-classical economics are unable to explain the price history of the American candy bar in the twentieth century. Market competition remained strong among candy-makers—in some respects, stronger than ever before. But it was no longer primarily price competition, and its effect on prices was the reverse of what neo-classical economic theory would lead us to expect. The more competitive the candy market became in America during the twentieth century, the more prices rose.[20]

Economist Slawson argued that there was little difference in pricing strategies used for candy bars, automobiles, airline tickets, and other goods and services. He developed a model of a new "competitive inflation" to describe a world of growing complexity in pricing decisions by corporate sellers, and of increasing uncertainties for the individual buyer. Those trends in turn represented a shift in the distribution of knowledge and power in the marketplace. Sellers operated increasingly at an advantage over buyers. When that happened, prices went up.

In all of these ways, the great inflation of the twentieth century differed from every price-revolution that had preceded it. Its velocity, mass, and momentum were greater than those that came before.

❧ The Troubles of Our Times

In 1962, the price-revolution entered a new stage. After a period of comparatively slow increase during the late 1950s, inflation began to accelerate. This was a global movement. It appeared at about the same time in many nations: Austria (1962), Denmark (1962), Ireland (1962), Norway (1962), Sweden (1962), Belgium (1963), Italy (1963), Switzerland (1963), the Netherlands (1964), United Kingdom (1964), Yugoslavia (1964), Germany (1965), and the United States (1965).[1]

The epicenter of this new movement was in western Europe, which had recovered very rapidly from the catastrophe of the second World War. After a recession in 1957–59, most European economies were flourishing. Unemployment fell to record lows in 1961: below 4 percent in Denmark and Italy; 3 percent in Austria and Norway; 2 percent in Britain and Spain; barely 1 percent in Germany and Switzerland.[2]

This economic prosperity had a strong political effect. Many western nations took a turn to the left. The results included the presidencies of John Kennedy and Lyndon Johnson in the United States (1961), the "Opening to the Left" in Italy (1961), the election of a Labour government in Britain (1964), and the emergence of the "Great Coalition" in Germany (1966). European labor movements became more aggressive and more successful, winning large wage settlements in these years.[3]

It was during this halcyon era of high prosperity and full employment that rates of inflation began to accelerate. Japanese consumer prices, for example, had increased less than one percent a year from 1955 to 1959. In the 1960s, they began to climb more rapidly, at more than five percent each year. Producer price increases in Japan were smaller, but still substantial.[4]

Rates of gain varied from one nation and monetary system to another in the early 1960s. The pace of inflation was very low in Switzerland (2.3%), West Germany (2.4%) and the United States (2.5%). It was higher in Sweden (3.6%), Britain (3.6%), France (4.4%) and India (4.5%). The highest rates were in Latin America, and the Middle East. No nations were exempt.[5]

Price rises remained comparatively moderate in the North American economy, which restrained the world inflation-rate until 1965. Then they also began to accelerate, partly because President Lyndon Johnson and his advisors made a major miscalculation. The Johnson administration decided to expand public spending for social welfare in the United States and simultaneously fight a major war in Southeast Asia, without a large increase in taxes. In the journalistic jargon of the day, they believed that the booming American economy could supply both "guns and butter" at the same time.

The result was a large increase in public spending, on top of growing aggregate demand in the private sector. American prices began to rise more rapidly, especially prices for food and farm products. The annual rate of inflation in the United States trebled from 1961 to 1966.

Many scholars mistakenly remember the Vietnam War as the pivotal event in the acceleration of inflation during the 1960s. In fact, the surge began a few years earlier, in another part of the world. The fiscal policies of the Johnson administration had an impact because they reinforced an existing trend and increased its momentum.[6]

The roots of the price-revolution ran deep in the 20th century. As in every other great wave, the rapid increase of world population and the growth of aggregate demand were the primary cause of price increases. The world economy was more productive than ever before, and its rate of growth was the highest in history. But it could not keep up with demand. In the United States, whenever capacity-utilization rose above 80 percent, the rate of inflation accelerated. When it fell below that level, as it did from time to time, inflation subsided.

A similar pattern appeared in the association between prices and unemployment. When the unemployment rate fell below 6 percent, the rate of inflation advanced more rapidly. When unemployment rose above that level, inflation retreated. Clearly, the price-revolution of the twentieth century was embedded in demographic trends and economic structures.

As early as 1966, American leaders began to show concern about rising prices and acted forcefully to restrain them. The expansion of the money supply (M-1) was brought to a dead halt in the second quarter of 1966. Interest rates were raised deliberately to their highest levels in half a century, in what was called the credit crunch of 1966. An economist observes that this was "the first occasion in the post World War II period that the Fed sharply cut back monetary growth and caused rapid and, for a time, large increases in interest rates."[7]

As these policies took effect, the prosperous American economy skidded into a brief "mini-recession" in 1967. But inflation did not end. Consumer prices continued to climb, and by 1968 the buoyant American economy began to boom again. As inflationary pressures mounted, public officials in the Johnson administration and the Federal Reserve Board once again adopted policies of economic restraint. They tightened credit, applied various fiscal restrictions, drove interest rates higher, increased taxes by a 10 percent surcharge on incomes, and curbed monetary growth in early 1969.

These measures were deliberately intended to create what was called a "policy recession." They succeeded all too well. In 1969, anti-inflationary measures began to have an effect, but not precisely the one that was intended. After the long boom of the 1960s, the American economy went into steep decline, dragging other nations with it. The recession of 1968–71, writes economist Robert Gordon, combined "the worst of three worlds." One might say that it combined the worst of five worlds. National product diminished. Unemployment rose sharply. The dollar fell against other currencies, and yet the American balance of payments rapidly deteriorated. Through it all, inflation stubbornly persisted in a new combination with economic stagnation, which American economist Paul Samuelson may have been the first to call "stagflation."[8]

Neoclassical economists were baffled by stagflation. Some believed it to be an unprecedented anomaly. In fact, stagflation had

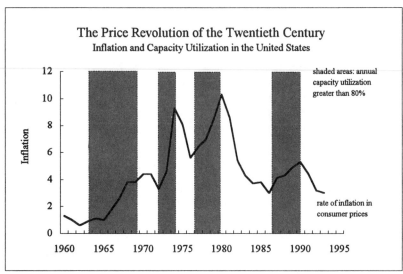

The Price Revolution of the Twentieth Century
Inflation and Capacity Utilization in the United States

Figure 4.14 shows the relationship between inflation and the use of manufacturing capacity in the United States from 1960 to 1993. When capacity-utilization rose above 8 percent, rates of inflation generally increased. When capacity-utilization fell below 8 percent, inflation tended to fall. Sources: *Historical Statistics of the United States* (1976), E135; *Statistical Abstract of the United States* (1993) table 757; capacity utilization, *ibid.*, (1976) table 1250; (1988) table 1250; (1993) table 1261.

happened in the later stages of every price-revolution from the thirteenth century to our own time.

When President Richard Nixon came to office, he was forced to deal with an economy in deep disarray. In response to stagflation, this highly conservative president amazed his friends and gratified his enemies by suddenly becoming a convert to the interventionist economics of John Maynard Keynes. ''Now I am a Keynesian,'' Nixon told an astonished television journalist, Howard K. Smith. The president's ''new economic policy'' combined a strong dose of Keynesian fiscal stimuli with an unprecedented system of peacetime price and wage controls.

These measures proved immensely popular with most Americans. National polls consistently showed strong public support for price controls. The economy began to revive, and inflation rapidly diminished from 5 percent in 1970 to 3 percent in 1972.[9]

But despite their general popularity, price and wage controls had powerful enemies in the United States. They were strongly opposed on theoretical grounds by neoclassical economists. At the same time they

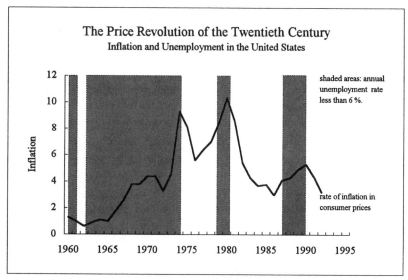

The Price Revolution of the Twentieth Century
Inflation and Unemployment in the United States

Figure 4.15 shows that the rate of inflation generally increased when unemployment fell below 6 percent. The rate of inflation commonly declined when unemployment rose above that level. The sources include: for inflation, *Historical Statistics of the United States* (1976) E135; *Statistical Abstract of the United States* (1993) table 757; for unemployment, *ibid.*, (1976) table 558; (1988) table 605; (1993) table 652.

were strenuously resisted by leaders of big labor and big business, and also by their many friends and protectors in both political parties. These small but vocal elites mounted effective campaigns—insisting over and over again that ''price controls don't work,'' that ''regulation is unfair,'' and that restraints would be destructive of economic growth.

All of those arguments were false. Short-term price and wage controls had worked well in recent applications. They were less unfair than unrestrained inflation, and did far less damage to economic growth than anti-inflationary tools such as interest-rate manipulation and policy recessions. But the anti-regulatory arguments were often repeated and widely believed. Powerful interests lobbied incessantly for an end to price and wage controls, until both Congress and the Nixon administration gave way. Controls were relaxed prematurely, while inflationary pressures remained strong.

Once more prices began to advance rapidly. This time, leaders of the administration tried to restrain them by a policy of moral suasion called ''jawboning'' in the jargon of the day. The only discernible effect of jawboning was an inflation of rhetoric that kept pace with rising prices. The cost of living kept on climbing.

Later in his beleaguered presidency, Nixon wanted to freeze prices again. His neoclassical economic advisers firmly resisted that idea. Herbert Stein remembers: ''I warned him, citing Heraclitus, that you can't step in the same river twice.'' Nixon replied, ''you can if it's frozen.'' But controls had become politically untenable, whatever their economic merits may have been.[10]

ᘖ Price Volatility: Oil Shocks and Commodity Surges, 1973–80

Then came an entirely unexpected event, of the sort that happens frequently in price history and yet can never be predicted. In October 1973, the state of Israel was attacked without warning by its Arab neighbors on the Jewish holiday called Yom Kippur. At the same time, Arab nations placed an embargo on oil as part of their war effort. A hitherto ineffective cartel called the Organization of Petroleum Exporting Countries (OPEC), agreed to raise the benchmark price of Saudi ''marker crude'' oil from $3 to $5.11 a barrel. This measure was meant to be a strategic weapon against Israel and her western allies. It proved to be highly successful—so much so that in January 1974 OPEC raised prices again, to the dizzy height of $11.65 a barrel. The Arab cartel also tried to stop the flow of oil altogether to the United States and the Netherlands as a special punishment for their support of Israel.

These acts were not unprecedented. Twice before the Arab states had tried to use oil as a strategic weapon. Twice the United States had stabilized prices by drawing on its vast petroleum reserves. By 1973, however, the American reserves were nearly gone, and the United States had become a heavy importer of foreign oil. It was powerless to stop OPEC by anything short of military action, which for a time was seriously considered by the Nixon administration. Within a few months, oil prices quadrupled.

The American reaction, writes oil expert John M. Blair, ''approached pure panic.'' Governments, corporations, and individuals were entirely unprepared for this turn of events. Many American families and institutions found their budgets strained beyond the breaking point. In Europe, energy-poor industries collapsed. Unemployment soared. The worst suffering occurred in the third world, where

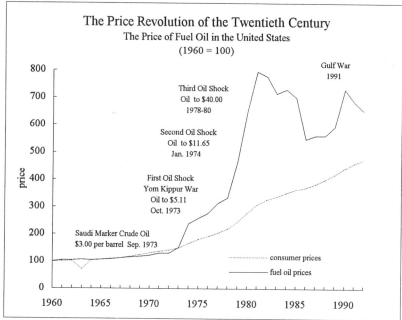

Figure 4.16 compares the cost of fuel oil with consumer prices in the United States (1960=100). The source is the *Statistical Abstract of the United States* (1993), table 756.

fragile economies were cruelly shattered by the actions of the OPEC cartel.[11]

The success of OPEC was made possible by fundamental economic forces. By 1973, the world had become highly vulnerable to commodity cartels. Twenty years of postwar prosperity and accelerating population growth had created heavy demand for raw materials. Oil was not unique in that respect. During the decade of the 1970s, the prices of many commodities rose even more rapidly than petroleum. Some surged to their highest levels in modern history. In 1980, as the price of oil climbed to $40 a barrel, tin reached $8 a pound, silver peaked at $54 an ounce and gold rose to $875 an ounce. Other raw materials such as hides, rubber, cotton, and grain also rose to high levels.

The velocity of these trends accelerated after 1973. In the United States, the Consumer Price Index registered an increase of 11 percent in 1974. Producer prices rose even more rapidly, to 18.9 percent in the same year. This "double-digit inflation" as it came to be called, was at that time the highest peacetime price-surge in American history.[12]

In 1975, President Gerald Ford convened an urgent "summit meeting" of leading economists to discuss the problem of inflation. John Kenneth Galbraith was present. "There was full professional agreement on only one remedy," Galbraith remembered, "that government regulations should be reviewed to remove any obvious impediments to market competition. For practical effect, this was no better than the President's own prescription, which was the wearing of buttons inscribed with the insignia WIN, for Whip Inflation Now."[13]

Inflation moderated in 1976–77, largely because of the disruption of the world economy and the decline of demand, but annual price increases continued in the range of 6 percent—an exceptionally high level by historic standards. The stubborn persistence of inflation, and the recent failure of so many policies created a painful dilemma for national leaders.

In the United States, the new Carter administration acted on the advice of neo-classical economists and promoted a new idea called "deregulation," partly in the hope of removing regulatory "floors" under price and wages. The effect of "deregulation" did not as a rule remove the floors themselves. It merely removed control of them from the public to the private sector. Inflation continued, now in company with growing inequalities of income. During the late 1970s, consumer prices in the United States accelerated sharply yet again, in another surge of increasing volatility. Once more the OPEC cartel played a leading role. In 1978–79, it ruthlessly raised the price of oil to such a height that the United States was paying nearly $100 billions a year to oil-producing nations. The annual rate of inflation in consumer prices reached 13.5 percent in 1980, a new peacetime record in American history.

American inflation, high as it was by historical standards, remained below the global average. A survey by the International Monetary Fund in 1979–80 found that consumer prices were rising in every nation for which data was available. The smallest rates of inflation that year were in Switzerland, Burma, and Saudi Arabia. The highest rates were in Israel, Turkey and Latin America. The United States experienced price increases of 12.8 percent, very high by the measure of its own experience, but below the International Monetary Fund's estimated "world inflation rate" of 15.6 percent that year. The price-revolution of the twentieth century was a global movement, with local variations.[14]

World Inflation in the Late 1970s
Annual Increase in Consumer Prices, 3d Quarter 1979–3d Quarter 1980

Developed Nations		Latin American Nations	
United States	12.8	Argentina	c88.0
Canada	10.6	Brazil	85.5
Australia	10.2	Chile	32.9
Japan	8.4	Colombia	26.3
New Zealand	16.3	Costa Rica	19.3
Austria	6.9	Ecuador	13.2
Belgium	6.5	El Salvador	19.6
Denmark	11.5	Guatemala	11.2
Finland	12.1	Mexico	28.4
France	13.6	Trinidad	15.8
Germany	5.3	Venezuela	23.4
Ireland	18.9	*Asian Nations*	
Italy	21.8	Bangladesh	10.1
Netherlands	7.1	Burma	c1.0
Norway	12.2	India	10.9
Spain	14.8	Korea	28.7
Sweden	13.6	Malaysia	7.9
Switzerland	3.8	Pakistan	11.1
United Kingdom	16.4	Philippines	14.8
Southern Europe		Singapore	8.1
Greece	24.5	Sri Lanka	28.9
Portugal	15.3	Thailand	19.0
Yugoslavia	19.2	*Middle Eastern Nations*	
African Nations		Egypt	c25.0
Kenya	13.5	Israel	132.7
Madagascar	11.7	Jordan	11.4
Senegal	6.1	Syria	c20.0
South Africa	12.2	Saudi Arabia	c2.0
Tunisia	8.9	Iran	c22.0
Zaire	c50.0	Turkey	108.3
Ghana	c67.0	*Developed Nations*	11.7
Ivory Coast	c10.0		
Morocco	c9.8	*World*	15.6
Cameroon	c11.0		

Figure 4.17. Source: *International Financial Statistics* 34 (1981) 45.

The tightly controlled Communist economies of eastern Europe were also caught up in the great wave, but in a different way. Prices and wages were held ruthlessly in check by the instruments of a totalitarian state, but state planners were not able to restrain the pressures of aggregate demand. The result was the development of rationing, the Communist alternative to inflation. In the western world, rising prices were themselves a system of market-rationing which allocated scarce resources to those who were willing and able to pay higher prices. The Communist system substituted state-rationing for market-rationing. Throughout eastern Europe the same scenes were enacted. Long queues, empty shops, and meatless meals became the Marxist surrogate for price-inflation. State-rationing, continued year after year, engendered problems of deep corruption in Communist nations. Corrupt regimes that ruled in the name of the people rapidly lost their moral legitimacy.

Free-market nations tried to protect themselves against inflation by adopting autarchic policies, with consequences that caused major economic problems throughout the world. The leading example was Japan, which was highly vulnerable to commodity cartels. To pay its soaring oil bills, the Japanese flooded the world market with exports. In America alone, the total value of Japanese goods rose from five billion dollars in 1970 to thirty billions only a decade later. At the same time, the Japanese actively discouraged imports to their own economy. The result was the growth of large imbalances in international trade, and the collapse of many American industries. Unemployment surged in the United States, while inflation continued at high levels.

In 1979–80, the liberal Democratic administration of Jimmy Carter declared inflation to be the nation's "number one problem." On the advice of economists, and in alliance with Chairman Paul Volcker, a deeply conservative banker who headed the Federal Reserve Board, a southern Populist president adopted highly repressive economic policies. Interest rates were raised to record heights. The money supply was restrained. Taxes were allowed to reach the highest peacetime levels in American history, mainly as a consequence of inflationary "bracket creep," which carried most Americans into higher tax brackets. A major effort was made to reduce American dependence on foreign oil. In the last months of the Carter administration these policies began to take effect. The American economy faltered and turned sharply downward. Inflation began to subside. But new problems began to appear.

Major instabilities developed in commodity markets. The United States and other nations had responded to rising the cost of energy by increasing domestic production of oil, by shifting to other fuels, and by reducing demand for energy. These measures succeeded beyond expectations. Their effect was to solve one problem by creating another—the energy glut of the 1980s. Suddenly, the world found itself awash in oil. Energy prices fell sharply, and petroleum-producing regions such as Texas and Alberta fell into deep depressions.

The oil glut of the 1980s caught governments and corporations by surprise. A symbol of massive miscalculations by high executives in the major oil corporations and shipping companies was long rows of idle supertankers, rusting at their moorings in Norwegian fjords during the early 1980s. These ships had been ordered during the OPEC oil famine. They had been completed just in time for the glut that followed. Many were among the largest ships ever constructed. Some were destined never to sail except to the breakers' yards. The shipbuilding industry had expanded to meet the demand for these new ships. Now it found itself with excess capacity, and collapsed with a resounding crash throughout the world.[15]

Similar reversals also occurred in other sectors of the world economy, notably in agriculture. During the early 1970s, high food prices had sent production soaring. American farmers borrowed heavily to increase production. Then, in the 1980s, the world found itself producing more food than it could consume. American farmers were faced with saturated markets, heavy debts, and excess capacity. They began to go bankrupt in numbers unprecedented even in the Great Depression. Meanwhile, politically powerful European farmers, encouraged by price supports, kept producing a vast surplus which was purchased by the European Economic Community and stored in "butter mountains" and "wine lakes." India and other developing nations, with the aid of new farming methods in the "green revolution," also began to produce more food than they consumed, and agricultural markets were glutted round the world.

Market-instability was intensified by the acts of private speculators. The effect of increasing wealth concentration was to increase the supply of surplus capital, which shifted rapidly from one investment opportunity to another throughout the world in search of profit. The increasing liquidity and volatility of markets created opportunities that were aggressively pursued, sometimes less for profit than for sport. Some of these speculations succeeded; others failed; all of them together contributed to the growing instability of the world economy.

An example was the silver bubble of the 1970s. In 1973, the Hunt family of Texas, at that time possibly the richest family in America, decided to buy precious metals as a hedge against inflation. Gold could not be held by private citizens in the United States at that time, and so the Hunts began to buy silver in enormous quantity, perhaps even hoping to corner the world silver market—a wild speculation reminiscent of Colebrook's alum scheme in the price-revolution of the eighteenth century. Silver prices surged from $1.94 an ounce in 1973 to $50.35 in 1980. The corner failed, and the Hunt family fell deep in debt. By 1987, their liabilities had grown to nearly $2.5 billion, against assets of $1.5 billion. America's richest family slipped to the edge of bankruptcy, and the shock waves spread through the economy.[16]

After 1981, the Reagan administration created new opportunities for speculators and corporate raiders by relaxing antitrust rules and promoting business deregulation. "Hostile takeovers" and "leveraged buyouts" multiplied at a rapid rate, often with catastrophic consequences for corporations, jobs, communities, and individuals. In the economically depressed state of Maine, for example, what remained of the shoe industry was dealt a heavy blow by takeovers. In the fragile economy of the American Middle West, small industrial corporations were destroyed by the same process. Healthy corporations with strong balance sheets, cash reserves, and an active sense of civic responsibility were specially at risk. Some of the best and most responsible American companies such as Dayton-Hudson and Phillips Petroleum, outstanding corporate citizens with strong balance sheets, were compelled assume crushing debt in an effort to fight off hostile takeovers. The result of this activity was growing instability in the economic life of the nation.

In the mid-1980s, the new electronic technology of securities markets increased speculative instabilities of another kind. Chicago's Mercantile Exchange invented futures-trading in stocks, with lower margin requirements than the stock exchanges themselves. This created opportunities for traders to shift their money back and forth from stocks to stock futures, and to extract large profits from small disparities. The work was done by "programmed trading," in which computers sent automatic signals to buy and sell when stocks and stock-futures reached predetermined levels. Programmed trading increased the volatility of securities markets. Buffers that had been invented after the Great Depression were unable to restrain this new technology. Stock values soared in 1987, and Wall Street became a great casino. Millions of small investors were caught up in the speculative mania.

The day of reckoning came on October 19, 1987. The New York stock market suddenly crashed. The same processes of programmed trading that had brought the market to dizzy heights, now sent it tumbling down again in its worst collapse since 1929. Panic-stricken investors rushed to sell large quantities of stock, often at a heavy loss. The Dow Jones industrial average plunged 500 points, and billions of dollars vanished in an afternoon.

On the morning after, some experts explained that the collapse was merely a massive correction of grossly inflated stock-prices. They did not ask how the inflation had happened in the first place. Others believed that the crash was caused by programmed trading in stock futures on commodity exchanges where margin requirements were low or nonexistent. Many small investors concluded that financial markets had become corrupt casinos, in which the games were rigged by insiders.

After the crash, the confidence of investors collapsed, and the stock market was unable to serve its primary economic function of mobilizing capital for investment. In 1988, more than 100 major American corporations found themselves unable to issue new stock offerings for their capital needs. Neither the securities industry nor the Reagan administration were able to agree on regulatory reforms. In the two years that followed the Crash of 1987, Congress and the federal government failed to enact a single substantive reform for securities markets.

❧ The Cost of Anti-Inflation:
Price Fears and Policy Recessions, 1980–95

In the 1980s, the battered world economy slipped into another recession. This one was deep—the deepest since the 1930s. It was marked by excess capacity and plummeting commodity prices. Producer prices of food and raw materials fell steeply from 1981 to 1986, reaching their lowest levels since the Great Depression. Oil declined from $40 a barrel to $8 in 1986. Tin dropped from $8 a pound to $2.50; copper slipped from $1 to 45 cents; silver plummeted from $54 to less than $5 an ounce. But even in the very depth of this recession, consumer prices continued their inexorable advance. Inflation slowed, but did not cease.[17]

When the major industrial economies began to revive, prices of raw materials started to climb again. In 1987, the price of oil doubled. Cotton and lead trebled. Strong upward trends appeared in the price of copper, nickel, aluminum, wool, hides and rubber. Overall, commodity prices rose by nearly one-third in a single year, and further increases followed in 1988.[18]

A large part of this increase was due to hoarding, in fear of higher prices ahead. Economic forecasters predicted further price increases, and an inflationary psychology rapidly strengthened throughout the world. Fear of inflation began to be more disruptive than inflation itself. The expectation of rising prices caused prices to rise higher.[19]

By 1989, as producer prices were rising sharply, world leaders openly discussed the need for driving the economies of the industrial world into a yet another "policy recession." They did so at a time when markets and economies were deeply unstable. Governments worked to "cool" their economies by raising interest rates. In the United States, the Federal Funds Rate was driven up from 6.7 percent in 1987 to 9.2 percent in 1990. Consumer interest rates climbed much higher. Other fiscal and monetary measures were also adopted, but now that price controls were discredited, the remedy for double-digit inflation was double-digit interest.

This policy of using high interest rates to control high inflation had many economic and social effects. It increased inequality, discouraged investment, diminished productivity, reduced demand, and drove up unemployment. Ironically, in some ways it also promoted inflation. The cost of housing, for example, rose sharply in part because home construction was inflated by builders' capital costs, which increased with the rate of interest. Interest-rate manipulation was a very powerful instrument of economic policy. Its impact was much broader than it was meant to be.

The result was yet another recession in 1990–91. In that year, the United States had negative rates of economic growth, falling per capita income, and growing unemployment. The rate of inflation slowed from 5.4 percent in 1990 to 3 percent in 1992. Economists and politicians declared that inflation was "under control." It wasn't. Even in the midst of the recession, consumer prices continued to climb. The rate of gain even in this recession remained higher than the average inflation in any previous price-revolution in world history.

So steep was the recession in 1990–91 that the managers of the American economy, in fear of a full-blown depression, shifted suddenly from the brake to the accelerator. Interest rates were driven down to historic lows. The Federal Funds Rate dropped from 9.2 percent in 1989 to 3.5 percent in 1992.

Industrial economies began to revive, first in America (1992), then in Europe (1993); but this was the halfway prosperity that had happened in the late stages of every price-revolution. Many workers remained jobless. In May 1994, rates of unemployment were above 6 percent in the United States, 8 percent in Germany, 9 percent in Great Britain, 11 percent in Italy, 12 percent in France, 13 percent in Belgium, 24 percent in Spain, and 50 percent in South Africa. These were the official rates. The true numbers were higher, and even they did not begin to measure the social costs. For every worker without a job there were others who had been unemployed in the recent past, and many more who feared that they might be jobless in the immediate future.

The social cost of anti-inflationary policies had become more destructive than inflation itself. Opportunities diminished. Inequalities increased. The principal victims were not a class but a generation— young people who had no hope for the future and no memory of better times in the past. The result was a rapid growth of alienation, anomie, confusion, and despair.

Through it all, consumer prices kept on climbing. Economic managers nervously shifted their weight from accelerators to brakes, then back to accelerators and once more to brakes. Inflation diminished but did not disappear. In early 1995, prices rose at annual rates of 4 percent in Germany, 6 percent in Britain and Switzerland, 8 percent in Italy and Spain. Lower rates prevailed in Japan and the United States, where some observers argued that inflation had been conquered. It was not so. Prices continued to outpace wages. Real income fell, and families were desperately hard pressed. Institutions of many kinds operated under heavy fiscal strain, and struggled to balance their budgets at heavy social cost.

?➤ Growing Imbalances

These stresses rose directly from the structure of the price-revolution itself. Every great wave had been much the same that way. In the late stages of these long movements, severe strains began to develop within social systems. The damage was done not by price-inflation itself, but by disparities in its operation.

Some prices inflated more rapidly than others. Price-relatives were much the same as in every long wave since the middle ages. Once again, as thrice before, soaring prices of food and energy and raw materials had led the inflationary advance. Prices of manufactured products such as cars, textiles, appliances, toys, leisure goods, and furniture all lagged behind. The cause was the same as in every other price-revolution. The consequences fell most cruelly upon the poor, who paid a large proportion of their income for food, fuel and shelter.[20]

Suffering was compounded by wage-movements after 1975. During the early and middle decades of the twentieth century, workers had done better than in previous price-revolutions. In the United States real wages kept rising through most of the period from 1896 to 1975.[21] The cause was to be found in a combination of union activity, minimum wage laws, productivity gains, and social welfare legislation.[22] During the early 1970s, that trend reversed. Real wages fell sharply after 1973, dropped again from 1978 to 1982, and declined once more from 1984

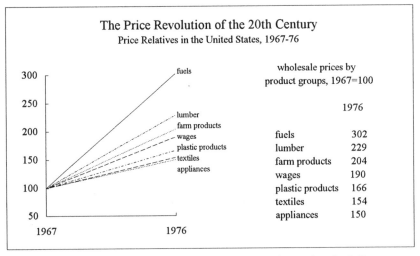

Figure 4.18 shows a pattern of price relatives in the 20th century that was broadly similar to earlier price revolutions, but different in important details. Once again the cost of energy, raw materials and farm products led the advance. Once more, wages and manufactures lagged behind. Two differences separated the 20th century price revolution from its predecessors. The cost of food increased less rapidly, re, relative to other raw materials; and wages rose a little more rapidly in relative terms, though still falling behind the cost of living. The source is *Statistical Abstract of the United States* (1978) 765.

to 1996. Broadly similar trends were evident in both white collar and blue collar jobs.[23]

While real wages fell, returns to capital rose more rapidly than the general price level. This was most dramatically so for landed capital. The cost of rent and real estate in the United States multiplied sixfold from 1960 to 1992, while the consumer price index increased three-fold. Prime real estate went up tenfold or more. On Manhattan's Upper East Side, a cooperative apartment that had gone for $60,000 in 1968 rose as high as $600,000 twenty years later. In Boston suburbs with good schools, modest homes that sold for $20,000 in 1965 brought $400,000 in 1986. Similar trends occurred in western Europe and east Asia. In Tokyo, prime commercial real estate rose so high that it was sold by the square meter, at prices between $200,000 and $300,000 for an area 40 inches on a side.[24]

Interest rates also increased more rapidly than prices. During the

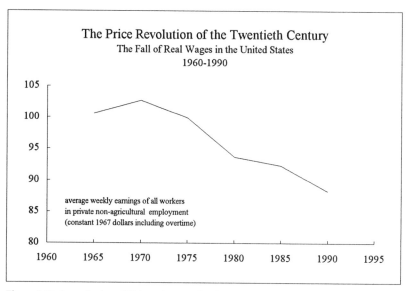

Figure 4.19 shows the long fall in real wages that began *circa* 1970, and continued with brief reversals to 1996. The price revolution of the twentieth century had differed from its predecessors in the rise of real wages before 1970. Thereafter, it conformed to the common pattern. Returns to labor fell for American workers, both blue collar and white collar, while returns to capital increased. The result was a growth of inequality that appears in figure 4.22 below. The source is the U.S. Bureau of Labor Statistics, *Employment and Earnings* (1992); *Statistical Abstract of the United States*, (1976), table 590); (1981), table 676; (1993), table 667.

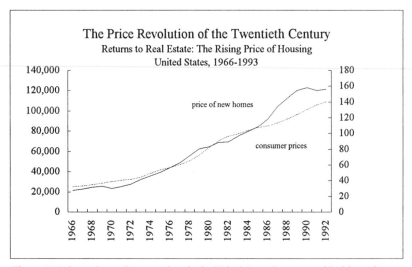

The Price Revolution of the Twentieth Century
Returns to Real Estate: The Rising Price of Housing
United States, 1966-1993

Figure 4.20 shows that real estate values in the United States kept pace with rising prices to 1985, then rose more rapidly. It compares the median sale price of new privately owned one-family houses in the United States, 1970-92, with consumer prices, indexed to 1982-84=100. The sources are *Statistical Abstract of the United States* (1993), tables 756, 1225; U. S. Dept. of Housing and Urban Development, *New One-Family Houses Sold* (1994).

early years of the twentieth century, interest had fluctuated more or less in proportion to the cost of living. In the 1960s, a different pattern appeared. Rates of interest on home mortgages trebled in fifteen years. In New England, mortgage rates rose from 5 per cent in 1965 to 16 per cent by 1979, a rate of increase half again higher than consumer prices in the same period. Consumer loans and credit-card interest went above 20 per cent.

In other price-revolutions, rates of interest had risen more rapidly than prices, but this time another factor was also at work. During the late twentieth century, interest rates were deliberately driven up as a way of managing the economy and controlling inflation. When prices accelerated, the central banks raised interest rates to depress demand. In periods of recession, interest rates were driven down to stimulate economic growth.

That, at least, was the idea. In practice the policy was distorted by a classic example of a "ratchet-effect," which allowed rates to move more freely up than down. When the Federal Reserve Board raised interest rates in the United States, retail bankers instantly passed on the increase to their borrowers. When the Fed lowered interest, the banks

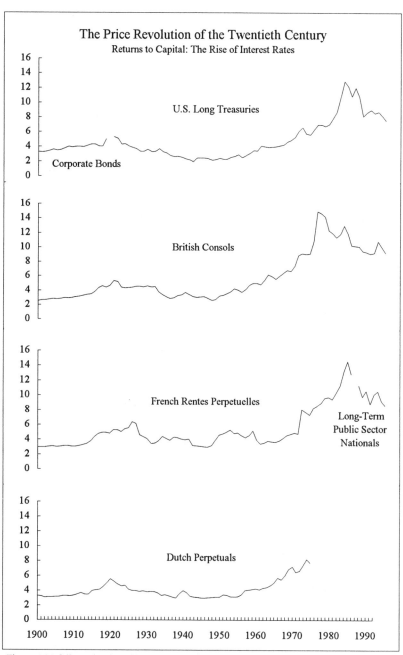

The Price Revolution of the Twentieth Century
Returns to Capital: The Rise of Interest Rates

U.S. Long Treasuries

Corporate Bonds

British Consols

French Rentes Perpetuelles

Long-Term
Public Sector
Nationals

Dutch Perpetuals

1900   1910   1920   1930   1940   1950   1960   1970   1980   1990

Figure 4.21 follows the rise of interest rates, which exceeded the pace of price inflation during the twentieth century. The sources are Homer, *History of Interest Rates,* 343-63, 416-17, 434-35, 448-49; *Statistical Abstract of the United States,* (1981-93); *Annuaire Statistique de la France* (1984-93); Great Britain, *Annual Abstract of Statistics* (1984-93).

were slower to follow suit. From 1970 to 1981, for example, the Federal Funds Rate rose from 7.2 to 16.4 percent, and the cost of a conventional fixed-rate, long-term mortgage went from 8.6 to 16.6 percent. But when the Federal Reserve reduced its discount rates from 9.2 to 3.5 percent (1989–92), the cost of fifteen-year fixed mortgages fell very little, from 9.7 to 7.8 percent. This ratcheting of rates reinforced the upward secular trend.

When real wages fell and real returns to capital increased, the social consequences were inexorable. Inequality increased. In the United States this trend began *circa* 1968.[25] Great fortunes grew steadily greater, and the upper middle class also flourished, while poverty and homelessness increased. The upper third of the nation gained ground; the lower two thirds fell behind. The work force was increas-

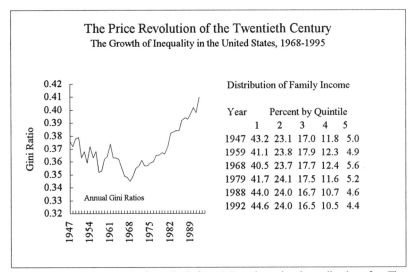

The Price Revolution of the Twentieth Century
The Growth of Inequality in the United States, 1968-1995

Distribution of Family Income

Year	Percent by Quintile				
	1	2	3	4	5
1947	43.2	23.1	17.0	11.8	5.0
1959	41.1	23.8	17.9	12.3	4.9
1968	40.5	23.7	17.7	12.4	5.6
1979	41.7	24.1	17.5	11.6	5.2
1988	44.0	24.0	16.7	10.7	4.6
1992	44.6	24.0	16.5	10.5	4.4

Figure 4.22 shows the growth of equality before 1968, and growing inequality thereafter. The graph includes annual Gini ratios for the distribution of income. The Gini ratio is a measure of concentration in which .00 represents perfect equality and .99 is perfect inequality (the upper percentile owns everything). The table to the right lists income shares for six specific years.

Data are from surveys by the Census Bureau, the oldest and best annual series on income distribution in the United States. They are useful as trend-indicators, but understate levels of inequality by omitting unrelated individuals (whose income is less equally distributed), and by excluding capital gains (which in 1992 raised the top quintile's share from 44.6 to 50 percent).

Sources are *Current Population Reports*, series P-60; *Historical Statistics of the United States* (1976), series G85-90; *Statistical Abstract of the United States* (various issues); and Lynn A. Karoly, "The Trend in Inequality among Families, Individuals, and Workers in the United States: Twenty-Five Year Perspective," in Sheldon Danziger and Peter Gottschalk, eds., *Uneven Tides: Rising Inequality in America* (New York, 1993), 27.

ingly polarized into two labor markets. The upper market offered high pay, fringe benefits, and long tenure; the lower market was for jobs with low pay, no fringes, and frequent layoffs.[26]

America in the late twentieth century was becoming two nations. In New York City, the contrast between wealth and poverty had always been great. Now it became increasingly visible, and more extreme than ever before. Studies by the author and his students found that after 1975, Gini ratios of wealth inequality reached their highest levels in four centuries of American history. Inequality of income also climbed steeply from 1968 to 1996.

On a bitter cold Saturday evening in the winter of 1986, the author remembers seeing crowds of opulent shoppers strolling on Madison Avenue, while homeless men and women in filthy rags lay silently on steam grates, next to battered shopping carts that held all their worldly goods. In 1989, Manhattan boutiques sold mink coats for four-year-old children ("a steal at $1,200"), while homeless children slept in the streets and subways. Similar sights were to be seen in other cities.[27]

Growing imbalances of another kind weakened the powers of governments and private institutions, when they were needed most. Fiscal and monetary disparities developed in public and private institutions. In the United States, President Ronald Reagan repeatedly overruled his advisors and refused to raise taxes, while he increased spending. As a consequence, the revenue of the federal government lagged far behind its expenditures, and the national debt increased at an unprecedented rate. In eight years, the Reagan administration increased the national debt more than all previous presidencies combined.[28]

The American national debt, large as it may have been, was only a small part of total indebtedness in the United States. While federal indebtedness soared above $1 trillion, private individual debt rose beyond $2 trillion, and debts owed by business corporations—the most profligate borrowers of all—exceeded $3 trillion. By 1987, the United States had become the world's leading debtor nation. This mountain of debt created dangerous imbalances in the American financial system. In Illinois, Texas, California and New York, some of the nation's biggest banks failed during the 1980s. Government intervention succeeded in preventing a general collapse, but by 1989 the American banking system had become the hostage of economic fortune. Any sort of setback—an international crisis, an economic recession, a rogue trader, or a run of bad weather—threatened major disaster.

Even more unstable than the banks were savings and loan associations. After deregulation, these institutions were so badly managed that by 1988 more than 500 were near bankruptcy, and the price of solvency was a huge taxpayer "bailout" which deepened Federal deficits. Investigators calculated that half of the losses were caused in part by fraud.

Instabilities also developed in international trade. The economic policies of the leading western nations differed profoundly in the 1980s. In the United States, the Reagan administration adopted "supply-side" policies which sought to stimulate the economy by deregulation, tax cuts and other incentives. Other nations such as Japan and Germany on the other hand, pursued a policy of slow growth, balanced budgets, strict regulation, and conservative management. These policies made a difference in rates of economic growth, which in turn distorted international trade. The American economy imported vast quantities of foreign goods, but found comparatively static or even shrinking markets abroad. As a consequence, imbalances increased in American foreign trade.

These trade imbalances contributed to monetary disorders. The Nixon administration had deregulated the international monetary system, destroying the Bretton Woods agreement in 1971–73, and allowing exchange rates to float. After it did so the international monetary system became increasingly unstable. The Reagan administration drove down the dollar relative to other currencies, in hopes of making American products more competitive. The dollar lost more than half of its value against several major currencies. Exports from the United States sluggishly revived, but Americans continued to import foreign products in large quantity, and their cost in devalued dollars was greater than before. The result in 1988 was the growth of imported inflation—a price surge led by rises in the cost of clothing (much of it made abroad) and other imported goods. American trade policy thus contributed directly to inflation and instability.

So also did monetary policy. Many government officials throughout the free world became monetarists in the 1970s. Major efforts were made by the Federal Reserve Board in the United States and the Bank of England in the United Kingdom to stabilize their disordered economies by regulating the money supply. These efforts were not successful, and actually increased instabilities. Economist Milton Friedman raged against the errors of his own disciples, repeatedly accusing the governors of the Federal Reserve System and the Bank of England of grievous incompetence. But John Kenneth Galbraith comments, "An economic policy, it might be pointed out in response, needs to be within the competence, however limited, of those available to administer it.'' A major problem was the complexity of factors that constrained monetary decision-making—domestic politics, international conditions, class interests, and social policy.[29]

Other sources of instability in the world included the acts of well-meaning economic planners who tried to stabilize the disordered world economy. Like generals trained to fight the last war, they tended to think in terms of past crises while new ones developed around them. A classic example was the Thatcher government in Britain. During the 1970s, that nation had suffered from chronic slow growth, soaring prices, massive unemployment and industrial disintegration. In 1986, recovery began at last. The British economy began to grow more rapidly than it had done for many years, but only a few months into the recovery, the British government became deeply concerned about the dangers of inflation. As the economy struggled painfully to its feet after decades of decline, an editorial in the *London Times* asked, ''Is the economy in danger of overheating?'' A few days later, the government deliberately drove up interest rates to ''cool'' it. The cause of their concern was the memory of double-digit inflation; the effect was to retard a fragile recovery and revive unemployment, in a nation where more than 15 percent of the work force were without a job.[30]

Economic instability in general, and inflation in particular, took a heavy toll in human suffering. Crime increased rapidly around the world during the period from 1965 to 1993. In the United States homicide rates rose in a series of surges that peaked in 1974, 1980, and 1991. These movements correlated very closely with rates of inflation. Similar patterns also appeared in theft and robbery. It should be understood that the primary cause was not inflation, but the stress that inflation caused. In the United States, crime had also tended to increase in the depth of the great depression, when prices were falling, but material stress was also very high. Nevertheless, in the penultimate stage of every price-revolution, price-surges caused crime-surges. This pattern appeared in the fourteenth century, the sixteenth century, the eighteenth century and again in the late twentieth century. Periods of price equilibrium, on the other hand, were marked by sustained decline in crime rates in the early years of each price-revolution.

Similar patterns appeared in the use of drugs and drink. In the United States, consumption of alcohol and the use of drugs both tended to rise during the 1960s and 1970s in a series of surges that correlated with the rate of inflation in consumer prices. Similar tendencies had

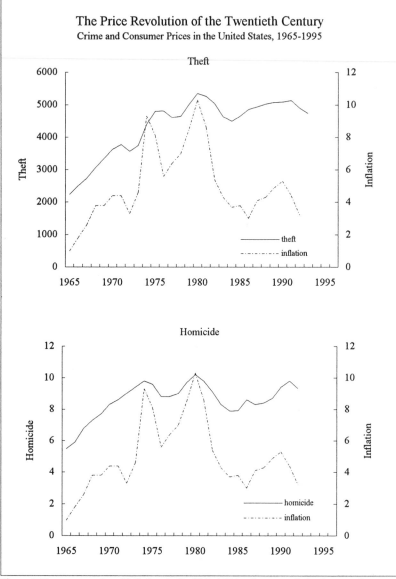

The Price Revolution of the Twentieth Century
Crime and Consumer Prices in the United States, 1965-1995

Figure 4.23 compares rates of inflation in the United States (more precisely, the annual percent increase in a fixed-weight price index of personal consumption expenditures), with rates of homicide (annual cases of murder and nonnegligent manslaughter known to the police per 100,000 population), and with annual rates of theft (theft, larceny and burglary known to the police, per 100,000 population). The sources include *Historical Statistics of the United States* (1976) series H972; *Statistical Abstract of the United States* (1976), table 248; (1981), table 293; (1988), table 263; (1993), table 300; and Federal Bureau of Investigation, *Uniform Crime Reports* (1993-94).

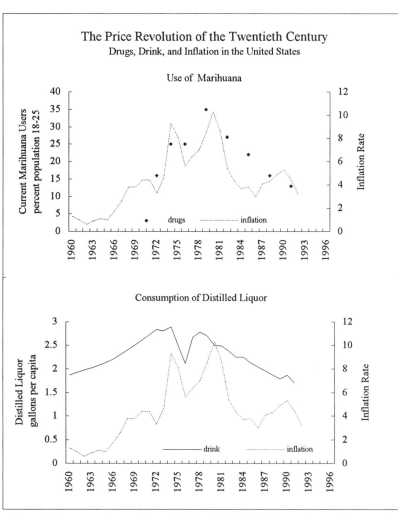

The Price Revolution of the Twentieth Century
Drugs, Drink, and Inflation in the United States

Use of Marihuana

Consumption of Distilled Liquor

Figure 4.24 compares the annual rate of inflation in the United States with annual consumption of distilled liquor per capita (population 18 and older); and also with the proportion of young adults (aged 18-25) who described themselves as "current users" of marihuana. Broadly similar trends (with variations) also appeared for the use of heroin, cocaine, hallucinogens, and inhalants; and for beer and wine. The source for liquor consumption is the Economic Research Service, U.S. Dept. of Agriculture; for drug use, the National Household Survey on Drug Abuse. Both are reported in *Statistical Abstract of the United States* (1981), tables 199, 1429; (1981), tables 180, 186; (1993), tables 208, 220. Readers should note that liquor consumption and drug use peaked when real incomes were falling rapidly, prices were surging and unemployment was increasing. A comparable surge in drinking (to the highest recorded levels in American history) occurred in similar circumstances during the climactic years of the eighteenth century price revolution . A long decline in alcohol consumption coincided with the Victorian equilibrium. See figure 3.30.

occurred in the United States during the price-revolution of the eighteenth century. The Victorian equilibrium, on the other hand, was marked by a sustained decline in alcohol consumption, and in the United States by a decline in drug use after 1830.

Another linkage appeared between price movements and family disruption. In the United States, the proportion of children born outside of marriage increased in proportion to the movement of consumer prices. This trend had also appeared in every earlier price-revolution for which evidence survives. It was very strong in the eighteenth century, and appeared also in fragmentary sources for the sixteenth century. Here again periods of price equilibrium were marked by countertrends. Material instability, and high rates of inflation placed heavy stresses on families as well as individuals. In short, the three trends that Americans identified as the most urgent social problems facing the nation—crime, drugs and family disruption—all correlated with rates of inflation.

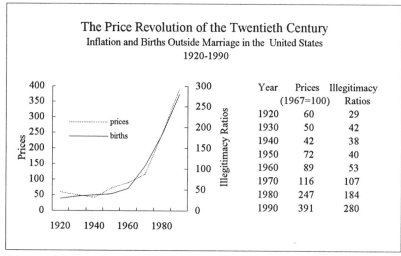

The Price Revolution of the Twentieth Century
Inflation and Births Outside Marriage in the United States
1920-1990

Year	Prices (1967=100)	Illegitimacy Ratios
1920	60	29
1930	50	42
1940	42	38
1950	72	40
1960	89	53
1970	116	107
1980	247	184
1990	391	280

Figure 4.25 compares annual illegitimacy ratios (births to unwed women per 1000 total live births in the United States) with consumer prices (1967=100). Sources include Daniel Scott Smith, "The Long Cycle in American Illegitimacy and Prenuptial Pregnancy," in Peter Laslett, Karla Osterveen, and Richard M. Smith, eds., *Bastardy and Its Comparative History* (Cambridge, 1980), 363-66; P. Cutright, "Illegitimacy in the United States, 1920-68," in R. Parke Jr., and C. F. Westoff, eds., *Demographic and Social Aspects of Population Growth* (Washington, 1972), 383; *Statistical Abstract of the United States* (1993), tables 101, 102, 756; *Historical Statistics of the United States* (1976), series E135.

❧ The Crisis of the Late Twentieth Century

In the 1980s and 1990s, material tensions approached the breaking point. Everywhere in the world, established orders came under heavy strain. Entire systems began to collapse, in a sequence of events that was similar to the climax of every other price-revolution since the Middle Ages. The crisis took different forms from one region to another, but every part of the world was caught up in it.

The people of Africa experienced the crisis in its most catastrophic form. Here the imbalances had become most extreme. After independence, the growth of population had accelerated sharply, and economic development had lagged far behind. In 1988, the twenty poorest nations of sub-Saharan Africa all had negative rates of economic growth. Per capita product fell from $324 to $270 a year. By 1990, much of Africa was in the grip of a classic Malthusian crisis, on a scale that Europe had not known since the fourteenth century.[31]

Sir William Osler observed that "humanity has but three great enemies: fever, famine and war." All were abroad in Africa. Famine stalked the Sahel. In Somalia, governments collapsed, order disintegrated; a large part of the nation was reduced to starvation, while warlords murdered relief workers who came to help. In Uganda and Zaire new epidemic diseases appeared in forms more terrible even than the plagues of the 14th century. In Rwanda and Burundi, tribal war led to mass murder of entire populations.

Even in the midst of crisis, there were countervailing tendencies. Nations such as Ghana built strong institutions and maintained them. The people of South Africa ended their system of apartheid, and struggled to construct a genuinely multiracial society. But in South Africa, half the work force was unemployed, and social stresses were very great. By 1996 Africa below the Sahara was in the grip of a general crisis as severe as any the world had ever seen.[32]

In eastern Europe, the general crisis caused one of the most dramatic reversals in modern history. In the 1980s, leaders of communist regimes found themselves under heavy stress in many ways at once. They felt themselves to be threatened from abroad by an American government that had become increasingly bellicose, and was spending heavily on armaments—even what appeared to be first-strike nuclear weapons, designed to "decapitate" command and control systems in the Soviet Union. At the same time, aging socialist economies were unable to maintain earlier rates of economic growth, and their citizens were demanding higher standards of living. The increasing ossification of the Soviet system coincided with the late stages of a global price-revolution, and with growing scarcities throughout the world. The result, as we have seen, was price-rationing in capitalist countries and state-rationing in the communist nations. Price-rationing was cruel in the west, but state-rationing was worse. It became grossly corrupt, and made a mockery of the ideals on which socialist systems were founded. The ruling few lived well; the many subsisted miserably. The rapid growth of corruption and inequality destroyed the moral legitimacy of the socialist states at the same time that the great wave eroded their material base. Any one of these problems alone was a serious threat to the standing system. All of them together were fatal.

The result was not reform but revolution. To the amazement of the West, Communist states suddenly began to fall apart. The first was Poland, where a union of shipyard workers who called themselves Solidarity founded a movement for national liberation. Their leader, Lech Walesa, declared in his Nobel speech of 1983, ''He who once became aware of the power of Solidarity and who breathed the air of freedom will not be crushed.''

Then to everyone's astonishment, the government of one of the world's two superpowers collapsed. In 1987 Mikhail Gorbachev tried to reform the Soviet system by *perestroika,* or restructuring. ''The new is knocking at every door,'' said Gorbachev. Soon it was coming in through the windows. His reforms ended in revolution, which destroyed the communist system. Marxism was discredited, and the Soviet Union disintegrated.[33]

In eastern Europe every other Marxist system came crashing down. A painful period followed. Old ethnic rivalries that had been suppressed by Communist regimes exploded into war. A new and very difficult economic transition from socialism to free market economics caused negative rates of growth, hyperinflation, disorder, crime, and severe suffering. But open institutions rapidly began to develop in eastern Europe. The new regimes were very shaky, and suffered from the same stresses that had brought down their predecessors. Their future remained in doubt.

In another part of the world, the crisis took a different form. From Afghanistan to Algeria, the many nations of Islam were in turmoil during the 1980s and 1990s. After World War II, modern secular elites had ruled them with a mix of Islamic and Western ideas. Rates of

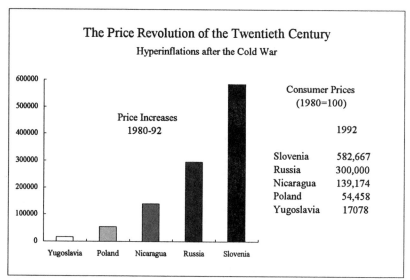

The Price Revolution of the Twentieth Century
Hyperinflations after the Cold War

Price Increases 1980-92

	Consumer Prices (1980=100) 1992
Slovenia	582,667
Russia	300,000
Nicaragua	139,174
Poland	54,458
Yugoslavia	17078

Figure 4.26 shows levels of hyperinflation in five former Socialist nations, 1992. Sources include United Nations, *Demographic Yearbook* (1993) 336-53; Grzegorz W. Kolodko, Danuta Gotz-Kozierkiewicz, and Elzbieta Skrzeszewska-Paczek, *Hyperinflation and Stabilization in Postsocialist Economies* (Boston and Dordrecht, 1992).

economic growth were high, but the increase of population was higher. With the exception of oil-rich Arab sheikdoms, Islam experienced the same economic stresses that were felt around the world. The price-revolution took its toll. The cost of living surged. Real wages fell. Inequalities increased. The teeming urban slums of this vast region were among the worst in the world.

Many in Islam blamed their troubles on western values. Fundamentalist movements began to sweep the Islamic world. One by one, the secular regimes were attacked, and some were destroyed. In 1979, Iran's Pahlevi dynasty fell from power. In 1981, Egypt's secular leader Anwar Sadat was assassinated. A secular socialist regime in Afghanistan was destroyed by a fundamentalist revolution. Islamic insurgencies developed in six of the former Soviet republics. In 1992, Algeria's Islamic Salvation Front won an election, but was prevented from taking power. The result was civil war, and the murder of hundreds of secular Algerian leaders. In 1993, Islamic fundamentalists in Turkey set fire to a hotel where secular leaders were meeting. Forty died in the flames. The Palestinian people turned to Islamic fundamentalism. Their aging secular leaders in desperation made peace with

Israel, but there was no peace. In 1996, the general crisis had barely begun in the Middle East. Its outcome was in doubt.

In Latin America during the Cold War, the superpowers had fostered the growth of client tyrannies both of the left and right. These predatory regimes made war upon their own people. The results included civil war in central America, a corrupt Communist dictatorship in Cuba, revolution from the right in Chile, the "disappearances" in Argentina, and the boat people of Haiti. The economics of tyranny in Latin America were catastrophic. The results were social exploitation, political corruption, and some of the worst hyperinflation in the modern world.

In the 1980s, new trends began to appear. As the Cold War ended, the superpowers withdrew their support of tyranny in Latin America. The people of the region rose against the systems that had oppressed them. One by one, the tyrannies began to collapse. By 1996, all but one Latin American nation were living under democracy and the rule of law. The general crisis in this region destroyed a system of tyranny and oppression. But here again the new and more open regimes were themselves very fragile, and the outcome was uncertain.

Even the strongest national economies showed signs of severe stress in the 1990s. A case in point was Japan, which for a generation had been perceived to be the most dynamic and successful economy in the world. In the early 1990s, signs of trouble began to appear. Increasing pressure was brought on Japan by competitors in Asia, and trading partners in America. A crisis of economic confidence developed within Japan itself. Labor costs were high; productivity gains lagged behind those of other nations. By 1994–95, Japan had negative rates of economic growth. The Japanese stock market fell sharply, and individual investors suffered huge losses. By 1995, the economic stress was so severe that the nation as a whole began to experience extended price deflation.

A growing spirit of cultural alienation began to develop in Japan, similar to that in other nations throughout the world. Religious cults grew rapidly. A militant Buddhist cult that called itself Aum Shinrikyo, who believed that the universe would end in 1997, began in their madness to manufacture a deadly nerve gas called Sarin. In March 1995, they released some of it in a crowded Japanese subway, killing eleven commuters and injuring hundreds more. The police struck quickly. Cult leader Shoko Asahara was arrested, but the incident brought home the vulnerability of modern industrial societies.

Supporters of Aum Shinrikyo included some of Japan's most highly educated young people who dedicated their talent and discipline to the destruction of their own nation. This terrible event could have happened anywhere. That it happened even in Japan demonstrated the depth and breadth of problems that existed in all industrial societies.

The events of the late twentieth century increasingly resembled price-revolutions in the past. Once again, world systems were in crisis. This was a crisis not only in the conventional sense of a moment when things go wrong, but also in the classical sense of a time when things hang in the balance.

When these words were written in the Spring of 1996, the outcome was very much in doubt, but some trends were clear enough. Environing conditions that had set the price-revolution in motion were changing rapidly. Rates of pouplation-growth were plummeting throughout the world. Total numbers of people continued to rise, but rates of gain were coming down. By 1996, some nations approached zero-growth. Other nations from the West Indies to eastern Europe had negative growth.[34]

As the pace of population-growth diminished, rates of inflation also fell in the 1990s, with a speed that took experts by surprise. Inflation forecasts were repeatedly revised downward, but not fast enough to keep pace with the new trends. In 1994, economic forecasters around the world swallowed hard and predicted that prices would rise only 3.5 percent the next year. In fact, they rose 2.6 percent. A journalist who studied the accuracy of economic forecasts observed in 1995, "Over the past couple of years, inflation has been consistently lower than expected in Britain and America."[35]

So strong was the decline of prices by 1996 that several leading economists asserted that the age of inflation was at an end. American economist Lester Thurow called it an "extinct volcano." British economist Roger Bootle wrote thoughtfully about "the death of inflation" and a coming "zero-era." Japanese economists and businessmen spoke more ominously of "price destruction." These judgments were premature. Prices continued to rise in most nations, though at a slower pace. Inflation was still institutionalized in economic systems.[36]

On the other side, central bankers continued to act on the belief that inflation was still the greatest danger. When economic systems showed signs of reviving, they raised interest rates, slowed expansion of the money supply, and "cooled" economies in other ways. For many years, central bankers had functioned as heroic inflation-fighters.

Reflexive inflation-fighting was also institutionalized in economic systems—more so than inflation itself.

The results were the same as before. In 1996, inflation was declining, but far from dead. Anti-inflationary policies added to the miseries that inflation itself had caused. The consequences continued in the 1990s: falling real wages, rising inequality, diminished economic growth, and increasing instability in political and social systems.

All that was happening in the Spring of 1996, when this book went to press. The end of the story has not been written. It could end in many different ways. So fragile were the major trends that contingencies of various kinds threatened to disrupt them. A major war in the Middle East or eastern Europe or some other trouble spot could reignite inflation. A collapse of overvalued security markets could cause panic, depression and deep deflation.

In a time of crisis, when so many possibilities were hanging in the narrow balance, much depended on the wisdom of our choices. Wise choices in turn required intelligent leaders and informed electorates. But intelligence and wisdom and even the information that we needed most were not much in evidence in national capitals throughout the world.

As the great wave of the twentieth century approached its climax, the condition of many nations called to mind a Melville novel, or perhaps a Masefield poem. The ship of state raced onward, through high seas and heavy weather. All sails were set, and her helm was lashed to the course that she had long been steering. On the quarterdeck, several parties of myopic navigators squinted dimly at the dark clouds behind them. Somewhere below was their amiable captain, who wanted mainly to be loved by his sullen crew. The first-class passengers amused themselves in their opulent cabins, knowing little of the suffering in steerage, and nothing of the dangers that surrounded them. On deck amidships, a lone bookish traveler turned his collar against the wind, leaned precariously across the lee rail, and tried to read the signs in the sky.

CONCLUSION
&. Between Past and Future

Chaos, Cosmos! Cosmos, Chaos!
    Who can tell how all will end?
Read the wide world's annals, you,
    and take their wisdom for your friend.

Forward then, but still remember how
    the course of Time will swerve,
Crook and turn upon itself in many a
    backward streaming curve.

—Alfred Tennyson[1]

WORKS ON THIS subject often end with a book of Revelations, or at least a chapter of Jeremiah, in which the reader is warned that we are heading for disaster—unless the author's ideas are speedily enacted. These dark prophecies find a growing market with modern readers, who appear to have an insatiable appetite for predictions of their own impending doom.

Even when prophecies fail, they are merely updated and sell briskly once again. They call to mind the career of the Reverend Samuel Miller, a Baptist minister in nineteenth century New England, who predicted that the world would end no later than December 31, 1843. When the fatal day approached, the Prophet discovered an error in his computations. He announced that the last trump had been rescheduled to March 21, 1844. His followers grew to many hundreds. They donned special "resurrection robes" and gathered to await the day of judgment. But Samuel Miller found another mistake in his arithmetic, and postponed the end of the world once again, this time to October 22, 1844. The faithful were undeterred. Their numbers rose so high that on the appointed day, business came to a halt in parts of New

235

England. But Samuel Miller revised his numbers yet again and went on prophesying until his end arrived—without warning—in 1849.[2]

Those who believe that the economic future has been revealed to them should remember the story of Samuel Miller. They might also reflect on the wisdom of John Kenneth Galbraith, who observes that "the most common qualification of the economic forecaster is not in knowing, but in not knowing that he does not know. His greatest advantage is that all predictions, right or wrong, are soon forgotten."[3]

Historians have special reasons for caution, for they will recall the fate of earlier attempts to know the future. They also have problems enough with the past. Further, they understand that predictions fail not because historical knowledge is limited, but because of the nature of history itself.

We are not merely the objects of history but also its agents. The future is determined partly by free choices that people willfully make, often in unexpected ways. These human choices are not always rational. They flow from hopes and fears, truths and errors, memories and dreams. They are unpredictable, and sometimes unimaginable, before they are made.

The history of prices offers many examples. No economic forecaster could have predicted (or even imagined) that a president as conservative as Richard Nixon would become a convert to Keynesian economics in 1971, or that a president as liberal as Jimmy Carter would adopt conservative fiscal policies in 1978, or that any president in his right mind would have embraced the "supply-side" nostrums called Reaganomics in 1981. Each of these individual choices made a difference in the history of prices. All of them were freely made—sometimes defiantly against reason, interest and the economic odds. As long as this is so, history will never be a predictive science.[4]

Nevertheless, if powers of prophecy are denied to us, there are other important links between the past and future. The study of history can never tell us with certainty what will happen next, but it gives us the benefit of much hard-won experience in the past. It also helps us to know our intentions for the future. To those ends, let us review the patterns that we have found, and think of the choices before us.

❧ Price Revolutions: Structural Similarities

This inquiry began with a problem of historical description about price movements in the modern world. Its primary purpose was to describe the main lines of change through the past eight hundred years. The central finding may be summarized in a sentence. We found evidence of four price-revolutions since the twelfth century: four very long waves of rising prices, punctuated by long periods of comparative price-equilibrium. This is not a cyclical pattern. Price revolutions have no fixed and regular periodicity. Some were as short as eighty years; others as long as 180 years. They differed in duration, velocity, magnitude, and momentum.

At the same time, these long movements shared several properties in common. All had a common wave-structure, and started in much the same way. The first stage was one of silent beginnings and slow advances. Prices rose slowly in a period of prolonged prosperity. Magnitudes of increase remained within the range of previous fluctuations. At first the long wave appeared to be merely another short-run event. Only later did it emerge as a new secular tendency.

The novelty of the new trend consisted not only in the fact of inflation but also in its form. The pattern of price-relatives was specially revealing. Food and fuel led the upward movement. Manufactured goods and services lagged behind. These patterns indicated that the prime mover was excess aggregate demand, generated by an acceleration of population growth, or by rising living standards, or both.

These trends were the product of individual choices. Men and women deliberately chose to marry early. They freely decided to have more children, because material conditions were improving and the world seemed a better place to raise a family. People demanded and at first received a higher standard of living, because there was an expanding market for their labor. The first stage of every price-revolution was marked by material progress, cultural confidence, and optimism for the future.

The second stage was very different. It began when prices broke through the boundaries of the previous equilibrium. This tended to happen when other events intervened—commonly wars of ambition that arose from the hubris of the preceding period. Examples included the rivalry between emperors and popes in the thirteenth century; the state-building conflicts of the late fifteenth and early sixteenth centuries; the dynastic and imperial struggles of the mid-eighteenth century; and the world wars of the twentieth century. These events sent prices surging up and down again, in a pattern that was both a symptom and a cause of instability. The consequences included political disorder, social disruption, and a growing mood of cultural anxiety.

The third stage began when people discovered the fact of price-inflation as a long-term trend, and began to think of it as an inexorable condition. They responded to this discovery by making choices that drove prices still higher. Governments and individuals expanded the supply of money and increased the velocity of its circulation. In each successive wave, price-inflation became more elaborately institutionalized.

A fourth stage began as this new institutionalized inflation took hold. Prices went higher, and became highly unstable. They began to surge and decline in movements of increasing volatility. Severe price shocks were felt in commodity movements. The money supply was alternately expanded and contracted. Financial markets became unstable. Government spending grew faster than revenue, and public debt increased at a rapid rate. In every price-revolution, the strongest nation-states suffered severely from fiscal stresses: Spain in the sixteenth century, France in the eighteenth century, and the United States in the twentieth century.

Other imbalances were even more dangerous. Wages, which had at first kept up with prices, now lagged behind. Returns to labor declined while returns to land and capital increased. The rich grew richer. People of middling estates lost ground. The poor suffered terribly. Inequalities of wealth and income increased. So also did hunger, homelessness, crime, violence, drink, drugs, and family disruption.

These material events had cultural consequences. In literature and the arts, the penultimate stage of every price-revolution was an era of dark visions and restless dreams. This a time of lost faith in institutions. It was also a period of desperate search for spiritual values. Sects and cults, often very angry and irrational, multiplied rapidly. Intellectuals turned furiously against their environing societies. Young people, uncertain of both the future and the past, gave way to alienation and cultural anomie.

Finally, the great wave crested and broke with shattering force, in a cultural crisis that included demographic contraction, economic collapse, political revolution, international war and social violence. These events relieved the pressures that had set the price-revolution in motion. The first result was a rapid fall of prices, rents and interest. This short but very sharp deflation was followed by an era of equilibrium that persisted for seventy or eighty years. Long-term inflation ceased. Prices stabilized, then declined further, and stabilized once more. Real wages began to rise, but returns to capital and land fell.

The recovery of equilibrium had important social consequences.

At first, inequalities continued to grow, as a lag effect of the preceding price revolution. But as the new dynamics took hold, inequality began to diminish. Times were better for laborers, artisans, and ordinary people. Landowners were hard pressed, but economic conditions improved for most people. Families grew stronger. Crime rates fell. Consumption of drugs and drink diminished. Foreign wars became less frequent and less violent, but internal wars of unification became more common and more successful.

Each period of equilibrium had a distinct cultural character. All were marked in their later stages by the emergence of ideas of order and harmony such as appeared in the Renaissance of the twelfth century, the Italian Renaissance of the *quattrocento,* the Enlightenment of the early eighteenth century, and the Victorian era.

After many years of equilibrium and comparative peace, population began to grow more rapidly. Standards of living improved. Prices, rents and interest started to rise again. As aggregate demand mounted, a new wave began. The next price-revolution was not precisely the same, but it was similar in many ways. As Mark Twain observed, history does not repeat itself, but it rhymes.

❧ Sequential Differences

Even as all price-revolutions shared a common wave-structure, they differed from one another in duration, magnitude, and range. These differences were not random variations. They comprised a coherent process of historical development from one great wave to the next. Since the twelfth century, price-revolutions have succeeded one another in a continuous sequence of historical change.

Several sequential patterns of this sort can be identified. The most obvious was a change in rates of change. From one wave to the next, average annual rates of price-inflation tended to increase geometrically: 0.5 percent in the price-revolution of the thirteenth century; a little above 1 percent in the very long wave of the sixteenth century; nearly 2 percent in the shorter wave of the eighteenth century; and at least 4 percent in the price-revolution of the twentieth century. This acceleration was caused by the expansion of markets, and by the institutionalization of price-increases.[5]

Second, as rates of change increased, a larger proportion of total price gains became concentrated in the later stages of each price-revolution. In the medieval price-revolution, absolute magnitudes of gain were comparatively even in their distribution through time. In the price-revolution of the twentieth century, more than half of the total increase in prices from 1896 to 1996 happened after 1970. Nine-tenths of it came after 1945. This pattern was caused by acceleration in rates of price-change from one price-revolution to another.[6]

Third, the range of annual fluctuations diminished from one wave to the next. In the medieval price-revolution, these gyrations were very violent and dangerous, mainly as a consequence of changing harvest conditions. Food prices tended also to be less stable when people lived closer to the margin of subsistence. In each subsequent price-revolution, those movements became less extreme, and fluctuations were damped down. The growth of production created surpluses, which functioned as price-cushions. The expansion of markets and the improvement of communications also diminished the disruptive effect of local scarcities and seasonal oscillations.

Fourth, from one wave to another, the final stage of cultural crisis became progressively less catastrophic. The medieval price-revolution ended in the massive famines and epidemics of the fourteenth century. The second wave culminated in the general crisis of the seventeenth century. This was the only period after the Black Death when the population of Europe declined, but not as much as in the fourteenth century. The third wave had its climax in an age of world revolutions (1776–1815), a time of many troubles, but population continued to increase. The price-revolution of the twentieth century has yet to reach its climax.

Fifth, as each successive crisis grew less severe in demographic terms, it became more sweeping in its social consequences. Every general crisis caused a social revolution, and the radicalism of these events increased through time. The crisis of the fourteenth century did much to end villeinage in western Europe, and to transform societies based on conquest and subjugation into customary systems of orders and estates. The general crisis of the seventeenth century transformed political systems and expanded the rule of law in Britain, America and Europe. The revolutionary crisis of the eighteenth and early nineteenth centuries (1776–1815) made public institutions in America and Europe more responsive to the will of the people, and more protective of their individual rights. It also transformed systems of social orders into classes. The great wave of the twentieth century has not yet reached its end, but it has already caused the collapse of totalitarian systems of the left (eastern Europe) and the right (Latin America), as well as sweeping social and economic reforms in many nations. Every general crisis in modern history has improved the condition of ordinary people. It has also enlarged ideas of human dignity, freedom, and the rule of law. This tendency has become more powerful in each successive wave.

To summarize, each price-revolution developed through five stages: slow beginnings in a period of high prosperity; a period of surge and decline; a time of discovery and institutionalization; an era of growing imbalances and increasing instability; and finally a general crisis. The climax was followed by a fall of prices, recovery of stability, and a long period of comparative price equilibrium. The social and cultural impact of these movements changed from one great wave to another. Velocity increased and variability declined. Each successive price-revolution became less catastrophic in its demographic consequences, but more sweeping in its social impact.

❧ Problems of Cause: Seven Models

These descriptive patterns raise many causal problems. What set the price-revolutions in motion? What processes shaped their distinctive structure? Fernand Braudel, one of the few historians to consider these questions, pronounced them "impossible" to solve. Certainly it is true that conventional models of explanation in history and economics do not work well when applied to this problem.[7]

Seven causal models are dominant in the historical literature: monetarist, Malthusian, Marxist, agrarian, neoclassical, environmental, and historicist. All have much to teach us, but none has solved the problem of explaining the origin and development of price-revolutions in a rounded way.[8]

The most simple and straight-forward explanation of price-revolutions is the monetarist model, which holds that price levels are determined by the quantity and velocity of money in circulation. This explanation has major strengths, and has made an important contribution to knowledge. Much research has established beyond doubt that monetary factors make a major difference in price levels. But when monetarist models are introduced as the first cause of price-revolutions, difficulties appear. The timing is never quite right. The price-revolution of the sixteenth century, for example, began as early as 1475, thirty years before the first American treasure reached Europe, and fifty years before it began to flow in quantity.[9]

Further, a monetarist model cannot account for many aspects of a price-revolution. It alone cannot explain the movement of price-relatives, or the disparity between prices and wage movements, or the difference in returns to labor and capital. It does not help us to understand why prices and interest rates tend to rise together in long inflations—the Gibson paradox, which is a major problem for monetarists.

A monetary explanation cannot tell us why people choose to expand the money supply in the first place, or why they do so in some periods more than others. Increases in the supply of money are not suddenly visited upon history as Zeus came to Danae, in a shower of gold. People deliberately decide to change the size of the money supply, for one reason or another. In the history of these events there is always a prior cause.

Moreover, the monetarist model works better for some periods than others. It does well for middle and later stages of price revolutions, but badly for early stages, and for periods of price equilibrium. Its explanatory power increases when it is used as an historical variable rather than a theoretical constant. In some periods, monetary forces are strong and overriding. In others they are weak and secondary.

Altogether, Wilhelm Abel observes from long and careful study that "Long-term trends in the price of grain . . . cannot be explained adequately by fluctuations in the circulation of money, though that has been attempted since the time of Jean Bodin (1568). Even when improved forms of the simple quantity theory are summoned to the rescue, the discrepancies of time apparent in the course of the price movements remain inexplicable."[10]

In short, a monetary model is a necessary and important part of any causal explanation of price-revolutions, but it is not a sufficient explanation. Monetarism alone won't do.

A second causal explanation is the Malthusian model, which centers on imbalances between economic and demographic growth. Here again, the approach of Malthus has much to teach us. Correlations between price-movements and population-growth are strong in most periods of world history. Many historians (not all of them) believe that a Malthusian model closely fits the evidence of the medieval price-revolution, and especially the general crisis of the fourteenth century.

Some apply it with equal confidence to the general crisis in Europe during the seventeenth century, and to Africa in the twentieth century. But most scholars also agree that for the period after Malthus published his *Essays on Population* (1798), his model no longer fits the historical facts in the Western world. From the late eighteenth century to our own time, European crises tended to develop from structural imbalances and systemic instabilities long before Malthusian "positive checks" came into play. This difference suggests that population pressures operated in conjunction with other factors that a Malthusian model alone does not consider. Malthusian (and neo-Malthusian) approaches help to make sense of many aspects of the problem. Like monetary models, they are a necessary part of any explanation of price-revolutions, but insufficient to the general explanatory task at hand.

Third, Marxist explanations are still favored by many academic historians in America and Europe, even after the collapse of Marxism as a ruling ideology throughout the world. At first glance, some parts of the wave-pattern seem to fit a Marxist frame. Changes in systems of production had a major impact on movements of prices, wages, rents and interest. Also, the imbalances that developed in each great wave rose in part from class-differences, and engendered class-conflicts in their turn. These patterns were strong in the late medieval and early modern eras. Many scholars, Marxist and non-Marxist alike, believe that the climax of the medieval price-revolution was part of a "crisis of feudalism" and a shift from one stage of production to another. Others have offered similar interpretations for the price-revolution of the sixteenth century, and some have tried to make sense of the long wave of the 20th century as a crisis of capitalism.

On closer scrutiny, however, major difficulties appear in the Marxist model. Tests of chronology show that the four waves of the modern era do not sit comfortably with the three systems of production that dominate Marxist analysis. Patterns such as "price scissors" which Marxist scholars believe to have been caused uniquely by the "crisis of feudalism" also appeared in every price-revolution. Events in the twentieth century that Marxists called the crisis of capitalism were a total catastrophe for socialism. Capitalist systems survived them; socialist systems collapsed.

Further, much of the historic role that Marxists assign to systems of production belongs to structures of exchange, and other material and cultural relations. Altogether, price revolutions and price-equilibria do not correlate with Marxist models of change in the organization of the means of production.

Marxist models remain heuristically useful in many ways. They prompt us to remember that history is about all humanity, not merely small elites. They remind us that class-relations are an important part of our problem, and they teach us to think in terms of long processes and large systems. But in conceptual terms, Marxist models are too narrow. In terms of chronology and historical fact, they are also mistaken.

A fourth model seeks an explanation for long waves in rhythms of agricultural production. The leading work is that of Ernest Labrousse, who argued that price fluctuations in the French economy were driven by the size of harvests, in which short crops sent up the price of grain, reduced the income of farmers, and caused the poor to spend a larger part of their meager wages on bread. These factors were thought to have caused the market for industrial goods to shrink, and to have created a general depression, which continued until better harvests brought lower prices and recovery. Other agrarian models of high complexity have been developed by the great German scholar Wilhelm Abel.[11]

This approach has many strengths. It works best for the time and place where they were invented: the history of rural Europe from the sixteenth to the eighteenth centuries. It helps to explain the movement of price-relatives, rents and wages in every price-revolution, and adds to our understanding of that distinctive combination of hard times and high prices which occurred in every general crisis.

But it does not work for the great wave of the twentieth century, or for North and South America in the early modern period. Another major weakness is its difficulty in explaining why harvest variations had very different consequences according to their timing within each great wave. Scarcities in early stages of a price-revolution, and in periods of price-equilibrium, did not have results as catastrophic as in periods of general crisis. The short harvests of the 1690s, though very severe, had nothing like the consequences of scarcity in the 1780s. To account for these disparities, one must move beyond the boundaries of an agrarian model.[12]

Yet another explanation might be sought in models of neoclassical economics, and especially in its laws of supply and demand. This approach is helpful in many ways. The rise and fall of prices may be understood as commonly the result of changes in levels of aggregate demand. Monetary models also have a neoclassical foundation, in their organizing idea of money as a commodity whose value fluctuates inversely with its supply. In these and other ways, neoclassical models have much to teach us about how a price-system works.

They are less successful in explaining why its workings change from one historical period to another. They help us to think clearly about price-movements as a function of supply and demand, but they do not explain why demand changes. They can help to model a great wave, but they cannot tell us why it begins, or why it develops its distinctive wave-structure, or why it suddenly comes to an end.

A French scholar observes from long experience that no historical problem of the *long durée* can be solved by economics alone. One might equally say that it cannot be solved by history alone. History and economics must advance together, if either is to advance at all. The nomothetic methods of economic theory and the idiographic tools of historical inquiry are complementary.[13]

Another approach to our problem is broadly ecological. It holds that great waves were set in motion by changes in environmental conditions. Many scholars through the years have tried to link changes in the earth's climate and solar activity to price movements and general crises. Recently in climate-history, there has been much learned discussion of a cold period in the fourteenth century, of the Maunder minimum and solar flares during the seventeenth century, and of the "Little Ice Age" in the late eighteenth and early nineteenth centuries.[14]

All of these episodes appear at first sight to correlate with our major periods of crisis in Europe, and also in Asia, Africa, America and Oceania. Earlier global crises of the same sort have also been identified by ancient historians and paleontologists. Further research may reinforce them.

But in the modern period, ecological models run into difficulties when they are studied in detail. Chronology is the critical problem. The European crisis of the seventeenth century, for example, overlapped with the period of the Maunder minimum, but began fifty years earlier. In the late seventeenth, eighteenth and nineteenth centuries, the several distinct cold periods that are collectively called the Little Ice Age show a strong correlation with short-run fluctuations, but not with secular trends. In 1979, a gathering of meteorologists, paleobotanists, chemists, physicists and historians at Harvard University generally concluded that changes in climate do not correlate closely with long-term economic change.[15]

Beyond doubt, climatic events were precipitants of crisis in 1315, in the 1590s and in the 1780s. They also functioned as powerful cata- lysts at various points in the wave sequence. But in light of present knowledge, environmental changes do not appear to have been the prime-movers of price movements in the modern era. This may change with further research, but at present ecological models are more useful in explaining fluctuations around the central trend, than in accounting for the trend itself.

Finally, there are historicist models which seek to explain things in their particulars. They begin with the idea that each historical event is unique, and seek to explain it in terms of special circumstances, distinctive details, and inner complexities. When historicists try to put the pieces together, they use a method of aggregation without general- ization. The classic example was British historian H. A. L. Fisher who asserted that all of history is one great fact, about which there can be no generalization.

On the subject of price revolutions, historicists have helped us to understand that each great wave was a unique event, and that details made a difference. But historicism cannot explain a general pattern that has recurred many times since the middle ages.

Each of these seven causal strategies helps to explain important aspects of our problem. None suffices to resolve it. The explanatory task at hand requires another approach which might combine their strengths and correct their weaknesses. Somehow, such an explanation should integrate ecological, demographic, social, monetarist and eco- nomic factors. It should do so without dissolving into an indiscriminate pluralism, or degenerating into *ad hoc* explanations. It should account for both similarities and differences between price-revolutions. How might this be done?

✎ Another Causal Model: Autogenous Change

One promising possibility centers on the internal dynamics of price- revolutions themselves. It begins with an idea of a culture as a complex web of causal relationships which link material structures, cultural values, and individual actions. It also builds upon an idea of history as a sequence of contingencies, in the special sense of people making choices, and choices making a difference. Two vital elements in this approach are ideas of contingency and choice.

Let us begin in the late stages of a price equilibrium, when prices are more or less stable, real wages are rising, rents and interest rates are falling, social stability is increasing, material conditions are improving, and cultural expectations are growing brighter. In these periods, people begin to make major choices in different ways. They decide to marry earlier. They choose to have more children. They also make economic decisions in a different way, expanding the scale of their ambition and the scope of their activity. These choices are made not entirely or even primarily for reasons that can be explained in material terms, but because of changes in cultural mood and expectation.

The result of these choices is that aggregate demand grows more rapidly than supply. As it does so, the general price-level begins to rise. Some prices increase faster than others. Food, energy, and shelter lead the trend, partly because their supply is less elastic, and partly because demand grows more rapidly for life's necessities. The prices of industrial products increase more slowly, because they are more easily produced in greater volume. Price relatives show their distinctive patterns. Rents and interest rates begin to climb, as demand grows for land and money. Real wages keep up at first but then begin to lag behind, partly because population growth has expanded the supply of labor, and partly because the dynamics of change favor people with positional goods.

For a time these trends develop within the same range of fluctuations as in the preceding period of equilibrium. When they move beyond that range, and become visible as a new secular trend, individuals and institutions make another set of decisions. By and large, they respond to inflation by making individual and collective choices that cause more inflation. The stock of money is deliberately enlarged to meet growing demand. Capitalists charge higher rates. Landlords raise the rent. Real wages fall farther behind. The cultural mood begins to change in a new way; there is a growing sense of material uncertainty and moral confusion.

The combined effect of these tendencies is to create growing imbalances within the cultural system. As returns to capital rise, and returns to labor fall, inequality increases in the distribution of wealth and income. These inequalities in turn create a problem of poverty and homelessness. They put a heavy strain on social relationships and intensify class conflicts.

This leads to another set of choices. Everyone tries to find a measure of protection or to profit from changing circumstances. People who possess power and wealth are best able to do so. For example, they demand tax-reductions and often receive them. Taxation becomes more regressive and public revenues fall behind expenditures. Fiscal imbalances develop. Public deficits increase, the cost of debt service rises, and governments are reduced to near-insolvency, and the springs of public action are weakened. The cultural mood changes once more, with a growing awareness of limits on human effort and a spreading sense of social pessimism—even social despair. Other imbalances begin to have similar consequences as people exercise choices in different ways.

These imbalances create instabilities. Prices surge and decline in swings of increasing amplitude. Markets of many kinds—capital markets, commodity markets, labor markets—become dangerously unstable. Production and productivity decline or stagnate, while prices continue to rise; together these trends create stagflation. Political instability increases, and with it comes social disorder, internal violence and international war. The cultural system becomes dangerously unstable; internal conflicts of value and identity grow more intense.

Things are specially hard for young people, who find it difficult to get good jobs, or start a family. They also have choices to make. Some decide to have children anyway, outside of marriage. The proportion of children born and raised outside marriage increases rapidly. Other young people turn against social institutions, or merely turn away from them. Crime increases. The consumption of drugs and drink goes up. People of age and wealth have very different experiences, and do not understand why their own children are so troubled. But the young and the poor, especially the working poor, are driven to despair.

Finally, a triggering event that might have caused a minor disturbance in another era creates a major crisis. The trigger itself might be a change in the weather—the heavy rains of the early fourteenth century, or the cold years of the eighteenth century, or drought in the twentieth century. It might be an epidemic or a war. It could be a malevolent monarch, or an incompetent president, or an irresponsible demagogue, or a dictator who is driven only by his own malevolence. More often—and most dangerously—it is a combination of disasters. Whatever they might be, these small events have sweeping consequences. They disrupt a cultural system that is dangerously unstable.

They tend to do so by straining the social fabric in several different directions at once. Established social fabrics are very strong and tough, and tenacious of their being. They are also highly resilient, and commonly deal successfully with stress. The danger comes when they are stressed in several ways at once. This is what happens in moments of general crisis. The result is a protracted period of political disorder, social conflict, economic disruption, demographic contraction and cultural despair.

This general crisis relieves the pressures that set the price revolution in motion. Afterward, the economic trends run in reverse. Demand falls and price-deflation follows. Real wages begin to rise. Interest and rent fall. Inequality continues for a time (the lag of effect of the last change-regime). There are other lag-effects, as people continue for a time to think in terms of the preceding period. But the new trends quickly take hold. As they do so, equality increases a little, or at least ceases to grow greater. A period of equilibrium develops, and the cultural mood becomes more positive. Population increases, and aggregate demand begins to grow. The pattern begins again.

Each of these stages develops from a sequence of choices that are framed by environing conditions. The choices are freely made, but they become part of the context for the next set of decisions. The interaction of individual choices have collective consequences which nobody intends or desires. This is specially so in the later stages of price revolutions. In a free market, individual responses to inflation commonly cause more inflation. Individual defenses against economic instability cause an economy to become more unstable.

This process might be called the irrationality of the market. It is so in the sense that it converts rational individual choices into collective results that are profoundly irrational. Far from being a benign or beneficent force, the market when left to itself is an unstable system that has repeatedly caused the disruption of social and economic systems in the past eight hundred years.

In important ways, the structure of this contingent process has changed through time. The balance between individual and institutional choices has tended to shift, and causal patterns have become more complex. The earliest wave in the thirteenth century was primarily a matter of population pressing against resources. In the second wave, monetary factors became more powerful and added strongly to demographic pressures—a tendency that Bodin and others were quick to notice. The third wave added yet another layer of institutional complexity in structural determinants such as the Speenhamland system, the banking system and securities exchanges, and also more complex dynamics of population growth and accelerating economic growth. The fourth wave contributed other layers of institutional complexity in regulatory floors without ceilings, administered prices, competitive inflation, wage-price spirals, other things.

This pattern of growing structural complexity may be understood as a process of increasing human intervention, with both negative and positive results. One consequence was that price-revolutions tend to move more rapidly. Another was that their destructive consequences are much reduced. Magnitudes of demographic disaster diminished from price-revolution to the next, but the intensity of social conflict increased. The structure of contingency is an historical variable, but it always operates as a web of expanding individual choices within a cultural frame.

These complex processes, and the great waves that they set in motion, have had many consequences. In material terms, they have been a powerful determinant of wealth and income distribution—not the only factor, but one of the more important. The later stages of every price-revolution were always a time when inequalities of wealth and income increased, primarily because of disparities in the movements of prices, wages, rents, interest and production. The late years of every price-equilibrium were marked by comparative stability in the distribution of wealth and income, and sometimes by the growth of equality.[16]

Other social consequences appear in rates of violent crime. In the late stages of every price-revolution, and especially during general crises, rates of homicide increase sharply in surges that correlate closely with price movements. The growth of crime in our own time has commonly been explained in other ways—notably the failure of law-enforcement, and the decline of moral values. These answers are tautological. The question is, why does enforcement fail? Why do moral values decline? An answer may be found in material and cultural conditions, and in processes of contingency and choice. In the latter stages of every great wave, price movements and crime rates are so intimately linked that they appear to move as statistical shadows.

Yet another social result appears in indicators of family decay, especially births outside of marriage. In general these trends rise during price-revolutions, and fall during periods of price equilibrium. The association is very strong in the twentieth century, and reaches as far into the past as the evidence runs. It has been observed and measured from the sixteenth century to the present.

The great waves, and the deeper movements which they represented, also have had a major impact on the main lines of cultural history. The timing of major trends in intellectual history coincided closely with the rhythm of price revolutions. Periods of price-equilibrium also correlate with the renaissance of the twelfth century, the renaissance of the fifteenth century, the enlightenment, and the Victorian era. The causal relationship was complex. Intellectual trends were certainly not mechanical reflexes of price movements. Rather, both the history of prices and ideas were parallel expressions of cultural conditions in the broadest sense, and of the individual choices conditioned by those cultures, that set the great waves in motion and were the instrument of their development.

This model understands price-revolutions as autogenous, self-generating processes. It is an historical idea, in each stage contains within itself the seed of the next, and the one after that. The causal sequence is not fixed and rigid in its determinism. It develops as a chain of individual choices, and as a consequence its structure changes from one great wave to the next.

❧ Retrospect and Prospect

Still the hardest questions remain. Where are we heading? What does the future hold for us? The study of history does not give us the answers to these questions. It cannot reveal the future. But it helps us to understand the present and very recent past.

The evidence of this inquiry tells us that we are living in the late stages of a very long price-revolution, perhaps in the critical stage. It also tells us that these are global processes. Our destiny is now closely linked to the condition of all humanity. The patterns of the past also suggest that what will happen in the future depends in no small degree on the choices that we make. Human beings do not hold everything in our hands, but our collective power to shape historical processes has grown enormously in the past eight hundred years. We can use this power wisely or foolishly. Our choices will make a difference for our children and grandchildren, and for generations yet unborn.

But what should be done? What individual choices should we make? What should we do collectively? As always, some believe that the best policy is to do nothing and let the market make its own correction. This argument was made as early as the fourteenth century. When medieval civilization was collapsing around him, the Canon of Bridlington spoke against an ordinance on prices. He believed that the "fruitfulness or sterility of all living things are in the power of God alone, from which it follows that the fertility of the soil and not the will of man must determine the price.'' Much the same attitude is shared today by those who substitute the theology of the free market for the Canon of Bridlington's power of God.[17]

Those who believe in the beneficence of a free market are correct in one tenet of their faith. It is true that the play of the market will in time correct almost any imaginable price-distortion. But to put our trust in the market is to ignore some hard historical facts. The free market restored equilibrium in the fourteenth century, but only after the Black Death. It did so again in the seventeenth century, but not until a general crisis had destroyed the peace of Europe. The free market recovered its equilibrium in the Victorian era, but only after the slaughter of the Napoleonic Wars. In short, the laisser-faire prescription, ''let the free market take its course'' has in the past eight hundred years created human suffering on a scale that is unacceptable. It is also unnecessary.

A second historical fact also tends to be missed by believers in the free market. In economic history, equilibrium is the exception rather than the. rule. A free market restores equilibrium only to break it down again, and to set in motion a new sequence of imbalances and insta-bilities with all the troubles that follow in their train. In the full span of modern history, most free markets have been in profound disequi-librium most of the time—often dangerous and destructive disequilib-rium.

A third fact is also frequently forgotten. In our complex and highly integrated modern economies, there are no truly free markets any more. The free market in the twentieth century is an economic fiction, much like the state of nature in the political theory of the eighteenth century. Markets today are highly regulated and actively manipulated by both public and private instruments. The real question is not whether we should interfere with the market, but what sort of interference we should make, and who will make it, and what its extent will be.

If we must intervene in the operation of the market, the question changes. How and when and to what ends should we intervene? Should we seek to suppress inflation as our primary goal? Here again, learned opinion is deeply divided. On the subject of long-term inflation in particular, many economists believe that rising prices are not neces-sarily a bad thing. Some think that they may even be a good thing, or at least better than the alternative. A few are convinced that fear of infla-tion has been more destructive than inflation itself, and that policies designed to restrain rising prices have done major damage to modern economies. Others take the opposite view, and insist that we have done too little to control a major scourge of modern society.

To study this problem in historical perspective is to see it in a different light. Long inflations, or more precisely the social and economic forces that long inflations represent, have caused profound human suffering on a massive scale. The major problem is not inflation itself. It is rather the imbalances, instabilities and inequities that have been associated with inflation.

The historical record of the past eight hundred years shows that ordinary people are right to fear inflation, for they have been its victims—more so then elites. And ordinary people who live in free societies have a special reason for concern. During the turbulent decade from 1963 to 1973, forty nations suffered from rates of inflation above 15 per cent. A recent study has shown that thirty-eight of those forty countries abolished or abridged democratic institutions in one way or another. A society that seeks to make its political decisions by open elections, and also hopes regulate its economic decisions by the operation of the free market, is specially vulnerable to the effect of unstable prices.[18]

Price revolutions and the long-term inflation that they engendered have caused major social problems in the past eight centuries. But there is another difficulty. Recent anti-inflationary policies have also done major damage in other ways, and sometimes even in the same ways. If both inflation and anti-inflationary policies have caused trouble, what should we do? Here are five suggestions.

❧ Learning to Think of the Long Run

First, we should learn to think historically about our condition. History is not only about the past. It is also about change and continuity. Most of all it is about the long run. The two leading errors of economic planning are to impose short-term thinking on long-term problems, and to adopt atemporal and anachronistic policies which do not recognize that the world has changed. It is an axiom of military history that generals are trained to fight the last war. In economic history, planners and managers are taught to prevent the last crisis from happening again. The next one is always different.

When we think historically about the problem of price-revolutions in particular, two important conclusions emerge. First, price-movements are historical processes; their magnitude, structure, cause and consequences have been highly variable. Second, these variations are patterned in ways that we are only beginning to understand. Many heads of government, leaders of corporations, business managers, economic theorists, and private investors have very little historical understanding of economic processes which they confront. Ideas and solutions are drawn from one set of historical circumstances (often very recent) and applied to others where they do not fit. The corrective is not merely historical knowledge. It is also historical thinking.

To that end we need to educate our leaders in politics, business, journalism, academe and every sector of society. We should help them to think in larger terms about the long run, and to expand the horizons of decision-making. This is especially the case in the United States, where we also need to educate every citizen to think in larger terms about the problems before us.

≥ Expanding Contextual Knowledge

Second, we need more information about long trends and large contexts. Our world is overwhelmed by information, but it is not the information that we most urgently require. Public and private agencies churn out immense quantities of economic data, mostly to monitor short-term movements within national boundaries. The vast statistical inquiries of United States government center on events of the past week, or month, or quarter. Every month, new sets of economic indicators are given to the public—producer prices, consumer prices, growth rates, foreign trade, housing starts, automobile sales, boxcar loadings, pork-belly contracts.

In a world of increasing economic volatility, these reports become front-page stories. We study them as closely as our ancestors examined their soothsayers' bones, and with as much effect. Last month's indicators have little meaning until they are set within a context that is broader than the month before. That sort of contextual knowledge is much neglected today. We need more of it. At present, long-term research on a large scale is left to individual scholars working alone in a primitive academic cottage industry. This division of labor makes no sense. Our major institutions should take up the work of information-gathering on a larger scale.

Unhappily, as these words are being written, data-gathering of this sort is being reduced rather than expanded. In the United States, Congress has cut the research budgets of the Securities and Exchange Commission, the Bureau of Economic Analysis, the Bureau of Labor Statistics, and other data-gathering agencies, at a time when information is needed most. The New York *Times* observes, "the theory seems to be that if government does not know what it is doing it will be tempted to meddle less with private industry. . . . More likely, it will still meddle, only less wisely."[19]

ঽ Economic Policy

The growth of knowledge might help us to invent better instruments for the management of modern economies. We have recently made much progress in that respect. During the past half-century, many new regulatory tools have been put to work with high success.

Prominent among them are monetary tools. Major gains have been made in the design of monetary policy, in the development of monetary institutions, and in the monetary education of electorates and elites. The importance of all this is now very clear. A sound and disciplined monetary policy, rigorously applied, is fundamental to the health of a modern economy.

Important progress has been made in the use of interest rates as a way of regulating an economic system. This method was first applied on a large scale by the Federal Reserve Board as recently as 1966. In three decades it has become an indispensable instrument of economic policy throughout the world.

We have been less successful in the realm of fiscal policy—that is, the use of public revenue and public spending as tools of economic planning. Here we were doing better a generation ago. The fiscal problems today are more nearly intractable, and solutions remain elusive. In the United States, the nadir of fiscal policy was reached during the Reagan administration (1981–89), when a Democratic Congress and a Republican presidency combined to create a larger national debt than did all other presidencies put together. We learned painfully from that experience; both the Bush and Clinton presidencies have done at least a little better. But major fiscal problems remain. They are compounded by demagogues of both the right and left, by irresponsible and cynical journalists, and by millions of Americans who demand low taxes and high services at the same time. We must urgently put our fiscal house in order, if we wish to recover the use of an economic instrument that helps in many ways.

Existing monetary and fiscal tools are all necessary instruments of economic policy—but they are not sufficient to the task at hand. They are powerful weapons, and yet very blunt and crude. Sometimes their use has been counterproductive. When inflation threatens, for example, central bankers seek to "cool" the economy in various ways—commonly, by driving up interest rates. The side effects of these methods are sometimes worse than the problems they are meant to solve.

Part of the problem are the central bankers who have tried to control inflation by "cooling an overheated economy" and even by creating deliberate "policy recessions." They bring to mind physicians in the eighteenth century who sought to heal their patients by bleeding, sweating, blistering, and purging. The remedy was sometimes more destructive than the disease. In Europe and America, anti-inflationary policies have reduced economic growth, diminished real wages, and increased inequities of many kinds. We can do better.

An important first step is to study the historical dynamics of a price revolution. To do so is to discover, for example, that great waves did their worst social and economic damage not by long, slow inflations but by short, sudden price-surges, which always developed in the late stages of every price-revolution. Wages commonly fell behind prices mostly in surge periods. Crime waves developed in the same way. These surge-patterns are an opportunity as well as a problem. They allow the application of strong but carefully targeted policies and tools for short periods and specific purposes when surges are developing.

Two such tools come quickly to mind. Price surges of specific commodities could be diminished by the use of commodity reserves. Stockpiles of major commodities might be expanded on the model of the American strategic oil reserve, and used to cushion sudden price shocks. Such an instrument would have little effect on long-term inflation, but it might dampen destructive surges more effectively than indiscriminate methods of "cooling the economy" or "policy recessions." This is not merely hypothetical. During the Gulf War, President Bush used successfully a small part of the Petroleum Reserve that way. President Clinton did so again on April 29, 1996, in the face of surging gas prices. The amounts of oil released were small by the measure of consumption, but the impact was larger than experts expected. We might organize a new Federal Commodity Board, to deliver our political leaders from temptation in election years.

Another tool of economic management would be a standby system of price controls, carefully designed for limited, short-term use in periods of sudden price surge. It is often repeated that price-controls "don't work." This economic dogma is very much mistaken. Twice in the past half-century, short-term price-controls have worked very well in the United States to diminish the momentum of dangerous price surges without disrupting economic growth.

With ingenuity and an open mind, economists should be able to refine these instruments and invent others more appealing to neoclassical tastes. In a world of uncertainty we need more refined, more controlled, and more flexible methods which in the phrase of historian Daniel Boorstin are "open to the unexpected." Their purpose should be to enlarge our capacity for choice rather than to restrict it; to work with market forces rather than against them. The important thing is to create better instruments than the crude tools we presently possess.[20]

ё▲ Social Policy

Price-revolutions also create major social problems that require attention. Most dangerous are material inequities that develop in the late stages of every great wave—never more so than in our own time. From 1968 to 1996, inequality of wealth and income have increased rapidly—as in every price-revolution since the thirteenth century. The results, then and now, were disastrous not only for the poor who were the principal victims, but for entire social systems. This is an urgent problem. If we neglect it, we shall pay a heavy price. The growth of material inequality diminishes economic growth, disrupts social order, and does grave injury to the social fabric. Everyone suffers from its effects—poor and rich alike.

All this is within our power to control. The laws and economic policies of every nation have a strong impact on the distribution of wealth and income. One may observe their effect by comparing one nation with another. During the mid-1980s, the poorest 20 percent of West German families received 13 percent of household income. In the United States, the poorest 20 percent recieved 6 percent of household income.[21]

In a dynamic economy, a more equitable distribution of income and wealth might be achieved not by confiscation or direct transfer, but by more subtle and less intrusive means. It is not necessary to make the rich poorer, so that the poor may grow richer. There are better ways. Expanded educational investment would help people to acquire more marketable skills and higher-paying jobs. Enlarged housing programs might help more people own their homes. Revised health and social security programs might shift our primary reliance from income-subsidies at the end of life to capital-accumulation early in the life cycle. Enlightened tax policies might halt the shift toward regressive taxes that are now falling increasingly on the poor. Inventive employment policies could protect the right to work and promote job security within a free labor market. With a little imagination, all this can be done by mixed public and private effort within the frame of capitalist, free-market economics—if we have the political will to make the effort.

Everything hinges on our political will. That in turn requires a shared sense of collective responsibility for our economic and social condition. We are all in this together. Our prevailing ideology stresses individual freedom and a tradition of minimal government. This way of thinking is central to our culture, and should be, but it represents only one side of our American heritage. The founders of our republic often wrote of the "liberty of America" to manage its affairs by collective effort. Their idea of freedom was better balanced than ours. Our ancestors clearly understood the vital role of collective effort in the cause of freedom. It is time that we remembered too.

APPENDIX A
₰ Price Revolutions in the Ancient World

This inquiry centered on modern Western history from the twelfth century to the present, primarily because the sources are still very thin for other cultures and earlier periods. Only scattered data survive from the more distant past. These materials, however limited, clearly show that price-revolutions occurred repeatedly in ancient and early medieval history.

In the valleys of the Tigris and Euphrates, price-records survive abundantly from the civilizations of ancient Mesopotamia. "The vast majority of excavated cuneiform tables deal with economic activities," writes historian Howard Farber. These sources supply much information about prices, wages, and money through a period much longer than the span of modern history. Farber himself studied Babylonian price movements from 1894 to 1595 B.C. He found evidence of a price-revolution, *circa* 1750–1684 B.C., which

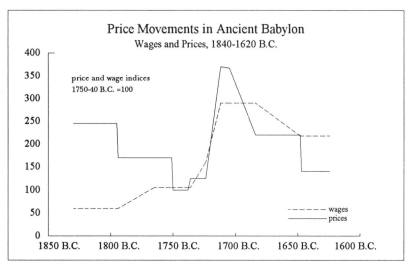

Price Movements in Ancient Babylon
Wages and Prices, 1840-1620 B.C.

price and wage indices
1750-40 B.C. =100

Figure 5.01 shows evidence of a price-revolution in Mesopotamia *circa* 1740-1680 B.C., when commodity prices rose sharply and wages lagged behind. This period was preceded by an era of price-equilibrium (1840-1750 B.C.), when prices were stable or falling and real wages rose. The last years of this equilibrium coincided with the reign of Hammurapi (1793-1750 B.C.), with its great cultural and legal achievements. The price-index used here is composed of prices for slaves, oil, barley, oxen, cattle, land, and house rentals. The wage index is for wages in silver. Both indices are converted to the common base of 1750-40 B.C.=100. The source is Howard Farber, "A Price and Wage Study in Northern Babylonia during the Old Babylonian Period," *Journal of the Social and Economic History of the Orient* 21 (1978) 1-51.

closely resembled similar events in the modern world. Price-relatives and price-wage movements were much the same as in the four great waves that we have studied. The reign of Hammurapi (*circa* 1793–1750 B.C.) coincided with the later stages of price-equilibrium, which showed the same combination of stable or declining prices and rising wages as in the equilibria modern era (Howard Farber, ''A Price and Wage Study for Northern Babylonia during the Old Babylonian Period,'' *Journal of the Economic and Social History of the Orient* 21 [1978] 1–51).

In ancient Egypt, scholars have found evidence of great waves in population movements, fluctuations of the Nile, the dynastic rhythm of Egyptian history, and the careers of individual leaders. All of these patterns interlocked. See Angelo Segré, *Circolazione monetaria e prèzzi nel mondo antico ed in particolare Egitto* (Rome, 1922); Karl Butzer, *Early Hydraulic Civilization in Egypt* (Chicago, 1976).

Other studies have been made of price movements and money in Greece. Here again historians have found evidence of recurrent price-revolutions, punctuated by periods of price-decline and comparative price equilibrium. Greek prices appear to have been comparatively stable during the fifth century before the birth of Christ. The troubled fourth century experienced a price

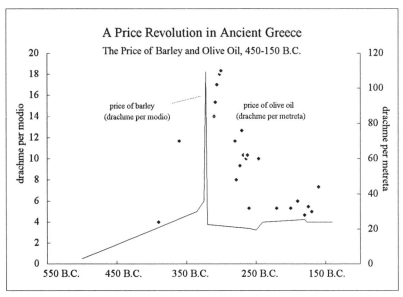

Figure 5.02 reports the results of two studies, both of which find evidence of a price revolution in the ancient world during the fourth and third centuries before the birth of Christ. These data for Greece are from Angelo Segre, *Circolazione monetaria e prèzzi nel mondo antico ed in particolare Egitto* (Rome, 1922), 164-173; and Lydia Spaventa de Novellis, *I prèzzi in Grècia e a Ròma nell'antichità* (Rome, 1934), 49-53.

revolution. (Lydia Spaventa de Novellis, *I prèzzi in Grecia e a Roma nell' antichità* (Rome, 1934), 101–2.

The people of ancient Rome experienced repeated price-revolutions, which closely coincided with the rhythm of Roman political history. One great wave reached its climax in a major time of troubles for the early republic, *circa* 240–210 B.C. Another coincided with the collapse of the republican institutions. In between, there was an intervening period of comparative price stability.

The Roman empire experienced a great wave of inflation in the second and third centuries A.D., when the price of wheat in some parts of the empire rose more than fifty-fold in less than a century. A study by Richard Duncan-Jones found that maximum wheat prices in Lower Egypt rose from 11 drachmas in private transactions before 100 A.D., to 200 drachmas, *circa* 201–300 A.D. Median prices increased more moderately from 8 to 16 drachmas in the same period. The rate of increase declined at the end of the third century. It rose again in yet another price revolution during the fourth century, from Constantine to Julian, *circa* 324–360 A.D., then fell and rose once more in the fifth century.

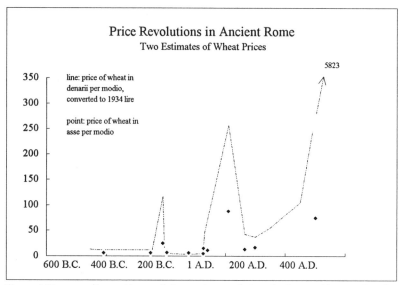

Price Revolutions in Ancient Rome
Two Estimates of Wheat Prices

Figure 5.03 summarizes evidence of three price revolutions in Roman history. The first happened in the Roman Republic, and coincided with similar events in ancient Greece, *circa* 300 B.C. (see figure 5.02). The second came at the end of the republic. The third occurred in the Empire during the third century A.D., a time of political and economic collapse. Sources are Lydia Spaventa de Novellis, *I prèzzi in Grècia e a Ròma nell' antichità* (Rome, 1934) 101-102; Jacobs, "Preis," 464.

Among many studies of Roman price movements is A. H. M. Jones, "Inflation in the Roman Empire," *Economic History Review* 2d ser. 5 (1953) 293–318; revised and corrected in P. A. Brunt, ed., *The Roman Economy: Studies in Ancient Economic and Administrative History* (Oxford, 1974), 187–229. More data are collected in Richard Duncan-Jones, *The Economy of the Roman Empire: Quantitative Studies* (Cambridge, 1974); *idem*, "The Price of Wheat in Lower Egypt," in *Structure and Scale in the Roman Economy* (Cambridge, 1990), 143–56; *idem*, "The Price of Wheat in Roman Egypt under the Principate," *Chiron* 8 (1978) 541–60. Also helpful are F. M. Heichelheim, "New Light on Currency and Inflation in Hellenistic-Roman Times, from Inscriptions and Papyri," *Economic History* 10 (1935) 1–11; Daniel Sperber, *Roman Palestine, 200–400: Money and Prices* (Ramat-gan, 1974); J. A. Straus, "Le prix des esclaves dans les papyrus d'époque romaine trouvée dans l'Egypte," *ZPE* 11 (1973) 289–95; G. Rickman, *The Corn Supply of Ancient Rome* (Oxford, 1980); S. Bolin, *State and Currency in the Roman Empire up to A.D. 300* (Stockholm, 1958). Much price data appear in Tenney Frank, ed., *An Economic Survey of Ancient Rome* (Baltimore, 1933–40; J. Kolendo, "L'arrêt de l'afflux des monnaies romaines dans le 'Barbaricum' sous Septime-Sévère," *Les Dévaluations à Rome* (Rome, n.d.) II, 169–72.

After the fall of Rome, price-movements became more difficult to fol-

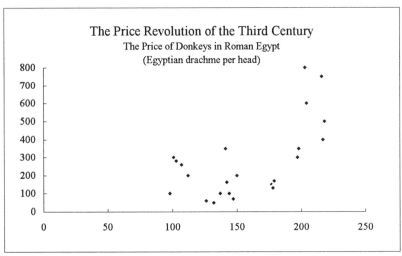

Figure 5.04 shows evidence that the price revolution in the third century A.D. was felt in Roman Egypt. Other inquiries have yielded similar results. The source is H.-J. Drexhage, "Eselpreise im römischen Ägypten: ein Beitrag zum Binnenhandel," *Münsterische Beiträge zur antiken Handelsgeschichte* 5 (1986), 34-48.

low. Scattered data show a long wave of rising prices during the tenth century. Livestock prices in Portugal appear to have doubled from A.D. 940 to 1000, and then to have stabilized in the eleventh century. If this evidence is reliable, there was an early medieval price-revolution in the tenth century, and a period of price-equilibrium in the eleventh century. One study finds supporting evidence in England of the emergence of a market economy during the period between the accession of King Alfred (871) and the death of Edgar (975). Thereafter, the quantity of silver coinage increased very rapidly from 975 to 1010.

See Claudio Sanchez-Albornez, *El precio de la vida en el reino Astur-Leones hace mil años* (Buenos Aires, 1945), 40–41; S. R. H. Jones, "Transaction Costs, Institutional Change, and the Emergence of a Market Economy in Later Anglo-Saxon England," *Economic History Review* 2d ser. 46 (1993) 658–78; P. Grierson and M. Blackburn, *Medieval European Coinage* (Cambridge, 1986); P. Grierson, "Commerce in the Dark Ages, A Critique of the Evidence," Royal Historical Society *Transactions* 5th ser. 9 (1959) 123–40.

Islamic prices also appear to have moved in great waves from the founding of Islam to the eleventh century. See Eliyahu Ashtor, *Histoire des prix et des salaires dans l'Orient medieval* (Paris, 1969); M. de Bouard, "Problèmes des subsistence dans un état médiévale; le marché et les prix des

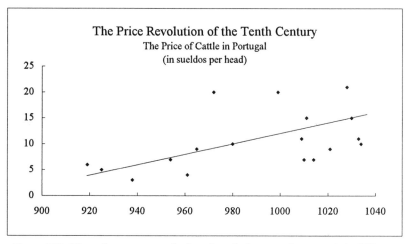

The Price Revolution of the Tenth Century
The Price of Cattle in Portugal
(in sueldos per head)

Figure 5.05 follows the movement of prices through the most obscure period of Western history. A price list (not a price series) for the early Middle Ages shows evidence of a price revolution in the tenth and early eleventh centuries. The source is Claudio Sánchez-Albornez, *El precio de la vida en el reino Astur-Leone's hace mil ano* (Buenos Aires, 1945), 40-41. A copy of this rare and charming work is in the New York Public Library. It shows similar trends in Galicia, Castille, and Asturia.

céréales au royaume angevin de Sicile," *Annales E.S.C.* 10 (1938) 483; Robert Latouche, *Les origines de l'économie occidentale* (Paris, 1956); A. Blanchet, *Les trésors de monnaies romaines et les invasions germaniques* (Paris, 1910); Claudio Sanchez-Albornez, *El precio de la vida en el reino Astur-Leones hace mil años* (Buenos Aires, 1945); Marc Bloch, "Le probleme de l'or au Moyen Age," *Annales* 5 (1933) 1–34.

Definitive conclusions require further study, but it is clear that price revolutions occurred repeatedly through the past four thousand years. Their timing correlates with population growth, cultural movements, and dynastic rhythms in ancient and early medieval history.

APPENDIX B

❧ The Crisis of the Fourteenth Century: A World Event?

Was the medieval price-revolution limited to Western civilization, or was it a world movement? Learned opinion is divided on this problem, and the price-records that might settle the question are very difficult to find outside Europe for the thirteenth century. But much empirical evidence is now available for the crisis of the fourteenth century. It suggests that Europe was not unique in its experiences. Parallel trends with similar timing appeared in many parts of the world.

In China, the great Sung dynasty collapsed in a prolonged time of troubles during the late thirteenth and fourteenth centuries. From 1279 to 1367, that country was ruled by Mongols from the steppes of Asia. China had seven emperors in thirty-eight years (1295–33). Most ruled by terror and died by violence. This time of troubles was merely a prelude to one of the darkest and most disastrous periods in China's history (1333–68), when a great empire collapsed into anarchy.

The population of China fell sharply during the fourteenth century, in a decline that coincided with the crisis in the medieval West. The leading causes of death in Asia appear to have been different in detail from those in Europe. China experienced its own distinctive combination of social violence, economic collapse, political chaos, massive famine, and catastrophic floods.

Perhaps the leading cause of suffering were the depredations of the Mongols. Their great leader Genghis Khan once remarked, "The greatest joy is to conquer one's enemies, to pursue them, to seize their property, to see their daughters in tears, to ride their horses, to possess their daughters and wives." A Mongol minister named Bayan proposed to restore order by killing all people named Chang, Wang, Liu, Li and Chao—the most common names in China. This intended holocaust was beyond the capacity even of the Mongols, but large numbers were slaughtered.

The crisis of this era was a pivot point in the history of China. Historian Mark Elvin calls it the great "turning point in the fourteenth century." This was an era of sweeping transformation in Chinese culture. It was also a moment of deep change that began a long process of isolation and decline, which continued into the twentieth century. Through that period, price-movements showed a rhythm of long waves that were similar, though not identical, to those in the West.

Similar rhythms also appeared in other civilizations. In Africa, the great empire of Mali collapsed during the late fourteenth century. Its trading center at Sigilmassa was destroyed by Taureg warriors in 1362, and commerce with Europe was interrupted.

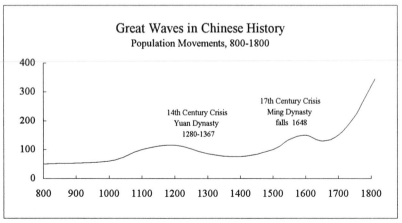

Great Waves in Chinese History
Population Movements, 800-1800

Figure 5.06 finds evidence of great waves in the demographic history of China. Sharp declines occurred in the fourteenth and seventeenth centuries. The timing was much the same as in Europe. Sources include Ping-ti Ho, *Studies on the Population of China, 1368-1953* (Cambridge, 1959).

In India, the Delhi Sultanate of Turko-Afghan rulers had grown from the eleventh century to its maximum under Sultan Muhammad bin Tughluq (1325–51), when it ruled nearly all the Indian subcontinent except the extreme south. After 1334, it rapidly disintegrated; by 1344, its revenues had fallen by 90 percent, and the Delhi Sultanate disintegrated.

The fourteenth century was also a period of major discontinuity in American history. In the Valley of Mexico, the classic Toltec culture collapsed in this period. The Aztecs, who like the Mongols and the Taureg were violent barbarians from the north, took possession of Lake Texcoco circa 1345. In South America, the pre-Inca states disintegrated in the fourteenth century and gave the Incas their opportunity to begin to create their great empire in the late fourteenth and early fifteenth centuries.

In the Pacific, the fourteenth century was also an important pivot-point for the history of oceanic cultures. The expansion of Polynesia, which had begun as early as the ninth century, came to a sudden end in the fourteenth century. The great Polynesian navigators had advanced as far as New Zealand, but they were unable to go farther, and failed to reach Tasmania and Australia.

There was no Black Death or Mongol horde in Polynesia. The research of New Zealand scientist A. T. Wilson yields evidence that the cause may have been a change in climate. His analysis of isotope ratios in calcium carbonate deposits shows evidence of an onset of an unusually cold period, with increased Pacific storms of such a magnitude as to deter even ocean voyagers as skilled as the Polynesians.

These global events tell us that their ætiology was not specific to a single culture, or to a particular agent such as the Black Death. They must have developed from a larger cause that affected virtually every part of the inhabited world.

Some historians find evidence of a change in world climate during the fourteenth century. During the preceding three hundred years—the tenth, eleventh and twelfth centuries—the weather had become increasingly warm. The growing season grew longer, crops became larger, and the carrying capacity of the environment increased. In the later years of the thirteenth century, these climatic trends reversed. The climate turned unusually cold, wet, windy and unstable.

The fact that these trends appeared as far apart as northern Europe, eastern Asia, western Africa and the south Pacific is evidence that the cause is unlikely to have been merely a change in meteorological circulation patterns, as some have suspected. Others believe that it rose from a change in the relationship between the earth and the sun—a decline in solar radiation, or perhaps a thickening of the earth's atmosphere, or possibly a cloud of cosmic dust that passed through the galaxy and blocked the passage of energy from the sun to the earth.

Some cultures suffered more than others in this era of crisis and catastrophe. The Christian West may have suffered worst of all. Here we find evidence that climate-events may be part of the explanation, but not the whole of it. Other causal factors, perhaps of greater power, were internal to the western culture, and important to the rhythm of its history.

Further, some cultures emerged stronger from the catastrophe of the fourteenth century while others were fatally weakened. During the fourteenth century, Islamic world-civilization entered a long decline from which it did not begin to recover until the twentieth century, nearly six hundred years later. The West was unique in its response to the crisis of the fourteenth century, though not in the crisis itself. Its open institutions made it more vulnerable, but also more resilient. The sources of its vulnerability in the fourteenth century were also the foundation of its future strength.

For relevant materials in the history of China, see Ping-ti Ho, *Studies on the Population of China, 1368–1953* (Cambridge, 1959, 1967); Mark Elvin, *The Pattern of the Chinese Past: A Social and Economic Interpretation* (Stanford, 1973); R. Hartwell, ''A Cycle of Economic Change in Imperial China: Coal and Iron in North-east China, 750–1350,'' *Journal of the Economic and Social History of the Orient* 10 (1967); M. Cartier, ''Notes sur l'histoire des prix en Chine du XIVe au XVIIe siècle,'' *Annales E.S.C.* 24 (1969) 1876–89; *idem*, ''Les importations de métaux monetaires en Chine: Essai sur la conjoncture chinoise,'' *ibid.*, 36 (1981) 454–66; P. Liu and K. Huang, ''Population Change and Economic Development in Mainland China since 1400,'' in C. Hou and T. Yu, eds., *Modern Chinese Economic History* (Taipei, 1977),

61–81; C. P. Fitzgerald, *China, A Short Cultural History* (New York, 1935, 1972), 432; Ch'uan Han-sheng, "Sung-Ming chien pai-yin kou-mai-li ti pien-tung chi ch'i yuan-yin" ["Fluctuations in the purchasing power of silver at their cause from the Sung to the Ming dynasties"], *Hsin-ya-hseuh-pao* [*New Asian Journal*] 8 (1967) 157–86, with a summary in English; M. Cartier, "Notes sur l'histoire des prix en Chine du XIVe au XVIIe siècle," [1368–1644] *Annales E.S.C.* 24 (1969) 1876–89; *idem,* "Les importations de métaux monetaires en Chine: Essai sur la conjoncture Chinoise," *ibid.,* 36 (1981) 454–66; W. S. Atwell, "Notes on Silver, Foreign Trade, and the Late Ming Economy," *Ch'ing shih wen-ti* 3 (1977) 1–33; *idem* "International Bullion Flows and the Chinese Economy, *circa* 1530–1650," *Past & Present* 95 (1982) 68–90; P. Liu and K. Huang, "Population Change and Economic Development in Mainland China since 1400," in C. Hou and T. Yu, eds., *Modern Chinese Economic History* (Taipei, 1977), 61–81; Yeh-chien Wang, "The Secular Trend of Prices during the Ch'ing Period," *Journal of the Institute of Chinese Studies of the Chinese University of Hong Kong,* 5 (1972) 364.

For Africa, see M. Malowist, "The Social and Economic Stability of the Western Sudan in the Middle Ages," *Past & Present* 33 (1966) 3–15; E. W. Bovill, *The Golden Trade of the Moors* (Oxford, 1958); J. Devisse, "Routes de Commerce et échanges en Afrique occidentale en relation avec la Méditerranée," *Revue d'histoire économique et sociale* 1 (1972) 42–73, 357–97.

For evidence of a global change in climate, see A. T. Wilson, "Isotope Evidence for Past Climatic and Environmental Change," *Journal of Interdisciplinary History* 10 (1980) 241–50.

APPENDIX C
ટ♣ The Seventeenth Century: A World Crisis?

In the year 1649, an English pamphleteer invented a fictional "interview" in the Elysian Fields between two newly arrived heads of state: Charles I of England and the Sultan Ibraham, who had been emperor of the Ottoman Turks. Both had just been executed by their angry subjects. The shades of these murdered monarchs met in the afterworld, and commiserated with one another on their common fate. (Lord Kinross, *Ottoman Centuries; The Rise and Fall of the Turkish Empire* [New York, 1977], 19, 317).

Other rulers might well have joined that ghostly conversation. More than a few met violent ends during the general crisis of the seventeenth century. This event was not limited to Europe. It developed in every part of the inhabited world.

China's Ming dynasty, which had come to power in the crisis of the fourteenth century, collapsed in the seventeenth century. Its disintegration was so complete that a bandit chieftain named Lu Tzu-ch'eng took control of the capital city of Beijing. The humiliation of the ruling dynasty was so great that the last Ming emperor hanged himself in 1644. During the mid-seventeenth century, the Chinese people suffered severely from famine, disease and disorder. Demographic evidence shows clearly that these were not routine miseries of a sort that were visited upon every generation. The population of China fell in the seventeenth century for the first time since the crisis of the fourteenth century—a pattern very similar to that in Europe.

India also experienced a time of troubles in the same period. Here too, the early seventeenth century was an era of economic stagnation, rising prices, falling population, growing inequality, hunger and pestilence. In 1616, bubonic plague returned to the subcontinent. Millions of Indians sickened and starved while the Mogul emperor Shah Jahan (1628–58) built the beautiful Taj Mahal at great expense for his wife—a testament of private love and material inequality. In 1658 Shah Jahan was deposed and imprisoned. After his death in that same year, a civil war broke out among his sons. Religious strife became intense, and the Mogul Empire began to disintegrate. This event opened the way for European conquest of the Indian subcontinent.

In sub-Saharan Africa, the Bornu Empire and the Mangding Empire both collapsed. In the Middle East, the Persian Empire began to disintegrate after the death of the great Shah Abbas (1587–1629). The Ottoman Empire decayed rapidly in the reign of Sultan Murad the Maniac, a sadistic madman who ruled from 1623 to 1640. He was followed by Ibrahim the Wretched, who went quietly insane. In 1648, the unfortunate Ibrahim was overthrown and executed—hence his Elysian conversation with Charles I, who was beheaded in 1649.

Persistent unrest also occurred in the American colonies of New England, New France, Virginia, New Spain, New Netherland, Brazil, and the Caribbean islands. The strife that developed in the New World throughout the seventeenth century has been interpreted by colonial historians in parochial ways, as consequences of local events. These events were also part of global trends in the period from 1618 to 1650. The crisis of the seventeenth century was a time of troubles throughout the world.

APPENDIX D
⁂ America and Europe: One Conjuncture or Two?

In 1963, a leading economic historian posed a problem about the movement of prices in America and Europe. Ruggiero Romano suggested that major price-trends in the Old World were fundamentally different from those in the New World. In his own pathbreaking inquiries into the economic history of Latin America, he reported evidence that during the eighteenth century prices were stagnant in the Spanish and Portuguese colonies, that a chronic shortage of money existed, and capital accumulation and economic growth lagged behind Europe. From this pattern Romano concluded that there was an "inverse movement of prices in Ibero-America and Europe." He also suggested that New France and British America were similar to Latin America in their price trends. See Ruggiero Romano, "Movimento de los precios y desarrollo económico: El caso de Sudamérica en el siglo XVIII," *Desarrollo Económico* 3 (1963) 31–43; and *idem*, "Some Considerations on the History of Prices in Colonial Latin America," in Lyman L. Johnson and Enrique Tandeter, eds., *Essays on the Price History of Eighteenth-Century Latin America* (Albuquerque, 1990), 35–71.

Romano's pioneering thesis has inspired much research on the price history of Latin America during the eighteenth century. The evidence is now beginning to flow in some abundance. Most of it suggests that Latin American price movements were a variation on European trends, but not an inverse pattern.

The debate centers on the eighteenth century. In that period, the reader will remember that European prices had showed no upward trend until the decade 1730–40. Thereafter they rose until the early nineteenth century. In the Spanish and Portuguese colonies, prices fell or remained on the same level until 1750, and continued to do so in some places such as Salvador and Potosí until as the 1780s. But in Mexico, Chile, and other parts of Latin America, prices were generally rising from the 1760s. By the late 1780s, the price-revolution of the eighteenth century was operating broadly there. Historian John Coatsworth writes of Latin America in general that "in all cases for which there are data, commodity prices were rising in the 1790s and during the war years that followed." See John H. Coatsworth, "Economic History and the History of Prices," in Johnson and Tandeter, eds., *Essays on the Price History of Eighteenth-Century Latin America*, 22.

In New France, price-trends were very similar, with a rising tendency during the late eighteenth century, and surges during the period from 1793 to 1817. See F. Ouellet and J. Hamelin, *Le mouvement des prix agricoles dans la province de Quebec (1760–1815)* (n.p., n.d.; *idem,* "La crise agricole dans le Bas-Canada," *Etudes Rurales* 7 (1962) 36–57.

In the United States, many inquiries have found the same trends and timing as in western Europe. This pattern appears in the wholesale price indices of Warren and Pearson, the research of Arthur Cole, in the Bezanson index of wholesale prices in Philadelphia, and the Taylor index of wholesale prices in Charleston, South Carolina. Similar patterns also appear in the research of Winifred Rothenberg on agricultural prices in New England. The evidence appears in George F. Warren and Frank A. Pearson, *Prices* (New York, 1933), 11–27; Arthur H. Cole, *Wholesale Commodity Prices in the United States, 1700–1861* (Cambridge, 1938) 153–67; Anne Bezanson, Robert D. Gray and Miriam Hussey, *Wholesale Prices in Philadelphia, 1749–1861* (Philadelphia, 1936), 392; George Rogers Taylor, "Wholesale Commodity Prices at Charleston, S.C., 1732–1791," *Journal of Economic History* 4 (1932) 356–77; *idem,* "Wholesale Commodity Prices at Charleston, S.C., 1796–1861," *ibid.,* supplement, 848–68; Winifred Rothenberg, *From Market Places to a Market Economy; The Transformation of Rural Massachusetts, 1750–1850* (Chicago, 1992); *idem,* "The Market and Massachusetts Farmers, 1750–1855," *Journal of Economic History* 41 (1981) 283–314; *idem,* "A Price Index for Rural Massachusetts, 1750–1855," *ibid.* 39 (1979) 975–1001.

Price series in some parts of Latin America come closer to the Romano model, and everywhere there were differences between colonial price movements and those of Europe. Small markets for locally traded commodities showed various idiosyncracies. Prices movements for manufactured products moved differently in the early years of colonial history. The dependency of many colonies on the price of a single dominant staple crop caused differences as well. But these patterns were variations on the central theme. Throughout the Atlantic world in the eighteenth century there was one great conjuncture, not two.

APPENDIX E
🍂 Cycles and Waves

Frank Manuel once remarked that every idea of history comes down to either the circle or the line. One might add that most models of price history are either the cycle or the wave. This inquiry centers on a wave-model, which has become increasingly dominant in the literature, because it solves many conceptual problems. In historical scholarship, waves of the past are the wave of the future.

Most early research on recurrent price movements was very different in its purpose. It was mainly a search for cycles rather than waves. Many scholars have gone looking for cycles in price movements, and few have been disappointed. Learned journals called *Cycles, Kyklos, Futures,* and *Technological Forecasting and Social Change* have published essays that report evidence of many different cyclical rhythms in modern history. They include Kondratieff cycles (with a period of fifty years), Kuznets "long swings" (twenty to twenty-five years), Labrousse "intercycles" (ten to twelve years), Juglar trade cycles (seven to eight years), and Kitchin business cycles (three to four years).

The largest and most controversial literature is about Kondratieff cycles, which are sometimes mistakenly called long waves. They are thought to have caused major depressions every half century, *circa* 1815, 1870, 1929, and 1970. The seminal monograph was written by Nikolai D. Kondratieff, head of the Moscow Institute for Business Cycle Research, and published in Russian in 1925. A German translation appeared as "Die langen Wellen der Konjunktur," *Archiv für Sozialwissenschaft und Sozialpolitik* 56 (1926) 573–609. An abridged English translation was published in *The Review of Economic Statistics* 17 (1935) 161–72. A complete English text is in *Review* 2 (1979) 519–62. The model was elaborated by Kondratieff in *The Long Wave Cycle* (1928, rpt., New York, 1984).

As Kondratieff himself was careful to point out, similar models had been put forward by A. Spiethoff in *Handwörterbuch der Staatswissenschaft* (1923). They had also been discussed by two Dutch socialists: S. de Wolff in "Prosperitats-und Depressionsperioden," *Lebendige Marxismus* (Jena, 1924); and even earlier by C. van Gelderen, "Springvloed: Beschouwingen over industrieele ontwikkeling en Prijsbeweging," *De Niewe Tijd* 18 (1913).

Marxist critics, including Trotsky and many Old Bolsheviks, condemned Kondratieff cycles as an economic heresy. In 1930, Kondratieff was sent to Siberia, where he died in a Communist concentration camp. See Richard B. Day, "The Theory of Long Waves: Kondratieff, Trotsky, and Mandel," *New*

Left Review 99 (1976) 67–82. An excellent historiographical essay on the diffusion of Kondratieff's work is Jean-Louis Escudier, "Kondratieff et l'histoire économique Française," *Annales E.S.C.* 48 (1993) 359–83.

French and German historians have always been much interested in Kondratieff cycles, more so than their American and British colleagues. Extended discussions include Gaston Imbert, *Des mouvements de longue durée Kondratieff* (Aix en Provence, 1959), and Ulrich Weinstock, *Das Problem der Kondratieff-Zyklen* (Berlin, 1964).

In the English-speaking world, historians have contributed comparatively little to this subject, but social scientists have written at length upon it. Interest surged during the 1930s in works such as Joseph Schumpeter, *Business Cycles* (New York, 1939); then declined, and revived in the 1970s. The best introduction to a large literature is Joshua S. Goldstein, *Long Cycles: Prosperity and War in the Modern Age* (New Haven, 1988), a careful, honest and thought-provoking work which analyzes 33 attempts by various scholars to test the existence of the Kondratieff cycle, mostly with positive results. Goldstein's excellent bibliography also lists hundreds of works, not so much by historians, but by political scientists and sociologists on various aspects of this question. For other discussions, see Donald V. Etz, "The Kondratieff Wave: A Review," *Cycles* (1973) 73–74; J. J. Van Duijn, *The Long Wave in Economic Life* (1979, rpt., Boston, 1983); John C. Soper, *The Long Swing in Historical Perspective* (New York, 1978); Casper Van Ewijk, "A Spectral Analysis of the Kondratieff Cycle," *Kyklos* 35 (1982) 468–99; T. Kitwood, "A Farewell Wave to the Theory of Long Waves," *Universities Quarterly—Culture, Education and Society* 38 (1984) 158–78; Irma Adelman, "Long Cycles: Fact or Artifact?" *American Economic Review* 55 (1965) 444–63; R. Hamil, "Is the Wave of the Future a Kondratieff?" *Futurist* 13 (1979) 381–84; J. P. Harkness, "A Spectral Analysis of the Long Swing Hypothesis in Canada," *Review of Economics and Statistics* 50 (1968) 429–36; Rainer Metz, "'Long Waves' in English and German Economic Historical Series from the Middle of the Sixteenth to the Middle of the Twentieth Century," in Rainer Fremdling and Patrick K. O'Brien, eds., *Productivity in the Economies of Europe* (Stuttgart, 1983) 175–219; *idem,* "Long Waves in Coinage and Grain Price-Series from the Fifteenth to the Eighteenth Century," *Review* 7 (1984) 599–647; Paolo S. Labini, "Le problème des cycles économiques de longue durée," *Economie appliquée* 3 (1950) 481–95; Jos. Delbeke, "Recent Long-Wave Theories: A Critical Survey," *Futures* 13 (1981) 246–57; M. N. Cleary and G. D. Hobbs, "The Fifty-Year Cycle: A Look at the Empirical Evidence," in Christopher Freeman, ed., *Long Waves in the World Economy* (London, 1983); Heinz-Dieter Haustein and Erich Neuwirth, "Long Waves in World Industrial Production, Energy Consumption, Innovations, Inventions and Patents and Their Identification by Spectral Analysis," *Technological*

Forecasting and Social Change 22 (1982) 53–89; Ghalib M. Baqir, "The Long Wave Cycles and Re-Industrialization," *International Journal of Social Economics* 8 (1981) 117–23; K. Eklund, "Long Waves in the Development of Capitalism?" *Kyklos* 33 (1980) 383–419; Hans Bieshaar and Alfred Kleinknecht, "Kondratieff Waves in Aggregate Output?" *Konjunktur Politik* 30 (1984); David M. Gordon, "Stages of Accumulation and Long Economic Cycles," in Terence K. Hopkins and Immanuel Wallerstein, eds., *Processes of the World System* (Beverly Hills, Calif., 1980); Alfred Kleinknecht, "Innovation, Accumulation and Crisis: Waves in Economic Development," *Review* 4 (1981) 683–711; Ernest Mandel, *Long Waves of Capitalist Development* (Cambridge, 1980).

The literature on Kondratieff's long cycles, for all its abundance, has a shallow empirical base. Many historians continue to doubt the very existence of Kondratieff cycles. Skepticism centers on the period from 1873 to 1893, for if the economic downturns in those years were no more severe than those of 1819, 1826, 1837 and 1859, then the Kondratieff pattern loses much of its salience and most of its shape. See S. B. Saul, *The Myth of the Great Depression, 1873–1896* (London, 1896); and Solomos Solomou, "Kondratieff Waves in the World Economy, 1850–1913," *Journal of Economic History* 46 (1986) 165–69.

Another weakness appeared in the 1970s when many Kondratieff-minded scholars predicted a "coming collapse of capitalism" that stubbornly refused to come, despite many dire warnings. See, e.g., Jay W. Forrester, "We're Headed for Another Depression," *Fortune* Jan.16, 1978; Geoffrey Barraclough, "The End of an Era," *New York Review of Books* 21 (1974) 14–20; and Cesare Marchetti, "Recession 1983: Ten More Years To Go?" *Technological Forecasting and Social Change* 24 (1983) 331–42.

Evidence for a Kondratieff pattern in earlier periods of history is even weaker than in the modern era. Kondratieff himself believed that his cycles did not occur before 1790. Other scholars have claimed to find evidence of the same rhythm throughout the modern and even the medieval era, but the empirical evidence is very soft.

My own judgment is that a cycle of approximately fifty or sixty years does in fact appear in many social indicators, and has been confirmed by various statistical methods including business cycle analysis, trend deviation, moving averages, and spectral analysis, to name but a few. But this pattern is not stronger than other cyclical rhythms, and it is much weaker than the secular trend with which it is sometimes confused. Kondratieff's "long wave" may be merely a multiple of generational "long swings," which move round the secular trend and vary broadly from one swing to the next in timing and intensity. Much of the energy devoted by American social scientists to the study of the Kondratieff cycle has been misdirected. Their efforts might be more usefully applied to the examination of recurrent wave-like secular trends which have more solid foundations in historical fact, though less predictive power.

Shorter cycles of thirty years also have been found in farm prices and harvest fluctuations by Beveridge, Goubert, and many recent writers on the world economy in the twentieth century. This pattern is sometimes (but not always) associated with solar activity. It has not been rigorously tested and is not generally accepted by most economists or historians today. But it keeps being rediscovered in descriptive studies. Cf. Stanley Jevons, "The Solar Period and the Price of Corn," in Jevons, ed., *Investigations in Currency and Finance* (London, 1884).

Kuznets cycles or "long swings" of approximately twenty years have been much discussed by American economists, but this pattern has not been so interesting to European scholars or so visible in the history of their nations. See Simon Kuznets, *Secular Movements in Production and Prices* (Boston, 1930); "Long Swings in the Growth of Population and Related Economic Variables," *Proceedings of the American Philosophical Society* 102 (1958) 25–52; Arthur F. Burns, *Production Trends in the United States since 1970* (New York, 1934); Moses Abramowitz, "Resource and Output Trends in the United States since 1870," *American Economic Review* 46 (1956) 5–23; Brinley Thomas, *Migration and Economic Growth* (Cambridge, 1954); John C. Soper, "Myth and Reality in Economic Time Series: The Long Swing Revisited," *Southern Economic Journal* 41 (1975) 570–79. This rhythm is sometimes thought to be demographic in its origin, but Friedman and Schwartz argue in *Monetary Trends in the United States and United Kingdom*, 599–621, that long swings are episodic in their origin and monetary in their expression. Many economists agree with them.

The Labrousse cycle (or intercycle) of roughly 10 or 12 years is much favored by European historians but rarely appears in American scholarship. It has been used in studies of French history.

Juglar cycles or trade cycles (7 or 8 years) have been found by many scholars—by Goubert in Beauvais, Parenti in Tuscany, Spooner in Udine, Hauser in Paris. The classic work is Clément Juglar, *Des crises commerciales et leur retour périodiques en France, en Angleterre, et aux Etats-Unis* (1889) rpt. New York, 1967).

Kitchin cycles or business cycles (3.5 years, or forty months) were first observed in the American economy during the nineteenth and twentieth centuries, and also in Europe during our own time. The classical text is Joseph Kitchin, "Cycles and Trends in Economic Factors," *Review of Economics and Statistics* 5 (1923) 10–16. They are sometimes called "inventory cycles" and are thought to rise from the structure of modern business enterprise. But several historians have also reported them in price data as early as the fifteenth century, and Pierre Chaunu has discovered them in the rhythm of Séville's transatlantic trade.

For general discussions of business cycles, see Wesley C. Mitchell, *Business Cycles* (New York, 1927); Arthur F. Burns and Wesley C. Mitchell, *Measuring Business Cycles* (New York, 1946); Joseph A. Schumpeter, *Business Cycles: A Theoretical, Historical and Statistical Analysis of the Capitalist Process* (New York, 1939); Geoffrey H. Moore, *The Cyclical Behavior of Prices* (Washington, 1971). Historians will find a rapport with E. R. Dewey and E. F. Dakin, *Cycles: The Science of Prediction* (New York, 1950), which argues that these rhythms are themselves variable through time and space—a conclusion that is certainly correct.

Cyclical patterns are often extracted from the data by "detrending" a time series—that is, by removing the secular trend so as to expose fluctuations more clearly. The great waves in this work are not extracted by filtering or detrending the data. They are the secular trends, and appear on the surface of the evidence. For problems of method, leading works are James D. Hamilton, *Time Series Analysis* (Princeton, 1994), and T. W. Anderson, *The Statistical Analysis of Time Series* (New York, 1971). Also helpful is Nathaniel J. Mass, *Economic Cycles: An Analysis of Underlying Causes* (Cambridge, Mass., 1975).

APPENDIX F
ᐓ Toward a Discrimination of Inflations

The many uses of the word "inflation" make an interesting study in scholarly semantics. The term has been defined in different ways. Some of the most common meanings incorporate a particular theory of inflation in such a way as to exclude all other theories. The result is a family of mutually contradictory theory-driven definitions. Each of them claims a universal validity. All are more unitary than the phenomenon that they purport to describe.

An amusing example appears in *Webster's New World Dictionary*. The second college edition of this work offers two contradictory theory-centered definitions on the same page. The term "inflation" itself is defined as "an increase in the amount of money in circulation, resulting in a relatively sharp and sudden fall in its value and rise in prices." Just below it is "inflationary spiral," which is defined as a "continuous and accelerating rise in the prices of goods and services, primarily due to the interaction of increases in wages and costs."

One of these definitions insists that inflation is exclusively a monetary phenomenon, caused by an expansion in the money supply. The other requires us to subscribe to a "cost-push" model. These theoretical definitions are narrow and specific. They are also mutually exclusive. If the "cost-push" model is correct, then inflation is not always caused by an increase in the amount of money in circulation.

Further, both definitions also include specific historical descriptions of inflation. One of them demands that we think of inflation as "sharp and sudden." Another insists that inflationary spirals are "continuous and accelerating." These historical models of inflation are not only at odds with one another. They are also mistaken, both in general historical terms and in their specific theoretical linkages. Monetary inflations are not necessarily "short and sharp." Wage-price inflations are not always "continuous and accelerating."

These usages often recur in learned discourse. It is very common for American economists to define the term "inflation" in exclusively monetary terms, and then to use it to describe an historical process which is not exclusively monetary in its cause.

An example is an assertion by American economist Alan Blinder that inflation is "always and everywhere primarily a monetary phenomenon" (New York *Times*, February 19, 1984). Many of his colleagues agree with this statement. There is no necessary error in it. As long as it is confined within the constraining context of monetarist theory, Blinder's statement is not merely

278

true but tautological. Given certain theoretical assumptions, a rise in prices can always be translated into monetary terms. If the discussion were exclusively theoretical, there is no error here. The trouble comes when the term is defined in this way, and then used to describe the operative cause of an actual rise of prices in the real world—where price-increases sometimes have a monetary cause, but often rise from other roots.

Outside of the learned professions, the word inflation is understood in other ways. In ordinary speech, it tends to be an omnibus term for any sort of increase in prices generally (which is not the same as an economist's idea of the "general price level").

Professional usage in the learned disciplines seems to be shifting in this direction. Increasingly, historians and economists are growing more eclectic in their ideas of inflation. Two economists, Paul Samuelson and William Nordhaus, write, "Like illnesses, inflations occur for many reasons." They divide inflations into three types, mainly by speed of advance: "moderate inflation" as in the industrial nations during the late twentieth century (1–10 percent), "galloping inflation" as in Latin America or Israel during the same period (10–1000 percent), and "hyperinflation" as in post-Wilhelmine Germany (1000 percent or more). This taxonomy brings to mind a mortality bill by an eighteenth-century New England physician who believed that all forms of disease shared a single etiology, and who classified deaths as "sudden" or "slow." This is a primitive idea in medicine and history, but sometimes it has its uses.

Another and better approach is to make a discrimination of price-inflations not by velocity but by cause. Historians tend to think of inflations in pluralistic terms, as rising from a broad variety of causal conditions. At least seven types of inflation might be distinguished by cause.

One common variety of price inflation is caused by an expansion of the money supply. This is sometimes a slow creeping movement. It can also become a sudden surge of hyperinflation, of which the classic example is the German inflation of 1922–23. When the infant Weimar Republic was unable to meet its obligations by taxes or loans, it deliberately resorted to the printing press. The number of German marks in circulation rose from 5,807 trillion in January 1922 to 202 trillion-trillion in December 1923, a number so large that it requires 30 digits: 202,232,341,000,000,000,000,000,000,000 marks. As a consequence, the wholesale price index in Germany rose from 100 in 1913 to 142 trillion in 1923. German burghers who suffered through this event told the story of a man who went to a grocery store with a wheelbarrow full of money to pay for his family's food. A thief stopped him, threw away the money, and stole the wheelbarrow. What was still more dramatic about the German inflation was its sudden end. Monetary stability was restored in 1924 by the issue of a new currency that was very stable. The German hyperinflation of 1922–23 had many social and political consequences, but it did not become embedded in the structure of the economy, and disappeared when the inflated marks were withdrawn from circulation. There have been many monetary inflations of this sort, and other monetary inflations of a more gradual variety.

A second type of inflation rises from increases in aggregate demand. One common example is war-inflation. Government spending for military purposes has often stimulated demand throughout an economy, at the same time that a shift of workers from productive labor into the armed forces causes a decline in aggregate supply. Other demand-inflations have risen from population growth, particularly when the general population increases more rapidly than the work force. In the twentieth century, demand-inflations have also been caused by rising expectations, and by higher standards of living.

A third form of inflation is caused by contractions in supply—for example, by runs of bad weather which drive up agricultural prices. This happening was very common in medieval and early modern Europe, when a large proportion of family income was spent on grain and other farm products. The supply shock of reduced harvests reverberated through the entire economy.

A fourth variety is cost-push inflation. It occurs when wages and prices begin to spiral upward, each driving the other in its turn. This mechanism was clearly operating in the middle stages of the price-revolution of the twentieth century.

A fifth variety might be called the inflation of administered prices. It has happened in the United States as a result of collusive price-fixing in oligopolistic industries. Recent examples include the manipulation of oil prices by OPEC nations during the 1970s. Oil shocks had an impact on general price levels through the world economy.

A sixth variety might be called bubble-inflation, caused by a surge of speculative activity, which when it rises rapidly and reaches broadly through an economy, distorts price levels in a general way. Examples might include the Dutch tulip mania in 1634 and the French Mississippi Bubble in 1717.

A seventh variety might be called the "inflationary-expectations" model. It occurs when people begin to raise prices not because of actual changes in supply or demand or costs or the size of the money supply, but out of fear that some such change might happen.

These different types inflation often coexist. In actual practice, price-revolutions are complex phenomena that characteristically include many different types of inflation. Most have begun as demand-inflations, to which the effects of monetary-inflation, supply-inflation, and administered-inflation are later added, and have the effect of reinforcing the momentum of the price revolution.

It is interesting to observe that the effect of short-term inflations varies according to their timing within price-revolutions and price equilibria. For example, the inflation associated with the Civil War, the Crimean War and the Franco-Prussian Wars in the nineteenth century did not cause a permanent elevation of price levels. Prices surged during the wars, then rapidly declined in the peace. In the United States by the 1880s, prices had returned to levels of the late 1850s. During the major wars of the twentieth century things were a little different. Inflation surged after America joined the World War I in 1917, then declined after 1919, but not to prewar levels. After World War II, Korea, and Vietnam, war-inflations were not followed by a decline at all. Prices continued to climb. What was different here was the underlying dynamic of the price system.

All of this suggests a need for price theory that incorporates a component of historical thinking, and also for historical models that include a generous measure of economic theory. Historical trends and contexts make a major difference. So also do the dynamic relationships that are modeled in economic theory.

Economics is what Windelband called a nomothetic discipline. It seeks knowledge through generalization. History is an idiographic discipline. It studies things in their particulars. The two approaches are different, but also complementary. Together they can help us understand the many varieties of price-inflation, and also their common characteristics.

APPENDIX G
& Money of Exchange and Money of Account

A student of price history must confront a vast diversity of monetary units in the world—not merely in the variety of coins and paper currency, but also in the structure of monetary systems themselves. In the early modern era, these systems were in some ways more complex than those of our own time.

One dimension of that complexity appeared in the difference between two types of monies: money of exchange and money of account. Alexander Justice wrote in 1707, "Money in general is divided into two sorts, imaginary and real." (*A General Treatise of Monies and Exchanges* [London, 1707], 1; quoted in John J. McCusker, *Money and Exchange in Europe and America, 1600–1775: A Handbook* [Chapel Hill, 1978], 3).

Justice's "real money" is money of exchange. It is issued by virtually all sovereign states and consists of coins and paper that pass physically from hand to hand. Justice's "imaginary money" is called money of account. It exists only as an idea, and is used in bookkeeping and credit transactions.

The distinction between real and imaginary money seems unnatural and absurd to Americans today, who use the dollar as both money of exchange and as money of account. But practices were different in earlier periods. Real money and imaginary money existed side by side.

A case in point was eighteenth-century England, and English-speaking North America. Money of exchange consisted primarily of two coins: the silver shilling and the golden guinea, which was worth twenty-one shillings. There was also a silver crown (worth five shillings), and various other coins of smaller denominations.

At the same time, the most important money of account was a different unit: the pound sterling, worth twenty shillings or 240 pence. This was "imaginary money." Pounds did not actually exist as coins or paper currency until the nineteenth century, but they were the standard money of account throughout the English-speaking world for many years. In the United States, elderly people continued to keep their books in pounds sterling as late as the 1830s, half a century after independence.

By the mid-nineteenth century, Americans abandoned this dual system. But even today the people of Britain still use different money of exchange and money of account. By a curious irony of monetary history the major units reversed their roles in Britain. The pound sterling became the leading money of exchange—first in the form of elegant banknotes, then small and clumsy coins of base metal that make a dreary clunking sound when dropped on a modern plastic counter. Guineas, on the other hand, have become a money of account. They rarely circulate but are used to reckon prices of luxury items. As recently as 1990, the author was billed in guineas by a private physician in Harley Street, but the bill was settled by the passing of pounds. Rolls Royce automobiles and tickets to opulent Commemoration Balls in Oxford Colleges are priced in guineas but paid in pounds.

Dual systems of this sort were widespread in the early modern era. Their complexity was compounded by multiple moneys of account. The great merchant banks of medieval Italy kept their books in imaginary money of account, which had a value that was unique to each house. This "banco money" rose and fell with the reputation of each banking house, even where monetary units were nominally the same.

The difference in value between one money of account and another was called by Italian bankers the *aggio,* or premium. That word entered common usage throughout Western world. It was often written *agio* in French, German, Spanish and English, and is still used in Europe.

Money of exchange also had many complexities. It consisted mostly of silver coin in medieval Europe. During the late medieval and early modern era a bimetallic standard was widely adopted. Gold and silver coins were minted in great variety, but a few units of value became common through many monetary systems. In the seventeenth and eighteenth centuries, roughly the same value attached to the French écu, the Spanish peso, the Dutch rijks-daalder, the German Reichsthaler, and, a little later, the Yankee dollar. All were worth about five English shillings, or one-quarter of an English pound.

England's golden guinea (after 1726) was approximately equivalent to the French louis d'or, which was also called the "French guinea." Before 1726, the louis d'or and Spanish pistole were about the same. Dutch and German ducats were roughly equal to Portuguese escudos, at a little less than half an English pound.

All of these coins passed current in every nation. When a British general fell overboard near Boston, his baggage was found to contain 694⅝ joannes, 37 moidores, 300 English guineas, 8½ pistoles, 1 French guinea, 1 dollar, 1 copper halfpenny, 26 "small heart" bits of silver, 6 pieces of gold, and 7 small pieces of silver. It was common for raw unminted lumps of gold and silver to be used as money. Value was determined by weight of gold or silver, measured in grains and later grams of precious metal. See W. T. Baxter, *The House of Hancock; Business in Boston, 1724–1775* [Cambridge, 1945], 15, 17–21.

In our contemporary world, money of exchange has become predominantly paper currency. This trend began as early as the seventeenth and eighteenth centuries in countries where gold and silver coins were very rare: New England, New France, Scandinavia and parts of eastern Europe.

Small farmers in Massachusetts did most of their business without money of exchange. They maintained a dense web of mutual charge accounts among themselves in a system that has been called bookkeeping barter. Changing monetary values in their account books closely matched the movement of money of exchange throughout the Atlantic world. During the price revolution of the eighteenth century, similar rates of inflation appeared in both "imaginary money" and "real money." See Winifred Rothenberg, *From Market Places to a Market Economy; The Transformation of Rural Massachusetts, 1750–1850* (Chicago, 1992); *idem,* "The Market and Massachusetts Farmers, 1750–1855," *Journal of Economic History* 41 (1981) 283–314; *idem,* "A Price Index for Rural Massachusetts, 1750–1855," *ibid.* 39 (1979) 975–1001; and for bookkeeping barter see Baxter, *House of Hancock,* 17–21.

Excellent works of reference on monetary systems include Peter Spufford (with the assistance of Wendy Wilkinson and Sarah Tolley), *Handbook of Medieval Exchange* (London, 1986); and John J. McCusker, *Money and Exchange in Europe and America, 1600–1775: A Handbook* (Chapel Hill, 1978). Another work on exchange in Europe from the late fifteenth century is in progress by Frank C. Spooner.

APPENDIX H
Nominal Prices and Silver Equivalents

How should prices be represented? What units should be used? Most scholars measure prices in standard monetary equivalents. That conventional practice has been followed in this work, with a few exceptions noted in this appendix. But other social and agricultural historians have sometimes reckoned prices differently in an effort to remove the effect of monetary fluctuations, and in particular to control for the effect of monetary debasement.

The silver-content in money of exchange was frequently altered by public authorities and private individuals. Monarchs and mint–masters changed the amount of precious metal in their coins: sometimes by debasements which reduced the content of precious metal; other times by recoinages which increased it. England's Edward III, for example, repeatedly shrank the silver content of an English penny: twenty-two grains in 1334, twenty in 1344, eighteen in 1351. Henry IV reduced it further to fifteen in 1411, and Edward IV took it down to twelve grains in 1464. Other kings went the other way. Henry VII, founder of a new Tudor dynasty, wished to establish the legitimacy of his reign by improving its coinage in silver content, technical excellence, and artistic merit. His son Henry VIII reversed that policy. In the words of historian Charles Oman, he converted "the finest, best executed and most handsome coinage in Europe" into "the most disreputable money that had been seen since the days of Stephen—the gold heavily alloyed, the so-called silver ill-struck and turning black and brown as the base metal came to the surface." (Charles Oman, *Coinage of England* [Oxford, 1931, 244]; Glyn Davies, *A History of Money* [Cardiff, 1994], 192–93).

Private individuals also debased gold and silver coins that passed through their hands. The crudest and most common method was to clip, shave, or file away part of the metal and pass what remained as if it were the intact coin. This ancient practice is the reason why modern coins are still minted with a distinctive pattern around their edges. A more subtle method of debasement was to wash or "sweat" a coin, so as to remove some of its gold or silver by chemical means. The most laborious technique was to cut the coin through its edge into two narrow discs, remove the center, and rejoin them. A merchant, money-changer or even small storekeeper in the early modern era had to keep his own scales and use them with great care.

In early projects of price history, some scholars tried to correct for monetary instability of this sort by reckoning prices not in monetary units but in grams or grains of pure silver. The pathbreaking British price historian Thorold Rogers did this. His example was followed by German agrarian historian

Wilhelm Abel, who computed his grain prices in kilograms of pure silver. Abel was mainly interested in harvest conditions, which he wished to study by a method that would remove the effect of currency debasements and recoinages.

Other price historians have followed Rogers and Abel, notably Fernand Braudel and Frank Spooner. But most have not done so. Increasingly, price historians work with nominal monetary units. One of the most meticulous of medieval price scholars, David L. Farmer, explains the reason why. "I have not followed J. E. T. Rogers and others in attempting to express medieval prices in terms of constant weights of silver," he wrote. "Such exercises ignore the value of silver relative to the stock in the economy in which it circulates" ("Prices and Wages, 1350–1500," in Joan Thirsk, ed., *Agrarian History of England and Wales,* III, 441).

Scholars will continue to disagree on this problem. This book supplies estimates by both methods for the price-revolutions of the Middle Ages, as well as for the sixteenth century and the eighteenth century, so that readers may judge the result. They will find that the two methods of representing prices make little difference for an understanding of long-term secular change.

Farmer himself attempted to measure the effect of debasements and recoinages more directly, and found that the many English debasements of silver pennies between 1334 and 1464 had little impact on long secular trends in price levels. He concluded that changes in 1344 and 1351 "were followed by livestock prices slightly higher than usual for a year or two after each devaluation. . . . But later changes in the weight of silver in the penny seem to have had little effect on prices" (*ibid.,* 440–41).

Altogether, indicators of the timing, direction, and spatial diffusion of major price-movements yield broadly similar results, no matter whether one uses the prevailing gold and silver currencies of the time or their equivalents in pure silver. Patterns of short-term fluctuation in commodity prices around the secular trend were more apt to show the effect of debasements; but the trend itself, as well as price relatives, wage-price movements, and the movement of rent and interest are much the same by the two methods.

APPENDIX I

❧ Returns to Capital:
Interest Rates as Historical Indicators

As a measure of changing returns to capital, the empirical indicator used throughout this inquiry is the annual rate of interest as it has changed through time. Here I have followed the work of Sidney Homer, an American lawyer and investment counselor who worked in the securities market for many years, and made it his hobby to study the history of interest rates throughout the world, which he did with great care. Many scholars and leaders in the American securities industry lent their expertise to his project. Among them were Henry Kaufman, Arthur Burns, and Marshall Dunn (Sidney Homer, *A History of Interest Rates* (1963, 2d. ed., New Brunswick, N.J., 1977).

From the broad range of materials that Homer collected, I have tried to assemble a set of indicators that have six qualities in common. First, they are specific to a time and place. Second, they are high-grade securities, issued either by leading governments, or by established private institutions. Third, they are securities that are actively bought and sold in financial markets. Fourth, market yields are preferred to nominal yields. Fifth, a range of securities is used wherever possible: long and short, public and private. Sixth, where possible they have been drawn from multiple national economies.

With a few exceptions, data that meet these criteria may be found from the fifteenth century to the present, but not earlier. I have not been able to make much headway on the movement of interest in the medieval price revolution. Scattered scraps of evidence suggest that the patterns were similar to subsequent great waves, but more work needs to be done on this question.

Other questions of high complexity will come quickly to mind. It would be good to know more about the relation between price revolutions and capital-formation, capital-accumulation, and patterns of change in the structure and function of capital markets. All this must be left to later inquiries and larger books.

APPENDIX J
ᶛ Returns to Labor: Real Wages and Living Standards

A difficult problem in this inquiry is to find a method of measuring returns to labor through four price revolutions. The most simple and straightforward way is to compute real wages: that is, money wages adjusted by an index of consumer prices. The result of this computation is yet another index, commonly expressed as a ratio of the purchasing power of wages in any given year to their purchasing power in a single benchmark year. This solution has been standard for many generations and is employed throughout this work.

Many scholars have criticized the use of real wages for this purpose. They have done so with good reason. Economists and historians agree that even the most refined indices of real wages are not in themselves an accurate measure of returns to labor. They are even less satisfactory as an indicator of changing standards of living. Here are a few of many problems.

First, standard series of money wages tend to have structural distortions in wage coverage itself. Long-running wage series tend to bias the inquiry toward workers whose employment is more stable than that of the labor force as a whole. This distortion was specially strong in the late medieval and early modern historiography. In twentieth century statistics, the same bias is still present, but not so strong. Its net effect in a study of secular change is to understate long-term improvement of wages before the twentieth century.

Second, wage series tend to omit unreported earnings in the "gray economy." As wages are increasingly taxed in many nations, and employment is subject to regulations of growing complexity, the gray labor market has grown larger during the twentieth century. Many of these unreported jobs tend to be more poorly paid than those that are reported. In studies of secular change, this problem causes an underestimate of growth in aggregate returns to labor, but an overestimate of average hourly money wages and real wages in the twentieth century.

Third, real wages are commonly computed only from money wages, and take no account of income in kind. A large part of returns to labor in the medieval and early modern periods consisted of income in kind. This assumption, to my knowledge, has never been tested empirically for long periods. The problem can only be solved by the use of personal documents (diaries, private accounts, etc.), which are limited to literate populations. In any case, a bias toward money wages understates returns to labor in every period. The magnitude of this distortion is greatest in earlier periods; the effect is to overstate long-term improvement in returns to labor by excluding a form of income that was relatively larger in the past.

Fourth, wage series in themselves tell us nothing about the extent of unemployment or underemployment. Returns to labor should properly include not only hourly or daily earnings but also the changing proportion of hours and days actually worked. Some twentieth-century studies have introduced corrections for this problem. Stanley Lebergott compiled a series of average annual returns of employees in the United States. He adjusted money earnings for unemployment, then deflated both series by consumer prices. The result was two series: real wages of workers when employed, and real wages of workers "after deduction for unemployment." But his correction did not fully account for underemployment, as distinct from unemployment. See Stanley Lebergott, *Manpower in Economic Growth: The American Record since 1800* (New York, 1964). Both unemployment and underemployment were widespread in the past. Many scholars believe that underemployment in particular was much greater in earlier periods than it is today. Its forms have changed through time. In eighteenth-century France, for example, laborers were often not able to work on religious feast days. This problem has not seemed important to secular scholars, but each year there were 111 feast days in France under the old regime. See George E. Rudé, "Prices, Wages and Popular Movements in Paris during the French Revolution," *Economic History Review* 2d ser. 6 (1953–54), 248n.

Fifth, feminists rightly complain of a strong gender-bias in wage indices, which commonly omit the work of women who are not formally in the labor market. How does one estimate the real wages of housewives? Their inclusion poses difficult problems of measurement, and their omission leads to heavy overstatement of real wages per worker. The same problem exists for the unpaid but often very arduous labor of other household members. As more women enter the work force, and fewer children work within the family, the secular effect of this bias is to understate the improvement of real wages in the past century.

Sixth, wage series do not tell us enough about actual living conditions and the standard of living as they have changed through time. There are two problems here. One is conceptual: how is one to define a standard of living? The second is empirical: how should it be measured? Two very able Scottish historians sum up: "We should reiterate the point that any study of the standard of the standard of living is beset with very substantial technical difficulties for the historian, that the study of wages makes up only part of it, and the study of male wages a smaller part still. Income is earned in several ways, and by all the household, so the only fully legitimate way into the problem is through the examination of a total household economy" (A. J. S. Gibson and T. C. Smout, *Prices, Food and Wages in Scotland, 1550–1780* [Cambridge, 1995], 356).

But this requirement creates other problems. The "examination of a total household economy" is fraught with difficulty. The evidence itself is much less than total, especially for medieval households. Problems of inference are abundant. Estimates have often been distorted by gross ideological biases in the "standard of living" debate that has raged in economic and social history for many years.

For excellent discussions of the problem see Christopher Dyer, *Standards of Living in the Later Middle Ages; Social Change in England, c. 1200–1520* (Cambridge, 1989); and D. Woodward, "Wage Rates and Living Standards in Pre-Industrial England," *Past and Present* 91 (1981) 28–45.

For the time being, it is necessary to confine this inquiry to real wages alone, but the limits of this indicator should be clearly understood. It refers only to the purchasing power of money wages for a fixed unit of time, without regard to unemployment, underemployment, unpaid labor, the gray market or the total household economy. It tells us only how the purchasing power of a fixed unit of labor changed through time in terms of a basket of prices. Future inquiries will undoubtedly be able to do better, but for the present this is as far as we can go in a study of long-term secular change in returns to labor.

APPENDIX K
?▲ Measures of Wealth and Income Distribution

Many different statistical methods have been used to measure the distribution of income and wealth. They present complex problems of bias in their construction, and are not easily compared with one another.

Most common and straight-forward are what might be called "upper quantile" methods. They estimate the size-shares of the richest 1 percent or 5 percent or 10 percent, or other top quantiles of the population. Another common measure of a similar type is the Pareto distribution, which calculates the slope of the upper tail of wealth or income holders. These techniques tell us much about patterns of distribution at the top of a wealth-order, but the coverage of all these approaches is biased toward the most affluent classes in a society.

Another favorite device is the Lorenz curve, which is created by plotting the cumulative distribution of wealth for an entire population on the x axis, against the cumulative proportion of the population holding that wealth on the y axis. If wealth is perfectly equal in its distribution, the result is a straight diagonal line, showing that 25 percent of the population owns 25 percent of the wealth, 50 percent owns 50 percent, etc. Where inequality exists, the plot becomes a curve, which moves away from the diagonal line as inequality increases.

Many methods have been invented for summarizing the shape of a Lorenz curve in a single statistic. Chief among them is the Gini ratio, which measures the area between the line of equality and the curve of inequality, as a ratio of the total area below the line. Where perfect equality exists, the line of equality and the curve coincide, and the Gini ratio is zero. Where perfect inequality exists (that is, the upper unit owns everything), the Gini ratio approaches 1.00. In general, the geometry of a Gini ratio tends to give more representation to middling groups, and less to the bottom and top.

Another measure of inequality has been invented by British economist A. B. Atkinson to correct these biases of coverage. It is an index that includes a constant which can be set at different levels, so as to give more or less weight to upper groups, or lower ones. In common practice, the constants are arbitrarily set at several different values and multiple results are given so as to provide different perspectives. Atkinson's index has become popular among economists, but it is rarely used by historians because it is not as accessible to general readers.

Other measures include the coefficient of variation, various applications of the standard deviation, mean/median ratios, and mean deviations. These tools are very crude and lacking in resolution.

Which measure should one use? A pluralist solution is adopted here, so as to combine clarity and comprehension. Where possible, this inquiry seeks to combine for any given distribution a Lorenz curve, a Gini ratio, and an attached table that lists the proportion of wealth held by each decile of the population. This combination (which can be compressed into a very small space) supplies easily accessible data for the top, middle and lower strata, and also gives the most widely used single summary statistic. The presentation also uses both tabular and graphic representations. The result combines clarity, precision, accessibility and comprehension for different readers.

Unhappily it cannot be used in every instance because of source limits. In some cases only Gini ratios, top quantile shares and zero holders are available.

APPENDIX L
‽ Price Revolutions and Inequality

Why are some people rich and others poor? What is the cause of material inequality? How has inequality changed through time? What, if anything, can or should we do about it? These eternal questions have given rise to many models of inequality, which differ both as theoretical propositions and empirical descriptions. Several leading models might be summarized in a few sentences, and then compared with evidence that we have found in this inquiry.

‽ Uniformity Models:
Pareto's Law, Lassalle's Conjecture, and Bowley's Law

One set of theories are uniformity models. They describe inequality as more or less constant in history and explain it as the inexorable result of something fixed and fundamental in human nature or the social condition.

The leading uniformity theory is Pareto's Law. It takes its name from Vilfredo Pareto (1848–1923), an Italian scholar who studied income statistics in many nations, and concluded that the pattern of inequality was a curve of constant shape for all incomes, all countries, and all periods of history. Pareto's Law is an equation that may be written in the form of:

$$\log N = \log A - a \log X$$

where X is income of a given size, N is the number of people with that income or more, and A is an empirical constant. When plotted on a double-log graph, the result is a line with a slope of a.

Pareto believed that the slope of a was always approximately 1.5 for upper income-holders. He concluded that this statistical regularity was a law of inequality, which derived mainly from biological differences in the distribution of human ability. It is interesting that Pareto himself was born to the nobility of Genoa. In later life he embraced many social causes, but his attitudes remained aristocratic, and his law has found many supporters on the political right. It has been used to prove that inequality is natural and inexorable.

Another and very different uniformity theory might be called Lassalle's Conjecture, or the Monte Carlo model. It comes not from the right but from the left, and takes its name from Ferdinand Lassalle, a German socialist with a sense of humor, who observed a statistical similarity between the distribution of wealth in European society and the distribution of winners at the roulette table in Monte Carlo. He framed a proposition that both results were ruled by the laws of chance, and would continue to be so until socialism shut down the game. Lassalle's idea of inequality was a constant curve of probability.

A third uniformity model is known to economists of advanced years as Bowley's Law. It bears the name of Arthur Bowley, a British statistician who constructed some of the earliest estimates of national income for the United Kingdom. Bowley discovered evidence that income shares of capital and labor remained approximately constant in Britain through the late nineteenth and early twentieth centuries. This finding was called Bowley's Law, which John Maynard Keynes celebrated as "one of the most surprising, yet best established facts in the whole range of economic statistics." Bowley also reported evidence that the distribution of incomes among individual workers in Britain remained stable over a period of nearly a century. His model was extended to individual income-shares, as well as to factor shares between labor and capital. See Y. S. Brenner, Hartmut Kaelbe and Mark Thomas, eds., *Income Distribution in Historical Perspective* (Cambridge, 1991), 35; A. L. Bowley, *Wages in the United Kingdom in the Nineteenth Century* (Cambridge, 1900); *idem, Wages and Income in the United Kingdom since 1860* (Cambridge, 1937).

ᡒᡐ Continuity Models: Persistent Cultural Values

Most historians reject the idea of uniformity in all periods and places, but some have developed models of continuity of a sort that can coexist with patterns of change through time, and with variation from one culture to another. A theory of continuity in regard to inequality appears in one of my own works, *Albion's Seed* (Oxford, 1989). This work reports empirical evidence that very different patterns of wealth-inequality developed in the various cultural regions of British America during the seventeenth and eighteenth centuries. These relative differences in wealth-distribution within American regions have persisted for many generations, and cannot be explained by material or environmental factors. They could only have arisen from enduring cultural values and institutional processes.

ᡒᡐ Ecological Models: Environmental Conditions

Other historical models give more attention to ecological and material conditions. An example is the work of Jackson Turner Main, who studied the distribution of wealth in early America and concluded that patterns of wealth inequality were "not so much cultural as social and economic" in their origin.

He believed that frontier conditions supported equality during the seventeenth, eighteenth and nineteenth centuries, while urbanization and commercialization caused inequality. See Jackson Turner Main, *The Social Structure of Revolutionary America* (Princeton, 1965), 286; *idem, Society and Economy in Colonial Connecticut* (Princeton, 1985), 376.

≥ Population Models: Malthus and Population Growth

Another theory of inequality derives from the work of Thomas Malthus and academic Malthusians. This is a change-model. It holds that the growth of population promotes the growth of inequality in a variety of ways. It expands the supply of labor relative to demand, lowers wages as more people compete for jobs, and drives the poor to the margin of subsistence. This theory has been widely accepted by economic historians of the medieval and early modern world. It has also been applied to global trends in the modern era. See Michael Postan, *The Medieval Economy and Society* (1972, Harmondsworth, 1975), 40, 275).

≥ Dialectical Models: Systems of Production and Exchange

Yet another set of theories holds that inequality has increased or diminished through time as a consequence of structural changes in economic systems. Among them are Marxist theories, which assert that inequality of wealth and income is determined principally by ownership of means of production. Two of Karl Marx's most creative ideas were his "law of capitalist accumulation" and his theory of surplus value, which holds that as productivity increases above subsistence, capitalist owners appropriate to themselves "surplus value" above the value equal to labor's subsistence, thereby increasing inequality.

Many Marxist writers have theorized that inequality increases with the growth of capitalism—that is, with private ownership of the means of production. A related theory is the argument that inequality has increased with the separation of capital and labor in the industrial revolution. Many Marxist historians believe that inequality increased rapidly during the industrial revolution from the eighteenth to the twentieth century.

In the United States, non-Marxist historians on the left have developed a related theory of inequality which attributes its growth not primarily to changes in systems of production but to processes of exchange and in particular to "market revolutions." They believe that the effect of an expanding free market within a capitalist system was thought to cause a growth of inequality. The precise linkages were apt to be a little fuzzy, but in general it has been argued that the effect of ''commercialization'' has been to create larger and more integrated markets in which the rich became richer, and inequality increased.

ஐ Economic Models: Growth-Processes and the Kuznets Curve

A very different theory of inequality has been invented by neo-classical economists. It is called the Kuznets model, after the work of American economist Simon Kuznets. Like many econometric historians, Kuznets was interested primarily in the problem of economic growth and development, and studied changes in inequality primarily in relation to those processes. The Kuznets model hypothesized that as ''traditional'' agricultural economies developed into ''modern'' industrial systems, inequality at first increased and then declined in a curve that resembled an inverted *U*. Kuznets and his colleagues found many mechanisms to explain this pattern. One of them, which Kuznets himself suggested, was the role of intersectoral shifts. In early stages of development, some workers moved into more highly paid jobs in sectors of the economy which had higher productivity. Other workers remained behind, and inequality increased. In later stages of economic growth, workers who had been left behind also made that same sectoral transition, and inequality diminished. Another mechanism was demographic: increasing rates of population growth in early stages; declining rates thereafter. A third factor was an acceleration in later stages of education and economic skills. See Jeffrey C. Williamson and Peter H. Lindert, *American Inequality, A Macroeconomic History* [New York, 1980]; Jeffrey C. Williamson, *Did British Capitalism Breed Inequality?* [Boston, 1985])

ஐ Cyclical Models: Life Cycle Theories

An interesting theory of inequality centers on individuals rather than economies. One such approach developed from the work of B. S. Rowntree on poverty in the city of York, England (*Poverty, A Study of Town Life* [London, 1899]). He found that distribution of income and wealth varied through the life cycle. Laborers in York lived through periods of poverty and comparative affluence, with poverty occurring in childhood, early adulthood and old age, and affluence in late youth and middle age. Other scholars have found different life-cycle rhythms of income and wealth for blue-collar and white-collar workers, and have linked this approach to differences of class, education, job-type, ethnicity, and race. These findings have been aggregated into macroeconomic theories that changes in age-composition, skill-distribution, and educational attainment have changed the distribution of wealth and income in entire social and economic systems.

⅋ Institutional Models:
The Welfare State and the Robin Hood Paradox

Historians commonly believe that laws, institutions, reform movements, and conservative counter-movements have made a major difference in the distribution of wealth and income. Most liberal textbooks in American history (which is to say, most textbooks) have been written around the belief that Franklin Roosevelt's New Deal and Lyndon Johnson's war on poverty caused an increase in equality, and that the Robber Barons and Republican presidents before 1932 and after 1968 caused inequality to grow. These ideas rest on the idea that laws and institutions make a difference.

A very different institutional model comes from economic historian Peter Lindert, who has framed the counterhypothesis called the "Robin Hood Paradox," which holds that "across time and jurisdictions, redistribution toward the poor is least given when most needed . . . Robin Hood shows up least when needed most." ("Toward a Comparative History of Income and Wealth Inequality," in Brenner, Kaelbe and Thomas, eds., *Income Distribution in Historical Perspective*," 226–29

⅋ Empirical Evidence

Which of these many theories of inequality is correct? Altogether, evidence now in hand is strong enough to support several generalizations

First, the uniformity models are mistaken. Pareto's Law, Lassalle's Conjecture and Bowley's Law all derived from early data, mainly for the mid-nineteenth and early twentieth centuries. That era was a period of comparatively little change in wealth and income distribution and appeared to confirm these models. But subsequent research yielded very different results. More evidence accumulated from the 1930s to 1968; most of it found growing of equality in that period. Yet more data is now available from 1968 to 1996, and shows the opposite trend in that period: a rapid increase in inequality. Projects of historical research have been completed for earlier periods. By and large they find evidence of growing inequality in the late eighteenth and early nineteenth centuries, stability in the late nineteenth and early twentieth centuries, growing equality in the mid-twentieth century, and growing inequality thereafter. All of this evidence supports a firm conclusion. The history of inequality is the history of change.

Further, there is strong evidence that wealth and income distribution have varied broadly one culture to another, and that some of these relative differences are remained highly persistent through time, even as change has occurred everywhere in levels and trends. Even within the narrow limits of American history, for example, the range of regional and local differences in inequality is nearly as broad as the limits of possibility. In terms of Gini ratios (where .00 equals perfect equality and .99 represents perfect inequality), the first distribution of lands in Roger Williams's Rhode Island Plantation briefly approached zero, but the distribution of land in Adams County, Mississippi, on the eve of the Civil War was above .95. Relative differences of that sort have persisted between northern and southern regions of the United States for two centuries. From these findings one may draw a second conclusion. Elements of cultural persistence have coexisted with patterns of change.

How do these combinations of change and persistence compare with leading theories of inequality? In general, one may say that most of the leading theorists of inequality have accurately described inequality-trends in the half-century or century before they wrote. But all were mistaken in building a universal theory on that narrow historical base. This conclusion holds for Malthus, Ricardo and Marx; for Lassalle, Pareto and Bowley; for Kuznets, Williamson and Lindert. All testified truly to their own immediate historical experience, but erred in over-generalizing to other periods.

It is well known, for example, that the relationship between population and wealth changed fundamentally just after Malthus published his work; that the relationship between capitalism and distribution was transformed after Marx. In the same way, the Kuznets-Williamson-Lindert inverted-U model appears to fit the facts from the mid-nineteenth to the mid-twentieth century, but not from the 1960s to our own time.

Other theories of inequality have been falsified by historical research. The institutional models fail the test of chronology. Inequality did not increase in the age of the Robber Barons. It did not diminish after 1968. Recent theoretical models of a market revolution as the driver of inequality during the nineteenth century fail every test, both for the timing of market-growth and inequality. The Robin Hood paradox works in the 1980s, but not in the 1930s. The idea that capitalism caused inequality is also incorrect in the same way: it works for some periods, but not for others. In terms of chronology the history of capitalism and the history of inequality do not coincide. In short, all of the theoretical models listed above are unsupported by historical evidence.

This evidence suggests the possibility of another theory. Let us look again at the descriptive patterns. In the past five centuries the predominant change pattern is not precisely linear or cyclical. Levels of inequality have tended to rise and fall in long wavelike movements. In what is now the northern United States, patterns appear to have been more or less as follows: 1630–1670, growing inequality; 1680–1730, growing equality; 1740–1840,

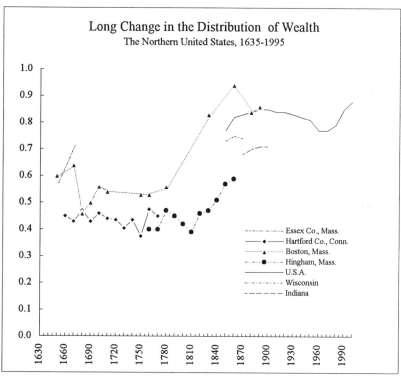

Long Change in the Distribution of Wealth
The Northern United States, 1635-1995

Legend:
- ·············· Essex Co., Mass.
- ——◆—— Hartford Co., Conn.
- ············▲ Boston, Mass.
- –·–●·–· Hingham, Mass.
- ———— U.S.A.
- –·–·–·– Wisconsin
- – – – – – Indiana

Figure 5.07 summarizes many studies of wealth-distribution in the northern United States. It finds three periods of growing inequality which coincide with later stages of price revolutions and early years of price equilibria: 1630-1670, 1760-1850, and 1968-1996+. It also finds two periods of stability or increasing equality which coincide with the later phases of price equilibria and the early stages of price revolutions: 1680-1760, and 1860-1968.

All time series are analyses of estates in probate except Hingham (taxable wealth), and the U.S.A. (census data and household surveys). All are computed as Gini ratios except Hingham, which is the size-share of the top ten percent. A Gini ratio is a measure of distribution, which ranges from .00 (perfect equality) to .99 (perfect inequality, where the top percentile owns everything).

Sources include Jeffrey G. Williamson and Peter H. Lindert, *American Inequality; A Macroeconomic History* (Madison, 1964); Lee Soltow, "Distribution of Income and Wealth," in Glenn Porter ed., *Encyclopedia of American Economic History*, III, 1087-1102; *idem, Men and Wealth in the United States, 1850-1870* (New Haven, 1975); *idem, Patterns of Wealthholding in Wisconsin since 1850* (Madison, 1971); W. I. King, *Wealth and Income of the People of the United States* (New York, 1915); Daniel Scott Smith, "Population, Family, and Society in Hingham..." (diss., Univ. of California at Berkeley, 1973); Donald Koch, "Income Distribution and Political Structure in Seventeenth-Century Salem," *Essex Institute Historical Collections* 105 (1969) 50-71; Jackson Turner Main, *Society and Economy in Colonial Connecticut* (Princeton, 1985).

growing inequality; 1850–1932, fluctuations on a fixed plateau; 1932–68, growing equality; 1968–96+, growing inequality.

The main lines of change in European data are more obscure. But in England, inequality increased during the sixteenth and early seventeenth centuries, diminished in the late seventeenth and early eighteenth centuries, increased again from the mid-eighteenth century to the mid-nineteenth century, fluctuated on the same plane *circa* 1850–1930, declined in the mid-twentieth century, and have been rising in the late twentieth century. In summary, British trends are broadly similar to those in the United States.

We find a wave pattern in the wealth-histories of both nations. These waves do not synchronize exactly with price-revolutions and price-equilibria. But if one lags price-movements against inequality-trends, then a correlation begins to emerge. In descriptive terms it might be summarized as follows. The later stages of every price revolution and the early stages of each equilibrium were periods when inequality increased. On the other hand, the latter stages of each equilibrium, and the early stages of each price revolution were marked by stability or decline in levels of inequality. These trends appear to have recurred in every price revolution since the late middle ages.

This descriptive pattern strongly suggests a theory of inequality. First, changes in relative returns to capital and labor were caused by the dynamics of price revolutions and price equilibria as discussed in the main body of this work. Second, changes in the distribution of income were caused by those prior changes in relative returns to labor and capital, lagged in time. Third, changes in wealth-distribution were caused by changes in income-distribution, also lagged in time. All of this would explain a correlation between price revolutions and inequality, but one that is offset in time, with strong inertial effects. This theory also suggests many obvious possibilities for the regulation of inequality. Here again, a wave-pattern is an opportunity for a policy-maker in a free society.

APPENDIX M
ဆ Price Revolutions and Family Disintegration

One of the great social questions in the late twentieth century is about the disintegration of the family. A particular source of concern is the rapid rise of births outside marriage, which in the United States increased from 3.5 percent in 1940 to 28 percent in 1990. These estimates refer to the entire American population. Among African Americans, the proportion of births to unwed mothers was 65 percent in 1990, and climbing. Similar trends (with different magnitudes) appeared in many nations. By the 1990s, the proportion of babies born outside of marriage was higher in Britain and some European nations than in America. See U. S. National Center for Health Statistics, *Vital Statistics of the United States* (1995); *Statistical Abstract of the United States* (1993), table 101.

By 1990 the problem of family disintegration had reached crisis proportions and became profoundly destructive of individual lives. Many studies have found that children born to unwed mothers are more likely to get into serious trouble in later life. By comparison with children in complete families, children born outside of marriage are less likely to stay in school or keep out of jail. They are less able to find a good job, or any job, or to be able to hold a job. They are also less likely to become married themselves, but more likely to have children of their own outside of wedlock.

ဆ The Problem of Cause

Why has this happened? Why have births outside marriage so greatly increased? In the United States, most answers to these questions have come from politicians, journalists, and social scientists. They think of the problem as something unique to our own time, and seek an explanation that is rooted in the twentieth century.

Opinion on the right holds that the modern social welfare system is largely responsible by paying unmarried women who have babies, and by giving them more attention in motherhood than they would otherwise receive. Observers on the left believe that the cause is poverty and exploitation of the poor by the institutions of ''late capitalist society.'' Others think that the cause is a general decline in the structure of ''family values,'' or a disintegration of systems of social control, or a disruption of processes of socialization, caused by a crisis of western civilization during the twentieth century. Many believe that the problem is specific to minorities which British historian Peter Laslett brutally calls ''the bastardy-prone sub-society.''

This problem looks very different when it is studied in a broad historical perspective. We are not the first generation to face the problem of family disintegration on a massive scale. Much historical research has been done on births outside of marriage in America and Europe, from the sixteenth century to the present. Many scholars have also studied the history of prenuptial pregnancy, which yields similar (but not identical) patterns of change. The results are summarized in Peter Laslett, Karla Oosterveen, and Richard Smith, eds., *Bastardy and Its Comparative History: Studies in the History of Illegitimacy and Marital Nonconformism in Britain, France, Germany, Sweden, North America, Jamaica, and Japan* (Cambridge, Mass., 1980); and in Daniel Scott Smith and Michael Hindus, "Premarital Pregnancy in America, 1640–1971: An Overview and Interpretation," *Journal of Interdisciplinary History* 5 (1975) 537–70.

?❧ Patterns of Long Term Change

On the question of long-term change, these studies yield similar results. Three times in the span of modern history, conceptions outside marriage and births to unwed mothers have surged to very high levels. The first of these waves occurred in the late sixteenth and early seventeenth centuries, and reached its peak *circa* 1600. The second wave started in the early eighteenth century (earlier in England), and crested in the late eighteenth and early nineteenth centuries. The third wave began in the early twentieth century (*ca.* 1900), and is still in progress as this work goes to press in 1996.

These three waves alternated with other long periods when illegitimacy and prenuptial pregnancy declined and stabilized at low levels. One such period occurred in the mid- and late seventeenth century. Another happened in the nineteenth century, from about 1830 to 1900.

In this long historical pattern of alternating surges and declines, the magnitudes of change were very large. Studies of illegitimacy in England, for example, find that the proportion of births outside of marriage rose in peak periods as high as 10 percent (and much higher in some regions) during the seventeenth and eighteenth centuries. During the period of decline from 1650 to 1750, they fell below 1 percent.

The range of prenuptial pregnancy rates in the United States was even greater. In some New England towns as many as 40 percent of brides were pregnant at the end of the eighteenth century. During the mid-nineteenth century, prenuptial pregnancy in New England fell below 5 percent, as it had also done in the seventeenth century. These findings have been replicated in many studies. The results vary in detail by region and ethnic group, but secular trends are broadly similar.

Why? What set these waves in motion? What brought them to an end? Causal theories favored by social scientists and journalists in the late twentieth

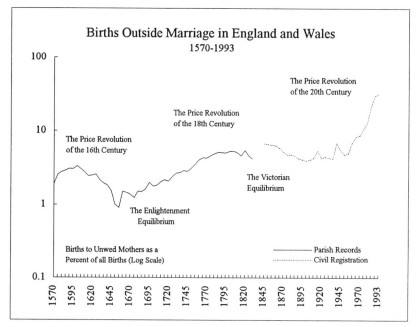

Figure 5.08 summarizes the results of a research project by the Cambridge Group for the History of Population and Social Structure on illegitimacy from 1570 to 1975, and civil registration data on the proportion of births outside marriage to 1993. Illegitimacy ratios are births to unwed mothers as a percent of all births, here presented as quinquennial means of annual data. The proportion of births outside marriage in Great Britain was 30.1 percent in 1990. The source is Peter Laslett, Karla Osterveen, and Richard M. Smith, eds., *Bastardy and Its Comparative History* (Cambridge, 1980), 14-17; *Annual Abstract of Statistics* 130 (1994) series 2.17; (1995) series 2.14.

century cannot answer these questions. Our modern system of social welfare might possibly be suspected as the cause of the third wave, but certainly not of the first or second. Further, an expansion of social welfare institutions happened in the nineteenth and very early twentieth centuries when rates of illegitimacy were falling. The "crisis of late capitalism" explanation fails in the same way. Earlier waves of family disintegration occurred before capitalist systems had fully developed. The idea of a "bastardy-prone sub-society" does not help to explain historical trends, for in each wave births outside marriage tended to increase in nearly all social groups.

ૠ Family Disintegration and Price Revolutions

To understand the root of this problem, we need to study it in a broader historical context. An important causal clue may appear in the fact that secular trends in births outside marriage and in prenuptial pregnancy synchronize closely with the rhythm of long-term price movements. The three long surges in births outside of marriage all coincided with price revolutions. The two declines occurred in eras of price equilibrium (see figures 3.11 and 3.29 and 4.25).

This correlation certainly does not prove that price movements themselves were the proximate cause of family disintegration, but it establishes beyond reasonable doubt an association of some kind. Skeptics must explain away three broad wave-surges, two wave-troughs, and a very tight chronology.

Several causal models come quickly to mind. One possibility would be a direct and simple causal connection between material stress and family stress—that is, between wage-price disparities, employment uncertainties, etc., and family disintegration. Another possibility would be a more complex causal sequence from material disequilibria to cultural anomie. Yet another would be a material disruption of systems of socialization and social control. A fourth would be a linkage to population-growth, in which price movements and births outside marriage are both consequences of a common cause.

In any case, three conclusions are clear enough. First, the crisis of family disintegration in the late twentieth century is not a unique event, and cannot be understood merely by reference to conditions in our time alone. Second, the strength of correlations between economic and demographic trends tells us that recurrent waves of family disintegration in the sixteenth, eighteenth and twentieth centuries were not random variations; neither were the periods of decline of illegitimacy in the late seventeenth century and again in the nineteenth century. These movements were part of a larger pattern. Third, the evidence strongly suggests that the rise of births outside marriage will reverse sometime in the near future.

In the meantime, the historical evidence also suggests that policies for control of the problem should center on the material and cultural stresses that impinge on young lives in the penultimate periods of price revolutions: that is, on price-wage differentials, on employment prospects for young people, and on the strength of socializing institutions such as schools and families. The welfare system is not the primary problem. Neither is it capitalism in general, or cultural values as a whole. The root of the problem is not the weakness of family values, but the difficulty that young people have in realizing them. This is specially so during the late stages of price revolutions.

It need not happen. Our own children and grandchildren have become the victims of historical processes that are now increasingly within our power to control by a common effort—if only we have the collective will and wisdom to do so.

APPENDIX N

𝕚 Price Revolutions and Personal Violence

During the late twentieth century, when crime was rapidly increasing throughout the Western world, many scholars turned their attention to its history. Much of the learned literature centered on the difficulty of drawing any substantive conclusions from historical records of crime and criminal prosecutions. But for all the deficiencies of the data, substantive patterns began to emerge. The evidence for some of these findings is very robust (more so with each new monograph), and several major historical discoveries have been made. Let us confine our attention mainly to the history of homicide, which presents fewer problems of reporting and source-bias than other crimes. Some of the leading findings are as follows.

𝕚 Secular Trends: The Long Decline of Violent Crime

First, studies mainly in England but also in other nations have found that rates of violent crime were much higher in the Middle Ages than in the modern era—higher by a different order of magnitude. Ten local studies of homicide in thirteenth-century England yield an average annual homicide rate of approximately 20 per 100,000 during the thirteenth century. By comparison, the homicide rate in modern Britain was about 1 per 100,000 in 1981 and 0.3 per 100,000 in 1951. See T. R. Gurr, "Historical Trends in Violent Crime: A Critical Review of the Evidence," *Crime and Justice: An Annual Review of Research* 3 [1981] 313. Population estimates are problematic here, but not so much so as to undercut the main conclusion.

Second, many studies of later historical periods have made the concomitant discovery of a very long secular decline in violent crime through the early modern era. In the English counties of Kent, Surrey, Sussex and Essex, recorded rates of homicide moved decisively downward. They were approximately 6 or 7 per 100,000 in the mid-sixteenth century, 2 or 3 in the mid-eighteenth century, and 1 in the mid-twentieth century. See J. S. Cockburn, "Patterns of Violence in English Society: Homicides in Kent, 1560–1985," *Past and Present* 130 [1991] 70–106; J. M. Beattie, "The Pattern of Crime in England, 1660–1800," *Past and Present* 62 (1974) 47–95; A. A. Sharpe, "Domestic Homicide in Early Modern England," *Historical Journal* 24 (1981) 34; Joel Samaha, *Law and Order in Historical Perspective: The Case of Elizabethan Essex* (New York, 1974), 20.

This long secular decline in homicide is not an artifact of measurement. It runs counter to the improvement of recordkeeping, and to the growing intolerance of personal violence. It is also diametrically opposed to the widespread belief of sociologists and criminologists in the mid-twentieth century that high crime rates are an artifact of modernity.

ᏓᎾ Trend Reversals: Four Crime Waves in the Past Millennium

Yet another important pattern has also emerged from the data. This long downward trend in personal violence was continuous, but not constant. Four times it reversed during the past eight centuries, in strong and sustained countertendencies that continued for many years. We have been fated to live through one of these counter-movements. Personal violence ceased falling and rose sharply to a peak during the early fourteenth century, the early seventeenth century, the late eighteenth century, and the late twentieth century. See Lawrence Stone, "Interpersonal Violence in English Society," *Past and Present* 101 (1983) 26–31.

In England, the first and greatest of these four crime waves happened during the crisis of the fourteenth century. In the years from 1310 to 1348, homicide rates rose to the highest levels in recorded English history, far above the high normal range of the thirteenth century, and higher than they would ever be again. In the town of Oxford, the annual murder rate rose as high as 110 per 100,000 during the fourteenth century. This extraordinary peak was not representative of homicide rates throughout England. Even in our own time, Oxford for all its dreaming spires and serene college quads is still a rough town on Saturday nights when the pubs close and crowds of workers, students, and skinheads collide in the ancient streets. Even so, one study finds that during the dark years of the fourteenth century, medieval Oxford was approximately a hundred times more dangerous than the modern town. See Carl I. Hammer, "Patterns of Violence in a Medieval University Town," *Past and Present* 78 [1978] 3–23.

After the crisis of the fourteenth century, homicide rates in England began to fall, and they kept on falling for nearly two centuries (*circa* 1350–1550). Despite persistent political instability, personal violence greatly declined in this period.

Then the trend reversed again. From approximately 1550 to 1650, a second great crime wave occurred in England. Murder rates doubled in Kent, trebled in Essex, and multiplied very rapidly in other parts of Britain. They reached their peak during the early seventeenth century.

Rates of personal violence began to fall again in a long decline that continued through the late seventeenth century to approximately 1730. This

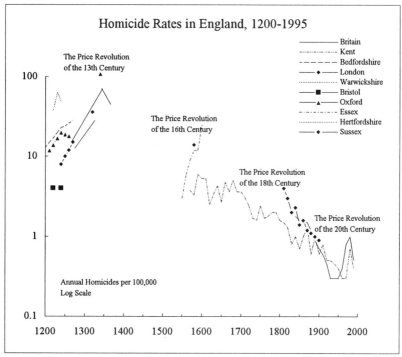

Homicide Rates in England, 1200-1995

The Price Revolution
of the 13th Century

The Price Revolution
of the 16th Century

The Price Revolution
of the 18th Century

The Price Revolution
of the 20th Century

Britain
Kent
Bedfordshire
London
Warwickshire
Bristol
Oxford
Essex
Hertfordshire
Sussex

100

10

1

0.1

Annual Homicides per 100,000
Log Scale

1200 1300 1400 1500 1600 1700 1800 1900 2000

Figure 5.09 summarizes many studies of homicide in England. It finds evidence of a long secular decline in personal violence. This trend was interrupted by strong upward surges in the fourteenth, sixteenth and twentieth centuries; by a more moderate rise in the eighteenth century; and by smaller and short-lived increases in other periods of stress (1680s, 1860s, etc.). Little evidence exists for the period from 1350 to 1530.

The many problems of source-bias in the evidence are discussed in Ted R. Gurr, "Historical Trends in Violent Crime: A Critical Review of the Evidence," *Crime and Justice* 3 (1981) 295-352, the first attempt to draw this material together. Population estimates are also full of difficulty, especially for the Middle Ages.

Other general studies reach similar conclusions as to level and trend. All stress the long decline, and also note (as did Gurr) strong upward surges in the fourteenth, sixteenth and twentieth centuries. See Lawrence Stone, "Interpersonal Violence in English Society, 1300-1983," *Past & Present* 102 (1983) 206-215; J. A. Sharpe, "The History of Violence in England: Some Observations," *Past & Present* 108 (1985) 216-54.

Specific studies include James B. Given, *Society and Homicide in Thirteenth-Century England* (Stanford, 1977); J. S. Cockburn, "Patterns of Violence in English Society: Homicides in Kent, 1560-1985," *Past & Present* 130 (1991) 70-106); Joel Samaha, *Law and Order in Historical Perspective: The Case of Elizabethan Essex* (New York, 1974); V. A. C. Gatrell, "The Decline of Theft and Violence in Victorian and Edwardian England," in Gatrell, et al., *Crime and the Law* (London, 1980), 342-45.

An excellent survey and bibliography of the very large literature is J. A. Sharpe, "The History of Crime in England, c. 1300-1914, An Overview of Recent Publications," *British Journal of Criminology* 28 (1988) 254-67.

307

downward movement was interrupted during the 1690s, when homicides and other crimes rose very sharply. This was a short surge rather than a new secular trend. It soon subsided, and rates of violent crime resumed their long fall.

A third crime wave followed in the eighteenth century. It was not as strong as other upward movements had been, but it was clearly evident in homicide rates, and more visible in respect to other crimes. In Staffordshire, indictments for theft increased sixfold from the 1760s to the 1790s. In Wiltshire, prosecutions for violations of the game laws multiplied by a factor of seven from the 1760s to the 1790s. See J. S. Cockburn, ed., *Crime in England, 1550–1800* (Princeton, 1977), 226; Douglas Hay, "War, Dearth and Theft in the Eighteenth Century: The Record of the English Courts," *Past and Present* 95 (1982) 125.

This surge reached its climax in the late eighteenth and early nineteenth centuries, then reversed. By 1830, rates of violent crime were falling in England, and in many nations. This decline, once begun, continued with a few interruptions through the Victorian era and well into the early twentieth century. It persisted as late as 1930 in Stockholm, 1940 in Sydney and Chicago, 1950 in London, and 1960 in Calcutta.

In the mid-twentieth century, a fourth crime wave began, and rapidly overswept most nations throughout the world. Dates varied in detail, but crime rates were rising everywhere by 1960, and surged to very high levels after 1970. The magnitude of this increase was very large. Homicide rates in some American cities approached the highest levels of the fourteenth century. In 1991, homicides per 100,000 population were approximately 5 in St. Paul, 8 in Seattle, 20 in Boston, 30 in New York, 40 in Baltimore, 50 in Atlanta, 60 in Detroit, 70 in New Orleans, and 80 in Washington. So dangerous were the streets of the nation's capital that it was not safe to walk Pennsylvania Avenue between the White House and the Capitol after dark. In 1991, the most powerful nation in the world was unable to keep order within a few hundred yards of the presidential mansion (*Statistical Abstract of the United States* [1993] table 303).

Then the pattern of change reversed yet again. In the 1990s crime rates were falling rapidly in the United States. Some learned observers believed that this decline marked the beginning of a new secular trend. Others thought that the crime wave of the twentieth century had yet to run its course.

This evidence comes mostly from Britain and the United States. Did similar patterns prevail in other nations? The broad answer is yes. Many local variations appeared in levels of crime, but temporal trends were similar in many nations.

?● Crime Waves and Price Revolutions

When the history of personal violence is compared with price movements through the past eight centuries, a striking paradox appears. The secular trends have moved in opposite directions. Crime rates have come down since the twelfth century; prices have gone up. But even as these long trends were opposed in their secular tendency, they were similar in timing and closely interlocked in rhythm and structure of change.

The complexity of this association clearly appears in a comparison of prices and murder in England. Homicide rates showed a strong downward tendency during periods of price-equilibrium (1350–1490, 1650–1730, and 1830–1900). Those declines continued into the early years of each price revolution (1490–1550, 1730–1760, 1900–1940). The downward trends reversed in later stages of price revolutions. Homicide rates began to increase, then surged to very high levels in years of crisis (1310–48, 1610–50, 1780–1820, and 1965–95).

The conjunction between these trends was most striking in critical periods, when price revolution approached its climax. Four times since the twelfth century, a similar sequence of events occurred. Prices began to surge and returns to capital kept pace with inflation, but wages lagged behind and inequalities of wealth increased. When all of these things happened, crime rates also increased sharply. Most major price surges were followed by crime surges, so closely that the two movements often appeared as statistical shadows. This pattern of association has been replicated in many different studies by scholars who were unaware of trends in other periods and places.

?● Questions of Cause: Four Theories of Crime

This complex association of price movements and crime waves holds important clues for the cause of crime, for the consequences of price revolutions, and for the structure of historical change in general.

Four theories of crime tend to dominate the debate. Two of these ideas are favored by conservative writers. One holds that crime is an act of rational choice, and rises from a prospect of gain. The remedy is to raise the cost of committing crime and to reduce its benefits by tougher penalties.

Another conservative theory begins differently but ends in a similar conclusion. It holds that crime rises mainly from crime-prone subgroups that are not susceptible to reform. The remedy is repression: capital punishment and long-term imprisonment.

Progressive observers tend to think of crime in two different ways. One theory that is favored by the left holds that crime is caused by oppression and exploitation. Marxist versions of this idea (still popular in the universities) argue that crime is a response to capitalist exploitation in particular. The remedy is social reform. Liberal versions center on the individual rehabilitation of the criminal.

Another theory much favored on the left is that crime waves are in large part the figments of overheated conservative imaginations, and are themselves instruments of social control. One scholar writes, "It is tempting to suggest that the historian should study at least some types of crime in the past in terms of 'enforcement waves' rather than 'crime waves.'" Another scholar suggests that we should think in terms of "control waves." See J. A. Sharpe, *Crime in Seventeenth-Century England: A County Study* (Cambridge, 1983) 210; and Jason Ditton, *Controlology: Beyond a New Criminology* (n.p., 1979).

All of these theories have elements of truth, but none of them encompasses the subject. It is certainly the case that "enforcement waves" exist, but they cannot explain away the existence of crime waves. The evidence of homicides, for example, derives not only from the police and courts, but also from public health records. Each of these empirical sources is problematic in its own way, but all of them clearly show similar wave-patterns that could not possibly be artifacts of measurement. Crime is something real in the world; so also are crime-waves and the long secular decline of criminal violence.

The progressive idea that crime is a reflex of capitalist exploitation works no better. The history of crime does not correlate with the history of capitalism. In general, as capitalist institutions developed during the eighteenth, nineteenth and twentieth centuries, crime rates declined. Further, some of the most violent crime waves in the late twentieth century occurred in socialist societies.

Conservative theories of crime work no better than those of progressives. Much work has shown that tougher penalties and restraints do deter crime in some degree, but are never the dominant causal agents that conservatives claim them to be. The stubborn rise of the murder rate in twentieth century America, even as many states returned to capital punishment, tells us that other factors were more powerful.

The conservative idea that criminal violence rises from crime-prone subgroups also is true in one sense but false in another. It is certainly the case that rates of personal violence vary broadly from one culture to another. This is clearly the case in the United States. Differences in homicide rates are greater between American regions than between European nations. But these differences are more evident in levels than trends. When rates of personal violence increased in late twentieth-century America, they did so in every part of the country. One striking property of the crime waves in the late stages of each price revolution is that they tend to appear in all regions, city and class. Always the poor and underprivileged were more likely to be the perpetrators of crime, and also its victims. But crime waves touched all groups, and regions and nations. The question is why, and what might be done about it.

The search for another explanation might begin with close study of the empirical evidence, which holds many causal clues. Let us begin by observing that crime waves correlate with surging prices. It is important to observe that many kinds of crime increase in these periods of economic stress. When the cost of living soars, theft increases sharply. Some people steal to survive. Others steal to get ahead in hard times when other avenues are blocked. The material linkages are very strong.

At the same time, when prices surge, homicides also increase. Increasingly in the modern world, the victims tend to be friends, neighbors, lovers and family members. In many of these acts of personal violence, prospects of material gain are not the primary cause. These are irrational acts. They are driven by passion, anger, jealousy, and fear. In them we may see another classic mechanism, long familiar to social science, of frustration and aggression. Deterrents are powerless to prevent this sort of personal violence, which explodes in periods of high stress without any rational calculus of material gain.

The remedy for these two tendencies cannot be either a conservative policy of repression and deterrence alone, or a liberal program of social reform. The control of crime requires a more complex and subtle policy that combines elements of deterrence for crimes of ambition, repression for hardened criminals, and another strategy for crimes of frustration and pain. This other strategy might include broadly conceived but narrowly targeted programs to provide short-term employment training in periods of stress and similar programs that are meant to keep hope alive. This can only be done by a combination of public and private effort, in which governments, educational institutions, and private corporations work together, unconstrained by ideologies of both the left and right.

One of the major conclusions to emerge from a study of price movements and crime waves is that surges are a large part of the phenomenon. A surge-pattern offers an opportunity for targeting a policy in temporal terms. To do so, planners must learn to think more rigorously and more historically about the problems before us.

APPENDIX O
𝕒 Economics and History

> The reason of a thing is not to be enquired after, till you are
> sure the thing itself be so. We commonly are at *what's the*
> *reason of it?* before we are sure of the thing.
> —John Selden, *Table Talk,* 1689

A primary purpose of this project is descriptive. One of its organizing assumptions is that a task of empirical description may be undertaken without an apparatus of theory. This idea breaks in a fundamental way with an epistemic orthodoxy that has dominated the disciplines of American social science since the late 1940s. So universal has this orthodoxy become in the United States that scholars who work within it are unaware that any other mode of thinking is even possible.

In American universities, a social scientist is free to adopt almost any style of dress, demeanor, life-style, sexual preference, or political ideology, no matter how bizarre or preposterous the choice may be. But graduate students are required to embrace the conventional epistemology of their disciplines, on pain of expulsion from the guild. If they dare to think about the world in any other way, their work is judged "unsound," and they are sent upon their way.

The orthodox epistemology of American social science may be summarized in a sentence. It holds that every explicit description rests upon implicit theoretical assumptions that create the criteria for selecting the things to be described. It teaches that nothing can be understood, or even perceived, without reference to a theory. This epistemology argues not merely that theory-centered thinking is a valid form of social science. It insists that theory is the only form.

Within this body of belief, the central idea of "theory" varies broadly from one social science to another. In economics, a theory is commonly understood as an "if . . . then . . . ." proposition; that is, a statement in the form of "if x, then y." In sociology, a theory is commonly a paradigm model. In history, it sometimes becomes a sequence of narrative statements. However it is conceived, theory-framing and theory-testing became the consuming obsession of American social science during the mid-twentieth century.

The emergence of this epistemic orthodoxy in the United States may be dated to the decade 1945–55, when it appeared simultaneously in manifestos by economists, sociologists, anthropologists, psychologists and historians. In economics, a leading example was an important essay called ''Measurement without Theory,'' published by Tjalling Koopmans in 1947. Koopmans argued that empirical measurement of *any* phenomenon was ''impossible'' without fixed ''theoretical preconceptions.'' Further, he asserted (inconsistently) that measurement without theory was trivial and useless, because ''conclusions relevant to the guidance of economic policies cannot be drawn.'' Koopmans was not content merely to defend the importance of theoretical knowledge in economics. He wished to deny the value of economic knowledge in any other form and to condemn any colleague who sought to attain it in a different way. See Tjalling C. Koopmans, ''Measurement without Theory,'' *Review of Economics and Statistics* 29 (1947) 161–72.

Similar arguments were simultaneously made in the other social sciences. An example in sociology was Serge Timasheff's manifesto called *Sociological Theory* (1955), which argued that ''without theory directing their interpretation and arrangement, facts are almost meaningless.'' Timasheff's sociological colleagues argued among themselves about how theorizing might best be done. Talcott Parsons favored the construction of grand theory. Robert Merton argued for ''theories of the middle range.'' But here again, in sociology as well as in economics, the new orthodoxy insisted that theory was not merely one form of meaningful thought. It was thought to be the only form. All others were dismissed by Timasheff as ''almost meaningless.''

The practical effect of this new orthodoxy was profound. It radically changed the work that social scientists actually did. During the 1930s, for example, an earlier generation of economists had labored at large projects of empirical description such as Koopmans's review-essay specifically condemned. An example was the work of the International Committee on Prices, which compiled comprehensive and very valuable time series on price movements through the past millennium. After 1950, this work came to an end. Mechanical data-gathering continued in government agencies, but creative projects of empirical description by leading scholars passed out of fashion.

In American sociology, something similar happened. During the 1920s, 1930s, and 1940s, sociologists had produced many powerful works of empirical description. Chief among them were community studies such as the Lynds' two *Middletown* volumes (1929–37), Lloyd Warner's *Yankee City* series, and Sidney Goldstein's *Norristown* study. As the new epistemic orthodoxy took hold, these projects were gradually abandoned, and sociological monographs became narrow tests of specific ''theoretical'' propositions. Larger works tended to be ruminations on theory in general. For a generation, theory-bound inquiry became the central and even the exclusive business of American social scientists.

The effect of this revolution was both positive and negative. Monographs became more coherent in their conceptual apparatus, and more rigorous as well. But a price was paid for these advances. Inquiry became narrowly blinkered by theoretical assumptions, which often proved to be circular in their structure and increasingly ignorant of the world that they purported to explain. As a consequence, social science became increasingly remote from social reality. The theory-centered epistemology of social science began by stimulating thought; it ended by stultifying it.

During the 1970s and 1980s, a growing chorus of self-criticism began to be heard from younger social scientists. In economics, for example, Lester Thurow in 1983 complained that his discipline had become a closed world. "In economics today," he wrote, "theory has become an ideology rather than a set of working hypotheses used to understand the behavior of the economy found in the real world . . . in my mind, mainstream American economics reflect more an academic need for an internal theoretical consistency and rigor than it reflects observable measurable realities in the world."

Similar arguments were also made by sociologists such as Alvin Gouldner. For the most part, however, these critics did not argue against theory in general. They inveighed against theories of which they disapproved. Even among the iconoclasts, the epistemic orthodoxy remained intact. Nevertheless, their critiques were symptoms of a malaise that was deeply felt during the late 1970s and early 1980s.

Ironically, at the same time that this epistemic orthodoxy established itself in social science, its assumptions were being challenged by epistemologists and cognitive scientists in a body of scholarship that is potentially revolutionary for social inquiry. One example of this work is the epistemology of Fred Dretske, who draws a helpful distinction between two epistemic operations that he calls "seeing" and "knowing." Dretske argues that there is a "visual ability" which is "an endowment relatively free from the influence of education, past experience, linguistic sophistication, and conceptual dexterity." He offers the example of a "bewildered savage, transplanted suddenly from his native environment to a Manhattan subway station, [who] can witness the arrival of the 3:45 express as clearly as the bored commuter. Ignorance of X does not impair one's vision of X; if it did, total ignorance would be largely irreparable." See Fred I. Dretske, *Seeing and Knowing* (Chicago, 1969), 8.

Dretske argues that "seeing" in this special sense can take place not only between an observer and a physical object, but also between an observer and an historical event. "Not only can books, cats, trees, automobiles, buildings, shadows and people be seen in the way that I have just depicted," he writes, "but also such items as battles, departures, signals, ceremonies, games, accidents, stabbings, performances, escapes and gestures. . . . Events as well as objects (and things such as shadows) can be seen in this way. . . . Events are movements and occurrences; they involve a moment or change" (14–15).

This simple act of brute perception is fundamental to our experience of the world. We use it every day. In purely practical terms, we can scarcely exist without it. But in the formal inquiries of social science and social history, its operations have been suppressed by a relativist epistemology which insists that there is no seeing without knowing, no description without explanation, no observation without prior belief, and no measurement without theory.

Seeing is, indeed, very different from knowing. Its product is information rather than meaning. Information, Dretske teaches us, is "an objective commodity, something whose generation, transmission and reception do not require or in any way presuppose interpretative process," and it can be attained by a process that is "logically independent of whatever beliefs we may possess" (17). He is wrong on the first point, but right on the second.

The present work is organized on the assumption that there are at least two very different forms of cognition: seeing-observing and knowing-believing. American social scientists in the twentieth century have been taught to do the second and to despise the first. They are trained to know and believe but not to see and observe. They are told to seek meaning rather than information. Most of all they are taught that the perception of social phenomena is necessarily theory-bound and that any other sort of cognition is insignificant or even impossible.

Much important work is done within this theoretical frame, but it does not exhaust the epistemic possibilities. There are other ways to study the world. American historian John Day, who has been formally trained in the very different epistemology of the French *Annales* School, offers a valuable suggestion in that respect. In a recent "essai d'autohistoire," Day distinguishes between two types of historical epistemology: that of what he calls the American "cliometric school" and that of the French *Annalists*. American cliometricians, he observes, begin with a theory—a hypothetico-deductive "if . . . then . . . " model. French *Annalists* begin with a *problematique*—a set of questions that are more open-ended and carefully set within a specific cultural and historical context. "Ce marriage de convenance entre pratique et theorie en histoire [de l'école des cliometricians Americains]," John Day writes, "contraste a mon sens avec la bonne entente entre pratique et problematique qui characterise les grands historiens de l'Ecole des Annales." See John Day, "Terres, marchés et monnaies en Italie et en Sardaigne du XIIe au XVIIIe siècle," *Histoire, Economie et Société* 2 (1983) 187–203.

These *problematiques* are more than merely problems. They are frames of inquiry that include a set of empirical questions, together with the epistemic apparatus necessary to answer them. In short, a *problematique* is not merely an object of inquiry. It is also a method and even an epistemology.

How does *problematique* differ from theory? In terms of grammar, a theory is a declarative statement. A *problematique* is an interrogative statement. Theory-bound research begins with an assertion; if the theory is sound, that assertion is proven to be correct. Problem-centered research starts with a question; if the problem is sound, then the question can be answered in many different ways according to the evidence. A *problematique* always has an open end. A theory, by the very nature of its entailed proposition, "if *x*, then *y*," always has a closed end.

There is also another difference between theory and *problematique*. A theoretical statement is a universal generalization. It commonly takes the form of an assertion that whenever *x* exists, then *y* must always follow. A *problematique*, on the other hand, can be tailored to historical circumstances.

Further, in actual practice, a theory-bound research design commonly commits the fallacy of many questions. That is, it asks two or more questions but demands a single answer. A *problematique* can be more exact, more flexible and also more rigorous. Its rigor is that of erotetic logic, which is the logic of questions and answers, as distinct from the logic of statements. See A. and M. Prior, "Erotetic Logic," *Philosophical Review* 64 (1955) 43–59; and Nuel D. Belknap Jr. and Thomas B. Steel Jr., *The Logic of Questions and Answers* (New Haven, 1976).

For all of these reasons, the frame of this inquiry has been constructed in terms of a problem rather than a theory. It is organized around a set of interrogative questions rather than declarative statements: What has been the pattern of secular change in price levels? How have price-fluctuations and price-relatives changed through time? How have real wages, rents and interest rates changed?

To adopt this problem-centered approach is not to deny the possibility of theory-driven inquiry. It is rather to assert the possibility and value of another kind of seeing and knowing. It is to suggest that historians and economists should study their Kipling at an impressionable age, and might be taught to play Kim's Game. They should not be compelled to choose theory-bound research as the only acceptable form of inquiry. There are other ways.

NOTES

≈ Preface

1. "De tous les appareils enregistreurs, capables de révéler a l'historian les mouvements profonds de l'economie, les phénomènes monétaires sont sans doute le plus sensible. Mais ne leur reconnaitre que cette valeur de symptôme serait manquer à leur rendre pleine justice; ils ont eté et sont, à leur tour, des causes; quelque chose comme un sismographe qui, non content de signaler les tremblements de terre, parfois les provoquerait." Marc Bloch, "Le problème de l'or au moyen age," *Annales d'Histoire Économique et Sociale"* 5 (1935) 1.

2. Daniel J. Boorstin, "Enlarging the Historian's Vocabulary," in R. W. Fogel and S. L. Engerman, eds., *The Reinterpretation of American Economic History* (New York, 1971), xi–xiv.

3. The author's favorite price lists for this period appear in Claudio Sanchez-Albornez, *El precio de la vide en el reino Astor-Leones hace mil años* (Buenos Aires, 1945). A copy of this rare and happy work, one of the few price compilations that can be read purely for pleasure, is in the New York Public Library.

4. See bibliography for a survey of these materials.

≈ Introduction

1. "Aufschwung im 13 Jahrhundert . . . Abschwung im Spätmittel-alter . . . Aufschwung im 16 Jahrhundert brach im 17 Jahrhundert ab; ein dritter Aufschwung im 18 Jahrhundert . . . Was bedeuten diese Wellen?" Wilhelm Abel, *Agrarkrisen und Agrarkonjunktur: Eine Geschichte der Land und Ernährungswirtschaft Mitteleuropas seit dem höhen Mittelalter* (Hamburg and Berlin, 1935, 1956, 1966, 1978), 13–14; an English edition, much revised, has been published as *Agricultural Fluctuations in Europe from the Thirteenth to the Twentieth Centuries* (London and New York, 1980).

2. Ernest Henry Phelps-Brown and Sheila V. Hopkins, "Seven Centuries of the Prices of Consumables, Compared with Builders' Wage-Rates," *Economica* 23 (1956) 296–314; *idem*, "Seven Centuries of Building Wages,"

ibid., 22 (1955) 195–206; *idem, A Perspective of Wages and Prices* (London, 1981). This is a weighted "market-basket" index, which includes grain, vegetables, meat, fish, butter, cheese, drink, fuel, light, and textiles. The weights are held constant throughout the series (80 percent for food; the rest for fuel and textiles), but specific products are changed to match consumption patterns.

3. Wilhelm Abel, *Agrarkrisen und Agrarkonjunktur*; François Simiand, *Les fluctuations économiques à longue période et la crise mondiale* (Paris, 1932); *idem, Recherches anciennes et nouvelles sur le mouvement général des prix du XVIᵉ au XIXᵉ siècle* (Paris, 1932); Jenny Griziotti-Kretschmann, *Il problema del trend sècolare nelle fluttuazioni dei prèzzi* (Pavia, 1935).

4. Fernand Braudel, *Civilization and Capitalism, 15th–18th Century*, vol. 3, *The Perspective of the World* (New York, 1984), 76–80, 82; for the response of American reviewers, see, e.g., Charles Kindleberger in the *New York Times*. I met the same response in 1980, when I first published an essay summarizing the main lines of my work on this subject. See D. H. Fischer, "Chronic Inflation: The Long View," *Journal of the Institute for Socioeconomic Studies* 5 (1980) 81–103. Attitudes at last are changing.

5. Alan Blinder, *New York Times,* 19 Feb. 1984.

6. Lester C. Thurow, *The Zero Sum Society* (New York, 1980), 43.

7. Here again waves and cycles behave differently. Academic interest in economic cycles tends to be countercyclical, but the study of waves increases as the wave-crest comes near.

8. Many cyclical rhythms have been found in modern history. For a survey of a very large literature by social scientists on long cycles—mainly fifty-year Kondratieff cycles or multiples of those units. See Joshua S. Goldstein, *Long Cycles: Prosperity and War in the Modern Age* (New Haven, 1988); the literature on this subject is discussed in Appendix E and the bibliography.

9. See appendix O.

10. Herbert Stein, *Presidential Economics* (rev. ed. N.Y., 1985), 222.

?◆ The Medieval Price Revolution

1. Robert Branner, ed., *Chartres Cathedral* (New York, 1969), 93.

2. The deans received rents from stalls in the porch of the cathedral; the canons were given the income from the south cloister. In a charter of May 26, 1224, the canons succeeded in moving the money-changers from the porch to the south cloister: "Each and every one of us, personages as well as canons of Chartres, who had assembled to elect a dean, are agreed that the stalls of the moneychangers, which are customarily in the porch be set up in the cloister to the south, between the steps of the church and the main tower, so that all the

dues from the stalls and the house in which they have been set up and the moneychangers themselves might belong to the Chapter, and that they might remain without hindrance, as heretofore, in the possession of the Chapter, in the place where they have been set up this day. . . . Executed in the year of the Lord 1224, the month of May, on the octave of the Lord's ascension.'' Ernest de Lépinois, *Cartulaire de Notre Dame de Chartres* (n.p., 1862) II, 103; Robert Branner, ed., *Chartres Cathedral* (New York, 1969), 98–99.

3. Charles Homer Haskins, *The Renaissance of the Twelfth Century* (Cambridge, 1927); G. Pare *et al.*, *La renaissance du XIIᵉ siècle: Les écoles et l'enseignement* (Paris, 1933); Robert L. Benson and Giles Constable, eds., *Renaissance and Renewal in the Twelfth Century* (Cambridge, Mass., 1982); R. W. Southern, *The Making of the Middle Ages* (New Haven, 1953); J. L. Bolton, *The Medieval English Economy, 1150–1500* (London, 1980), 82–179.

4. This is the estimate of Carl Richard Brühl, *Palatium und Civitas: Studien zur Profantopographie spätantiker Civitates von 3. bis zum 13. Jahrhundert* (Cologne, 1975), I, 19. A more conservative reckoning appears in R. W. Southern, ''The Schools of Paris and the School of Chartres,'' in Benson and Constable, eds., *Renaissance and Renewal in the Twelfth Century*, 119.

5. In the Romagna, Herlihy found that the most common articles of substitute money were books. ''At Ravenna,'' Herlihy writes, ''they dominate exchange throughout the eleventh century.'' One wonders what the rate of exchange might have been between authors and fields. ''Treasure Hoards in the Italian Economy, 960–1139,'' *Economic History Review* 2d ser. 10 (1957) 4.

6. *Ibid.*, 5.

7. William Beveridge, *Prices and Wages in England from the Twelfth to the Nineteenth Century* (London, 1939); also *idem*, ''Wages in Winchester Manors,'' *Economic History Review* 7 (1936–37) 22–43; and *idem*, ''Westminster Wages in the Manorial Era,'' *Economic History Review* 2d ser. 8 (1955–56) 18–35.

8. The beginning date of the medieval price revolution is one of the more difficult empirical problems in this project, for it antedates most major price series. Some historians believe that prices had been rising as early as the tenth century, after the last of the major barbarian invasions. But a major discontinuity appears in English price movements during the period 1181–1200. Evidence from Exchequer Pipe Rolls and Winchester Pipe Rolls shows a moderate upturn in the price of grain and livestock, followed by a small decline in the period 1190–99, and then a surge in the period 1200–02, which D. L. Farmer describes as a ''violent disturbance in the prices of all commodities.'' Thereafter the long inflation was clearly underway. See D. L. Farmer, ''Prices and Wages,'' in Joan Thirsk, ed., *The Agrarian History of England*

and Wales, vol. 2, 1042–1350 (Cambridge, 1988), 717–19, 787–817; *idem,* "Some Price Fluctuations in Angevin England," *Economic History Review* 2d ser. 9 (1956–57) 34–43; *idem,* "Some Grain Price Movements in Thirteenth-Century England," *Economic History Review* 2d ser. 10 (1957–58) 207–20; Norman S. B. Gras, *The Evolution of the English Corn Market from the Twelfth to the Eighteenth Century* (Cambridge, Mass., 1915), 11–17; and P. D. A. Harvey, "The English Inflation of 1180," *Past & Present* 61 (1973) 3–30.

For France, George Duby finds evidence of "an important qualitative change in the 1180s, and there to fix one of the main turning-points in European economic history"; *The Early Growth of the European Economy: Warriors and Peasants from the Seventh to the Twelfth Century* (Ithaca, 1974), 263.

In Italy the pattern is less clear; see David Herlihy, "The Agrarian Revolution in Southern France and Italy, 801–1150," *Speculum* 33 (1958) 23–41; *idem,* "The History of the Rural Seignury in Italy, 751–1200," *Agricultural History* 33 (1959) 1–14.

9. M. M. Postan, *Medieval Economy and Society: An Economic History of Britain in the Middle Ages* (London, 1972; Pelican ed., 1975), 257; *idem,* "Economic Foundations of Medieval Society," in *Essays on Medieval Agriculture and General Problems of the Medieval Economy* (Cambridge, 1973), 2–27.

10. Postan, *Medieval Economy and Society,* chap. 13.

11. Abel, *Agrarkrisen und Agrarkonjunktur,* 27–41.

12. In medieval Picardy, Fossier found that in families with children, the number of sons per family increased sharply, *circa* 1175:

Period	Sons per Family
1075–1100	2.53
1100–1125	2.26
1125–1150	2.35
1150–1175	2.46
1175–1200	2.70
1200–1225	2.77
1225–1250	2.62
1250–1275	2.54
1275–1300	2.66

The annual growth rate accelerated from 0.28 percent in the period 1150–75, to 0.72 percent in 1175–1200. Life expectancy at birth was probably in the range of forty to fifty in this exceptionally healthy era. No reliable record survives of daughters, who were regarded as "trop aléatoire pour être notée." Robert Fossier, *La terre et les hommes en Picardie, jusqu'a la fin du XIIIᵉ siècle* (2 vols., Paris and Louvain, 1968), I, 282–92.

An English study found a similar pattern: a rate of population growth from 1209 to 1311 of 0.85 percent per year—higher than in eighteenth century England, and nearly as high as in some developing nations in the twentieth century. See J. Z. Titow, "Some Evidence of Thirteenth Century Population Increase," *Economic History Review* 2d ser. 14 (1961) 220.

For other research that confirms this pattern, see Duby, *Early Growth of the European Economy*, 182; Josiah Russell, *The Control of Late Ancient and Medieval Population* (Philadelphia, 1985), 20; *idem*, "Recent Advances in Medieval Demography," *Speculum* 45 (1965) 84–101; *idem*, "Aspects démographiques des débuts de la féodalité," *Annales* 20 (1965) 1118–27.

13. This estimate comes from a comparison of manorial surveys in the period 1260–1315, with census data from 1801 to 1951, as reported in H. E. Hallam, "Population Density in Medieval Fenland," *Economic History Review* 14 (1961) 71–79; *idem*, "Some Thirteenth Century Censuses," *ibid.*, 10 (1957) 340–61; and *idem*, *Rural England, 1066–1348* (Brighton, 1981), 245–50; similar findings are reported in H. P. R. Finberg, *Tavistock Abbey* (Cambridge, 1951); W. G. Hoskins and H. P. R. Finberg, *Devonshire Studies* (London, 1952); H. P. R. Finberg, *Gloucestershire* (London, 1955); W. G. Hoskins, *Leicestershire* (London, 1957); Edward Miller, *The Abbey and Bishopric of Ely* (Cambridge, 1951); J. B. Harley, "Population Trends and Agricultural Developments from the Warwickshire Hundred Rolls of 1279," *Economic History Review* 2d ser. 11 (1958) 8–18. For similar trends in other parts of Europe, see Enrico Fiume, "Sui rapporti economici tra città e contado nell'età communale," *Archivio Storico Italiano* 114 (1956) 18–68; Georges Duby, *L'economie rurale et la vie des campagnes dans l'Occident Médiéval* (2 vols., Paris, 1962).

14. For evidence of falling female age at marriage see David Herlihy, "The Medieval Marriage Market," *Medieval and Renaissance Studies* 6 (1976) 3–27; *idem*, "The Generation in Medieval History," *Viator* 5 (1974) 347–64. Herlihy finds that male age at marriage increased in this period; but the age of the female is critical for changes in fertility levels.

15. Postan, *Medieval Economy and Society*; J. Z. Titow, *English Rural Society, 1200–1350* (London, 1969). On the problem of population estimates for England, see G. Ohlin, "No Safety in Numbers: Some Pitfalls in Historical Statistics," in H. Rosovsky, ed., *Industrialization in Two Systems: Essays in Honor of Alexander Gershenkron* (New York, 1966), 70–81. See also M. M. Postan, "Some Economic Evidence of Declining Population in the Later Middle Ages," *Economic History Review* 2d ser. 2 (1950) 221–46; Julian Cornwall, "English Population in the Early Sixteenth Century," *Economic History Review* 2d ser. 23 (1970) 32–44; Clyde George Read, "Price Data and European Economic History: England, 1300–1600" (thesis, University of Washington, 1972); Mavis Mate, "High Prices in Early Fourteenth-

Century England: Causes and Consequences,'' *Economic History Review* 28 (1975) 1–16.

16. These estimates were computed by the author from data in James E. Thorold Rogers, *A History of Agriculture and Prices in England* . . . (7 vols., Oxford, 1866–1902, rpt. Vaduz, 1963), I, 1259–1400.

17. Jean Gimpel, *The Medieval Machine: The Industrial Revolution of the Middle Ages* (New York, 1976), 82–84.

18. Abel, *Agrarkrisen und Agrarkonjunktur,* chap. 1.

19. Median prices in solidi for body armor in medieval Italy were as follows:

Year	Coif	Hauberk	Cuirass	Panceria
1182				65/0
1191				48/4
1192		152/0		
1203				30/0
1211	32/0			
1213	27/0			
1216		123/0		
1220				64/0
1222			50/0	80/0
1224	20/6		46/0	50/0
1225			58/0	45/0
1226			46/0	
1228				65/0
1238	16/0			
1239		120/0	50/0	60/0
1240			60/0	60/0
1241			60/0	60/0
1242			50/0	60/0
1243			60/0	
1244			50/0	
1248			45/0	60/0
1249			60/0	
1250			60/0	40/0
1251	20/0		60/0	
1252			45/0	
1253		133/4	58/9	
1254		120/0		50/0

A coif was an iron skullcap or mail hood or both; a hauberk was a long tunic of chain mail; a cuirass was commonly but not invariably a breastplate, and a panceria was the companion piece of a cuirass. These data are taken from William N. Bonds, ''Some Industrial Price Movements in Medieval Genoa (1155–1255),'' *Explorations in Entrepreneurial History* 7 (1969–70) 123–139; see also Henrietta M. Larson, ''The Armor Business in the Middle

Ages,'' *Business History Review* 14 (1940) 49–64; and C. F. ffoulkes, ''European Arms and Armor,'' in G. Barraclough, ed., *Social Life in Early England* (London, 1960), 124–38.

20. Postan, *Medieval Economy and Society*, 253–76; *idem*, ''Some Economic Evidence of Declining Population in the Later Middle Ages.'' An important study is Christopher Dyer, *Standards of Living in the Later Middle Ages: Social Change in England c. 1200–1520* (Cambridge, 1989), 101–103.

Historians refer to disparities between agricultural and industrial prices as a pattern of ''price scissors,'' which cut one way during the price revolutions, when landlords and money-lenders gained, and laborers and artisans lost. The scissors cut the other way during periods of price equilibrium, when landlords and money-lenders lost, and artisans and laborers gained from the movement of price relatives.

Some Marxist scholars believe the ''price scissors'' to have been peculiar to a feudal economy. Others draw similar conclusions about capitalist economies. This was not the case. The cruelest cuts of all were a variant on price scissors in socialist economies of the twentieth century, as discussed below.

Further, similar price relatives appeared in the price revolutions of the sixteenth, eighteenth and twentieth centuries, as we will see. See Guy Bois, *Crise du feodalisme: économie rurale et démographie en Normandie orientale du début du 14ᵉ siècle au milieu du 16ᵉ siècle* (Paris, 1976), 85–88.

21. Markets of known date were founded as follows in twenty one English counties:

Region	1200–1224	1225–1249	1250–1274	1275–1299	1300–1324	1325–1349
East Anglia	17	43	71	21	26	16
South of England	13	10	12	3	10	2
Southwest	8	11	14	18	10	1
East Midlands	11	12	20	6	19	3
West Midlands	25	22	34	11	13	12
North	18	21	63	25	37	16
Total	92	119	214	84	115	50

Markets of unknown date are not included. R. H. Britnell, ''The Proliferation of Markets in England, 1200–1349,'' *Economic History Review* 2d ser. 34 (1981) 209–21.

22. E. M. Carus-Wilson, ''An Industrial Revolution of the Thirteenth Century,'' *Economic History Review* 11 (1941) 39–60; Rolf Sprandel, ''La production du fer au Moyen Age,'' *Annales* 24 (1969) 305–21.

23. Abel, *Agrarkrisen und Agrarkonjunktur*, chap. 1; F. Curschmann, ''Hungersnöte in Mittelalter. Ein Beitrag zur deutschen Wirtschaftsgeschichte

des 8. bis 13. Jahrhunderts,'' *Leipziger Studien aus dem Gebiete der Geschichte* 6 (1900) 1.

24. Marc Bloch, "Le probleme de l'or au Moyen Age,'' *Annales d'Histoire Économique et Sociale* 5 (1933) 1–34; a translation appears in *Land and Work in Medieval Europe: Selected Papers by Marc Bloch* (tr. J. E. Anderson; Berkeley and Los Angeles, 1967), 186–229. Also important is a companion piece by Bloch, translated by Anderson as "Natural Economy or Money Economy: A Pseudo–Dilemma,'' *ibid.*, 230–41.

25. Pierre Vilar, *A History of Gold and Money 1450–1920* (Barcelona, 1969; English tr. London, 1976), 19.

26. C. C. Patterson, "Silver Stocks and Losses in Ancient and Medieval Times,'' *Economic History Review* 2d ser. 25 (1972) 205–35; the estimate of three hundred tons is from D. M. Metcalf, "English Monetary History in the Time of Offa: A Reply,'' *Numismatic Circular* 71 (1963) 1651.

27. J. R. Strayer, "The Crusades of Louis IX,'' in K. M. Setton, ed., *A History of the Crusades* (Philadelphia, 1962), II, chap. 14.

28. Robert S. Lopez writes, "Silver had been mined in various European regions throughout the early Middle Ages; the opening of the Goslar mines had been one of the earliest signs of the long trend of growth in the tenth century; Freiburg, probably the richest source, had been developed in the twelfth century. The thirteenth was marked by intensive exploitation of old mines but not blessed by important new discoveries; and there were symptoms of increasing difficulties in securing the larger amounts demanded by the growing hunger for silver. In Italy, the inferior mines of Tuscany and Sardinia were tapped, and water-driven hammers were introduced to exploit the poorer ores of Trentino; in Germany, Goslar passed its peak and Freiburg was nearing exhaustion.'' Robert S. Lopez, "Back to Gold, 1252,'' *Economic History Review* 2d ser. 9 (1956) 219–40, 233.

29. Patterson, "Silver Stocks and Losses,'' 230.

30. Mate, "High Prices in the Early Fourteenth Century,'' 2.

31. Two excellent and very thoughtful essays on this subject are N. J. Mayhew, "Money and Prices in England from Henry II to Edward III,'' *Agricultural History Review* 35 (1987) 121–32; and A. R. Bridbury, "Thirteenth-Century Prices and the Money Supply,'' *ibid.*, 33 (1985) 1–21. Bridbury and Mayhew believe that the expansion of the money supply began earlier, circa 1280, and that a "sudden late-twelfth century surge has every appearance of monetary inflation.'' (Mayhew, 129).

I read the price-series of Thorold Rogers and David Farmer differently (as did Rogers and Farmer themselves), as a gradual rise in prices, except for a very violent price-surge during a period from 1201 to 1205, which was time of extreme bad weather. W. L. Warren writes of that time, "the rivers froze after Christmas and the Thames could be crossed on foot. The ground was so hard that no ploughshare could bite into it until March. The winter sowings were almost ruined by the ferocity of the cold; vegetables and herbage shriveled up. When spring finally came . . . corn was selling at famine prices. Oats fetched ten times the normal price, and men were paying half a mark for a few pence worth of peas or beans. A sorry land was England in 1204–05." W. L. Warren, *King John* (London, 1961), 105.

32. On florins and ducats, a good survey appears in Frederic Lane, *Venice, a Maritime Republic* (Baltimore, 1973), which summarizes many years of study on this subject; see also *idem,* "Le vecchie monete di conto veneziane ed il ritorno all'ore," *Atto dell Instituto Veneto di Scienze Letre ed Arti; Classe di Scienzi Morali, Letter, ed Arti* 117 (1958–59) 49–78; A. M. Watson, "Back to Gold and Silver," *Economic History Review* 2d ser. 20 (1967) 1–34.

33. Lopez describes a "boom of contracts of exchange and bank transfers between 1248 and 1255." "Back to Gold," 232.

34. Carlo M. Cipolla, "Currency Depreciation in Medieval Europe," *Economic History Review* 2d ser. 15 (1963) 417.

35. On the fall of real wages, see Postan, "Some Economic Evidence of Declining Population," 221–46; Phelps-Brown and Hopkins, "Seven Centuries of the Prices of Consumables, Compared with Builders' Wage-Rates," 296–314; and Abel, *Agrarkrisen und Agrarkonjunktur,* 40–41.

36. Georges d'Avenel, *Histoire économique de la proprieté, des salarires des denrées et de tous les prix en general depuis l'an 1200 jusqu'en l'an 1800* (7 vols., Paris, 1894–1926), III, 317.

37. *The Chronicle of Jocelin of Brakelond,* ed. H. E. Butler (London, 1949), 59.

38. Carus-Wilson, "Industrial Revolution of the Thirteenth Century," 54.

39. Carlo M. Cipolla, *Money, Prices, and Civilization in the Mediterranean World: Fifth to Seventeenth Century* (Princeton, 1956), 63–65; Sidney Homer, *A History of Interest Rates* (New Brunswick, 1963) 94–99.

40. Cipolla, *Money, Prices, and Civilization,* chap. 3.

41. "It is generally agreed that the thirteenth century witnessed an economic crisis that led to the impoverishment of the population." Alfred N. May, "An Index of Thirteenth-Century Peasant Impoverishment? Manor Court Fines," *Economic History Review* 2d ser. 26 (1973) 397; Titow, *English Rural Society,* 64–96.

42. Rohault de Fleury, *Mémoire sur les instruments de la Passion de N.-S.J.-C.* (Paris, 1870), 213, 357.

43. J. Z. Titow, *Winchester Yields* (Cambridge, 1972); Mate, "High Prices in Early Fourteenth-Century England," 8.

44. A running tabulation of *disettes* appears in M. E. Levasseur, *Les prix aperçu de l'histoire économique de la valeur et du revenu de la terre, en France du commencement du XIIe siècle à la fin du XVIIIe, avec un appendice*

sur le prix du froment et sur les disettes depuis l'an 1200 jusqu'a l'an 1891 (Paris, 1893), appendix.

45. D'Avenel, *Histoire* . . . *de tous les prix*, III, 183.

46. D. L. Farmer, "Some Livestock Price Movements in Thirteenth-Century England," *Economic History Review*, 2d ser. 22 (1969) 1–16. Postan, in an appended note to *Medieval Economy and Society*, 280–81, expresses strong skepticism about the thesis that recoinages made a difference in price levels. He writes: "The upsurge of prices which Mr. Farmer noted in the years following some of the recoinages does not occur in the years following other recoinages. Between 1150 and 1300, recoinages occurred at least six times, from 1156–9, 1181, 1205, 1247, 1279 and 1299, yet some of these do not appear to have had any effect on prices, especially 1181, 1205 and 1299." Postan appears to have been mistaken about the recoinages of 1205 and 1299, but he may have been correct about 1181. On balance, the weight of Farmer's evidence is greater than Postan's skepticism. See also D. L. Farmer, "Some Grain Price Movements in Thirteenth-Century England, *Economic History Review* 2d ser. 10 (1957–58) 207.

47. Mate, "High Prices in Early Fourteenth-Century England," 5.

48. *Ibid.*

49. Michael Prestwich, "Early Fourteenth-Century Exchange Rates," *Economic History Review* 32 (1979) 470–82.

50. Raymond de Roover, *The Rise and Decline of the Medici Bank* (Cambridge, 1963; New York, 1966), 2.

51. Mario Chiaudano, "I Rothschild del Dugento: La Gran Tavola di Orlando Buonsignori," *Bullettino Sienese di Storia Patria* 42 (1935), 103–42; William M. Bowsky, *The Finance of the Commune of Siena, 1287–1355* (Oxford, 1970); *idem, A Medieval Italian Commune: Siena Under the Nine, 1287–1355* (Berkeley, 1981).

❧ The Crisis of the Fourteenth Century

1. A quantitative study appears in Hugues Neveux, "Bonnes et mauvaises récoltes du XIVᵉ au XIXᵉ siècle: Jalons pour une enquête systématique," *Revue d'Histoire Économique et Sociale* 53 (1975) 177–92. There were many local exceptions. Tuscany appears to have escaped the ravages of this great famine but was hit severely a few years later.

2. Ian Kershaw, "The Great Famine and Agrarian Crisis in England, 1315–1322," *Past & Present* 59 (1973) 3–50; Elisabeth Carpentier, "Famines et epidemies dans l'histoire du XIVᵉ siècle," *Annales* 17 (1962) 1062–92; David Herlihy, "Population, Plague, and Social Change in Rural Pistoia, 1201–1430," *Economic History Review*, 2d ser. 18 (1965) 225–44; H. S.

Lucas, "The Great European Famine of 1315–1317," *Speculum* 15 (1930) 343; H. V. Weveke, "La famine de l'an 1316 en Flandre et dans les regions voisines," *Revue du Nord* 41 (1950) 5.

For a quantitative study of the diet of harvest workers by decade, 1250–1430, see Christopher Dyer, "Changes in Diet in the Late Middle Ages: The Case of Harvest Workers," *Agricultural History Review* 36 (1988) 21–37.

3. Lucas, "Great European Famine of 1315–1317," 61.

4. *Ibid.*, 58.

5. *Ibid.*, 57–58.

6. *Ibid.*, 66.

7. A. R. Bridbury, "Before the Black Death," *Economic History Review* 2d ser. 30 (1977) 393–410.

8. J. R. Maddicott, "The English Peasantry and the Demands of the Crown, 1294–1341," *Past & Present* supplement 1 (1975), rpt. in T. H. Aston, ed., *Landlords, Peasants and Politics in Medieval England* (Cambridge, 1987), 285–359; E. Miller, "War, Taxation, and the English Economy of the Late Thirteenth and Early Fourteenth Centuries," in J. M. Winter, ed., *War and Economic Development* (Cambridge, 1975); J. O. Prestwich, "War and Finance in the Anglo-Norman State," Royal Historical Society *Transactions* 5th ser. 4 (1954) 19–44; K. B. McFarlane, "War, the Economy, and Social Change," *Past & Present* 22 (1962) 3–35.

9. This is the conclusion of Guy Bois, no friend of Malthusian models. He writes, "The chronology of the fall in the revenues of the landed seignury shows a remarkable correspondence with the movement of population." This was specially the case with petty nobles; great seigneurs did much better. Bois observes: "On the one hand, the privileged position of the recipients of dues from seigneurial monopolies and tithes is obvious. Their revenues offered particular resistance to the erosion that threatened from all sides. They even derived benefit from the price rises of the thirteenth and sixteenth centuries. On the other hand stood the mass of small landlords drawing the best part of their incomes from the rent from their peasant tenures." See *The Crisis of Feudalism: Economy and Society in Eastern Normandy c. 1300–1500* (1976; Cambridge, 1984), 221, 236–37.

10. Edouard Perroy, "Les crises du XIVᵉ siècle," *Annales* 4 (1949) 167–182; R. H. Hilton, "Y eut-il une crise générale de feodalité?" *Annales* 6 (1951) 23–30; Robert Boutrouche, *La crise d'une societé* (Paris, 1947). A popular account appears in Barbara Tuchman, *A Distant Mirror: The Calamitous Fourteenth Century* (New York, 1978), a lively narrative of military and political events centered on a knight of France, Euguerrand de Coucy VII.

11. Philip Ziegler, *The Black Death* (New York, 1969) 35.

12. Colin McEvedy and Richard Jones, *Atlas of World Population History* (New York, 1978), 24–25.

13. Guy Bois believes that these "price scissors" were "an original form of price movements peculiar to the feudal economy." This interpretation is central to his Marxist analysis of the "crisis of feudalism." But similar scissor-like movements also appeared after the climax of other great waves and are not unique to any one of them. Further, these wave-movements in crises cannot be made to correlate with Marxist stages of production unless that taxonomy is changed in fundamental ways. There is an interpretative opportunity here, for a post-Marxist historian. See Bois, *Crise du feodalisme,* 92.

⁊ The Equilibrium of the Renaissance

1. For contextual essays, see R. S. Lopez and H. A. Miskimin, "The Economic Depression of the Renaissance," *Economic History Review* 2nd ser. 14 (1962) 408–26; Leopold Genicot, "Crisis: From the Middle Ages to Modern Times," *Cambridge Economic History of Europe,* I, 678–94.

2. This account is drawn from David Herlihy, *Medieval and Renaissance Pistoia: The Social History of an Italian Town, 1200–1430* (New Haven, 1967); and idem, "Population, Plague, and Social Change in Rural Pistoia," *Economic History Review* 2d ser. 18 (1965) 225–44.

3. Tuchman, *Distant Mirror,* 166.

4. C. A. Christensen, "Aendringerne i landsbyens oslashkonimiske og sociale strukur i det 14 og 15 århundrede," *Historisk Tidskrifft* 12 (1964) 346.

This is what German scholars call the *Wüstungsproblem,* the "problem of the deserted villages," a major historiographical issue in many European nations. Part of the problem is about how many villages were deserted by their inhabitants, and precisely when the desertion took place. See Maurice Beresford and John B. Hurst, *Deserted Medieval Villages* (London, 1971); A. Holmsen, "Desertion of Farms around Oslo in the late Middle Ages," *Scandinavian Economic History Review* 10 (1962) 165; Wilhelm Abel, *Die Wüstungen des ausgehenden Mittelalters* (2d ed., 1955); J. F. Pesez and E. Le Roy Ladurie, "Les villages desertes en France: Vue d'ensembles," *Annales* 20 (1965) 257.

5. A leading authority on this subject is John Day, "The Great Bullion Famine of the Fifteenth Century," *Past & Present* 29 (1978) 3–54; reprinted with many other essays in idem, *The Medieval Market Economy* (Oxford, 1987).

6. The price of wheat (in grains of silver) changed as follows in England, according to evidence drawn from the estates of the Bishops of Winchester:

Period	Price of Wheat in Grains of Silver (per quarter)	(1310–19 = 100)
1300–1319	1734	100
1320–1329	1547	90
1340–1359	1372	79
1360–1379	1308?	89
1380–1399	1113	65
1400–1419	1188	68
1420–1439	1107	64
1440–1459	926	53
1460–1479	812	47

Source: M. M. Postan, "Some Economic Evidence of
Declining Population in the Later Middle Ages," 226.

7. N. J. Mayhew, "Numismatic Evidence and Falling Prices in the Fourteenth Century," *Economic History Review* 2d ser. 27 (1974) 1–15; H. A. Miskimin, "Monetary Movements and Market Structure—Forces for Contraction in Fourteenth- and Fifteenth-Century England," *Journal of Economic History* 2d ser. 24 (1964) 470–490; J. Schreiner, *Pest og prisfall i Senmiddelalderen* (Oslo, 1948); H. van Werveke, "Essor et déclin de la Flandre," in *Studi in onore di Gino Luzzato* (Milan, 1950).

8. Herlihy, *Medieval and Renaissance Pistoia*; Beveridge, "Wages in the Winchester Manors"; *idem,* "Westminister Wages in the Manorial Era"; D. Woodward, "Wage Rates and Living Standards in Pre-Industrial England," *Past & Present* 91 (1981) 28–46.

Important new evidence of qualitative change in the labor market after the Black Death appears in Dyer, *Standards of Living,* 222–33, and Simon A. C. Penn and Christopher Dyer, "Wages and Earnings in Late Medieval England: Evidence from the Enforcement of the Labour Laws," *Economic History Review* 2d ser. 43 (1990) 356–76.

9. Samuel Cohn, *The Laboring Classes of Renaissance Florence* (New York, 1980); Richard C. Trexler, *The Spiritual Power: Republican Florence under the Interdict* (Brill, 1974).

10. E. Powell, *The Rising in East Anglia in 1381* (Cambridge, 1896).

11. Postan, *Medieval Economy and Society,* 173; H. L. Gray, "The Commutation in Villein Services in England before the Black Death," *English Historical Review* 29 (1914) 625–56; R. H. Hilton, "Freedom and Villeinage in England," *Past & Present* 31 (1965) 3–19; T. W. Page, *The End of Villeinage in England* (New York, 1900).

12. Herlihy, *Medieval and Renaissance Pistoia,* 146–47.

13. For many years, the Renaissance was thought to be the product of high prosperity. That idea was challenged by R. S. Lopez and H. A. Mis-

kimin, who argued that the Renaissance was actually a time of economic depression. The Lopez-Miskimin model fits the period from 1348 to 1405 in Italy, and also the early fifteenth century in northern Europe. But the Italian *quattrocento* is better understood as an era of economic equilibrium with comparatively stable prices, falling rent and interest, and rising wages. That equilibrium became an important underpinning of the Renaissance; see Lopez and H. A. Miskimin, "Economic Depression of the Renaissance"; Carlo M. Cipolla, "Economic Depression of the Renaissance?" with rejoinders by Lopez and Miskimin, *Economic History Review* 2d ser. 16 (1964) 519–529; C. Barbagallo, "La crisi economico-sociale dell'Italia della Renascenza," *Nouva Rivista Storica* 34 (1950) and 35 (1951). For fiscal movements, see Josef Rosen, "Prices and Public Finance in Basel, 1360–1535," *Economic History Review,* 2d ser. 25 (1972) 1–17.

14. Bois, *Crise du feodalisme,* 284–308.

15. M. M. Postan, "The Fifteenth Century," *Economic History Review* 9 (1938–39) 160–67; Perroy, "Les Crises du XIVᵉ siècle".

16. One study shows that wages in Rouen rose for hand workers from 20 pence in 1399–1407 to 27 pence in 1469–78; wages of masons rose from two shillings sixpence to four shillings or four shillings sixpence in the same period. At the same time, the price of grain in hours of labor fell 40 to 50 percent. See Guy Bois, "La prix du froment à Rouen au XVᵉ siècle," *Annales* 23 (1968) 1262–82; for England, see J. Hatcher, *Population and the English Economy* (London, 1977).

17. The Mediterranean moment was made possible by favorable climatological conditions, which have changed profoundly in this region. The territories of Spain, Italy, Greece, and Turkey, which today are baked dry by the summer sun, were in the fifteenth century more moist, because of changing atmospheric circulation systems. Small changes in precipitation had a large impact upon the carrying capacity of the environment. See J. Vicens Vives, *Manual de historia economica de España* (Barcelona, 1959).

18. The estimate of 870,000 deaths was made by Theodoros Spandugino, and is accepted by Franz Babinger, *Mehmed the Conqueror and His Time* (Princeton, 1978), 431; a lively survey is Lord Kinross, *The Ottoman Centuries; The Rise and Fall of the Turkish Empire* (New York, 1977).

19. This process may be said to have begun in 1405, with the acquisition of Padua, Bessano, Vicenza, and Verona; it reached its limit with the annexation of Rovigo in 1484; thereafter, the boundaries of Venice changed little until the conquest of the republic by Napoleon in 1797.

20. Lane, Venice, 289.

21. De Roover, *Rise and Decline of the Medici Bank*; Richard A. Goldthwaite, *The Building of Renaissance Florence: An Economic and Social History* (Baltimore, 1980), 29–66; idem, *Private Wealth in Renaissance Florence* (Princeton, 1968).

22. Goldthwaite, *Building of Renaissance Florence*, 328–29; *idem*, "I prèzzi del grano a Firenze dal XIV al XVI secolo," *Quaderni Storici* 28 (1975) 5–36.

23. Pico della Mirandola, "Oration on the Dignity of Man," in Ernst Cassirer, Paul Oscar Kristeller, and John Herman Randall, Jr., eds., *The Renaissance Philosophy of Man* (Chicago, 1948), 225.

24. Hans Baron argues that the work of Gregorio Dati, Leonardo Bruni and Poggio Bracciolini all reveal "the attitude of mind from which sprang the ideas of equilibrium and balance-of-power—just so, the picture of the *urbs florentina* as the geometric center of the surrounding countryside is a striking anticipation of the ideal of the 'perfect city,' and of what has been called the 'geometrical spirit' of the Renaissance." See Baron, *The Crisis of Early Italian Renaissance* (2d ed., New York, 1966), 202. His discussion of dates begins on xxv.

Other scholars had introduced this interpretation long before Baron; see., e.g., William Shepherd, *The Life of Poggio Bracciolini* (Liverpool, 1837), 458–461. But Baron developed it in a rounded way.

ᘒ The Price Revolution of the Sixteenth Century

1. Livy, *History*, 45.40.1ff.

2. The Medici family spent 663,755 florins on buildings, charities and taxes in the period from 1434 to 1471, not counting household expenses. Rates of spending were also very high from 1471 to 1491, but Cosimo had been even more generous than Lorenzo. De Roover, *Rise and Decline of the Medici Bank*, 371n.

3. Francesco Guicciardini, *The History of Florence* (New York, 1970), 68–69. This work was written in 1508–9 and first published in the nineteenth century.

4. *Ibid.*, 69.

5. Richard C. Trexler, *Public Life in Renaissance Florence* (New York, 1980), 452; de Roover, *Rise and Decline of the Medici Bank*, 371.

6. Trexler, *Public Life in Renaissance Florence*, 458.

7. D. Weinstein, *Savonarola and Florence: Prophecy and Patriotism in the Renaissance* (Princeton, 1970)

8. Roberto Ridolfi, *The Life of Girolamo Savonarola* (New York, 1959), 184.

9. *Ibid.*, 191.

10. Girolamo Savonarola to Alberto Savonarola, 24 July 1497, in *ibid.*, 207.

11. Pasquali Villari, *Life and Times of Girolamo Savonarola* (London, 1888), 758.

12. Ferdinand Schevill, *Medieval and Renaissance Florence* (1936, New York, 1965), 456.

13. Ingrid Hammarström, "The 'Price Revolution' of the Sixteenth Century: Some Swedish Evidence," *Scandinavian Economic History Review* 5 (1957) 118–54.

14. Georg Wiebe, in *Zur Geschichte der Preisrevolution des XVI und XVII Jahrhunderts* (Leipzig, 1895). The historical literature on the "price-revolution of the sixteenth century" is very large. That subject was given a strong monetarist cast by the American economist Earl Hamilton, who argued that the cause of the price-revolution was the influx of large amounts of American silver and gold into Europe. Hamilton's research appears in *American Treasure and the Price Revolution in Spain, 1501–1650* (Cambridge, Mass., 1934); and *Money, Prices and Wages in Valencia, Aragon and Navarre, 1651–1800* (Cambridge, Mass., 1947).

This monetarist model was at first widely accepted by economic and social historians. Fernand Braudel, in his *grand thèse* on *The Mediterranean and the Mediterranean World in the Age of Philip II* (1946), wrote enthusiastically (and erroneously, as we shall see) "There is no possible doubt about the influx of gold and silver from the New World. . . . The coincidence of the curve of influx of precious metals from America and the curve of prices throughout the sixteenth century is so clear that there seems to be a physical, mechanical link between the two."

After Braudel wrote those words, the preponderant weight of historical opinion shifted away from this position. One historian even questioned whether there was a price-revolution at all in the sixteenth century. Carlo Cipolla, in "The So-Called 'Price Revolution': Reflections on the 'Italian Situation,'" (in Peter Burke, ed., *Economy and Society in Early Modern Europe; Essays from Annales* [New York, 1972], pp. 42–46) argued that the inflation of the sixteenth century was not much greater than that which occurred in what he called the "century of monetary stability" from 1791 to 1912. That erroneous conclusion rests upon an error of chronology. Cipolla defined his "century of monetary stability" to include not only the Victorian equilibrium but also the climax of the great wave of the eighteenth century and the beginning of the great wave of the twentieth. Further, he defined the price revolution of the sixteenth century in such a way as to rule out one of its most inflationary stages. When these errors are corrected, Cipolla's thesis collapses, and the "so-called" price revolution of the sixteenth century survives his skepticism.

Most recent historians of this subject have accepted the descriptive reality of the price-revolution, but have challenged Hamilton's monetarist explanation in varying degrees. This revisionary literature has been collected in two anthologies by Peter Burke (cited above) and Peter Ramsay, *The Price Revolution in Sixteenth-Century England* (London, 1971). Specially useful are essays by C. Verlinden, J. Craeybeckx and E. Scholliers on the price revolution in Belgium; Stanislas Hoszowski on Austria, Yugoslavia and Poland; Z. P. Bach on Hungary, and Marian Laowist on economic movements throughout Europe. One of the most helpful contributions is Ingrid Hammarström's excellent essay, "The 'Price Revolution' of the Sixteenth Century: Some Swedish Evidence," *Scandinavian Economic History Review* 5 (1957) 118–54. Also of value are J. Nadal Oller, "La revolución de los precios españoles en el siglo XVI," *Hispania* 19 (1959) 503–29; J.H. Elliott, *The Old World and the New, 1492–1650* (Cambridge, 1970), pp. 54–78, which is specially perceptive on the question of contemporary understandings of the price-revolution; and Perez Zagorin, *Rebels and Rulers, 1500–1600* (2 vols., Cambridge, 1982), I, 122–39.

The best overview remains Fernand P. Braudel and Frank C. Spooner, "Prices in Europe from 1450 to 1750," in E. E. Rich and C. H. Wilson, eds., *The Cambridge Economic History of Europe*, vol. 4, *The Economy of Expanding Europe in the Sixteenth and Seventeenth Centuries*, (Cambridge, 1967), 378–486, which revises Braudel's earlier views. Another major study that qualifies the Hamilton thesis in important ways is Michel Morineau, *Incroyables gazettes et fabuleux métaux; Les retours des trésors américains d'après les gazettes hollandaises (XVIe–XVIIIe siècles)* (Paris and London, 1985); also *idem*, "Des métaux précieux américains et de leur influence au XVIIe et XVIII siècle," *Bulletin de la societé d'histoire moderne et contemporaine* XV (1977) 2–95; and *idem*, "Histoire sans frontières: prix régionaux, prix nationaux, prix internationaux," *Annales E.S.C.* 24 (1969).

15. Deane, "Inflation in History," 3; J. D. Gould calculates that silver prices in England trebled from 1540 to 1640—an annual geometric increase of 1.1 percent. Other estimates yield slightly higher results. See J. D. Gould, "The Price Revolution Reconsidered," *Economic History Review* 2d ser. 17 (1964) 249–66.

16. Readers will find in these data the "pennant pattern" that is often observed in stock prices. For a discussion of flag and pennant patterns, see John Downes and Jordan Elliot Goodman, *Barron's Finance and Investment Handbook* (Woodbury, N.Y., 1986), 269, 387.

17. Solid quantitative evidence is lacking in English demographic history before the development of the parish registration system in 1538. But there is general agreement on the general trends, with continuing dispute as to the inflection points. Postan's estimate, many years ago, still appears to be correct. See E. A. Wrigley and R. S. Schofield, *The Population History of England, 1541–1871* (Cambridge, 1981), 566; Cornwall, "English Population in the Early Sixteenth Century," 32–44; M. M. Postan "Some Economic Evidence of Declining Population," 11.

18. Guy Bois estimates that median age at marriage in Normandy during the early and mid-sixteenth century was in the range of 21 to 22 years, well

below levels in France during the seventeenth century, for both urban and rural populations; the Hajnal thesis requires qualification in this period; see Bois, *Crise du Feodalisme,* 330–31.

19. Evidence of rapid population growth appears in Italian city states, where household size is estimated as follows from a variety of sources:

Year	Verona	Florence	Palermo	Arezzo	Prato	Bologna
1380		3.7				
1395	3.7					3.5
1425	3.7					
1427		3.8		3.5	3.7	
1456	5.2					
1470		4.6				
1479			4.9			
1502	5.9					
1551		6.4				
1561		7.3				
1591			6.8			

Sources include David Herlihy, "The Population of Verona in the First Century of Venetian Rule," in J.R. Hale, ed., *Renaissance Florence* (London, 1973), 91–120; for complaints of overcrowding see Abel, *Agricultural Fluctuations,* 99.

20. Emmanuel Le Roy Ladurie, *The Peasants of Languedoc* (Urbana, 1974), 56.

21. One of the first scholars to observe this pattern of price relatives in a systematic way was F. Simiand, in *Recherches anciennes et nouvelles sur le mouvement général des prix du XVIe au XIXe siècle* (Paris, 1932); this finding has been replicated many times, and is a key to the structure of the great wave. Some have argued that agricultural products rose swiftly because "they were coming most rapidly into markets." But this is not the case by comparison with industrial products, which were equally subject to market forces. The difference was in the disparities of demand which developed from demographic trends, and in different supply elasticities.

22. The only contrary finding that I have seen is in Steve Rappaport's excellent study of prices paid by London Livery Companies, which finds that the price of firewood faggots in London rose slowly in the sixteenth century. He concludes that the cause may have been a shift from wood to coal in London; imports of coal increased 400 percent in the reign of Queen Elizabeth I. In other parts of England, wood prices rose three times faster than in London. See Steve Rappaport, *Worlds within Worlds: Structures of Life in Sixteenth-Century London* (Cambridge, 1989), 144–45.

23. Hoszowski, "Central Europe and the Price Revolution," 91.

24. Hoszowski writes that in Poland, "prices rose without a break from

between 1521 and 1530 until 1550, when they had already reached a high level. The reason is that Poland was the greatest cereal exporter; the rise took place there before the invasion of American 'treasure' and the great upheavals that followed it throughout Europe.'' (Hoszowski, "Central Europe and the Sixteenth- and Seventeenth-Century Price Revolution," p. 91).

25. On the problem of relative prices, see especially F. Simiand, *Recherches anciennes et nouvelles sur le mouvement general des prix du XVIe au XIXe siecle* (Paris, 1932), pp. 114–138. See also essays by Hammarström, Brenner and Gould cited above.

26. "An Act to Restrain the Carrying of Corn, Victuals and Wood over the Sea," in R. H. Tawney and Eileen Power, eds., *Tudor Economic Documents* (3 vols., London, 1924) I, 150–52.

27. In England, one study of prices and wages yields the following result (1550 = 100):

Year	Food Prices	Skilled Wages	Unskilled Wages
1550	100	100	100
1600	244	160	114
1650	316	226	171

These data are from Y. S. Brenner, "The Inflation of Prices in England, 1551–1650," *Economic History Review* 15 (1962) 266–84; other enquiries have obtained similar results.

28. The pathbreaking work on price-wage differentials was done by German scholars, particularly M. J. Elsas, *Umriss einer Geschichte der Preise und Löhne in Deutschland vom ausgehenden Mittelalter bis zum Beginn des neunzehnten Jahrhunderts* (Leiden, 1936–1949), a series of price studies centered on six German cities. Virtually every other study also reports a fall of real wages in the sixteenth century; see Ramsay, *The Price Revolution in Sixteenth Century England*, 14, 17; Abel, *Agrarkrisen und Agrarkonjunktur*, pp. 129–131; E. Scholliers, *De Lebensstandaard in de XVe en XVe eeuw to te Anwerpen* (Antwerp, 1960); D. Bartolini, "Prèzzi e salari nel Commune di Portugruaro durante il secolo XVI," *Annali di Statistica* 2d ser., I (1878). A rare exception is Verlinden, Craeybeckx and Scholliers, "Price and Wage Movements in Belgium," who argue (78) that wages hovered very near the level of subsistence throughout the period.

Hoszowski also reports variations in eastern Europe on the timing of wage movements. In Austria wages rose slowly in the early 16th century, but faster thereafter. In Poland the pattern was the reverse: comparatively rapid increases before 1550; slower movements after that date. Hoszowski concludes that in general "workmen's wages rose much more slowly than the prices of crops." See Stanislas Hoszowski, "Central Europe and the Price Revolution," 92–93.

29. In Antwerp, the market rate for short term commercial loans in the period 1530–50 was 4–13 percent; in the latter part of the century low-interest loans tended to disappear, and rates were in the range of 7–12 percent. The same pattern also appeared in Lyons. Loans to penurious princes commonly carried prodigiously high charges. The house of Fugger, for example, charged the Hapsburgs as much as 52 percent for short term loans.

At the other extreme, usury laws and strict municipal regulation held nominal interest rates on annuities to very low levels. But these securities traded far below par, much like deep-discount securities in today's bond market. See Sidney Homer, *History of Interest Rates* (2d. ed., New Brunswick, 1977), 104–32.

30. Eric Kerridge, "The Movement of Rent, 1540–1640," *Economic History Review*, 2d ser., 6 (1953–54) 16–34.

31. *Ibid.*, 16.

32. *Ibid.*

33. Hoszowski, "Central Europe and the Price Revolution," 97–98.

34. H. G. Koenigsberger, "Property and the Price Revolution (Hainault, 1474–1573)," *Economic History Review*, 2d ser., 9 (1956) 1–15.

35. Wiebe reckoned that silver stocks in Europe were 9,190,000 kilograms in 1544, 21,400,000 in 1600 and 31,270,000 in 1660. At the same dates, the supply of gold was 815,000 kilos, 1,192,000 and 1,580,000 respectively; see G. Wiebe, *Zur Geschichte der Preisrevolution des XVI. und XVII. Jahrhunderts* (Leipzig, 1895), 260. Braudel and Spooner estimated by three different methods that world stocks of precious metal in 1550 were 3,564.5 tons of gold, and 37,427.3 tons of silver ("Prices in Europe," 444).

36. Many European price series show that the price-revolution began at various dates between 1470 and 1510, but American treasure did not arrive in Europe until 1503, and did not begin to expand in a rapid or sustained manner until after 1526. See Hamilton, *American Treasure*, 34–35; Y. S. Brenner, "The Inflation of Prices in Early Sixteenth Century England," *Economic History Review* 14 (1961) 225–39; *idem*, "The Inflation of Prices in England, 1551–1650," *ibid.*, 15 (1962) 266–84; C. E. Challis, "Spanish Bullion and Monetary Inflation in England in the Later Sixteenth Century," *Journal of European Economic History* 4 (1975) 381–92; R. A. Doughty, "Industrial Prices and Inflation in Southern England, 1401–1640," *Explorations in Economic History* 12 (1975) 177–92; J. Blum, "Prices in Russia in the Sixteenth Century," *Journal of Economic History* 16 (1956) 182–99; Hammarström, "The 'Price Revolution' of the Sixteenth Century: Some Swedish Evidence," 118–54.

37. The bulk of American silver arrived in Spain after 1580. Of total imports from 1531 to 1660, only 15 percent (2.6 million kilograms) came in the fifty years from 1531 to 1580; approximately 67 percent (11.6 million kilos) came in the fifty years from 1581 to 1630; 17 percent (2.9 million kgs.)

arrived in the thirty-one years from 1630 to 1660; Vicens Vives, *An Economic History of Spain,* 323; see also J. Nadal Oller, "La revolución de los precios españoles en el siglo XVI," *Hispania* 19 (1959) 503–29.

38. The rhythm of change in price levels and in the money supply in England during the sixteenth century has been elaborately studied. In the period 1542–51, both gold and silver coins were debased several times under both Henry VIII and Edward VI; then, from 1551 to 1560, the silver coinage was several times reduced in quantity and raised in content of precious metal. See J. D. Gould, *The Great Debasement* (Oxford, 1970).

These episodes have been closely examined in one of the most controlled historical tests of a monistic monetarist model. The results of that test are conceded to constitute a "contradiction of the basic hypothesis" even by a monetarist as convinced as Anna Schwartz. She acknowledges that in sixteenth-century England the movement of prices failed to reflect "the behavior of money stock per unit of output." ("Secular Price Change in Historical Perspective," *Journal of Money, Credit and Banking* 5 (1973) 243–69.

Similar difficulties also appear in other attempts to correlate the movement of prices with the stock of money. See, for France and Belgium, J. Lejeune, *La formation du capitalisme moderne dans la principauté de Liège au XVIe siècle* (Liege, 1939), 196; for Austria, Poland and Bohemia, Stanislas Hoszowski, "Central Europe and the Sixteenth-Seventeenth Century Price Revolution," in Burke, ed., *Economy and Society in Early Modern Europe,* 94–95. Even in Spain, Hamilton himself noted that the curves diverge at the beginning of the sixteenth century; see *American Treasure,* 511.

An excellent study of high importance by Michel Morineau also finds that the flow of American treasure continued at high levels in the late seventeenth century, when prices were falling. See Morineau, *Incroyables gazettes et fabuleux métaux,* 563.

All of these authors conclude that the rise of prices was linked in important ways to the quantity of money and specifically to American treasure. They also agree that the quantity of money was not the only cause. All but Hamilton think that it was not the first cause. Many believe it was not the most important cause.

39. These tests were developed at the University of Michigan by Adon and Jeanne Gordus, and extended by a French team at the Centre Ernest Babelon in Orléans. The first tests were based on analysis of gold content in Potosí silver; later a method of neutron-activation analysis was used to detect trace elements of indium, which is present in Andean silver.

See Adon A. Gordus, Jeanne P. Gordus, Emmanuel Le Roy Ladurie and D. Richet, "Le Potosí et la physique nucléaire," *Annales E. S. C.* 27 (1972) 1235–56; Adon A. Gordus and Jeanne P. Gordus, "Identification of Potosí Silver Usage in Sixteenth–Seventeenth Century European Coinage through Gold-Impurity Content of Coins," in W. L. Bischoff, ed., *The Coinage of El*

Perú (New York, 1989) 21–22; *idem,* "Potosí Silver and Coinage of Early Modern Europe," in Hermann Kellenbenz, ed., *Precious Metals in the Age of Expansion; Papers of the XIVth International Congress of the Historical Sciences* (Stuttgart, 1981) 225–242; Emmanuel Le Roy Ladurie et al., "Sur les traces de árgent du Potosí," *Annales E.S.C.* 45 (1990) 483–505; Dennis O. Flynn, "A New Perspective on the Spanish Price Revolution: The Monetary Approach to the Balance of Payments," *Explorations in Economic History* 15 (1978) 388–406.

40. J. D. Gould, "The Price Revolution Reconsidered," *Economic History Review,* 2d ser. 17 (1965) 249–266; Ingrid Hammarström, "The 'Price Revolution' of the Sixteenth Century," Y. S. Brenner, "The Inflation of Prices in Early Sixteenth Century England," 225–39; *idem,* "The Inflation of Prices in England, 1551–1650," 266–84.

41. John U. Nef, "Silver Production in Central Europe, 1450–1618," *Journal of Political Economy* 20 (1941) 575–91. An heroic attempt to place the history of precious metals in a global context appears in Frank C. Spooner, *The International Economy and Monetary Movements in France, 1493–1725* (Cambridge, Mass., 1972) pp. 9–86. Spooner concludes that gold was the dominant metal in Europe from 1400 to about 1450; that silver became dominant from 1450 to the early seventeenth century; and that thereafter a pluralistic monetary system prevailed: gold, silver, copper and credit. Spooner identifies major flows of silver from central Europe, gold from Africa, gold and silver from Mexico and Peru, copper from Hungary, Sweden and Japan. As the supply of each metal expanded its price fell, and the price of other metals rose in movements of great complexity. By studying these price relatives, Spooner is able to establish a chronology with remarkable precision, but the critical monetarist problem of quantity remains elusive; and the problem of velocity is even more difficult.

42. Blum, "Prices in Russia," 188.

43. Frank Spooner has estimated the quantity of coinage in France, and correlated it with wheat prices in Paris from 1520 to 1680. The results are most interesting. Annual fluctuations in wheat prices were not closely associated with the quantity of money coined each year. But when Spooner compared prices with a moving average of annual coinage through the period 1522–1680, he obtained a high correlation (approximately .70) between the two series. This association grew even tighter when the moving average of total coinage was lagged by five years.

But what is most interesting for our wave model is that the the coefficients of correlation between coinage and prices were highest in the period 1551–1610. They were lower and very mixed in 1522–1550, and tended to disappear altogether in 1611–1680.

Spooner's evidence is complex, and problems of interpretation are full of difficulty on these questions. Nevertheless, two general conclusions appear to emerge. First, the quantity of the money supply clearly had an effect upon price levels in France. Second, that effect was not constant through time: it was strongest and most consistent in the middle and later stages of the price-revolution, and comparatively weak and erratic in the first and last stages.

Spooner himself interprets his own results somewhat differently, but in a manner consistent with this analysis. "In general," he writes, "the comparison of the two series of coinage and prices cannot be said to show a highly significant correlation. . . . On the other hand, in the longer term, an association exists between periods of violent price changes and periods of heavy coinage. This remains roughly valid for the inflation of the second half of the sixteenth century, when coinage reached a peak in 1587. It also remains pertinent for the period 1625–1657, covering the great recoinages of the 1630's and early 1640's. . . . Monetary flows cannot have been wholly responsible for the movement of prices; they were important but their causal nature must not be overstressed. In this, prudence is necessary." See Frank C. Spooner, *The International Economy and Monetary Movements in France, 1493–1725* (Cambridge, 1972), pp. 274–80.

44. Marjorie Grice-Hutchinson, *The School of Salamanca: Readings in Spanish Monetary Theory, 1544–1605* (Oxford, 1952), 91; H. Hauser, ed., *La response de Jean Bodin à M. de Malestroit, 1568* (Paris, 1932); other early expressions of the quantity theory include Noel du Fail, *Balivernes et contes d'Entrepal* (1548); Gomara, *Annals of the Emperor Charles V* (1557); [Thomas Smith?], *Discourse of the Common Weal* (London, 1581); Gerard de Malynes, *A Treatise of the Canker of England's Commonwealth* (London?, 1601); and the same author's *England's View, in the Unmasking of Two Paradoxes; with a Replication unto the Answer of Maister John Bodine* (London, 1603). Some of these works are discussed in A. E. Munroe, *Monetary Theory before Adam Smith* (1923; New York, 1966); Claude Nicolet, "Les variations des prix et la 'théorie quantitative de la monnaie' à Rome, de Cicéron à Pline l'Ancien," *Annales E. S. C.* 26 (1971), 1203–27.

45. Tawney and Power, *Tudor Economic Documents*, I, 74.

46. George Hakewill, *An Apologie or Declaration of the Power and Providence of God in the Government of the World* (2d ed., Oxford, 1630); quoted in F. J. Fisher, "Influenza and Inflation in Tudor England," *Economic History Review* 2d ser. 18 (1965) 120–21.

47. John H. Elliott, *Imperial Spain, 1469–1716* (1963; New York, 1966), 205.

48. For a summary of this work see the various essays in Bob Scribner and Gerhard Benecke, *The German Peasant War of 1525—New Viewpoints* (London, 1979). Of fourteen essays in this volume, mostly by young German scholars, the majority find close links between the peasants' war and the price-revolution.

49. Pieter Geyl, *The Revolt of the Netherlands, 1555–1609* (1932; 2d ed., London, 1966), 94.

50. This is the conclusion of three leading historians. "It will no longer do to cut off religious or political aspects of sixteenth-century life from economic factors," they write, and offer evidence of a "link between the iconoclast movement and the high price of grain." See Verlinden, Craeybeckx and Scholliers, "Price and Wage Movements in Belgium in the Sixteenth Century," 68.

51. Barry E. Supple, *Commercial Crisis and Change in England, 1600–1642: A Study in the Instability of a Mercantile Economy* (Cambridge, 1959).

52. Brenner computed decennial averages and standard deviations of English grain prices (in shillings per quarter) as follows:

Decade	Mean	Standard Deviation
1451–1460	5.75	0.92
1461–1470	5.53	1.32
1471–1480	5.43	0.96
1481–1490	6.48	1.61
1491–1500	5.37	0.97
1501–1510	6.04	1.39
1511–1520	7.40	1.61
1521–1530	8.07	2.39
1531–1540	8.31	1.75
1541–1550	11.38	4.02

The source is Y. S. Brenner, "The Inflation of Prices in Early Sixteenth-Century England," 231–232.

53. Lane, *Venice,* 332.

54. This is the argument of F. J. Fisher, "Influenza and Inflation in Tudor England," *Economic History Review* 2d ser. 18 (1965) 120–29.

55. In Haarlem, Dutch scholar Lauris Jansz wrote a play called *Van't Coren* ("About Corn") dated November 4, 1565, which was furious attack on "monopolists." See Verlinden, Craeybeckx and Scholliers, "Price and Wage Movements in Belgium in the Sixteenth Century," 67.

56. Blum, "Prices in Russia," 199.

57. Albert Feaveryear, *The Pound Sterling: A History of English Money* (2d ed., rev. by E. Victor Morgan, Oxford, 1963), 63.

58. R. B. Outhwaite, *Inflation in Tudor and Stuart England* (1969; 2d ed., 1982) 54; W. R. Scott, *The Constitution and Finance of English, Scottish and Irish Joint-Stock Companies to 1720* (3 vols., Cambridge, 1912) I, 78–85.

59. Jaime Vicens Vives, *An Economic History of Spain* (Princeton, 1969), 384.

60. J.H. Elliott, *Imperial Spain, 1469–1716* (New York, 1966), 197,

207–8, 228, 260, 265, 283–4, 287, 329, 352; see also *idem, The Old World and the New, 1492–1650* (Cambridge, England, 1970) 54–78.
    61. Outhwaite, *Inflation in Tudor and Stuart England,* 45.

☙ The Crisis of the Seventeenth Century

    1. The general crisis of the seventeenth century is a historiographic issue of high complexity. The idea appears to have been suggested by English Marxist Eric J. Hobsbawm, who argued that a "general crisis" continued from the early seventeenth century into the early eighteenth century, and that it can be explained by an "elaborated or modified version of the Marxist model of economic development;" that is, a revolutionary transformation from feudal to capitalist stages.
    Other historians accept the idea of a general crisis, but interpret it in different ways. In 1960, the English conservative Hugh Trevor-Roper argued that this event was "a crisis not of . . . the system of production, but of the State, or rather of the relation of the State to society." Agrarian historians such as Slicher van Bath and Wilhelm Abel suggested that the crisis was one that occurred periodically in the agricultural system of western Europe. Historical demographers believed that the general crisis was "a revival of famines, plagues, and crises of subsistence." Environmental historian Victor Skipp approached the crisis of the seventeenth century "not merely in terms of the struggle of class against class, man against man, but with mindfulness of the wider, often sadder, yet surely essential, ecological perspective." T. K. Rabb saw it as a crisis of value and belief.
    A few skeptics do not think that there was a "general crisis" in any of these meanings. Perez Zagorin and A. D. Lublinskaya believe that the disturbances of the seventeenth century were not exceptionally severe and that they were disconnected events, broadly distributed through space and time.
    There are at least three issues here. The first is whether or not there was a systemic crisis in the seventeenth century. The answer to this descriptive question is certainly in the affirmative. The clearest evidence is demographic. The early seventeenth century was the only period in European history since the Black Death when population declined. To this demographic evidence, economic data might be added primarily in the form of price and wage and rent movements. The political aspect of this question is more doubtful, because we do not have a calculus of controlled comparison for political disturbances. Nevertheless, as to both wars and revolutions, the list of seventeenth century disturbances in the period 1610–60 seems to this observer far greater both in number and magnitude than those of any comparable period in the sixteenth century. Recent attempts to compile "statistics of deadly quarrels" confirm this conclusion.

The second question is when exactly the crisis of the seventeenth century happened. Various dates have been assigned in the period from 1550 to 1715. The evidence is strongest for the years from 1610 to 1660. Most historians accept these dates, or something like them. The third question is whether the disturbances of the seventeenth century may be explained as Hobsbawm's Marxist crisis in the system of production, or Trevor-Roper's crisis in the relation of state and society, or Abel's agrarian crisis, or the demographers' population crisis, or Flinn's environmental crisis, or Rabb's cultural crisis. In the judgment of this historian, the last five interpretations are correct, but none is broad enough to encompass the event. The purpose of the present work is to offer another model that might survive this test.

See Eric Hobsbawm, "The Overall Crisis of the European Economy in the Seventeenth Century," *Past and Present* 5 (1954) 33–53; Trevor Aston, ed., *Crisis in Europe, 1560–1660* (London, 1965); Geoffrey Parker and Lesley M. Smith, eds., *The General Crisis of the Seventeenth Century* (London, 1978, 1985); Victor Skipp, *Crisis and Development: An Ecological Case Study of the Forest of Arden, 1570–1694* (Cambridge, 1978); Zagorin, *Rebels and Rulers,* especially I, 122–39; Theodore K. Rabb, *The Struggle for Stability in Early Modern Europe* (New York, 1975).

2. On the question of when the price-revolution reached its climax, readers will find different answers in the literature. René Baehrel found that prices in Provence ceased rising and began to fall during the 1590s; see *Une croissance: La basse Provence rurale . . .* (Paris, 1961). Pierre Goubert, on the other hand, concluded that in Beauvais the turning point came later, in the mid-seventeenth century. Spooner and Braudel suggest that the great wave crested in southern Europe during the 1590s and in northern Europe during the second quarter of the seventeenth century. The evidence collected for the present work shows in many areas a double peak, both very high.

3. Supple, *Commercial Crisis and Change in England, 1600–1642;* 23,52, *passim*; J. D. Gould, "The Trade Depression of the Early 1620s," *Economic History Review* 2d ser. 7 (1954) 81–90; "The Trade Crisis of the Early 1620s and English Economic Thought," *Journal of Economic History* 15 (1955) 121–33.

4. Le Roy Ladurie found "late or very late wine harvests" in "seven successive years: 1591, 1592, 1593, 1594, 1595, 1596, and 1597 . . . [the 1590s are] the coldest decade from this point of view since the beginning of the sixteenth century." Emmanuel Le Roy Ladurie, *Times of Feast, Times of Famine* (1967; New York, 1971), 67.

5. Gustaf Utterstrom, "Climatic Fluctuations and Population Problems in Early Modern History," *Scandinavian Economic History Review* 3 (1955) 27–28.

6. Andrew Appleby, *Famine in Tudor and Stuart England* (Stanford, 1978), 133–54.

7. He adds, "Recent work has demonstrated that its effects cannot be dissociated from those of famine." François Lebrun, "Les crises démographiques en France aux XVIIe et XVIIIe siècles," *Annales* 35 (1980) 205–25.

8. Parker and Smith, eds., *The General Crisis*, 10–11; Sancho de Moncada, *Restauración politica de España*, ed. J. Vilar (1619; reprinted Madrid, 1974.

9. Ruggiero Romano, "Between the Sixteenth and Seventeenth Centuries: The Economic Crisis of 1619–22," in Parker and Smith, eds., *General Crisis* 165–225; Huguette and Pierre Chaunu, *Séville et l'Atlantique (1504–1650)* (7 vols., Paris, 1955–57); Nina Ellinger Bang, *Tabeller over Skibsfart og Varentransport gennem Oresund, 1497–1660* (3 vols., Copenhagen, 1906–23); F. C. Lane, "La marine marchande et le trafic maritime de Venise . . . ," in *Les Sources de l'histoire maritime . . .* (Paris, 1962); Supple, *Commercial Crisis and Change in England, 1600–1642*; S. C. van Kampen, *De Rotterdamse particuliere Scheepsbouw in de tijd van de Republiek* (Assen, 1953); J. C. van Dillen, *Bronnen tot de Geschiedenis van het Bedriffsleven en het Gildewezen van Amsterdam* (2 vols., The Hague, 1929–33).

10. *Cambridge Economic History of Europe*, IV, 42.

11. *Ibid.*, IV, 44.

12. Some scholars believe that war was a spur to economic growth; others take the opposite position. See Braudel, *Mediterranean*, 1:409; John U. Nef, "War and Economic Progress, 1540–1640," *Economic History Review* 12 (1942) 13–38; *idem, War and Human Progress* (Cambridge, Mass., 1950); Niels Steensgaard, "The Seventeenth-century Crisis," Parker and Smith, eds., *The General Crisis of the Seventeenth Century*, 26–56, 39; originally published as "Det syttende Arhundredes Krise," *Historisk Tidsskrift* 12 (1970) 475–504.

13. Steensgaard, "Seventeenth Century Crisis," 42.

14. R. Pillorget, *Les mouvements insurrectionnels de Provence . . .* (Paris, 1975); most scholars agree that economic grievances were central to these movements, often operating in combination with other issues of a political or religious nature; R. Mousnier, *Peasant Uprisings* (London, 1971).

15. Rabb, *Struggle for Stability*, 38.

16. Parker and Smith, *General Crisis*, 17.

✐ The Equilibrium of the Enlightenment

1. One of the best general reviews of the evidence is still Abel, *Agrarkrisen und Agrarkonjunktur*, 152–81, "Abschwung und Depression." But what Abel calls stagnation and depression might be understood more

accurately as equilibrium. He studied his subject from the perspective of the landowner. Others had different experiences.

2. *Ibid.*, 166.

3. Phelps-Brown and Hopkins, "Seven Centuries of the Prices of Consumables, Compared with Builders' Wage-Rates," 196–315.

4. D'Avenel, *Histoire économique de . . . tous les prix en general,* 3:508. The evidence in this pioneering work has been criticized, and techniques of price compilation are now much more refined in many ways. But d'Avenel's broad conclusions are generally confirmed by subsequent research.

5. H. J. Habakkuk, "The Long-Term Rate of Interest and the Price of Land in the Seventeenth Century," *Economic History Review* 1 (1952–53) 27.

6. Homer, *History of Interest Rates,* 142, 155.

7. *Ibid,* 305.

8. A. J. S. Gibson and T. C. Smout, *Prices, Food, and Wages in Scotland, 1550–1780* (Cambridge, 1995) 170; E. Jutikkala, "The Great Finnish Famine in 1696–7," *Scandinavian Economic History Review* 3 (1955) 48–63; R. E. Tyson, "Famine in Aberdeenshire, 1695–1699: Anatomy of a Crisis," in D. Stevenson, ed., *From Lairds to Louns: County and Burgh Life in Aberdeen, 1600–1800* (Aberdeen, 1986), 32–51.

9. Emmanuel Le Roy Ladurie, *Paysans de Languedoc* (Paris, 1966, 1969), 290–91, tr. by John Day as *The Peasants of Languedoc* (Urbana, 1974), 244. Why did France suffer more than England? Appleby finds that in France most grain prices tended to fluctuate together, but in England they rarely rose or fell as one. He concludes that English agriculture was more diversified than that of France. It is also probable that per capita income was higher in England, and that the margin of subsistence was not as narrow as in France.

10. On the history of *dissettes,* see Levasseur, *Les prix aperçu de l'histoire économique,* appendix

11. Morineau writes, "La seconde moitié du XVIIᵉ siècle ne saurait plus être regardé comme l'aride désert sans or ni argent que l'on a souvent décrit." Morineau, *Incroyables gazettes,* 566. Morineau's series for the arrival of American treasure in Europe appears in *ibid., 563,* and in "Des métaux prècieux américains."

12. Voltaire, *The Age of Louis XIV,* tr. Martyn P. Pollack (London, 1962), 349; Ernest Labrousse *et al., Histoire économique et sociale de la France,* vol. 2, *Les derniers temps de l'age seigneurial aux préludes de l'age industriel (1660–1789)* (Paris, 1970), 393–95.

13. On bills of exchange, see Raymond De Roover, *L'évolution de la lettre de change* (Paris, 1952); John J. McCusker, *Money and Exchange in Europe and America, 1600–1775: A Handbook* (Chapel Hill, 1978), 19.

14. Louis Dermigny, "Circuits de l'argent et mileux d'affaires au

XVIIIe siècle," *Review Historique* 112 (1954) 239–278; and *idem*, "Une carte monetaire de la France au XVIIIe siècle," *Annales E.S.C.* 10 (1955) 480–93; McCusker, *Money and Exchange in Europe and America, 1600–1775* 87; Fernand Braudel and Frank C. Spooner, "Prices in Europe from 1450 to 1750" in E. E. Rich and C. H. Wilson, eds., *The Cambridge Economic History of Europe*, vol. 4, *The Economy of Expanding Europe in the Sixteenth and Seventeenth Centuries*, (Cambridge, 1967), 378–486.

15. Wrigley and Schofield, *Population History of England, 1541–1871*, appendix A.3.

16. A summary of evidence from more than 200 family reconstitution projects in England, France, the Low Countries, Scandinavia, Germany, and Italy, appears in Michael W. Flinn, *The European Demographic System, 1500–1820* (Baltimore, 1981), 102–37.

17. Albert Soboul, Guy Lemarchand, and Michele Fogel, *Le siècle des lumières* (2 vols., Paris, 1977), 1:230–79; especially chap. 4, "l'apparente stabilité agricole."

18. Canadian economist Harold Innis was one of the first to explain that this was so because marginal returns increased when labor and capital were transferred from Europe to America. For example, a fixed unit of a fisherman's labor became more productive when it was shifted from the North Sea to the Grand Banks. The same pattern also appeared in agriculture, extractive industry, and many branches of commerce and manufacturing.

19. Plumb dated this great transition "very near the year 1700." Other scholars found its beginnings in the English Restoration of 1660, or in the Glorious Revolution of 1688. To refine Prof. Plumb's analogy, the water became ice in a series of freezings and thawings. See J. H. Plumb, *The Growth of Political Stability in England, 1675–1725* (Harmondsworth and Baltimore, 1967), 13.

20. Alekssandr A. Kizevetter, "Portrait of an Enlightened Autocrat," in Mare Raeff, ed., *Catherine the Great: A Profile* (New York, 1972), 3.

21. He dated this period as the century that began with the founding of the French Academy (1635) or the birth of Louis XIV (1639); Voltaire, *Essai sur les moeurs et l'esprit des nations* (Paris, 1756), of which the last part was called *Le Siècle de Louis XIV* (London, 1926), 2.

22. Edward Gibbon, *Autobiography*, ed. M. M. Reese (London, 1970), 15.

23. The rationalism of the early Enlightenment has been mocked in the twentieth century by cynics, skeptics, and relativists who take a perverse pleasure in demonstrating the contradictions of an eighteenth-century faith in the sovereign power of reason. The *philosophes* of the Enlightenment, were they transported to our own time, would be much amused by this attitude. They would be quick to point out the absurdity of reasoned arguments for the omnipotence of irrationality in human affairs, and the fatuity of a fashionable

academic industry that uses empirical evidence to support the dogmas of radical skepticism and historical relativism.

24. C. B. A. Behrens, *Society, Government, and the Enlightenment: The Experiences of Eighteenth-Century France and Prussia* (London, 1985), 160.

25. Patrick Chorley, *Oil, Silk, and Enlightenment: Economic Problems in Eighteenth-Century Naples* (Naples, 1965), 9.

26. Jean Ehrard, *"L'idée de nature en France a l'aube des lumières* (Paris, 1963; édition Flammarion, 1970), 43.

৯ The Price Revolution of the Eighteenth Century

1. Pierre Gaxotte, *Paris au XVIIIe siècle* (Paris, 1968); Leon Bernard, *The Emerging City: Paris in the Age of Louis XIV* (Durham, 1970); Orest Ranum, *Paris in the Age of Absolutism: An Essay* (New York, 1968); Jean Aymar Pignaniol de la Force, *Description de Paris* (8 vols., Paris, 1742); Robert Henard, *La rue Saint-Honoré* (2 vols., Paris, 1908); A. de Boislisle, "Notice historiques sur la place des Victoires et sur la place Vendôme," *Memoires de la Societé de l'histoire de Paris et de l'Ile-de France* 15 (1888).

2. Edmond Jean François Barbier, *Chronique de la régence et du règne de Louis XV, 1718–1763* (8 series in 123 parts, Paris, 1857) II, 80.

3. In Paris, an inflection-point appears as early as 1710, in a set of price series by Jean Tits-Dieuaide, "L'evolution du prix du blé dans quelques villes d'Europe occidentale du XVe au XVIIIe siècle," *Annales E. S. C.* 42 (1987) 529–48. Other price-historians have placed the turning point in or about the year 1729.

4. *Ibid.*, figure 1, p. 543; Anne Bezanson et al., *Prices in Colonial Pennsylvania, 1720–1775* (Philadelphia, 1935) 422–24; Phelps-Brown and Hopkins, *Perspective of Wages and Prices,* 30.

The inflection-point for the price-revolution of the 18th century varies from one price series to another, according to commodity, currency, method, and place. In general, earlier dates appear for urban grain prices in nominal currency. The inflection-points came a little later for rural prices of mixed commodities in silver equivalents.

5. B. A. Holderness, "Prices, Productivity, and Output," in Joan Thirsk, ed., *The Agrarian History of England and Wales,* vol. 6, *1750–1850* (Cambridge, 1989), 84–274; A. H. John, "Statistical Appendix," in *ibid.,* 973–1155; Peter J. Bowden, "Agricultural Prices, Wages, Farm Profits, and Rents," in *ibid.,* vol. 5.2, *1640–1750,* (Cambridge, 1985), 84–274; "Statistics," in *ibid.,* 827–902; Abel, *Agrarkrisen und Agrarkonjunktur* appendix.

6. Winifred Rothenberg, *From Market Places to a Market Economy; The Transformation of Rural Massachusetts, 1750–1850* (Chicago, 1992); *idem,* "The Market and Massachusetts Farmers, 1750–1855," *Journal of*

Economic History 41 (1981) 283–314; *idem,* "A Price Index for Rural Massachusetts, 1750–1855," *ibid.* 39 (1979) 975–1001; for the British officer's money and the system of "bookkeeping barter," see W. T. Baxter, *The House of Hancock: Business in Boston, 1724–1775* (Cambridge, 1945), 15, 17–21.

7. F. Ouellet and J. Hamelin, *Le mouvement des prix agricoles dans la province de Quebec (1760–1815)* n.p., n.d.; *idem,* "La crise agricole dans le Bas-Canada," *Etudes Rurales* 7 (1962) 36–57; John H. Coatsworth, "Economic History and the History of Prices," in Lyman L. Johnson and Enrique Tandeter, eds., *Essays on the Price History of Eighteenth-Century Latin America* (Albuquerque, 1990), 22.

Ruggiero Romano suggests a different reading of Latin American evidence: an "inverse movement of prices in Ibero-America and Europe." The evidence in Johnson and Tandeter is rather more mixed, and suggests a variation on the patterns that appear in Europe and North America. Cf. Ruggiero Romano, "Movimento de los precios y desarrollo económico: El caso de Sudamérica en el siglo XVIII," *Desarrollo Económico* 3 (1963) 31–43; and *idem,* "Some Considerations on the History of Prices in Colonial Latin America," in Johnson and Tandeter, eds., *Essays on the price History of Eighteenth-Century Latin America,* 35–71.

8. M. Cartier, "Notes sur l'histoire des prix en Chine du XIVe au XVIIe siècle," *Annales E.S.C.* 24 (1969) 1876–89; idem, "Les importations de métaux monetaires en Chine: Essai sur la conjoncture chinoise," *ibid.,* 36 (1981) 454–66; P. Liu and K. Huang, "Population Change and Economic Development in Mainland China since 1400," in C. Hou and T. Yu, eds., *Modern Chinese Economic History* (Taipei, 1977), 61–81.

9. The price of English coal per chaldron rose from 21 shillings in 1687 to 82 shillings in 1813. Wheat increased from 21 shillings in 1731 to 126 shillings in 1800 and went even higher by 1812. For price relatives and the rise of energy prices in the eighteenth century, see Beveridge, *Prices and Wages in England from the Twelfth to the Nineteenth Century,* 434–36.

In France the pattern of price relatives was much the same. On the subject of firewood, Labrousse writes, "La hausse de longue durée est la plus forte de toutes celles que nous avons observée sur le marché des produits [dans le] XVIIIe siècle: elle atteint 91% . . . L'amplitude de la hausse . . . parait imputable en grande partie a des disboisements massifs." See C. E. Labrousse, *Esquisse du mouvement des prix et des revenus en France au XVIIIe siècle* (2 vols., Paris 1933), and *La crise de l'économie française a la fin de l'ancien régime et au debout de la Revolution* (Paris, 1944), 343–47.

10. It might be noted that agricultural price relatives appear to have correlated with the proportion of each commodity traded in the market. Thus, a larger fraction of cheaper grains and beans were consumed by their producers than was the case with other foodstocks.

11. Wrigley and Schofield, *Population History of England, 1541–1871;* 402–7; also D. V. Glass, "Population and Population Movements in England

and Wales, 1700–1850;'' and Louis Henry, ''The Population of France in the Eighteenth Century,'' both in D. V. Glass and D. E. C. Eversley, eds., *Population and History* (London, 1965), 140, 434–56.

12. Abel, *Agricultural Fluctuations*, 192.

13. Family reconstitution projects have obtained the following mean age at first marriage for women in this period: four parishes in West Flanders, 1680–1739, 23.6; sixteen parishes in Yorkshire, 1662–1714, 23.6; five parishes in Nottinghamshire, 1701–36, 24.3; two parishes in Bas Quercy, 1700–39, 23.7; two parishes in Germany, 1691–1750, 25.7. Higher ages appeared in urban populations and in Scandinavia; lower ages were common in American colonies. Age at last birth and age-specific intramarital fertility in later child-bearing years also rose moderately in this period. The evidence is brought together in Flinn, *European Demographic System, 1500–1820.*

14. Georges Lefebvre, *Les paysans du nord pendant la révolution française* (Bari, 1959), chaps. 2–6; similar evidence appears in Robert Gross, *The Minutemen and Their World* (New York, 1976), 68–108.

15. Esther Boserup, *The Conditions of Agricultural Growth* (London, 1965); *idem, Population and Technological Change: A Study of Long-Term Trends* (Chicago, 1981).

16. Labrousse, *Esquisse du mouvement des prix*, II, 393–95.

17. On commercial paper, see Baxter, *House of Hancock*; A. H. John, ''Insurance Investment and the London Money Market of the Eighteenth Century,'' *Economica* new ser. 20 (1953) 137.

18. Eli Heckscher, ''The Bank of Sweden . . . ,'' in J. G. Dillen, ed., *History of the Principal Public Banks* (The Hague, 1934), 1760; Richard A. Lester, *Monetary Experiments: Early American and Recent Scandinavian* (Princeton, 1939); Joseph Ernst, *Money and Politics in America, 1755–1775* (Chapel Hill, 1973); Bruce D. Smith, ''American Colonial Monetary Regimes: The Failure of the Quantity Theory and Some Evidence in Favour of an Alternative View,'' *Canadian Journal of Economics* 18 (1985) 531–56.

19. Homer, *History of Interest Rates*, 160.

20. Decennial means of interest rates on long-term British securities (old 3 percent annuities before 1752 and 3 percent consols thereafter) increased as follows from 1730 to 1789:

Decade	Decennial Mean
1730–39	3.05%
1740–49	3.22%
1750–59	3.13%
1760–69	3.47%
1770–79	3.75%
1780–89	4.64%

The source is Homer, *History of Interest Rates*, 162, 177.

21. Christopher Clay, "The Price of Freehold Land in the Later Seventeenth and Eighteenth Centuries," *Economic History Review* 2d ser. 27 (1974) 173–89; Abel, *Agricultural Fluctuations,* 212–15; Arthur Young, *An Enquiry into the Progressive Value of Money in England* (London, 1812); d'Avenel, *Histoire économique,* 2: 508; D. Zolla, "Les variations du revenu et du prix des terres en France au XVIIᵉ et au XVIIIᵉ siècle, *Annales de l'Ecole Libre des Sciences Politiques* (1893–94).

22. A summary of the evidence appears in Abel, *Agricultural Fluctuations,* 199; see also Elizabeth W. Gilboy, *Wages in Eighteenth Century England* (Cambridge, 1934), 117–18.

23. A. P. Usher, "The General Course of Wheat Prices in France, 1350–1788," *Review of Economic Statistics* 12 (1930) 162; Gilboy, "Cost of Living and Real Wages in Eighteenth-Century England," 135.

24. Robert Jenkins (fl. 1731–38) appeared before Parliament in 1738 and testified that while sailing on the high seas from Jamaica to London, he was boarded by a Spanish garda-costa who seized his cargo, lashed him to the mast and tortured him by tearing off his ear. When asked what he had felt while "in the hands of such barbarians," he replied that he had "committed his soul to God and his cause to his country." Other evidence later suggested that he may have lost his ear in an English pillory, but patriotism ran high, and a powerful West Indian lobby demanded action. In 1739, war was declared, "amidst the rejoicings of the mob, the ringing of bells, and the Prince of Wales toasting the multitude from a city tavern." (Temperley in Royal Historical Society *Transactions* 3d ser. 3; G. Hertz, afterward Sir Gerald Berkeley Hurst, *British Imperialism in the Eighteenth Century*; Basil Williams, *The Whig Supremacy, 1714–1760* (Oxford, 1939; 2d ed., rev. by C. H. Stuart, 1962), 210.

25. Usher, "General Course of Wheat Prices," 162; Gilboy, "Cost of Living," 135; Ruth Crandall, "Wholesale Commodity Prices in Boston during the Eighteenth Century," *Review of Economic Statistics* 16 (1934) 117–82.

26. M. W. Flinn, "Trends in Real Wages, 1750–1850," *Economic History Review* 2d ser. 27 (1954) 397–413; also G. N. Von Tunzelmann, "Trends in Real Wages, 1750–1850, Revisited," *ibid.,* 33–49; E. W. Gilboy, *Wages in Eighteenth Century England* (Cambridge, Mass., 1934).

27. Eleanor Barber, *The Bourgeoisie in Eighteenth-Century France*; Robert R. Palmer, *The Age of Democratic Revolution* (2 vols., Princeton, 1959–64), I, 459; Martin Göhring, *Weg und Sieg der modernen Staatsidee in Frankreich* (Tübingen, 1947).

28. *Reflections on the Present High Price of Provisions, and the Complaints and Disturbances Arising Therefrom* (London, 1766). A copy of this pamphlet is in the New York Public Library.

29. The livre became the franc in the Revolution; in 1789, the exchange rate was five livres to the U.S. dollar.

30. Homer, *History of Interest Rates*, 169.

31. L. Stuart Sutherland, "Sir George Colebrooke's World Corner in Alum, 1771–73," *Economic History* 3 (1936) 237–58.

32. Charles P. Kindleberger, *Manias, Panics, and Crashes: A History of Financial Crises* (New York, 1978), 84, 122–24.

33. The importance of price movements in the Swiss revolutions is discussed in Patrick O'Mara, "Geneva in the Eighteenth Century: A Socioeconomic Study of the Bourgeois City" (thesis, University of California at Berkeley, 1956).

34. David Hackett Fischer, *Paul Revere's Ride* (New York, 1994), 76–77.

ᐧᐟ The Revolutionary Crisis

1. Le Roy Ladurie, *Times of Feast, Times of Famine*, 72.

2. Labrousse, *Esquisse du mouvement des prix*, II, 598.

3. Jean Egret, *The French Prerevolution, 1787–1788* (1962; Chicago, 1977), 31–59.

4. Georges Lefebvre, *The Great Fear of 1789* (New York, 1973), 10; Lefebvre errs in his belief that the industrial and commercial depression of the 1780s was a French phenomenon, caused by the reduction of customs barriers and a flood of English imports. In fact the English economy was also much depressed, and that of America as well.

5. This anecdote was recorded in the *Gazette Nationale, ou Le Moniteur Universel*, 15 July 1790; P. M. Zall, *Benjamin Franklin Laughing* (Berkeley, 1980), 162.

6. "Let them eat cake" ("Qu'ils mangent de la brioche") was attributed to "a great princess" in the sixth book of Rousseau's *Confessions*. This work was drafted at least two years before the Queen came to France in 1770; the other statements appear in Lefebvre, *Great Fear*, 37.

7. George E. Rudé, "Prices, Wages, and Popular Movements in Paris during the French Revolution," *Economic History Review* 2d ser., 6 (1954) 246–67.

8. Of 954 people granted the honor of "vainqueur de la Bastille," occupations are known for 661. Of that number, five-sixths were artisans, masters or journeymen or shopkeepers; the rest were mainly bourgeois; Jacques Godechot, *The Taking of the Bastille* (1965, N.Y., 1970); G. Durieux, *Vainqueurs de la Bastille* (Paris, 1911), on the price of grain and the Bastille, see Georges Lefebvre, "Le mouvement des prix et les origines de la Révolution française," *Annales Historiques de la Révolution Française* 14 (1937) 289–329.

9. George Rudé, "Prices, Wages, and Popular Movements," 246.

10. Price movements and political events in France, were associated as follows, from 1787 to 1815:

Period	Price and Real Wage Movements	Political Events
1788–1789	Surging prices; falling wages	Revolution begins
1790–1791	Stable prices; rising wages	Constitutional monarchy
1792–1793	Surging prices; falling wages	Jacobins to power; Louis XVI killed; Terror
1793–1794	Stable prices; stable wages; price and wage controls	Jacobin dictatorship
1794–1795	Riots against wage controls	Thermidor: Jacobins fall; Robespierre killed
1795–1801	Surging prices; falling wages	Directorate; Consulate
1801–1805	Stable prices; rising wages	Peace in Europe
1805–1812	Surging prices; falling wages	Napoleonic Wars

For general discussion of these relationships see Lefebvre, "Le mouvement des prix et les origines de la Révolution française," 289–329; Rudé, "Prices, Wages, and Popular Movements," 247–67.

11. Still the best short survey of world revolution in this period is Jacques Godechot, *Les révolutions, 1770–1799* (Paris, 1963); this work also is valuable for its historiography and copious bibliography. For more extended accounts see idem, *La grande nation* (2 vols., Paris, 1956); and especially Palmer, *Age of Democratic Revolution.*

12. Palmer, *Age of Democratic Revolution,* I,178.

13. On hyperinflations in the eighteenth century, see Seymour E. Harris, *The Assignats* (Cambridge, 1930); and Anne Bezanson, *Prices and Inflation during the American Revolution: Pennsylvania, 1770–1790* (Philadelphia, 1951).

14. Emmanuel Coppieters, *English Bank Note Circulation, 1694–1954* (The Hague, 1955), 13–34; Bray Hammond, *Banks and Politics in America from the Revolution to the Civil War* (Princeton, 1957); statistics for the United States appear in J. Van Fenstermaker, *The Development of American Commercial Banking, 1782–1837* (Kent, Ohio, 1965); a survey of events in France appears in Labrousse et al., *Histoire économique et sociale de la France* 2:367–410.

15. Lyman L. Johnson, "The Price History of Buenos Aires during the Viceregal Period," and Richard L. Garner, "Prices and Wages in Eighteenth-Century Mexico," both in Johnson and Tandeter, eds., *Essays on the Price History of Eighteenth-Century Latin America* (Albuquerque, 1995), 164–65, 80–81; Sevket Pamuk, "Money in the Ottoman Empire, 1326–1914," in Halil Inalcik and Donald Quataert, eds., *An Economic and Social History of the Ottoman Empire, 1300–1914* (Cambridge, 1994) 970; Charles Issawi, *The Economic History of Turkey, 1880–1914* (Chicago, 1980).

16. A contrary finding is reported by Tits-Dieuaide, who writes that wheat prices in European cities increased two or three times faster in the sixteenth century than in the eighteenth. The problem here is that her eighteenth-century series are not coequal with the price revolution; they begin as early as 1703, thirty years before the beginning of the long inflation, and end in the period 1753–90, before its climax. See Jean Tits-Dieuaide, "L'evolution du prix."

Overall, during the price-revolution of the sixteenth century, prices quintupled in 180 years, at an annual rate of 1 percent. In the price-revolution of the eighteenth-century, an index of English consumables increased by a factor of 3.6 from their nadir in 1734 to their peak in 1813—an annual rate of increase of approximately 1.7 percent.

17. Joel Mokyr and N. Eugene Savin, "Stagflation in Historical Perspective: The Napoleonic Wars Revisited," *Research in Economic History* 4 (1979) 198–259; G. Hueckel, "War and the British Economy, 1793–1815: A General Equilibrium Analysis," *Explorations in Economic History* 10 (1973) 365–96; N. J. Silberling, "British Prices and Business Cycles, 1779–1850," *Review of Economic Statistics* 5 (1923) 223–60; Eli Heckscher, *The Continental Blockade: An Economic Interpretation* (Oxford, 1922); A. K. Cairncross and B. Weber, "Fluctuations in Building in Great Britain, 1785–1849," *Economic History Review* 2d ser. 7 (1956) 283–97; A. C. Clauder, *American Commerce as Affected by the Wars of the French Revolution and Napoleon, 1793–1812* (Philadelphia, 1932).

18. Once again, the cost of energy was by far the most inflationary. One set of estimates for American wholesale prices shows the following increases from 1790 to 1814 (1790 = 100):

Commodities	Index
Fuel and lighting	552.6
Building materials	197.1
Metals	187.8
Food	174.0
Farm products	165.7

These data were computed from Warren and Pearson wholesale price indices in *Historical Statistics of the United States,* series E52–63.

19. John P. Post, *The Last Great Subsistence Crisis in the Western World* (Baltimore, 1977).

&❧ The Victorian Equilibrium

1. Francois Crouzet, *L'économie de la Grande Bretagne victorianne,* translated by Anthony Forster as *The Victorian Economy* (New York, 1982),

is a good overview of British economic history of the nineteenth century. Other major works include R. Floud and D. McCloskey, *The Economic History of Britain since 1700* (2 vols., Cambridge, 1981); E. J. Hobsbawm, *Industry and Empire from 1750 to the Present Day* (London, 1968); P. Mathias, *The First Industrial Nation: An Economic History of Britain, 1700–1914* (London, 1959); P. Deane and W. A. Cole, *British Economic Growth, 1688–1956* (2d ed., Cambridge, 1967). Still instructive is a great masterwork, J. H. Clapham, *An Economic History of Modern Britain* (3 vols., Cambridge, 1926–38).

Works comparing English and European economic development in the nineteenth century include P. K. O'Brien and C. K. Kyder, *Economic Growth in Britain and France, 1780–1914: Two Paths to the Twentieth Century* (London, 1978); Charles P. Kindleberger, *Economic Growth in France and Britain, 1851–1950* (Cambridge, Mass., 1964); Simon Kuznets, *Modern Economic Growth: Rate, Structure, and Spread* (New Haven, 1966); and David S. Landes, *The Unbound Prometheus: Technological Change and Industrial Development in Western Europe from 1750 to the Present* (Cambridge, 1970).

2. Namier writes, "There was undoubtedly also an economic and social background to the revolution [of 1848]. Lean harvests in 1846 and 1847, and the potato disease, were causing intense misery in most parts of the Continent. Agrarian riots occurred in France, where 1847 was long remembered as 'l'année du pain cher.' " But most histories give little attention to this aspect of the revolutionary movement. Lewis Namier, *1848: The Revolution of the Intellectuals* (1946; Garden City, 1964), 3; see also Priscilla Robertson, *Revolutions of 1848: A Social History* (New York, 1952), 56; Georges Duveau, *1848: The Making of a Revolution* (1965; New York, 1967).

3. On German economic history, see Helmut Böhme, *Deutschlands Weg zur Grossmacht . . .* (Cologne and Berlin, 1966); Wolfram Fischer, *Wirtschaft und Gesellschaft im Zeitalter der Industrialisierung . . .* (Gottingen, 1972); Fritz Stern, *Bismarck, Bleichroder, and the Building of the German Empire* (New York, 1977); and Franz Schnabel, *Deutsche Geschichte im neunzehnten Jahrhundert* (4 vols., Freiberg, 1954).

4. Even the strongest surveys of American economic history in the past generation give little attention to price movements; see, for example, Lance Davis *et al.*, *American Economic Growth: An Economist's History of the United States* (New York, 1972), 363–65; and Douglass C. North, *Growth and Welfare in the American Past: A New Economic History* (Englewood Cliffs, N.J., 1966), which defines the American economy as a "price system" rather than a "planning system" (p. 8) but largely ignores the history of price movements.

5. E. M. Coulter, *The Confederate States of America* (Baton Rouge, 1950), 155.

6. See above, figures 1.02, 1.18, 2.02, 2.14, 3.02, 3.13.

7. Abel, *Agrarkrisen und Agrarkonjunktur,* 258.

8. Phelps-Brown and Hopkins, "Seven Centuries of the Prices of Consumables, Compared with Builders' Wage-Rates"; for Germany see Abel, *Agrarkrisen und Agrarkonjunktur,* 244–64; for Sweden see Lennart Jörberg, *A History of Prices in Sweden, 1732–1914,* II, 334–49.

9. For real wages in the United States during the nineteenth century, see *Historical Statistics of the United States,* average annual and daily earnings of nonfarm employees, 1860–1900, series D735–38; and daily wage rates on the Erie Canal, series D718–21; and wage rates of artisans, laborers, and agricultural workers in the Philadelphia area, 1785–1830, series D715–17; also Peter H. Lindert and Jeffrey G. Williamson, "Three Centuries of Wealth Inequality," *Research in Economic History* 1 (1976) 69–122.

10. Stephan Thernstrom, *Poverty and Progress: Social Mobility in a Nineteenth-Century City* (Cambridge, 1964), 20.

11. Ulrich B. Phillips, *American Negro Slavery* (Baton Rouge, 1966), 371.

12. Homer, *History of Interest Rates,* 181–215.

13. *Ibid.,* 216–173; J. M. Fachan, *Histoire de la rente française* (Paris, 1904); Leonidas J. Loutchitch, *Des variations du taux de l'intérêt en France de 1800 a nos jours* (Paris, 1930).

14. Homer, *History of Interest Rates,* 205; Robert Blake, *Disraeli* (Anchor ed., New York, 1968), 295, 405, 716, 157, passim.

15. Abel, *Agrarkrisen und Agrarkonjuntur,* 237, 283.

16. Wrigley and Schofield, *Population History of England, 1541–1871,* 402–12. To call this revolution "economic" betrays a material bias that is stronger in the observer than the event. The revolution was other things before it became economic, but in other respects the interpretation is sound.

17. Davis, et al., *American Economic Growth,* chaps. 1–3; Kuznets, *Modern Economic Growth;* N. F. R. Crafts, *British Economic Growth during the Industrial Revolution* (Oxford, 1985); John J. McCusker and Russell R. Menard, *The Economy of British America* (Chapel Hill, 1985).

18. Kindleberger, *Manias, Panics, and Crashes;* 15, passim.

19. Peter Temin, *The Jacksonian Economy* (New York, 1969). These generalizations are in some respects at variance with Temin's conclusions but consistent with his evidence. It is also interesting to observe that wholesale prices and specie supplies tended to move in unison, but consumer prices actually fell as the money supply increased sharply.

20. H. H. Lamb, *Climate: Present, Past, and Future* (2 vols., London, 1977), II, 481.

21. Byron Farwell, *Queen Victoria's Little Wars* (New York, 1972), 364–71.

22. Fernand Braudel, *Capitalism and Material Life, 1400–1800* (London, 1973), 332.

23. Walter E. Houghton, *The Victorian Frame of Mind, 1830–1870* (New Haven, 1957), a valuable work, though it makes too much of similarities between Victorian and post-Victorian thought; G. M. Young, *Victorian England: Portrait of an Age* (New York, 1954).

↨ The Price Revolution of the Twentieth Century

1. For a general cultural history of this transformation, see Jan Romein, *The Watershed between Two Eras: Europe in 1900* (Middletown, 1978), a work of high importance in modern historiography.

2. An intelligent discussion of the "battle of the standards" appears in Richard Hofstadter's introduction to William H. Harvey, *Coin's Financial School* (Cambridge, 1963), 1–80.

3. G. L. Bach, *The New Inflation; Causes, Effects, Cures* (Providence, 1973), 4,5.

4. *Financial Review* (1898) 1; Harold U. Faulkner, *The Decline of Laissez Faire*, 22.

5. Vilar, *A History of Gold and Money, 1450–1920*, 328, 352.

6. Many studies have shown that, once the long wave began, changes in the stock of money correlated roughly (very roughly) with price movements. Price movements and the money supply were associated as follows from 1890–1978:

Period	Annual Percentage Rate of Growth			
	Stock of Money	Prices	Real GNP	Ratio Money to Nominal GNP
1890–1913	6.04	0.82	3.97	1.25
1913–1923	8.44	5.33	2.33	0.78
1923–1929	4.03	0.23	3.41	0.85
1929–1939	0.56	−1.58	0.28	1.86
1939–1948	12.23	6.79	4.84	0.60
1948–1967	4.24	2.05	3.87	−1.68
1967–1978	8.51	6.11	2.76	−0.36
1890–1978	6.11	2.53	3.24	0.34

See also Milton Friedman and Anna Jacobson Schwartz, *A Monetary History of the United States, 1867–1960* (Princeton, 1963), 91; and W. Arthur Lewis, *Growth and Fluctuations, 1870–1913* (London, 1978), 91.

7. World population has been estimated at 900 million in 1800, 1.2 billion in 1850, 1.625 billion in 1900, and 2.5 billion in 1950. The rate of increase was approximately the same in 1800–1850 (33 percent) and 1850–1900 (35 percent). From 1900–1950, the rate of gain was 54 percent, despite

the horrific cost of two world wars. McEvedy and Jones, *Atlas of World Population History*, 342–43.

The important causal linkage was not to population growth alone but to the acceleration of population growth, relative to the pace of economic growth. The equilibrium of the Victorian era had also been a time of world population growth but at a slower rate, and in a stable relationship to economic change.

8. Quoted in W. David Slawson, *The New Inflation* (Princeton, 1981), 6.

9. Geoffrey Barraclough, *An Introduction to Contemporary History* (Baltimore, 1967), chaps. 3, 4.

10. John Stevenson, *British Society, 1914–1945* (Harmondsworth, 1984), 46–102; Arthur Marwick, *The Deluge: British Society and the First World War* (1965).

11. Carl T. Holtfrerich, "Political Factors of the German Inflation, 1914–1923," in Nathan Schmukler and Edward Marcus, eds., *Inflation Through the Ages: Economic, Social, Psychological, and Historical Aspects* (New York, 1983), 400–16; Gordon Craig, *Germany, 1866–1945* (New York, 1978), 342–57.

12. A. J. P. Taylor, *English History, 1914–1945* (Oxford, 1965), 171.

13. R. A. C. Parker, *Struggle for Survival; The History of the Second World War* (Oxford, 1989), 76.

14. *Historical Statistics of the U.S.* (1976), series F4, 224.

15. Prisoner of war camps created their own internal economies in which cigarettes commonly functioned as money. Prices tended to fluctuate with the supply of tobacco, in a classical example of the monetarist model. But changing levels of aggregate demand also played a role.

16. *Historical Statistics of the United States* (1976), series E, 135. The two exceptional years were 1949 and 1955.

17. Eric F. Goldman, *The Crucial Decade and After: America, 1945–1960* (New York, 1973), 25–26, 46–47.

18. Structural interpretations of inflation include those of Gardiner Means in "Simultaneous Inflation and Unemployment," in Means *et al.*, *The Roots of Inflation: The International Crisis* (New York, 1975), 19–27; also the many works of Robert Heilbruner.

19. Slawson, *New Inflation*, 51.

20. Slawson, *New Inflation*, also *idem*, "Price Controls for a Peacetime Economy," *Harvard Law Review* 84 (1971) 1090–1107; and *idem*, "Fighting Stagflation with the Wrong Weapons," *Princeton Alumni Weekly*, 23 Feb. 1983, 33–38. For other "new inflation" theories, see Robert Lekachman, *Economists at Bay* (New York, 1976); Dudley Jackson, H. A. Turner, and Frank Wilkinson, *Do Trade Unions Cause Inflation?* (Cambridge, 1974); and Bach, *New Inflation*.

ᨀ The Troubles of Our Times

1. B. R. Mitchell, *European Historical Statistics, 1750–1975* (2nd rev. ed., New York, 1981), 777.
2. *Ibid.*, series C2, 177–80.
3. Charles S. Maier, "Inflation and Stagnation as Politics and History," in Leon N. Lindberg and Charles S. Maier, eds., *The Politics of Inflation and Economic Stagnation* (Washington, 1985), 3–24.
4. Kozo Yamamura, "The Cost of Rapid Growth and Capitalist Democracy in Japan," in Lindberg and Maier, eds., *Politics of Inflation and Economic Stagnation*, 467–508.
5. Arthur B. Laffer, "The Phenomenon of Worldwide Inflation: A Study of International Market Integration," in Meisselman and Laffer, eds., *The Phenomenon of Worldwide Inflation* 27–52.
6. In 1979, American economist Lester Thurow advised his colleagues that they could not hope to understand the inflation that was then surging to high levels in the United States without entering a distant realm that he quaintly called "the long ago." By "the long ago" he meant the year 1965. This observation was part of an argument commonly made by American economists, that the great inflation of the late twentieth century had its origin in fiscal and monetary decisions made during the Vietnam War. This was mistaken in at least three ways at once. The price revolution began seventy years earlier. Even the surge of the 1960s began before the United States sent large numbers of troops to Vietnam, and in another part of the world. Lester C. Thurow, *The Zero Sum Society* (New York, 1980), 43.
7. Rudiger Dornbusch and Stanley Fischer, *Macroeconomics* (New York, 1978), 316.
8. Robert Aaron Gordon, *Economic Instability and Growth: The American Record* (New York, 1974), 170.
9. The Nixon price and wage controls were imposed in three phases: phase I, August-November, 1971, prices, wages, and rents frozen for ninety days; phase II, November, 1971 to 1973, prices and wages controlled by a Pay Board and Price Commission; phase III; prices and wages restrained by largely voluntary restraints except in food, health, and construction industries, where mandatory controls continued until 1974. The impact of these measures may be seen in the following annual rates of change in price levels and economic indicators.

Year & Quarter	Output per Hour	Wages per Hour	Unit Labor Costs	Consumer Prices	Wholesale Prices
1966	3.5	6.1	2.4	2.9	3.3
1967	1.6	5.7	4.0	2.9	0.2
1968	2.9	7.3	4.3	4.2	2.5

(continued)

(continued)

Year & Quarter	Output per Hour	Wages per Hour	Unit Labor Costs	Consumer Prices	Wholesale Prices
1969	−0.2	7.0	7.2	5.4	3.9
1970	0.7	7.2	6.5	5.9	3.7
1971:1	7.4	9.1	1.5	3.1	5.5
2	3.2	7.5	4.2	4.4	4.7
3	2.5	5.2	2.5	4.0	3.2
4	4.7	4.9	0.3	2.3	0.3
1972:1	5.2	9.1	3.8	3.3	7.9
2	5.1	4.6	−0.5	3.3	4.2
3	6.6	6.1	−0.4	3.6	5.9
4	4.3	7.4	3.0	3.5	4.4

Source: Gordon, *Economic Instability and Growth*, 165, 190–92. Neoclassical economists insist that inflation would have diminished anyway, but there can be little doubt that controls worked by reducing inflationary expectations, profit margins, and aggregate demand.

10. Stein, *Presidential Economics*, 186.

11. John M. Blair, *The Control of Oil* (New York, 1976), 264. Blair points out that the crisis became more severe because it came on top of an artificial domestic shortage that had been deliberately created by the Exxon corporation and other major corporations, who were trying to break the competition of discount dealers in the United States and independent Libyan suppliers. This conjunction of events, he writes, "set the stage for a virtual explosion of prices" (254).

12. *Statistical Abstract of the United States* (1984), tables 801, 810.

13. John Kenneth Galbraith, *Economics in Perspective* (Boston, 1987), 270.

14. *International Financial Statistics* 34 (1981) 45.

15. Robert Mabro, ed., *The 1986 Oil Price Crisis: Economic Effects and Policy Responses* (Oxford, 1988).

16. John A. Jenkins, "The Hunt Brothers: Battling a Billion Dollar Debt," *New York Times Magazine*, 27 Sept. 1987.

17. *New York Times*, 15 Sept. 1986.

18. Part of this increase was caused by the fall of the dollar. But a multi-currency index of commodity prices kept by the *Economist* in London showed an increase of 16 percent in 1986–87. *New York Times*, 15 Sept. 1985.

19. *Ibid.*

20. *Statistical Abstract of the United States* (1984), tables 771, 772, 773, 775, 779, 780, 781, 782.

21. *Boston Globe* Oct. 4, 1987; *Statistical Abstract of the United States* (1984), 745; (1993) 1225.

22. Real wages are not an entirely accurate indicator of returns to labor.

One must also add levels of employment to the level of wages. Unemployment became a chronic problem in western economies, and reduced the real returns to labor, especially in the United States, where unions and corporations favored comparatively high wages even at the price of high unemployment. When unemployment is taken into consideration, the movement of real returns to labor may be more nearly comparable to that in previous price- revolutions. *Statistical Abstract of the United States,* (1981), tables 606, 607.

The classic study of the relation between unemployment and inflation and the source of the Phillips curve is A. W. Phillips, "The Relation between Unemployment and the Rate of Change of Money Wage Rates in the United Kingdom, 1861–1957," *Economica* 25 (1958) 183–299.

23. In the United States, from 1970 to 1992, average hourly and weekly dollars in constant (1982) dollars declined as follows:

	1970	1980	1985	1990	1992
Hourly earnings	8.03	7.78	7.77	7.52	7.43
Weekly earnings	298	275	271	259	255

Source: *Statistical Abstract of the United States* (1993), table 667.

24. *Boston Globe,* 4 Oct. 1987; *Statistical Abstract of the United States* (1984), 745; (1993), 1225.

25. Jeffrey G. Williamson and Peter H. Lindert, *American Inequality: A Macroeconomic History* (New York, 1980); James D. Smith, *Modeling the Distribution and Intergenerational Transmission of Wealth,* National Bureau of Economic Research, *Studies in Income and Wealth,* vol. 46 (Chicago, 1980); Gabriel Kolko, *Wealth and Power in America* (New York, 1962).

26. Frank Levy, *Dollars and Dreams: The Changing American Income Distribution* (New York, 1987), 1–22; U.S. Bureau of the Census, *Household Wealth and Asset Ownership: 1984, Current Population Reports, Household Economic Studies,* P–70, no. 7 (Washington, 1986).

27. *New York Times,* 6 Jan. 1980.

28. This flowed from a promise that President Reagan incautiously made in the election of 1984, that he would not raise taxes. The American electorate tends to be cynical about campaign promises, but studies have shown that politicians commonly try very hard to keep them, even at the cost of rigid adherence to wrongheaded policies that would have been abandoned if honor were not at stake. The Reagan presidency's stubborn refusal to increase taxes in the face of fiscal disaster was a classic case in point.

29. Galbraith, *Economics in Perspective,* 272–273.

30. *London Times,* ca. 23–28 July 1987. Another factor was an obsession with the Phillips curve, with its trade-offs between unemployment and inflation. The Thatcher government, with its middle-class constituency, feared the latter more than the former.

31. *New York Times* 9 June 1988.

32. Harvey Cushing, *The Life of Sir William Osler*, vol. 1, chap. 14.

33. Mikhail Gorbachev, *Perestroika: New Thinking for Our Country and the World* (New York, 1987), 85.

34. The work of Maris Vinovskis has been specially important in studying population decline.

35. "What Happened to Inflation?" *Economist*, 16–22 Sept. 1995, 85.

36. Lester C. Thurow, *The Future of Capitalism: How Today's Economic Forces Shape Tomorrow's World* (New York, 1996), 185–193; Roger Bootle, *The Death of Inflation: Surviving and Thriving in the Zero Era* (London, 1996), 3–31.

❧ Conclusion

1. Alfred, Lord Tennyson, "Locksley Hall, Sixty Years After, Etc.," in *Poems and Plays of Tennyson* (Modern Library ed., New York, 1938), 833–840.

2. Silvester Bliss, *Memoir of William Miller* (n.p., 1853); Ruth Alden Dean, *The Miller Heresy, Millenialism, and American Culture* (Philadelphia, 1987); David Tallmadge Arthur, *Come Out of Babylon: A Study of Millerite Separatism and Denominationalism, 1840–1865* (Rochester, 1970).

3. Galbraith, *Economics in Perspective*, 4.

4. See Stein, *Presidential Economics*, on Nixon's administration as "conservative men with liberal ideas," the increasing conservatism of Jimmy Carter, and the absurdity of Reaganomics.

5. In estimates of average rates of gain, much depends on periodization. These estimates are calculated from the point of inflection (ca. 1180, 1470, 1730, and 1896), to the maximum.

6. Mitchell, *European Historical Statistics, 1750–1975*, 772–76.

7. Braudel made these problems more difficult to solve by two errors in his own work. He entangled the pattern of great waves with Kondratieff cycles, which are certainly a second-order problem, and possibly a non-problem. He also limited his inquiries too narrowly in time and space. For a discussion of Kondratieff cycles see appendix E.

8. Fernand Braudel, *Perspective of the World* (1979; New York, 1984), 82.

9. See pp. 82.

10. Abel, *Agrarkrisen und Agrarkonjunktur*, 292.

11. Labrousse, *Esquisse du mouvement des prix, La crise de l'économie française*, the same argument is made by a student of Labrousse, M. A. Chabert, *Essai sur les mouvements des prix et des revenus en France de 1798 à 1820* (Paris, 1949); Abel, *Agrarkrisen und Agrarkonjunktur*, 1–16, 292–97.

12. For other complaints see David Landes, "The Statistical Study of French Crises," *Journal of Economic History* 10 (1950) 195–211.

13. André Marchal, quoted in Braudel, *Perspective of the World*, 76.

14. John Eddy, "The 'Maunder Minimum': Sunspots and Climate in the Reign of Louis XIV," in Parker and Smith, eds., *General Crisis* 226–69.

15. Robert I. Rotberg and Theodore K. Rabb, eds., *Climate and History: Studies in Interdisciplinary History* (Princeton, 1981); compare especially essays by Jan De Vries and Christian Pfister, with author attempting to find a mediating position (pp. 19–50, 85–116, 241–50).

16. There are at least three other explanations of wealth distribution in the literature: the Pareto model, which attributes inequality mainly to constant genetic factors; the Marxist model, which links it to long movements in the organization of the means of production; and the Kuznets "inverted U model," which argues that inequality increases when more economic growth begins and diminishes as rapid growth continues. None of these models fits the empirical patterns of change in wealth distribution. See S. Robinson, "A Note on the U Hypothesis Relating Income Inequality and Economic Development," *American Economic Review* 66 (1976) 437–40; Williamson and Lindert, *American Inequality*, 281–94 and Appendix L, above.

17. Quoted in May McKisack, *The Fourteenth Century, 1307–1399* (Oxford, 1959), 50.

18. C. Lowell Harris, *Inflation: Long-Term Problems, Proceedings of the Academy of Political Science*, 31 (New York, 1975).

19. *New York Times*, Oct. 4, 1995. At present the various data-gathering agencies of the U.S. government have compiled only one single series of statistical data through the full span of American history—a set of population estimates that are grossly inaccurate through the first two centuries. There are no comprehensive price or wage series for American economic history before 1890, except those compiled by individual scholars; no comprehensive data on production except for the past century; and no satisfactory data on wealth distribution for any period of American history. These historical data are necessary to give context and meaning to current indicators.

20. Hugh Rockoff, "Price and Wage Controls in Four Wartime Periods," *Journal of Economic History* 41 (1981) 381–401.

21. Levy, *Dollars and Dreams*, 13n.

BIBLIOGRAPHY
ᴈ Published Sources for the History of Prices

> The historian of prices must possess or control three separate
> techniques at least, those of the archivist, of the statistician,
> and of Sherlock Holmes.
>
> —William Beveridge, 1929

THE AMERICAN ECONOMIST Thurston Adams began his research
on the history of prices in Vermont by inviting the people of that state to
send him farmers' account books from the period 1790–1840. He was
amazed to receive four tons of records.

This embarrassment of riches exists very generally in the history of
prices. No definitive bibliography exists for this subject, partly because of the
vast abundance of primary and secondary materials. The most recent general
bibliographies published separately in English appeared more than eighty
years ago: the New York Public Library's *List of Works in the Library Relating to Prices* (New York, 1902) and Hermann H. B. Meyer, *Select List of
References on the Cost of Living and Prices* (Washington, 1910). More restricted in coverage are economic bibliographies such as Paul Wasserman,
Sources of Commodity Prices (New York, 1959), and Joe S. Bain, *Literature
on Price Policy and Related Topics, 1933–1947; A Selective Bibliography*
(Berkeley, 1947).

Historical bibliographies appear in Ruggiero Romano, ed., *I Prèzzi in
Europa dal XVIII sècolo a òggi* (Turin, 1967), 569–90, which is specially
helpful on the large and very rich Italian journal literature. An excellent
bibliography is attached to Georges and Geneviève Frêche, *Les prix des
grains, des vins et des légumes à Toulouse (1486–1868): Extraits des Mercuriales suivis d'une bibliographie d'histoire des prix* (Paris, 1967), which was
meant to supplement bibliographies in C. E. Labrousse, *Esquisse du mouvement des prix et revenus en France, au XVIIIe siècle* (Paris, 1933), 5, 11–12,

363

650–64. These two works are very strong for the rich harvest of monographs that appeared in France. German bibliographies have been published in the works of Alfred Jacobs and Wilhelm Abel, cited below. Many local studies cited in these works are not repeated here. Also useful is W. H. Chaloner and R. C. Richardson, *Bibliography of British Economic and Social History* (Manchester, 1984); and Derek H. Aldcroft and Richard Rodger, *Bibliography of European Economic and Social History* (Manchester, 1984), which is limited to literature in English for the modern period. A second edition appeared in 1992. Bibliographies also appear in various volumes of the *Cambridge Economic History of Europe,* especially volume 4, 605–15. A *Price History Newsletter* (1984) has been issued by the American historian John McCusker. Specialized bibliographies are noted below.

The following survey of printed materials is far from definitive, but it attempts to include major published works of general interest on the history of prices. Inevitably many titles have been missed. Additions and corrections are welcome for future editions. The bibliography is divided into the following parts:

primary sources
   mercuriales
   price currents
   historical compilations
   serial publications
   materials on the analysis of primary sources

secondary sources
   general works
   economic theory
   social theory
   historical models
   general works on related subjects

period-specific secondary sources
   ancient civilizations
   the medieval price-revolution
   the crisis of the fourteenth century
   the equilibrium of the Renaissance
   the price-revolution of the sixteenth century
   the crisis of the seventeenth century
   the equilibrium of the Enlightenment
   the price-revolution of the eighteenth century
   the revolutionary crisis
   the Victorian equilibrium
   the price-revolution of the twentieth century

੩ Mercuriales

The growth of the literature on prices has an historical rhythm which is linked to price-revolutions themselves. The first important serial publications appeared during the price-revolution of the sixteenth century, when price records began to be compiled in weekly or monthly market surveys called *mercuriales*. The earliest long series known to the author were kept in the city of Toulouse and have been published in Georges and Geneviève Frêche, *Les prix des grains, des vins et des légumes à Toulouse (1486–1868)*, cited above. Another run of *mercuriales* exists for Paris from as early as 1520. They are analyzed in Micheline Baulant[-Duchaillut] and Jean Meuvret, *Prix des céréales extraits de la mercuriale de Paris (1520–1698)* (2 vols., Paris, 1960–62). Yet another set of mercuriales for seven market towns in the northern part of the Ile-de-France is published in J. Dupaquier, M. Lachiver and J. Meuvret, *Mercuriales du pays de France et du Vexin Français, 1640–1792* (Paris, 1968).

A large journal literature on these sources, with major contributions by Marc Bloch, Pierre Chaunu, C. E. Labrousse, and others, is surveyed by George and Geneviève Frêche. To their excellent bibliography might be added Jean Georges, "Les mercuriales d'Angoulême, de Cognac et de Jarnac (1593–1797)," *Bulletin et Memoires de la Societé d'Histoire et Archeologie de la Charente* 64 (1920); J. C. Humblot, "Les mercuriales de Langres du XVᵉ au XIX² siècle," *Revue de Champagne et de Brie* 9 (1897); R. Vaschalde, "Les mercuriales du Vivarais," *Bulletin de la Societé d'Agriculture du Departement de l'Ardèche* (1874); Abbé Merle, "Mercuriales de la Grenette de Boen au XVIIᵉ et au XVIIIᵉ siècle," *Bulletin de la Diana* 24 (1931); Jean Meuvret, "Les prix des grains à Paris au XVᵉ siècle et les origines de la mercuriale," *Paris et Ile-de-France* 2 (1960) 283–311; Franz Irsigler, "La mercuriale de Cologne (1531–1797): Structure de marché et conjoncture des prix céréaliers," *Annales E.S.C.* 33 (1978) 93–114. On methodological problems, see C. E. Labrousse, "Comment controler les mercuriales? Le test de concordance," *Annales d'Histoire Sociale* 2 (1940) 117–30.

੩ Price Currents

As early as the 1580s, small newspapers called *price currents* began to appear in Antwerp, Amsterdam, Hamburg, and other commercial centers of western Europe. They spread slowly to the English-speaking world, not appearing in London until the late seventeenth century, or in America until the late eighteenth. By the mid-nineteenth century, *price currents* were published in European colonies throughout the world, from Havana to Hong Kong and Calcutta. During the 1950s, a very good set of *price currents* was buried in the basement of the Maryland Historical Society, where the author discovered them as a schoolboy and spent happy hours turning their musty pages when he was supposed to be conjugating his Latin verbs.

During the eighteenth and early nineteenth centuries, prices were also reported in general newspapers and magazines. Contemporary essayists commonly derived their economic data from these sources, which in many commercial centers have not been systematically collected and published. Discussions of these materials appear in Jacob M. Price, "Notes on Some London Price Currents, 1667–1715," *Economic History Review* 2d ser. 7 (1954–55) 240–50; *idem*, "A Note on the Circulation of the London Press, 1704–1714," *Bulletin of the Institute of Historical Research* 31 (1958) 215–24; N. W. Posthumus, "Lijst van documenten," *Economisch-Historisch Jaarboek* 13 (1927) xliii–lx; L. W. Hanson, *Contemporary Printed Sources for British and Irish Economic History, 1701–1750* (Cambridge, 1963); and John J. McCusker, *Money and Exchange in Europe and America, 1600–1775: A Handbook* (Chapel Hill, 1978).

?▲ Early Historical Compilations

The modern historiography of prices came of age in the mid-nineteenth century with the publication of the first large-scale national compilation in England by Thomas Tooke and William Newmarch, *History of Prices and of the State of the Circulation from 1792 to 1856* (6 vols., London, 1838–57).

This work inspired other large projects in England, France, and Germany. The first of them was James E. Thorold Rogers, *A History of Agriculture and Prices in England from the Year after the Oxford Parliament (1259) to the Commencement of the Continental War (1793) Compiled Entirely from Original and Contemporaneous Records* (7 vols., Oxford, 1866–1902). A critique appears in Paul Mantoux, "Le livre de Thorold Rogers sur l'histoire des prix et l'emploi des documents statistiques pour la période antérieure au XIXᵉ siècle," *Bulletin de la Societé d'Histoire Moderne* (1903).

Rogers was followed by Georges d'Avenel, *Histoire Économique de la proprieté, des salaires, des denrées, et tous les prix en général depuis l'an 1200 jusqu'en l'an 1800* (7 vols., Paris, 1894–1926); and Georg Wiebe, *Zur Geschichte der Preisrevolution des XVI und XVII Jahrhunderts* (1894, Leipzig, 1895).

These scholars brought together large quantities of data from the manuscript records of manors, universities, monasteries, etc., as well as from *price currents* and individual account books. Their methods were later criticized for lack of rigor. D'Avenel was thought to have compiled his sources without discriminating sufficiently as to quality or place of origin. Rogers was accused of methodological errors by the standards of subsequent research. Wiebe was criticized for having relied in some instances on secondary sources of doubtful merit. Nevertheless, these pathbreaking works put the history of prices upon a new empirical foundation. They were also among the first to discover the major patterns of secular change that are discussed in this work. Much of the data they collected remains useful and even indispensable today.

During the early twentieth century, much scholarship in economics took the form of price compilations. The *Review of Economic Statistics* was crowded with contributions on price history and methodological essays on problems of concordance, series-splicing, weighting, and indexing.

The most important product of this research appeared in the 1920s, when American scholar Earl Hamilton began to publish the results of his inquiries on Spanish prices and American treasure—an immense feat of learning. Hamilton's work was controversial from the start. It was intensely criticized by American economic historians such as John U. Nef and extravagantly praised by British economist John Maynard Keynes.

Serious weaknesses have become apparent with subsequent research: notably its misreading of periods of price-revolution as good times, and price-equilibria as bad times. Fernand Braudel has written of his conversations with Hamilton at Simancas in 1927. The American scholar said, "in the sixteenth century, every wound heals, every breakdown can be repaired, every lapse can be made good." This was true of economic elites, and also of ordinary folk in the early years of price-revolutions. But for most people, most of the time, the opposite was the case. It was only after the work of Henry Phelps-Brown that historians took a broader view, and began to understand that the material condition of most people grew better in periods of price-equilibrium and worse in times of price-revolution.

That elitist bias was very strong in Earl Hamilton's work, as it was in the early work of Fernand Braudel and Wilhelm Abel and most other historians of that generation. Even so, Hamilton's scholarship was held in deservedly high respect by most colleagues who worked on related subjects, especially by French historians who would later be known as the *Annales* school. Half a century after it began to appear, Hamilton's work retains its reputation, even among historians who do not share its social or its monetarist assumptions. It remains a monument of careful scholarship.

Earl Hamilton's success, and the catastrophic failure of the world economy in 1929, stimulated a surge of interest in price history. The result was the founding in 1930–31 of the International Scientific Committee on the History of Prices, the largest and most sustained effort at international collaboration historians have ever undertaken. The initiative came from William Beveridge in England. Coordinated projects were undertaken in France by Henri Hauser, in Germany by Moritz Elsas, in Austria by A. F. Pribram, in the Netherlands by Nicolaas Posthumus, in Denmark by Astrid Friis and Kristoff Glamann, and in the United States by Arthur Harrison Cole.

The international committee on prices recommended standard procedures, drew up a list of twenty five types of commodities, and agreed on base periods for the computation of price indices. Despite these attempts to achieve common standards, individual price histories sponsored by the committee differed in many ways. Some were content merely to compile lists of nominal prices; others converted their data into silver equivalents—a procedure the committee recommended. Some works were based on institutional records; others on published price lists. Most works were national in scope but tended to be based upon data from a comparatively small number of sources. Even so, rapid progress was made in the publication of price materials, until World War II intervened. This work is discussed in Henri Hauser, "Un comité internationale d'enquête sur l'histoire des prix," *Annales d'Histoire Économique et Socialé* 2 (1930) 384–85; and Arthur Harrison Cole, "American Research in Price History," University of Pennsylvania Bicentennial Conference, *Studies in Economics and Industrial Relations* (Philadelphia, 1941). A history of this effort is Arthur H. Cole and Ruth Crandall, "The International Scientific Committee on Price History," *Journal of Economic History* 24 (1964) 381–88.

During the 1920s and 1930s, many leading historians throughout the world devoted themselves to problems of price history. The great French historian Marc Bloch did much of his work on medieval money and prices. Young Italian scholar-intellectuals became price historians; among them were Amintore Fanfani and Luigi Einaudi, who would later occupy the highest political offices in their nation. The brilliant British polymath Lord Beveridge was deeply interested in the history of prices and made a major contribution. His original purposes were far removed from those of most price historians. "My own interest in the subject," Beveridge wrote, " . . . arose not from general considerations but from the belief that the study of prices could be used to throw a light upon the problem of periodicity of harvests and so of weather."

Whatever Beveridge's purposes may have been, his scholarship was excellent, and his flair and imagination appeared in one of the most lively methodological essays to flow from a scholar's pen, "A Statistical Crime of the Seventeenth Century," *Journal of Economic and Business History* 4 (1929) 528, a discourse on techniques of price history, centering on a fraud in the fixing of wheat prices at Exeter. A lively and intelligent study of this extraordinary figure is José Harris, *William Beveridge: A Biography* (Oxford, 1977).

In the 1920s and 1930s, historians were not alone in this work. Leading economists throughout the world also studied descriptive problems of price history. They included François Simiand in France; Alfred Marshall and John Maynard Keynes in Britain; Irving Fisher, Earl Hamilton, and Simon Kuznets in the United States; and Nikolai Kondratieff in the Soviet Union. All were drawn to the subject by a faith in the possibility of objective knowledge about historical change and a belief that economics was an inductive science.

After World War II, a major discontinuity occurred in the study of price history. With the spread of historical relativism, the ideal of objectivity faded in many disciplines. At the same time, an epistemic revolution spread rapidly through the discipline of economics. In 1947, economist Tjalling Koopmans published a pivotal essay, which strenuously attacked the compilation of price records for their own sake. Koopmans argued that empirical observation of any phenomenon is "impossible" without "theoretical preconceptions" and that measurement without theory is useless because "conclusions relevant to the guidance of economic policies cannot be drawn." (Tjalling C. Koopmans, "Measurement without Theory," *Review of Economics and Statistics* 29 [1947] 161–72). Koopman's argument was mistaken in its epistemology and fallacious in its logic (see appendix O above), but it captured perfectly a new academic attitude in economics and the social sciences. This new orthodoxy was widely accepted in America especially. It caused a radical change in the work that economists actually did.

In the United States, large open-ended projects of empirical description on price history came to an end. Prices continued to be studied, but in a very different way, mainly as part of the process of "testing" specific theories. Open descriptive inquiries on price movements were banished to the periphery of economic research in the United States (see appendix O).

In Europe, the trend was different. Projects of empirical description in price history became more important after 1945, not less so. This was so in Britain, where Sir Henry Phelps-Brown and Sheila Hopkins made a seminal contribution by carefully constructing long series of English wages and "consumable" prices, which put the entire problem in a new perspective by bringing home the experience of ordinary people. It is striking to observe that the Phelps-Brown-Hopkins indices are now very heavily used by American economists who insist on the uselessness of "measurement without theory."

Price history also had a central place in the work of the French *Annales* school, which devoted much attention to the subject. The major conceptual apparatus of the *Annales* school, and in particular its concepts of "longue durée", "conjuncture," and "structure," was drawn from the history of prices. The epistemology of the Annalists centered on the study of problems and *"problematiques,"* not on the theories and "theory-testing" of American economics and social science. A *problematique* was not merely the problem itself but also an apparatus of methods for its study and a critique of previous attempts at its solution. Each of these epistemic approaches had strengths and weaknesses. Both made major contributions to knowledge.

The profound differences between American and European scholarship in this generation have been discussed by John Day, an American trained in the methods of the *Annales* school. In his "autohistoire," Day observes that where American economic historians are trained to begin with a theory, *Annalists* are taught to start with a problem. "Ce marriage de convenance," he writes, "entre pratique et théorie en histoire [de l'école des cliometricians Americains], contraste a mon sens avec la bonne entente entre pratique et problematique qui characterise les grands historiens de l'École des Annales." See John Day, "Terres, marchés et monnaies en Italie et en Sardaigne du XIIème au XVIIIème siecle," *Histoire Économie et Société* II (1983) 187–203.

The major *problematiques* of the *Annales* school kept the history of prices at the heart of its historiography. European monographs in social history gave much attention to price movements, both as indicators of change and as sources of inferential knowledge about other subjects. European scholars achieved a new level of sophistication in the construction of historical price series, a labor that Americans have been encouraged mistakenly to despise as inferior to "theory-testing." Leading examples include the work of Ernest Labrousse in France, Astrid Friis in Denmark, Nicolaas Posthumus in the Netherlands, and especially Lennart Jörberg's *History of Prices in Sweden, 1732–1914* (2 vols., Lund, 1972), a model work that is more comprehensive, more rigorous, and also more analytic than previous compilations. Price history continued to be a progressive science in Europe, while it languished in the theory-centered social sciences of North America.

These countertendencies in Europe and the United States have had important substantive consequences for the progress of historical knowledge. French monographs in social history routinely examine price movements with close attention. American monographs tend to ignore them. Price history is almost entirely absent from the social history of New England, except for the excellent work of my able student Winifred Rothenberg noted below. It has appeared only in works of the Chesapeake school, especially the excellent scholarship of Russell Menard who gives much attention to the prices of tobacco and slaves.

A comparison of articles in the American *Journal of Economic History* with leading European journals shows that American economic historians have recently shown comparatively little interest in studying price movements for their own sake. The result has been a lost generation of price historiography in the United States and a failure of institutional memory about price movements in the past.

This is also the case with historians who work in other fields. Every early American historian with whom I discussed this work expressed entire ignorance of the fact that prices were rising in the eighteenth century. All American economists whom I consulted believed that inflation in the twentieth century began with Lyndon Johnson and the war in Vietnam. Most scholars in both disciplines were aware of the price-revolution in the sixteenth century, but nearly all believed that it was a simple reflex of the supply of American treasure in Europe. None remembered the medieval price revolution. Even medievalists expressed surprise and even skepticism, until they were invited to examine the data, which was largely unknown to them.

This state of affairs is beginning to change. We are already seeing a revival of interest in price history by young American economists and historians, in new scholarship of unprecedented creativity and refinement. The starting point for the next generation will be the excellent corpus of scholarship in price history that was so laboriously produced in the past.

?⋆ Historical Compilations by Place

A large body of published primary sources on the history of prices is available in many nations. These materials are divisible into two parts: historical compilations and current surveys. General works and local studies of long duration are listed here by continent and nation. More specialized studies, limited to a single great wave or equilibrium, will be listed in later sections of the bibliography. For a general survey of quantitative sources, see Val R. Lorwin and Jacob M. Price, eds., *The Dimensions of the Past: Materials, Problems, and Opportunities for Quantitative Work in History* (New Haven, 1972).

?⋆ International Historical Compilations

B. R. Mitchell, *European Historical Statistics, 1750–1975* (1975, 1980, 2d rev. ed., New York, 1980); *idem, International Historical Statistics: Africa and Asia* (New York, 1982); *idem, International Historical Statistics: The Americas and Australasia* (London, 1983). New editions of these works (1995) are updated to 1988.

Another compendium, issued by the Organization for Economic Cooperation and Development, is *Consumer Price Indices: Sources and Methods and Historical Statistics* (Paris, 1980).

?⋆ Continental Compilations: Europe

Most European price history has appeared in national and local studies, but two broad European works contain much primary material. One of them is Wilhelm Abel, *Agrarkrisen und Agrarkonjunktur in Mittel Europa vom 13 bis zum 19 Jahrhundert* (Berlin, 1935; new eds. 1966, 1978), English translation by Olive Ordish as *Agricultural Fluctuations in Europe* (London, 1980); an appendix includes data for prices of wheat and rye in silver for fourteen

German localities from 1341 to 1935, and also price data for six European nations. The English edition has a forword and a second bibliography of English-language materials by Joan Thirsk.

Another continental work of high importance is Fernand P. Braudel and Frank Spooner, "Prices in Europe from 1450 to 1750," *The Cambridge Economic History of Europe* (Cambridge, 1967), 4:378–486. This major interpretative essay brings together much European data, drawn mostly from local studies listed below.

ᨃ Latin America

In Latin America more than Europe, many publications with primary material are continental rather than national in scope. A brief but helpful survey is E. Florescano, "La historia de los precios en la época colonial de Hispanoamérica: Tendencias, métodos de trabajos y objetivos," *Latino-América: Anuario de Estudios Latinamericanos* (1968) 111–29.

In a class by itself is Ruggiero Romano, "Movimento de los precios y desarrollo económico: El caso de Sudamérica en el siglo XVIII," *Desarrollo Económico* 3 (1963) 31–43; *idem,* "Mouvement de prix et développement économique: le cas de l'Amerique du Sud au XVIIIᵉ siècle," *2e Conference Internationale d'Histoire Économique, Aix-en-Provence, 1962* (The Hague, 1962) 2:141–53; *idem, Historia colonial hispanio-americana e historia de los precios* (Santiago, 1963); *idem,* "Some Considerations on the History of Prices in Colonial Latin America," in Lyman L. Johnson and Enrique Tandeter, eds., *Essays on the Price History of Eighteenth-Century Latin America* (Albuquerque, 1990), 35–72. Romano argues a thesis that price trends in Latin America were the opposite of those in Europe (see appendix D).

Johnson and Tandeter include twelve essays, most of which take issue with Romano. A broad perspective also appears in Steven A. Mange, "Commodity Price Movements in the Andes and La Plata during the Seventeenth and Eighteenth Centuries" (thesis, Chicago, 1988).

ᨃ National Compilations: Argentina

Historical price series appear in Lyman L. Johnson, "The Price History of Buenos Aires during the Viceregal Period," in Lyman L. Johnson and Enrique Tandeter, eds., *Essays on the Price History of Eighteenth-Century Latin America* (Albuquerque, 1990), 137–72; Juan Alvarez, *Temas de historia económica Argentina* (Buenos Aires, 1929); Direccion General de Estadistica, *Precios unitarios dearticulos de consuma y servicios, capital federal y provincia, 1901–1963* (2 vols., Buenos Aires, 1964–65?)

❧ Australia

Prices are included in in Jennifer A. S. Finlayson, *Historical Statistics of Australia* (Canberra, 1970). Still useful is Douglas B. Copland, *Currency and Prices in Australia* (Adelaide, 1921).

❧ Austria

A. F. Pribram et al., *Materielen zur Geschichte der Preise und Löhne in Osterreich* (Vienna, 1938) is the leading collection of historical prices for Austria. It is based mainly on institutional prices. Other studies include Luschin von Ebengreuth, *Vorschlage und Erfordernisse für eine Geschichte der Preise und Löhne in Osterreich* (Vienna, 1874); K. T. Inama-Sternegg, *Beiträge zur Geschichte der Preise* (Vienna, 1873); idem, "Die Quellen der historischen Preisstatistik," *Statistiche Monatschriften* 12 (1886); Alois Gehart, *Statistik in Osterreich, 1918–1938: Eine Bibliographie* (Vienna, 1984). Price records for Austria-Hungary were also published by B. Von Jankovich in *Bulletin de l'Institut Internationale de Statistique* 19 (1911).

❧ Belgium: General Studies

H. van Houtte, *Documents pour servir à une histoire des prix de 1381 à 1794* (Brussels, 1902) was a pathbreaking effort.

The inquiries of the second generation yielded M. Peeters, "Les prix et les rendements de l'agriculture belge de 1791 à 1935," *Bulletin des Sciences Économiques de Louvain* (1936) 22–48; F. Michelotte, "L'évolution des prix de détail en Belgique de 1830 à 1913," *Bulletin de l'Institute de Recherche Economique* (Louvain, 1937); and François Loots, "Les mouvements fondamentaux des prix en gros en Belgique de 1822 à 1913," *Bulletin de l'Institut des Sciences économiques* 8 (1936) 23–47.

Postwar studies include P. Schöller, "La transformation économique de la Belgique de 1832 à 1844," *Bulletin de l'Institute de Recherche Économique* (Louvain, 1948) and, for the price revolution of the sixteenth century, C. Verlinden, J. Craeybeckx, and J. Scholliers, "Mouvements des prix et salaires en Belgique au XVIᵉ siècle," *Annales E.S.C.* 10 (1955) 173–98. *Cahiers d'histoire des prix* (Louvain, published by the Inter-University Center for the History of Prices and Wages in Belgium, 1956–58) includes bibliographical materials.

❧ Belgium: Local Studies

[Antwerp] E. Scholliers, *Loon arbied en Honger de Levensstandaard in de XVᵉ en XVIᵉ eeuw te Antwerpen* (Antwerp, 1960).

[Antwerp] H. Van der Wee, *The Growth of the Antwerp Market and the European Economy* (3 vols., Louvain, 1963); *idem*, "Prices and Wages as Development Variables: a Comparison between England and the Southern Netherlands, 1400–1700," *Acta Historiae Neerlandicae* 10 (1978).

[Brabant] C. Verlinden et al., "Dokumenten voor de Geschiedenis van Prijzen en Lonen in Vlaandaeren en Brabant (XVᵉ–XVIIIᵉ eeuw)" (4 vols. in 5, Bruges, 1959–73); *idem, Documents pour l'histoire des prix et salaires (XIVᵉ–XIXᵉ siècles)* (Bruges, 1965).

[Brabant] M.-J. Tits-Dieuaide, *La formation des prix céréaliers en Brabant et en Flandre au XVᵉ siècle* (Brussels, 1975).

[Namur] L. Genicot, "Les prix du froment à Namur de 1773 à 1840," *Annales de la Societé Archéologique de Namur* 43 (1938–39) 129.

[Namur, etc.] J. Ruwet et al., *Marché des cereales à Ruremonde, Luxembourg, Namur et Diest aux XVIIᵉ et XVIIIᵉ siècles* (Louvain, 1966).

J. Ruwet, *L'agriculture et les classes rurales au pays Herve sous l'ancien régime* (Liége, 1943).

❧ Bolivia

Enrique Tandeter and Nathan Wachtel, "Prices and Agricultural Production: Potosí and Charcas in the Eighteenth Century," in Lyman L. Johnson and Enrique Tandeter, eds., *Essays on the Price History of Eighteenth-Century Latin America* (Albuquerque, 1995), 201–76.

Brooke Larson, "Rural Rhythms of Class Conflict in Eighteenth-Century Cochabamba," in Lyman L. Johnson and Enrique Tandeter, *Essays on the Price History of Eighteenth-Century Latin America* (Albuquerque, 1990), 277–308.

José Maria Dalence, *Bosquejo estadístico de Bolivia* (Chuquisaca, 1851).

W. L. Schurz, *Bolivia: A Commercial and Industrial Handbook* (Washington, 1921).

United Nations Economic Commission, *El desarrollo económico de Bolivia* (Mexico, 1957), includes data from the 1920s to the 1950s.

Cornelius H. Zondag, *The Bolivian Economy* (New York, 1966) publishes data for the period 1952–65.

❧ Brazil

Dauril Alden, "Price Movements in Brazil before, during, and after the Gold Boom, with Special Reference to the Salvador Market [*circa* 1670–1769]," in Lyman L. Johnson and Enrique Tandeter, eds., *Essays on the Price History of Eighteenth-Century Latin America* (Albuquerque, 1990), 335–72.

H. Johnson Jr., "A Preliminary Inquiry into Money, Prices, and Wages in Rio de Janeiro, 1763–1823," in Dauril Alden, ed., *Colonial Roots of Modern Brazil; Papers of the Newberry Library Conference* (Berkeley, 1973), 230–83.

Katia M. de Queiros Mattoso, "Conjoncture et société au Brésil à la fin de XVIIIᵉ siècle. Prix et salaire à la veille de revolution de alfaiates, Bahia, 1798," *Cahiers des Ameriques Latines* 5 (1970) 3–53.

Mirceu Buescu, *300 anos de inflaçâo* (Rio de Janeiro, 1973).

Armin K. Ludwig, *Brazil: A Handbook of Historical Statistics* (Boston, 1985).

❧ Canada

F. Ouellet and J. Hamelin, "Le mouvement des prix agricoles dans la province de Quebec (1760–1815)," n.p., n.d.; *idem,* "La crise agricole dans le Bas-Canada," *Études Rurales* 7 (1962) 36–57.

H. Michel et al., *Statistical Contributions to Canadian Economic History* (2 vols., Toronto, 1931), includes statistics on banking, foreign trade, and prices.

M. C. Urquhart and Kenneth A. Buckley, *Historical Statistics of Canada* (Toronto, 1965).

F. H. Leacy, ed., *Historical Statistics of Canada* (Ottawa, 1983).

Newfoundland Statistics Agency, *Historical Statistics of Newfoundland and Labrador* (St. Johns, 1970).

❧ Chile

Ruggiero Romano, "Une économie coloniale: le Chili au XVIIIᵉ siècle," *Annales E.S.C.* 15 (1960) 259–85; *idem,* "Historia colonial hispano-Americana e historia de los precios," in *Tres lecciones inaugurales* (Santiago de Chile, 1963).

José Manuel Larraín, "Gross National Product and Prices: The Chilean Case in the Seventeenth and Eighteenth Centuries," in Lyman L. Johnson and Enrique Tandeter, eds., *Essays on the Price History of Eighteenth-Century*

Latin America (Albuquerque, 1990), 109–136; *idem*, "Movimento de precios en Santiago de Chile, 1749–1808," *Jahrbuch für Geschichte von Staatwirtschaft und Gesellschaft Latinamerikas* 17 (1980) 199–259.

Armando de Ramón and José Manuel Larraín, *Origines de la vida económica chilena*, (Santiago, 1982), includes price series from 1659 to 1808.

Marcello Carmagnani, *Les mecanismes de la vie économique dans une societé coloniale: Le Chile* (Paris, 1973), with much statistical data for the period 1680–1830; *idem, El salariado minero en Chile colonial: au desarrollo en una sociedad provincial: el Norte Chico, 1690–1800* (Santiago de Chile, 1963).

Markos J. Mamalakis, *Historical Statistics of Chile* (5 vols. to date, Westport, Conn., 1978–85 +), includes prices from 1860 to 1982.

⁂ China

Period-specific price histories with primary data from the fourteenth to the twentieth centuries include:

Ch'uan Han-sheng, "Sung-Ming chien pai-yin kou-mai-li ti pien-tung chi ch'i yuan-yin" [Fluctuations in the purchasing power of silver and their cause from the Sung to the Ming dynasties] *Hsin-ya-hseuh-pao* [New Asian Journal] 8 (1967) 157–86, with a summary in English.

M. Cartier, "Notes sur l'histoire des prix en Chine du XIVᵉ au XVIIᵉ siècle," [1368–1644] *Annales E. S. C.* 24 (1969) 1876–89; *idem*, "Les importations de metaux monetaires en Chine: Essai sur la conjoncture chinoise," *ibid*. 36 (1981) 454–66.

W. S. Atwell, "Notes on Silver, Foreign Trade, and the Late Ming Economy," *Ch'ing shih wen-ti*' 3 (1977) 1–33; *idem*, "International Bullion Flows and the Chinese Economy, *circa* 1530–1650," *Past & Present* 95 (1982) 68–90.

P. Liu and K. Huang, "Population Change and Economic Development in Mainland China since 1400," in C. Hou and T. Yu, eds., *Modern Chinese Economic History* (Taipei, 1977), 61–81.

Yeh-chien Wang, "The Secular Trend of Prices during the Ch'ing Period," *Journal of the Institute of Chinese Studies of the Chinese University of Hong Kong* 5 (1972) 364, covers the period 1644–1912.

Nankai University Committee on Social and Economic Research, *Wholesale Prices and Price Index Numbers in North China, 1913 to 1929* (Tientsin, 1929).

Franklin L. Ho, *Index Numbers of the Quantities and Prices of Imports and Exports and the Barter Terms of Trade in China, 1867–1928* (Tientsin, 1930).

L. L. Chang, "Farm Prices in Wuchin, Kangsu, China," *Chinese Economic Journal* 10 (1932) 449–512.
Hsin Ying, *Price Problems of Communist China* (Kowloon, 1963).

?♣ Congo (Democratic Republic)

The leading work is Leon H. Dupriez et al., *Diffusion du progres et convergence des prix; études internationales; le cas Congo-belgique, 1900–1960; la formation du systeme des prix et salaires dans une economie dualiste* (2 vols., Louvain 1966–70).

?♣ Cuba

Susan Schroeder, *Cuba: A Handbook of Historical Statistics* (Boston, 1982), includes prices.

?♣ Czechoslovakia

Stanislas Hoszowski, "L'Europe centrale devant la révolution des prix," *Annales E.S.C.* 16 (1961) 441–56, cites studies by J. Janacek, A. Mika, and J. Novotny which I have not seen.

?♣ Denmark

A general work of exceptionally high quality is Astrid Friis and Kristof Glamann, *A History of Prices and Wages in Denmark, 1660–1800* (Copenhagen and London, 1958), vol. 1 only published to date. It is based on assizes and *price currents* in Copenhagen.

Two pioneering projects by Danish economists are William Scharling, *Pengenes synkende Vaerdi* (Copenhagen, 1869); and *idem* and V. Falbe-Hansen, *Danmarks Statistik* (6 vols., Copenhagen, 1878–91).

A. Nielsen, "Dänische Preise, 1650–1750," in *Jahrbuch für Nationalökonomie und Statistik* 31 (1906) 289–347.

L. Rumur, "Assessed Average Market Prices and the Prices of Cereal Grains in Denmark, 1600–1850," *Scandinavian Economic History Review* 18 (1970) 33–65.

For later periods, see Jorgen Pedersen and O. Strange Petersen, *An Analysis of Price Behaviour during the Period 1855–1913* (Copenhagen and London, 1938); Jorgen Pedersen, *Arbejdslønnen i Danmark under skiftende Konjunkturer, c. 1850–1913* (Copenhagen, 1913), a history of wages in Den-

mark; and K. Bjerke and N. Ussing, *Studier over Danmarks National Produkt, 1870–1950* (Copenhagen, 1958).
A methodological work with particular attention to Danish materials is P. Thestrup, *The Standard of Living in Copenhagen, 1730–1800: Some Methods of Measurement* (Copenhagen, 1971).

ໃ▲ Finland

"Markegangspris i Finland 1731–1870," [Market Prices in Finland] *Statistika Oversitkter* (1926). I have not been able to find this work in American libraries.

ໃ▲ France: General Studies

Vicomte Georges d'Avenel, *Histoire économique de la proprieté, des salaires, des denrées, et tous les prix en général depuis l'an 1200 jusqu'en l'an 1800* (7 vols., Paris, 1894–1926), an immense compilation, much criticized by academic price historians. Jörberg writes in his great history of Swedish prices, "D'Avenel's enormous collection of material is considered today to be almost worthless, since prices are assembled from widely different sources and widely separated geographical areas." (p. 4).
Nevertheless, many of d'Avenel's descriptive findings have been confirmed by subsequent work, and he is still worth reading for his interpretative insights, grace, good humor, ripe learning, and especially for a knowledge of men and the world that is often missing in works of higher technical proficiency. D'Avenel also published *Les enseignements de l'histoire des prix* (Paris, 1925) and *Histoire de la fortune française: la fortune privée à travers sept siècles* (Paris, 1927).
A critique of d'Avenel's work appears in René Jouanne, *Les monographes normandes et l'histoire des prix* (Caen, 1931). A critique of the critique is Lucien Febvre, "Chiffres faux, courbes vraies?" *Annales d'Histoire Économique et Sociale* 4 (1932) 585–86, a title that succinctly summarizes the weaknesses and strengths of d'Avenel's work.
Abbott Payson Usher, "The General Course of Wheat Prices in France: 1350–1788," *Review of Economic Statistics* 12 (1930) 159–69; this essay was a statistical supplement to the same author's *The History of the Grain Trade in France, 1400–1710* (Cambridge, 1913).
François Simiand, *Recherches anciennes et nouvelles sur le mouvement général des prix du XVIe au XIXe siècle* (Paris, 1932); other works by Simiand are listed below.
C. E. Labrousse, *Esquisse du mouvement des prix et des revenus en*

France au XVIIIe siècle (2 vols., Paris, 1933); *La crise de l'économie française à la fin de l'ancien régime et au début de la Révolution* (Paris, 1944), still the indispensable work on the price revolution of the eighteenth century; *idem*, Ruggiero Romano, and F.-G. Dreyfus, *Le prix du froment en France au temps de la monnaie stable (1726–1913)* (Paris, 1970), includes data on Belgium, Netherlands, Germany, Switzerland, and Italy during periods of French occupation.

Henri Hauser, *Recherches et documents sur l'histoire des prix en France de 1500 à 1800* (Paris, 1936).

A. Chabert, *Essai sur les mouvements des prix et des revenus en France de 1798 à 1820* (Paris, 1945); *idem, Essai sur les mouvements des revenus et l'activité économique en France de 1798 à 1820* (Paris, 1949).

Jean Fourastié, *Documents pour l'histoire et la theorie des prix: Series statistiques réunies et élaborées* (Paris, 1958).

J. Marczewski and J. C. Toutain, *Histoire quantitative de l'économie française* (2 vols., Paris, 1961), covers the period 1700–1958.

🕮 France: Local Studies

[Alsace] A. C. Hanauer, *Études économiques sur l'Alsace ancienne et modern* (2 vols., Paris, 1876–78).

[Anjou] Victor Dauphin, *Recherche pour servir à l'histoire des prix des céréales et du vin en Anjou sous l'ancien régime* (Paris, 1934).

[Berry] F. Gay, "Production, prix et renaitabilité de terre en Berry au XVIIIe siècle," *Revue d'Histoire Économique et Sociale* 36 (1958) 399–411.

[Beziers] Emmanuel Le Roy Ladurie, *Les Paysans de Languedoc* (2 vols., Paris, 1966), with price series on 2:820–22.

[Châteaudun] A. de Belfort, "Prix moyen des grains vendus sur le marché de Châteaudun depuis l'année 1583," *Bulletin de la Societé Dunoise* 1 (1864–69) 161–70.

[Douai] Monique Mestayer, "Les prix du blé et de l'avoine à Douai de 1329 à 1793," *Revue du Nord* 45 (1963) 157–76.

[Forèze] Vicomte de Meaux, "Note sur le cours des céréales en Forèze de 1363 à 1698," *Bulletin de la Societé de la Diana,* 11 (1899–1900).

[Gâtinais] Leopold Nottin, *Recherches sur les variations des prix dans la Gâtinais du XVIe au XIXe siècle* (Paris, 1935).

[Marseilles] Ruggiero Romano, *Commerce et prix du blé a Marseille au XVIIIe siècle* (Paris, 1956).

[Montdidier] V. de Beauville, *Histoire de la ville de Montdidier* (3 vols., Paris, 1857).

[Orleans] P. Mantellier, "Mémoire sur la valeur des principales denrées et marchandises qui se vendaient ou se consommaient en la ville d'Orléans au cours des XIVᵉ, XVᵉ, XVIᵉ, XVIIᵉ, et XVIIIᵉ siècles," *Mémoires de la Societé Archeologique et Historique de l'Orléans* 5 (1862) 103–496.

[Paris] Micheline Baulant, "Le prix des grains à Paris de 1431 à 1789," *Annales E.S.C.* 23 (1968) 537–40.

[Paris] Jeanne Singer-Kérel, *Le coût de la vie à Paris de 1840 à 1954* (Paris, 1961).

[Picardy] P. Deyon, *Contribution à l'étude des revenus fonciers en Picardie, les fermages de l'Hotel-Dieu d'Amiens et leurs variations de 1515 à 1789* (Lille, 1967).

[Poitiers] Duffaud, *Note sur le prix des grains à Poitiers depuis trois siècles* (Paris, 1861)

[Poitou] P. Raveau, *Essai sur la situation économique et l'état social en Poitou, au XVIᵉ siècle* (Paris, 1931); *idem, "*La crise des prix au XVIᵉ siècle en Poitou,"* Revue Historique* 54 (1929) 1–44, 168–93.

[Provence] René Baehrel, *Une croissance: La Basse-Provence rurale (fin XVIᵉ siècle-1789)* (2 vols., Paris, 1961).

[Toulouse] Georges Frêche and Geneviève Frêche, *Lex prix des grains, des vins et des légumes à Toulouse (1486–1868: Extraits des mercuriales suivis d'une bibliographie d'histoire des prix* (Paris, 1967).

[Valenciennes] G. Sivery, "L'évolution du prix du blé à Valenciennes," *Revue du Nord* 17 (1965) 177–94.

Other local studies of prices in France are listed in bibliographies to Frêche and Frêche, cited for [Toulouse] above; and Labrousse, *Esquisse,* pp. 5 (note 4), 11–12 (note 17), 650–64.

❧ Germany: General Studies

L. Keller, "Zur Geschichte der Preisbewegung in Deutschland während der Jahre 1466–1525," *Jahrbücher für Nationalökonomie und Statistik* 34 (1879) 181–207.

Georg Wiebe, *Zur Geschichte der Preisrevolution des XVI und XVII Jahrhunderts* (1894, Leipzig, 1895).

J. Hansen, *Beiträge zur Geschichte des Gretreidehandels der Freien und Hansestadt* (Lübeck, 1912).

Moritz J. Elsas, *Umriss eine Geschichte der Preise und Löhne in Deutschland vom ausgehenden Mittelalter bis zum Beginn des neunzehnten Jahrhunderts* (2 vols. in 3, Leiden, 1936–49), the standard work.

A. Jacobs and H. Richter, "Die Grosshandelpreise in Deutschland von 1792 bis 1934," *Sonderhefte des Institute fur Konjunkturforschung,* no. 37 (Berlin, 1935).

Gerd Hohorst *et al. Materialien zur Statistik des Kaiserreichs, 1870–1914* (Munich, 1975).

G. Bry, *Wages in Germany, 1871–1945* (Princeton, 1960).
H. Wiese, "Der Rinderhandel im Nordwesteuropaischen Kustenggebiet vom Beginn des 19 Jahrhunderts" (dissertation, Gottingen, 1963).

⁇ Germany: Local Studies

[Alsace] A. C. Hanauer, *Études économiques sur l'Alsace ancienne et modern* (2 vols., Paris, 1876–78).
[Berlin] W. Naude and A. Skalweig, *Die Getreidehandelspolitik. . . Acta Borussica* (Berlin, 1896, 1910).
[Brunswick] An original series from primary data appears in Abel, *Agrarkrisen und Agrarkonjunktur*, appendix.
[Chemnitz] Rudolph Strauss, "Löhne und Preise in Deutschland, 1750 bis 1850," *Jahrbuch fur Wirtschaftsgeschichte* (1963) 1:189–219; 2:212–36; 3:257–64; 4:263–80; (1964) 1:271–80; 4:307–17; (1965) 1:233–49.
[Cologne] Dietrich Ebeling and Franz Irsigler, *Getreideumsatz, Getreide-und Brotpreise in Köln, 1369–1797* (Cologne, 1976); Franz Irsigler, *Kölner Wirtschaft im Spätmittelalter, Zwei Jahrtausende Kölner Wirtschaft* (Cologne, 1975).
[Gottingen, etc.] H. Kullak-Ublick, *Die Wechsellagen und Entwicklung der Landwirtschaft im südlichen Niedersachen vom 15 bis 18 Jahrhundert* (Göttingen, 1953).
[Halle] J. Conrad, "Die Preisentwicklung der gewöhnlichsten Nährungsmittel in Halle a/S von 1731–1878," *Jahrbücher für Nationalökonomie und Statistik* 34 (1879) 83–180.
[Kaiserswerth] C. Bone, "Frucht-, Fleisch- und Brotpreise in der Stadt Kaiserswerth," *Beiträge zur Geschichte die Niederrheins* 5 (1890) 154–60.
[Leipzig] O. Dittmann, *Die Getreidepreise in der Stadt. Leipzig im 17., 18. und 19. Jahrhundert* (Leipzig, 1889); E. E. Koehler, "Haushaltsrechnungen des Georgenhauses zu Leipzig; Preise, Löhne . . ." *Jahrbuch für Wirtschafts-Geschichte* (1967), 4:347–409.
[Mainz] Francois G. Dreyfus, "Beitrag zu den Preisbewegungen im Oberrheingebiet im 18 Jahrhundert," *Vierteljahrshrift für Sozial und Wirtschaftsgeschichte* 47 (1960) 245–56.
[Mannheim] E. Hofmann, "Die Milchpreis in Mannheim," *Jahrbuch für Nationalökonomie und Statistik* 108 (1917) 639–43; also "Die Eierpreise in Mannheim," *ibid.* 109 (1917) 69–76; and "Die Salzpreise in Mannheim . . . ," *ibid.* 111 (1918) 591–605.
[Meissen] H. E. Pietzsch, *Wechsellagen der Landwirtschaft im Amte Meissen während des 16. und 17. Jahrhunderts* (Gottingen, 1950).
[Munich] M. J. Elsas, "Price Data from Munich, 1500–1700," *Economic Journal Supplement* 3 (1934–37).

[Ostfriesland] O. Aden, "Entwicklung und Wechsellagen ausgewählter Gewerbe in Ostfriesland von der Mitte des 18. bis zum Ausgang des 19. Jahrhunderts" (thesis, Gottingen, 1963); partly published in _Abhandlungen und Vorträge zur Geschichte Ostfrieslands_ 40 (1964).

[Prussia] U. Eggert, "Die Bewegung der Holzpreise und Tagelohnsätze in der preussischen Staats forsten von 1800–1879," _Zeitschrift der Königlich Preussische Statistiche Bureau_ 23 (1883).

[Quedlinberg] Willi Schulz, "Löhne und Preise 1750 bis 1850 nach den Akten und Rechnungsbelegen des Stadtarchivs Quedlinberg," _Jahrbuch für Wirtschaftsgeschichte_ (1967), 4:347–409.

[Saxony] Johannes Falke, "Geschichtliche Statistik der Preise im Königreich Sachsen," _Jahrbücher für Nationalökonomie und Statistik_ 13 (1869) 364–95; 16 (1871) 1–71.

[Schleswig-Holstein] Emil Waschinski, _Währung, Preisentwicklung und Kaufkraft des Geldes in Schleswig-Holstein von 1226–1864_ (2 vols., Neumünster, 1952–59).

Many other local German studies are listed in bibliographies to various editions of Abel, _Agrarkrisen und Agrarkonjunktur_, and in Jacobs, "Preisgeschichte," cited above.

ﾞﾞ Hungary

I. N. Kiss, "Money, Prices, Values, and Purchasing Power from the Sixteenth to the Eightenth Century," _Journal of European Economic History_ 9 (1980).

R. Horvath, "Monetary Inflation in Hungary during the Napoleonic Wars," _Journal of European Economic History_ 5 (1976); _idem_ "The Interdependence of Economic and Demographic Development in Hungary (from the mid-eighteenth to the mid-nineteenth centuries)," in _Proceedings of the Fourth International Economic History Conference, Bloomington, 1968_ (Paris, 1973).

L. Katus, "Economic Growth in Hungary during the Age of Dualism, 1867–1918, A Quantitative Analysis" _Studia Historica_ 62 (1970)

E. Pamlenyi, ed., _Social-Economic Researches on the History of East Central Europe_ (Budapest, 1980)

ﾞﾞ India

J. J. Brennig, "Silver in Seventeenth-Century Surat: Money Circulation and the Price Revolution in Mughal India," in John F. Richards, ed., _Precious_

Metals in the Later Medieval and Early Modern World (Durham, 1983), 477–96.

John F. Richards, ed., *The Imperial Monetary System of Mughal India* (Delhi, 1987).

Aziza Hazan, "En Inde aux XVIᵉ et XVIIᵉ siècles: Trésors Américains, monnaie d'argent et prix dans l'empire Mogol," *Annales E.S.C.* 24 (1969) 835–859, includes data from 1556 to 1705.

India Department of Commercial Intelligence and Statistics, *Index Numbers of Indian Prices, 1861–1926* (Calcutta, 1928).

Tirthankar Roy, "Price Movements in Early Twentieth-Century India," *Economic History Review* 2d ser. 48 (1995) 118–33, includes price series from 1900 to 1933, and 1953 to 1987.

Lakshini Narain, *Price Movements in India, 1929–1957* (Meerut, 1957).

David Singh, *Inflationary Price Trends in India since 1939* (Bombay, 1957; 2d ed., New York, 1961).

ἐ▲ Ireland

Edward Nevin, *The Irish Price Level: A Comparative Study* (Dublin, 1962).

C. St. J. Oherlihy, *A Statistical Study of Wages, Prices, and Employment in the Irish Manufacturing Sector* (Dublin, 1966).

Wm. E. Vaughan and André J. Fitzpatrick, *Irish Historical Statistics,* vol. 1, *Population* (Dublin, 1978); a subsequent volume is promised on Irish prices.

ἐ▲ Italy: General Studies

V. Magaldi and R. Fabris, "Notizie storiche e statistiche sui prèzzi e salari nei secoli XIII–XVIII nelle città di Milano, Venezia, Genova, Firenze, Pisa, Lucca, Mantova e Forli," *Annali di Statistica* 2d ser. 3 (1878) 5–106.

Vittorio Franchini, *Contributo alla storia dei prèzzi in Italia. Documenti economici del secolo XVIII* (Roma, 1928); *idem, Di talune neglette fonti per la ricostruzione dei valori delle cose all' inizio delle Signorie in Italia* (Milan, 1928).

ἐ▲ Italy: Local and Regional Studies

[Bari] Carlo Massa, "Il prèzzo del grano e dell'orzo in Terra di Bari (1419–1727)," *Atti dell'Accademia Pontaniana* 38 (1908); *idem,* "I salari agricoli in Terra di Bari (1447–1733)," *Atti dell'Accademia Pontaninana* 42 (1912); *idem*, "I salari di mestiere in Terra di Bari dal 1449 al 1732," *Giornale degli Economisti* 42 (1911) 553–76; *idem*, "Costo dei trasporti in Terra di Bari (1542–1722)," *Giornale degli economisti* 55 (1917) 331–39; *idem, I salari agricoli in Terra di Bari (1447–1733)* (n.p., 1911); *idem, Il prèzzo e il commercio degli oli d'oliva di Gallipoli et Bari* (Trani, 1897); *idem*, "Paghe di professionisti, d'impiegati e di cambii militari in Terra di Bari dal 1491 al 1715," *Cose di Puglia* (Bari, 1911); *idem, Bari nel secolo XVII* (Bari, 1903); *idem, La industria della pesce nella Provincia di Bari* (Trani, 1900).

[Bassano] Gabriele Lombardini, *Pane e denaro a Bassano: Prèzzi del grano politica dell approvigionamento dei cereali tra il 1501 e il 1799* (Venice, 1963).

[Florence] Giuseppi Parenti, *Prime ricerche sulla rivoluzione dei prèzzi in Firenze* (Florence, 1949).

[Florence] Richard A. Goldthwaite, "I prèzzi del grano a Firenze dal XIV al XVI secolo," *Quaderni Storici* 10 (1975) 5–36.

[Genoa] Paolo Maria Arcari and Ettore Rossi, "I prèzzi a Genova dal XII al XV secolo," *La Vita Economica Italiana* 2d ser. 8 (1933) 53–87.

[Milan] G. Ferrario, *Statistica medica di Milano dal secolo XV fino ai nostri giorni escluso il militare* (Milan, 1840).

[Milan] Amintore Fanfani, "La rivoluzione dei prèzzi a Milano nel XVI e XVII secolo," *Giornale degli Economisti e Rivista di Statistica* 72 (1932) 465–82; *idem, Indagini sulla rivoluzione dei prezzi* (Milan, 1940).

[Milan] Aldo de Maddalena, *Prèzzi e aspetti di mercato in Milano durante il secolo XVII* (Milan, 1950); *idem, Prèzzi e mercedi a Milano dal 1701 al 1860* (2 vols., Milan, 1974).

[Milan] Commune di Milano, *I prèzzi dei generi alimentari in Milano dal 1798 al 1918* (Milano, 1919).

[Modena] Gian Luigi Basini, *Sul mercato di Modena tra cinque e seicento: Prèzzi e salari* (Milan, 1974); *idem, L'uomo e il pane . . .* (Milan, 1970); *idem, Zecca e monete a Modena nei secoli XVI e XVII* (Parma, 1967).

[Naples] Giuseppe Coniglio, "La rivoluzione dei prèzzi nella città di Napoli nei secoli XVI e XVII," *Atti della IXa riunione scientifica a Roma 1950* (Rome, 1952).

[Naples] Nunzio Federico Faraglia, *Storia dei prèzzi in Napoli dal 1131 al 1860* (Bologna, 1983).

[Naples] Pietro Lonardo, *Contributo alla storia dei pèzzi nelle province napoletane* (Santa Maria Capua Vetere, 1904).

[Naples] Ruggiero Romano, *Prèzzi e salari e servizi a Napoli nel secolo XVIII [1734–1806]* (Milan, 1965).

[Pavia] Giuseppe Medici, "Tentativo di recostruire un numero indice dei prèzzi dei prodotti cerealicoli per la zona agraria dell'Alto Pavese e per il periodo dal 1784 al 1930,'' *Annali dell'Osservatorio di Economia Agraria per la Lombardia* 1 (1930).

[Pistoia] Armando Sapori, *Per la storia dei prèzzi a Pistoia; il quaderno dei conti un capitano di Custo[d]ia nel 1339* (Pistoia, 1928; an offprint is in the Baker Library, Harvard Business School); *idem*, ''Per la storia dei prèzzi a Pistoia,'' *Bulletino storico pistoiese* 29 (1927); 30 (1928).

[Rome] Comte de Tournon, *Études statistiques sur Rome* (3 vols., Paris, 1831).

[Siena] Giuseppe Parenti, *Prezzi e mercato del grano a Siena, 1546–1765* (Florence, 1942).

[Sicily] Antonio Petino, *La questione del commercio del grani in Sicilia nel settecento* (Catania, 1946); *idem, I prèzzi del grano, dell'orzo, dell'olio, del vino, del cacio a Catania dal 1512 al 1630* (Milan, 1949).

[Venice and Venetia] Dario Bartolini, ''Prèzzi di alcuni derrate e salari correnti in Venezia ed in alcune città della Dalmatia a del Levante, durante gli anni 1486 a 1490,'' *Annali di Statistica* 2d ser. 19 (1881); *idem*, ''Prèzzi e salari nel commune di Portugruaro durante il secolo XVI,'' *Annali di Statistica* 2d ser. 1 (1878) 194–204; *idem*, ''La metida del frumento, vino ed oglio dal 1670 al 1685 nel commune di Portugruaro,'' *Annali di Statistica* 2d ser. 7 (1879); *idem*, ''Nota intorno alla 'metida' o 'calamiere' nel Veneto,'' *Annali di Statistica* 3d ser. (1882); *idem, Contribuzione per una storia dei prèzzi e salari* (Rome, 1881).

[Venice] M. Aymard, *Venise, Raguse et le commerce du blé pendant la seconde moitié du XVIᵉ siècle* (Paris, 1966).

Other Italian local studies are listed in the bibliography to Ruggiero Romano, ed., *I prèzzi in Europa dal XIII secolo a oggi* (Turin, 1967), 569–90.

≈ Japan

Kokisha Asakuri and Chiaki Nishiyama, eds., *A Monetary Analysis and History of the Japanese Economy, 1868–1970* (Tokyo, 1974).

Kakujiro Yamasaki, *The Effect of the World War upon Commerce and Industry in Japan* (New Haven, 1929), includes prices, ca. 1914–1929.

Supreme Commander for the Allied Powers, *Staple Food Prices in Japan, 1930–1948* (Tokyo, 1949).

Bank of Japan, Statistics Department, *Hundred Year Statistics of the Japanese Economy* (Tokyo, 1966).

Kazushi Ohkawa et al., *Estimates of Long-Term Economic Statistics of Japan since 1968* (Tokyo, 1965).

ᵭ Luxembourg

J. Ruwet et al, *Marché des céréales à Ruremonde, Luxembourg, Namur et Diest aux XVIIᵉ et XVIIIᵉ siècles* (Louvain, 1966).

ᵭ Madagascar

Frederic L. Pryor, *Income Distribution and Economic Development in Madagascar: Some Historical Statistics* (Washington, World Bank, 1988).

ᵭ Mali

Pascal J. Imperato and Eleanor M. Imperato, *Mali: A Handbook of Historical Statistics* (Boston, 1982).

ᵭ Malawi

Frederic L. Pryor, *Income Distribution and Economic Development in Malawi: Some Historical Statistics* (Washington, World Bank, 1988).

ᵭ Mexico

A large literature includes Woodrow Wilson Borah and Sherburne F. Cook, *Price Trends of Some Basic Commodities in Central Mexico, 1531–1570* (Berkeley and Los Angeles, 1958); Enrique Florescano, *Precios del maíz y crisis agrícolas en México (1708–1810)* (Mexico City, 1969, 1971); Richard L. Garner, "Price Trends in Eighteenth-Century Mexico," *Hispanic American Historical Review* 65 (1985); and *idem,* "Prices and Wages in Eighteenth-Century Mexico," in Lyman L. Johnson and Enrique Tandeter, eds., *Essays on the Price History of Eighteenth-Century Latin America* (Albuquerque, 1995), 73–108.

ᵭ Netherlands: General Studies

Nicolaas W. Posthumus, *Inquiry into the History of Prices in Holland* (2 vols., Leiden, 1946–64). This major work is based largely upon Amsterdam *price currents,* of which Posthumus collected more than two thousand, and also upon institutional records. "The most detailed price history which has hitherto been published," writes Lennart Jörberg in his *History of Prices in Sweden* 1:5.

Jan de Vries, *The Dutch Rural Economy in the Golden Age, 1500–1700* (New Haven, 1974), contains original series on rental values; idem, "An Inquiry into the Behavior of Wages in the Dutch Republic and the Southern Netherlands, 1580–1800," *Acta Historiae Neerlandicae* 10 (1978).

Netherlands Central Bureau voor de Statistiek, *75 Jarr Statistiek van Nederland* (The Hague, 1955), includes prices from 1900 to 1975; headings in Dutch and English.

ᓬ Netherlands: Local Studies

[Amsterdam] Besides Posthumus see P. J. Middelhoven, "Auctions at Amsterdam of Northern European Pinewood: A Contribution to the History of Prices in the Netherlands," *Low Countries Yearbook* 13 (1980).

[Arnhem] M. K. Heringa, "Overzicht van Marktprijzen van Granen te Arnhem in de jaren 1544–1901," *Bijdragen tot de Statistiek van Nederland* 26 (1903).

[Overjissel] B. H. Slicher van Bath, *Een Samenleving on der Spanning: Geschiedenis van het Platteland in Overjissel* (n.p., 1957).

[Utrecht] J. A. Sillem, *Tabellen van Marktprijzen van Granen te Utrecht in de Jaren 1393 tot 1644*, (Amsterdam, 1901).

ᓬ New Zealand

James W. McIlraith, *The Course of Prices in New Zealand* [1861–1910] (Wellington, 1911).

Malcolm Frasier, *Prices: An Inquiry into Prices in New Zealand, 1891–1919* (Wellington, 1920).

Gerald I. Bloomfield, *New Zealand: A Handbook of Historical Statistics* (Boston, 1984).

ᓬ Ottoman Empire (see also Turkey)

Ömer Lütfi Barkan, "The Price Revolution of the Sixteenth Century: A Turning Point in the Economic History of the Near East," *International Journal of Middle East Studies* 6 (1975) 3–28; "Die 'Preisrevolution' im osmanischen Reich wahrend der zweiten Hälfte des 16. Jahrhunderts," *Sudost-Forschungen* 42 (1983) 169–81.

Sevket Pamuk, "Money in the Ottoman Empire, 1326–1914," in Halil

Inalcik and Donald Quataert, eds., *An Economic and Social History of the Ottoman Empire, 1300–1914* (Cambridge, 1994) 970–75.
Justin McCarthy, ed., *The Arab World, Turkey, and the Balkans (1878–1914): A Handbook of Historical Statistics* (Boston, 1982).

ஃ Pakistan

Central Statistical Office, *Twenty-Five Years of Pakistan in Statistics, 1947–1972* (Karachi, 1972).

ஃ Peru

G. Lohmann Villena, *Apuntaciónes sobre el curso de los precios de los articulos de primera necesidad en Lima durante el siglo XVI* (Lima, 1961).
Luis Miguel Glave and Maria Isabel Remy, *Estructura agraria y vida rural en una region andina: Ollantay-tambo entre los siglos XVI y XIX* (Cuzco, 1983).
Pablo Macera and Rosario Jiméniz, "Precios: Lima, 1667–1738" (mimeograph, Lima, n.d.); Pablo Macera and Rosa Boccolini, "Precios de locs Colegios de ka Cia de Jesu's, Arequipa, 1627–1767" (mimeograph, Lima, 1975).
Paul Gootenberg, "*Carneros y Chuño:* Price Levels in Nineteenth-Century Peru" (unpublished ms., 1988).
Kendall Brown, "Price Movements in Eighteenth-Century Peru: An Overview," in Lyman L. Johnson and Enrique Tandeter, eds., *Essays on the Price History of Eighteenth-Century Latin America* (Albuquerque, 1995), 173–200.

ஃ Philippines

Pierre Chaunu, *Les Philippines et le Pacifique des Ibériques* (Paris, 1960).

ஃ Poland

F. Bujak, *Badania z dziejow spolecznych i gospodarczych (Recherches sur l'histoire sociale et economique* (Lwow and Poznan, 1928–49); includes price data in vols 4:13–17, 21–22, 24–25.
[Cracow] J. Pelc, *Ceny w Krakowie w latach 1369–1600* (Lwow, 1935);

E. Tomaszewski, *Ceny w Krakowie w latach 1601–1795* (Lwow, 1934); Frêche and Frêche report a French edition, *idem, Les prix à Cracovie de 1601 à 1795* (Lwow, 1934), not seen.

[Gdansk] J. Pelc, *Ceny w Gdańsku w XVI i XVII wieku* (Lwow, 1937); Tadeusz Furtac, *Ceny w Gdańsku w latach 1701–1815* (Lwow, 1935).

[Lublin] W. Adamczyk, *Ceny w Lublinie od XVI do końca XVIII wieku* (Lwow, 1935).

[Lvov] Stanislas Hoszowski, *Ceny we Lwowie w XVI i XVII wieku* (Lwow, 1928), French tr. *Les prix a Lwow* (Paris, 1954); Stanislas Hoszowski, *Ceny we Lwowie w latach, 1701–1914* (Lwow, 1934).

[Warsaw] W. Adamczyk, *Ceny w Warszawie w XVI i XVII wieku* (Lwow, 1938); S. Siegel, *Ceny a Warzawie w latch 1701–1815* (Lwow, 1936).

ᡧ Portugal

V. M. Godinho, *Prix et monnaies au Portugal, 1750–1850,* (Paris, 1955).

F. Mauro, *Le Portugal et l'Atlantique au XVIIᵉ siècle (1570–1670)* (Paris, 1957).

Joel Serrão, ed., *Dicionário de História de Portugal* (4 vols., Lisbon, 1971), includes historical statistics and prices.

R. de Moraes Soares, "Resumo historico dos preços de cereaes e outros generos alimentares no continento do Reino," *Archivo Rural* 2 (1859) 436–40, 462–66.

[Lisbon] A. Silbert, "Contribution a l'étude du mouvement du prix des céréales à Lisbonne (du milieu du XVIIIᵉ au milieu du XIXᵉ siècle," *Revista de Economia* (1953) 65–80.

Frêche and Frêche also cite local studies by Albade de Bacal and F. M. Alves on prices in Braganza, and by A. d'Ayres Lanca Pereira on the economic history of Beja. I have not seen these works.

ᡧ Russia

V. O. Klutchevsky [*sic*], *Le rouble russe des XVIᵉ et XVIIᵉ siècles, et son rapport avec le rouble actuel: Essais et études* (St. Petersburg, 1918).

A. G. Mankov, *Le mouvement des prix dans l'état Russe du XVIᵉ siècle,* (Paris, 1957); a summary of Mankov's work for English readers is Jerome Blum, "Prices in Russia in the Sixteenth Century," *Journal of Economic History* 16 (1956) 182–99.

Boris Mironov, "The 'Price Revolution' in Eighteenth-Century Russia," *Soviet Studies in History* 11 (1973) 325–52; *idem,* "Le mouvement des prix des céréales en Russie du XVIIIᵉ siècle au début du XXᵉ siècle,'' *Annales E.S.C.* 41 (1986) 217–51. In the reign of Peter I, Russia became the first nation in Europe to collect monthly information on grain prices for all its provinces. Mironov's research rests upon these data, which run unbroken from 1707 to 1914. This essay summarizes the author's thesis at Leningrad and many other monographs. It also includes a bibliography.

V. N. Jakovchevsky, *Kupechesky kapital v feodal' no-krepostnicheskoi* (Moscow, 1959); partly translated as "I prèzzi ed il profitto commerciale nella Russia feudal-servile," in Romano, ed., *I prèzzi in Europa dall XIII secolo a oggi*, 447–80; a study of prices in Russia during the eighteenth and nineteenth centuries.

W. M. Pintner, "Inflation in Russia during the Crimean War Period," *Slavic Review* 18 (1959) 81–87.

A. Roger Clarke and J. I. Matko, *Soviet Economic Facts, 1917–81* (2d ed., London, 1983).

A. Bergson, "Prices of Basic Industrial Products in the U.S.S.R., 1928–1950," *Journal of Political Economy* 64 (1956); idem, *Basic Industrial Prices in the U.S.S.R. 1928–56: Twenty-five Branch Series and Their Aggregation* (Santa Monica, 1956).

I. B. Kravis and J. Mintzes, "Food Prices in the Soviet Union, 1936–1950," *Review of Economics and Statistics* 32 (1950) 164–68.

M. C. Kaser, "Soviet Statistics of Wages and Prices," *Soviet Studies* 7 (1955–56).

☙ Scotland: *see* United Kingdom

☙ Spain: General Studies

Earl J. Hamilton, *American Treasure and the Price Revolution in Spain, 1501–1650* (Cambridge, Mass., 1934); idem, *Money, Prices, and Wages in Valencia, Aragon, and Navarre, 1351–1500* (Cambridge, Mass., 1936); idem, *War and Prices in Spain, 1651–1800* (Cambridge, Mass., 1947).

Juan Sardà, *La politicia monetaria y las fluctuaciones de la economia Española en el siglo XIX* (Madrid, 1948); idem, "Spanish Prices in the Nineteenth Century," *Quarterly Journal of Economics* 62 (1948) 143–59.

N. Sanchez-Albornoz, "En Espagne au XIXᵉ siècle, géographie des prix," *Melanges Antony Babel* (Geneva, 1963), 2:179–91.

Higinio Paris Equilaz, *El movimiento de precios en España* (Madrid, 1943), prices from 1913 to 1942.

૨જ Spain: Local Studies

[Andalusia] Earl J. Hamilton, "American Treasure and Andalusian Prices, 1503–1660 . . . " *Journal of Economic and Business History* 1 (1928) 1–35.
[Barcelona] E. Giralt-Raventos, "En torno al precio del trigo en Barcelona durante el siglo XVI," *Hispania* 18 (1958).
[Catalonia] P. Vilar, *La catalogne dans l'Espagne moderne* (3 vols., Paris, 1962).
[Seville] Pierre and Hugette Chaunu, *Seville et l'Atlantique,* cited above.

૨જ Sweden

Lennart Jörberg, *A History of Prices in Sweden, 1732–1914* (2 vols., Lund, 1972). A remarkably comprehensive work, based mainly on market price scales prepared for the valuation of commodities used to meet tax obligations. From these data, Lennart was able to compile price series for sixty-three commodities in thirty regions of Sweden. The second volume adds statistical analysis. No other nation has been so comprehensively studied.
Gunnar Myrdal, *The Cost of Living in Sweden, 1830–1930* (London, 1933).
K. Amark, "En Svensk prishistorisk studie," *Ekonomisk Tidskrift* 12 (1921); idem, "En svensk prisindex für aren 1860–1913," *Kommersiella Meddelanden,* 3 (1921) 18.
Eli Heckscher, *Sveridges ekonomiska Historia fran Gustav Vasa* (Stockholm, 1936).
Statistika Centralbyran, *Historisk Statistik för Sverige* (Stockholm, 1955, 1972).

૨જ Sri Lanka

Patrick Peebles, *Sri Lanka: A Handbook of Historical Statistics* (Boston, 1982).

૨જ Switzerland

Vettiger, *Die Agrare Preispolitik des Kantons Basel im 18 Jahrhundert* (Weinfelden, 1941), not found.
Francois G. Dreyfus, "Beitrag zu den Preisbewegungen im Oberrhein-

gebiet im 18 Jahrhundert,'' *Vierteljahrshrift für Sozial- und Wirtschaftsgeschichte* 47 (1960) 245–56.
Emil Notz, *Die säkulare entwicklung der Kaufkraft des geldes für Basel
in den perioden 1800–1833 und 1892–1923* (Jena, 1925).

ล*ะ* Thailand

Constance M. Wilson, *Thailand: A Handbook of Historical Statistics*
(Boston, 1983).

ล*ะ* Turkey; *see also* Ottoman Empire

Charles Issawi, *The Economic History of Turkey, 1880–1914* (Chicago,
1980).

ล*ะ* United Kingdom: General Studies

B. R. Mitchell and Phyllis Deane, *Abstract of British Historical Statistics*
(Cambridge, 1962); B. R. Mitchell and H. G. Jones, *Second Abstract of
British Historical Statistics* (Cambridge, 1971).
A. L. Bowley and G. H. Wood, ''The Statistics of Wages in the United
Kingdom during the Last Hundred Years,'' *Journal of the Royal Statistical
Society* 61 (1898) 702–22.
Charles H. Feinstein, *Key Statistics of the British Economy, 1900–1962*
(London, 1965).

ล*ะ* United Kingdom: England

W. Fleetwood, *Chronicum Preciosum: or, an Account of English Money,
the Price of corn and other commodities in the last 600 years in a Letter to a
Student in the University of Oxford* (London, 1707).
W. F. Lloyd, *Prices of Corn in Oxford in the Beginning of the Fourteenth
Century; also from the Year 1583 to the Present Time* (Oxford, 1830).
Thomas Tooke and William Newmarch, *History of Prices and of the
State of the Circulation from 1792 to 1856* (6 vols., London, 1838–57).
James E. Thorold Rogers, *A History of Agriculture and Prices in En-
gland from the Year after the Oxford Parliament (1259) to the Commencement
of the Continental War (1793) Compiled Entirely from Original and Contem-
poraneous Records* (7 vols., Oxford, 1866–1902; rpt. Vaduz, 1963); *idem,
Six Centuries of Work and Wages* (2 vols., London, 1884); subsequent studies

have found errors in this work. Early volumes lumped together data for different types of purchase and sale, which was especially a problem for livestock. Rogers was also not as careful about weights and measures as subsequent studies. But Farmer observes, "Rogers's price and wage series have been fundamental . . . and in some respects they are unlikely ever to be supplanted." For a critique see Paul Mantoux, "Le livre de Thorold Rogers sur l'histoire des prix et l'emploi des documents statistiques pour la période antérieure au XIXᵉ siècle," *Bulletin de la Societé d'Histoire Moderne* (1903); much thoughtful discussion of Thorold Rogers is scattered through the writings of the English economist Alfred Marshall.

J. Kirkland, *Three Centuries of Prices of Wheat, Flour, and Bread* (London, 1917).

Abbott Payson Usher, "Price of Wheat and Commodity Price Indexes for England, 1259–1930," *Review of Economic Statistics* 13 (1931) 103–13, includes a continuous series for wheat prices throughout the period, and two broken commodity indices that generally show the same pattern as Phelps-Brown and Hopkins.

G. N. Clark, *Guide to English Commercial Statistics, 1696–1782* (London, 1938).

William Beveridge, *Prices and Wages in England from the Twelfth to the Nineteenth Century* (London, 1939), vol. I (all published), institutional prices; *idem*, "A Statistical Crime of the Seventeenth Century," *Journal of Economic and Business History* 1 (1928–29) 503–33; *idem*, "Wages on the Winchester Manors," *Economic History Review* 7 (1936) 22–43; "Westminster Wages in the Manorial Era," *Economic History Review* 2d ser. 8 (1955–6) 18–35; "Wheat Measures in the Winchester Rolls," *Economic Journal, Economic History Supplement* 2 (1930–33); "The Yield and Price of Corn in the Middle Ages," *Economic Journal, Economic History Supplement* 1 (1926–29) 162–66; "Wheat Prices and Rainfall in Western Europe," *Journal of the Royal Statistical Society* 85 (1922) 418–54; "Weather and Harvest Cycles," *Economic Journal* 31 (1921) 421–53. All this was the product of a team effort under the auspices of the International Committee on Wages and Prices; its work is very careful and cautious, but only a small part of its materials have been published. The manuscripts are in the British Library of Political and Economic Science.

Ernest Henry Phelps–Brown and Sheila V. Hopkins, "Seven Centuries of Building Wages," *Economica* 22 (1955) 195–206; *idem*, "Seven Centuries of the Prices of Consumables, Compared with Builders' Wage-Rates," *Economica* 23 (1956) 196–314; "Wage-Rates and Prices: Evidence for Population Pressure in the Sixteenth Century," *Economica* 24 (1957) 289–306; *idem*, "Builders' Wage-Rates, Prices, and Population: Some Further Evidence," *Economica* 26 (1959) 18–38; *idem*, "Seven Centuries of Wages and Prices: Some Earlier Estimates," *Economica* 28 (1961) 30–36; *idem, A Perspective of Wages and Prices* (London, 1981); *idem,* "The Course of Wage Rates in Five Countries, 1860–1939," *Oxford Economic Papers* (1950) 226–96; E. H. Phelps-Brown and S. A. Ozga, "Economic Growth and the Price Level," *Economic Journal* 65 (1955) 1–18; E. H. Phelps-Brown and M. H. Browne, *A Century of Pay* (New York, 1968); a critique appears in Robert A. Doughty, "Industrial Prices and Inflation in Southern England, 1401–1640," *Explorations in Economic History* 12 (1975) 177–92.

Joan Thirsk et al., eds., *The Agrarian History of England and Wales,* esp. vol. 2, 1042–1350 (Cambridge, 1988); vol. 3, 1348–1500 (1991); vol. 4, 1500–1640; vol. 5, 1640–1750 (1985); vol. 6, 1750–1850 (1989); vol. 8, 1914–39 (1978). Each volume includes chapters and appended data series on prices and wages, and much related material.

ẽ▲ United Kingdom: Scotland

J. S. Moore, "Prices and Wages in Scotland, 1450–1860," an un-published survey of sources, issued as a report to the British Social Science Research Council, Report HR 400/1 (1970)

Rosalind Mitchison, "The Movement of Scottish Corn Prices in the seventeenth and eighteenth Century," *Economic History Review* 18 (1965) 278–91, an excellent pioneering study of Scottish price movements.

Elizabeth Gemmill and Nicholas Mayhew, *Changing Values in Medieval Scotland* (Cambridge, forthcoming) will survey prices and wages in the medieval and early modern eras to ca. 1550.

A. J. S. Gibson and T. C. Smout, *Prices, Food, and Wages in Scotland, 1550–1780* (Cambridge, 1995); *idem,* A. J. S. Gibson, and T. C. Smout, "Regional Prices and Market Regions: The Evolution of the Early Modern Scottish Grain Market," *Economic History Review* 48 (1995) 258–82.

ẽ▲ United States: General Studies

G. F. Warren and F. A. Pearson, *Wholesale Prices for 213 Years, 1720–1932* (Ithaca, N.Y. 1932).

Arthur Harrison Cole, *Wholesale Commodity Prices in the United States, 1700–1861* (Cambridge, Mass., 1938), with statistical supplement; Walter B. Smith and Arthur Harrison Cole, *Fluctuations in American Business, 1790–1860* (Cambridge, Mass., 1935).

United States Bureau of the Census, *Historical Statistics of the United States, Colonial Times to 1970* (1949; 3d ed., Washington, 1976); a collaborative venture of the Census Bureau and the Social Science Research Council, much in need of root-and-branch revision.

Dorothy S. Brady, "Price Deflators for Final Product Estimates," in *idem*, ed., *Output, Employment, and Productivity in the United States after 1800* (Princeton, 1966), 91–115.

Ethel Hoover, "Retail Prices after 1850," and John W. Kendrick, "Retail Prices after 1850: Comment on Hoover," in William N. Parker, ed., *Trends in the American Economy in the Nineteenth Century* (Princeton, 1960), 141–86, 186–90.

Paul A. David and Peter Solar, "A Bicentenary Contribution to the Cost of Living in America," *Research in American Economic History* 2 (1977) 1–80.

Donald R. Adams Jr., "Some Evidence on English and American Wage Rates, 1790–1830," *Journal of Economic History* 30 (1970) 499–520.

Albert Rees, *Real Wages in Manufacturing, 1890–1914* (Princeton, 1961).

ᨸ United States: New England

Three generations of price history have been done in New England. The first was undertaken by a pioneer in historical statistics, Carroll Wright, who published his results in a work issued by the Massachusetts Bureau of Statistics, *History of Prices and Wages in Massachusetts: 1752–1883* ed. Carroll D. Wright (Boston, 1885).

The second generation worked in the context of the international price history committee. One major study is Ruth Crandall, ed., "Wholesale Commodity Prices in Boston during the Eighteenth Century," *Review of Economic Statistics* 16 (1934) 117–28, 178–83. Another is Thurston M. Adams, "Prices Paid by Vermont Farmers for Goods and Services and Received by Them for Farm Products, 1790–1940; Wages of Vermont Farm Labor, 1790–1940" *Vermont Agricultural Station Bulletin no. 507* (Burlington, 1944). This is a study of "on the farm" prices from farmers' account books. A copy is in the American Antiquarian Society, Worcester.

In the third generation, the leading works are by Winifred Rothenberg, "A Price Index for Rural Massachusetts, 1750–1855," *Journal of Economic History* 39 (1979) 975–1001; *idem*, "Markets and Massachusetts Farmers, 1750–1855," *ibid.* 41 (1981) 283–314; *idem*, "The Emergence of Capital Markets in Rural Massachusetts, 1730–1838," *ibid.* 45 (1985) 781–808; *idem*, "The Emergence of Farm Labor Markets and the Transformation of the Rural Economy: Massachusetts, 1750–1855," *ibid*, 48 (1988) 537–66; *idem*, *From Market-Places to a Market Economy: The Transformation of Rural Massachusetts, 1750–1850* (Chicago, 1992), a much revised version of the author's Brandeis dissertation, with much material on commodity, capital, and labor markets.

ᶟ҉ United States: Middle States

The major work was done in the 1930s by a team headed by Anne
Bezanson. Its findings were published as Anne Bezanson et al., *Prices in
Colonial Pennsylvania* (Philadelphia, 1935); Anne Bezanson et al., *Prices
and Inflation during the American Revolution: Pennsylvania, 1770–1790*
(Philadelphia, 1951); Anne Bezanson et al., *Wholesale Prices in Phila-
delphia, 1784–1861* (Philadelphia, 1936); Anne Bezanson, "Inflation and
Controls in Pennsylvania, 1774–1779," *Tasks of Economic History*, 8 (1948).
On wage movements there is Donald R. Adams Jr., "Wage Rates in the Early
National Period: Philadelphia, 1785–1830," *Economic History Review* 27
(1968) 404–26.

ᶟ҉ United States: The South

There is no general work on the history of prices in the American South.
Special studies include Russell R. Menard, "Farm Prices of Maryland To-
bacco, 1659–1710," *Maryland Historical Review* 68 (1973) 83–85; *idem*, "A
Note on Chesapeake Tobacco Prices, 1618–1660," *Virginia Magazine of
History and Biography* 89 (1976) 401–10; Jacob Price, *France and the Chesa-
peake* (2 vols., Ann Arbor, 1973), which includes tobacco prices before 1791;
Donald R. Adams Jr., "Prices and Wages in Maryland, 1750–1850," *Journal
of Economic History* 46 (1986) 625–47; A. G. Peterson, "Historical Study of
Prices Received by Producers of Farm Products in Virginia, 1801–1927,"
Technical Bulletin of the Virginia Polytechnic Institute (1929); George Rogers
Taylor, "Wholesale Commodity Prices at Charleston, South Carolina, 1732–
1791," *Journal of Economic History* 4 (1921–22) 356–77; "Wholesale Commodity Prices at Charleston, South Carolina, 1796–1801," *ibid.* 848–67, plus
appended unpaged tables.

ᶟ҉ United States: The West

The standard compilation is Thomas Senior Berry, *Western Prices before
1861: A Study of the Cincinnati Market* (Cambridge, 1943). Specialized com-
pilations include Henry Ellis White, *An Economic Study of Wholesale Prices
at Cincinnati, 1844–1914* (Ithaca, 1935); Howard Houk, *A Century of Indiana
Farm Prices, 1841 to 1941* (Lafayette, Ind., 1943); George Rogers Taylor,
"Prices in the Mississippi Valley preceding the War of 1812," *Journal of
Economic and Business History* 3 (1930) 148–63; Thomas Senior Berry, *Early
California: Gold, Prices, and Trade* (Richmond, 1984).

❧ Venezuela

Robert J. Ferry, "The Price of Cacao, Its Export, and Rebellion in Eighteenth-Century Caracas," in Lyman L. Johnson and Enrique Tandeter, eds., *Essays on the Price History of Eighteenth-Century Latin America* (Albuquerque, 1990), 309–34.

❧ Yugoslavia

J. Tadic, *Organizacija dubrowaczkog pomortstwa u XVI veku* (Belgrade, 1949); *idem*, "Les archives économiques de Raguse," *Annales E.S.C.* 16 (1961) 1168–75.

❧ Serial Publications

During the nineteenth century, many nations began to issue statistical yearbooks which often included prices and wages. These compendia contain strong biases. Most governments have used their statistical reports as political instruments, to minimize their problems and exaggerate their strengths. Communist regimes treated social statistics alternately as state secrets and ideological weapons. Capitalist nations have tended to suppress statistics of wealth distribution.

Nevertheless, statistical yearbooks and other serial publications remain historical sources of high importance. Coverage of prices, wages, GNP deflators, etc., has steadily improved in these works. So also has the accuracy of the data.

The oldest national statistical yearbook in continuous publication is Britain's *Annual Abstract of Statistics*, which first appeared in 1854, together with a volume summarizing data from 1840 to 1853. France began to publish annual statistical abstracts in 1876. Italy and the United States followed in 1878, Germany in 1880, and the Netherlands in 1881. During the twentieth century these compilations have begun to appear in most nations throughout the world.

Except in French- and Spanish-speaking nations, most yearbooks now tend to appear in multilingual or bilingual editions. As recently as 1939, the international language of statistics was French. After 1945 it rapidly became English, and is increasingly so throughout the world. Today several non-English-speaking nations publish their statistical yearbooks in English alone. The leading materials are as follows.

🞜 Bibliographical Guides

Jacqueline Wasserman O'Brien and Stephen R. Wasserman, *Statistics Sources* (2 vols., Detroit, 1989+), annual; a bibliography of current statistical materials, bibliographies, and online statistical data throughout the world.

🞜 International Compilations

United Nations, *Statistical Yearbook* and *Monthly Bulletin of Statistics* (1947+); *Monthly Commodity Price Bulletin* (1969+); *Yearbook of Labour Statistics* (1950+) and *Monthly Bulletin of Labor Statistics* (1950+).

International Monetary Fund, *International Financial Statistics* (1948+), monthly and annual.

OECD, *Main Economic Indicators* (1965+), monthly.

🞜 National Compilations: Australia

Commonwealth Bureau of Census and Statistics, *Official Yearbook of the Commonwealth of Australia,* from 1908 (Canberra, 1908+), annual. The first volume includes data from 1901 to 1907 and some statistics from 1780.

🞜 Austria

Statistische Zentralkommission, *Tafeln zur Statistik der Osterreichischen Monarchie,* 1842–59 (Vienna, n.d.).

Statistisches Zentralkommission, *Statistisches Jahrbuch der Osterreichisches Monarchie,* 1861–80 (Vienna, 1861–81), annual; *idem, Osterreichisches Statistisches Handbuch,* 1882–1917 (Vienna, 1882–1917), annual.

Statistiches Zentralamt, *Statistisches Jahrbuch für Osterreich,* 1919–36 (Vienna, 1919–36), annual. Publication was suspended after the *Anschluss.*

Statistiches Zentralamt, *Statistisches Handbuch für die Republik Osterreich,* 1950+ (Vienna, 1950+), mostly annual.

🞜 Belgium

Institut National de Statistique, *Annuaire statistique de la Belgique,* 1870+ (Brussels, 1870+) mostly annual; title varies: from 1912 to 1959 (vols. 42–80) it was published as *Annuaire statistique de la Belgique et du Congo belge.*

ᘔ Brazil

Conselho Nacional de Estatistica, *Anuario estatistico do Brasil,* quinquennial from 1908/12 to 1970, annual from 1971 (Rio de Janeiro and Brasilias, 1913 +).

ᘔ Bulgaria

Glavna Direktsiia na Statistikata, *Statisticheski Godishnik na Tsarstvo Bulgari,* also issued in French as *Annuaire statistique du Royaume de Bulgarie,* 1910–42, mostly annual (Sofia, 1909–41); *idem, Statistickeski Godishnik na Narodnata Republika Bulgariia,* annual, 1947/48 + (Sofia, 1948 +), also issued in English as *Statistical Yearbook of the People's Republic of Bulgaria,* irregular, 1962 + (Sofia, 1962 +).

ᘔ Canada

Census and Statistics Office, *Canada Yearbook,* 1905 + (Ottawa, 1906 +), annual, text in English and French; *idem, Prices and Price Indexes* (1918–52) mostly annual, text in English and French; *idem, Prices and Price Indexes,* (Ottowa, 1952 +), monthly, text in English and French.

ᘔ Chile

Dirección General da Estadistica, *Anuario estadistico,* mostly annual, 1848/58–1925 (Santiago, 1860 +); *Estadistica anual,* mostly annual, 1928 + (Santiago, 1928 +).

ᘔ China

China Yearbook, unofficial compilation, annual, 1912–39, (London, New York, and Tientsin, 1912–39).
Chinese Yearbook, mostly annual, 1935/36–1944/45 (Chungking, 1935–46).
State Statistical Bureau, *Statistical Yearbook of China,* annual, 1981 + (English language edition distributed by Oxford University Press, 1982 +); the 1986 edition includes consumer prices from 1950.

❧ Czechoslovakia

Statni urad statisticky, *Manuel Statistique de la Republicque Tcheco-slovaque,* annual, (Prague, 1920–32).
Statisticka Rocenka Ceskoslovenske Socialisticke Republiky, annual, 1934–38.
Statistical Handbook of the Czech Republic, 1942 (London, 1942).
Statisticka Prirucka Slovenska, 1947–48.
Statisticka Rocenka Ceskoslovenske Socialisticke Republiky, annual, (Prague, 1953–89).
Statisticka Rocenka Ceske a Slovenske Federativni Republicky, annual, (Prague, 1990 +)

❧ Denmark

Statistiske Bureau, *Statistisk aarbog,* annual from 1892 (Copenhagen, 1896 +); text in Danish and French to 1951, Danish and English thereafter.

❧ Finland

Stattika Centralbyran, *Suomen Tilastollinen Vuosikinja,* mostly annual, 1879 + (Helsinki, 1883 +); text in Finnish, Swedish, and French 1934–52; Finnish, Swedish, and English 1953 + .

❧ France

Institut National de la Statistique et des Études Économiques, *Annuaire statistique de la France,* mostly annual, 1876 + (Paris, 1876).

❧ Germany

Statistiches Reichsamt, *Statistisches Jahrbuch für das Deutsches Reich,* annual, 1880–1940/1 (Berlin, 1880–1941).
Federal Republic of Germany, Statistiches Bundesamt, *Statistiches Jahrbuch für die Bundesrepublik Deutschland,* annual, 1952 + (Bonn, 1952 +); an abridged edition, *Handbook of Statistics for the Federal Republic of Germany* (Stuttgart, 1961 +), is published triennially in English.
Staatliche Zentralverwaltüng für Statistik, *Statistiches Jahrbuch der Deutschen Demokratischen Republik,* annual (Berlin, 1955–90); also issued in

English as *East German Statistical Yearbook*. Absorbed by the *Statistiches Jahrbuch* from 1991.

⅏ Greece

Ethnike Statistike Hyperesia, *Statistike epeteristes Hellados* [Statistical Yearbook of Greece], annual from 1930 (Athens, 1931 +), suspended 1940–1953; text in Greek and French 1930–1939, Greek and English 1954 +; issuing agency and title vary.

⅏ Hungary

Kozponti Statisztikai Hivatal *Magyar Statistikai Evkonyv*, annual, 1871–90 (Budapest, 1870–90); *idem, Magyar Statistikai Evkonyv Uj Folyam* annual, 1893–1942 (Budapest, 1892–1941); *idem, Magyar Statistikai Evkonyv*, mostly annual, 1949–55 + (Budapest, 1957 +).

⅏ Iceland

Tolfraedihandbok, annual (Reykjavik, 1930 +).

⅏ India

India Office, *Statistical Abstract Relating to British India,* irregular, (London, 1840–1918).

Department of Commercial Intelligence and Statistics, *Statistical Abstract for British India,* annual, (Calcutta, 1920–47).

Central Statistical Organization, *Statistical Abstract of India,* annual, 1949 + (Delhi, 1950 +).

⅏ Indonesia

Dutch East Indies, *Centraal Kantoor voor de Statistiek,* 1922/23–39 (Batavia, 1924–40).

Indonesia Central Office of Statistics, *Statistical Abstracts,* irregular, 1955/56 (Djakarta, 1956 +).

ᶻ᷒ Italy

Istituto Centrale di Statistica, *Annuario Statistico Italiano*, 1878+ (Rome, 1878+), mostly annual.

ᶻ᷒ Japan

Sorifu Tokeikyoku, *Resumé statistique de l'Empire du Japon*, 1884–1940 (Tokyo, 1887–1940), mostly annual, published in Japanese and French.
Prime Minister's Office, Bureau of Statistics, *Japan Statistical Yearbook*, 1949+ (Tokyo, 1949+), published in Japanese and English.
Prime Minister's Office, Bureau of Statistics, *Annual Report on the Retail Price Survey* (1964+), published in Japanese and English.

ᶻ᷒ Korea

National Bureau of Statistics, *Annual Report of the Price Survey* (Seoul, 1961+), published in Korean and English.

ᶻ᷒ Mexico

Dirección General de Estadistica, *Anuario estadistico de los Estados Unidos Mexicanos*, 1893+ (Mexico City, 1894+), not issued 1908–20, 1931–37.

ᶻ᷒ Netherlands

Central Bureau voor de Statistick, *Statisches Jaarboekje* (1851–80), mostly annual; *idem, Jaarcijfers voor Nederlanden Statistical Yearbook of the Netherlands*, 1881+ (The Hague, 1882+), mostly annual; published in Dutch and French 1884–1939, Dutch and German 1940–42, Dutch and English 1943–68; English alone, 1969+.

ᶻ᷒ New Zealand

Census and Statistics Office, *Statistics of the Dominion of New Zealand* (1853–1920), irregular; *idem, New Zealand Official Yearbook*, 1891+ (Wellington, 1892+), annual.

Census and Statistics Department, *Report on Prices, Wages, and Labour Statistics of New Zealand for the Year*. . . . (Wellington, 1946+), mostly annual.

?⚘ Nigeria

Federal Office of Statistics, *Annual Abstract of Statistics*, 1960+ (Lagos, 1960+).

?⚘ Norway

Statistisk Sentralbyra, *Statistisk Arbok*, 1880+ (Oslo, 1881+), mostly annual.

?⚘ Poland

Glowny Urzad Statystyczny, *Rocznik Statystyczny*, irregularly published since 1920/21 (Warsaw, 1922). From 1920 to 1938 the text was in Polish and French; from 1946+ issued also in German, Russian, and in English as *The Statistical Yearbook of Poland*.

?⚘ Portugal

Instituto Nacional de Estatística, *Anuário estatístico de Portugal*, 1875+ (Lisbon, 1875+), annual; text in Portuguese and French.

?⚘ Romania

Directiunea Statisticei Generale, *Buletin Statistic Romaniei*, 1892–1911.
Directia Centrala de Statistica, *Anuarul Statistic al Romaniei*, 1902+ (Bucharest, 1904–41, 1957+) annual; includes English translations.

?⚘ Russia

Statistika Rossieskoie Imperie (1887–1904).
Annuaire de la Russie (1904–1911).

Narodnoe Khoziaistvo SSSR, *Statistikii Sbornik,* 1923–90 (Moscow, 1923–90), also issued in an English edition; *idem, Statisticheskii Ezhedgodnik,* 1955+ (Moscow, 1956–90).
Narodnoe Khoziaistvo, Rossiiskoi Federatsii, *Statisticheskii Ezhedgodnik,* 1992+ (Moscow, 1992+).

ﻙ Serbia

   Matériaux pur la Statistique du Serbie (1888–1896).
   Annuaire Statistique du Royaume de Serbie (1895–1908).

ﻙ Spain

   Instituto Nacional de Estadistica, *Anuario Estadistico de España,* 1858+ (Madrid, 1859–67, 1911–35, 1942+), mostly annual.

ﻙ Sweden

   Statistiska Centralbyran, *Statistisk Tidskrift: Sveriges Officielle Statistea* (Stockholm, 1860–1913), title varies.
   Statistika Centralbyran, *Statistik arsbok för Sverige,* 1914+ (Stockholm, 1914+) annual; text in Swedish, French, and English to 1951, Swedish and English thereafter.

ﻙ Switzerland

   Statistisches Jahrbuch der Schweiz: Annuaire Statistique de la Suisse, 1891+ (Bern, 1891–96, 1898+); mostly annual; some volumes include thirty-year summaries of statistical data; a statistical atlas of Switzerland was issued in place of the volume for 1897.

ﻙ United Kingdom

   Central Statistical Office, *Annual Abstract of Statistics,* annual from 1854; the oldest national statistical yearbook in continuous publication. Most volumes include data for the preceding fifteen years. The first volume (1854) includes statistical material for the period 1840–53.
   Social Trends (London, HMSO) (1970+).

ᑫ United States

Bureau of the Census, *Statistical Abstract of the United States,* 1878+ (Washington, 1878+), annual.

Bureau of Labor Statistics, *Producer Prices and Price Indexes* (Washington, 1902+), monthly and annual, with historical compilations from 1890; idem, *Monthly Labor Review* and *Handbook of Labor Statistics* (Washington, 1904+), consumer prices and price indexes, monthly and annual, in various formats from 1904, with historical compilations from 1890.

ᑫ Yugoslavia

Savezni Zavod za Statistiku i Evidenciju, *Statisticki Godisnjak* [Statistical Yearbook] 1929–39 (Belgrade, 1929–39), mostly annual, issued in Serbian and French; idem, *Godisnjak Jugoslavije* [Yearbook of Yugoslavia], 1954+; *Statiosticki Godisnjak Jugoslavije* (Belgrade, 1955+), issued in Serbo-Croatian, Russian and English.

ᑫ Analysis of Primary Materials: Historical Metrology

Many learned disciplines contribute to the history of prices. Indispensable is the science of historical metrology; that is, the study of weights and measures. The literature of this field is surveyed in Z. Herkov and M. Kurelac, *Bibliographia Metrologiae Historiae* (2 vols., Zagreb, 1971–73).

Standard works include Ronald E. Zupko, *A Dictionary of English Weights and Measures from Anglo-Saxon Times to the Nineteenth Century* (Madison, 1968); *idem, Italian Weights and Measures from the Middle Ages to the Nineteenth Century* (*Memoirs of the American Philosophical Society;* vol. 145, Philadelphia, 1981); Horace Doursther, *Dictionnaire universel des poids et mesures anciens et modernes, contenant des tables des monnaies de tous les pays,* an older but still useful work (Brussels, 1840; rpt. Amsterdam, 1965); M. Bloch, "Prix et mesures . . . ," *Annales d'Histoire Économique et Sociale* 2 (Paris, 1930) 385–86; A. Machabey, *Poids et mesures du Languedoc et des provinces voisines* (Toulouse, 1953); A. E. Berriman, *Historical Metrology* (New York, 1953); John J. McCusker, "Weights and Measures in the Colonial Sugar Trade . . . ," *William and Mary Quarterly* 3d ser. 30 (1973) 599–624; *idem,* "Les équivalents métriques des poids et mesures du commerce colonial aux XVIIe et XVIIIe siècles," *Revue française d'Histoire d'Outre-Mer* (1974) 349–65; M. H. Sauvaire, "Matériaux pour servir à l'histoire de la numismatique et de la métrologie musulmanes," *Journal Asiatique* 8th ser. 10 (1887).

A large literature has developed on the measurement of prices and the construction of price series, particularly with regard to questions of quality-change. Leading works include Zvi Griliches, ed., *Price Indexes and Quality Change* (Cambridge, 1971); P. A. Armknecht and D. E. Weyback, "Adjustments for Quality Change in the U.S. Consumer Price Index," *Journal of Official Statistics* 2 (1989) 107–23; Robert J. Gordon, *The Measurement of Durable Goods Prices* (Chicago, 1990); various publications of the U.S. Department of Labor, Bureau of Labor Statistics, including Sarah Gousen, *Producer Price Measurement: Concepts and Methods* (Washington, 1986), and *BLS Handbook of Methods for Surveys and Studies* (Washington, 1988). An important collection of essays is Murray F. Foss, Marilyn E. Manser, and Allan H. Young, eds., *Price Measurements and Their Uses* (Chicago, 1993).

❧ Secondary Sources: General Works

Michel Morineau has described the history of prices as an "histoire sans frontières." More than most other other fields of historical scholarship, its major problems have been studied in a collaborative way by scholars of many nations, in a spirit that transcends differences of ideology.

Since 1945, however, one nation has dominated the field. Four groups of French historians have made the most important contributions to price history in the second half of the twentieth century.

The most active is the *Annales* school, which takes its name from the journal that has become one of the most important outlets for research on the history of prices, as well as the most influential historical journal in the twentieth century. One of its founders, Marc Bloch, contributed many essays including "Le problème d'histoire des prix: Comment recueillir les anciens prix?" *Annales d'Histoire Économique et Sociale* 3 (1931) 227–28; idem, "Le salaire et les fluctuations économiques à longue période," *Revue Historique* 173 (1934); idem, "L'histoire des prix: Remarques critiques," *Annales d'Histoire Sociale* 1 (1939) 141–51; idem, "Prix, monnaies, courbes," *Annales E.S.C.* 1 (1946) 355–57; idem, "Deux lettres," *Annales E.S.C.* 2 (1947) 364–66.

The co-founder of *Annales*, Lucien Febvre, also addressed larger problems of price history in "Le problème historique des prix," *Annales d'Histoire Économique et Sociale* 2 (1930) 67–80.

Another *annalist* who has contributed many writings on this subject through the years is René Baehrel. His essays include "Economie et histoire: À propos des prix," in *Eventail de l'histoire: Hommage à Lucien Febvre* (2 vols., Paris, 1953); idem, "Prix, superficies, statistique, croissances," *Annales E.S.C.* 16 (1961) 699–722; idem, "L'exemple d'un exemple: Histoire statistique et prix italiens," *Annales E.S.C.* 9 (1954) 213–26; idem,

"Pitié pour elle et pour eux," *Annales E.S.C.* 10 (1955) 55–62; *idem* and J. A. Faber, "Prix nominaux, prix metalliques et formule d'Irving Fisher . . ." *Annales E.S.C.* 17 (1962) 732–36.

A second school of French historiography, separate from the *Annales* group but increasingly overlapping, derives from an older tradition of French economic history. It is represented by the work of Henri Hauser, "Statistici storici di fronte alla storia dei prèzzi," *Rivista Internazionale di Scienze Sociali* 45 (1937) 874–882; *idem*, "L'histoire des prix: Controverse et méthode," *Annales d'Histoire Économique et Sociale* 8 (1936) 163–66.

A scholar of high importance was François Simiand, who did much to link an empirical method with broad conceptual model-building in the history of prices and wages. One of his most important works is *Le salaire, l'évolution sociale et la monnaie* (Paris, 1932).

Another central figure in this tradition is Ernest Labrousse. His two major works are *Esquisse du mouvement des prix et des revenus en France au XVIIIᵉ siècle*, preface by H. Sée and R. Picard (2 vols., Paris, 1933; rpt. 1984); and *La crise de l'économie française à la fin de l'Ancien Régime et au début de la Revolution* (Paris, 1944, new edition, 1990). This was the first volume, the only one published, of a projected multi-volume work subtitled *Aperçus généraux*. Labrousse also published many shorter essays, including "Observations complémentaires sur les sources et la methodologie pratique de l'histoire des prix et salaires au XVIIIᵉ siècle," *Revue d'Histoire Économique et Sociale* 24 (1938) 292–308; *idem*, "Le mouvement des prix au XVIIIᵉ siècle: les sources et leur emploi," *Bulletin de la Societé d'Histoire Moderne* (1937). A large part of the influence of Labrousse derived from his role as teacher. After World War II, he trained an entire generation of French economic historians. A study of his life and work is Jean-Yves Grenier and Bernard Lepetit, "L'experience historique, à propos de C.-E. Labrousse," *Annales E.S.C.* 44 (1989) 1337–60. Still other economic approaches are taken by Alfred Marc, *L'évolution des prix depuis cent ans* (Paris, 1958).

A third group of French historians have come to the subject mainly from numismatics and the study of money. A prolific scholar in this group is Pierre Vilar, who has given us "Histoire des prix, histoire géneérale," *Annales E.S.C.* 4 (1949) 29–45; "Remarques sur l'histoire des prix," *Annales E.S.C.* 16 (1961) 110–15; and *A History of Gold and Money, 1450–1920* (London, 1976); see also Jean Meuvret, "Simple mise au point," *Annales E.S.C.* 10 (1955) 48–54.

A fourth group are French demographic historians, associated with the Institut National d'Etudes Demographiques. Their leader Louis Henry invented a new method of demographic history by "family reconstitution," which has spread widely through the academic world. Many of their monographs include a chapter on prices, which are prominent in their analysis of demographic problems.

These various French schools had a great influence in Belgium, Italy, and Spain. Belgian historians have made many excellent contributions to price history. See Herman Van Der Wee, "Prix et salaires: Introduction methodologique," *Cahiers d'Histoire des Prix* 1 (1956).

Italian scholars also have taken a leading role in this field. Prominent among them are Luigi Einaudi, "Schemi statistichi e dubbi storici," *Rivista di Storia Economica* 5 (1940); *idem,* "Dei criteri informatori della storia dei prèzzi; questo devono essere espressi in peso d'argento o d'oro o negli idoli usati dagli uomini?" in Ruggiero Romano, ed., *I prèzzi in Europa dal XIII secolo a oggi* (Turin, 1967), 505–17; *idem,* "Storia dei salari e storia dei prèzzi," *Rivista Storica Italiana* 138 (1965) 311–20; and *idem,* "Introduzione," to *Prèzzi in Europa.* Other Italian price historians of high importance include Amintore Fanfani and Ruggiero Romano, whose many publications are listed above and below.

Among many contributions by German historians are C. W. Asher, *Die Geschichte und Bestimung der Preise* (Dresden, 1858–59); Ernst Wagemann, *Konjunkturlehre: eine Grundlegung zur Lehre vom Rhythmus der Wirtschaft* (Berlin, 1928); Moritz L. Elsas, "Zur Methode des Preisgeschichte," *Zeitschrift für die Geschichte Staatswissenschaft* 94 (1933); Hermann Klauer, *Gold produktion und Preisniveau: Versuch einer Kritik der monataren Theorie der langen Wellen* (Berlin, 1941); and Alfred Jacobs, "Preisgeschichte," in *Handwörterbuch der Sozialwissenschaften* (Gottingen, 1964), 8: 459–476.

A Marxist perspective from eastern Europe appears in Witold Kula, "Histoire et économie: la longue durée," *Annales E.S.C.* 15 (1960) 48–54.

American historians have contributed less than their European colleagues to the conceptual literature of price historiography. Exceptions include Earl Hamilton, "The Use and Misuse of Price History," *Journal of Economic History* 4 (1944) supplement, 47–60; Walt Rostow, "Histoire et sciences sociales: La longue durée," *Annales E.S.C.* 14 (1959) 710–14; Eric E. Lampard, "The Price System and Economic Change: A Commentary on Theory and History," *Journal of Economic History* 20 (1960) 617–37.

&. Long-Term Secular Trends: French, German, and Italian Models

On the problem of secular trends in price history, the literature in France, Germany, and Italy is fundamentally different in its descriptive patterns from that in Britain and the United States.

Two classic works were written by French economist François Simiand in the 1930s. In *Les fluctuations économiques à longue période et la crise mondiale* (Paris, 1932) and especially *Recherches anciennes et nouvelles sur le mouvement général des prix du XVIe au XIXe siècle* (Paris, 1932), Simiand described a secular pattern of price movements roughly similar to the great waves in this book, but not precisely the same. Working from the data of Thorold Rogers, d'Avenel, and others, he concluded that prices had tended to move in a series of long surges ("hausse majeure") and declines ("baisse majeure"), which he called alpha and beta phases. Simiand guessed that the prime mover was change in the supply of precious metal but cautioned against a premature monetarist model. For discussions of Simiand's work, see M. Levy-Leboyer, "L'Heritage de Simiand: Prix, profit et termes d'échange au XIXᵉ siècles," *Revue Historique* 243 (1970) 77–120; F. Crouzet, "The Economic History of Modern Europe," *Journal of Economic History* 31 (1971) 135–52.

Simiand's work had a major influence on French price historians C-E. Labrousse and his student M. A. Chabert, who also found a rhythm of alpha and beta phases but argued that price fluctuations were regulated mainly by the size of harvests. See C.-E. Labrousse, *Esquisse du mouvement des prix et des revenus en France au XVIIIᵉ siècle* (Paris, 1932); *idem, La crise de l'économie française à la fin de l'Ancien Régime et au début de la Révolution* (Paris, 1944); M. A. Chabert, *Essai sur les mouvements des prix et des revenus en France de 1798 à 1820* (Paris, 1949).

Simiand's "alpha-beta" phases and Labrousse's conception of agrarian rhythms were combined by German historian Wilhelm Abel into a broad secular pattern of "conjunctures" and "crises" in which periods of prosperity alternated with long depressions. Abel built a stronger empirical base than Simiand by constructing indices of grain prices computed in silver equivalents. In this evidence, Abel found a pattern of "long-term trends" almost identical in their timing with the great waves in this book, but different in their substance and cause. He believed that price revolutions were periods of prosperity, and price equilibria were eras of depression. Further, he concluded that until the nineteenth century, the cause of these secular trends was change in the "density of population." Abel observed that "until the mid-nineteenth century prices and income developed exactly as Malthus had predicted." See *Agrarkrisen und Agrarkonjunktur: Eine Geschichte der Land und Ernähr-ungswirtschaft Mitteleuropas seit dem höhen Mittelalter* (Hamburg and Berlin, 1935, 1966, 1978). The third edition of this work, much revised, is translated as *Agricultural Fluctuations in Europe from the Thirteenth to the Twentieth Centuries* (London and New York, 1980).

At the same time that Abel produced this work, other European scholars built different structures of interpretation on Simiand's base. Three such works were J. Lescure, *Hausses et baisses de prix de longue durée* (Paris, 1933, 1935); Robert Marjolin, *Prix, monnaie et production: Essai sur les mouvements économiques de longue durée* (Paris, 1941); and Marie Kerhuel, *Les mouvements de longue durée des prix* (Rennes, 1935).

Marie Kerhuel in particular developed an approach distinct from

Simiand's monetary model, Labrousse's harvest fluctuations, and Abel's Malthusian-Ricardian approach. She stressed the cultural correlates of price movements. This subject has been so totally neglected by American scholars that one of the few copies of Marie Kerhuel's thesis available in the United States (in the economics collection of Widener Library, Harvard University) had never been borrowed or even read in fifty years, until I took it off the shelves for this inquiry. Its brittle pages were still uncut.

One of the most intelligent and creative analyses of long-term price movements is to be found in the work of Italian historian Jenny Griziotti-Kretschmann, *Il problema del trend secolare nelle fluttuazioni dei prezzi* (Pavia, 1935, Pubblicazioni della R. Universitá di Pavia, no. 54), a thesis supported by empirical data published separately in the same author's "Ricerche sulle fluttuazioni economiche di lungadurate," *Giornale degli Economisti* 73 (1933) 461–508. Griziotti-Kretschmann found that long price movements did not conform to the Kondratieff pattern, and did not correlate with world production of gold and silver, and were not caused primarily by population movements, but rose instead from a "structural transformation in economic and political systems."

The work of Griziotti-Kretschmann was far ahead of its time. It was highly regarded by European scholars and heavily used by Fernand Braudel and others, but it is so little known to American scholars that the copy in Harvard's Widener Library had not been borrowed for twenty-two years before it was taken out in the course of this inquiry.

Various elements of Kondratieff's waves, Simiand's alpha-beta phases, Labrousse's harvest rhythms, Abel's agrarian *konjunktur,* Kerhuel's cultural correlates, and Griziotti-Kretschmann's *lungadurata* caused by "structural transformation in economic and political systems"—were brought together by Fernand Braudel in three classic works of modern historiography: *The Mediterranean and the Mediterranean World in the Age of Philip II* (2 vols., 1949; 2d ed., 1966, New York, 1972); *Capitalism and Material Life, 1400–1800* (New York, 1967) plus *Afterthoughts on Material Civilization and Capitalism* (Baltimore, 1977); and especially *Civilization and Capitalism, Fifteenth-Eighteenth Century* (3 vols., New York, 1982–84).

These books display the great strengths of the *Annales* school: breadth of comprehension, depth of insight, maturity of judgment, flair and creativity. English-speaking scholars (e.g., Charles Kindleberger in the *New York Times*, and Bernard Bailyn in the *Journal of Economic History*) have fairly complained of vagueness, contradiction, and incoherence, but for most readers (including this one) the strengths remain predominant.

In the third volume of *Civilization and Capitalism* Fernand Braudel recognized a secular trend similar in timing to the great waves of this book, but he jumbled it together with Kondratieff cycles, Simiand phases, and Labrousse intercycles, made no systematic attempt to reconcile these movements or to discuss them in detail, and dismissed the problem of analyzing and explaining the secular trend as an "impossible" task. Despite those deficiencies, these works are full of insight and deserve their reputation as masterworks of modern scholarship. A helpful discussion is Samuel Kinser, "Annaliste Paradigm? The Geohistorical Structuralism of Fernand Braudel," *American Historical Review* 86 (1981) 63–105.

Throughout his career, Braudel also contributed many essays and monographs on problems of price history, including "Monnaies et Civilisations: De l'or du Soudan à l'argent d'Amerique," *Annales E.S.C.* 1 (1946) 9–22; *idem*, "Histoire et sciences sociales: La longue durée," *Annales E.S.C.* 4 (1958) 725–53; *idem* and Frank Spooner, "Prices in Europe from 1450 to 1750," in M. M. Postan et al., *The Cambridge Economic History of Europe*, vol. 4, (E. E. Rich and C. H. Wilson, eds. Cambridge, 1967), 378–486, a work of larger significance than its title suggests.

Among the most important histories of the "longue durée" have been local or localized studies—another genre in which the *Annales* school has led the world. The classical works are Pierre Goubert, *Beauvais et le Beauvaisis de 1600 à 1730. Contribution à l'histoire sociale de la France du XVIIe siécle* (2 vols., Paris, 1960); Emmanuel Le Roy Ladurie, *Les paysans de Languedoc* (Paris, 1966); Pierre Vilar, *La Catalogne dans l'Espagne moderne: Recherches sur les fondements économiques des structures nationales* (3 vols., Paris, 1962); Pierre Léon, *La naissance de la grande industrie en Dauphiné fin du XVIIe siècle—1869* (2 vols., Paris, 1954); P. Deyon, *Amiens, capitale provinciale* . . . (Paris, 1967); and Pierre and Huguette Chaunu, *Seville et l'Atlantique (1504–1650)* (8 vols., Paris, 1955–60), the ultimate *grand thèse*. These works are familiar to American social historians, but the *problematiques* that inspired them are not well understood.

❧ Long-Term Secular Trends: Two Italian Dissenters

One historian has challenged the model of long waves and has even disputed the existence of the most familiar long wave: the price revolution of the sixteenth century. Carlo Cipolla, in "The So-Called 'Price Revolution': Reflections on the 'Italian Situation,'" (in Peter Burke, ed., *Economy and Society in Early Modern Europe: Essays from Annales* [New York, 1972], 42–46) argues that the inflation of the sixteenth century was not much greater than that which occurred in what he called the "century of monetary stability" from 1791 to 1912.

Cipolla is mistaken. He defined his "century of monetary stability" to include not only the Victorian equilibrium but also the end of the great wave of the eighteenth century and the beginning of the great wave of the twentieth. Further, he defined the price revolution of the sixteenth century in such a way as to rule out one of its most inflationary stages. When these errors are corrected Cipolla's thesis collapses, and the "so-called" price revolution of the sixteenth century survives his skepticism.

Another approach is that of Ruggiero Romano, "Movimento de los precios y desarrollo económico: el caso de Sudamérica en el siglo XVIII," *Desarrollo Económico* 3 (1963) 31–43; *idem,* "Some Considerations on the History of Prices in Colonial Latin America," in Lyman L. Johnson and Enrique Tandeter, eds., *Essays on the Price History of Eighteenth-Century Latin America* (Albuquerque, 1990), 35–72. Ruggiero Romano proposed the thesis that the long waves of Simiand, Abel, etc., occurred in Europe but not in Latin America. He suggested the existence of a distinctive "American conjuncture" or secular trend, in many ways opposite of European tendencies.

It was an ingenious theory, but the evidence of American price movements compiled in Johnson and Tandeter in general does not support it. A few local patterns in Latin America offer some support for Romano; ironically, price movements in the mining center of Potosí were closest to his American conjuncture and farthest from the European norm. But most Latin American series indicated that the price revolutions of the sixteenth and twentieth centuries were operative in Latin America. So also was the price wave of the eighteenth century in its later and most inflationary stage. As evidence accumulates throughout the world, great waves appear increasingly to be global movements, with important regional variations.

❧ Long-Term Secular Trends: A British Contribution

The most important British contribution to price history was made by Henry Phelps-Brown, a civil servant and scholar who held the chair of economics of labor at the London School of Economics. In the early 1950s he came upon a copy of H.O. Meredith's *Economic History of England* and discovered two pull-out graphs at the back of the book. One displayed the wages of a carpenter and a farm worker in England for every decade from 1270 to 1890. The other graph showed their purchasing power in terms of wheat prices. Meredith concluded that real wages were higher in the fifteenth century than at any other time until the nineteenth. "This challenged investigation," Phelps-Brown recalled. He went to work with Sheila Hopkins (Mrs. L. S. Presnell), and the results were carefully constructed indices of "consumable prices" and real wages from 1264 to 1954, in publications cited among primary sources above.

Phelps-Brown's work is best known for its price series, which are now beginning to be reproduced in American economics textbooks such as the most recent edition of Samuelson and Nordhaus. But the most important finding was the wage series, which gave a new meaning to the main lines of change. It shifted the perspective on price movements from propertied elites to the experience of ordinary people. Hamilton, Abel, Fourastié, and Grandamy all had been aware that a gap had opened between prices and wages during the price revolution of the sixteenth century. But Braudel remembers that it was due "particularly to the published research of E. H. Phelps-Brown and Sheila Hopkins" that scholars became aware of an actual "drop in real wages." (*The Perspective of the World,* III, 87). This discovery revised many earlier interpretative judgments by Abel, Hamilton and Braudel himself of social and economic conditions in various stages of price revolutions. It opened the way for the interpretation that appears in this book.

ᴥ Long-Term Secular Trends: American and British Writings

English-speaking scholars who have written at length about long-term secular movements in price history have tended to depart from the conventional models of Continental scholarship. Many have worked out their own synthetic models in a variety of ways. Four of these syntheses show something of the range and diversity of the work in Britain and the United States, and also its distinctive character and limits.

Phyllis Deane, "Inflation in History," in David F. Heathfield, ed., *Perspectives on Inflation: Models and Policies,* (London, 1979), 1–37 is an historical overview of price movements. Deane, whose scholarship centers on the economic history of Britain, derives a general synthesis mainly from British materials. She identifies three periods of rising prices: the price revolution of the sixteenth century, which she dates 1500–1650; the war inflation of 1793–1815 (that is, the crest of the third wave); and the "twentieth-century inflation." The author was not aware of the medieval price revolution or of the long rise of prices in the mid-eighteenth century. She assigned a different cause to each inflation, a classic historicist conclusion.

Another and very different approach appears in the work of Rondo Cameron, an able and learned American economic historian who developed an original historical model in "The Logistic of European Economic History: A Note on Historical Periodization," *Journal of European Economic History* 2 (1973) 145–48; "Europe's General Logistic," *Comparative Studies in Society and History* 12 (1975) 452–62; "Economic History, Pure and Applied," *Journal of Economic History* 36 (1976) 3–27; and *A Concise Economic History of the World from Paleolithic Times to the Present* (1989; 2d ed., New York, 1993), an excellent and very graceful survey of world history from an economic perspective. Cameron organizes his understanding of modern European history into a sequence of three "logistics" or logistic curves of development: the first running from the ninth to the fourteenth century; the second from the late fifteenth to the seventeenth century; and the third from the mid-eighteenth to the second quarter of the twentieth. His periodization derives mainly from patterns of population growth and from his understanding of rhythms of economic growth. Cameron's model is similar in timing to our price revolutions in the period from the twelfth century to the mid-seventeenth, but differs in its reading of the evidence from the late eighteenth to the late twentieth century.

A third approach from a business perspective appears in R. G. Lipsey, "Does Money Always Depreciate?" *Lloyd's Bank Review*, October 1960, 1–13. Lipsey asks if inflation would have been a betting proposition for a businessman from 1275 to 1949. He concludes that if the businessman had used a fifty-year "time horizon," an inflationary assumption would have been "a fairly good bet" throughout that period except in the fourteenth and nineteenth centuries. If, however, a ten-year horizon is used, then it would have been a bad bet in most decades during the fourteenth, fifteenth, seventeenth and nineteenth centuries. That judgment is roughly (very roughly) consistent with the rhythm of price revolutions, but its use of fixed periods of analysis masks the main lines of change.

A fourth attempt to make sense of the subject is Anna J. Schwartz, "Secular Price Change in Historical Perspective," *Journal of Money, Credit, and Banking* 5 (1973) 243–69. Schwartz covers a large territory in time and space, mainly in an effort to validate a monetarist interpretation of price movements. She argues that "episodes of rising prices have alternated with episodes of declining prices apparently for as long as money has been used." But her empirical grasp of price movements was faulty—a mix of long price-waves in the sixteenth and twentieth centuries and climactic price surges in other waves. Schwartz concluded that "long-run price changes consistently parallel the monetary changes, with one exception for England in the sixteenth century," But the author had very little evidence of long-term change in the quantity of money before the late nineteenth century except for sixteenth-century England. She recognized no other pattern in price movements beyond that of the monetary model. Critiques of her essay have been published by Lance Davis and Paul B. Trescott in the *Journal of Money, Credit, and Banking* 5.2 (1973) 269–71. Davis is generally hostile to Schwartz's monetary model and offers a series of ad hoc explanations for individual price movements. Trescott complains of a lack of empirical rigor in the monetarist model and adds an interesting attempt at correlation between prices and the money supply in the United States from 1870 to 1970. Anna Schwartz in response protests against the poverty of "ad hoc" explanations.

Attempts to generalize primarily from American price movements appear in George F. Warren and Frank A. Pearson, *Prices* (New York, 1933), an able and still informative work which is marred by ignorance of trends outside the United States before the twentieth century. A critique appears in Charles O. Hardy, *The Warren-Pearson Price Theory* (Washington, 1935).

Another American study is Walter W. Haines, "The Myth of Continuous Inflation: United States Experience, 1700–1980," in Schmukler and Marcus, eds., *Inflation through the Ages*, 183–204, which also interprets the history of prices as a discontinuous sequence of episodic movements. This Anglo-American literature is very different from that of French, German, and Italian scholars, in both its empirical base and its conceptual models.

In the late twentieth century, English-speaking scholars began at last to come to terms with the European literature. A leader in this effort is sociologist Jack A. Goldstone. In "The Cause of Long-Waves in Early Modern Economic History," *Research in Economic History* 6 (1991) 51–92, Goldstone has the descriptive evidence firmly in hand. He builds beyond European scholarship by adding data on long waves in Asia and the Middle East. His explanatory model is unstable and tends to shift from broad ideas of institutional structure to a narrow emphasis on mortality experiences, which will not bear the weight that he wishes to put on them. Overall, however, Goldstone's work is an important contribution, both in its breadth of insight and in its attempt to link economic tendencies to social and demographic processes. Another useful work is Don Pearlberg, *An Analysis and History of Inflation* (Westport, Conn., 1993), a survey of both long-term price movements and hyperinflations.

⅍ Descriptive Patterns: Cycles

On substantive patterns of change in price history, the literature might be divided into two parts: studies of long-term secular change and discussions of cyclical movements. By far the largest body of literature is about cycles. The journals called *Cycles, Kyklos, Futures*, and *Technological Forecasting and Social Change* publish many essays that discuss a variety of cyclical rhythms, including Kondratieff "long waves" (50 years), Kuznets "long swings" (20 to 25 years), Labrousse "intercycles" (10 to 12 years), Juglar trade cycles (7 to 8 years), and Kitchin business cycles (3 to 4 years).

The largest and most controversial literature is about Kondratieff waves (often called long waves), which are thought to cause major depressions every half century (ca. 1815, 1870, 1929, and 1970). The seminal monograph was written by Nikolai D. Kondratieff, head of the Moscow Institute for Business Cycle Research, and published in Russian in 1925. A German translation appeared as "Die Langen Wellen der Konjunktur," *Archiv für Sozialwissenschaft und Sozialpolitik* 56 (1926) 573–609. An abridged English translation was published in *The Review of Economic Statistics* 17 (1935) 161–72. A complete English text is in *Review* 2 (1979) 519–62. The model was elaborated by Kondratieff in *The Long Wave Cycle* (1928; rpt. New York, 1984).

As Kondratieff himself was careful to point out, similar models had been set forward by A. Spiethoff in *Handwörterbuch der Staatswissenschaft* (1923); and by two Dutch socialists, S. de Wolff in "Prosperitats-und Depressionsperioden," *Lebendige Marxismus* (Jena, 1924); and even earlier by C. van Gelderen, "Springvloed: Beschouwingen over industrieele ontwikkeling en Prijsbeweging," *De Niewe Tijd* 18 (1913). Among Marxists, Kondratieff waves were condemned as heresy and were denounced by Trotsky and many Old Bolsheviks. In 1930, Kondratieff was sent to Siberia, where he died in a Communist concentration camp. See Richard B. Day, "The Theory of Long Waves: Kondratieff, Trotsky, and Mandel," *New Left Review* 99 (1976) 67–82. An excellent historiographical essay on the diffusion of Kondratieff's work is Jean-Louis Escudier, "Kondratieff et l'histoire économique Française," *Annales E.S.C.* (1993) 359–83.

French and German historians have always been much interested in Kondratieff waves—more so than their American and British colleagues. Extended discussions include Gaston Imbert, *Des mouvements de longue durée Kondratieff* (Aix en Provence, 1959); Ulrich Weinstock, *Das Problem der Kondratieff-Zyklen* (Berlin, 1964); and Jean-Louis Escudier, "Kondratieff et l'histoire économique française," *Annales E.S.C.* (1993) 359–83.

In the English-speaking world, interest surged during the 1930s in works such as Joseph Schumpeter, *Business Cycles* (New York, 1939), then declined, and revived in the 1970s. The best introduction to a large literature is Joshua S. Goldstein, *Long Cycles: Prosperity and War in the Modern Age* (New Haven, 1988), a careful, honest, and thought-provoking work that analyzes thirty-three attempts by various scholars to test the existence of the Kondratieff wave, mostly with positive results. Goldstein's excellent bibliography also lists hundreds of works by political scientists and sociologists on various aspects of this question. For other discussions, see Donald V. Etz, "The Kondratieff Wave: A Review," *Cycles* (1973) 73–74; J. J. Van Duijn, *The Long Wave in Economic Life* (1979; rpt. Boston, 1983); John C. Soper, *The Long Swing in Historical Perspective* (New York, 1978); Casper Van Ewijk, "A Spectral Analysis of the Kondratieff Cycle," *Kyklos* 35 (1982) 468–99; T. Kitwood, "A Farewell Wave to the Theory of Long Waves," *Universities Quarterly—Culture, Education, and Society* 38 (1984) 158–78; Irma Adelman, "Long Cycles: Fact or Artifact?" *American Economic Review* 55 (1965) 444–63; R. Hamil, "Is the Wave of the Future a Kondratieff?" *Futurist* 13 (1979) 381–84; J. P. Harkness, "A Spectral Analysis of the Long Swing Hypothesis in Canada," *Review of Economics and Statistics* 50 (1968) 429–36; Rainer Metz, "'Long Waves' in English and German Economic Historical Series from the Middle of the Sixteenth to the Middle of the Twentieth Century," in Rainer Fremdling and Patrick K. O'Brien, eds., *Productivity in the Economies of Europe* (Stuttgart, 1983), 175–219; *idem.*, "Long Waves in Coinage and Grain Price-Series from the Fifteenth to the Eighteenth Century," *Review* 7 (1984) 599–647; Paolo S. Labini, "Le problème des cycles économiques de longue durée,'' *Economie Appliquée* 3 (1950) 481–95; Jos. Delbeke, ''Recent Long-Wave Theories: A Critical Survey,'' *Futures* 13 (1981) 246–57; M. N. Cleary and G. D. Hobbs, ''The Fifty-Year Cycle: A Look at the Empirical Evidence,'' in Christopher Freeman, ed., *Long Waves in the World Economy* (London, 1983); Heinz-Deiter Haustein and Erich Neuwirth, ''Long Waves in World Industrial Production, Energy Consumption, Innovations, Inventions, and Patents and Their Identification by Spectral Analysis,'' *Technological Forecasting and Social Change* 22 (1982) 53–89; Ghalib M. Baqir, ''The Long Wave Cycles and Re-Industrialization,'' *International Journal of Social Economics* 8 (1981) 117–23; Klas. Eklund, ''Long Waves in the Development of Capitalism?'' *Kyklos* 33 (1980) 383–419; Hans Bieshaar and Alfred Kleinknecht, ''Kondratieff Waves in Aggregate Output?'' *Konjunktur Politik* 30 (1984); David M. Gordon, ''Stages of Accumulation and Long Economic Cycles,'' in Terence K. Hopkins and Immanuel Wallerstein, eds., *Processes of the World System* (Beverly Hills, 1980); Alfred Kleinknecht, ''Innovation, Accumulation, and Crisis: Waves in Economic Development,'' *Review* 4 (1981) 683–711; Ernest Mandel, *Long Waves of Capitalist Development* (Cambridge, 1980).

This scholarship on Kondratieff's long cycles, for all its abundance, has a shallow empirical base. Many historians and economists continue to doubt the very existence of Kondratieff waves. Skepticism centers on the period from 1873 to 1893, for if the economic downturns in those years were no more severe than those of 1819, 1826, 1837, and 1859, then the fifty- (or sixty-) year Kondratieff pattern as such loses much of its salience and most of its shape. See S. B. Saul, *The Myth of the Great Depression, 1873–1896* (London, 1896); and Solomos Solomou, ''Kondratieff Waves in the World Economy, 1850–1913,'' *Journal of Economic History* 46 (1986) 165–69.

Another weakness appeared in the 1970s, when many Kondratieff-minded scholars predicted a ''coming collapse of capitalism,'' which stubbornly refused to come. See, e.g., Jay W. Forrester, ''We're Headed for Another Depression,'' *Fortune*, 16 Jan. 1978; Geoffrey Barraclough, ''The End of an Era,'' *New York Review of Books* 21 (1974) 14–20; and Cesare Marchetti, ''Recession 1983: Ten More Years to Go?'' *Technological Forecasting and Social Change* 24 (1983) 331–42.

Evidence for a Kondratieff pattern in earlier periods of history is even weaker than in the modern era. Kondratieff himself believed that his waves did not occur before 1790. Other scholars have claimed to find evidence of the same rhythm throughout the modern and even the medieval era, but here again the empirical evidence is very soft.

My own judgment is that a fifty- or sixty-year cycle does in fact appear in many social indicators and has been confirmed by various statistical methods including business cycle analysis, trend deviation, moving averages, and spectral analysis, to name but a few. But this pattern is not substantively stronger than many other cyclical rhythms, and much weaker than the secular trend with which it is sometimes confused. Kondratieff's "long wave" may be merely a multiple of generational "long swings," which move round the secular trend and vary broadly in their timing and intensity from one swing to the next. Much of the energy devoted by American social scientists to the study of the Kondratieff wave has been misdirected. Their efforts might be more usefully applied to the examination of secular trends—which have a more solid foundation in historical fact, though less predictive power.

Shorter cycles of thirty years and fifteen years also have been found in farm prices and harvest fluctuations by Beveridge, Goubert, and many recent writers on the world economy in the twentieth century. This pattern is often (but not always) associated with solar activity. It has not been rigorously tested and is not generally accepted by most economists or historians today. But it keeps being rediscovered in descriptive studies. See, e.g., Stanley Jevons, "The Solar Period and the Price of Corn," in *Investigations in Currency and Finance* (London, 1884).

Kuznets cycles or "long swings" of approximately twenty years have been much discussed by American economists, but this pattern has not been so interesting to European scholars or so visible in the history of their nations. See Simon Kuznets, *Secular Movements in Production and Prices* (Boston, 1930); *idem,* "Long Swings in the Growth of Population and Related Economic Variables," *Proceedings of the American Philosophical Society* 102 (1958) 25–52; Arthur F. Burns, *Production Trends in the United States since 1870* (New York, 1934); Moses Abramowitz, "Resource and Output Trends in the United States since 1870," *American Economic Review* 46 (1956) 5–23; Brinley Thomas, *Migration and Economic Growth* (Cambridge, 1954); John C. Soper, "Myth and Reality in Economic Time Series: The Long Swing Revisited," *Southern Economic Journal* 41 (1975) 570–79. This rhythm is sometimes thought to be demographic in its origin, but Friedman and Schwartz argue in *Monetary Trends in the United States and United Kingdom* (599–621) that long swings are episodic in their origin and monetary in their expression. Many economists agreed with them.

On the other hand, the Labrousse cycle (or intercycle) of roughly ten or twelve years is much favored by European historians but rarely appears in American scholarship.

Juglar cycles or trade cycles (seven to eight years) have been found by many scholars—by Goubert in Beauvais, Parenti in Tuscany, Spooner in Udine, Hauser in Paris. The classic work is Clément Juglar, *Des crises commerciales et leur retour périodiques en France, en Angleterre et aux États-Unis* (Paris, 1889); rpt. New York, 1967).

Kitchin cycles or business cycles (3.5 years, or forty months) were first observed in the American economy during the nineteenth and twentieth centuries, and also in Europe during our own time. The classical text is Joseph

Kitchin, "Cycles and Trends in Economic Factors," *Review of Economics and Statistics* 5 (1923) 10–16. They are sometimes called "inventory cycles" and are thought to rise from the structure of modern business enterprise. Several historians have also reported them in price data as early as the fifteenth century, and Pierre Chaunu has discovered them in Seville's transatlantic trade.

For general discussions of business cycles, see Wesley C. Mitchell, *Business Cycles* (New York, 1927); Arthur F. Burns and Wesley C. Mitchell, *Measuring Business Cycles* (New York, 1946); Joseph A. Schumpeter, *Business Cycles: A Theoretical, Historical, and Statistical Analysis of the Capitalist Process* (New York, 1939); Geoffrey H. Moore, *The Cyclical Behavior of Prices* (Washington, 1971). Historians will find a rapport with E. R. Dewey and E. F. Dakin, *Cycles: The Science of Prediction* (New York, 1949), which argues that cyclical rhythms are themselves variable through time and space— a conclusion that is certainly correct.

For problems of method, an excellent work is James D. Hamilton, *Time Series Analysis* (Princeton, 1994). Also useful are T. W. Anderson, *The Statistical Analysis of Time Series* (New York, 1971), and Nathaniel J. Mass, *Economic Cycles: An Analysis of Underlying Causes* (Cambridge, Mass., 1975).

☙ Movements of Wages, Rents and Interest

These various cyclical and linear interpretations may also be found in the general literature on wages, interest, rents, and wealth distribution. The classic works include François Simiand, *Le salaire; L'évolution sociale et la monnaie* (3 vols., Paris, 1932); J. R. Hicks, *The Theory of Wages* (London, 1932); J. Kuczynski, *Die Geschichte der Lage der Arbeiter in Deutschland von 1800 bis in die Gegenwart* (Berlin, 3d ed., 1947); idem, *Die Geschichte der Lage der Arbeiter unter dem Kapitalismus* (Berlin, 1960–1963); P. Wolff and F. Mauro, *Histoire générale du travail* (Paris, 1960). There is no general history of wages in English, but much information appears in Stanley Lebergott, *Manpower in Economic Growth* (New York, 1964). Many specialized studies are listed below.

On the history of interest, the standard work is Sidney Homer, *A History of Interest Rates* (2d ed., New Brunswick, 1977). A classic treatise is Knut Wicksell, *Interest and Prices* (London, 1936).

For the history of rent, see G. Postel-Vinay, *La rente foncière dans le capitalisme agricole* (Paris, 1974); and J. Jacquart, "La rente foncière, indice conjoncturel?" *Revue Historique* 253 (1975) 355–76. There is no general history of rent or land prices for Britain or the United States—a major gap in the literature. Many specialized studies are listed below.

For patterns of wealth and income distribution over the long run in the United States, see Jeffrey H. Williamson and Peter H. Lindert, *American Inequality: A Macroeconomic History* (New York, 1980), with a good bibliography; and Lee Soltow, *Men and Wealth in the United States, 1850–1870* (New Haven, 1975).

Studies of Britain include Jeffrey G. Williamson, *Did British Capitalism Breed Inequality?* (Boston, 1985), which cites many other studies by the same author; E. H. Phelps-Brown, *The Inequality of Pay* (Berkeley, 1977); A. J. Harrison and A. B. Atkinson, *The Distribution of Personal Wealth in Britain* (Cambridge, 1978); and A. B. Atkinson, *The Economics of Inequality* (Oxford, 1975).

For other nations, Y. S. Brenner, Hartmut Kaelbe, and Mark Thomas, *Income Distribution in Historical Perspective* (Cambridge, 1991) includes essays on Australia, Austria, Belgium, Germany, and Sweden, with a full list of references. M. Schnitzer, *Income Distribution: A Comparative Study* (New York, 1974) looks at the United States, Germany, Sweden, and Japan. Also helpful are many studies by Harold Lydall, notably *A Theory of Income Distribution* (Oxford, 1979); and J. Söderberg, "Trends in Inequality in Sweden, 1700–1914," *Historical Social Research* 21 (1987) 58–78.

?⬤ Money

On the history of money the literature is even larger than on prices, and of course strongly monetarist in its interpretation. The leading bibliography is Philip Grierson, *Bibliographie numismatique* (2d ed., Brussels, 1979). The standard overviews are Philip Grierson, *Numismatics* (Oxford, 1975) and John Porteus, *Coins in History* (London, 1969). A useful survey is Glyn Davies, *A History of Money from Ancient Times to the Present Day* (Cardiff, 1994).

On the history of precious metals, see Adon A. Gordus and Jeanne P. Gordus, "Potosí Silver and Coinage of Early Modern Europe," in Hermann Kellenbenz, ed., *Precious metals in the Age of Expansion: Papers of the Fourteenth International Congress of the Historical Sciences* (Stuttgart, 1981) 225–242; and Emmanuel Le Roy Ladurie et al., "Sur les traces de 'argent du Potosí,'" *Annales E.S.C.* (1990) 483–505.

For medieval numismatics, the best beginning is Peter Spufford, *Money and Its Use in Medieval Europe* (Cambridge, 1986), and *idem,* "Coinage and Currency," in *Cambridge Economic History of Europe,* (2d ed., Cambridge, 1987), 2:1788–863, both with appended tables on medieval money and excellent bibliographies. Peter Spufford, with the assistance of Wendy Wilkinson and Sarah Tolley, has also compiled a very useful *Handbook of Medieval Exchange* (London, 1986), with a full introduction on money and exchange, a listing of exchange rates by European region, and an excellent bibliography.

For the Renaissance and the modern era, an outstanding work is Frederic C. Lane and Reinhold C. Mueller, *Money and Banking in Medieval and Renaissance Venice*, vol. 1, *Coins and Moneys of Account* (Baltimore, 1985), a work broader than its title, with a full bibliography. Other major studies of high quality include Peter Spufford, *Monetary Problems and Policies in the Burgundian Netherlands, 1433–1496* (Leiden, 1970); Frank C. Spooner, *The International Economy and Monetary Movements in France, 1493–1725* (Cambridge, 1972); John Day, ed., *Études d'histoire monétaire XIIᵉ–XIXᵉ siècles* (Lille, 1984); Carlo M. Cipolla, *Money, Prices, and Civilization in the Mediterranean World: Fifth to Seventeenth Century* (Princeton, 1956); *idem, La moneta a Firenze nel cinquecento* (Bologna, 1987); B. H. Michell, "The Impact of Sudden Accessions of Treasure upon Prices and Real Wages," *Canadian Journal of Economics and Social Science* 12 (1946); J. L. Laughlin, *Money, Credit, and Prices* (Chicago, 1951); John J. McCusker, *Money and Exchange in Europe and America, 1600–1775: A Handbook* (Chapel Hill, 1978), with bibliographical notes; and many works of Milton Friedman and Anna J. Schwartz, cited below. A handbook on money and exchange in Europe during the modern period is coming from Frank Spooner.

On particular currencies, there is R. Sédillot, *Le franc: histoire d'une monnaie des origines à nos jours* (Paris, 1953); A. Blanchet and A. Dieudonné, *Manuel de numismatique française* (4 vols., Paris, 1912–36); Albert Feaveryear, *The Pound Sterling: A History of English Money* (2d ed. rev., Oxford, 1963); W. C. Mitchell, *A History of the Greenbacks* (Chicago, 1903); Octavio Gil Farres, *Historia de la moneda española* (2d ed., Madrid, 1976); Kirsten Bendixen, *Denmark's Money* (Copenhagen, 1967); A. Lohr, *Osterreichische Geldgeschichte* (Vienna, 1946); I. G. Spasskij, *The Russian Monetary System* (3d ed., Leningrad, 1962; Eng., Amsterdam, 1967).

On the problem of money of account, see Marc Bloch, "La monnaie de compte," *Annales d'Histoire Économique et Sociale* (1935); *idem*, "Le problème de la monnaie de compte," *ibid.* (1938); Luigi Einaudi, "The Theory of Imaginary Money from Charlemagne to the French Revolution," in F. C. Lane and J. C. Riemersma, eds., *Enterprise and Secular Change* (Homewood, Ill., 1953) 229–61. Good discussions appear in Lane and Mueller and McCusker above.

A major work on "bookkeeping barter," of a more general importance than its title implies, is W. T. Baxter, *The House of Hancock: Business in Boston, 1724–1775* (Cambridge, 1945).

❧ Population

Indispensable to this inquiry are general works on historical demography, which tend to explain price movements as the result of changes in population growth. Leading works include D. V. Glass and D. E. C. Eversley, *Population in History: Essays in Historical Demography* (London, 1965; rpt. 1974); W. R. Lee, ed., *European Demography and Economic Growth* (London, 1979); R. D. Lee, ed., *Population Patterns in the Past* (New York, 1977); R. J. Mols, *Introduction à la demographie historique des villes d'Europe du XIVe au XVIIIe siècle* (3 vols., Gembloux, 1954–56); and Michael W. Flinn, *The European Demographic System, 1500–1820* (Baltimore, 1981) with an excellent bibliography of more than seven hundred works in demographic history.

National studies of general interest include J. C. Russell, *British Medieval Population* (Albuquerque, 1948); E. A. Wrigley and R. S. Schofield, *The Population History of England, 1541–1871* (Cambridge, 1981), an indispensable work; Julius Beloch, *Bevölkerungsgeschichte Italiens* (3 vols., Berlin, 1937–61); and Maris A. Vinovskis, ed., *Studies in American Historical Demography* (New York, 1979), with a bibliography (pp. 21–25).

On methods and models of demographic analysis, the best introduction is still George W. Barclay, *Techniques of Population Analysis* (New York, 1958), now unhappily out of print; also Nathan Keyfitz and Wilhelm Flieger, *Population: Facts and Methods of Demography* (San Francisco, 1971); and Alfred Sauvy, *General Theory of Population* (1966; London, 1969).

❧ Climate and Environment

Also important for the study of prices is the literature on climate and ecological change. Here the leading works are Robert I. Rotberg and Theodore K. Rabb, eds., *Climate and History: Studies in Interdisciplinary History* (Princeton, 1981); H. H. Lamb, *Climate: Past, Present, and Future* (2 vols., New York, 1972, 1977); idem, *Climate, History, and the Modern World* (London, 1982); T. M. L. Wigley, M. J. Ingram, and G. Farmer, eds., *Climate and History: Studies in Past Climates and Their Impact on Man* (Cambridge, 1981); Emmanuel Le Roy Ladurie, *Times of Feast, Times of Famine: A History of Climate since the Year 1000* (1967; New York, 1971); Reid Bryson and Thomas J. Murray, *Climates of Hunger* (Madison, 1977); A. S. Goudie, *Environmental Change* (Oxford, 1977); Patrick Richard Galloway, *Population, Prices, and Weather in Preindustrial Europe* (Berkeley, 1987); W. Dansgaard, "One Thousand Centuries of Climatic Record from Camp Century on the Greenland Ice Sheet," *Science* 166 (1969) 377–81; Christian Pfister, "Fluctuations climatiques et prix céréaliers en Europe du XVIe au XXe siècle," *Annales E.S.C.* 43 (1988) 25–53.

On the historical geography of price movements, the classic work is

P. Hall, ed., *Von Thünen's Isolated State: An English Edition of De Isolierte Staat* (Oxford, 1966). Von Thünen rings continue to resonate in a large literature of economic geography and are sometimes observed by a study of prices; see J. R. Peet, "The Spatial Expansion of Commercial Agriculture in the Nineteenth Century: A Von Thünen Interpretation," *Economic Geography* 45 (1969) 283–300.

ᴥ Economic Growth

The central problem in economic historiography during the 1960s and 1970s was to describe and explain processes of economic growth. A large literature was created, which in the United States showed little interest in prices except as they impinged upon the measurement of national product. Nevertheless, this literature bears upon price history in many ways. Among general works, a classic is Simon Kuznets, *Modern Economic Growth: Rate, Structure, and Spread* (New Haven, 1966), *idem, The Economic Growth of Nations* (Cambridge, 1971); also E. F. Denison, *Why Growth Rates Differ* (Washington, 1967).

Most of this literature centers on national economies. For Britain, the leading works include Phyllis Deane and W. A. Cole, *British Economic Growth (1688–1959)* (Cambridge, 1964); R. C. Floud and D. N. McCloskey, eds., *The Economic History of Britain since 1700* (Cambridge, 1981 +). A revisionist work is N. F. R. Crafts, *British Economic Growth during the Industrial Revolution* (Oxford, 1985).

On the United States, see John J. McCusker and Russell R. Menard, *The Economy of British America, 1607–1789* (Chapel Hill, 1985); Douglass C. North, Terry L. Anderson, and Peter J. Hill, *Growth and Welfare in the American Past: A New Economic History* (3d ed., Englewood Cliffs, N.J., 1983); Lance E. Davis et al., *American Economic Growth: An Economist's History of the United States* (New York, 1972).

On Italy, the best survey is in Ruggiero Romano and Corrado Vivanti, eds., *Storia d'Italia* (Torin, 1973 +), a magisterial multivolume work that includes both period volumes and topical histories on economic subjects.

On the low countries a national economic history that gives much attention to prices is J. A. van Houtte, *An Economic History of the Low Countries* (New York, 1977).

Still a standard work on Sweden is Eli F. Hecksher, *Sevriges ekonomiska historia fran Gustava Vasa* (2 vols. in 4, Stockholm, 1935–49).

For Switzerland, see Antony Babel, *Histoire économique de Geneve des origines au début du XVIe siècle* (2 vols., Geneva, 1963).

🕿 Agriculture

On agriculture and price history see B. H. Slicher van Bath, *The Agrarian History of Western Europe: A.D. 500–1850* (London, 1963); E. Kerridge, *The Agricultural Revolution* (Paris, 1967); J. D. Chambers and G. E. Mingay, *The Agricultural Revolution, 1750–1880* (London, 1966); E. Boserup, *The Conditions of Agricultural Growth* (Chicago, 1965); national and regional histories include Joan Thirsk et al., eds., *The Agrarian History of England and Wales* (8 vols., Cambridge, 1967 +); J. C. Toutain, *Le produit de l'agriculture française de 1700 à 1958* (Paris, 1961); and Wilhelm Abel, *Agricultural Fluctuations in Europe* (London, 1980), which is specially helpful for central Europe; the English edition includes an additional bibliography on English agricultural history.

A general history of agriculture in the United States remains to be written; the leading works are still Lewis C. Gray, *History of Agriculture in the Southern United States to 1860* (2 vols., 1933; rpt. Washington, 1958), a work of remarkable scholarship; Percy W. Bidwell and John I. Falconer, *History of Agriculture in the Northern United States, 1620–1860* (1925; rpt. New York, 1941); Paul Gates, *The Farmer's Age: Agriculture, 1815–1860* (New York, 1960); Fred A. Shannon, *The Farmer's Last Frontier: Agriculture, 1860–1897* (New York, 1963).

On harvest fluctuations, see W. G. Hoskins, "Harvest Fluctuation and English Economic Life, 1480–1619," *Agricultural History Review* 12 (1964) 28–46; *idem*, "Harvest Fluctuations and English Economic Life, 1620–1759," *Agricultural History Review* 16 (1968) 15–31; C. Walford, "Famines of the World, Past and Present," *Journal of the Royal Statistical Society* 42 (1879).

🕿 Technology, Energy, and Transportation

On technology and long-term change, a very large literature includes John A. Clark et al., "Long Waves, Inventions, and Innovations," in Christopher Freeman, ed., *Long Waves in the World Economy* (London, 1983), 164–82; David Dickson, "Technology and Cycles of Boom and Bust," *Science* 219 (1983) 933–36; Alan Graham and Peter M. Senge, "A Long-Wave Hypothesis of Innovation," *Technological Forecasting and Social Change* 17 (1980) 283–311; Alfred Kleinknecht, "Observations on the Schumpeterian Swarming of Innovations," *Futures* 13 (1981) 293–307; Derek J. De Solla Price, "Is Technology Historically Independent of Science? A Study in Statistical Historiography," *Technology and Culture* 6 (1965) 568; an expression of skepticism appears in Nathan Rosenberg, "Technological

Innovation and Long Waves,'' *Cambridge Journal of Economics* 8 (1984) 7–24.

On secular trends in the history of energy, see Matthew Edel, ''Energy and the Long Swing,'' *Review of Radical Political Economics* 15 (1983) 115–30; George F. Ray, ''Energy and the Long Cycles,'' *Energy Economics* 5 (1983) 3–8.

On transportation and the long run, see Walter Isard, ''A Neglected Cycle: The Transport-Building Cycle,'' *Review of Economic Statistics* 24 (1942) 149–58; *idem,* ''Transport Development and Building Cycles,'' *Quarterly Journal of Economics* (1942) 90–112.

ࣈ War, Politics, and Imperialism

On war and long-term economic movements, see Albert Bergesen, ''Cycles of War in the Reproduction of the World Economy,'' in Paul M. Johnson and William R. Thompson, eds., *Rhythms in Politics and Economics* (New York, 1985), 313–32; Paul P. Craig and Kenneth E. F. Watt, ''The Kondratieff Cycle and War: How Close Is the Connection?'' *Futurist* 19 (1985) 25–28; Edward R. Dewey, ''Evidence of Cyclic Patterns in an Index of International Battles, 600 *B.C.–A.D.* 1957'' *Cycles* 21 (1970) 121–58; Charles F. Doran and Wes Parsons, ''War and the Cycle of Relative Power,'' *American Political Science Review* 74 (1980) 947–65; L. L.Farrar Jr., ''Cycles of War: Historical Speculations on Future International Violence,'' *International Interactions* 3 (1977) 161–79; Joshua Goldstein, *Long Cycles,* cited above; *idem,* ''Kondratieff Waves as War Cycles,'' *International Studies Quarterly* 29 (1985) 411–44; Richard K. Hoskins, *War Cycles, Peace Cycles* (Lynchburg, Va. 1985); J. S. Lee, ''The Periodic Recurrence of Internecine Wars in China,'' *China Journal* 14 (1931) 111–15, 159–63; Lewis F. Richardson, *Statistics of Deadly Quarrels* (Pittsburgh, 1960); Albert Rose, ''Wars, Innovations and Long Cycles,'' *American Economic Review* 31 (1941) 105–07; J. David Singer and Melvin Small, *The Wages of War, 1816–1965* (New York, 1972); Melvin Small and J. David Singer, *Resort to Arms: International and Civil Wars, 1816–1980* (Beverly Hills, 1982)

On the rhythm of imperialism, see Albert Bergeson, ''Cycles of Formal Colonial Rule,'' in Terence K. Hopkins and Immanuel Wallerstein, eds., *Processes of the World System* (Beverly Hills, 1980); *idem,* and Ronald Schoenberg, ''Long Waves of Colonial Expansion and Contraction, 1415–1969,'' in Albert Bergeson, ed., *Studies of the Modern World-System* (New York, 1980).

৯ৠ Culture

On culture and the long run, see John Langrish, "Cycles of Optimism in Design," *Design Studies* 3 (1982) 153–56; J. Zvi Namenwirth, "The Wheels of Time and the Interdependence of Value Change in America," *Journal of Interdisciplinary History* 3 (1973) 649–83; *idem* and J. Zvi Namenwirth and Harold D. Lasswell, *The Changing Language of American Values: A Computer Study of Selected Party Platforms* (Beverly Hills, 1970).

৯ৠ General Works on Price Movements: Economic Theory

The index to an economics textbook of 565 pages by Donald McCloskey contains the following entry: "price, pp. 11, 1–565." In the largest sense, all economic theory is about price movements. For readers uninitiated in this discipline, the best starting point is a good textbook, of which there are many. Among broad surveys, Paul Samuelson and William D. Nordhaus, *Economics* (14th ed., New York, 1990), is a graceful and good-humored introduction.

The academic discipline of economics is divided in two parts. Macroeconomics studies the aggregate "behavior" of economic systems and what some economists call "absolute price levels." Microeconomics is about individual choices in the market, mostly by two mythical decision makers, the "consumer" and the "firm."

Outstanding among textbooks on macroeconomics is Rudiger Dornbusch and Stanley Fischer, *Macroeconomics* (New York, 1978), which has the merit for historians of including chapters that explicitly apply theoretical models to historical events since 1960.

Specially relevant here is Charles W. Calomiris and Christopher Hanes, "Historical Macroeconomics and American Macroeconomic History," *National Bureau of Economic Research Working Papers* no.4935 (1994), 1–77, which argues for "an historical definition of the economy" in a "path-dependent way." The authors give much attention to Kuznets cycles, which are often called "long swings," but they have nothing to say about price revolutions, which would have strengthened their substantive case. Calomiris and Hanes are much interested in "aggregate-demand shocks," which produce "endogenous changes in aggregate supply." They add a bibliography, which is a helpful guide to recent economic literature on long swings, a subject that has come to life in the 1990s.

Among microeconomic texts, Donald N. McCloskey, *The Applied Theory of Prices* (New York, 1982) is fun to read and might be specially recommended to students of history. Its author is an economic historian with a sense of humor and an awareness of the human dimensions of his subject.

On price movements in general and the problem of inflation in particular, economists have generated a vast literature which offers many different theoretical models of price movements. Two empirical essays on changing fashions in economic thought are Paul Bairoch and Bouda Etemad, "La litérature périodique d'histoire économique contemporaine," *Annales E.S.C.* 42 (1987) 369–401; and George Stigler, "Statistical Studies of Economic Thought," in *Essays in the History of Economics* (Chicago, 1965), 31–50.

Among the leading schools of thought in the United States are various monetarist approaches, Keynesian theories, neoclassical cost-push and demand-pull models, administered price theory, new inflation or competitive inflation theories, sociopolitical models, and rational expectations theories.

Many economists in America today believe that price movements are determined primarily by variations in the supply of money. The classic statement of the monetarist model in the early twentieth century was Irving Fisher, *The Purchasing Power of Money* (New York, 1911, 1920, 1922, rpt. 1963); also *idem, Appreciation and Interest* (New York, 1896), *The Rate of Interest* (New York, 1907), and *The Theory of Interest* (New York, 1930). For a memoir of this remarkable, very interesting and unjustly maligned man, see Irving Norton Fisher, *My Father—Irving Fisher* (New York, 1956).

The next generation of monetarists was led by Milton Friedman. In Isaiah Berlin's disjunction between the hedgehog who knows one thing and the fox who knows many things, Friedman is a classic example of the academic hedgehog at work. His many works include "The Quantity Theory of Money: A Restatement," in Milton Friedman, ed., *Studies in the Quantity Theory of Money* (Chicago, 1956); *The Optimum Quantity Theory of Money and Other Essays* (Chicago, 1969); "The Role of Monetary Policy," *American Economic Review* 58 (1968) 1–17. His major empirical work was published in a series of monographs: *A Monetary History of the United States* (Princeton, 1963), *Monetary Statistics of the United States* (New York, 1970), and *Monetary Trends in the United States and the United Kingdom: Their Relation to Income, Prices, and Interest Rates, 1867–1975* (Chicago, 1982). Also important is Phillip Cagan, *Determinants and Effects of Change in the Stock of Money, 1875–1960* (New York, 1965).

Another and more eclectic generation of monetary theory appears in Robert J. Barro and Stanley Fischer, "Recent Developments in Monetary Theory," *Journal of Monetary Economics* 2 (1976) 151–55. Barro has also given us "Government Spending, Interest Rates, Prices, and Budget Deficits in the United Kingdom, 1701–1918," *Journal of Monetary Economics* 20 (1987) 221–48; and Robert J. Barro and R. G. King, "Time-Separable Preferences and Intertemporal-Substitution Models of Business Cycles," *Quarterly Journal of Economics* 99 (1984) 817–39.

For critiques of monetarism, see Robert J. Gordon, ed., *Milton Friedman's Monetary Framework: A Debate with His Critics* (Chicago, 1974);

R. J. Ball, *Inflation and the Theory of Money* (London, 1964); Harry G. Johnson, *Inflation and the Monetarist Controversy* (Amsterdam, 1972–1976).

Keynesian models of price movements tend to differ from other approaches in their assumption that the movement of prices, wages, rents, and interest are "sticky" in various ways. See John Maynard Keynes, *A Tract on Monetary Reform* (London, 1923); *idem, A Treatise on Money* (New York, 1930); *idem, The General Theory of Employment, Interest, and Money* (London, 1936). The standard biography is R. F. Harrod, *The Life of John Maynard Keynes* (London, 1963). For Keynesian approaches in America see Seymour Harris, *The New Economics:Keynes' Influence on Theory and Public Policy* (London, 1947); James Tobin, *The New Economics One Decade Older* (Princeton, 1974); John Kenneth Galbraith, *A Theory of Price Control* (Cambridge, 1952); *idem, Money* (Boston, 1975); R. Clower and A. Leijonhufvud, "The Coordination of Economic Activities: A Keynesian Perspective," *American Economic Review* 65 (1975) 182–88; Sidney Weintraub, "The Keynesian Theory of Inflation: The Two Faces of Janus," *International Economic Review* 1 (1960); Axel Leijonhufvud, *On Keynesian Economics and the Economics of Keynes* (New York, 1968); Herschel Grossman, "Was Keynes a 'Keynesian'?" *Journal of Economic Literature* 10 (1972) 26–35; Robert J. Barro, "Second Thoughts on Keynesian Economics," *American Economic Review* 69 (1979) 54–59.

Neoclassical cost-push and demand-pull inflation models were developed in Richard T. Selden, "Cost-Push versus Demand-Pull Inflation, 1955–57," *Journal of Political Economy* 67 (1959) 1–20; Robert J. Gordon, "The Demand For and Supply of Inflation," *Journal of Law and Economics* 18 (1975) 871–74; *idem,* "Alternative Responses of Policy to External Supply Shocks," *Brookings Papers on Economic Activity* 1 (1975) 183–204; Robert E. Lucas, "Some International Evidence on Output Inflation Trade-Offs," *American Economic Review* 63 (1973) 326–34.

On administered price models and oligopoly theory, which hold that prices are determined in part by the distribution of economic power, see Gardiner Means, *Industrial Prices and Their Relative Inflexibility,* Senate Document 13, 74th Cong., 1st session (1935); *idem et al., The Structure of the American Economy* (Washington, 1939); Paul M. Sweezy, "Demand under Conditions of Oligopoly," *Journal of Political Economy* 47 (1939) 569–73; U.S. Congress, Senate Subcommittee on Antitrust and Monopoly, *Administered Prices,* 86th Cong., 1st session (1959). On administered prices and excess demand, a suggestive essay is Martin S. Feldstein, "The Rising Price of Physicians' Services," *Review of Economics and Statistics* 52 (1970) 121–33.

"New inflation" models appear in W. David Slawson, *The New Inflation: The Collapse of Free Markets* (Princeton, 1981); and Frank C. Ripley and Lydia Segal, "Price Determination in 395 Manufacturing Industries," *Review of Economics and Statistics* 55 (1973) 263–71.

Sociopolitical models of inflation include Fred Hirsch and John H. Goldthorpe, *The Political Economy of Inflation* (Cambridge, Mass., 1978); Leon N. Lindberg and Charles S. Maier, *The Politics of Inflation and Economic Stagnation* (Washington, 1985); and Paul Peretz, "The Political Economy of Inflation" (thesis, Chicago, 1976).

Rational expectations theory hypothesizes that economic decisions are made not so much in response to past prices themselves as to perceptions of present and future prices in a world of incomplete information. This idea was put forward in John Muth, "Rational Expectations and the Theory of Price Movements," *Econometrica* 29 (1961) 315–35. It is examined in Milton Friedman, "The Role of Monetary Policy," *American Economic Review* 58 (1968) 1–17; R. M. Solow, *Price Expectations and the Behaviour of the Price Level* (Manchester, 1969); S. J. Turnovsky and M. L. Wachter, "A Test of the 'Expectations Hypothesis' Using Directly Observed Wage and Price Expectations," *Review of Economics and Statistics* 54 (1972) 47–54; Stephen Figlewski and Paul Wachtel, "The Formation of Inflationary Expectations," *Review of Economics and Statistics* 63 (1981) 1–10; Clifford F. Thies, "Interest Rates and Expected Inflation, 1831–1914: A Rational Expectations Approach," *Southern Economic Journal* 51 (1985) 1107–20.

Eclectic works include Gottfried Haberler, *Inflation: Its Causes and Cures* (Washington, 1966); Gardiner Means et al., *The Roots of Inflation* (New York, 1975); J. Popkin, ed., *Analysis of Inflation, 1965–1974* (Cambridge, 1974); K. K. F. Zawadzki, *The Economics of Inflationary Processes* (London, 1965).

Other theoretical writings have centered on specific problems, including stagflation, disinflation, deflation, hyperinflation, long-term inflation, global inflation, the economic consequences of inflation, methods of controlling inflation, price and wage controls, price relatives, price and wage movements, prices and income distribution, prices and interest, prices and employment, or prices and interest.

On stagflation, a difficult problem for neoclassical economics, see A. S. Blinder, *Economic Policy and the Great Stagflation* (New York, 1981); Karl Brunner et al., "Stagflation, Persistent Unemployment, and the Permanence of Economic Shocks," *Journal of Monetary Economics* 6 (1980) 467–92; Mokyr and Savin, "Stagflation in Historical Perspective," cited above; Mancur Olsen, *The Rise and Decline of Nations: Economic Growth, Stagflation, and Social Rigidities* (New Haven, 1982).

Disinflation and deflation are periodically rediscovered as theoretical problems; see, e.g., Olivier Wormser, *Déflation et dévaluation; Étude comparée de leurs effets sur les prix* (Paris, 1938); Donald Franklin, "Risks of deflation," *Banker* 136 (1986) 47.

Hyperinflation as a theoretical problem is studied from a monetarist perspective by Phillip Cagan, "The Monetary Dynamics of Hyperinflation," in Milton Friedman, ed., *Studies in the Quantity Theory of Money* (Chicago, 1956), 3–24.

Long-term inflation is the subject of Phillip Cagan, *Persistent Inflation: Historical and Policy Essays* (New York, 1979); and G. L. Bach, *The New Inflation: Causes, Effects, Cures* (Providence, 1958, 1973, 1974). Also useful are James Tobin, "Inflation: Monetary and Structural Causes and Cures"; Paul Beckerman, "Inflation and Inflation Feedback"; David Colander, "Towards a Real Theory of Inflation"; Thomas F. Wilson, "Institutional Change as a Source of Excessive Monetary Expansion"; Y. S. Brenner, "Sources of Inflation: Old and New"; Edward Marcus, "Inflation, the Terms of Trade, and National Income Estimates"; Patricia F. Bowers, "A Theoretical Analysis of the Exchange Process and Inflation"; Hyman P. Minsky, "Institutional Roots of American Inflation"; all in Schmukler and Marcus, eds., *Inflation through the Ages*, 3–146, 265–77.

Global inflation is explored in Michael R. Darby et al., *The International Transmission of Inflation* (Chicago, 1985), a monetarist approach; N. Kaldor, "Inflation and Recession in the World Economy," *Economic Journal* 86 (1976) 703–14; D. I. Meiselman and A. B. Laffer, eds., *The Phenomenon of Worldwide Inflation* (Washington, 1975); A. J. Brown, *The Great Inflation, 1939–51* (London, 1955); idem, *World Inflation since 1950* (Cambridge, 1985); Geoffrey Maynard and W. van Ryckegham, eds., *A World of Inflation* (New York, 1975); Gardner Ackley, *Stemming World Inflation* (Paris, 1971).

The consequences of inflation are discussed in Gardner Ackley, "The Costs of Inflation," *American Economic Review* 68 (1978) 149–54; James Tobin and Leonard Ross, "Living with Inflation," *New York Review of Books*, 6 May 1971, 23–24; K. K. Kurihara, ed., *Post-Keynesian Economics* (Aldershot, 1955, 1993); George Terborgh, *Essays on Inflation* (Washington, 1971).

On methods of controlling inflation, two leading works in a large literature are Arthur Okun and G. L. Perry, eds., *Curing Chronic Inflation* (Washington, 1978); Robert M. Solow and Paul M. Samuelson, "Analytical Aspects of Anti-Inflation Policy," *American Economic Review* 50 (1960) 177–94; see also from a very different perspective Richard Portes, "The Control of Inflation: Lessons from East European Experience," *Economica* 44 (1977) 109–29.

The effect of price and wage controls is studied in Hugh Rockoff, "Price and Wage Controls in Four Wartime Periods," *Journal of Economic History* 41 (1981) 381–401, which finds that controls worked better than many neoclassical economists believe; similar conclusions appear in Orley Ashenfelter and Robert S. Smith, "Compliance with the Minimum Wage Law," *Journal of Political Economy* 87 (1979) 333–50; a study of variability in effectiveness is Charles C. Cox, "The Enforcement of Public Price Controls," *Journal of Politial Economy* 88 (1980) 887–916.

On the problem of price relatives and the classical problem of Ricardian distribution and Marshallian scissors, see L. Pasinetti, "A Mathematical Formulation of the Ricardian System," *Review of Economic Studies* 27 (1960) 78–98; Ronald Findlay, "Relative Prices, Growth, and Trade in a Simple Ricardian System," *Economica* 41 (1974) 1–13; Daniel R. Vining and Thomas C. Elwertowski, "The Relationship between Relative Prices and the General Price Level," *American Economic Review* 66 (1976) 699–708; Mario I. Blejer and Leonardo Liederman, "On the Real Effects of Inflation and Relative-Price Variability: Some Empirical Evidence," *Review of Economics and Statistics* 62 (1980) 539–44, which explores the consequences of relative price variability for production and employment; Richard W. Parks, "Inflation and Relative Price Variability," *Journal of Political Economy* 86 (1978) 79–95; Michael D. Bordo, "The Effects of Monetary Change on Relative Commodity Prices and the Role of Long-Term Contracts," *Journal of Political Economy* 88 (1980) 1088–1109; Paul H. Earl, *Inflation and the Structure of Industrial Prices* (Lexington, 1973).

On inflation and wages, see A. A. Alchian and R. A. Kessel, "The Meaning and Validity of the Inflation-Induced Lag of Wages behind Prices," *American Economic Review* 50 (1960) 43–66; T. Cargill, "An Empirical Investigation of the Wage-Lag Hypothesis," *ibid.* 59 (1969) 806–16; Arnold H. Packer and Seong H. Park, "Distortions in Relative Wages and Shifts in the Phillips Curve," *Review of Economics and Statistics* 56 (1973) 16–22.

Barry Eichengreen, "Macroeconomics and History," in Alexander J. Field, ed., *The Future of Economic History* (Boston, 1987) 43–90, observes (48) that "no one has as yet provided a satisfying macroeconomic explanation for sixteenth-century real wage and relative price trends."

On inflation and the distribution of income and wealth, see E. Budd and D. Seiders, "The Impact of Inflation on the Distribution of Income and Wealth," *American Economic Review* 61 (1971) 128–38; G. L. Bach and A. Ando, "The Redistributional Effects of Inflation," *Review of Economics and Statistics* 39 (1957) 1–13; G. L. Bach and James B. Stephenson, "Inflation and the Redistribution of Wealth," *Review of Economics and Statistics* 66 (1974) 1–13; Andrew F. Brimmer, "Inflation and Income Distribution in the United States," *Review of Economics and Statistics* 53 (1971) 37–48; R. G. Hollister and J. L. Palmer, "The Impact of Inflation on the Poor," in K. E. Boulding and M. Pfaff, eds., *Redistribution to the Rich and the Poor: The Grants Economics of Income Distribution* (Belmont, Calif., 1972); J. Muellbauer, "Prices and Inequality: The United Kingdom Experience," *Economic Journal* 84 (1974) 32–55; Paul Peretz, *The Political Economy of Inflation,* cited above; Edward N. Wolff, "The Distributional Effects of the 1969–1975 Inflation on Holdings of Household Wealth in the United States,"

Review of Income and Wealth 25 (1979) 195–207; Lindert and Williamson, *American Inequality: A Macroeconomic History,* 136–38.

Many economists believe that inflation is associated with egalitarian trends, but this refers mainly to evidence from 1939 to 1970, an anomalous period in the history of prices. Very different patterns appeared before 1920 and after 1970. Others argue that "the redistributional effects are more complex than isoften suggested" and that "simple conclusions that inflation is good for the rich and bad for the poor need to be viewed with considerable doubt" (Bach and Stephenson, 13), but these judgments also lack historical depth.

On inflation and employment, the classic essay is A. W. Phillips, "The Relation between Unemployment and the Rate of Change in Money Wage Rates in the United Kingdom, 1861–1957," *Economica* 25 (1958) 283–99. For further discussion, see John A. James, "The Stability of Nineteenth-Century Phillips Curve Relationship," *Explorations in Economic History* 26 (1989) 117–34; Erik Aerts and Barry Eichengreen, eds., *Unemployment and Underemployment in Historical Perspective* (Leuven, 1990). Other contributions include Milton Friedman, "Nobel Lecture: Inflation and Unemployment," *Journal of Political Economy* 85 (1977) 451–472; James Tobin, "Inflation and Unemployment," presidential address, *American Economic Review* 62 (1972) 1–18; Charles C. Holt et al., *The Unemployment-Inflation Dilemma: A Manpower Solution* (Washington, 1971); George L. Perry, *Unemployment, Money Wage Rates, and Inflation* (Cambridge, 1966). Helpful bibliographical notes on inflation and unemployment appear in Maynard and van Ryckeghem, eds., *A World of Inflation,* 42–44 and Gerald W. Scully, "Static vs. Dynamic Phillips Curves," *Review of Economics and Statistics* 56 (1974) 387–90.

A thorn in monetarist flesh is the Gibson paradox: that is, the tendency for prices and interest rates to rise and fall together. Every monetarist of my acquaintance can explain it away, but it keeps coming back again. This problem has spawned a large literature. See Gerald P. Dwyer Jr., "An Explanation of the Gibson Paradox" (thesis, Chicago, 1979); Robert J. Shiller and Jeremy Siegel, "The Gibson Paradox and Historical Movements in Interest Rates," *Journal of Political Economy,* 85 (1977) 891–907; C. Knick Harley, "The Interest Rate and Prices in Britain, 1873–1913: A Study of the Gibson Paradox," *Explorations in Economic History* 14 (1977) 69–89.

❧ General Works on Price Movements: Social Theory

Another body of theoretical writings has been produced by social scientists and social historians. This literature is divisible into three large groups that might be called Malthusian, Marxist, and Smithian.

The first of these schools of thought follows in the footsteps of Malthus. Many scholars believe that price movements are driven mainly by endogenous demographic trends. Malthusians believe that population growth tends to force farm prices and rents up while sending industrial prices and wages down. Others hold that population movements are themselves constrained by social and cultural systems—an approach taken in this book. But the idea of endogenous demographic determinants is very strong in the literature of social science. British historians took the lead in developing this model, primarily with reference to medieval trends. Among the early general statements was M. M. Postan, "[Section 3, Histoire économique;] Moyen âge," *IXe Congrès internationale des sciences historiques, . . . Rapports* (2 vols., Paris, 1950–51) vol. 1; rpt. in M. M. Postan, *Essays on Medieval Agriculture and General Problems of the Medieval Economy* (Cambridge, 1973), and many other writings cited below. A Malthusian model was also applied to modern history in H. J. Habbakuk, "The Economic History of Modern Britain," *Journal of Economic History* 18 (1958) 488–501; rpt. in D. V. Glass and D. E. C. Eversley, *Population in History* (London, 1965), 147–58. Habbakuk asserted, "For those who care for the overmastering pattern, the elements are evidently there for a heroically simplified version of English history before the nineteenth century in which the long-term movements in prices, in income distribution, in investment, in real wages, and in migration are dominated by changes in the growth of population."

A similar approach was developed in the early modern period by the great French historian Emmanuel Le Roy Ladurie in his *grand thèse, Les paysans de Languedoc* (Paris, 1966), and his inaugural lecture at the College de France, "L'histoire immobile," *Annales E.S.C.* 29 (1974) 675.

Another Malthusian contribution of high importance has been made by the American economic demographer Ronald Demos Lee, in *Econometric Studies of Topics in Demographic History* (New York, 1978), and "A Historical Perspective on Economic Aspects of the Population Explosion: The Case of Preindustrial England," in Richard A. Easterlin, ed., *Population and Economic Change in Developing Countries* (National Bureau Comm. for Economic Research Conference Report no. 30 [1980]; rpt. Chicago, 1987), 517–66. Lee concludes from a cross-spectral analysis of the Cambridge group's population estimates and the Phelps-Brown and Hopkins wage series that the English economy easily absorbed changes in rates of population growth of about 0.4 percent a year but that "deviations of population size above or below this trend line, however, had dramatic consequences." He also believes that demographic changes were themselves autonomous—a conclusion not firmly grounded.

Some American economists believe that the Malthusian model is fundamentally mistaken when it is developed into an argument that an increase in population causes the general price level to rise. Joel Mokyr, for example, insists that "other things equal, the effect of population growth is deflationary." This hypothesis is developed in "Discussion," *Journal of Economic History* 44 (1984) 341–3. On this issue opinion is divided among Malthusians themselves.

A different critique of Malthusian theory comes from Marxist historians, who believe that the prime movers of price movements are changes in modes of production and class relations. Marxist models have enjoyed a revival among some historians in the Western world during the 1970s and 1980s, at a time when young scholars in eastern Europe, the Soviet Union, and China were turning away from them. Marxist explanations are specially popular among historians of the early modern era as a way of making sense of transformations in that period.

One body of Marxist theory seeks to explain economic trends primarily in terms of the transition from one stage of production to another—and especially from feudalism to capitalism. This approach stimulated a lively theoretical debate in the 1950s, which centered on the conceptualization of feudal and capital systems and the causes of their transformation. The movement of prices and especially wages became an important issue in this debate. The central work was Maurice Dobb, *Studies in the Development of Capitalism* (London, 1943; rpt. 1963, 1972). After a critique was published by American Marxist Paul Sweezy in *Science and Society* in 1950, a controversy continued in various Marxist journals. Thirteen essays including Sweezy's are reprinted in Rodney Hilton, ed., *The Transition from Feudalism to Capitalism* (London, 1976, 1978).

Another body of theoretical literature centers on the relative merits of Marxist and Malthusian models. An important essay is Robert Brenner, "Agrarian Class Structure and Economic Development in Pre-Industrial Europe," *Past and Present* 70 (1976), a Marxist attack on "demographic determinism" in general and on the work of Emmanuel Le Roy Ladurie in particular. Brenner insists that "it is the structure of class relations, of class power, which will determine the manner and degree to which particular demographic and commercial changes will effect long-term trends in the distribution of income and economic growth—not vice versa." This uncompromising thesis stimulated many articles by academic Marxists and Antimarxists in *Past & Present*, from which ten are reprinted in T. H. Aston and C. H. E. Philpin, eds., *The Brenner Debate: Agrarian Class Structure and Economic Development in Pre-Industrial Europe* (Cambridge, 1985).

Yet another theoretical debate among Marxists has developed around Immanuel Wallerstein's "world-systems" model, an ambitious and thoughtful attempt to combine Braudel's *problematique* with a Marxist model of historical development and the epistemology of American sociology. The results are set forward in Immanuel Wallerstein, *The Modern World-System* (2 vols., New York, 1974, 1989); also *idem*, "Kondratieff Up or Kondratieff

Down?'' *Review* 2 (1979) 663–73; "Economic Cycles and Socialist Policies," *Futures* 16 (1984) 579–85; "Long Waves as Capitalist Process," *Review* 7 (1984) 559–75.

A very different school of historical theory seeks to explain economic and social trends primarily in terms of systems of exchange and market relationships. It is stigmatized by Marxists as "Smithian," or worse, "neo-Smithian." The leading work is by American economic historians Douglas North and Robert Thomas, *The Rise of the West World* (Cambridge, 1973); *idem*, "The Rise and Fall of the Manorial System: A Theoretical Model," *Journal of Economic History* 31 (1971) 777–803.

Critiques of this approach include Alexander James Field, "The Problem with Neoclassical Institutional Economics: A Critique with Special Reference to the North / Thomas Model of Pre-1500 Europe," *Explorations in Economic History* 18 (1981) 174–98. See also R. Brenner, "The Origins of Capitalist Development: A Critique of Neo-Smithian Marxism," *New Left Review* 104 (1977).

❧ Catastrophe Studies

Of relevance to the study of the last stage of each price revolution is a growing literature on crisis and catastrophe. A pioneering work is Pitirim Sorokin, *Man and Society in Calamity: The effects of War, revolution, Famine, pestilence upon Human Mind, Behavior, Social Organization . . .* (New York, 1946). An interesting French journal has been devoted to this subject. It was founded as *Materiaux pour l'Etude des Calamités* in 1925, and became the *Revue pour l'Étude des Calamités* in 1938. Cultural and social approaches to the study of catastrophe are explored in Paul Hugger, "Elemente einer Ethnologie der Katastrophe in der Schweiz," *Zeitschrift für Volkskunde* 86 (1990) 25–36; and Wieland Jäger, *Katastrophe und Gesellschaft Grundlegung und Kritik von Modellen der Katastrophensoziologie.* Other works include Kai T. Erikson, *A New Species of Trouble: Explorations in Disaster, Trauma, and Community* (New York, 1994); John I. Clarke, ed., *Population and Disaster* (Oxford, 1989).

❧ The Ancient World

General works on money in the ancient world, with some attention to prices, include A. R. Burns, *Money and Monetary Policy in Early Times* (London, 1927); François Lenormant, *La monnaie dans l'antiquité* (3 vols., Paris, 1878–79); L. Incarnati, *Moneta e scambio nell'antichitá a nell' alto medioevo* (Roma, 1953).

A starting point for studies of the rhythm of ancient history is Rein Taagepera, "Size and Duration of Empires: Growth-Decline Curves, 3000 to 600 B.C.," *Social Science Research* 7 (1978) 180–96; *idem*, "Size and Duration of Empires: Growth-Decline Curves, 600 B.C. to 600 A.D.," *Social Science History* 3 (1979) 115–38.

✥ Price Movements in Mesopotamia

Specialized studies on money and prices in Mesopotamia include Henry F. Lutz, "Price Fluctations in Ancient Babylonia," *Journal of Economic and Business History* 4 (1931–32) 335–55; Howard Farber, "An Examination of Long-Term Fluctuations in Prices and Wages for North Babylonia during the Old Babylonian Period," (thesis, Northern Illinois University, 1974); *idem*, "A Price and Wage Study for Northern Babylonia during the Old Babylonian Period," *Journal of the Economic and Social History of the Orient* 21 (1978) 1–51; W. H. Dubberstein, "Comparative Prices in Later Babylonia (625–400)," *American Journal of Semitic Languages and Literatures* 56 (1938) 21–72; B. Meissner, *Warenpreise in Babylonien* (Berlin, 1936).

✥ Egyptian Prices

Leading works include Angelo Segré, *Circolazione monetaria e prèzzi nel mondo antico ed in particolare Egitto* (Rome, 1922); J. J. Janssen, *Commodity Prices from the Ramessid Period: An Economic Study of the Village of Necropolis Workmen at Thebes* (Leiden, 1975); Karl Butzer, *Early Hydraulic Civilization in Egypt* (Chicago, 1976); T. Reekmans, "The Ptolemaic Copper Inflation 220–173 B.C.," *Studia Hellenistica* 7 (1951) 61; *idem*, "Economic and Social Repercussions of the Ptolemaic Copper Inflation," *Chronique d'Égypte* 24 (1949) 324; and for Roman Egypt, J. A. Straus, "Le prix des esclaves dans les papyrus d'époque romaine trouvés dans, l'Egypte," *Zeitschrift für Papyrologie und Epigraphik* 11 (1973) 289–95; A. K. Bowman, "The Economy of Egypt in the Earlier Fourth Century," in C. E. King, ed., *Imperial Revenue, Expenditure, and Monetary Policy in the Fourth Century* A.D. (Oxford, 1980) 23–40; Roger S. Bagnall, *Currency and Inflation in Fourth-Century Egypt* (Chico, Calif., 1985).

✥ Prices in Ancient Greece

Greek prices are discussed in Alfred Jacobs, "Preis (1) Preisgeschichte," *Handwörterbuch der Sozialwissenschaften* (Gottingen, 1964), 8:459–76, an excellent short survey of price movements in classical Greece (600–169 B.C.) and Rome (456 B.C. to A.D. 301), with a bibliography. A pathbreaking attempt at a price history of ancient Greece is Lydia Spaventa de Novellis, *I prèzzi in Grecia e a Roma nell'antichità* (Rome, 1934); a copy of this work is in the New York Public Library. Also helpful are Gustave Glotz, *La travail dans la Grèce ancienne* (Paris, 1920; Eng. tr., New York, 1926); M. I. Finley, *Studies in Land and Credit in Ancient Athens, 500–200 B.C.* (New Brunswick, 1952); Chester G. Starr, *The Economic and Social Growth of Ancient Greece, 800–500 B.C.* (New York, 1977); K. Christ, "Die Griechen und das Geld," *Saeculum* 15 (1964) 214–29; M. J. Price et al., *Essays in Greek Coinage Presented to Stanley Robinson* (Oxford, 1968); L. Lacroix, "La monnaie grecque et les problèmes de la circulation monétaire," *Bulletin de la Classe des Lettres, Academie Royale Belgique* 55 (1969) 169–80.

ᘓ Rome

On Roman prices there is a large literature. Some material on prices appears in Michael Rostovtzeff, *The Social and Economic History of the Roman Empire* (2 vols., Oxford, 1926; rpt. 1957); much more is in Tenney Frank, ed., *An Economic Survey of Ancient Rome* (Baltimore, 1933–40).

An important survey is A. H. M. Jones, "Inflation under the Roman Empire," *Economic History Review* 2d ser. 5 (1953) 293–318; a second edition, revised and corrected, appears in P. A. Brunt, ed., *The Roman Economy: Studies in Ancient Economic and Administrative History* (Oxford, 1974), 187–229.

Much data is collected in Richard Duncan-Jones, *The Economy of the Roman Empire: Quantitative Studies* (Cambridge, 1974); idem, "The Price of Wheat in Lower Egypt," in *Structure and Scale in the Roman Economy* (Cambridge, 1990), 143–56; idem, "The Price of Wheat in Roman Egypt under the Principate," *Chiron* 8 (1978) 541–60; J. Kolendo, "L'arrêt de l'afflux des monnaies romaines dans le 'Barbaricum' sous Septime-Sévère," *Les Dévaluations à Rome* 2 (Rome) 169–72.

Also useful are G. Rickman, *The Corn Supply of Ancient Rome* (Oxford, 1980); S. Bolin, *State and Currency in the Roman Empire up to A.D. 300* (Stockholm, 1958); F. M. Heichelheim, "New Light on Currency and Inflation in Hellenistic-Roman Times, from Inscriptions and Papyri," *Economic History* 10 (1935) 1–11; Sture Bolin, *State and Currency in the Roman Empire to 300 A.D.* (Stockholm, 1958); P. Louis, *Ancient Rome at Work* (London, 1927); H. Mattingly, *Roman Coins from the Earliest Times to the Fall of the Western Empire* (New York, 1928).

Period-specific studies include Claude Nicolet, "Les variations des prix et la 'théorie quantitative de la monnaie à Rome, de Cicéron à Pline l'Ancien," *Annales E.S.C.* 26 (1971) 1203–27; Z. Yaveta, "Fluctuations monétaires et condition de la plébe à la fin de la République," *Recherches sur les societes anciennes* (Caen, 1971); Tenney Frank, "The Financial Crisis of 33 A.D." *American Journal of Philology* 56 (1935) 336–41; L. C. West, "The Coinage of Diocletian and the Edict on Prices," in P. R. Coleman-Norton, ed., *Studies in Roman Economic and Social History in Honor of Allen Chester Johnson* (Princeton, 1951), 290–302; Marta Giacchero, ed., *Edictum Diocletiani et collegarum de pretiis rerum venalium . . .* (Genoa, 1974); C. R. Whittaker, "Inflation and the Economy in the Fourth Century A.D.," in C. E. King, ed., *Imperial Revenue, Expenditure, and Monetary Policy in the Fourth Century A.D.* (Oxford, 1980), 1–22; M. Fulford, "Coin Circulation and Mint Activity in the Late Roman Empire: Some Economic Implications," *Archaeological Journal* 135 (1978) 67–114.

❧ Palestine

Prices in Palestine are examined in Daniel Sperber, *Roman Palestine, 200–400: Money and Prices* (Ramat-gan, 1974); A. Kindler, ed., *The Patterns of Monetary Development in Phoencia and Palestine in Antiquity* (Jerusalem, 1963).

❧ Byzantium

For the eastern empire and Byzantine history, see G. Ostrogorsky, "Löhne und Preise in Byzanz," *Byzantische Zeitschrift* 23 (1932), Italian trans. in Romano, *I prèzzi in Europa*, 47–85; H. Antoniadis-Bibicou, "Demographie, salaires et prix à Byzance au XIᵉ siècle," *Annales E.S.C.* 27 (1972) 215–46; D. A. Zakythinos, *Crise monétaire et crise économique à Byzance du XIIIᵉ au XVᵉ siècle* (Athens, 1948); Michael F. Hendy, *Studies in the Byzantine Monetary Economy, c. 300–1450* (Cambridge, 1985); Angeliki Laiou-Thomadakis, *Peasant Society in the Late Byzantine Empire: A Social and Demographic Study* (Princeton, 1977); A. L. Harvey, "The Growth of the Byzantine Rural Economy (thesis, Birmingham, 1983); A. M. Andréadés, "De la monnaie et de la puissance d'achat des métaux précieux dans l'empire byzantin," *Byzantion* 1 (1924) 75–115; C. Morrison, "La dévaluation de la monnaie byzantine au XIᵉ siècle: Essai d'interprétation," *Travaux et Mémoires* 6 (1976) 3–48; Franz Dölger, *Beitrage zur Geschichte der byzantinischen Finanzverwaltung* (Darmstadt, 1927).

ᨑ Islam

For Islamic prices and wages the leading authority is Eliyahu Ashtor, *Historie des prix et des salaires dans l'Orient médiéval* (Paris, 1969); tr. as *A Social and Economic History of the Near East in the Middle Ages* (London, 1976); *idem, Les métaux precieux et la balance des payements du Proche-Orient à la fin de la basse époque* (Paris, 1971); *idem, The Medieval Near East: Social and Economic History* (London, 1978), a collection of essays on prices, wage and interest movements; *idem,* "La recherche des prix dans l'Orient médiéale," *Studia Islamica* 21 (1964); *idem,* "Prix et salaires dans l'Espagne musulmane aux Xe et XIe siècles," *Annales E.S.C.* 20 (1965) 664–79; "Matériaux pur l'histoire des prix dans l'Egypte médiévale," *Journal of the Economic and Social History of the Orient* 6 (1963) 158–89; *idem,* "Le coût de la vie dans l'Egypte médiévale," *Journal of the Economic and Social History of the Orient* 3 (1960) 56–77; *idem,* "Le coût de la vie dans la Syrie médiévale," *Arabica* 8 (1961) 59–73; *idem,* "Le coût de la vie en Palestine au Moyen Age," in *L. A. Mayer Memorial Volume,* 154–64; also published in *Eretz-Israel* 7 (1963); also *idem,* "Prix et salaires à l'époque mamlouke," *Revue des Études Islamiques* (1949) 49–94; *idem,* "Essai sur les prix et les salaires dans l'empire califien," *Rivista degli Studi Orientale* 36 (1961) 19–69; *idem,* "L'évolution des prix dans le Proche-orient à la basse-époque, *Journal of Economic and Social History of the Orient* 4 (1961) 15–46.

Especially strong on the demographic and ecological history of Islam is Xavier de Planhol's excellent *Les fondements géographiques de l'histoire de l'Islam* (Paris, 1968). For a fiscal perspective see H. Rabie, *The Financial System of Egypt, A.H. 564–741 / A.D. 1169–1341* (London, 1972); William Popper, *Egypt and Syria under the Circassian Sultans (1382–1468 A.D.)* (Berkeley, 1955).

ᨑ Ancient Africa

Useful works include M. Malowist, "The Social and Economic Stability of the Western Sudan in the Middle Ages," *Past & Present* 33 (1966) 3–15; E. W. Bovill, *The Golden Trade of the Moors* (Oxford, 1958); and J. Devisse, "Routes de Commerce et échanges en Afrique occidentale en relation avec la Méditerranée," *Revue d'histoire économique et sociale* 1 (1972) 42–73, 357–97.

ﾆﾑ Polynesia

A. T. Wilson, "Isotope Evidence for Past Climatic and Environmental Change," *Journal of Interdisciplinary History* 10 (1980) 241–50, is an important work on climate and historical change in Oceania.

ﾆﾑ East Asia

General works on East Asian civilizations before the modern era include Ping-ti Ho, *Studies on the Population of China, 1368–1953* (1959, 2d ed., Cambridge, 1967); Mark Elvin, *The Pattern of the Chinese Past; A Social and Economic Interpretation* (London, 1973); P. Liu and K. Huang, "Population Change and Economic Development in Mainland China since 1400," in C. Hou and T. Yu, eds., *Modern Chinese Economic History* (Taipei, 1977), 61–81. An older but still useful survey is C. P. Fitzgerald, *China, A Short Cultural History* (New York, 1935, 1972).

Period-specific studies are R. Hartwell, "A Cycle of Economic Change in Imperial China: Coal and Iron in North-east China, 750–1350," *Journal of the Economic and Social History of the Orient* 10 (1967)

On the Sung and Ming periods, there are M. Cartier, "Notes sur l'histoire des prix en Chine du XIVᵉ au XVIIᵉ siècle," *Annales E. S. C.* 24 (1969) 1876–89; *idem*, "Les importations de métaux monetaires en Chine: Essai sur la conjoncture chinoise," *ibid.*, 36 (1981) 454–66; Ch'uan Han-sheng, "Sung-Ming chien pai-yin kou-mai-li ti pien-tung chi ch'i yuan-yin," ["Fluctuations in the purchasing power of silver at their cause from the Sung to the Ming dynasties,"] *Hsin-ya-hseuh-pao* [*New Asian Journal*] 8 (1967) 157–86, with a summary in English; M. Cartier, "Notes sur l'histoire des prix en Chine du XIVe au XVIIe siècle," [1368–1644] *Annales E. S. C.* 24 (1969) 1876–89; *idem*, "Les importations de métaux monetaires en Chine: Essai sur la conjoncture Chinoise," *ibid.*, 36 (1981) 454–66; W. S. Atwell, "Notes on Silver, Foreign Trade, and the Late Ming Economy," *Ch'ing shih wen-ti* 3 (1977) 1–33; *idem* "International Bullion Flows and the Chinese Economy, *circa* 1530–1650," *Past & Present* 95 (1982) 68–90.

For the Ching period, see Yeh-chien Wang, "The Secular Trend of Prices during the Ch'ing Period," *Journal of the Institute of Chinese Studies of the Chinese University of Hong Kong*, 5 (1972) 364; Han-sheng Ch'uan and Richard A. Kraus, *Mid-Ch'ing Rice Markets and Trade: An Essay in Price History* (Cambridge, 1975).

❧ The Western World in the Early Middle Ages

On the early medieval West, Rosamond McKitterick, ed., *The New Cambridge Medieval History*, vol 2, c. 700–c. 900 (Cambridge, 1995), has chapters on economic organization by Adriaan Verhulst (481-509) and on money and coinage by Mark Blackburn (538–62) but nothing on prices.

Price lists for this period appear in Claudio Sánchez-Albornoz, *El precio de la vida en el reino astur-leone's hace mil Años* (Buenos Aires, 1945), a rare work that can be found in the New York Public Library.

General works of economic history on this period include Robert Latouche, *Les origines de l'économie occidentale IVᵉ–XIᵉ siècle* (Paris, 1956); and Georges Duby, *The Early Growth of the European Economy: Warriors and Peasants from the Seventh to the Twelfth Century* (Ithaca, 1978).

Other works centering on the question of subsistence and commerce include P. Grierson, "Commerce in the Dark Ages: A Critique of the Evidence," *Royal Historical Society Transactions* 9 (1959) 123–40; R. Hodges, *Dark Age Economics: The Origins of Towns and Trade, A.D. 600–1000* (London, 1982); S. R. H. Jones, "Transaction Costs, Institutional Change, and the Emergence of a Market Economy in Later Anglo-Saxon England," *Economic History Review* 46 (1993) 658–78; P. Grierson, "Commerce in the Dark Ages: A Critique of the Evidence," *Royal Historical Society Transactions* 5th ser. 9 (1959) 123–40; M. de Bouard, "Problemes des Subsistence dans un État medievale: le marché et les prix des céréales au royaume angevin de Sicile," *Annales d'Histoire Économique et Sociale* 10 (1938) 483.

On money and coinage, see P. Grierson and M. Blackburn, *Medieval European Coinage* (Cambridge, 1986); A. Blanchet, *Les tresors de monnaies romaines et les invasions germaniques* (Paris, 1900); Marc Bloch, "Le probleme de l'or au moyen age," *Annales d'Histoire Économique et Sociale* 5 (1933) 1–34, Eng. tr. in *Land and Work in Mediaeval Europe: Selected Papers by Marc Bloch* (Berkeley, 1967), 186–229; Carlo Cipolla, "Currency Depreciation in Medieval Europe," *Economic History Review* 2d ser. 15 (1962–63) 413–22.

❧ The Medieval Price Revolution

General works include Georges Duby, *L'économie rurale et la vie des campagnes dans l'Occident médiéval* (2 vols., Paris, 1962), trans. C. Postan as *Rural Economy and Country Life in the Medieval West* (London, 1968); idem, *The Early Growth of the European Economy: Warriors and Peasants from the Seventh to the Twelfth Century* (Ithaca, 1974) with a "bibliographical guide"; M. M. Postan, *The Medieval Economy and Society: An Economic History of Britain in the Middle Ages* (London, 1972); *idem,* "Economic

Foundations of Medieval Society,'' in *idem, Essays on Medieval Agriculture and General Problems of the Medieval Economy* (Cambridge, 1973), 2–27; *idem, Medieval Economy and Society* (1972); J. Z. Titow, *English Rural Society, 1200–1350* (London, 1969); H. E. Hallam, *Rural England, 1066–1348* (Brighton, 1981); Edward Miller, "England in the Twelfth and Thirteenth Centuries: An Economic Contrast?" *Economic History Review* 2d ser. 24 (1971) 1–14.

A heroic attempt to model the main lines of medieval economic history appears in Richard H. Britnell and Bruce M. S. Campbell eds., *A Commercialising Economy: England 1086 to c. 1300* (Manchester, 1995). Graeme Donald Snooks, "The Dynamic Role of the Market in the Anglo-Norman Economy and Beyond, 1086–1300," *ibid.*, 27–54, discusses great waves in prices, population, domestic product, and product per capita from the eleventh century to the present. Nicholas Mayhew, "Modelling Medieval Monetisation," *ibid.*, 55–77, offers a very different estimate of medieval domestic product. The disparity derives from different readings of Domesday evidence. We are still a long way from closure on questions of economic growth in the middle ages.

Major local studies of general interest in France include Robert Fossier's excellent *La terre et les hommes en Picardie, jusqu'a la fin du XIIIe siècle* (2 vols., Paris and Louvain, 1968); Y. Bezard, *La vie rurale dans le sud de la région parisienne* (Paris, 1929); A. Fierro, "Un cycle démographique: Dauphiny et Faucigny du XIVe aux XIXe siècle," *Annales E.S.C.* (1969); Joseph Strayer, "Economic Conditions in the Country of Beaumont-le-Roger, 1261–1313," *Speculum* 26 (1951) 277–87; Ph. Wolff, *Commerces et marchands de Toulouse (vers 1350–vers 1450)* (Plon, 1954); J. Yver, "Remarques sur l'évolution de quelques prix en Normandie aux XIVe et XVe siècles," *Revue d'Histoire du Droit Français et Étranger* 4 (1958) 145–54; G. Fourquin, *Les campagnes de la région parisienne à la fin du moyen age* (Paris, 1964); G. Lesage, *Marseille Angevine* (Paris, 1950).

Among Belgian and Dutch local histories there are L. Genicot, *L'economie rurale namuroise au bas Moyen Age, 1199–1429* (Louvain, 1960); G. Sivery, *Structures agraires et vie rurale dans le Hainaut à la fin du Moyen Age* (Lille, 1973); N. DePauw, ed., *Ypre jeghen Poperinghe angeande den verbonden: Gedingsstukken der XIVde eeuw nopens het laken* (Ghent, 1899); G. Des Marez and E. De Sagher, eds. *Comptes de la ville d'Ypres de 1267 à 1329* (2 vols. Brussels, 1909).

English local studies include H. P. R. Finberg, *Tavistock Abbey: A Study in the Social and Economic History of Devon* (Cambridge, 1951; 2d ed., Newton Abbot, 1969); W. G. Hoskins and H. P. R. Finberg, *Devonshire Studies* (London, 1952); H. P. R. Finberg, *Gloucestershire* (London, 1955); W. G. Hoskins, *Leicestershire* (London, 1970); Edward Miller, *The Abbey and Bishopric of Ely* (Cambridge, 1951); J. B. Harley, "Population Trends and Agricultural Developments from the Warwickshire Hundred Rolls of 1279," *Economic History Review* 2d ser. 11 (1958) 8–18; Frances Davenport, *The Economic Development of a Norfolk Manor, 1086–1565* (Cambridge, 1906); E, Miller, *The Abbey and Bishopric of Ely: The Social History of an Ecclesiastical Estate from the Tenth Century to the Early Fourteenth Century* (Cambridge, 1951); Alan Everitt, *Continuity and Colonization: The Evolution of Kentish Settlement* (Leicester, 1986); J. Hatcher, *Rural Economy and Society in Medieval Cornwall, 1300–1500* (Cambridge, 1970); H. E. Hallam, *Settlement and Society: A Study of the Early Agrarian History of South Lincolnshire* (Cambridge, 1965); *idem, Rural England, 1066–1348* (Brighton, 1981).

Italian studies include H. Bresc, *Un monde méditerranéean: économie et société en Sicilie, 1300–1450* (2 vols., Rome, 1986).

For Spain there is C. Dufourcq, *L'Espagne catalane et le maghrib aux XIIIᵉ et XIVᵉ siècles* . . . (Paris, 1966).

For demographic trends in medieval Europe, see J. Z. Titow, "Some Evidence of the Thirteenth-Century Population Increase," *Economic History Review* 14 (1961) 218–23; Josiah Russell, *Late Ancient and Medieval Population,* 20; *idem,* "Recent Advances in Medieval Demography," *Speculum* 45 (1965) 84–101; *idem,* "Aspects démographiques des débuts de la féodalité," *Annales E.S.C.,* 20 (1965) 1118–27; a critique of Russell's estimates appears in G. Ohlin, "No Safety in Numbers: Some Pitfalls in Historical Statistics," in H. Rosovsky, ed., *Industrialization in Two Systems: Essays in Honor of Alexander Gershenkron* (New York, 1966), 70–81. Other essays include M. M. Postan, "Some Economic Evidence of Declining Population in the Later Middle Ages," *Economic History Review* 2d ser. 2 (1950) 221–46; Julian Cornwall, "English Population in the Early Sixteenth Century," *Economic History Review,* 2d ser. 23 (1970) 32–44; H. E. Hallam, "Population Density in Medieval Fenland," *Economic History Review* 14 (1961) 71–79; and "Some Thirteenth-Century Censuses," *ibid.* 10 (1957) 340–61; *idem, Rural England, 1066–1348* (Brighton, 1981), 245–50; H. E. Hallam, "Population Movements in England, 1086–1350," in Hallam, ed., *The Agrarian History of England and Wales* (Cambridge, 1988), II, 508–593; Enrico Fiume, "Sui rapporti economici tra cittá e contado nell' etá communale," *Archivio Storico Italiano* 114 (1956) 18–68; David Herlihy, "The Medieval Marriage Market," *Medieval and Renaissance Studies* 6 (1976) 3–27; *idem,* "The Generation in Medieval History," *Viator* 5 (1974) 347–64; E. Baratier, "La démographie Provençale au XIIIᵉ et XIVᵉ siècle (Paris, 1961).

On medieval price movements, the literature is most abundant for England. Besides William Beveridge, *Prices and Wages in England from the Twelfth to the Nineteenth Century* cited above; *idem,* "The Yield and Price of Corn in the Middle Ages," *Economic Journal, Economic History Supplement* 1 (1926–29) 162–66; A. L. Poole, "Livestock Prices in the Twelfth Century," *English Historical Review* 55 (1940) 284–95; M. M. Postan and J. Titow, "Heriots and Prices on Winchester Manors," *Economic History Review* 2d ser. 11 (1959) 392–411; J. Longden, "Statistical Notes on Winchester Heriots," *Economic History Review* 2d ser. 11 (1959) 412–17. The best and most comprehensive studies of English medieval prices are those of D. L. Farmer (University of Saskatchewan): "Some Price Fluctuations in Angevin England," *Economic History Review* 2d ser. 9 (1956–57) 34–43; "Some Grain Price Movements in Thirteenth-Century England," *Economic History Review* 2d ser. 10 (1957) 207–20; "Some Livestock Price Movements in Thirteenth-Century England," *Economic History Review* 2d ser. 22 (1969) 1–16; "Crop Yields, Prices, and Wages in Medieval England," *Studies in Medieval and Renaissance History* 6 (1983) 117–55; "Grain Yields on Westminster Abbey Manors, 1271–1410," *Canadian Journal of History* 18 (1981) 331–47; "Prices and Wages," in H. E. Hallam, ed., *The Agrarian History of England and Wales, vol. 2, 1042–1350* (Cambridge, 1988), 716–817; "Prices and Wages, 1350–1500," in E. Miller, ed., *The Agrarian History of England and Wales, vol. 3, 1348–1500* (Cambridge, 1988), 431–525.

Other price studies include Norman S. B. Gras, *The Evolution of the English Corn Market from the Twelfth to the Eighteenth Century* (Cambridge, Mass., 1915); T. H. Lloyd, "The Movement of Wool Prices in Medieval England," *Economic History Review* Supplement 6 (1973) 38–50; P. D. A. Harvey, "The English Inflation of 1180–1220," *Past and Present* 61 (1973) 3–30; Mavis Mate, "High Prices in Early Fourteenth-Century England: Causes and Consequences," *Economic History Review* 2d ser. 28 (1975) 1–16.

Specially helpful for price relatives is an unpublished thesis, Clyde George Reed, "Price Data and European Economic History: England, 1300–1600" (thesis, University of Washington, 1972).

The most comprehensive French study of the medieval price revolution is still d'Avenel, *Historique économique de la propriété, des salaires des denrées et de tous les prix en général depuis l'an 1200 jusqu'en l'an 1800*, cited above, vols. 2 and 3.

Especially helpful for Italian prices in this period are Gino Luzzatto, "Il costo della vita a Venezia nel Trecento," *Ateneo Veneto* 25 (1934); Michel de Bouard, "Problemes de subsistances dans un état médiéval: Le marché et les prix des céréales au Royaume angevin de Sicile: 1266–82," *Annales d'Histoire Économique et Sociale* 10 (1938); Raimondo Carta-Raspi, *L'economia della Sardegna medievale: scambi e prèzzi* (Cagliari, 1940); Magalde and Fabris, "Notizie storiche e statistiche sui prèzzi e salari nei secoli XIII–XVIII nelle città di Milano, Venezia, Genova, Firenze, Lucca, Mantova e Forli"; Faraglia, *Storia dei prèzzi in Napoli . . .* and Ettore Rossi and Paolo Maria Arcari, "I prèzzi a Genova dal XII al XV secolo," all cited above.

For central and eastern Europe, see, in addition to Abel, *Agrarkrisen und*

Agrarkonjunktur, cited above, Alfred Dieck, "Lebensmittelpreise in Mitteleuropa und im Vordern Orient zum 12. bis 17. Jahrhundert," *Zeitschrift für Agrargeschichte und Agrarsoziologie"* 2 (1955), Italian tr. in Romano, ed., *I prèzzi in Europa,* 143–50 *idem,* "Tauschobjekte, Preise und Löhne des Vorderen Orient und Mitteleuropas im Mittelalter und Nachmittelalter," *Forschungen und Fortshritte* 36 (1962); and Waschinski, *Wahrung, preisentwicklung . . . in Schleswig-Holstein,* cited above.

On wages, see William Beveridge, "Wages in Winchester Manors," *Economic History Review* 1st ser. 7 (1936–37) 22–43; *idem,* "Westminster Wages in the Manorial Era," *Economic History Review,* 2d ser. 8 (1955–56) 18–35; Douglas Knoop and G. P. Jones, "Masons' Wages in Medieval England," *Economic History* 2 (1933) 473–99; *idem, The Medieval Mason* (Manchester, 1967); L. F. Salzman, *Building in England down to 1540* (Oxford, 1952); R. Beissel, *Geldwert und Arbeitslohn im Mittelalter* (Freiburg in Breisgau, 1884); B. Geremek, *Le salariat dans l'artisanat parisien aux XIIIe–XVe siècles* (Paris, 1968); Etienne Robo, "Wages and Prices in the Hundred of Farnham in the Thirteenth Century," *Economic History* 3 (1934) 24–34; a discussion of wages appears in H. Thomas Johnson, "Cathedral Building and the Medieval Economy," *Explorations in Entrepreneurial History* 4 (1967) 191–210; B. W. E. Alford and M. Q. Smith, "The Economic Effects of Cathedral and Church Building in Medieval England: A Reply," *ibid.* 6 (1969) 158–69; H. Thomas Johnson, "The Economic Effects of Cathedral and Church Building in Medieval England: A Rejoinder," *ibid.,* 169–74.

On rent, see E. A. Kominskii, "Services and Money Rents in the Thirteenth Century," *Economic History Review* 5 (1935) 24–45; *idem,* "The Evolution of Feudal Rent in England from the Eleventhth to the Fifteenth Centuries," *Past & Present* 7 (1955) 12–36; *idem, Studies in the Agrarian History of England in the Thirteenth Century* (Oxford, 1956); Ronald Witt, "The Landlord and the Economic Revival of the Middle Ages in Northern Europe, 1000–1250," *American Historical Review* 76 (1971) 965–88; Brice Lyon, "Medieval Real Estate Developments and Freedom," *American Historical Review* 63 (1957) 47–61; P. D. A. Harvey, ed., *The Peasant Land Market in Medieval England* (Oxford, 1984); P. R. Hyams, "The Origins of a Peasant Land Market in England," *Economic History Review* 23 (1970) 18–31.

Rates of interest in medieval Europe are surveyed in Sidney Homer, *A History of Interest Rates* (New Brunswick, 1963), 94–99.

Monetary movements are explored in Marc Bloch, "Le problème de l'or au Moyen Age," *Annales d'Histoire Économique et Sociale* 5 (1933) 1–34, tr. J. E. Anderson in *Land and Work in Medieval Europe: Selected Papers by Marc Bloch* (Berkeley and Los Angeles, 1967), 186–229. Also important is a companion piece by Bloch, translated by Anderson as "Natural Economy or Money Economy: A Pseudo-Dilemma," in *ibid.,* 230–41.

A leading study is Peter Spufford, *Money and Its Use in Medieval Europe* (Cambridge, 1988). Other contributions to a large literature include Pierre Vilar, *A History of Gold and Money, 1450–1920* (London, 1976); Carlo M. Cipolla, *Money, Prices, and Civilization in the Mediterranean World: Fifth to Seventeenth Century* (Princeton, 1956), cited above; *idem*, "Currency Depreciation in Medieval Europe," *Economic History Review* 2d ser. 15 (1963) 413–22; Michael Prestwich, "Early Fourteenth-Century Exchange Rates," *Economic History Review* 2d ser. 32 (1979) 470–82; *idem*, "Edward I's Monetary Policies and Their Consequences," *Economic History Review* 2d ser. 22 (1969) 406–16; C. C. Patterson, "Silver Stocks and Losses in Ancient and Medieval Times," *Economic History Review* 2d ser. 25 (1972) 205–35; D. M. Metcalf, "English Monetary History in the Time of Offa: A Reply," *Numismatic Circular* 71 (1963) 1651; Frederic Lane, *Venice: A Maritime Republic* (Baltimore, 1973), in which the author summarizes many years of study on this subject; *idem*, "Le vecchie monete di conto Veneziane ed il ritorno dall'ore," *Atto dell Instituto Veneto di Scienze Letre ed Arti: Classe di Scienzi Morali, Letter, ed Arti* 117 (1958–59) 49–78. See also Robert S. Lopez, "Back to Gold, 1252," *Economic History Review* 2d ser. 9 (1956) 219–40; A. M. Watson, "Back to Gold and Silver," *Economic History Review* 2d ser. 20 (1967) 1–34; L. B. Robbert, "Monetary Flows: Venice, 1150–1400," in J. F. Richards, ed., *Precious Metals in the Later Medieval and Early Modern Worlds* (Durham, 1983), 274–93.

The problem of velocity is studied in N. J. Mayhew, "Population, Money Supply, and the Velocity of Circulation in England, 1300–1700," *Economic History Review* 2d ser. 48 (1995) 238–57; other important studies of medieval money and prices by the same author include: "Money and Prices in England from Henry II to Edward III," *Agricultural History Review* 35 (1987) 121–32; "Modelling Medieval Monetisation," in B. M. S. Campbell and R. H. Britnell, eds., *A Commercialising Economy: England, 1086–1300* (Manchester, 1995), 55–77.

On finance a classic work is Mario Chiaudano, "I Rothschild del Dugento: La Gran Tavola di Orlando Bonsignori," *Bullettino Senese di Storia Patria* 42 (1935) 103–42; William M. Bowsky, *The Finance of the Commune of Siena, 1287–1355* (Oxford, 1970); *idem*, *A Medieval Italian Commune: Siena Under the Nine, 1287–1355* (Berkeley, 1981).

On markets and commerce, see R. H. Britnell, "The Proliferation of Markets in England, 1200–1349," *Economic History Review* 2d ser. 34 (1981) 209–221; Richard Hodges, *Dark Age Economics: The Origins of Towns and Trade, A.D. 600–1000* (London, 1982); Raymond De Roover, "The Commercial Revolution of the Thirteenth Century," in F. C. Lane and J. Riemersma, eds. *Enterprise and Secular Change* (1953).

Industrialization in medieval Europe is the subject of E. M. Carus Wilson, "An Industrial Revolution of the Thirteenth Century," *Economic*

History Review 11 (1939) 39–60; Rolf Sprandel, "La production du fer au moyen age," *Annales E.S.C.* 24 (1969) 305–21; Jean Gimpel, *The Medieval Machine: The Industrial Revolution of the Middle Ages* (New York, 1976); William N. Bonds, "Some Industrial Price Movements in Medieval Genoa (1155–1255)," *Explorations in Entrepreneurial History* 7 (1969–70) 123–39; Henrietta M. Larson, "The Armor Business in the Middle Ages," *Business History Review* 14 (1940) 49–64; C. F. ffoulkes, "European Arms and Armor," in G. Barraclough, ed., *Social Life in Early England* (London, 1960) 124–38; F. Philippi, *Die erste Industrialisierung Deutschlands* (Munster, 1909); *idem, Das Eisengewerbe im Mittelalter* (Stuttgart, 1968).

On agriculture, see J. Z. Titow, *Winchester Yields: A Study in Medieval Agricultural Productivity* (Cambridge, 1972), which covers the period from 1209 to 1349; D. L. Farmer extends this series from 1350 to 1453 in "Grain Yields on the Winchester manors in the Later Middle Ages," *Economic History Review* 2d ser. 30 (1977) 555–66; E. A. Kominskii, *Studies in the Agrarian History of England in the Thirteenth Century* (Oxford, 1956); David Herlihy, "The Agrarian Revolution in Southern France and Italy, 801–1150," *Speculum* 33 (1958) 23–41; *idem*, "The History of the Rural Seignury in Italy, 751–1200," *Agricultural History* 33 (1959) 1–14.

For harvests and *disettes*, see E. Thorold Rogers, *A History of Agriculture and Prices in England*, vol. 1, *1259–1400*; Heinrich H. W. F. Curschmann, *Hungersnöte in Mittelalter. Ein Beitrag zur deutschen Wirtschaftsgeschichte des 8. bis 13. Jahrhunderts* (Leipzig, 1900); M. E. Levasseur, *Les prix aperçu de l'histoire économique de la valeur et du revenu de la terre, en France du commencement du XIIe siècle a la fin du XVIIIe, avec un appendice sur le prix du froment et sur les disettes depuis l'an 1200 jusqu'a l'an 1891* (Paris, 1893), appendix.

For the problem of poverty, see Alfred N. May, "An Index of Thirteenth-Century Peasant Impoverishment? Manor Court Fines," *Economic History Review* 2d ser. 26 (1973) 389–402.

On economic ethics in medieval Europe, there is a large literature. Much of it centers on the problem of just price. See Henri Garnier, *L'idée du juste prix chez les théologiens et canonistes du Moyen Age* (New York, 1973); Benjamin Nelson, "The Usurer and the Merchant Prince: Italian Businessmen and the Ecclesiastical Law of Restitution, 1100–1550," *Journal of Economic History* Supplement 7 (1947) 104–22; *idem, The Idea of Usury* (Princeton, 1949); T. P. McLaughlin, "The Teaching of the Canonists on Usury (Twelfth, Thirteenth, and Fourteenth Centuries)," *Medieval Studies* 1 (1939) 81–147; A. Sapori, "L'interesse del danaro a Firenze nel trecento (Dal testamento di un usuraio)," *Archivio Storico Italiano* 10 (1928) 161–86; and Noonan, *Usury*, cited above.

Various other aspects of the relationship between material and cultural history are explored in J. R. Strayer, "The Crusades of Louis IX," in

K. M. Setton, ed., *A History of the Crusades* (Philadelphia, 1962); Jocelin de Brakeland, *The Chronicle of Jocelin of Brakelond*, H. E. Butler ed., (London, 1949); Steven Epstein, *Wills and Wealth in Medieval Genoa, 1150–1250* (Cambridge, 1984).

On Chartres Cathedral, see Robert Branner, ed., *Chartres Cathedral* (New York, 1969); Lucien Merlet and Eugene de Lepinois, *Cartulaire de Notre-Dame de Chartres* (3 vols., Chartres, 1862–65) 2:103; Robert Branner, ed., *Chartres Cathedral* (New York, 1969); Charles Rohault de Fleury, *Memoire sur les instruments de la passion de N.-S. J.-C.* (Paris, 1870).

The renaissance of the twelfth century is discussed in Charles Homer Haskins, *The Renaissance of the Twelfth Century* (London, 1927); R. W. Southern, *The Making of the Middle Ages* (New Haven, 1953); Robert L. Benson and Giles Constable, eds., *Renaissance and Renewal in the Twelfth Century* (Cambridge, 1982); G. Pare et al., *La Renaissance du XIIᵉ Siècle: Les Écoles et l'Enseignement* (Paris, 1933); J. L. Bolton, *The Medieval English Economy, 1150–1500* (London, 1980); Carlrichard Brühl, *Palatium und Civitas: Studien zur Profantopographie spatantiker Civitates vom 3. bis 13. Jahrhundert* (Cologne, 1975), 1:19.

ᨠ The Crisis of the Fourteenth Century

The best starting point is Bruce M. S. Campbell, ed., *Before the Black Death: Studies in the 'Crisis' of the Early Fourteenth Century* (Manchester, 1991; rpt. 1992), with an excellent consolidated bibliography (209–26).

General studies include Edouard Perroy, "A l'origine d'une économie contractée: Les crises du XIVᵉ siècle," *Annales E.S.C.* 4 (1949) 167–82; trans. in Rondo Cameron, ed., *Essays in French Economic History* (Homewood, Ill., 1970); R. E. Lerner, *The Age of Adversity: The Fourteenth Century* (Ithaca, 1968); R. Boutruche, *Seignurie et féodalité* (2 vols., Paris, 1968); R. Delatouche, "La crise du XIVᵉ siècle en Europe occidentale," *Les Études Sociales* 28 (1959) 1–19; F. Graus, "Das spätmittelalter als Krisenzeit . . . ," *Mediaevalia Bohemica* Supplement 1 (Prague, 1969); *idem*, "Die Erste Krise des Feudalismus," *Zeitschrift für Geschichtswissenschaft* 3 (1955) 552–92; Cicely Howell, "Stability and Change, 1300–1700," *Journal of Peasant Studies* 2 (1975) 468–82; N. Hybel, *Crisis or Change: the Concept of Crisis in Light of the Agrarian Structural Reorganization in Late Medieval England* (Aarhus, 1989).

Many schools of interpretation exist: Malthusian, which puts stress on imbalances between population and the means of subsistence; Marxist, on the class structure and the means of production; monetarist, on changes in the money supply; market-centered, on structures of exchange; climatological, on weather events.

The Malthusian model of the crisis is developed in Michael Postan, *Essays on Medieval Agriculture and General Problems of the Medieval Economy* (Cambridge, 1973); and *idem, The Medieval Economy and Society: An Economic History of Britain in the Middle Ages* (Berkeley, 1972), cited above. A critique of the Postan thesis appears in Barbara F. Harvey, "The Population Trend in England between 1300 and 1348," *Transactions of the Royal Historical Society* 5th ser. 16 (1966) 23–42; and D. G. Watts, "Model for the Early Fourteenth Century," *Economic History Review* 20 (1967) 543–47, which argues that the Malthusian model does not appear to work if one omits the crisis years! Important discussions appear in Guy Bois, "Against the Neo-Malthusian Orthodoxy," *Past & Present* 79 (1978) 60–69. The thesis is restated in Edward Miller and John Hatcher, *Medieval Society and Economic Change, 1086–1348* (London, 1978), and M. M. Postan and John Hatcher, "Population and Class Relations in Feudal Society," *Past & Present* 78 (1978) 24–37. An argument for local complexity appears in H. E. Hallam, *Rural England, 1066–1348* (Brighton, 1981); *idem,* "The Postan Thesis," *Historical Studies* 15 (1972) 203–22; and Edward Britton, *The Community of the Vill* (Toronto, 1977). Much of this controversy centers on population trends in East Anglia; strong empirical evidence from there to support Postan is presented in L. R. Poos, "The Rural Population of Essex in the Later Middle Ages," *Economic History Review* 2d ser. 38 (1985) 515–30.

Marxist models include R. H. Hilton, "Y eut-il une crise générale de féodalité?" *Annales E.S.C.* 6 (1951) 23–30; E. A. Kosminskii, *Studies in the Agrarian History of England in the Thirteenth Century* (Oxford, 1956); Robert Brenner, "Agrarian Class Structure and Economic Development in Pre-Industrial Europe," *Past & Present* 70 (1976) 30–75; and Guy Bois, *Crise du féodalisme: économie rurale et démographie en Normandie orientale du début du XIVe siècle au milieu du XVIe siècle* (Paris, 1976); trans. as *The Crisis of Feudalism . . .* (Cambridge, 1984). For discussions of Marxist models in general and Brenner in particular, see Trevor Aston and C. H. E. Philpin, eds., *The Brenner Debate: Agrarian Class Structure and Economic Development in Pre-Industrial Europe* (Cambridge, 1985). A critique of Guy Bois is Emmanuel Le Roy Ladurie, "En Haute-Normandie: Malthus ou Marx?" *Annales E.S.C.* 33 (1978) 115–24. Marxist interpretations in the West have been much influenced by the work of a Polish scholar, W. Kula, *Théorie économique du système féodal: Pour un modéle de l'économie polonaise XVIe–XVIIIe siècles* (Paris, 1970); this study of a later period has had a major impact on Marxist medievalists.

For monetarist models see J. Schreiner, "Wages and Prices in England in the Later Middle Ages," *Scandinavian Economic History Review* 2 (1954) 61–73; Earl J. Hamilton, "The History of Prices before 1750," in *Rapports du XVe congrés international des sciences historiques* (Stockholm, 1960) 1:144–64, also separately issued (Stockholm, 1960); W. C. Robinson,

"Money, Population, and Economic Change in Late Medieval Europe," *Economic History Review* 2d ser. 12 (1959) 63–76; N. J. Mayhew, "Numismatic Evidence and Falling Prices in the Fourteenth Century," *Economic History Review* 2d ser. 27 (1974) 1–15; idem, "Money and Prices in England from Henry II to Edward III," *Agricultural History Review* 35 (1987) 121–32; and especially the work of the able American Annalist John Day, *The Medieval Market Economy* (Oxford, 1987); idem, "The Decline of a Money Economy: Sardinia in the Late Middle Ages," *Studia in memoria di Federico Melis* (Naples, 1978) 3:155–176; and idem, "Crise du féodalisme et conjunctures des prix à la fin du moyen age," *Annales E.S.C.* 34 (1979) 305–18. A critique of monetarist models in general and Day's review-essay in particular is Guy Bois, "Sur la monnaie et les prix a la fin du moyen age: réponse a John Day," *ibid.*, 319–23.

On market-centered models, exchange rates, balance of payments, and price surges there are Mavis Mate, "High Prices in Early Fourteenth-Century England: Causes and Consequences," *Economic History Review* 2d ser. 28 (1975) 1–16; idem, "The Impact of War on the Economy of Canterbury Cathedral Priory, 1294–1340," *Speculum* 57 (1982) 761–78; C. G. Reed, "Price Movements, Balance of Payments, Bullion Flows, and Unemployment in the Fourteenth and Fifteenth Centuries," *Journal of European Economic History* 8 (1979) 479–86; Michael Prestwich, "Early Fourteenth-Century Exchange Rates," *Economic History Review* 2d ser. 32 (1979) 470–82; Edward Ames, "The Sterling Crisis of 1337–1339," *Journal of Economic History* 25 (1965) 496–522; B. Kedar, *Merchants in Crisis: Genoese and Venetian men of Affairs and the Fourteenth-Century Depression* (New Haven, 1976).

A fourteenth-century equivalent of an administered price model may be inferred from P. D. A. Harvey, *A Medieval Oxfordshire Village: Cuxham, 1240–1400* (London, 1965).

For climatological models, see the works of Beveridge, cited above, and J. Z. Titow, "Evidence of Weather in the Account Rolls of the Bishopric of Winchester, 1209–1350," *Economic History Review* 2d ser. 12 (1960) 360–407; idem, "Le climat à travers les rôles de comptabilité de l'évêché de Winchester (1350–1450)," *Annales E.S.C.* 25 (1970) 312–50; C. E. Britton, *A Meteorological Chronology to A.D. 1450* (London, 1937); W. T. Bell and A. E. J. Ogilview, "Weather Compilations as a Source of Data for the Reconstruction of European Climate during the Medieval Period," *Climatic Change* 1 (1978) 331–48; H. E. Hallam, "The Climate of Eastern England, 1250–1350," *Agricultural History Review* 32 (1984) 124–32. Still useful is C. E. P. Brooks and J. Glasspole, *British Floods and Droughts* (London, 1928).

An ecological approach, stressing the history of agriculture and the contraction of arable land, is the subject of R. H. Britnell, "Agricultural Technology and the Margin of Cultivation in the Fourteenth Century," *Economic*

History Review 30 (1977) 53–66; J. Z. Titow, *Winchester Yields: A Study in Medieval Agricultural Productivity* (Cambridge, 1972); Alan R. H. Baker, "Evidence in the Nonarum Inquisitiones of Contracting Arable Lands in England during the Early Fourteenth Century," *Economic History Review* 2d ed. 19 (1966) 518–32; A. R. Lewis, "The Closing of the Medieval Frontier," *Speculum* 33 (1958) 475–83. On problems of marginality, see M. Bailey, "The Concept of the Margin in the Medieval English Economy" *Economic History Review* 2d ser. 42 (1989) 1–17; *idem, A Marginal Economy?: East Anglian Breckland in the Later Middle Ages* (Cambridge, 1989).

On famines, see Hugues Neveux, "Bonnes et mauvaises récoltes du XIVe au XIXe siècle: Jalons pour une enquête systématique," *Revue d'Histoire Économique et Sociale* 53 (1975); 177–92; Ian Kershaw, "The Great Famine and Agrarian Crisis in England, 1315–1322," *Past & Present* 59 (1973) 3–50; Elisabeth Carpentier, "Famines et epidemies dans l'histoire du XIVe siècle," *Annnales E.S.C.* 17 (1962) 1062–92; H. S. Lucas, "The Great European Famine of 1315, 1316, and 1317," *Speculum,* 15 (1930) 343–77; H. Van Werweke, "La famine de l'an 1316 en Flandre et dans les régions voisines," *Revue du Nord* 41 (1959) 5–14; A. R. Bridbury, "Before the Black Death," *Economic History Review* 2d ser. 30 (1977) 393–410; *idem,* "The Black Death," *Economic History Review* 2d ser. 26 (1973) 577–92; Marie-Josèphe Larenaudie, "Les famines en Languedoc aux XIVe et XVe siècles," *Annales du Midi* 64 (1952) 27–39; P. J. Capra, "Au sujet des famines en Acquitaine au XIVe siécle," *Revue Historique de Bordeaux et du Département de la Gironde* 4 (1955) 1–32; important evidence of the magnitude of the famines of 1315–17 appears in L. R. Poos, "The Rural Population of Essex in the Later Middle Ages," cited above; on Ireland, see M. E. Crawford, ed., *Famine: The Irish Experience, 900–1900* (Edinburgh, 1989), especially M. Lyons, "Weather, Famine, Pestilence, and Plague in Ireland, 900–1500," 31–74.

On nutrition, see C. Dyer, "Changes in Diet in the Later Middle Ages: the Case of Harvest Workers," *Agricultural History Review* 2d ser. 36 (1988) 21–37; and *Standards of Living in the Later Middle Ages: Social Change in England, c.1200–1520* (Cambridge, 1989).

The Black Death and its social and economic impact is the subject of Philip Ziegler, *The Black Death* (Harmondsworth, 1969), an excellent popular history. On cultural consequences of the Black Death, a classic study is Millard Meiss, *Painting in Florence and Siena after the Black Death: The Arts, Religion, and Society in the Mid-Fourteenth Century* (1951); New York, 1964). Two helpful essays are Elisabeth Carpentier, "La peste noire: Famines et épidemies au XIVe siècle," *Annales E.S.C.* 17 (1962) 1062–92; and František Graus, "Autour de la peste noire au XIVe siècle en Bohême," *Annales E.S.C.* 18 (1963) 720–24. A large literature on England includes A. E. Levett, "The Black Death on the Estates of the See of Winchester," *Oxford Studies in Social and Legal History* 5 (1916) 7–180; A. Ballard, "The Black Death on the Manors of Witney, Brightewell, and Downton," *ibid.*, 181–216; C. Creighton, *A History of Epidemics in Britain from A.D. 664 to the Extinction of Plague* (Cambridge, 1891); A. R. Bridbury, "The Black Death," *Economic History Review* 2d ser. 26 (1973) 577–92; J. D. F. Shrewsbury, *A History of Bubonic Plague in the British Isles* (Cambridge, 1970); C. Morris, "The Plague in Britain," *Historical Journal* 14 (1971) 205–15; J. Saltmarsh, "Plague and Economic Decline in England in the Later Middle Ages," *Cambridge Historical Journal* 7 (1941–43) 23–41; J. M. W. Bean, "Plague, Population, and Economic Decline in England in the Later Middle Ages," *Economic History Review* 2d ser. 15 (1963) 423–37; Mavis Mate, "Agrarian Economy after the Black Death: The Manors of Canterbury Cathedral Priory, 1348–91" *Economic History Review* 37 (1984) 341–55; Johan Schreiner, "Wages and Prices in England in the Later Middle Ages," *Scandinavian Economic History Review* 2 (1954) 61–73.

On France the leading work is J. N. Biraben, *Les hommes et la peste en France* (2 vols., Paris, 1975); also valuable are C. Prat, "La peste noire à Albi," *Annales du Midi* 64 (1952) 15–25; and M. Boudet and R. Grand, *Étude historique sur les épidémies de peste en Haute-Auvergne (XIV–XVIII siècle* (Paris, 1902). Important local and regional studies in Italy include David Herlihy, "Population, Plague, and Social Change in Rural Pistoia, 1201–1430," *Economic History Review* 2d ser. 18 (1965) 225–44; Elisabeth Carpentier, *Une ville devant la peste: Orvieto et la peste noire de 1348* (Paris, 1962).

On Spain there are Nicolás Cabrillana, "La crisis del siglio XIV en Castilla: La peste negra en el obisado de Palencia," *Hispania* 28 (1968) 245–58; Jaime Sobrequés Callicó, "La peste negra en la península ibérica," *Anuario de Estudios Medievales* 7 (1970–71) 67–102.

For northern and central Europe there are Johan Schreiner, *Pest og prisfall i Senmiddelalderen: et problem in Norsk Historie* (Oslo, 1948); H. Klein, "Das grosse Sterben von 1348/49 und seine Auswirkung auf die Beseidlung der Ostalpenländer," *Mitteilungen der Gesellschaft für Salzburger Landeskunde* 100 (1960) 91–170; R. Hoeniger, *Der Schwarze Tod in Deutschland* (Berlin, 1882).

On war and political troubles in this period, see J. R. Maddicott, "The English Peasantry and the Demands of the Crown, 1294–1341," *Past & Present* Supplement 1 (1975), rpt. T. H. Aston ed., *Landlords, Peasants and Politics in Medieval England* (Cambridge, 1987), 285–359; E. Miller, "War, Taxation, and the English Economy of the Late Thirteenth and Early Fourteenth Centuries," in J. M. Winter, ed., *War and Economic Development: Essays in Memory of David Joslin* (Cambridge, 1975), 11–31 ; J. O. Prestwich, "War and Finance in the Anglo-Norman State," *Royal Historical Society Transactions* 5th ser. 4 (1954) 19–44; K. B. MacFarlane, "England and the Hundred Years War," *Past & Present* 22 (1962) 3–17; Robert Boutruche,

La crise d'une societé: Seigneurs et paysans du Bordelais pendant la guerre de Cent Ans (Paris, 1947); *idem,* "La dévastation des campagnes pendant la guerre de Cent Ans et la reconstruction agricole de la France," *Publications de la Faculté des Lettres de l'Université de Strasbourg, Melanges* (Strasbourg, 1945), 125–63. Elena Lourie, "A Society Organized for War: Medieval Spain," *Past & Present* 35 (1966) 54–76; S. L. Waugh, "The Profits of Violence: The Minor Gentry in the Rebellion of 1321–1322 in Gloucestershire and Herefordshire," *Speculum* 52 (1977) 843–69.

On social disorders, see Philippe Wolff, "The 1391 Pogrom in Spain: Social Crisis or Not?" *Past & Present* 50 (1971) 4–18; P. Elman, "The Economic Causes of the Expulsion of the Jews in 1290," *Economic History Review* 2d ser. 7 (1936–37) 145–54; B. Geremek, "La lutte contre le vagabondage à Paris aux XIVᵉ et XVᵉ siècles," *Richerche storiche ed economiche in memoria di Corrado Bargello* (Naples, 1970), 2:213–36; M. Mollat and Philippe Wolff, *Ongles bleus, Jacques et Ciompi: Les révolutions populaires en Europe aux XIVᵉ et XVᵉ siècles* (Paris, 1970); L. Mirot, *Les insurrections urbaines au début du régne de Charles VI* (Paris, 1905); R. B. Dobson, *The Peasants' Revolt of 1381* (London, 1970); R. H. Hilton, "Peasant Movements in England before 1381," *Economic History Review* 2d ser. 2 (1949) 117–36; Charles Oman, *The Great Revolt of 1381,* ed. E. B. Fryde, (Oxford, 1969); Lauro Martines, ed., *Violence and Disorder in Italian Cities, 1200–1500* (Berkeley, 1972); William M. Bowsky, "The Medieval Commune and Internal Violence: Police Power and Public Safety in Siena, 1287–1355," *American Historical Review* 73 (1967) 1–17; R. Kieckhefer, *European Witch Trials: Their Foundations in Popular and Learned Culture, 1300–1500* (London, 1976).

On monetary policies, see Harry A. Miskimin, "Monetary Movements and Market Structure: Forces for Contraction in Fourteenth- and Fifteenth-Century England," *Journal of Economic History* 2d ser. 24 (1964) 470–90; C. G. Reed, "Price Movements, Balance of Payments, Bullion Flows, and Unemployment in the Fourteenth and Fifteenth Century," *Journal of European Economic History* 8 (1979) 479–86; Marc Bloch, *Esquisse d'une histoire monétaire de l'Europe* (Paris, 1954).

On politics and finance, see May McKisack, *The Fourteenth Century, 1307–1399* (Oxford, 1959); William M. Bowsky, *A Medieval Italian Commune: Siena under the Nine, 1287–1355* (Berkeley, 1981); *idem,* "The Impact of the Black Death upon Sienese Government and Society," *Speculum* 39 (1964) 1–34; *idem, The Finance of the Commune of Siena, 1287–1355* (Oxford, 1970).

Outside of Europe, there is much evidence of a world crisis in this era. On major discontinuities in the history of China during the fourteenth century, see especially Mark Elvin, *The Pattern of the Chinese Past; A Social and Economic Interpretation* (Stanford, 1973).

For the history of Africa in the fourteenth century, see M. Malowist, "The Social and Economic Stability of the Western Sudan in the Middle Ages," *Past & Present* 33 (1966) 3–15; E. W. Bovill, *The Golden Trade of the Moors* (London, 1958); J. Devisse, "Routes de commerce et échanges en Afrique occidentale en relation avec la Méditerranée," *Revue d'Histoire Économique et Sociale*, 1 (1972) 42–73, 357–97.

Discontinuities in the history of Oceania during the fourteenth century are discussed in A. T. Wilson, "Isotope Evidence for Past Climatic and Environmental Change," *Journal of Interdisciplinary History* 10 (1980) 241–50.

For the Middle East see Michael W. Dols, "Mortality of the Black Death in the Mamluk Empire," in A. L. Udovitch, *The Islamic Middle East, 700–1900: Studies in Economic and Social History* (Princeton, 1981), 397–428; Michael W. Dols, *The Black Death in the Middle East* (Princeton, 1977); and the works of Ashtor cited above.

A best-selling popular account of high quality is Barbara Tuchman, *A Distant Mirror: The Calamitous Fourteenth Century* (Franklin Center, Pa., 1978); for a gentle critique, see Geoffrey Barraclough's review in *The New Republic*.

❧ The Renaissance Equilibrium

General surveys of this period include Denys Hay, *The Italian Renaissance in Its Historical Background* (Cambridge, 1977); Eugene F. Rice, *The Foundations of Early Modern Europe* (New York, 1970); Brian Pullan, *A History of Early Renaissance Italy* (London, 1973); M. W. Ferguson et al., eds., *Rewriting the Renaissance* (Chicago, 1986). A useful work of reference is J. R. Hale, ed., *A Concise Encyclopaedia of the Italian Renaissance* (London, 1981).

On the historiography of the Renaissance, an enduring classic is W. K. Ferguson, *The Renaissance in Historical Thought: Five Centuries of Interpretation* (Boston, 1948); supplemented by *idem,* "The Reinterpretation of the Renaissance," in *Facets of the Renaissance* (New York, 1959), 1–18; *idem, The Renaissance: Six Essays* (New York, 1962); "Recent Trends in the Economic Historiography of the Renaissance," *Studies in the Renaissance* 7 (1960) 7–26; Tinsley Helton, *The Renaissance: A Reconsideration of the Theories and Interpretations of the Age* (Madison, 1961); Eric Cochrane, *Historians and Historiography in the Italian Renaissance* (Chicago, 1981).

A major work of cooperative scholarship is Ruggiero Romano and Corrado Vivanti eds., *Storia d'Italia* (6 vols., Turin, 1972–1977, especially vols. 2 & 3; also Denys Hay, ed., *Longman History of Italy,* especially Denys Hay and John Law, *Italy in the Age of Renaissance, 1380–1530* (London, 1989).

On major economic trends in this period, see R. S. Lopez and H. A.

Miskimin, "The Economic Depression of the Renaissance," *Economic History Review*, 2d ser. 14 (1962) 408–426; and a critique by Carlo M. Cipolla, "Economic Depression of the Renaissance?" with rejoinders by Lopez and Miskimin, *ibid.* 16 (1964) 519–24; C. Barbagallo, "La crisi economico-sociale dell'Italia della Rinascenza," *Nouva Rivista Storica* 34 (1950) 389–411, 35 (1951) 1–38; Leopold Genicot, "Crisis: From the Middle Ages to Modern Times," *Cambridge Economic History of Europe* 1:678–694; M. M. Postan, "The Fifteenth Century," *Economic History Review* 9 (1938–39) 160–67; F. Lutge, "Das 14–15 Jahrhundert in der Sozial und Wirtschaft Geschichte," *Jahrbucher für National Ekonomie und Statistik* (1950) 161–213; M. Mollat, "Y-a-t-il une économie de la Renaissance?" in *Actes du colloque sur la Renaissance* (Paris, 1958); Harry A. Miskimin, *The Economy of Early Renaissance Europe, 1300–1460* (Cambridge, 1975); idem, *The Economy of Later Renaissance Europe, 1460–1600* (Cambridge, 1977).

Demographic trends are discussed in M. M. Postan, "Some Economic Evidence of Declining Population in the Later Middle Ages," *Economic History Review* 2d ser. 2 (1950) 221–46; J. Hatcher, *Plague, Population, and the English Economy, 1348–1530* (London, 1977); E. F. Rice, "Recent Studies on the Population of Europe, 1348–1620," *Renaissance News* 18 (1965) 180–87.

On the problem of deserted villages in Europe, see C. A. Christensen, "Aendringerne i landsbyens økonimiske og sociale strukur i det 14. og 15. arhundrede," *Historisk Tidsskrift,* 12th ser. 1 (1964) 257–349, which includes a summary and conclusion in English; A. Holmsen, "Desertion of Farms around Oslo in the Late Middle Ages," *Scandinavian Economic History Review* 10 (1962) 165–202; Wilhelm Abel, *Die Wüstungen des ausgehenden Mittelalters* (2d ed. Stuttgart, 1955); idem, "Wüstungen und Preisfall im spätmittelalterlichen Europa," *Jahrbücher für Nationalökonomie und Statistik* 165 (1953) 380–427; J. F. Pesez and E. Le Roy Ladurie, "Les villages désertés en France: Vue d'ensembles," *Annales E.S.C.* 20 (1965) 257–90. On deserted villages in the British Isles, see Maurice Beresford, *The Lost Villages of England* (London 1954; rpt. 1965); Maurice Beresford and John G. Hurst, *Deserted Medieval Villages* (London, 1971); Maurice Beresford and J. K. Joseph, *Medieval England: An Aerial Survey* (Cambridge, 1979); Christopher Dyer, "Deserted Villages in the West Midlands," *Economic History Review* 2d ser. 35 (1982) 19–34; K. J. Allison et al., *The Deserted Villages of Oxfordshire* (Leicester University Department of English Local History, occasional paper no. 17, 1965); idem, *The Deserted Villages of Northamptonshire (ibid.,* 1966); K. J. Allison, "The Lost Villages of Norfolk," *Norfolk Archeology* 31 (1957) 116–62; and a very large literature in county archeology journals.

General and national works of economic and social history for Italy include Armando Sapori, *Studi di storia economica, secoli XIII–XIV–XV*

(3 vols., Florence, 1955, 1967), the collected essays of a distinguished economic historian; Gino Luzzatto, *An Economic History of Italy from the Fall of the Roman Empire to the Beginning of the Sixteenth Century* (New York, 1961); and Ruggiero Romano and Corrado Vivanti, eds., *Storia d'Italia*, vol. 2, *Dalla caduta dell'impero Romano al secolo XVIII* (2 parts, Turin, 1974), the most useful single work, with full bibliographical notes.

On relations between economic, social and cultural history, much of the best Italian historical scholarship in this period consists of local (or rather localized) studies. Of high quality on Florence are Marvin B. Becker, *Florence in Transition* (2 vols., Baltimore, 1967); Gene Brucker, *The Civic World of Early Renaissance Florence* (Princeton, 1977); *idem, Renaissance Florence* (Berkeley, 1983); Nicolai Rubinstein, *The Government of Florence under the Medici (1434 to 1494)* (Oxford, 1966); *idem, Florentine Studies: Politics and Society in Renaissance Florence* (Evanston, 1968); Lauro Martines, *The Social World of the Florentine Humanists, 1390–1460* (Princeton, 1963); *idem, Power and Imagination: City-States in renaissance Italy* (London, 1979); Frederick Antal, *Florentine Painting and Its Social Background* (London, 1948);

For the history of Venice, see Frederic C. Lane, *Venice* (Baltimore, 1973); Lane and Mueller, *Money and Banking in Medieval and Renaissance Venice*, cited above; Gino Luzzato, *Storia economica di Venezia dall XI al XVI secolo* (Venice, 1961); William J. Bouwsma, *Venice and the Defense of Republican Liberty* (Berkeley, 1968); J. R. Hale, ed., *Renaissance Venice* (London, 1973).

On Pistoia, a model work of social history is David Herlihy, *Medieval and Renaissance Pistoia: The Social History of an Italian Town, 1200–1430* (New Haven, 1967); and *idem,* "Population, Plague, and Social Change in Rural Pistoia," *Economic History Review* 2d ser. 18 (1965) 225–44.

Genoa also has been fortunate in its historians. Among the leading works are V. Vitale, *Il commune del podestà a Genova* (Milan, 1951); T. O. De Negri, *Storia di Genova* (Milan, 1968); J. Heers, *Gênes au XVᵉ siècle* (Paris, 1961); John Day, *Les douanes de Gênes, 1376–77* (2 vols., Paris, 1963).

For Pavia, there is D. Zanetti, *Problemi alimentari di una economica preindustriale* (Turin, 1964), with good price series for the *quattrocento*. For southern Italy and Sicily, see A. Petino, *Aspetti e momenti di politica granari a Catania ed in Sicilia nel quattrocento* (Catania, 1952). Major multivolume histories of Milan, Mantua, Verona, and Brescia were published in the 1960s, but I have not found full-scale modern histories of Bologna or Perugia.

On Iberia, the leading works are V. Magalhaes-Godinho, *L'economie de l'Empire portugais aux XVᵉ et XVIᵉ siècles* (Paris, 1969); A. Santamaria Arandez, *Aportacion al estudio de la economia de Valencia durante el siglo XV* (Valencia, 1966); and the works of Vicens and Elliott cited above.

Among many excellent French local studies are Guy Bois, *Crise du féodalisme*, cited above; P. Wolff, *Commerces et merchands de Toulouse, vers 1350–vers 1450* (Paris, 1954); *idem, Les estimes toulousianes des XIV et XV siècles* (Toulouse, 1956); G. Sivery, *Structures agraires et vie rurale dans Le Hainaut à la fin du Moyen Age* (Lille, 1973); Latouche, *La vie en Bas Quercy du XIVe au XVIIIe siècle* (Paris, 1923); John Day, "Prix agricoles en Méditerranée à la fin du XIV$^{e'}$me siècle (1382)," *Annales E.S.C.* 16 (1961) 629–56; Yvonne Bezard, *La vie rurale dans le sud de la region parisienne de 1450 à 1560* (Paris, 1929).

For England in the fifteenth century, see F. R. H. Du Boulay, *An Age of Ambition: English Society in the Late Middle Ages* (New York, 1970); R. M. Hilton, *The Economic Development of Some Leicestershire Estates in the Fourteenth and Fifteenth Centuries* (London, 1947); J. A. Raftis, *the Estates of Ramsay Abbey* (Toronto, 1957); J. W. F. Hill, *Medieval Lincoln* (Cambridge, 1948); *idem, Tudor and Stuart Lincoln* (Cambridge, 1956); A. L. Rowse, *Tudor Cornwall* (London, 1941).

In Scandinavia, a great classic of local history is A. Holmsen, *Eidsvoll Bygds Historie* (2 vols., Oslo, 1950–61).

On the low countries, see H. van der Wee, *The Growth of the Antwerp Market and the European Economy, Fourteenth-Sixteenth Centuries* (3 vols., Louvain, 1963).

For the rise of the Ottoman Empire, see Franz Babinger, *Mehmed the Conqueror and His Time* (Princeton, 1978), 431; a lively survey in English is Patrick Balfour, Baron Kinross, *The Ottoman Centuries: The Rise and Fall of the Turkish Empire* (New York, 1977).

Biographical approaches to economic history in this period include Frederic C. Lane, *Andrea Barbarigo, Merchant of Venice, 1418–1449* (Baltimore, 1944); Iris Origo, *The Merchant of Prato: Francesco di Marco Datini, 1335–1410* (London, 1957); Gene Brucker, ed., *Two Memoirs of Renaissance Florence: the Diaries of Buonaccorso Pitti and Gregorio Dati* (New York, 1967); Florence de Roover, "Andrea Banchi, Florentine Silk Manufacturer and Merchant in the Fifteenth Century," *Studies in Medieval and Renaissance History* 3 (1966) 223–85; Henri Lapeyre, *Une famille de marchands: Les Ruiz* (Paris, 1955); Gotz Freiherr von Pölnitz, *Die Fugger* (Frankfurt am Main, 1960).

On price movements, in addition to general works listed above by Elsas for Germany, Pribram for Austria, Verlinden for Belgium, and Beveridge and Rogers for Britain, there is also a monographic literature specific to this period. For Britain it includes D. L. Farmer, "Prices and Wages, 1350–1500" in Edward Miller, ed., *The Agrarian History of England and Wales, vol. 3, 1348–1500* (Cambridge, 1988), 431–525.

For France, there are "La prix du froment à Rouen au XVe siècle," *Annales E.S.C.* 23 (1968) 1262–82; J. Meuvret, "Les prix des grains à Paris au XVe siècle et les origines de la mercuriale," *Paris et Ile-de-France* 2

458   *Bibliography*

(1960) 283–311; M. Baulant, "Le prix des grains à Paris de 1431 à 1788," *Annales E.S.C.* 23 (1968) 520–40; Guy Bois, "Compatabilité et histoire des prix: Le prix de froment à Rouen au XVᵉ siècle," *Annales E.S.C.* 23 (1968) 1262–68.

For Belgium, there is G. Sivéry, "Les profits agricoles au bas Moyen Age," *Annales E.S.C.* 31 (1976) 626. The classic work on Spanish prices in this period is Earl J. Hamilton, *Money, Prices, and Wages in Valencia, Aragon, and Navarre, 1351–1500* (Cambridge, Mass., 1936). Also helpful is Boaz Shoshan, "Money Supply and Grain Prices in Fifteenth-Century Egypt," *Economic History Review"* 36 (1983) 47–67.

On wages, in addition to works of Abel, Beveridge, d'Avenel, Elsas, Farmer, Phelps-Brown, Pribram, and Scholliers cited above, see E. Perroy, "Wage Labour in France in the Later Middle Ages," *Economic History Review* 2d ser. 8 (1955) 232–39; R. H. Hilton, *The Decline of Serfdom in Medieval England* (London, 1969).

On the fall of rent, there is C. A. Christensen, "Krisen pa Slesvig Domkapitels jordegods," *Historisk Tidsskrift* 11th ser. 6 (1960) 161–244.

Money and interest in the fifteenth century is the subject of John Day, "The Great Bullion Famine of the Fifteenth Century," *Past & Present* 29 (1978) 3–54; see also N. J. Mayhew, "Numismatic Evidence and Falling Prices in the Fourteenth Century," *Economic History Review* 2d ser. 27 (1974) 1–15; H. A. Miskimin, "Monetary Movements and Market Structure—Forces for Contraction in Fourteenth- and Fifteenth-Century England," *Journal of Economic History* 24 (1964) 470–490; J. Schreiner, *Pest og Prisfall i Senmiddelalderen* (Oslo, 1948); H. van Werveke, "Essor et déclin de la Flandre," in *Studi in onore di Gino Luzzato* (Milan, 1950); Harry A. Miskimin, *Money and Power in Fifteenth-Century France* (New Haven, 1984); idem, *Money, Prices, and Foreign Exchange in Fourteenth-Century France* (New Haven, 1963); A. Mackay, *Money, Prices, and Politics in Fifteenth-Century Castile* (London, 1981); P. Spufford, *Monetary Problems and Policies in the Burgundian Netherlands, 1433–1496* (Leiden, 1970); John H. A. Munro, *Wool, Cloth, and Gold: The Struggle for Bullion in the Anglo-Burgundian Trade, 1340–1478* (Brussels and Toronto, 1972); J. Richards, ed., *Precious Metals in the Later Medieval and Early Modern Worlds* (Durham, 1983); Raymond de Roover, *The Bruges Money Market around 1400* (Brussels, 1968); and F. C. Lane and R. C. Mueller, *Money and Banking in Medieval and Renaissance Venice* (Baltimore, 1985), with a good bibliography of the vast literature on monetary history in this period.

Banking is the subject of Raymond de Roover, *The Medici Bank: Its Organization, Management, Operations, and Decline* (New York, 1948); and idem, *The Rise and Decline of the Medici Bank* (Cambridge, 1963); and on northern Europe, Richard Ehrenberg, *Capital and Finance in the Age of the Renaissance* (New York, n.d.).

For political economy and fiscal movements, see Josef Rosen, "Prices and Public Finance in Basel, 1360–1535," *Economic History Review*, 2d ser. 25 (1972) 1–17; Anthony Molho, *Florentine Public Finances in the Early Renaissance* (Cambridge, 1971); political structure is the subject of Nicolai Rubenstein, *the Government of Florence under the Medici, 1434–1494* (Oxford, 1966).

On social structure, see Samuel Cohn, *The Laboring Classes of Renaissance Florence* (New York, 1980); E. Powell, *The Rising in East Anglia in 1381* (Cambridge, 1896); M. M. Postan, *Medieval Economy and Society*, 173; T. W. Page, *The End of Villeinage in England* (New York, 1900); R. H. Hilton, *The English Peasantry in the Later Middle Ages* (Oxford, 1975); C. C. Dyer, "A Redistribution of Incomes in Fifteenth Century England," *Past & Present* 39 (1968) 11–33; G. A. Holmes, *The Estates of the Higher Nobility in Fourteenth-Century England* (Cambridge, 1957); Brian Pullan, *Rich and Poor in Renaissance Venice: The Social Institutions of a Catholic State, to 1620* (Oxford, 1971).

On cultural trends during the Renaissance, see Ernst Cassirer, Paul Oscar Kristeller, and John Herman Randall Jr., *The Renaissance Philosophy of Man* (Chicago, 1948), 225; and Hans Baron, *The Crisis of Early Italian Renaissance* (2d ed., Princeton, 1966) Many scholars before Baron had anticipated this interpretation; one of the first was William Shepherd, *The Life of Poggio Bracciolini* (Liverpool, 1837), 458–461.

On the relationship between economic and cultural history in the Renaissance there are two books by Richard A. Goldthwaite: *Private Wealth in Renaissance Florence: A Study of Four Families* (Princeton, 1968) and *The Building of Renaissance Florence: An Economic and Social History* (Baltimore, 1980).

ᏋᎧ The Price Revolution of the Sixteenth Century

The idea of a price revolution in the sixteenth century was developed by German historians in the late nineteenth century. The pioneering works are Georg Wiebe, *Zur Geschichte der Preisrevolution des XVI. und XVII. Jahrhunderts* (Leipzig, 1895) and Julius Moritz Bonn, *Spaniens Niedergang während der Preisrevolution des 16. Jahrhunderts* (Stuttgart, 1896). This idea has spawned a very large literature, in which one finds the same array of interpretations as in other great waves: monetarist, market-centered, Malthusian, Marxist, climatological, ecological.

For many years the conventional wisdom was predominantly monetarist, as a consequence of work by American price historian Earl Hamilton. His major studies were *American Treasure and the Price Revolution in Spain, 1501–1650* (Cambridge, Mass., 1934) and *Money, Prices, and Wages in Valencia, Aragon, and Navarre, 1651–1800* (Cambridge, Mass., 1947). A respectful critique appears in Fernand Braudel, "En relisant Earl J. Hamilton: De l'histoire d'Espagne à l'histoire des prix," *Annales E.S.C.* 6 (1951) 202–06.

Fernand Braudel himself used a monetarist model in *The Mediterranean and the Mediterranean World in the Age of Philip II* 2 vol. (1946, tr. Reynolds Sian, London, 1972–3; Berkeley, 1995). He revised this interpretation in favor of a more market-centered approach in F. P. Braudel and F. Spooner, "Prices in Europe from 1450 to 1750," *The Cambridge Economic History of Europe* (Cambridge, 1967), 4:378–486.

A major study that qualifies the Hamilton thesis in important ways is Michel Morineau, *Incroyables gazettes et fabuleux métaux; Les retours des trésors américains d'après les gazettes hollandaises (XVIe–XVIIIe siècles)* (Paris, New York, and London, 1985); *idem,* "Des métaux précieux américains et de leur influence au XVIIe et XVIIIe siècle," *Bulletin de la Societé d'Histoire Moderne et Contemporaine* 15 (1977) 2–95; *idem,* "Histoire sans frontières: prix régionaux, prix nationaux, prix internationaux," *Annales E.S.C.* 24 (1969) 403–21; and other essays listed in the excellent bibliography to *Incroyables gazettes.*

Other historians in the mid-twentieth century preferred a Malthusian explanation, in which the growth of population was thought to have driven the revolution in prices. Two useful collections of articles on this debate are Peter Burke, ed., *Economy and Society in Early Modern Europe: Essays from Annales* (New York, 1972) and Peter Ramsay, ed., *The Price Revolution in Sixteenth-Century England* (London, 1971). Critiques of the literature include D. O. Flynn, "The 'Population Thesis' View of Inflation versus Economics and History," in Eddy van Cauwenberghe and Franz Irsigler, eds., *Münzprägung, Geldumlauf und Wechselkurse* (Budapest, 1982) 362–82; and *idem,* "Use and Misuse of the Quantity Theory of Money in Early Modern Historiography," *ibid.,* 382–418. Also helpful is H. A. Miskimin, "Population Growth and the Price Revolution in England," *Journal of European Economic History* 4 (1975) 179–86.

Marxist models include Robert Brenner, "Agrarian Class Structure and Economic Development in Pre-Industrial Europe," *Past & Present* 70 (1976) 30–75; and Trevor Aston and C. H. E. Philpin, eds., *The Brenner Debate: Agrarian Class Structure and Economic Development in Pre-Industrial Europe* (New York, 1985). A sociological model with a strong Marxist interpretation appears in Immanuel Wallerstein, *The Modern World-System: Capitalist Agriculture and the Origins of the European World Economy in the Sixteenth-Century* (New York, 1974).

Other useful works from various perspectives include Alexandre Chabert, "Encore la révolution des prix au XVIᵉ siècle," *Annales E.S.C.* 12 (1957); A. V. Judges, "A Note on Prices in Shakespeare's Time," *A Companion to Shakespeare Studies* (Cambridge, 1934); Walter Achilles, "Getreidepreise und Getreidehandelsbeziehungen europäischer Raüme im 16. und 17. Jahrhundert," *Zeitschrift für Agrargeschichte und Agrarsoziologie* 7 (1959) 32–55.

Few major processes in modern history have been better documented than the price revolution of the sixteenth century. Even so, there are inevitably a few academic unbelievers. Various expressions of skepticism appear in M. Morineau, "D'Amsterdam à Seville: De quelle realité l'histoire des prix est-il le miroir?" *Annales E.S.C.* 23 (1968) 178–205; Carlo Cipolla, "La prétendu 'révolution des prix': réflexions sur l'expérience italienne," *Annales E.S.C.* 10 (1955) 212–16; an expanded English version appears in Burke, ed., *Economy and Society in Early Modern Europe*, 43–54.

Many studies of sixteenth-century price movements have been made of national economies. For Spain, they include in addition to the work of Hamilton cited above, J. Nadal Oller, "La revolución de los precios españoles en el siglo XVI: Estado actual de la cuestión," *Hispania* 19 (1959) 503–29; J. H. Elliott, *Imperial Spain, 1469–1716* (New York, 1966); idem, *The Old World and the New, 1492–1650* (Cambridge, 1970); idem, "The Decline of Spain," *Past & Present* 20 (1961) 52–75; Jaime Vives Vicens with Jorge Nadal Oller, *An Economic History of Spain* (Princeton, 1969); idem, *Approaches to the History of Spain* (Berkeley, 1967); Earl J. Hamilton, "American Treasure and Andalusian Prices, 1503–1600: A Study in the Spanish Price Revolution, " *Journal of Economic and Business History* 1 (1928) 1–35; Pierre Chaunu and Huguette Chaunu, *Seville et l'Atlantique (1504–1650)* (Paris, c1977); a summary of findings in this vast work appears in Pierre Chaunu and Huguette Chaunu, "Économie Atlantique, économie mondiale (1504–1640)," *Journal of World History* (1953–54) 91–104, tr. as "The Atlantic Economy and the World Economy," in Peter Earle, ed., *Essays in European Economic History, 1500–1800* (Oxford, 1974), 113–26; Renate Pieper, *Die Preisrevolution in Spanien, 1500–1640: Neuere Forschungsergebnisse* (Wiesbaden, 1985).

For the price revolution in Portugal, see V. M. Godinho, *Prix et monnaies au Portugal* (Paris, 1955); Damaião Peres, *Historia monetária de D. João III* (Lisbon, 1957).

On Italy, there are Gino Parenti, *Prime ricerche sulla rivoluzione dei prèzzi in Firenze* (Florence, 1939); idem, *Prèzzi e mercato del grano a Siena* (Florence, 1942); Lucien Febvre, "La révolution des prix à Florence," *Annales d'Histoire Sociale* 2 (1940) 239–42; Richard A. Goldthwaite, "I prèzzi del grano a Firenze dal XIV al XVI secolo," *Quaderni Storici* 10 (1975) 5–36; Amintore Fanfani, "La rivoluzione dei prèzzi a Milano nel XVI e XVII secoli," *Giornale degli Economisti e Rivista di Statistica* 72 (1932) 465–82; *idem, Indagini sulla rivoluzione dei prèzzi* (Milan, 1940); Henri Hauser, "La révolution des prix à Milan au XVIᵉ et au XVIIᵉ siècle," *Annales d'Histoire Économique et Sociale* 4 (1934) 465–82; Giuseppe Coniglio, *Il regno di Napoli al tempo di Carlo V* (Naples, 1951); *idem, Il viceregno di Napoli nel secolo XVII* (Rome, 1955); idem, "La rivoluzione dei prèzzi nella città di Napoli nei Secoli XVI e XVII," *Atti della IXa riunione scientifica della Società italiana di statistica (Roma, 7–8 gennaio 1950)* (Spoleto, 1952); Jean Delumeau, *vie économique et sociale de Rome dans la seconde moitié du XVIᵉ siècle* (2 vols., Paris, 1957–59); Gabriele Lombardini, *Pane e denaro a Bassano: Prèzzi del grano e politica dell'approvigionamento dei cereali tra il 1501 e il 1799* (Venice, 1963); D. Bartolini, "Prèzzi e salari nel Comune di Portugruaro durante il secolo XVI," *idem., Contribuzione per una storia dei prèzzi e salari;* "La metida del frumento, vino ed oglio dal 1670 al 1685 nel commune di Portuguaro," all cited above; I. Jacobetti, *Monete e prèzzi a Cremona dal XVI al XVII secola* (Cremona, 1965); Ubaldo Meroni, *Cremona Fedilissima, studi di storia economica e amministrativa di Cremona durante la dominazione spagnola* (Cremona 1951); Gianluigi Barni, "Prèzzi, mercato e calmiere del pesce al principio del secolo XVI," *La Martinella di Milano* 11–12 (1957); Gino Barbieri, "L'introduzione del mais dall'America e la storia dei prèzzi in Italia," *Saggi di storia economica italiana* (Bari and Naples, 1948); Jacopo Stainero, *Patria del Friuli restaurata* (Udine, 1595); Giuseppe Mira, "I prèzzi dei cereali a Como dal 1512 al 1658," *Rivista Internazionale di Scienze Sociali* 12 (1941) 195–211.

For England, a helpful survey is R. B. Outhwaite, *Inflation in Tudor and Stuart England* (London, Melbourne, 1969; 2d ed., 1982); see also Frieda A. Nicolas, "The Assize of Bread in London during the Sixteenth Century," *Economic History* 2 (1930–33) 323–47; Y. S. Brenner, "The Inflation of Prices in Early Sixteenth-Century England," *Economic History Review* 2d ser. 14 (1961) 225–39; idem, "The Inflation of Prices in England, 1551–1650," *ibid.* 15 (1962) 266–84; J. D. Gould, "Y. S. Brenner on Prices: A Comment," *Economic History Review* 2d ser. 16 (1963) 351–60; *idem,* "The Price Revolution Reconsidered," *Economic History Review* 2d ser. 17 (1964–65) 249–66; P. Bowden, "Agricultural Prices, Farm Profits, and Rents," in Joan Thirsk, ed., *Agrarian History of England and Wales,* vol. 4, 593–695; C. E. Challis, "Spanish Bullion and Monetary Inflation in England in the Later Sixteenth Century," *Journal of European Economic History* 4 (1975) 381–92; R. A. Doughty, "Industrial Prices and Inflation in Southern England, 1401–1640," *Explorations in Economic History* 12 (1975) 177–92; John U. Nef, "Prices and Industrial Capitalism in France and England, 1540–1640," *Economic History Review* 7 (1937) 155–85; P. J. Bowden, "Agricultural Prices, Wages, Farm Profits, and Rents, 1500–1640," in *Eco-*

nomic Change: Wages, Profits, and Rents, 1500–1750 (Cambridge, 1990), 13–115.

An excellent study of Scottish trends in this period is Alex J. S. Gibson and T. C. Smout, *Prices, Food, and Wages in Scotland, 1550–1780* (New York, 1995).

On France, see F. Simiand, *Recherches anciennes et nouvelles sur le mouvement général des prix du XVIe au XIXe siècle* (Paris, 1932); André Liautey, *La hausse des prix et la lutte contre la vie chère en France au 16e siècle* (Paris, 1921); Frank C. Spooner, *The International Economy and Monetary Movements in France, 1493–1725* (Cambridge, 1972); P. Raveau, *essai sur la situation économique et l'état social en Poitou, au XVIe siècle* (Paris, 1931); idem, "La crise des prix au XVIe siècle en Poitou," *Revue Historique* 54 (1929) 1–44, 268–93; *L'agriculture et les classes paysannes: La transformation de la propriété dans le haut Poitou au XVIe siècle* (Paris, 1926); P. Chaunu, "Sur le front de l'histoire des prix au XVIe siècle: De la Mercuriale de Paris au port d'Anvers," *Annales E.S.C.* 4 (1961) 791–803; Marcel Lachiver, "Pres des grains a' Paris et à Meulan dans la second moitié du XVIe siècle (1573–1586)," *Annales E.S.C.* 30 (1975) 140–150; Robert Latouche, "Le prix du blé à Grenoble du XVe au XVIIIe siècle," *Revue d'Histoire Économique et Sociale* 20 (1932) 337–51; Henri Hauser, "La question des prix et des monnaies en Bourgogne dans la seconde moitié du XVIe siècle," *Annales de Bourgogne* 4 (1932) 7–21.

For the Netherlands and Belgium, see E. Scholliers, *Loonarbied en Honger de Levens-Standaard in de XVe en XVIe eeuw te Antwerpen* (Antwerp, 1960); J. Lejeune, *La Formation du Capitalisme moderne dans la Principaute de Liege au XVIe siècle* (Paris, 1939); C. Verlinden, J. Craeybeckx, and E. Scholliers, "Price and Wage Movements in Belgium in the Sixteenth Century," in Peter Burke, ed., *Economy and Society in Early Modern Europe: Essays from Annales;* Jan de Vries, *The Dutch Rural Economy in the Golden Age, 1500–1700* (New Haven, 1974); J. Lejeune, *La formation du capitalisme moderne dans la principauté de Liége au XVI siècles* (Paris, 1939).

For Germany, see M. J. Elsas, *Umriss einer Geschichte der Preise und Löhne in Deutschland vom ausgehenden Mittelalter bis zum Beginn des neunzehnten Jahrhunderts* (Leiden, 1936–49), a series of price studies centered on six German cities; idem, "Price Data from Munich, 1500–1700," *Economic History* 3 (1935) 63–78; W. Koppe, "Zur preisrevolution des 16 Jahrhunderts in Holstein," *Zeitschrift der Gesellschaft für Schleswig-Holsteinsche Geschichte* (1955); Hans Helmut Wächter, *Ostpreussiche Domänenvorwerke im 16 und 17 Jahrhundert* (Würzburg, 1958); Otto Dittmann, *Die Getreidepreise im der Stadt Leipzig im XVI und XVII Jahrhundert* (Leipzig, 1889); Wilhelm Koppe, "Zur Preisrevolution des 16. Jahrhunderts in Holstein,'' *Zeitschrift der Gesellschaft für Schleswig-Holsteinische Geschichte* 79 (1955); Volkmar von Arnim, *Krisen und Konjunkturen der Landwirtshaft in Schleswig-Holstein vom 16 bis zum 18 Jahrhundert* (Neumünster, 1957).

For eastern Europe, see Stanislas Hoszowski, ''The Revolution of Prices in Poland in the sixteenth and seventeenth Centuries,'' *Acta Polonia Historica* 2 (1959) 7–16; *idem,* ''L'Europe centrale devant la révolution des prix,'' *Annales E.S.C.* (1961), partly tr. as ''Central Europe and the Sixteenth- and Seventeenth-Century Price Revolution,'' in Burke, ed., *Economy and Society in Early Modern Europe; Essays from Annales,* 84–103. The same anthology also includes essays by Z. P. Bach on Hungary and Marian Laowist on economic movements throughout Europe; see also Jan Szpak, *Rewolucja cen XVI wieku a funkcjonamie godpodarki dworskiej w starostwach Prus Krolewskich* (Cracow, 1982), with a full summary in English; Tibor Wittman, *Az 'arforrdalom' e's a vilagpiaci kopcsolatok kezdeti mozzanatai (1566–1618)* [The price revolution and fundamental factors in market relationships throughout the world] (Budapest, 1957); for Russia, see Jerome Blum, ''Prices in Russia in the Sixteenth Century,'' *Journal of Economic History* 16 (1956) 182–99.

Scandinavian prices are studied in Ingrid Hammarström's excellent essay, ''The 'Price Revolution of the Sixteenth Century': Some Swedish Evidence,'' *Scandinavian Economic History Review* 5 (1957) 118–54, which is also one of the best overviews of the price revolution in general.

On the Middle East, see O. L. Barkan, ''The Price Revolution of the Sixteenth Century: A Turning Point in the Economic History of the Near East,'' *International Journal of Middle Eastern Studies* 6 (1975) 3–28; and K. N. Chaudhuri, *Trade and Civilisation in the Indian Ocean: An Economic History from the Rise of Islam to 1750* (New York, 1985).

On price relatives, a valuable work is Clyde George Reed, ''Price Data and European Economic History: England, 1300–1600,'' (thesis, University of Washington, 1972); also R. A. Doughty, ''Industrial Prices and Inflation in Southern England, 1401–1640'' *Explorations in Economic History* 12 (1975) 177–92.

On rates of change and fluctuations, a helpful study is Jeanne Tits-Dieuaide, ''L'evolution du prix du blé dans quelques villes d'Europe occidentale du XVᵉ au XVIIIᵉ siècle,'' *Annales E.S.C.* 42 (1987) 529–48.

On wages and the cost of living, in addition to the work of Abel, Phelps-Brown, d'Avenel, and Gibson and Smout cited above, a major work is Steve Rappaport, *Worlds within Worlds: Structures of Life in Sixteenth-Century London* (New York and London, 1989). Older studies include B. L. Hutchins, ''Notes towards a History of London Wages,'' *Economic Journal* 9 (1899) 599–605, and 10 (1900) 103–4; E. H. Phelps-Brown and Sheila V. Hopkins, ''Wage-Rates and Prices: Evidence for Population Pressure in the Sixteenth

Century,'' *Economica* 24 (1957) 289–306; and *idem*, ''Builders' Wage Rates, Prices, and Population: Some Further Evidence,'' *Economica* 26 (1959) 18–38. An English study of wages that quarrels with the Phelps-Brown-Hopkins index is D. Woodward, ''Wage Rates and Living Standards in Pre-Industrial England,'' *Past & Present* 91 (1981) 28–46.

For wage movements in other nations, see Earl J. Hamilton, ''Wages and Subsistence on Spanish Treasure Ships, 1503–1660,'' *Journal of Political Economy* (1929); Hertha Hon-Firnberg, *Lohnarbeiter und freie Lohnarbeit im Mittelalter und zu Beginn der Neuzeit* (Baden b. Wein, 1935); M. Baulant, ''Les salaires du Bâtiment, 1490–1726,'' cited above; E. Scholliers, *De Levenstandaard in de XVe en XVIe eeuw to Antwerpen* (Antwerp, 1960); Aldo de Maddalena, ''Preise, Löhne unde Goldwesen im Verlauf der wirtschaftlichen Entwicklung Mailands,'' in Ingomar Bog, ed., *Wirtschaftliche und soziale Strukturen im saekularen Wandel* (Hanover, 1974); Brian Pullan, ''Wage Earners in the Venetian Economy, 1550–1630,'' *Economic History Review* 16 (1964) 407–26; Cristóbal Espejo, ''La carestia de la vida en el siglo XVI y medios de abarataria,'' *Revista de Archivos, Bibliotecas y Museos*, 24–25 (1920–21); B. H. Putnam, ''Northamptonshire Wage Assessment of 1560 and 1667,'' *Economic History Review* 1 (1927–28) 124–34.

On population movements, see Edward Anthony Wrigley and Roger S. Schofield, *The Population History of England, 1541–1871* (New York and Cambridge, 1989), 566; Julian Cornwall, ''English Population in the Early Sixteenth Century,'' *Economic History Review* 23 (1970) 32–44; M. M. Postan, ''Some Economic Evidence of Declining Population in the Later Middle Ages,'' *Economic History Review* 2d ser. 2 (1949–50) 221–46; F. J. Fisher, ''Influenza and Inflation in Tudor England,'' *Economic History Review* 2d ser. 18 (1965) 120–29.

On climate, in addition to the work of Le Roy Ladurie cited above, see Micheline Baulant, Emmanuel Le Roy Ladurie, and Michel Demonet, ''Une synthése provisoire: Les vendages du XVe au XIXe siècle,'' *Annales E.S.C.* 33 (1978) 763–71; Micheline Baulant and Emmanuel Le Roy Ladurie, ''Les dates de vendages au XVIe siècle . . . ,'' *Mélanges en l'honneur de Fernand Braudel: Methodologie de l'histoire et des sciences humaines* (Toulouse, 1973); C. Harrison, ''Grain Price Analysis and Harvest Qualities, 1465–1634,'' *Agricultural History Review* 19 (1971) 135–55.

Monetarist interpretations are revived with various shades of enthusiasm in Dennis O. Flynn, ''A New Perspective on the Spanish Price Revolution: The Monetary Approach to the Balance of Payments,'' *Explorations in Economic History* 15 (1978) 388–406; D. N. McCloskey, *Journal of Political Economy* 80 (1972) 1332–35; D. L. Gadiel and M. E. Falkus, ''Comment on the 'Price Revolution','' *Australian Economic History Review* 9 (1969) 9–16.

On the money supply the literature is very large; see, in addition to works of Hamilton cited above, C. H. Haring, ''American Gold and Silver Production in the First Half of the Sixteenth-Century," *Quarterly Journal of Economics* 29 (1915) 433–79; John U. Nef, "Silver Production in Central Europe, 1450–1618," *Journal of Political Economy* 49 (1914) 575–91; Fernand Braudel, "Monnaies et Civilisations: De l'or du Soudan à l'argent d'Amerique," *Annales E.S.C.* 1 (1946) 9–22; and A. Attman, *The Bullion Flow between Europe and the East, 1000–1750* (Goteborg, 1981).

English money is the subject of Albert Feaveryear, *The Pound Sterling: A History of English Money* (2d ed., revised by E. Victor Morgan, Oxford, 1963); G. D. Gould, *The Great Debasement* (Oxford, 1970); C. E. Challis, "Currency and the Economy in Mid-Tudor England," *Economic History Review* 25 (1972) 313–22; J. D. Gould, "The Great Debasement and the Supply of Money," *Australian Economic History Review* 13 (1973) 177–89; idem, "Currency and Exchange Rate in Sixteenth-Century England," *Journal of European Economic History* 2 (1973) 149–59; C. E. Challis, *The Tudor Coinage* (New York and Manchester, 1978); idem, *Currency and the Economy of Tudor and Early Stuart England* (Oxford, 1989); idem, ed., *A New History of the Royal Mint* (Cambridge, 1992).

On France the leading study is Frank C. Spooner, *The International Economy and Monetary Movements in France, 1493–1725* (Cambridge, Mass., 1972).

Italian monetary history in this period includes Carlo Cipolla, *La moneta a Firenze nel cinquecento* (Bologna, 1987); idem, *Mouvements monétaires dans l'état de Milan (1580–1700* (Paris, 1952); G. Pesce and G. Felloni, *Le monete genovesi* (Genoa, 1975).

The difficult problem of velocity, the most elusive term in the monetarist equation, is discussed in J. A. Goldstone, "Monetary versus Velocity Interpretation of the 'Price Revolution': A Comment," *Journal of Economic History* 51 (1991) 176–81; and N. J. Mayhew, "Population, Money Supply, and the Velocity of Circulation in England, 1300–1700," *Economic History Review* 2d ser., 48 (1995) 238–57.

Fiscal factors are discussed in Alvaro Castillo Pintado, "Dette flotante et dette consolidée en Espagne de 1557 à 1600," *Annales E.S.C.*, 18 (1963) 745–59; Charles J. Jago, "The Influence of Debt on the Relations between Crown and Aristocracy in Seventeenth-Century Castile," *Economic History Review* 2d ser. 26 (1973) 218–36; Ladislas Reitzer, "Some Observations on Castilian Commerce and Finance in the Sixteenth-Century," *Journal of Modern History* 32 (1960) 213–23; Bernard Schapper, *Les rentes au XVIe siècle: Histoire d'un instrument de crédit* (Paris, 1957).

On money and banking and means of payment, a pathbreaking work is Marie-Thérèse Boyer-Xambeu, Ghislain Deleplace, and Lucien Azodi, *Private Money & Public Currencies: the Sixteenth Century Challenge* (Paris, 1986; Eng. tr. Armonk, N.Y., 1994)

The movement of interest rates is followed in Sidney Homer, *A History of Interest Rates* (2d ed., New Brunswick, 1977).

For the history of land, rent, and real estate prices, see Eric Kerridge, "The Movement of Rent, 1540–1640," *Economic History Review* 2d ser. 6 (1953–54) 16–34; H. G. Koenigsberger, "Property and the Price Revolution (Hainault, 1474–1573)," *Economic History Review* 2d ser. 9 (1956) 1–15; David E. Vassberg, "The Sale of 'Tierras Baldías' in Sixteenth-Century Castile," *Journal of Modern History* 47 (1975) 629–54; idem, "The *Tierras Baldías:*Community Property and Public Lands in Sixteenth-Century Castile," *Agricultural History* 48 (1974) 383–401; D. Zolla, "Les variations du revenu et du prix des terres en France au XVIIᵉ et XVIIIᵉ siècles," *Annales de l'École Libre des Sciences Politiques* (1893–94); Helen Nader, "Noble Income in Sixteenth-Century Castile: The Case of the Marquises of Mondejar, 1480–1580," *Economic History Review* 2d ser. 30 (1977) 411–28; Emmanuel Le Roy Ladurie, "Changes in Parisian Rents from the End of the Middle Ages to the Eighteenth Century," in *The Territory of the Historian* (Chicago, 1973), 61–75.

Outstanding among many local and regional studies for this period are Emmanuel Le Roy Ladurie, *Les paysans de Languedoc* (2 vols., Paris, 1966) and Carla Rahn Phillips, *Ciudad Real, 1500–1700; Growth, Crisis, and Readjustment in the Spanish Economy* (Cambridge, 1979).

On social disturbances during the price revolution, see Bob Scribner and Gerhard Benecke, *The German Peasant War of 1525—New Viewpoints* (London, 1979); Pieter Geyl, *The Revolt of the Netherlands, 1555–1609* (1932, New York, 1966; 2d ed., London, 1966); Perez Zagorin, *Rebels and Rulers, 1500–1660* (2 vols., Cambridge, 1982), 1:122–39.

On contemporary responses and the development of monetary theory in the sixteenth-century, see Marjorie Grice-Hutchinson, *The School of Salamanca: Readings in Spanish Monetary Theory, 1544–1605* (Oxford, 1952); Jean Bodin, *La réponse de maistre Jean Bodin, Avocat en le Cour, au paradox de Monsieur Malestroit . . .* (1568; ed. Henri Hauser, Paris, 1932); idem, "Les 'Coutumes' considérees comme source de l'histoire des prix d'après Jean Bodin," *Revue d'Histoire Économique et Sociale* 19 (1931); other early expressions of the quantity theory include Noel du Fail, *Balivernes et contes d'Entrepal* (1548); Francisco Lopez de Gomara, *Annals of the Emperor Charles V* (Oxford, 1557); [Thomas Smith?] *Discourse of the Common Weal* (London, 1581); Gerard de Malynes, *A Treatise of the Canker of England's Commonwealth* (London?, 1601); and the same author's *England's View, in the Unmasking of two Paradoxes; with a Replication unto the Answer of Maister John Bodine* (1603, London; New York, 1972). Some of these works are discussed in A. E. Munroe, *Monetary Theory before Adam Smith* (1923; New York, 1966); R. H. Tawney and Eileen Power, *Tudor Economic Docu-*

ments (3 vols., London, 1924); George Hakewill, *An Apologie or Declaration of the Power and Providence of God in the Government of the World* (2d ed., Oxford, 1630); Paul Harsin, *les doctrine monétaires et finacières en France du XVIe au XVIIIe siècle* (Paris, 1928); J. Y. Le Branchu, *Ecrits notables sur la monnaie, XVIe siècle.*

Other relations between social and economic history are explored in C. G. A. Clay, *Economic Expansion and Social Change: England, 1500–1700* (Cambridge, 1984); J. A. Goldstone, "Urbanization and Inflation: Lessons from the English Price Revolution of the Sixteenth and Seventeenth Centuries," *American Journal of Sociology* 89 (1984) 1122–60.

On cultural and economic history, see William J. Callahan, *Honor, Commerce, and Industry in Eighteenth-Century Spain* (Boston, 1972); L. A. Clarkson, "Inflation and the Moral Order," *History Today* 36 (1986) 10–14; Frances Elizabeth Baldwin, *Sumptuary Legislation and Personal Regulation in England* (Baltimore, 1926).

⁂ The Crisis of the Seventeenth Century

General surveys of this subject include Roland Mousnier, *Les XVIe et XVIIe Siècles* (Paris, 1954, 4th ed. 1965; rev. ed. London, 1976); Henry Kamen, *The Iron Century: Social Change in Europe, 1550–1660* (1972, New York, rev. ed., London, 1976); and Theodore K. Rabb, *The Struggle for Stability in Early Modern Europe* (New York, 1975), with bibliographical notes and appendix.

Two indispensable anthologies of journal literature on the general crisis are Trevor Aston, ed., *Crisis in Europe, 1560–1660* (New York, 1965) and Geoffrey Parker and Lesley M. Smith, eds., *The General Crisis of the Seventeenth Century* (1978, London, 1985). Another major essay is Josef Polisensky, "The Thirty-Years' War and the Crises and Revolutions of Seventeenth-Century Europe," *Past & Present* 39 (1968) 34–63.

Historiographical essays include Theodore K. Rabb, "The Effects of the Thirty Years War on the German Economy," *Journal of Modern History* 34 (1962) 40–51; Sheilagh C. Ogilvie, "Historiographical Review: Germany and the Seventeenth Century Crisis," *Historical Journal* 35 (1992) 417–41; and John Theibault, "Towards a New Sociocultural History of the Rural World of Early Modern Germany" *Central European History* 24 (1991), 304–24.

The idea of a "general crisis" in the seventeenth century is challenged by E. H. Kossmann, "Trevor Roper's 'General Crisis,'" *Past & Present* 18 (1960) 8–11. With the progress of demographic and economic research, many scholars have now come to accept the idea of a general crisis in a sense more profound than political historians originally intended.

Marxist approaches appear in Eric Hobsbawm, "The Overall Crisis of the European Economy in the Seventeenth Century,'' *Past & Present* 5 (1954) 33–53; Immanuel Wallerstein, ''Y a-t-il une crise du XVIIᵉ siècle?'' *Annales E.S.C.* 34 (1979) 126–44; B. F. Porshnev, *Frantziia, Angliiskaia Revoliutsiia i Evropeiskaia Politika* (*v' Ceredina XVII*) (Moscow, 1970), from which excerpts for English readers appear in P. Dukes, ''Russia and Mid-Seventeenth Century Europe: Some Comments on the Work of B. F. Porschnev,'' *European Studies Review* 4 (1970) 81–88; Witold Kula, *Théorie économique du système féodal; Pour un modéle de l'économie polonaise XVIᵉ–XVIIIᵉ siècles* (Paris, 1970); Perry Anderson, *Lineages of the Absolutist State* (London, 1974); and Immanuel Wallerstein, *The Modern World-System* (New York, 1974).

Malthusian models appear in Pierre Goubert, ''Historical Demography and the Reinterpretation of Early Modern French History,'' *Journal of Interdisciplinary History* 1 (1970) 37–48; Wilhelm Abel, *Massenarmut und Hungerkrisen im vorindustriellen Europa* (Hamburg, 1974); Andrew Appleby, *Famine in Tudor and Stuart England* (Stanford, 1978); François Lebrun, ''Les crises démographiques en France aux XVIIᵉ at XVIIIᵉ siècles,'' *Annales E.S.C.* 35 (1980) 205–25; Luis Granjel, ''Las epidemias de peste en España durante el siglo XVII,'' *Cuadernos de Historia de la Medicina Española* 3 (1964) 19–40; Bernard Vincent, ''Les pestes dans le royaume de Grenade aux XVIᵉ et XVIIᵉ siècles,'' *Annales E.S.C.* 24 (1969) 1511–13. For a critique, see D. M. Palliser, ''Tawney's Century: Brave New World or Malthusian Trap?'' *Economic History Review* 2d ser. 35 (1982) 339–53; Carlo M. Cipolla, *Cristofano and the Plague: A Study in the History of Public Health in the Age of Galileo* (Berkeley, 1973); with a critique by George Rosen in *Renaissance Quarterly* 28 (1975) 83–86; B. Bennassar, *Recherches sur les grandes épidemies dans le nord de l'Espagne à la fin du XVIe siècle* (Paris, 1969);

An ecological approach within a broadly Malthusian frame appears in Victor Skipp, *Crisis and Development: An Ecological Case Study of the Forest of Arden, 1570–1694* (Cambridge, 1978). Models of exogenous climate change are explored in Emmanuel Le Roy Ladurie, *Times of Feast, Times of Famine: A History of Climate since the Year 1000* (Garden City, 1967; New York, 1971), Gustaf Utterstrom, ''Climatic Fluctuations and Population Problems in Early Modern History,'' *Scandinavian Economic History Review* 3 (1955) 27–28; and the works of H. H. Lamb, cited above.

For a cultural history of the crisis, see Theodore K. Rabb, *The Struggle for Stability in Early Modern Europe* (New York, 1975). Other works include Alexander Augustine Parker, *Literature and the Delinquent: The Picaresque Novel in Spain and Europe, 1599–1753* (Edinburgh, 1967); R. Mandrou, ''La baroque européen: Mentalité pathétique et révolution sociale,'' *Annales E.S.C.* 15 (1960) 898–914; G. Scholem, *Sabbatai Sevi: The Mystical Messiah, 1626–1676* (Princeton, 1973).

For one great work of literature in its historical context see Pierre Vilar,

"Le temps du Quichotte," *Europe* 34 (1956) 3–16, available to English readers as "The Age of Don Quixote," in Peter Earle, ed., *Essays in European Economic History, 1500–1800* (Oxford, 1974) 100–12; A classic of German literature by a German soldier (actually a regimental clerk) in the Thirty Years' War is H. J. C. von Grimmelhausen, *The Adventurous Simplicissimus* tr. A. S. Goodrick (Lincoln, 1962); a discussion is Hans Dieter Gebauer, *Grimmelshausens Bauerdarstellung: Literarische Sozialkritik und ihr Publikum* (Marburg, 1977).

Most local and regional studies tend to combine elements of these various Marxist, Malthusian, cultural approaches in pluralistic interpretations, which in the 1970s and 1980s were increasingly stressing material causes and cultural results. See, e.g., Carla Rahn Phillips, *Ciudad Real, 1500–1700,* cited above; William Hunt, *The Puritan Movement: The Coming of Revolution in an English County* [Essex] (Cambridge, Mass., 1983); Gerald Lyman Soliday, *A Community in Conflict: Frankfurt Society in the Seventeenth and Early Eighteenth Centuries* (Hanover, 1974); Emmanuel Le Roy Ladurie, *Paysans de Languedoc,* cited above; Pierre Goubert, *Beauvais et le Beauvaisis de 1600 à 1730* (Paris, 1960); B. Bennasar, *Valladolid au siècle d'or* (Paris, 1969); Rudolf Schlögl, *Bauern, Krieg, und Staat: Oberbayerische Bauernwirtschaft und frühmoderner Staat im 17. Jahrhundert* (Göttingen, 1988).

On economic aspects of the crisis, a good overview is Jan de Vries, *The Economy of Europe in an Age of Crisis, 1600–1750* (Cambridge, 1976); see also Carlo M. Cipolla, ed., *The Fontana Economic History of Europe,* vol. 2, *The Sixteenth and Seventeenth Centuries* (Glasgow, 1974; Hassocks and New York, 1976–77). Specially helpful is an excellent survey by Ruggiero Romano, "Tra XVI e XVII secolo. Una crisi economica: 1619–1622," *Rivista Storica Italiana* 74 (1962) 480–531, which is accessible to English readers as "Between the Sixteenth and Seventeenth Centuries: The Economic Crisis of 1619–22," in Parker and Smith, *General Crisis,* 165–225; see also Romano's "Encore la crise de 1619–1622," *Annales E.S.C.* 19 (1964) 31–37. Many useful essays on economic aspects of the crisis are brought together in Peter Earle, ed., *Essays in European Economic History* (Oxford, 1974). Some of the relevant economic data are published in Geoffrey Parker and C. H. Wilson, eds., *Introduction to the Sources of European Economic History, 1500–1800* (London, 1977).

Specialized economic studies include B. E. Supple, *Commercial Crisis and Change in England, 1600–1642: A Study in the Instability of a Mercantile Economy* (Cambridge, 1959); J. D. Gould, "The Trade Depression of the Early 1620s," *Economic History Review* 7 (1954) 81–90; *idem,* "The Trade Crisis of the Early 1620s and English Economic Thought," *Journal of Economic History* 15 (1955) 121–33; Rene Baehrel, *Une croissance: La Basse Provence rurale . . .* (Paris, 1961); Huguette Chaunu and Pierre Chaunu, *Séville et l'Atlantique (1504–1650)* (8 vols., Paris, 1955–59); Nina Ellinger

Bang, *Tabeller over Skibsfart og Varentransport gennem Oresund* (vols. I and 3, Copenhagen, 1906, 1923); F. C. Lane, "La marine marchande et le trafic maritime de Venise . . . ," in *Les Sources de l'Histoire Maritime* . . . (Paris, 1962); Jan de Vries, *The Dutch Rural Economy in the Golden Age, 1500–1700* (New Haven, 1974; S. C. van Kampen, *De Rotterdamse particuliere Scheepsbouw in de tijd van de Republiek* (Assen, 1953); Johannes Gerard van Dillen, *Bronnen tot de Geschiedenis van het Bedrijfsleven en het Gildewezen van Amsterdam* (3 vols., The Hague, 1929–33); Domenico Sella, "The Two Faces of the Lombard Economy in the Seventeenth Century," in Frederick Krantz and Paul M. Hohenberg, eds., *Failed Transitions in Modern Industrial Society* (Montreal, 1975), 11–15; R. Gaettens, *Die Zeit der Kipper und Wipper der Inflationem* (Munich, 1955); N. W. Posthumus, "The Tulip Mania in Holland in the Years 1636 and 1637," *Journal of Economic and Business History* I (1929) 434–55; Richard T. Rapp, *Industry and Economic Decline in Seventeenth-Century Venice* (Cambridge, 1976); L. Nottin, *Recherches sur les variations des prix dans le Gâtinais du XVIᵉ au XIXᵉ siècle* (Paris, 1935); E. Pannier, *Prix des grains sur le marché d'Abbeville depuis l'année 1590* (Abbeville, 1865); P. Chaunu, "Au XVIIᵉ siècle, rythmes et coupures: À propos de la Mercuriale de Paris," *Annales E.S.C.* 6 (1964) 1171; Jean Meuvret, "Conjuncture et crise au XVIIᵉ siècle: L'example des prix milanais," *Annales d'Histoire Économique et Sociale* 8 (1953) 215–219.

On political and social aspects of the general crisis, there is a very large literature. For general studies of internal disorder and revolution throughout Europe, see Roger Bigelow Merriman, *Six Contemporaneous Revolutions* (Oxford, 1938), the expansion of a lecture with the same title (Glasgow, 1937); also Jack P. Greene and Robert Forster, *Preconditions of Revolution in Early Modern Europe* (Baltimore, 1970); C. S. L. Davies, "Peasant Revolts in France and England: A Comparison," *Agricultural History Review* 21 (1973) 122–34; Roland Mousnier, *Fureurs paysannes: Les paysans dans les révoltes du XVIIᵉ Siècle (France, Russie, Chine)* (Paris, 1967, English tr., 1971); M. O. Gately, A. L. Moote, and J. E. Wills Jr., "Seventeenth-Century Peasant 'Furies': Some Problems of Comparative History," *Past & Present* 51 (1971) 63–80; a survey of this period from another perspective is Perez Zagorin, *Rebels and Rulers, 1500–1660* (2 vols., Cambridge, 1982).

The effect of war is a subject of historical controversy. Werner Sombart, *Krieg und Kapitalismus* (1913, Munich; New York, 1975) argued that war promoted economic development in this period; arguments to the contrary are in John U. Nef, "War and Economic Progress, 1540–1640," *Economic History Review* 12 (1942) 13–38; and *idem, War and Human Progress* (Cambridge, Mass., 1950); see also Frederic C. Lane, "Economic Consequences of Organized Violence," *Journal of Economic History* 18 (1958) 401–17. Another historiographical problem in this period concerns the effect of the crisis on warfare. For this question see Geoffrey Parker, "The 'Military

Revolution, 1560–1660': A Myth?'' *Journal of Modern History* 48 (1976) 195–214.

On the Thirty Years' War, the standard works are Günther Franz, *Der Dreissigjährige Kreig und das deutsche Volk* (4th ed., Stuttgart, 1978); Cecily Veronica Wedgwood, *The Thirty Years' War* (London, 1938); Siegfried H. Steinberg, *The Thirty Years' War and the Conflict for European Hegemeny, 1660–1660* (New York, 1966); Josef V. Polisensky, *The Thirty Years' War* (Berkeley, 1971); Henry Kamen, "The Economic and Social Consequences of the Thirty Years' War,'' *Past & Present* 39 (1968) 44–48; T. K. Rabb, "The Effects of the Thirty Years' War on the German Economy.'' *Journal of Modern History* 34 (1962) 40–51; F. L. Carsten, "Was There an Economic Decline in Germany before the Thirty Years' War?'' *English Historical Review* 71 (1956) 240–47; John C. Theibault, *German Villages in Crisis: Rural Life in Hesse-Kassel and the Thirty Years' War, 1580–1720* (Atlantic Highlands, N.J., 1995).

For internal disorder in France, see René Pillorget, *Les mouvements insurrectionnels de Provence entre 1596 et 1715* (Paris, 1975); Boris Porschnev, *Les soulèvements populaires en France de 1623 à 1648* (1948, French translation, Paris, 1963); Sal Alexander Westrich, *The Ormée of Bordeaux: A Revolution during the Fronde* (Baltimore, 1972); Phillip A. Knachel, *England and the Fronde* (Ithaca, 1967); Alanson Lloyd Moote, *The Revolt of the Judges: the Parlement of Paris and the Fronde, 1643–1652* (Princeton, 1972); Robert Mandrou, "Les soulèvements populaires et la société française du XVIIe siècle,'' *Annales E.S.C.* 14 (1959) 756–65; *idem, Classes et luttes de classes en France au début de XVIIe siècle* (Messina, 1965). Many essays are brought together in P. J. Coveney, ed., *France in Crisis, 1620–1675* (London, New York, 1977).

On the English civil wars the standard work is still S. R. Gardiner, *History of England from the Accession of James I to the Outbreak of the Civil War* (rev. ed., 10 vols., London, 1883–84); *idem, The Great Civil War* (rev. ed., 4 vols., London, 1893); *idem, History of the Commonwealth and Protectorate, 1649–1656* (rev. ed., London, 1903); continued by Charles Harding Firth, *The Last Years of the Protectorate, 1656–1658* (2 vols., London, 1909); and completed in Godfrey Davies, *The Restoration of Charles II, 1658–1660* (Oxford, 1969). More recent scholarship is surveyed in Christopher Hill, *Puritanism and Revolution* (London, 1958); Lawrence Stone, *The Causes of the English Revolution, 1529–1642* (London, 1972); John Morrill, *The Revolt of the Provinces* (London, 1976, 1980).

On revolutions within the English revolution, see G. E. Aylmer, ed., *The Levellers in the English Revolution* (Ithaca, 1975); Arthur Leslie Morton, *The World of the Ranters: Religious Radicalism in the English Revolution* (London, 1970); C. S. L. Davies, "Les révoltes populaires en Angleterre (1500–1700),'' *Annales E.S.C.* 24 (1969) 24–60; contemporary works of relevance here include R. Mentet de Salmonet, *Histoire des troubles de la Grande Bretagne* (Paris, 1649; English tr., London, 1735); Thomas Hobbes, *Leviathan* (London, 1651).

On English social structure, contemporary writings include Thomas Smith, *De Republica Anglorum* (1583), ed. Mary Dewar (Cambridge, 1982); William Harrison, *The Description of England* (1587), ed. George Edelen (Ithaca, 1968); Thomas Wilson, *The State of England, 1600*, ed. F. J. Fisher (1936).

On Spain, see Michel R. Weisser, *The Peasants of the Montes: the Roots of Rural Rebellion in Spain* (Chicago, 1976); J. H. Elliott, *The Revolt of the Catalans* (Cambridge, 1963); Sancho de Moncada, *Restauracion Politica de España* (1619, ed. J. Vilar (Madrid 1974); on the Portuguese revolution, H. V. Livermore, *A New History of Portugal* (Cambridge, 1969).

Italian disorders are examined in H. G. Koenigsberger, "The Revolt of Palermo in 1647," *Cambridge Historical Journal* 8 (1944–46) 133–47; *idem, Estates and Revolutions: Essays in Early Modern European History* (Ithaca, 1971); Rosario Villari, *La revolta antispagnola a Napoli, le origini (1585–1647)* (Bari, 1967).

For eastern Europe, see Jerzy Topolski, "Economic Decline in Poland from the Sixteenth to the Eighteenth Centuries," in Peter Earle, ed., *Essays in European Economic History* (Oxford, 1974); M. Malowist, *Croissance et regression en Europe, XIVᵉ–XVIIᵉ siècles* (Paris, 1972); M. Malowist, "Poland, Russia, and Western Trade in the Fifteenth to the Seventeenth Centuries," *Past & Present* 13 (1958) 26–41. On unrest in Hungary, see L. Makkai, "The Hungarian Puritans and the English Revolution," *Acta Historica* 5 (1958) 1–27.

For the time of troubles in Russia, see V. O. Kliuchevskii, *A Course in Russian History: The Seventeenth Century*, the third volume of a historical classic (1907; Chicago, 1968), which is organized around a crisis model.

On Scandinavia, see four works by Michael Roberts, *The Swedish Imperial Experience, 1560–1718* (Cambridge, 1979, 1984); *The Early Vasas: A History of Sweden, 1523–1611* (Cambridge, 1968); *Sweden as a Great Power: Government, Society and Foreign Policy, 1611–1697* (New York, 1968); and "Queen Christina and the General Crisis of the Seventeenth Century," *Past & Present* 22 (1962) 36–59.

For the seventeenth-century crisis outside Europe, see A. A. M. Adshead, "The Seventeenth-Century General Crisis in China," *France-Asie* 24 (1970) 251–65; E. J. Van Kley, "News from China: Seventeenth-Century European Notices of the Manchu Conquest," *Journal of Modern History* 45 (1973) 561–82; Ping-Ti Ho, *Studies on the Population of China, 1368–1953* (Cambridge, 1959), James Bunyon Parsons, *The Peasant Rebellions of the Late Ming Dynasty* (Tucson, 1970); Jonathan D. Spence, *The Death of Woman Wang* (New York, 1978); Helen Dunstan, "The Late Ming Epidemics: A Preliminary Survey,'' *Ch'ing-shih Wen-t'i* 3 (1975) 1–59; Ray Huang, *1587, A Year of No Significance: The Ming Dynasty in Decline* (New Haven, 1981).

On the general crisis in the Middle East, see Bruce McGowan, *Economic Life in Ottoman Europe: Taxation, Trade and the Struggle for Land, 1600–1800* (Cambridge, 1981); Murat Cizakca, ''Price History and the Bursa Silk Industry: A Study in Ottoman Industrial Decline, 1550–1650,'' *Journal of Economic History* 40 (1980) 533–50; Omer L. Barkan, ''The Social Consequences of Economic Crisis in Later Sixteenth-Century Turkey,'' in *Social Aspects of Economic Development* (Istanbul, 1964); *idem*, ''The Price Revolution of the Sixteenth-Century: A Turning Point in the Economic History of the Middle East,'' *International Journal of Middle East Studies* 6 (1975) 3–28.

On the general crisis in America, see P. Chaunu, ''Brésil et Atlantique au XVIIᵉ siècle,'' *Annales E.S.C.* 16 (1961) 1176–1207; Arthur Aiton, ''Early American Price-Fixing Legislation,'' *Michigan Law Review* 25 (1926); Chester L. Gutrie, ''Colonial Economy, Trade, Industry, and Labor in Seventeenth-Century Mexico City,'' *Revista de Historia de America* 5 (1939).

≥● The Equilibrium of the Enlightenment

Price and wage movements through this period are discussed in Wilhelm Abel, *Agrarkrisen und Agrarkonjunktur* who understands this era (mistakenly) as a time of prolonged depression but adds much to our understanding in other ways. This interpretation partly reflected movements in central Europe, which were less positive than in the Atlantic nations. Other studies show more positive patterns; see E. H. Phelps-Brown and Sheila Hopkins, ''Seven Centuries of the Prices of Consumables, Compared with Builders' Wage-Rates,'' *Economica* 23 (1956) 296–314; d'Avenel, *Histoire économique de . . . tous les prix en général*, vol. 2.

A comprehensive survey of price movements appears in Fernand Braudel and Frank C. Spooner, ''Prices in Europe from 1450 to 1750,'' in E. E. Rich and C. H. Wilson, eds., *The Cambridge Economic History of Europe, vol. 4, The Economy of Expanding Europe in the Sixteenth and Seventeenth Centuries* (Cambridge, 1967). But this work, for all its many merits, gives too much credence to Kondratieff models and alpha-beta phases, and too little to secular trends and relative prices.

For demographic trends the leading works include E. A. Wrigley and R. S. Schofield, *The Population History of England, 1541–1871: A Reconstruction* (Cambridge, 1981) and Michael W. Flinn, *The European Demographic System, 1500–1820* (Baltimore, 1981).

A good survey of economic history in this period is Jan de Vries, *The Economy of Europe in an Age of Crisis, 1600–1750*, cited above. For various national economies, see John J. McCusker and Russell R. Menard, *The Economy of British America, 1607–1789* (Chapel Hill, 1985); Ernest Labrousse et al., *Histoire économique et sociale de la France, vol. 2, Les derniers temps de l'age seigneurial aux préludes de l'age industriel (1660–1789)* (Paris, 1970); Jaime Vicens Vives, *An Economic History of Spain* (Princeton, 1969); Brian Pullen, ed., *Crisis and Change in the Venetian Economy in the Sixteenth and Seventeenth Centuries* (London, 1968); Jan de Vries, *The Dutch Rural Economy in the Golden Age* (New Haven, 1974); A. H. John, "Some Aspects of English Economic Growth in the First Half of the Eighteenth Century," *Economica* 28 (1961) 176–190; Patrick Chorley, *Oil, Silk, and Enlightenment: Economic Problems in Eighteenth Century Naples* (Naples, 1965).

Climate changes in this period are examined in John A. Eddy, "The 'Maunder Minimum': Sunspots and Climate in the Reign of Louis XIV," *Science* 92 (1976) 1189–1202, rpt. in Parker and Smith, *The General Crisis of the Seventeenth Century*, 226–68; this is a serious and important essay. On harvest fluctuations, see W. G. Hoskins, "Harvest Fluctuations and English Economic Life, 1620–1759," *Agriculture History Review* 16 (1968) 15–31.

On agricultural history, see R. V. Jackson, "Growth and Deceleration in English Agriculture, 1660–1780," *Economic History Review* 38 (1985) 333–51.

On price movements and markets, in addition to works cited above by Posthumus and Phelps-Brown and Hopkins, see C. W. J. Granger and C. M. Elliott, "A Fresh Look at Wheat Prices and Markets in the Eighteenth Century," *Economic History Review* 2d ser. 20 (1969) 257–65; Walter Achilles, "Getreidepreise und Getreide Handelsbeziehungen europäischer Räume im 16 und 17 Jahrhundert," *Zeitschrift für Agrargeschichte und Agrarsoziologie* 7 (1959) 32–55; Ursula M. Cowgill and H. B. Johnson Jr., "Grain Prices and Vital Statistics in a Portuguese Rural Parish, 1671–1720," *Journal of Bio-Social Science* 3 (1971) 321–29; M. Couturier, "La fixation des prix des grains et du pain à Chateauneuf-en-Thymerais: 1692–1741," *Histoire Locale Beauce et Perche* 3 (1961) 19–24; R. Meuvret, "Histoire de prix des céréales en France dans la seconde moitié du XVIIme siècle; Sources et publications," *Annales d'Histoire Sociale* 5 (1944) 27–44; idem., "Les mouvements des prix de 1661 à 1715 et leurs répercussions," *Journal de la Societé de Statistique de Paris* 85 (1944), rpt. in Romano, ed., *I prèzzi in Europa*, 315–29; Robert S. Smith, "Indigo Production and Trade in Colonial Guatemala," *Hispanic American Historical Review* 39 (1959); Raymond L. Lee, "Grain Legislation in Colonial Mexico," *Hispanic American Historical Review* (1947); E. Mireaux, *Une province français au temps du Grand Roi: La*

Brie (Paris, 1958); F. G. Dreyfus, "Remarques sur le mouvement des prix et la conjuncture en Allemagne de la second moitié du XVIIᵉ siècle," *Premiere Conference Internationale d'Histoire Économique, Contributions-Communications, Stockholm, 1960* (Paris, 1960); Marcello Boldrini, "Il prèzzo del pane in Matelica nel secolo XVII [1642–1694]," *Giornale degli Economisti* 61 (1921) 298–302; I have not seen J. A. Faber, "Graanhandel, graanprijzen en tarievenpolitiek in Nederland gedurende de tweede helft der zeventiende eeuw," *Tijdschricht voor Gescheidenis* (1962).

Wage movements and living standards may be followed in works of Abel, Phelps-Brown cited above, Micheline Baulant, "Les salaires du Bâtiment, 1490–1726," *Annales;* E. Scholliers, *De Levenstandaard in de XVᵉ en XVIᵉ eeuw te Antwerpen* (Antwerp, 1960); Aldo de Maddalena, "Preise, Löhne und Goldwesen im Verlauf der wirtschaftlichen Entwicklung Mailands," in Ingomar Bog, ed., *Wirtschaftliche und soziale Strukturen im saekularen Wandel* (Hanover, 1974); Jan de Vries, "Peasant Demand Patterns in Friesland, 1550–1750," in William N. Parker and E. L. Jones, eds., *European Peasants and Their Markets:Essays in Agrarian Economic History* (Princeton, 1975); E. J. Hamilton, "Prices and Wages at Paris under John Law's System," *Quarterly Journal of Economics* 51 (1936–37) 42–70; *idem,* "Prices and Wages in Southern France under John Law's System," *Journal of Economic History* 3 (1937) 441–61; Domenico Sella, *Salari e lavoro nell'edilizia lombardia durante il secolo XVII* (Pavia, 1968).

For rent, interest, and returns to capital, see H. J. Habakkuk, "The Long-Term Rate of Interest and the Price of Land in the Seventeenth Century," *Economic History Review* 5 (1952–53) 26–45; *idem,* "Economic Fortunes of English Landowners in the Seventeenth and Eighteenth Centuries," in E. M. Carus-Wilson, ed., *Essays in Economic History* (New York, 1966) 1:187–201; G. E. Mingay, "The Agricultural Depression, 1730–1750," *Economic History Review* 14 (1962) 323–38; D. Zolla, "Les variations du revenu et du prix des terres en France au XVIIᵉ et XVIIIᵉ siècles," *Annales de l'École Libre des Sciences Politiques* (1893–94).

On monetary movements, see Louis Dermigny, "Circuits de l'argent et mileux d'affaires au XVIIIᵉ siècle," *Review Historique* 112 (1954) 239–78; *idem,* "Une carte monetaire de la France au XVIIIᵉ siècle," *Annales E.S.C.* 10 (1955) 480–93; John J. McCusker, *Money and Exchange in Europe and America, 1600–1775: A Handbook* (Chapel Hill, 1978); J. K. Horsefield, *British Monetary Experiments, 1650–1710* (1960, London; New York, 1983), with an important review by T. S. Ashton in *Economic History Review* 2d ser. 13 (1960) 119–22.

On commerce, trade, and migration, see H. E. S. Fisher, "Anglo-Portuguese Trade, 1700–1770," *Economic History Review* 2d ser. 16 (1963) 219–33; V. M. Godinho, "Flottes de sucre et flottes de l'or, 1660–1770," *Annales E.S.C.* 5 (1950) 184–97; J. A. Faber, "The Decline of the Baltic

Grain Trade in the Second Half of the Seventeenth Century,'' *Acta Historiae Neerlandica* 1 (1966) 108–31.

Fiscal history is the subject of P. G. M. Dickson, *The Financial Revolution in England: A Study in the Development of Public Credit, 1688–1756* (London, 1967) and E. B. Schumpeter, ''English Prices and Public Finance, 1660–1822,'' *Review of Economic Statistics* 20 (1938) 21–37. The institutional structure of economic activity is the subject of W. R. Scott, *The Constitution and Finance of English, Scottish, and Irish Joint-Stock Companies to 1720* (3 vols., Cambridge, 1912).

On social history in this period many hundreds of local and regional studies have been completed by *Annales* historians in Europe and by students of the ''new social history'' in the United States. Annalists normally study price and wage movements; American social historians mostly do not (except the Chesapeake group), but all of these works remain useful. Among them are R. Baehrel on Provence, P. Deyon on Amiens, P. Goubert on Beauvais, Le Roy Ladurie on Languedoc, J. Meyer on Brittany, A. Poitrineau on Basse-Auvergne, F. Lebrun on Anjou, G. Frêche on the Toulouse area, P. St. Jacob on Burgundy, J. Dupâquier on Vexin, G. Lemarchand on Normandy, Thomas Sheppard on Lourmarin, Patrice Higonnet on Pont-de-Montvert, and John Day on Sardinia. For central Europe, there are studies by Gerald Soliday on Frankfurt-am-Main and Gerald Strauss on Nuremberg. In Belgium there is the work of E. Hélin on the Liége region, C. Bruneel on Brabant. In Britain, there is the work of D. C. Chambers on the Vale of Trent, W. G. Hoskins and his students on Leicestershire, V. Skipp on the Forest of Arden, David Hey on Myddle, Shropshire, Margaret Spufford on Cambridgeshire, and E. A. Wrigley and R. S. Schofield, on Colyton, Devon. In America, there is the work of Philip Greven on Andover, Mass., John Demos on Plymouth, Mass., Kenneth Lockridge on Dedham, Mass., Daniel Scott Smith on Hingham, Mass., Robert Gross on Concord, Mass., Linda Auwers on Windsor, Conn., Jessica Kross on Newtown, N.Y., Stephanie Wolff on Germantown, Pa., Allan Kulikoff on Prince George's County, Md., Darrett and Anita Rutman on Middlesex County, Va., and many other projects.

On the growth of political stability in this period, see C. B. A. Behrens, *Society, Government, and the Enlightenment: The Experiences of Eighteenth-Century France and Prussia* (London, 1985); Ronald W. Harris, *Absolutism and Enlightenment, 1660–1789* (London, 1964, 2d ed. 1967); John G. Gagliardo, *Enlightened Despotism* (New York, 1967). On England, see J. H. Plumb, *The Growth of Political Stability in England, 1675–1725* (London, 1967); Betty Kemp, *Kings and Commons, 1660–1832* (New York, 1957); E. N. Williams, *The Eighteenth-Century Constitution* (New York, 1960).

On France, the political historiography tends to stress the weakness of the old regime rather than its strengths; but see Roland E. Mousnier, *The Institu-*

tions of France under the Absolute Monarchy, 1598–1789 (2 vols., Chicago, 1979, 1984); Pierre Goubert, *Louis XIV and Twenty Million Frenchmen* (New York, 1970).

For Prussia, see Hans Rosenberg, *Bureaucracy, Aristocracy, and Autocracy* (Boston, 1966); Reinhold August Dorwart, *Administrative Reform of Frederick William I of Prussia* (Westport, 1953).

On Iberia, see Carl A. Hanson, *Economy and Society in Baroque Portugal, 1668–1703* (Minneapolis, 1981), which interprets this period as "an era of relative quiescence in Portuguese history . . . as in most nation-states, the General Crisis . . . was clearly resolved in favor of absolutism."

On cultural and intellectual history there is a very rich literature, which tends, however, to be careless in its chronology and confused in its assumption of social and economic trends. The classical work is Voltaire, *The Age of Louis XIV*, (tr. Martyn P. Pollack (London, 1962). In the twentieth century, many works have been written to deny that this period was truly an "age of reason." See, e.g., Carl Becker's witty but wrong-headed *The Heavenly City of the Eighteenth-Century Philosophers* (New Haven, 1932); Basil Willey, *The Eighteenth-Century Background* (New York, 1941); Lester Crocker, *An Age of Crisis: Man and World in Eighteenth-Century French Thought* (Baltimore, 1959); Frank Manuel, *The Eighteenth Century Confronts the Gods* (New York, 1967). A contrary argument appears in Ernst Cassirer, *The Philosophy of the Enlightenment* (Boston, 1951). Mediating models are developed in Albert Soboul, Guy Lemarchand, and Michele Fogel, *Le siècle des lumières* (2 vols., Paris, 1977); Paul Hazard, *The European Mind* (New York, 1963); Peter Gay, *The Enlightenment: An Interpretation* (2 vols., New York, 1966–69); Roger Mercier, *La réhabilitation de la nature humaine (1700–1750)* (Paris, 1980).

Among many helpful monographs are Jean Ehrard, *"L'idée de nature en France à l'aube des lumières* (Paris, 1963; Flammarion ed., 1970); Charles Vereker, *Eighteenth-Century Optimism* (Liverpool, 1967); William Letwin, *The Origin of Scientific Economics* (Garden City, 1963).

Some of the most important contributions to intellectual history in this period are biographies. Among them are Frank Manuel, *A Portrait of Sir Isaac Newton* (Cambridge, 1968); Maurice Cranston, *John Locke* (London, 1957; rpt. New York, 1979); Ronald Grimsley, *D'Alembert* (New York, 1963); Isabel Knight, *The Geometric Spirit: The Abbé de Condillac and the French Enlightenment* (New Haven, 1968); and Ira Wade, *The Intellectual Development of Voltaire* (Princeton, 1969).

⁊⬥ The Price Revolution of the Eighteenth Century

Most historians outside of France are not aware that there was a price revolution in the eighteenth century. The subject has been so little understood that when Boris Mironov picked up in Russia unmistakeable evidence of what looked to him like a price-revolution in the eighteenth century, he concluded that it was a delayed Russian extension of the price-revolution of the sixteenth century! See Boris Mironov, "The 'Price Revolution' in Eighteenth-Century Russia," *Soviet Studies in History* 11 (1973) 325–52;

General historical introductions to this period include Franco Venturi, *The End of the Old Regime in Europe, 1768–1776: The First Crisis,* tr. R. Burr Litchfield (Princeton, 1989); C. B. A. Behrens, *The Ancien Régime* (1967, New York, 1979); M. S. Anderson, *Europe in the Eighteenth Century, 1713–1783* (2d ed., London, 1976); Leonard Krieger, *Kings and Philosophers, 1689–1789* (New York, 1970); and Isser Woloch, *Eighteenth-Century Europe: Tradition and Progress, 1715–1789* (New York, 1982). Still useful are three volumes in the old Langer series: Penfield Roberts, *The Quest for Security, 1715–1740* (New York, 1947); Walter L. Dorn, *Competition for Empire, 1740–1763* (New York, 1940); and Leo Gershoy, *From Despotism to Revolution, 1761–1789* (New York, 1944); and two volumes in the French *Peuples et civilisations* series: P. Muret, *La prépondérance anglaise, 1713–1763* (Paris, 1937); and Philippe Sagnac, *La fin de l'ancien régime et la révolution Américaine, 1763–1789* (Paris, 1952). General works of economic and social history include Fernand Braudel, *Capitalism and Material Life, 1400–1800* (1967; New York, 1973); idem, *Afterthoughts on Material Civilization and Capitalism* (Baltimore, 1977); idem, *Civilization and Capitalism, Fifteenth-Eighteenth Century* (3 vols., 1979; New York, 1982–84); Pierre Chaunu, *La civilisation de l'Europe classique* (Paris, 1966).

On the economic history of England, see T. S. Ashton, *An Economic History of England: The Eighteenth Century* (London, 1955); idem, *Economic Fluctuations in England, 1700–1800* (Oxford, 1959).

For France, the leading works are Ernest Labrousse et al., *Histoire économique et sociale de la France* vol. 2, *1660–1789* (Paris, 1970); Roger Price, *The Economic Modernization of France* (New York, 1975); H. Sée, *La France économique et sociale au XVIIIe siècle* (1925, Paris, 1967); idem, *Esquisse d'une histoire économique et sociale de la France depuis les origines jusqu'à la guerre mondiale* (Paris, 1929); Marc Bloch, "La lutte pour l'individualisme agrare," *Annales d'Histoire Économique et Sociale* 2 (1930) 329–81, 511–56, which deals mainly with the eighteenth century.

On Italy, the best beginning is Giulio Einaudi, ed., *Storia d'Italia,* vol. 3, *Dal primo settecento all'unita* (Turin, 1973); specialized studies include Bruno Caizzi, *Industria, commercio e banca in Lombardia nel XVIII secolo* (Milan, 1968); Giuseppe Felloni, *Il mercato monetario in Piemonte nel secolo XVIII* (Milan, 1968); R. Burr Litchfield, "Les investissements commerciaux des patriciens florentins au XVIIIe siècle," *Annales E.S.C.* 14 (1969) 685–721; Giulio Giacchero, *Storia economica del Settecento genovese* (Genoa, 1951); Carlo Antonio Vianello, *Il settecento milanese* (Milan, 1934); R. Romano, *Prèzzi, salari e servizi a Napoli dal secolo XVIII (1734–1806)* (Milan, 1965).

On Spain, see Richard Herr, *the Eighteenth-Century Revolution in Spain* (Princeton, 1958); Jaime Carrera Pujal, *Historia de la economia española* (5 vols., Barcelona, 1943–47), devotes vols. 3–5 to the eighteenth century. A classic is G. Desdevises du Dezert, *L'Espagne de l'ancien régime* (3 vols., Paris, 1897–1904).

For central Europe, see W. H. Bruford, *Germany in the Eighteenth Century: The Social Background of the Literary Revival* (1935, Cambridge, 1968); Hermann Aubin and Wolfgang Zorn, eds., *Handbuch der deutschen Wirtschafts-und Sozialgeschichte* (2 vols., Stuttgart, 1971), 1:495–678; Otto Hintze, "Zur Agrarpolitik Friedrichs des Grossen," *Forschungen zur brandenburgischen Geschichte* 10 (1898) 275–309.

Eastern Europe in this era is studied in M. Confino, *Domaines et seigneurs en Russie vers la fin du XVIIIᵉ siècle* (Paris, 1963); Jerome Blum, *Lord and Peasant in Russia from the Ninth to the Nineteenth Century* (Princeton, 1961); Boris Mironov, "The 'Price Revolution' in Eighteenth-Century Russia," *Soviet Studies in History* 11 (1973) 325–52; *idem*, "Le mouvement des prix des céréales en Russie du XVIIIᵉ siècle au début du XXᵉ siècle," *Annales E.S.C.* 41 (1986) 217–51; and W. H. Reddaway, ed., *The Cambridge History of Poland* (Cambridge, 1941).

On northern Europe, the first volume of B. J. Hovde, *The Scandinavian Countries, 1720–1865* (Boston, 1943) is devoted to this period.

For the Middle East see, André Raymond, "The Economic Crisis of Egypt in the Eighteenth Century," in A. L. Udovitch, ed., *The Islamic Middle East, 700–1900: Studies in Economic and Social History* (Princeton, 1981), 687–709.

For America, John J. McCusker and Russell R. Menard, *The Economy of British America, 1607–1789* (1985, Chapel Hill, 1991) has an excellent bibliography. Also helpful are J. H. Parry, *Trade and Dominion: European Overseas Empires in the Eighteenth Century* (London, 1971); Richard B. Sheridan, *Sugar and Slavery: An Economic History of the British West Indies, 1623–1755* (Baltimore, 1974); Lyman L. Johnson and Enrique Tandeter, eds., *Essays on the Price History of Eighteenth-Century Latin America* (Albuquerque, 1990); Harold B. Johnson, "A Preliminary Inquiry into Money, Prices, and Wages in Rio de Janeiro, 1763–1823," in Dauril Alden, ed., *Colonial Roots of Modern Mexico* (Berkeley, 1973); Armando de Ramón and José de Larrain, *Origenes de la vida ecónomica Chilena, 1659–1808* (Santiago, 1982).

For localized studies it is interesting to compare Georges Lefebvre, *Les paysans du Nord pendant la Revolution Français* (Bari, 1959); Robert Gross, *The Minutemen and Their World* (New York, 1976); Patrick O'Mara, "Geneva in the Eighteenth Century: A Socioeconomic Study of the Bourgeois City," (thesis, Berkeley, 1956); Franklin L. Ford, *Strasbourg in Transition,*

1648–1789 (Cambridge, 1958); Thomas Sheppard, *Loumarin in the Eighteenth Century: A Study of a French Village* (Baltimore, 1971); Patrice Higonnet, *Pont-de-Montvert* (Cambridge, 1971); Olwen Hufton, *Bayeux in the Late Eighteenth Century* (Oxford, 1967); and Jeffrey Kaplow, *Elbeuf during the Revolutionary Period: History and Social Structure* (Baltimore, 1964). Demographic movements are discussed in E. A. Wrigley and R. S. Schofield, *The Population History of England, 1541–1871; A Reconstruction* (Cambridge, 1981), 402–7; also D. V. Glass, "Population and Population Movements in England and Wales, 1700–1850"; and Louis Henry, "The Population of France in the Eighteenth Century," in Glass and Eversley, eds., *Population and History* (London, 1965), 434–56; Michael W. Flinn, *The European Demographic System, 1500–1820* (Baltimore, 1981).

On harvest conditions and subsistence crises see John W. Rogers Jr., "Subsistence Crises and Political Economy in France at the End of the *Ancien Régime*," *Research in Economic History* 5 (1980) 249–301; David Landes, "The Statistical Study of French Crises," *Journal of Economic History* 10 (1950) 195–211; Emanuel Le Roy Ladurie, "Climat et recoltes au XVIIᵉ et XVIIIᵉ siècles," *Annales E.S.C.* 15 (1966) 434–65; Douglas Hay, "War, Dearth, and Theft in the Eighteenth Century: The Record of the English Courts," *Past & Present* 95 (1982) 117–60; J. Jenny, "Le prix du blé à Bourges en 1766: Un tumulte populaire," *Mémoires Union Societe Savantes, Bourges* 8 (1959–60) 49–122.

On price movements and markets in this era, much work has been done in France. The leading authority is still C.-E. Labrousse: *Esquisse du mouvement des prix et des revenus en France au XVIIIᵉ siècle* (2 vols., Paris 1933), idem, "Prix et structure regionale: Le froment dans les régions française, 1782–1790," *Annales d'Histoire Sociale* 2 (1940) 382–400; and *La crise de l'économie Française a la fin de l'ancien régime et au début de la Révolution* (Paris, 1943). Also helpful are A. P. Usher, *History of the Grain Trade in France, 1400–1710* (Cambridge, 1913), and idem, "The General Course of Wheat Prices in France, 1350–1788," *Review of Economic Statistics* 12 (1930) 159–69. Other studies of French prices include Georges Frêche, "Études statistiques sur le commerce céréalier de la France méridionale au XVIIIᵉ siècle," *Revue d'Histoire Économique et Sociale* 49 (1971) 5–43, 183–224; A. Danière, "Feudal Incomes and Demand Elasticity for Bread in Late Eighteenth-Century France," *Journal of Economic History* 18 (1958) 317–41; R. Latouche, *Le mouvements des prix en Dauphiné sous l'ancien régime; étude méthodologique* (Grenoble, 1934) and *Annales E.S.C.* 9 (1937) 110; A. Poitrineau, *La vie rurale en Basse-Auvergne au XVIIIᵉ siècle (1726–1789)* (2 vols., Paris, 1965); Ruggiero Romano, *Commerce et prix du blé à Marseille au XVIIIᵉ siècle* (Paris, 1956); P. de Saint-Jacob, *Les paysans de la Bourgogne du Nord au dernier siècle de l'Ancien Régime* (Paris, 1960); P. Saint-Jacob, "La question des prix en France à la fin de l'Ancien Régime, d'après les

contemporains,'' *Revue d'Histoire Économique et Sociale* 36 (1952) 133–46;
E. Sol, "Les céréales inférieures en Quercy (prix de 1751 à 1789)'' *Revue
d'Histoire Économique et Sociale* 4 (1938) 335–55; G. Afanasiev, *Le commerce des céréales en France au XVIIIe siècle* (Paris, 1894); J.
Letaconnoux, *Les subsistances et le commerce des grains en Bretagne au XVIIIe siècle*
(Rennes, 1909); Ernest Blin, *Le prix du blé à Avalon de 1756 à 1790* (Paris,
1945); F. G. Dreyfus, "Prix et population à Treves et à Mayence au XVIIIe
siècle,'' *Revue d'Histoire Économique et Sociale* 34 (1956) 241–61; Marie-
Jeanne Tits-Dieuaide, "L'evolution du prix du blé dans quelques villes d'Europe occidentale du XVe au XVIIIe siècle,'' *Annales E.S.C.* (1987) 529–48.

For price movements in other nations, see William Beveridge, *Prices and
Wages in England from the Twelfth to the Nineteenth Century* (London, 1939;
reissued New York, 1966); Earl J. Hamilton, *War and Prices in Spain, 1651–
1800* (Cambridge, Mass., 1947); Vitorino M. Godinho, *Prix et monnaies au
Portugal, 1750–1850* (Paris, 1955); Corrado Vivanti, "I prèzzi di alcuni
prodotti agricoli a Mantova nella seconda metà del XVIII secolo,'' *Bolletino
Storico Mantovano* 3 (1958) 499–518; P. J. Middelhoven, "Auctions at
Amsterdam of North European Pinewood, 1717–1808: A Contribution to the
History of Prices in the Netherlands,'' *Acta Historiae Neerlandicae* 13 (1980)
65–89; Astrid Friis and Kristof Glamann, *A History of Prices and Wages in
Denmark, 1660–1800* (Copenhagen, 1958); Tadeusz Furtak, *Ceny w Gdańsku
w latach 1701–1815* [A history of prices in Danzig-Gdansk] (Lemberg, 1935);
Ruth Crandall, "Wholesale Commodity Prices in Boston during the Eigh-
teenth Century,'' *Review of Economic Statistics* 16 (1934) 117–28; R. Cesse,
"La crisis agricola negli Stati Veneti a meta del secolo XVIII,'' *Estratto dal
Nouvo Archivo Veneto* n.s. 42; Giuseppe Prato, *La vita economica in Pie-
monte a mezzo il secolo XVIII* (Turin, 1908); Helena Madurowicz-Urbanska,
Ceny zbozaw zachodniej Malopolsce w Drugiej Polowie XVIII wieku (War-
saw, 1963); William S. Sachs, "Agricultural Conditions in the Northern
Colonies before the Revolution,'' *Journal of Economic History* 13 (1953)
274–90; V. N. Jakovchevsky, *Kupechesky kapital v feodal no-krepostnicesky
Rossii* [Prices and Profit in Feudal and Servile Russia] (Moscow, 1953), of
which pp. 77–103 and 193–201, with statistical materials, are translated in
Italian in Romano, ed., *Prèzzi in Europa*, 447–79; this is mainly a study of
Russian prices in the mid- and late eighteenth century. Abel also cites Paul von
Hedemann-Heespen, "Zur Sitten-und-Preisgeschichte des 18 Jahrhundert,''
*Die heimat. Monatsschrift des Vereins zur Pflege der Natur-und-Lands-
kunde in Schleswig-Holstein,* 21 (1911), which I have not seen.

On wage movements, see Elizabeth W. Gilboy, "The Cost of Living and
Real Wages in Eighteenth-Century England,'' *Review of Economic Statistics*
18 (1936) 134–43; *idem, Wages in Eighteenth-Century England* (Cambridge,
Mass., 1934, New York, 1969); M. W. Flinn, "Trends in Real Wages, 1750–

1850,'' *Economic History Review* 2d ser. 27 (1974) 395–413, with commentary in *ibid.* 29 (1976) 137–144; G. N. Von Tunzelmann, "Trends in Real Wages, 1750–1850, Revisited," *ibid.*, 33–49; Luigi Dal Pane, *Storia del lavoro in Italia dagli inizi del secolo XVIII al 1815* (Milan, 1958); F. W. Botham and E. H. Hunt, "Wages in Britain during the Industrial Revolution," *Economic History Review,* 2d ser. 40 (1987) 380–99; L. D. Schwarz, "The Standard of Living in the Long Run: London, 1700–1860," *Economic History Review* 38 (1985) 24–41; A. Verhaegan, "Note sur le trevail et les salaires en Belgique au XVIIIᵉ siècle," *Bulletin de l'Institut de Recherches Économiques et Sociales de l'Universite de Louvain* 19 (1953) 71–88; R. Keith Kelsall, "The General Trend of Real Wages in the North of England during the Eighteenth Century," *York Archaeological Journal* 33 (1936); *idem,* "The Wages of Northern Farm Labourers in the Mid-Eighteenth Century," *Economic History Review* 8 (1937) 80–81; Pierre Vilar, "Elan urbain et mouvement des salaires: Le cas de Barcelone au XVIIIᵉ siècle," *Revue d'Histoire Économique et Sociale* 28 (1950); E. H. Hunt, "Industrialization and Regional Inequality: Wages in Britain, 1760–1914," *Journal of Economic History* 46 (1986) 935–66; *idem* and F. W. Botham, "Wages in Britain during the Industrial Revolution," *Economic History Review* 2d ser. 40 (1987) 380–99; L. D. Schwarz, "Trends in Real Wage Rates, 1750–1790: A reply to Hunt and Botham," *Economic History Review,* 2d ser. 43 (1990) 90–98; J. Söderberg, "Real Wage Trends in Urban Europe, 1750–1850: Stockholm in Comparative Perspective," *Social History* 12 (1987) 155–76.

On problems of poverty, see Cissie Fairchilds, *Poverty and Charity in Aix-la-Provence, 1640–1789* (Baltimore, 1976).

For land prices, see Christopher Clay, "The Price of Freehold Land in the Later Seventeenth and Eighteenth Centuries," *Economic History Review* 2d ser. 27 (1974) 173–89; Arthur Young, *An Enquiry into the Progressive Value of Money in England* (London, 1812); Vicomte G. d'Avenel, *Histoire économique de la propriété des salaires, des denrées et de tous les prix . . . ,*vol. 2; Daniel Zolla, "Les variations du revenu et du prix des terres en France au XVIIᵉ et au XVIIIᵉ siècle, *Annales de l'École Libre des Sciences Politiques* 8 (1893), 9 (1894).

For returns to capital, see Homer, *History of Interest Rates,* cited above; Earl J. Hamilton, "Profit Inflation and the Industrial Revolution, 1751–1800," *Quarterly Journal of Economics* 56 (1941–42) 256–73.

Commercial conditions and finance are discussed in T. S. Ashton, *Economic Fluctuations in England,1700–1800* (Oxford, 1950); W. T. Baxter, *The House of Hancock* (Cambridge, Mass., 1945); A. H. John, "Insurance Investment and the London Money Market of the Eighteenth Century," *Economica* 20 (1953) 137–58, Eli Heckscher, "The Bank of Sweden . . . ," in

J. G. Dillen, ed., *History of the Principal Public Banks* (The Hague, 1934), 1760; P. G. M. Dickson, *The Financial Revolution in England: A Study in the Development of Public Credit, 1688–1756* (London, 1967).

On monetary movements, see Richard A. Lester, *Monetary Experiments: Early American and Recent Scandinavian* (Princeton, 1939); Joseph Ernst, *Money and Politics in America, 1755–1775* (Chapel Hill, 1973).

On speculative manias, see L. Stuart Sutherland, "Sir George Cole-brooke's World Corner in Alum, 1771–73," *Economic History* 3 (1936) 237–58; Stephan Skalweit, *Die Berliner Wirtschaftskrise von 1763 und ihre Hintergrunde* (Stuttgart, 1937); Charles P. Kindleberger, *Manias, Panics, and Crashes: A History of Financial Crises* (New York, 1978); Julian Hoppit, "Financial Crises in Eighteenth-Century England," *Economic History Review* 39 (1946) 39–58.

On industrialization, see Franklin Mendels, "Proto-Industrialization, the First Stage of the Industrialization Process," *Journal of Economic History* 32 (1972) 241–61; Paul Mantoux, *The Industrial Revolution in the Eighteenth Century* (London, 1928); Rudolf Braun, *Industrialisierung und Volksleben: Die Veränderungen der Lebensformen in einem ländlichen Industriegebiet vor 1800* (Zurich, 1960); Walther G. Hoffmann, *Wachstum und Wachstumformen der Englischen Industriewirtschaft von 1700 bis zur Gegenwart* (Jena, 1940), tr. as *British Industry, 1700–1950* (Oxford, 1955; New York, 1965); P. Lebrun, *L'industrie de la laine à Verviers pendant le XVIIIe et le début du XIXe siècle* (Liege, 1948).

Another change-indicator that shows a fundamental break in secular trends circa 1730–45 is internal migration. See Jan de Vries, *Barges and Capitalism: Passenger Transportation in the Dutch Economy (1632–1789)* (Utrecht, 1981), 221–232.

On the economic effect of war and military spending, see James C. Riley, *The Seven Years War and the Old Regime in France: The Economic and Financial Toll* (Princeton, 1986); also good on the "crisis of confidence" in the mid-eighteenth century.

For a contemporary discussions of the price revolution, see the anonymous English pamphlet *Reflections on the Present High Price of Provisions, and the Complaints and Disturbances Arising Therefrom* (London, 1766) in the Kress Collection, Baker Library, Harvard Business School. Other works include T. de Anzano, *Reflexiones económico-politicas sobre las causas de la alteración de Precios* (Saragossa, 1768); Nicholas F. Dupré de Saint Maur, *Essai su les monnaies, ou réflexions sur le rapport entre l'argent et les denrées* (Paris, 1746); idem, *Recherches sur la valeur des monnaies et sur les prix des grains, avant et après le Concile de Francfort* (Paris, 1762); Claude J. Herbert, *Essai sur la police générale des grains, sur leur prix et sur les effects de l'agriculture* (Paris, 1755); F. Messance, *Recherches sur le population* (Paris, 1766), which includes an appendix on the price of wheat in

England and France from 1674 to 1764; Gian Rinaldo Carli, *Delle monete e dell' istituzione delle zecche d' Italia* (4 vols., Pisa and Lucca, 1754–60); *idem, Del valore e della proporzione de' metalli monetati con i generi in Italia . . .* (Lucca, 1760); A. Zanon, *Dell' agricultura, dell' arti, e del commercio . . .* in *Lettere scelte sollàgricultura,* vol. 5 (Venice, 1765; Milan, 1804).

On the physiocrats, the leading work is G. Weulersee, *Le mouvement physiocratique en France de 1756 à 1770* (Paris, 1910); *La physiocratie à la fin de règne de Louis XV, 1770–1774* (Paris, 1959); *La physiocratie sous les ministères de Turgot et Necker, 1774–1781* (Paris, 1950); see also Ronald L. Meek, *The Economics of Physiocracy* (Cambridge, 1963); John W. Rogers Jr., "Opposition to the Physiocrats: A Study of Economic Thought and Policy in the Ancien Régime, 1750–1780," (thesis, Johns Hopkins, 1971).

On mercantilism the leading work is still Eli Heckscher, *Mercantilism* (2 vols., 1935, New York, 1983) and *idem, Revisions in Mercantilism,* ed. D. C. Coleman (London, 1969).

On the relationship between economic and cultural history, see John W. Van Cleve, *The Merchant in German Literature of the Enlightenment* (Chapel Hill, 1986).

For the problem of cultural discontinuity in the mid-eighteenth century, see Roger Mercier, *La réhabilitation de la nature humaine (1700–1750)* (Paris, 1980); T. D. Kendrick, *The Lisbon Earthquake* (London, 1956).

❧ The Revolutionary Crisis of 1789–1815

A good introduction is Jacques Godechot, *Les révolutions, 1770–1799* (1963, 4th ed. Paris, 1988), with extensive discussions of historiography and a copious bibliography. More detailed accounts are Jacques Godechot, *La grande nation* 2 vols. (1956, 2d ed. Paris, 1983); R. R. Palmer, *The Age of Democratic Revolution* (2 vols., Princeton, 1959–64); Martin Göhring, *Weg und Sieg der modernen Staatsidee in Frankreich* (Tubingen, 1947).

Histories of national economies in this period include, for Britain, A. D. Gayer, W. W. Rostow, and A. J. Schwartz, *The Growth and Fluctuations of the British Economy, 1790–1850* (1953; new ed., London, 1975); Phyllis Deane and W. A. Cole, *British Economic Growth, 1688–1959* (1962; 2d ed. Cambridge, 1969); R. C. Floud and D. N. McCloskey, eds., *The Economic History of Britain since 1700* (Cambridge, 1981); and N. F. R. Crafts, *British Economic Growth during the Industrial Revolution* (Oxford, 1985), a revisionist essay; and for Scotland, H. Hamilton, *Economic History of Scotland in the Eighteenth Century* (Oxford, 1963).

On France, Ernest Labrousse et al., *Histoire économique et sociale de la France* (Paris, 1970), vols. 2 and 3; M. Marion, *Histoire financière de la*

France depuis 1715 (Paris, 1914–25), vols. 2–4 cover the period from 1789 to 1818; Henri Sée, *Histoire économique de la France* (Paris, 1939).

For Germany, Hermann Aubin and Wolfgang Zorn, *Handbuch der deutschen Wirtschaftsundsozialgeschichte* (2 vols., Stuttgart, 1971).

For the United States in this period see Samuel Blodget, *Economica: A Statistical Manual for the United States of America* (Washington, 1806); Curtis P. Nettels, *The Emergence of a National Economy, 1775–1815* (New York, 1962); Stuart Bruchey, *The Roots of American Economic Growth, 1607–1861* (New York, 1965); Douglas North, *The Economic Growth of the United States, 1790–1860* (1961; New York, 1966); Claudia Goldin and Frank Lewis, "The Role of Exports in American Economic Growth during the Napoleonic Wars, 1793 to 1807," *Explorations in Economic History* 17 (1980) 6–25; Paul David, "The Growth of Real Product in the United States before 1840: New Evidence, Controlled Conjectures," *Journal of Economic History* 27 (1967) 151–97; Stanley L. Engerman and Robert E. Gallman, eds., *Long-Term Factors in American Economic Growth* (Chicago, 1986).

On the history of prices, see Winifred Rothenberg, "The Market and Massachusetts Farmers, 1750–1855," *Journal of Economic History* 41 (1981) 283–314; *idem*, "A Price Index for Rural Massachusetts, 1750–1855," *ibid.* 39 (1979) 975–1001; *idem*, "The Emergence of Capital Markets in Rural Massachusetts, 1730–1838," *ibid.* 45 (1985) 781–808; *idem*, "The Emergence of Farm Labor Markets and the Transformation of the Rural Economy: Massachusetts, 1750–1855," *ibid,* 48 (1988) 537–66; *idem, From Market-Places to a Market Economy: The Transformation of Rural Massachusetts, 1750–1850* (Chicago, 1992); Anne Bezanson, *Prices and Inflation during the American Revolution: Pennsylvania, 1770–1790* (Philadelphia, 1951); *idem et al., Wholesale Prices in Philadelphia, 1784–1861* (Philadelphia, 1936); *idem,* "Inflation and Controls in Pennsylvania, 1774–1779," *Tasks of Economic History* 8 (1948) 1–20; Arthur Harrison Cole, *Wholesale Commodity Prices in the United States, 1700–1861* (Cambridge, Mass., 1938); Walter B. Smith and Arthur Harrison Cole, *Fluctuations in American Business, 1790–1860* (Cambridge, Mass., 1935); George Rogers Taylor, "Wholesale Commodity Prices at Charleston, South Carolina, 1732–1791," *Journal of Economic History* 4 (1921–22) 356–77; "Wholesale Commodity Prices at Charleston, South Carolina, 1796–1801," *ibid.,* 848–67; Thomas Senior Berry, *Western Prices before 1861: A Study of the Cincinnati Market* (Cambridge, 1943); Harold V. Roelse, "Wholesale Prices in the United States, 1791–1801," *Quarterly Publications of the American Statistical Association* 15 (1917) 840–46.

On prices in France, C.-E. Labrousse, *Esquisse du mouvement des prix et des revenus en France au XVIIIe siècle* (2 vols., Paris, 1933) is still the indispensable work on the price revolution of the eighteenth century; see also C.-E. Labrousse, "Recherches sur l'histoire des prix en France de 1500 à

1800," *Revue d'Économie Politique* (1939); *idem*, "Un siècle et demi de hausse des prix agricoles (1726–1873): presentation d'un nouvel indice général des prix," *Revue Hhistorique* 65 (1940); *idem*, "Prix et structure régionale: le froment dans les régions françaises (1782–1790)," *Annales d'Histoire Sociale* 1 (1939); L. Dutil, *L'état économique du Languedoc à la fin de l'Ancien Régime, 1750–1789* (Paris, 1911); A. Achard, "Le prix du pain à Ambert, de 1774 à 1790," *Bulletin Historique et Scientifique de l'Auvergne* 57 (1937) 136–39; Georges Sangnier, *La crise du blé à Arras à la fin du XVIIIᵉ siècle, 1788–1796* (Fontenay-Le-Comte, 1943).

On English prices, in addition to the works of Tooke and Newmarch, Beveridge cited above, see N. J. Silberling, "British Prices and Business Cycles, 1779–1850," *Review of Economic Statistics* 5 (1923) 223–61; E. L. Jones, *Seasons and Prices: The Role of Weather in English Agricultural History* (London, 1964); W. W. Rostow, "Business Cycles, Harvests, and Politics, 1790–1850," *Journal of Economic History* 1 (1941) 206–21.

On prices in other nations, see Jean Meuvret, "La géographie des prix des céréales et les anciennes économies européennes: prix méditerranéens, prix continentaux, prix atlantiques à la fin du XVIIIᵉ siècle, *Revista da Economia* (1951); Anselmo Bernardino, "Contributo all storia dei prèzzi in Sardegna tra la fine del secolo XVIII e il principio del secolo XIX," *Giornale degli Economisti* 71 (1931) 423–43.

On wages, see M. W. Flinn, "Trends in Real Wages, 1750–1850," *Economic History Review* 2d ser. 27 (1974) 395–413; T. R. Gourvish, "Flinn and Real Wage Trends in Britain, 1750–1850: A Comment," *Economic History Review* 2d ser. 29 (1976) 136–42; G. N. Von Tunzelmann, "Trends in Real Wages, 1750–1850, Revisited," *Economic History Review* 2d ser. 32 (1979) 33–49; Valerie Morgan, "Agricultural Wage Rates in Late Eighteenth-Century Scotland," *Economic History Review* 24 (1971) 181–201; Donald R. Adams Jr., "Wage Rates in the Early National Period: Philadelphia, 1785–1830," *Journal of Economic History* 28 (1968) 404–26; *idem*, "Some Evidence on English and American Wage Rates, 1790–1830," *Journal of Economic History* 30 (1970) 499–520.

On the tangled "standard of living" debate, in which the effect of the Industrial Revolution has not been clearly distinguished from the secular trend, see Eric Hobsbawm, "The British Standard of Living, 1790–1850," *Economic History Review* 2d ser. 10 (1957) 46–68; *idem*, "The Rising Standard of Living in England, 1800–1850," *Economic History Review* 2d ser. 13 (1961) 397–416; and many subsequent contributions in A. J. Taylor, ed., *The Standard of Living in Britain during the Industrial Revolution* (London, 1975); F. Collier, *The Family Economy of the Working Class in the Cotton Industry, 1784–1833* (Manchester, 1965).

On social and economic conditions and the coming of the American Revolution, see Gary B. Nash, *The Urban Crucible: Social Change, Political*

Consciousness, and the Origins of the American Revolution (Cambridge, 1979); Marc Egnal and Joseph Ernst, "An Economic Interpretation of the American Revolution," *William and Mary Quarterly* 29 (1972) 3–32; Alfred Young, *The American Revolution: Explorations in the History of American Radicalism* (De Kalb, 1976); McCusker and Menard, *The Economy of British America*, 351–77; Richard B. Sheridan, "The British Credit Crisis of 1772 and the American Colonies," *Journal of Economic History* 20 (1960) 161–86.

For France, the relationship between prices, wages, and revolutionary events is discussed in Georges Lefebvre, "Le mouvement des prix et les origines de la Révolution française," *Annales Historiques de la Révolution Française* 9 (1937) 288–329; idem, "La crise économique en France à la fin de l'ancien régime, " *Annales E.S.C.* 1 (1946) 51–55; C.-E Labrousse, *La crise de l'économie française à la fin de l'ancien régime et au début de la révolution* (Paris, 1943); Philipe Sagnac, "La crise de l'économie en France à la fin de l'Ancien Régime," *Revue d'Histoire Économique et Sociale* (1950); P. de St-Jacob, "La question des prix en France à la fin de l'Ancien Régime, après les contemporains," *Revue d'Histoire Économique et Sociale* (1952) 133–46 George E. Rudé, "Prices, Wages, and Popular Movements in Paris during the French Revolution," *Economic History Review* 2d ser. 6 (1954) 246–267; George Lefebvre, "Les mouvement des prix et les origines de la Revolution Française," *Annales Historiques de la Revolution Francaise* 14 (1937) 289–329; Emmanuel LeRoy Ladurie, "Révoltes et contestations rurales en France de 1675 à 1788," *Annales E.S.C.* 29 (1974) 6–22; F. G. Dreyfus, "Prix et population à Mayence et à Tréves au XVIIIᵉ siècle," *Revue d'Histoire Économique et Sociale* (1956); Hubert C. Johnson, *The Midi in Revolution: A Study of Regional Political Diversity, 1789–1793* (Princeton, 1986); Roger Chartier, "Cultures, lumières, doléances: Les Cahiers de 1789," *Revue d'Histoire Moderne et Contemporaine* 28 (1981) 68–93; David Ringrose, *Transportation and Economic Stagnation in Spain, 1750–1850* (Durham, 1970).

On subsistence crises of the late eighteenth century, see J. Meuvret, "Les crises de subsistances et la démographie de la France d'Ancien Régime," *Population* 1 (1946) 643–50; idem, "Demographic Crisis in France from the Sixteenth to the Eighteenth Century," *Population in History*, 507–22; Walter M. Stern, "The Bread Crisis in Britain, 1795–96," *Economica* 31 (1964) 168–87; P. Vilar, "Réflexions sur le 'crise de l'ancien type,' 'inégalité des reécoltes,' et 'sous-développement,'" *Conjuncture économique, structures sociales: Hommage à Ernest Labrousse* (Paris, 1974); Jacques Godechot and S. Moncassin, "Démographie et subsistances en Languedoc du XVIIIᵉ siècle du XVIIIᵉ siècle au début au XIXᵉ," *Bulletin d'Histoire Économique et Sociale de la Révolution Française* (1965); D. Klingaman, "Food Surpluses and Deficits in the American Colonies, 1768–1772," *Journal of Economic History* 31 (1971) 553–69; Olwen Hufton, "Social Conflict and the Grain Supply in

Eighteenth-Century France," *Journal of Interdisciplinary History* 14 (1983) 305–09; G. Sangnier, *La crise du blé à Arras, à la fin du XVIIIe siècle (1788–1796)* (Fontenay-le-Comte, 1943). On the French financial crisis, see J. Bouchary, *Les manieurs d'argent à Paris à la fin du XVIIIe siècle* (2 vols., Paris, 1939–43) and *Les compagnies financières à Paris à la fin du XVIIIe siècle* (3 vols., Paris, 1940–42); L. Dermigny, "La France à la fin de l'Ancien Régime: une carte monétaire," *Annales E.S.C.* (1955) 480–93; J. F. Bosher, *French Finances, 1770–1795* (Cambridge, 1970).

The role of prices, wages, and subsistence in the outbreak of the French Revolution is also discussed in Jean Egret, *The French Prerevolution, 1787–1788* (1962; Chicago, 1977); Georges Lefebvre, *The Great Fear of 1789* (New York, 1973); Jacques Godechot, *The Taking of the Bastille, July 14th, 1789* (1965; New York, 1970); G. Durieux, *The Vainqueurs de la Bastille* (Paris, 1911); W. Sewell, *Work and Revolution in France* (Cambridge, 1980); E. Barber, *The Bourgeoisie in Eighteenth Century France* (Princeton, 1955).

Monetary movements in the revolutionary era are the subject of Seymour E. Harris, *The Assignats* (Cambridge, 1930); J. Morini–Combi, *Les assignats, révolution et inflation* (Paris, 1926); G. Hubrecht, *Les assignats dans le Haut-Rhin* (Strasbourg, 1931); idem, "Les assignats à Bordeaux du début de la Révolution," *Annales Historique de la Révolution Française* 16 (1939) 289–301; Jean Bouchary, *Les faux monayers sous la Révolution française* (Paris, 1946).

Continuing price problems after the Revolution are discussed in R. Schnerb, "La dépression économique sous le Directoire après la disparition du papier-monnaie," *Annales Historique de la Révolution Française* 11 (1934) 27–49; J. Bertrand, *La taxation des prix sous la Révolution française* (Paris, 1949); W. F. Shepard, *Price Control and the Reign of Terror: France, 1793–1795* (Berkeley, 1953); George Rudé and Albert Soboul, "Le maximum des salaires parisiens et la Révolution française," *Annales Historique de la Révolution Française* (1954) 1–22; Richard Cobb, "Politique et subsistance en l'an III, l'exemple du Havre," *Annales de Normandie* (1955) 135–59; idem, *Terreur et subsistances, 1793–1795* (Paris, 1965); O. Festy, *L'agriculture pendant la Révolution française: les conditions de production et de récolte des céréales (1789–1795)* (Paris, 1947).

On prices and political movements in other nations, see L. Dal Pane, *Lo Stato Pontificio e il movimento riformatore del settecento* (Milan, 1959); J. Vicens Vives, "Conjuntura economica y reformismo burgués: Dos factores en la evolucion de España del antiguo regimen," *Estudios de Historia Moderna* 4 (1954) 349–91; R. Werner, *L'approvisionnement en pain de la population du bas-Rhin et de l'armée du Rhin pendant la Revolution (1789–1797)* (Strasbourg, 1951).

On poverty there is a very large literature with different *problematiques* for France: Olwen Hufton, *The Poor of Eighteenth-Century France, 1750–1789* (Oxford, 1974) and Alan Forrest, *The French Revolution and the Poor* (New York, 1981), both with full bibliographies. For Britain, old Benthamite and Fabian interpretations of the poor law by Sir George Nichols, the Hammonds, and the Webbs are radically revised in Mark Blaug, "The Myth of the Old Poor Law and the Making of the New," *Journal of Economic History* 23 (1963) 151–84; this line of inquiry continues in James P. Huzel, "Malthus, the Poor Law, and Population in Early Nineteenth-Century England," *Economic History Review* 2d ser. 22 (1969) 430–52; *idem,* "The Demographic Impact of the Old Poor Law: More Reflections on Malthus," *Journal of Economic History* 2d ser. 33 (1980) 367–81; Donald McCloskey, "New Perspectives on the Old Poor Law," *Explorations in Economic History* 10 (1972–73) 419–36.

For the Napoleonic crisis, see A. Chabert, *Essai sur les mouvements des prix et des revenus en France de 1798 à 1820* (Paris, 1945–49); J. Norris, "British Wartime Inflation, 1793–1815: The Beginning of a Pragmatic Tradition," in B. M. Gough, ed., *In Search of the Visible Past* (Waterloo, 1975); Joel Mokyr and N. Eugene Savin, "Stagflation in Historical Perspective: The Napoleonic Wars Revisited," *Research in Economic History* 4 (1979) 198–259; Glenn Hueckel, "War and the British Economy, 1793–1815: A General Equilibrium Analysis," *Explorations in Economic History* 10 (1973) 365–96; *idem,* "Relative Prices and Supply Response in English Agriculture during the Napoleonic Wars," *Economic History Review* 2d ser. 29 (1976) 401–14; A. K. Cairncross and B. Weber, "Fluctuations in Building in Great Britain, 1785–1849," *Economic History Review* 9 (1956) 283–97; J. W. Anderson, "A Measure of the Effect of British Public Finance, 1793–1815," *Economic History Review;* Eli Heckscher, *The Continental Blockade: An Economic Interpretation* (Oxford, 1922); A. C. Clauder, *American Commerce as Affected by the Wars of the French Revolution and Napoleon, 1793–1812* (Philadelphia, 1932); W. F. Galpin, *The Grain Supply of England during the Napoleonic Period* (New York, 1925); R. Ruppenthal, "Denmark and the Continental System," *Journal of Modern History* 15 (1943) 7–23; E. Tarlé, *Le blocus continental et le royaume d'Italie* (Paris, 1931); C. Northcote Parkinson, ed., *The Trade Winds: A Study of British Overseas Trade during the French Wars, 1793–1815* (London, 1948).

On finance, banking, and interest rates, see N. J. Silberling, "British Financial Experience, 1790–1830," *Review of Economic Statistics* 1 (1919) 321–23; Emmanuel Coppieters, *English Bank Note Circulation, 1694–1954* (Louvain, 1955), 13–34; Bray Hammond, *Banks and Politics in America from the Revolution to the Civil War* (Princeton, 1957); statistics for the United States appear in J. Van Fenstermaker, *The Development of American Commercial Banking, 1782–1837* (Kent, Ohio, 1965).

On the relationship between prices and disorder in England, see Douglas

Hay, "War, Dearth, and Theft in the Eighteenth Century: The Record of the English Courts," *Past & Present* 95 (1982) 117–60.

Thomes Malthus and David Ricardo generalized the experiences of their time in *Essays on the Principles of Population* (1798) and *Principles of Political Economy and Taxation* (1817). A discussion appears in Samuel Hollander, "Ricardo's Analysis of the Profit Rate, 1813–15," *Economica* 40 (1973) 260–82; see also Edmond E. Lincoln, ed., *Du Pont de Nemours on the Dangers of Inflation* (a speech in the National Assembly, 25 Sep. 1790; Boston, 1950). Two classic contemporary accounts are by Arthur Young: *An Inquiry into the Progressive Value of Money in England* (London, 1812) and *An Enquiry into the Rise of Prices in Europe* (London, 1815). The relationship between economic and cultural movements appears in D. Mornet, *Les origines intellectuelles de la révolution française, 1715–1787* (Paris, 1933).

ॐ The Victorian Equilibrium

General works on European economic history in the nineteenth century include David S. Landes, *The Unbound Prometheus: Technological Change and Industrial Development in Western Europe from 1750 to the Present* (Cambridge, 1969); Charles P. Kindleberger, *Economic Growth in France and Britain, 1851–1950* (Cambridge, Mass., 1964); P. K. O'Brien and C. K. Kyder, *Economic Growth in Britain and France, 1780–1914: Two Paths to the Twentieth Century* (London, 1978); and Simon Kuznets, *Modern Economic Growth: Rate, Structure, and Spread* (New Haven, 1966).

On British economic history, general works include François Crouzet, *L'économie de la Grande Bretagne victorienne,* (Paris, 1978) tr. by Anthony Forster as *The Victorian Economy* (New York, 1982); Roderick Floud and Donald McCloskey, *The Economic History of Britain since 1700* (2 vols., Cambridge, 1981); Eric J. Hobsbawm, *Industry and Empire: An Economic History of Britain since 1750* (London, 1968); Peter Mathias, *The First Industrial Nation: An Economic History of Britain, 1700–1914* (London, 1969); Phyllis Deane and W. A. Cole, *British Economic Growth, 1688–1959* (2d ed., Cambridge, 1967); J. D. Chambers, *The Workshop of the World: British Economic History from 1820 to 1880* (London, 1961). Still instructive is J. H. Clapham, *An Economic History of Modern Britain* (3 vols., Cambridge, 1926–38). A revisonist interpretation appears in N. F. R. Crafts, *British Economic Growth during the Industrial Revolution* (Oxford, 1985). A classic contribution to price history in this period is Stanley Jevons, "On the Variation of Prices and the Value of Currency since 1782," *Journal of the Statistical Society of London* (1865).

The French economy is examined in Rondo Cameron, *France and the Economic Development of Europe, 1800–1914* (Princeton, 1961); *idem,*

"Profit, croissance et stagnation en France au XIXe siècle," *Economie Appli-quée* 10 (1957) 409–44; Shepherd B. Clough, "Retardative Factors in French Economic Development in the Nineteenth and Twentieth Centuries," *Journal of Economic History* 6 (1946) 91–102; N. Beaurieux, *Les prix du blé en France au XIXe siècle* (Paris, 1909).

For German economic history, a major synthesis of economic and political history is Helmut Böhme, *Deutschlands Weg zur Grossmacht . . .* (Cologne and Berlin, 1966). Also of high quality are Wolfram Fischer, *Wirtschaft und Gesellschaft im Zeitalter der Industrialisierung . . .* (Gottingen, 1972); Fritz Stern, *Bismarck, Bleichroder, and the Building of the German Empire* (New York, 1977); Franz Schnabel, *Deutsche Geschichte im neunzehnten Jahrhundert* (4 vols., Freiberg, 1927–37); W. G. Hoffman, *Das Wachstum der deutschen Wirtschaft seit der mitte des 19. Jahrhunderts* (Berlin, 1965; Tubingen, 1971).

The economic history of the United States is surveyed in Lance Davis et al., *American Economic Growth: An Economist's History of the United States* (New York, 1972), 363–65; and Douglass C. North, *Growth and Welfare in the American Past: a New Economic History* (3d ed., Englewood Cliffs, N.J., 1983). Specialized studies that give serious attention to price history include Peter Temin, *The Jacksonian Economy* (New York, 1969); Eugene M. Lerner, "Inflation in the Confederacy, 1861–65," in Milton Friedman, ed., *Studies in the Quantity Theory of Money* (Chicago, 1956); George E. Dickey, "Money, Prices, and Growth: The American Experience, 1860–1896" (thesis, Northwestern University, 1968).

On Italy, a general survey is Shepard B. Clough, *The Economic History of Modern Italy* (New York, 1964); on prices in Italy during the nineteenth century, many studies have been published in C. M. Cipolla et al., *Archivio economico dell'Unificazione italiana,* including P. Bandettini, "I prèzzi sul mercato di Firenze dal 1800 al 1890" (vol. 5, fasc. 1, 28–34); I. Delogu, "I prèzzi sui mercati di Cagliari e di Sassari dal 1818 al 1880" (vol. 9, fasc. 4, 20–24); G. Felloni, "I prèzzi sul mercato di Torino dal 1815 al 1890" (vol. 5, fasc. 2, 36–44); *idem,* "I prèzzi sul mercato di Genova dal 1815 al 1890" (vol. 7, fasc. 3, 126–34), A. de Maddalena, "I prèzzi . . . sul mercato di Milano," (vol. 5, fasc. 3, 36–44); A. Petino, "I prèzzi . . . sui mercati di Palermo a di Catania dal 1801 al 1890" (vol. 8, fasc. 5, 20–24); S. Pinchera, "I prèzzi . . . sui mercati dello Stato Pontifico (dal 1823 al 1860) e Roma (dal 1823 al 1890)" (vol. 5, fasc., 4, 32–34; and P. Spaggiari, "I prèzzi . . . sul mercato di Poarma dal 1821 al 1890" (vol. 8, fasc. 3, 24–34).

On Spain, there are Juan Sardá, *La politica monetaria y las fluctuaciones de la economia espannñola en el siglo XIX* (Madrid, 1948); Nicolás Sánchez Albornoz, *Las crisis de subsistencias de Espana en el siglo XIX* (Rosario, 1963); *idem,* "La formazione del mercato nazionale: Spagna e Italia," *Rivista*

Storica Italiana 85 (1973) 907–31; Pierre Conrad and Albert Lovett, "Problèmes de l'évaluation du coût de la vie en Espagne: 1. Le prix du pain depuis le milieu du XIXᵉ siècle: une source nouvelle," *Melanges de la Cas Velázquez* 5 (1965) 411–41; Juan J. Novara, *Contribución a la historia de los precios en Córdoba, 1887–1907* (Cordoba, 1968).

On the Middle East, a useful essay is Haim Gerber and Nachum T. Gross, "Inflation or Deflation in Nineteenth-Century Syria and Palestine," *Journal of Economic History* 40 (1980) 351–57.

On southern Asia, see K. N. Chaudhuri, ed., *The Economic Development of India under the East India Company, 1814–1858* (Cambridge, 1971); John Adams and Robert C. West, "Money, Prices, and Economic Development in India, 1861–1895," *Journal of Economic History* 39 (1979) 55–68.

On East Asia, pathbreaking works include M. Lee, *Economic History of China* (New York, 1921); Richard Henry Tawney, *Land and Labor in China* (New York, 1932); Albert Feuerwerker, *China's Early Industrialisation* . . . (Cambridge, 1958).

On Oceania, Australia, and New Zealand, see Edward O. G. Shann, *An Economic History of Australia* (London, 1930); N. G. Butlin, *Investment in Australian Economic Development, 1861–1900* (London, 1963); C. G. F. Simkin, *The Instability of a Dependent Economy* (London, 1951).

Much work has been done on economic fluctuations in the nineteenth century. A general study is Charles P. Kindleberger, *Manias, Panics, and Crashes: A History of Financial Crises* (New York, 1978). On specific crises, panics, and depressions, a large literature includes John D. Post, *The Last Great Subsistence Crisis in the Western World* (Baltimore, 1977), on the crisis of 1816; Murray N. Rothbard, *The Panic of 1819: Reactions and Policies* (New York, 1962); P. Gonnet, "Esquisse de la crise économique de 1827 à 1832," *Revue d'Histoire Économique et Sociale* 33 (1955) 249–92; R. C. O. Mathews, *A Study in Trade Cycle History: Economic Fluctuations in Great Britain, 1833–42* (Cambridge, 1954); Reginald Charles McGrane, *The Panic of 1837* (Chicago, 1924); Peter Temin, *The Jacksonian Economy* (New York, 1969); D. Morier Evans, *The Commercial Crisis, 1847–48* (1849, rpt. New York, 1968, 2d ed. 1969); Henry Grote Lewin, *The Railway Mania and its Aftermath, 1845–1852* (1936; rpt. New York, 1968); J. R. T. Hughes, *Fluctuations in Trade, Industry and Finance* (Oxford, 1960); George W. Van Vleck, *The Panic of 1857: An Analytical Study* (New York, 1943); D. Morier Evans, *History of the Commercial Crisis, 1857–1858, and the Stock Exchange Panic of 1859* (1859; rpt. New York, 1969); Hans Rosenberg, *Die Weltwirtschaftskrise von 1857–59* (Stuttgart, 1934); Wladimir d'Ormesson, *La grande crise mondiale de 1857* . . . (Paris, 1933); E. Ray McCartney, *Crisis of 1873* (Minneapolis, 1935); S. B. Saul, *The Myth of the Great Depression, 1873–1896* (London, 1969); W. Jett Lauck, *The Causes of the Panic of 1893* (Boston, 1907); H. S. Foxwell, "The American Crisis of 1907," in *Papers in*

Current Finance (London, 1919); Franco Bonelli, *La crisi del 1907* . . . (Turin, 1971).

On monetary trends, see Wesley C. Mitchell, *Gold, Prices, and Wages under the Greenback Standard* (Berkeley, 1908); Irwin Unger, *The Greenback Era* (Princeton, 1964); Robert Sharkey, *Money, Class, and Party* (Baltimore, 1959); Milton Friedman and Anna J. Schwartz, *A Monetary History of the United States, 1867–1960* (Princeton, 1963); idem, *Monetary Statistics of the United States* (New York, 1970); idem, *Monetary Trends in the United States and the United Kingdom: Their Relation to Income, Prices, and Interest Rates, 1867–1975* (Chicago, 1982); Larry T. Wimmer, ''The Gold Crisis of 1869,'' *Explorations in Economic History* 12 (1975) 105–22.

Banks and banking are discussed in Bray Hammond, *Banks and Politics in America from the Revolution to the Civil War* (Princeton, 1957); idem, *Sovereignty and an Empty Purse: Banks and Politics in the Civil War* (Princeton, 1970); Richard H. Timberlake, *The Origins of Central Banking in the United States* (Cambridge, 1978); and for quantitative data, J. Van Fenstermaker, ''The Development of American Commercial Banking, 1782–1837'' (thesis, Kent State University, 1965). Forrest Capie and Alan Webber, *A Monetary History of the United Kingdom, 1870–1982* (London, 1985) includes much data on British banking. See also Sir John Clapham, *The Bank of England, a History* 2 vol. (Cambridge, 1944); Walter Bagehot, *Lombard Street* (5th ed. London, 1873), a classic, which should be read in conjunction with Frank W. Fetter, ''A Historical Confusion in Bagehot's Lombard Street,'' *Economica* 34 (1967) 80–83; Robert Bigo, *Les banques francaises au cours de XIXᵉ siècle* (Paris, 1947).

General price studies include Ethel D. Hoover, ''Wholesale and Retail Prices in the Nineteenth Century,'' *Journal of Economic History* 18 (1958) 298–316; and Walt W. Rostow, ''Money and Prices: An Old Debate Revisited,'' (ms., Austin, 1978), an argument that price fluctuations were driven by ''real'' rather than monetary forces (mainly supply shocks). Monetarist rejoinders appear in Michael Bordo and Anna J. Schwartz, ''Money and Prices in the Nineteenth Century: An Old Debate Rejoined,'' *Journal of Economic History* 40 (1980) 61–67; idem, ''Money and Prices in the Nineteenth Century: Was Thomas Tooke Right?'' *Explorations in Economic History* 18 (1981) 97–127; C. Knick Harley, ''Prices and the Money Market in Britain, 1870–1913,'' *Explorations in Economic History* 14 (1977) 69–89; P. R. P. Coelho and J. F. Shepherd, ''Differences in Regional Prices: The United States, 1851–1880,'' *Journal of Economic History* 34 (1974) 555–91.

Specialized price studies include Ruth L. Cohen, *History of Milk Prices* (Oxford, 1936); W. Stanley Jevons, *The Coal Question* (1865, London, 2d ed. 1866); C. Knick Harley, ''Western Settlement and the Price of Wheat, 1872–1913,'' *Journal of Economic History* 36 (1978) 865–78; Thorstein Veblen, ''The Price of Wheat since 1867,'' *Journal of Political Economy* 1 (1892)

365–79; L. B. Zapoleon, *Geography of Wheat Prices* (USDA Bulletin no. 594, Washington, 1918); Robert C. Allen, "Accounting for Price Changes: American Steel Rails, 1879–1910," *Journal of Political Economy* 89 (1981) 512–28; Peter Temin, "The Causes of Cotton-Price Fluctuations in the 1830s," *Review of Economics and Statistics* 49 (1967) 463–70. The climatic optimum of the nineteenth century is examined in H. H. Lamb, *Climate: Present, Past and Future* (2 vols., London, 1977). Interest rates and returns to capital are the subject of J. M. Fachan, *Historique de la rente française* (Paris, 1904); Leonidas J. Loutchitch, *Des variations du taux de l'intérêt en France de 1800 à nos jours* (Paris, 1930); Clifford F. Thies, "Interest Rates and Expected Inflation, 1831–1914: A Rational Expectations Approach," *Southern Economic Journal* 51 (1985) 1107–20; Gene Smiley, "Interest Rate Movement in the United States, 1888–1913," *Journal of Economic History* 35 (1975) 591–620; C. Knick Harley, "The Interest Rate and Prices in Britain, 1873–1913: A Study of the Gibson Paradox," *Explorations in Economic History* 14 (1977) 69–89.

On rent and real estate prices, see F. M. L. Thompson, "The Land Market in the Nineteenth Century," *Oxford Economic Papers* 9 (1957) 285–308; E. M. Carus-Wilson, "A Century of Land Values: England and Wales [1781–1880]," in *idem, Essays in Economic History* (London, n.p.), 3:128–31; Avner Offer, "Ricardo's Paradox and the Movement of Rents in England, c. 1870–1910," *Journal of Economic History* 33 (1980) 236–52; Country Landowners' Association, *The Rent of Agricultural Land in England and Wales, 1890–1946* (London, 1949).

Wages are studied in J. Kucynski, *Die Geschichte der Lage der Arbeiter in Deutschland von 1800 bis in die gegenwart* (1947); *idem, Die Geschichte der Lage der Arbeiter unter dem Kapitalismus* (1960–63); P. Mombert, "Aus der Literatur über die soziale Frage und über die Arbeiterbewegung in Deutschland in der ersten Hälfte des 19. Jahrhunderts," *Archiv für die Geschichte der sozialismus über die Arbeiterbewegung* 9 (1921); A. W. Phillips, "The Relation between Unemployment and the Rate of Change in Money Wage Rates in the United Kingdom, 1861–1957," *Economica* 25 (1908) 283–99; Richard G. Lipsey, "The Relation between Unemployment and the Rate of Change in Money Wage Rates in the United Kingdom, 1861–1957: A Further Analysis," *Economica* 27 (1960) 1–31; E. H. Phelps-Brown and Sheila Hopkins, "The Course of Wage Rates in Five Countries, 1860–1939," *Oxford Economic Papers* (Oxford, 1950); Stanley Lebergott, *Manpower in Economic Growth: the American Record since 1800* (New York, 1964); Stephen DeCanio and Joel Mokyr, "Inflation and Wage Lag during the American Civil War," *Explorations in Economic History* 14 (1977) 311–36; P. R. P. Coelho and J. F. Shepherd, "Regional Differences in Real Wages: The United States, 1851–1880," *Explorations in Economic History* 13 (1976) 203–30; E. H. Hunt, *Regional Wage Variations in Britain, 1850–1914* (Oxford, 1973).

American slave prices, which tended to follow global trends in real wages, are charted in Ulrich B. Phillips, *American Negro Slavery* (Baton Rouge, 1966); see also Robert Fogel and Stanley Engerman, *Time on the Cross: The Economics of American Negro Slavery* (2 vols., Boston, 1974).

On unemployment, see Marie Dessauer, "Unemployment Records, 1849–59," *Economic History Review* 10 (1939–40) 38–43; and Alex Keyssar, *Out of Work; The First Century of Unemployment in Massachusetts* (Cambridge, 1986).

On wealth and income distribution, see Peter H. Lindert and Jeffrey G. Williamson, "Three Centuries of Wealth Inequality," *Research in Economic History* 1 (1976) 69–122; Stephen Thernstrom, *Poverty and Progress: Social Mobility in a Nineteenth-Century City* (Cambridge, 1964).

On cultural trends in the Victorian equilibrium, Walter E. Houghton, *The Victorian Frame of Mind, 1830–1870* (New Haven, 1957), is a valuable work though it makes too much of similarities between Victorian and post-Victorian thought; still useful for this inquiry are G. M. Young, *Victorian England: Portrait of an Age* (Garden City, 1954) and W. L. Burn, *The Age of Equipoise* (1964; New York, 1965).

?♣ The Price Revolution of the Twentieth Century

On the origins of the twentieth century price revolution, two general works are indispensable: Jan Romein, *The Watershed between Two Eras: Europe in 1900* (Middletown, 1978); Geoffrey Barraclough, *An Introduction to Contemporary History* (Harmondsworth, 1967).

The statistical evidence is summarized in B. R. Mitchell, *European Historical Statistics, 1750–1988* (3d ed., New York, 1992); idem, *International Historical Statistics: Africa and Asia* (New York, 1995); idem, *International Historical Statistics: The Americas and Australasia* (London, 1995); and national yearbooks listed above.

The global dimensions of price movements in the twentieth century are examined in Arthur B. Laffer, "The Phenomenon of Worldwide Inflation: A Study of International Market Integration," in David I. Meiselman and Arthur B. Laffer, eds., *The Phenomenon of Worldwide Inflation* (Washington, 1975), 27–52; A. J. Brown, *The Great Inflation, 1939–51* (London, 1955); idem, *World Inflation since 1950* (Cambridge, 1985); Geoffrey Maynard and W. van Ryckegham, eds., *A World of Inflation* (New York, 1975); Gardner Ackley, *Stemming World Inflation* (Paris, 1971); Charles S. Maier, *In Search of Stability: Explorations in Historical Political Economy* (Cambridge, 1987).

On the beginning of the price revolution of the twentieth century, two different interpretations appear in Milton Friedman and Anna Jacobson

Schwartz, *A Monetary History of the United States, 1867–1960* (Princeton, 1963) and W. Arthur Lewis, *Growth and Fluctuations, 1870–1913* (London, 1978). Still useful are J. L. Laughlin: "Gold and Prices, 1890–1907," *Journal of Political Economy* (1909) 257–71, and *idem* "Causes of the Changes in Prices since 1896," American Economic Association *Papers and Proceedings* (1911) 26–36.

On economic trends before 1914, a major work from a monetarist perspective is Michael Bordo, "The Effect of the Sources of Change in the Money Supply on the Level of Economic Activity" (thesis, Chicago, 1972). Other studies include Donald McCloskey and J. Richard Zecher, "How the Gold Standard Worked, 1880–1930," in J. A. Fraenkel and H. G. Johnson, eds., *The Monetary Approach to the Balance of Payments* (London, 1976); R. P. Higonnet, "Bank Deposits in the United Kingdom, 1870–1914," *Quarterly Journal of Economics* 20 (1957) 329–67; Austin H. Spencer, *An Examination of Relative Downward Industrial Price Flexibility, 1870–1921* (New York, 1978), on eastern Europe.

For the economic and social history of price movements during and after World War I, see John Stevenson, *British Society, 1914–1945* (London, 1984), 46–102; Arthur Marwick, *The Deluge: British Society and the First World War* (Boston, 1965); A. J. P. Taylor, *English History, 1914–1945* (New York, 1965); James Harvey Rogers, *The Process of Inflation in France, 1914–1927* (New York, 1929); Charles S. Maier, *Recasting Bourgeois Europe: Stabilization in France, Germany, and Italy in the Decade after World War I* (Princeton, 1975); Stephen A. Schuker, *The End of French Predominance in Europe: The Financial Crisis of 1924 and the Adoption of the Dawes Plan* (Chapel Hill, 1976); R. H. Tawney, "The Abolition of Economic Controls, 1918–21," *Economic History Review* 13 (1943) 1–30; Alice Coulon, *Recherches sur les origines du boom et de la crise de 1920* (Montlucon, 1946).

Germany's experience of hyperinflation has engendered a large literature; see Carl-Ludwig Holtfrerich, *The German Inflation, 1914–1923: Causes and Effects in International Perspective* (Berlin, 1986); "Political Factors of the German Inflation, 1914–1923," in Schmukler and Marcus, eds., *Inflation through the Ages: Economic, Social, Psychological, and Historical Aspects,* (New York, 1983) 400–416; Andreas Kunz, *Civil Servants and the Politics of Inflation in Germany, 1914–1924* (New York, 1986); Gordon Craig, *Germany, 1866–1945* (New York, 1978); Gerald Feldman, *Iron and Steel in the German Inflation, 1916–1923* (Princeton, 1977); K. Laursen and J. Pederson, *The German Inflation, 1918–1923* (Amsterdam, 1964); Gerald D. Feldman et al., *The German Inflation Reconsidered: A Preliminary Balance* (Berlin, 1982); *idem, The Experience of Inflation: International and Comparative Studies* (Berlin, 1984); *idem, Die Nachwirkungen der Inflation auf die deutschen Geschichte, 1924–1933* (Munich, 1985); *idem, The Great Disor-*

der: Politics, Economics, and Society in the German Inflation, 1914–1924 (New York, 1993).

For other hyperinflations in eastern and central Europe after World War I, see a valuable group of articles: György Ránki, "Inflation in Post-World War I East Central Europe" and "Inflation in Hungary"; Ljuben Berov, "Inflation and Deflation Policy in Bulgaria during the Period between World War I and World War II"; Mugur Isarescu, "Inflation in Romania during the Post-World War I Period"; Zbigniew Landau, "Inflation in Poland after World War I"; Alice Teichova, "A Comparative View of the Inflation of the 1920s in Austria and Czechoslovakia"; all in Schmukler and Marcus, eds., Inflation through the Ages, 475–571; also Z. S. Katsenellenbaum, Russian Currency and Banking, 1914–1924 (London, 1925); J. van Walre de Bordes, The Austrian Crown: Its Depreciation and Stabilization (London, 1924).

Price movements between the wars are discussed in Derek H. Aldcroft, Finanz und wirtschaftspolitsche Fragen der Zwischenkreigszeit (Berlin, 1973); Albert Sauvy, Histoire économique de la France entre les deux guerres (4 vols., Paris, 1965–75); Emile Moreau, Souvenirs d'un gouverneur de la Banque de France (Paris, 1954); Sidney Pollard, The Development of the British Economy, 1914–1950 (London, 1962).

For the great depression see John Kenneth Galbraith, The Great Crash, 1929 (Boston, 1955); Lester V. Chandler, America's Greatest Depression, 1929–1941 (New York, 1970); Murray N. Rothbard, America's Great Depression (Princeton, 1963; Kansas City, 1969); Karl Brunner, ed., The Great Depression Revisited (Boston, 1981); Peter Temin, Did Monetary Forces Cause the Great Depression? (New York, 1976).

On price movements during and after World War II see Arthur Joseph Brown, The Great Inflation, 1939–1951 (New York, 1983); Eric F. Goldman, The Crucial Decade and After: America, 1945–1960 (New York, 1966); Arthur Hanau, Die deutsche landwirtschaftliche Preis aud Marktpolitik im Zweiten Weltkreig (Stuttgart, 1975); John J. Klein, "German Money and Prices, 1932–44," in Milton Friedman, ed., Studies in the Quantity Theory of Money (Chicago, 1956); Henry S. Miller, Price Control in Fascist Italy (New York, 1938); Gail E. Makinin, "The Greek Hyperinflation and Stabilization of 1943–1946," Journal of Economic History 46 (1986) 755–807; and A. J. Brown, The Great Inflation, 1939–1951 (London, 1955); and Robert S. Morrison, The Real War on Inflation Has Not Begun . . . (Ashtabula, Ohio, 1982), which covers the period from 1937 to 1980; A fascinating sidelight is R. A. Radford, "The Economic Organization of a P.O.W. Camp," Economica 12 (1945).

The economic history of the United States since World War II is the subject of Robert Aaron Gordon, Economic Instability and Growth: The American Record (New York, 1974); Herbert Stein, Presidential Economics: The Making of Economic Policy from Roosevelt to Reagan and Beyond (rev.

ed., New York, 1985); Peter Bohley, *Die Recession der Jahre 1957–58 in den Vereinigten Staaten von Amerika* . . . (Berlin, 1963).

On price movements in Germany see Günter Schmölders, "The German Experience," in *Inflation: Long-Term Problems, Proceedings of the Academy of Political Science* 31 (1975), 201–211; Fritz Rahmeyer, *Sektorale Preisentwicklung in der Bundesrepublik Deutschland, 1951–1977: Eine theoretische und empirische Analyse* (Tubingen, 1983).

The Italian experience is the subject of Georgio Rota, *L'Inflazione in Italia, 1952–1974* (Turin, 1975). On Belgium, see L. H. Dupriez, *Monetary Reconstruction in Belgium* (New York, 1947). For Great Britain, see Paul Ormerod, "Alternative Models of Inflation in the United Kingdom . . . ," in Schmukler and Marcus, eds., *Inflation through the Ages*, 643–58.

On the Communist economies, see Wolfgang Teckenberg, "Economic Well-Being in the Soviet Union: Inflation and the Distribution of Resources," in Schmukler and Marcus, eds., *Inflation through the Ages*, 659–676; Jan Adam, *Wage Control and inflation in the Soviet Bloc Countries* (London, 1979); F. D. Holzman, "Soviet Inflationary Pressures, 1928–1957, Causes and Cures," *Quarterly Journal of Economics* 74 (1960) 167–88; Fyodor I. Kushnirsky, *Growth and Inflation in the Soviet Economy* (Boulder, 1989); Adam Martan, *Consumer Prices in Austria and Hungary, 1945–1972* (Vienna, 1974); Sofija Popov and Milena Jovicic, *Uticaj Licnih Dohodaka na Kretanje Cena* (Belgrade, 1971), with a summary and conclusion in English, a study of cost-push inflation in Yugoslavia; J. M. van Brabant, *Regional Price Formation in Eastern Europe* (Doedrecht, 1987), on price movements after 1945.

For China there is Ying Hsin, *The Price Problems of Communist China* (Kowloon, 1964).

On inflation in Latin America, see Walter Manuel Beveraggi Allendi, *La inflacion Argentina, 1946–1975* (Buenos Aires, 1975); Stefan Robeck, "The Brazilian Experience" and William P. Glade, "Prices in Mexico: From Stabilized to Destabilized Growth," in *Proceedings of the American Academy of Political Science* 31 (1975) 179–187, 188–200; R. C. Vogel, "The Dynamics of Inflation in Latin America," *American Economic Review* 64 (1974) 102–14; Susan M. Wachter, *Latin-American Inflation* (Lexington, Mass., 1976); Felipe Pazos, *Chronic Inflation in Latin America* (New York, 1972); Rosemary Thorp and Lawrence Whitehead, eds., *Inflation and Stabilisation in Latin America* (New York, 1979); John Williamson, ed., *Inflation and Indexation: Argentina, Brazil, and Israel* (Washington, 1985); Alain Ize and Gabriel Vera, *La inflacion en Mexico* (Mexico City, 1984).

On price trends in South Asia, Chandulal Nagindas Vakil, *War against Inflation: The Story of the Falling Rupee, 1943–1977* (Delhi, 1978); Yogesh C. Halan, "Inflation, Poverty and the Third World: India's Experience," in Schmukler and Marcus, eds., *Inflation through the Ages*, 625–42; R. J. Venkateshwaran, *The Tragedy of the Indian Rupee* (Bombay, 1968); John Latham, "Food Prices and Industrialization: Some Questions from Indian History," *IDS Bulletin* 9 (1978) 17–19.

For East Asia, see Kokishi Asakuri and Chiaki Nishiyama, eds., *A Monetary Analysis and History of the Japanese Economy, 1868–1970* (Tokyo, 1968); Gilbert Brown, *Korean Pricing Policies and Economic Development in the 1960s* (Baltimore, 1973).

For African trends, see Jean Phillipe Peemans, *Diffusion du progres économique et convergence des prix: Le cas Congo-Belgique, 1900–1960; la formation du systeme des prix et salaires sand une economie dualiste* (Louvain, 1968).

For Oceana, there is Bryan Haig, *Real Product, Income, and Relative Prices in Australia and the United Kingdom* (Canberra, 1968).

The price shocks of the 1970s are the subject of John M. Blair, *The Control of Oil* (New York, 1976); also interesting is Ali D. Johany, *The Myth of the OPEC Cartel: The Role of Saudi Arabia* (Dhahran, Saudi Arabia, University of Petroleum and Minerals, 1980).

On the new inflation, see Gardiner Means, "Simultaneous Inflation and Unemployment," in Means et al., *The Roots of Inflation,* (New York, 1975) 19–27; also the many works of Robert Heilbruner; W. David Slawson, *The New Inflation: The Collapse of Free Markets* (Princeton, 1981); also *idem,* "Price Controls for a Peacetime Economy," *Harvard Law Review* 84 (1971) 1090–1107; *idem,* "Fighting Stagflation with the Wrong Weapons," *Princeton Alumni Weekly,* 23 Feb. 1983, 33–38.

For other "new inflation" theories, see Robert Lekachman, *Economists at Bay* (New York, 1976); Dudley Jackson, H. A. Turner and Frank Wilkinson, *Do Trade Unions Cause Inflation?* (Cambridge, 1972); G. L. Bach, *The New Inflation: Causes, Effects, Cures* (Providence, R.I., 1973).

On economic policy and attempts to control inflation see Leonardo Leiderman and Lars E. O. Svensson, eds., *Inflation Targets* (London, 1995), a survey of policies and outcomes in nine nations. On the United States, a survey is Richard H. Timberlake, *Monetary Policy in the United States; An Intellectual and Institutional History* (Chicago, 1993). Two journalistic accounts include William Greider, *Secrets of the Temple; How the Federal Reserve Runs the Country* (New York, 1987) and Maxwell Newton, *The Fed* (New York, 1983).

For discussion of stagflation, see Alex McLeod, *The Fearsome Dilemma: Simultaneous Inflation and Unemployment* (Lanham, Md., 1984).

The attitudes of economists are discussed in Howard Ellis, *German Monetary Theory, 1905–1933* (Cambridge, 1934); John Kenneth Galbraith, *Economics in Perspective* (Boston, 1987); Lester C. Thurow, *The Zero Sum Society* (New York, 1981).

On prices and speculators in this period, see John A. Jenkins, "The Hunt

Brothers: Battling a Billion Dollar Debt,'' *New York Times Magazine,* 27 Sept. 1987.

On the cultural and social context of inflation, see Alejandro Conde Lopez, *Socio-economia de la inflacion* . . . (Madrid, 1973). The impact of inflation upon the youth culture of this era may be observed in Jonathon [*sic*] Green, *The Book of Rock Quotes* (New York, 1982); other discussions include George Katona, ''The Psychology of Inflation''; David J. Webber, '' . . . a Political Theory of Inflation''; Arthur J. Vidich, ''Social and Political Consequences of inflation . . . ''; Edwin T. Harwood, ''Toward a Sociology of Inflation''; Beth T. Niemi and Cynthia Lloyd, ''Inflation and female Labor Force Participation''; Wilhelmina A. Leigh, ''The Impact of Inflation upon Homeownership . . . ''; Bettina Berch, ''Inflation of Housework''; and Donald C. Snyder and Bradley R. Schiller, ''The Effect of Inflation on the Elderly''; all in Schmukler and Marcus, eds., *Inflation through the Ages,* 745–882.

On inflation and unemployment, the Phillips curve first appeared in A. W. Phillips, ''The Relation between Unemployment and the Rate of Change of Money Wage Rates in the United Kingdom, 1861–1957,'' *Economica* 25 (1958) 183–299.

On the distribution of wealth and income see A. B. Atkinson, *Unequal Shares—Wealth in Britain* (London, 1972); Peter Wiles, *Distribution of Income: East and West* (Amsterdam, 1974); Lee Soltow, ''Long-Run Changes in British Income Inequality,'' *Economic History Review* 21 (1968) 17–29; Jeffery G. Williamson and Peter H. Lindert, *American Inequality: A Macroeconomic History* (New York, 1980); Jeffrey G. Williamson, *Did British Capitalism Breed Inequality?* (Boston, 1985); Y. S. Brenner, Hartmut Kaelbe and Mark Thomas, eds., *Income Distribution in Historical Perspective* (Cambridge, 1991), 35; A. L. Bowley, *Wages in the United Kingdom in the Nineteenth Century* (Cambridge, 1900); *idem, Wages and Income in the United Kingdom since 1860* (Cambridge, 1937).

A very lively book might be written on attempts to predict price movements through the past century, from Samuel Benner, *Benner's Prophecies of Future Ups and Downs in Prices; What Years to Make Money on Pig-Iron, Hogs, Corn and Provisions* (Cincinnati, 1876) to Ravi Batra, *The Great Depression of 1990; Why It's Got to Happen—How to Protect Yourself* (New York, 1985, 1987).

On the decline of inflation in the 1990s, leading works include Roger Bootle, *The Death of Inflation: Surviving and Thriving in the Zero Era* (London, 1996); Lester C. Thurow, *The Future of Capitalism: How Today's Economic Forces Shape Tomorrow's World* (New York, 1996).

ACKNOWLEDGMENTS

This book began nearly forty years ago at The Johns Hopkins University, where I studied economic history with Frederic Chapin Lane. Fred, as I later came to know him, was a scholar of the old school. His special field was the Venetian economy during the late Middle Ages and the Renaissance. Mine was (and is) American history, but I took a graduate course with him and found myself deeply drawn to the example of his scholarship. One course led to another, and then to a doctoral field under his direction on the economic and social history of Florence and Venice in the fifteenth century.

Those who knew Frederic Lane will understand how it happened. He never attracted large numbers of students or reached a broad public, but he was a gifted teacher and a truly great scholar. Later he would be elected president of the American Historical Association as a testament of esteem by his colleagues.

Fred is now in his grave, but he is still a living presence in my world. I can see him in my mind's eye as I write these words—a tall, lean New England Yankee with a laconic manner, a long leathery face deeply seamed by his many years, and a thick mustache that bristled dangerously whenever I said something that he thought more than ordinarily obtuse. Fred's words were few. His manner was abrupt. He demanded a standard of performance that I had never met before, and trained his students in an old-fashioned way that has nearly vanished from my profession.

Fred introduced me to the old historical sciences that are nearly forgotten in America today: paleography, spaghistics, numismatics and diplomatics in the eighteenth-century sense. As a matter of course, he insisted on a command of the languages that one needed to study the history of Venice in the *quattrocento*—a good many languages altogether. There were written tests, followed by oral examinations in his office. I vividly remember one of those occasions more than forty years ago. It was late in the afternoon. The heavy curtains were drawn against the sun, and the room seemed as dark as a cave when I first entered it. Fred showed me to a seat near his desk. On a bookcase nearby was a dusty model of an old Venetian galley. The sharp tip of her sinister prow seemed to be pointed like a dagger in my direction. Fred was oblivious to these sensations. He rummaged happily through piles of old manuscripts, drew out one incomprehensible sheet after another, and demanded a sight translation. Sometimes my failures seemed to gratify him more than my successes, but we persevered. Fred labored to correct my many errors, and slowly the sinister Venetian galley disappeared into the gathering shadows of the afternoon. As the last rays of the setting sun slanted through the drawn curtains, Fred's mustache stopped bristling and began to twitch in a more hopeful way. Finally he looked up at me and said, "That will do, Fischer." It was the nearest thing to a word of praise that I ever had from him. I went reeling into the twilight as he called after me, "next week, nostro and vostro accounts."

After we studied methods of fifteenth-century Venetian accounting (a favorite subject of Fred's), he led me to the literature of economic theory. I had not studied economics before. An advisor at Princeton had told me at an impressionable age that economics was not a fit subject for a gentleman. "One must *have* one's money," he said to a penurious undergraduate, "but one need not *think* of it."

Fred dismissed that attitude with the contempt that it deserved. He approached economic theory in historical terms, and encouraged me to burrow into the Hutzler Collection, a wonderful library of economic theory that had been lovingly assembled by the owner of a Baltimore department store. I read the classics in first editions, a few with marginalia by their authors. Fred and I had urgent conversations on theoretical problems that are no longer urgent today—the theory of surplus value which he judged to be Karl Marx's only contribution to knowledge, and the monetarist theories of Irving Fisher and Earl Hamilton, whom Fred Lane knew and respected.

To work with Fred Lane was to meet the leading economic historians of his generation, who came from many nations to visit him. It was to share the camaraderie that still exists among an international fraternity. My thinking was strongly influenced by conversations with Michael Postan, a friend of Fred's who came to Baltimore in 1959. He was a small ginger-haired British medievalist who taught me his Malthusian approach to historical problems. His influence can be seen in the pages of this work.

Fred's friends included Fernand Braudel and the leading French historians of what would later be called the "*Annales* school." I did not hear that expression until much later in the 1960s. Fred knew them in another way. In 1958 and 1959 we studied the work of the martyred Marc Bloch and Lucien Febvre and Fernand Braudel not for their methods but for their results.

In Fred and his friends I met an ideal of disinterested scholarship that began with an act of faith that the pursuit of truth was a worthy end in itself. Today that idea is regarded with contempt by a "post-modern" generation (as it had been in the 1920s and 1930s). But Fred was a believer, and so am I. At Johns Hopkins I was lucky to study with other historians who were believers too: Owen Lattimore, Sidney Painter, Wilson Smith, and Vann Woodward. Fred was in that company. The integrity of his scholarship, and especially his way of combining breadth with rigor, has been a continuing inspiration to me.

In 1962, I finished my graduate work at Johns Hopkins and took a job at Brandeis. Shortly afterward, Fred retired and moved to his ancestral home in Massachusetts. I was able to arrange for him to join the faculty at Brandeis. He became my colleague, but always he remained my teacher. During the late

1960s, while working mainly in American history, I taught an occasional course on the history of Italy in the *quattrocento,* and in the 1970s began to teach a course on the main lines of change in modern history. Both grew very much from the work I had done with Fred Lane.

In 1979, those courses gave rise to a short essay that summarized the central themes of this book. The essay was commissioned by B. A. Rittersporn for *The Journal of the Institute of Socioeconomic Studies.* I am grateful for his encouragement, and for the generous support of Leonard M. Greene, president of the Institute of Socieconomic Studies in White Plains, New York.

Much of the research for this project was done in four great library systems: Harvard, the New York Public Library, Oxford and Brandeis. A special word of thanks is due to the Brandeis reference staff, the best I have ever known, who literally never failed to find the answer to many difficult questions.

My Brandeis students have as always taught their teacher more than he taught them. On this subject, I have learned much from Winifred Rothenberg whose dissertation I was privileged to direct. Winnie has done the best American price history of this generation. Her work is a model for us all.

While I was teaching at Oxford, I got to know Henry Phelps-Brown whose work revolutionized price history by centering it on the experience of ordinary people, and correcting the elitist bias that had dominated earlier scholarship. Henry Phelps-Brown was a distinguished British civil servant, and a great scholar who shared the same devotion to truth that I have found in so many other price historians. I learned much from our conversations, and my wife and I remember with pleasure the kindness and generosity with which Henry and Evelyn Phelps-Brown received two Americans who were far from home.

The first book-length draft of this work was presented to a conference on quantification in economics and history at California Institute of Technology. I remember with thanks the hospitality of our hosts in Pasadena, Morgan Kousser and Lance Davis, and also acknowledge with gratitude the advice and suggestions of the members of the conference—among them, David Galenson, Maris Vinovskis, and Daniel Scott Smith. After the conference, Claudia Goldin and Stanley Engerman generously took time from their busy schedules to read the manuscript. Special thanks are due to Samuel Cohn of the University of Glasgow, who also read the manuscript and shared his expertise in social and economic history of the early modern era. My good friend, John Rowett of Brasenose College, Oxford, had many constructive suggestions for the modern period.

Portions of this work were presented as a public lecture at Connecticut College, where I remember with thanks the hospitality of President Oakes Ames and members of the Department of History. Other ideas were tried out on students and history faculty at Oxford University. A revised draft was presented as a lecture at Dartmouth College in 1994.

At the Oxford University Press, my editor and friend of thirty years, Sheldon Meyer, read the manuscript and made many suggestions for its improvement. Joellyn Ausanka shepherded the book through the press, and India Cooper was a superb copy editor. Jeffrey Ward created the maps for the book, and it was a pleasure to collaborate with him. Greg Meyer helped us to get started on the graphs, and contributed to the project his expertise with the Excel program. Mark Fisher, Kimberly Gazes, Susan Hendricks, and Deborah Melnick worked as research assistants. Judy Brown and Ina Malaguti were as efficient as ever. My wife Judith took time from her busy career to help when deadlines loomed. Susanna, Anne, Fred, John, Ann, Will, Kate and my brother Miles Fischer contributed their encouragement and advice. My parents were as always an example of wisdom and support. This book is dedicated to them, as a small token of the love that all of their children and grandchildren feel for them.

Wayland, Massachusetts   D. H. F.
April 1996

CREDITS

Permission is gratefully acknowledged for the following: *Agricultural History Review*, for data in C. J. Harrison, "Grain Price Analysis and Harvest Qualities, 1465–1634," 19 (1971), 139–51.

Annales E.S.C., for data in Elisabeth Carpentier, "Autour de la peste noir," 17 (1962) 1062–92.

Cambridge University Press, for data in Michel Morineau, *Incroyables gazettes et fabuleux métaux* (1985); Margaret Spufford, *Contrasting Communities* (1974); Joan Thirsk, ed., *The Agrarian History of England and Wales* Vol. II, 1042–1350, H. E. Hallam, ed. (1988); and Vol. V, 1640–1750 (1985).

Economica, for data in Henry Phelps-Brown and Sheila V. Hopkins, "Seven Centuries of the Prices of Consumables compared with Builders' Wage Rates," 23 (1956) 311–314; and *idem*, "Wage Rates, Prices and Population Pressure," 26 (1959) 26, 35–37.

Harvard University press, for data in Earl Hamilton, *American Treasure and the Price Revolution in Spain* (1935); Barbara Hanawalt, *Crime and Conflict in English Communities* (1979); Peter Laslett, Karla Osterveen and Richard M. Smith, ed., *Bastardy and Its Comparative History* (1980); Frank Spooner, *The International Economy and Monetary Movements in France, 1493–1725* (1972); E. A. Wrigley and R. S. Schofield, *The Population History of England, 1541–1871* (1981).

Journal of the Social and Economic History of the Orient, for data in Howard Farber, "A Price and Wage Study in Northern Babylonia . . ." 21 (1978) 34.

Journal of Studies on Alcohol, Inc., for data in M. M. Hyman, M. A. Zimmermann, C. Guroli and A. Helrich, eds., *Drinkers, Drinking, and Alcohol-Related Mortality and Hospitalizations: A Statistical Compendium* (New Brunswick, 1980).

Münsterische Beiträge zur antiken Handelsgeschichte, for data in H.-J. Drexhage, "Eselpreis im römischen Ägypten: ein Beitrag zum Binnenhandel" 5 (1986) 34–48.

Northwestern University Press, for data in David Herlihy, "Santa Maria Impruneta," in Nicolai Rubenstein, ed., *Florentine Studies* (Evanston, 1968).

Princeton University Press, for data in J. S. Cockburn, ed., *Crime in England, 1550–1800* (1977)

Rand McNally, for base maps in R. R. Palmer, *Atlas of World History* (Chicago, 1957).

INDEX